Measurement and Evaluation in the Schools

BLAINE R. WORTHEN

WALTER R. BORG

KARL R. WHITE

Utah State University

Longman
New York & London

Measurement and Evaluation in the Schools

Longman, 10 Bank Street, White Plains, N.Y. 10606

Associated companies:
Longman Group Ltd., London
Longman Cheshire Pty., Melbourne
Longman Paul Pty., Auckland
Copp Clark Pitman, Toronto

Acquisitions editor: Kenneth J. Clinton
Sponsoring editor: Raymond T. O'Connell
Development editor: Virginia L. Blanford
Production editors: Cracom Corporation, Marcy Gray
Cover design: David Levy

Library of Congress Cataloging-in-Publication Data

Worthen, Blaine R.
    Measurement and evaluation in the schools
  Blaine R. Worthen, Walter R. Borg, Karl R. White.
      p.   cm.
    Includes bibliographical references and index.
    ISBN 0-582-28501-1
    1. Educational tests and measurements.   2. Educational tests and
  measurements—Design and construction.   I. Borg, Walter R.
  II. White, Karl.   III. Title.
  LB3051.W65   1993
  371.2′6—dc20   92-20856
                                                            CIP

1 2 3 4 5 6 7 8 9 10-HA-9695949392

To Walter R. Borg, whose passing impoverishes not only the field of educational research and measurement but also the worlds of all who knew him well. His keen intellect, extensive professional experience, impressive talent, delightful wit, and deep personal integrity are each uncommon; together they define Walter's uniqueness.

And to Marie R. Borg, his ever equal partner and inspiration.

Contents

CHAPTER 7 WHY WORRY ABOUT VALIDITY? VALID MEASURES PERMIT ACCURATE CONCLUSIONS 176

CHAPTER 8 CUTTING DOWN TEST SCORE POLLUTION: REDUCING THE INFLUENCE OF EXTRANEOUS FACTORS 197

SECTION THREE CONSTRUCTING NEW MEASURES: LEARNING TO USE A BLUEPRINT 231

CHAPTER 9 CONSTRUCTING YOUR OWN ACHIEVEMENT TESTS—DECIDING WHEN AND HOW TO DO SO 233

Preface

Measurement and evaluation play a pivotal role in today's schools. Indeed, these activities are commonplace in classrooms from nursery school to university. Determining what students have learned, what aptitude they possess for future learning, how well they are progressing toward specific educational goals, how they feel toward school, and what aspirations and interests they possess are only a few examples of the questions teachers and other educators use measurement and evaluation to answer.

To answer such questions, teachers, school administrators, psychologists, and counselors use tests, rating scales, observational records, questionnaires, and a wide array of other types of measurement instruments discussed in this book. Whatever the type of instrument chosen, the user must understand and apply sound measurement principles and practices to be certain that instrument is used correctly, rather than abused.

During the past decade, tests of educational achievement have increasingly come under fire because of widespread abuses in selecting, administering, and interpreting such tests. Yet public pressure for evidence that schools and teachers are effectively educating students makes it unlikely that testing efforts will be abandoned or decreased in the foreseeable future. This means that much of the responsibility for the quality of testing must be shouldered by test users, many of whom are not now being trained appropriately in educational testing procedures.

Consequently, classroom teachers, administrators, and counselors must be helped to better understand educational testing principles and practices if the quality of test use is to improve and the extent of test abuse to decline. It is no less reasonable to train educators and psychologists who work in schools to use tests effectively and efficiently than to train the surgeon in plying the scalpel deftly or the virologist in thoughtfully interpreting the world through a microscope.

ACKNOWLEDGMENTS

We express our appreciation to:

- Richard L. Sudweeks, for valuable insights and information that have contributed greatly to some portions of this book, and for his work in preparing the *Instructor's Manual*; we look forward to his collaboration on future editions;

- Our colleague Kenneth W. Merrell, for his creativity in designing and writing the *Student Exercise Manual* that accompanies this text;

- The following colleagues in measurement, whose reviews of the manuscript or portions of it resulted in immeasurable improvements:

  John Badgett, Slippery Rock University
  Kathryn Cochran, University of Northern Colorado
  Valerie Flynn, Aurora University
  Thomas Haladyna, Arizona State University
  James Impara, University of Nebraska
  Richard M. Jaeger, University of North Carolina at Greensboro
  Jason Millman, Cornell University
  Barbara Plake, University of Nebraska
  Todd Rogers, University of Alberta

- The officers in many test publishing companies and other commercial interests who provided us sample test copies and other materials reviewed in the preparation of this book and who have allowed reproduction of portions of those materials herein;

- Our colleagues who have allowed us to reprint excerpts or graphics that exceeded normal quotation privileges;

- Joyce Brinck, Vicki Anderson, Karen Ranson, Debra Peck, and Mary Ellen Heiner for their outstanding typing and proofreading of this manuscript, as well as myriad tasks associated with it;

- Vanessa Moss, Becky Valcarce, Philip Rodgers, David G. Gibson and Bradley W. Worthen for their excellent and insightful assistance in searching extant literature on testing and measurement to make certain no stones were left unturned in our effort to make this text current and relevant;

- Vicki Spandel, for her superb editorial assistance, which went far beyond technical editing to substantially improve the content and presentation;

- David G Gibson, Vanessa Moss, and Gregory Leopold whose careful reading of the final draft has enhanced its consistency and accuracy;

- Our wives, Barbara and Amy, without whose support and sacrifice this book could not have been written.

But most of all, we acknowledge our colleague, co-author, and friend, Walter R. Borg, who died before the final draft of this book was complete, but not before his chapters were largely completed. We regret he did not live to see the fruition of his efforts. We trust that those who have enjoyed Walter's other texts will discern his contribution to this one as well.

To the Instructor

If you are a professor who is familiar with the field of educational measurement, you may wonder why we would add another introductory measurement text to the many that aspire to be the standard in that area. There are numerous books that discuss measurement principles, issues in testing, reliability and validity, and the selection and construction of measurement instruments, but we believe the orientation and presentation of this text offers unique advantages.

AUDIENCES AND PURPOSES FOR THIS BOOK

This book is designed as a basic text for university or college preservice courses in educational measurement and evaluation, or related administration, curriculum, or teacher education courses designed to teach practitioners to apply measurement and evaluation tools and techniques. Our primary audience is, therefore, the same as that of other introductory measurement texts. But we also aspire to reach a second important audience that most measurement texts do not address—practicing educators (and those preparing for such roles)—who want a comprehensive but practical reference book to provide an overview of educational measurement and evaluation.

This book is intended to (1) familiarize its users with basic measurement and evaluation concepts, principles, and issues; (2) help readers learn to determine the quality and utility of an educational measure and to interpret correctly the results it produces; (3) provide practical guidelines for constructing and using new "home-grown" measures; (4) provide practical guidelines for finding, selecting, and using existing measures; and (5) advise readers on how to set up high quality school testing and evaluation programs.

CONTENT AND ORIENTATION OF THIS TEXT

Decisions about what to include in this book come largely from our experience teaching introductory measurement and evaluation courses at several universities, working in public schools, and using measurement instruments in collecting research and evaluation data for many educational studies.

Authors of other measurement texts similarly draw on their experience, consciously or unconsciously. But we have based the content also on what practicing educators view as important to know about educational measurement. First, to help us better focus the content of this text, two of us directed a study (Borg, Worthen, & Valcarce, 1986) in which 1,000 classroom teachers were asked to judge the importance of a variety of measurement topics. Second, other studies dealing with teachers' measurement skills or perceptions of the importance of measurement topics were reviewed (e.g., Gullickson, 1984, Green & Stager, 1985). Collectively, these studies prompted us not only to include most topics typically covered in introductory measurement texts but also to address several additional issues of current concern to educators such as "authentic" assessment approaches; national trends in achievement scores; minimum competency testing; use of tests to certify teacher competence; legal, ethical, social, and cultural issues in testing; how to set up school assessment and evaluation systems; and the use of microcomputers in classroom and school testing. Indeed, much of the material in Chapters 2, 3, 15, 21, and 22 covers current issues and practices that are important to a full understanding of measurement in today's classroom yet that are rarely covered in introductory measurement texts. We prefer to include this content, since instructors can then choose whether to require it of the entire class, have students cover it individually, or leave it for the student to pursue at some later date.

This text also differs from other introductory measurement texts in that we have restricted its focus to *educational* measurement and evaluation, treating measures that typically fall within the province of the psychologist only as they may have direct applications to education.

The book's general orientation is toward application, which has resulted in its being unashamedly practical in its approach. More than half of this volume is devoted directly to practical guidelines for using existing measures or constructing and using new measures. Checklists and step-by-step procedural guides are provided to help the beginner learn more quickly the fundamental skills involved in completing measurement tasks.

We make no pretense of covering all the interesting and potentially useful theoretical and methodological developments related to educational measurement and evaluation. We scarcely mention out-of-level testing, answer-until-correct procedures, item response theory, or dozens of other topics of which measurement specialists and even some more informed practitioners are fond. We acknowledge the usefulness and importance of such topics, but see them as less appropriate to the audiences we seek to serve. We make no apology for dealing with much that is simple. Our intent is to show how measurement principles can be applied straightforwardly to real-life situations confronted in the educator's day-to-day activities. We leave useful but more advanced concepts and techniques for the advanced graduate seminar and its accompanying text.

Space has not permitted us to treat several topics here in the depth we desired. Entire books are devoted to some of the topics that we deal with in a few pages, such as cultural biases in tests, or minimum competency testing. Yet since most educators take only a single course in measurement, such critical topics should not be omitted altogether.

Finally, we have devoted more space than most introductory measurement texts to the *context* in which testing occurs. We think it more important that teachers understand why tests are criticized and what issues spark current debates about testing than that they know how to use the Spearman-Brown formula to calculate test reliability.

PRESENTATION OF CONTENT

We have worked hard to make the content readable and useful. More specifically:

1. We use content and learning aids that employ generally accepted presentation techniques that can be readily used by most instructors and readily understood by most students.
2. We avoid jargon, esoteric language, and sophisticated statistical and mathematical treatments in favor of clear, straightforward language, uncomplicated examples, and simple calculations. We think students can learn the essentials of educational measurement and evaluation without learning to dislike the subject.
3. We reference a wide array of research studies in the expanding literature pertaining to educational measurement and evaluation in order to make this book both a useful reference source and a text. Although we include mostly up-to-date sources, we do not hesitate to refer students to some of the older sources that provide valuable information.
4. We attempt to avoid both awkwardness and sexism in the use of gender pronouns by using male and female pronouns in randomly assigned chapters, rather than forcing teachers or students to be plural in all our examples, or using the more stilted and awkward passive voice, or depending upon the tortured "s/he" or the laborious "his/her" constructions.

TEACHING AND LEARNING AIDS IN THE TEXT

To simplify use for instructors and students, the book is structured as follows:

1. Each section of the book begins with a *brief orientation.*
2. Each chapter begins with a *brief overview* of the chapter content.
3. Each chapter includes a list of *specific learner objectives,* presented immediately after the overview.

4. At the end of each chapter is a *brief self-check quiz*. You also will find *application problems* within most chapters. These few items and problems are designed to help students check their general understanding of the material covered in the chapter but are not intended to cover all chapter objectives.
5. Each chapter concludes with an *annotated list of suggested readings*.

ADDITIONAL AIDS FOR STUDENT AND INSTRUCTOR

To assist the instructor, the following ancillary materials have been developed for this text:

1. A *Student Exercise Manual* (Merrell, 1993) that contains, for each chapter:
   • A chapter summary
   • An outline of the chapter content
   • Exercises to help students define key terms
   • Multiple-choice and short-answer questions and activities to guide student study
2. An *Instructor's Manual* that includes:
   • Suggestions on presentation techniques to enhance instruction
   • Additional application exercises for student assignments
   • Test items for use in assessing student knowledge and skill in relation to each chapter
3. A *Computerized Test Item Bank*, including all items from the *Instructor's Manual*, on floppy disk to facilitate instructors' efforts to create tailored tests for their classes.

STUDENT PREREQUISITES

Our treatment of statistical techniques is as nontechnical as possible. We try to relate statistical techniques to the measurement context within which they are commonly associated, but avoid preoccupation with computation and formulas, which seem more appropriate for statistics courses. In our opinion, students should have at least one elementary course in statistics before taking this educational measurement course, but we have tried to make the book understandable to those who do not have a strong background in statistics.

SUGGESTIONS FOR IMPROVEMENT

We hope that this text will meet your needs and those of your students, and we want very much to receive your comments or suggestions, as we intend to update and modify future editions to make this work as helpful as possible to those who use it.

We have included a suggestion sheet at the end of the book for feedback from instructors and students. Each instructor and student is asked to give feedback on at least one chapter, although we would welcome comment on other chapters. The end of each chapter contains a brief set of instructions identifying (by first letter of surname) students specifically invited to make comments on that chapter. Please encourage your students to complete the suggestion sheet. It is designed to be torn out and mailed in.

We would especially appreciate your comments about the entire text or as many chapters as you see fit. With your help, we hope to make the next edition even more useful to you.

Blaine R. Worthen
Karl R. White

To the Student

The main goal of this book is to help you, the student in education or the practicing educator, to become skilled and confident in using educational measurement and evaluation techniques effectively in your chosen profession.

Educational measurement is becoming ever more complex and sophisticated, which makes it a more powerful influence in educational improvement, and increases the challenge of mastering the content in this field. We have tried to make the task easier by writing in clear, straightforward language, free of technical language, mathematical jargon, or formulas. So, don't go into "symbol shock" when you encounter something numerical in the text. Even if you are rusty in math, our approach should help you survive without too much pain.

To help you organize the field of educational measurement and evaluation in your own mind, we include an introduction to each part of the book and an overview and set of objectives for each chapter. The overview is designed to give you a quick overall picture of what you will learn in the chapter, while the objectives tell you the specific details to which you should attend. Not all objectives are of equal importance. Which are most important to you depends on your own goals—whether you are primarily interested in becoming a competent user of tests in the classroom or in making measurement a major part of your educational career.

Since many measurement concepts and techniques are difficult for the beginner to understand, we include examples to illustrate how these techniques have been applied in specific situations. To help you determine how well you have mastered its content, you will find a brief multiple-choice self-check test at the end of each chapter that covers a sample of the important content. Application problems are also included in appropriate chapters to help you determine whether you can apply concepts you have learned to practical problems and questions you will encounter. Together, the self-check test and application problems should be sufficient to help you decide whether you have mastered a chapter or should devote more study to it.

Also, in case you are not already aware of it, a separate *Student Exercise Manual* has been developed to assist you in understanding and applying the content of each chapter. This supplement to the text (Merrell, 1993) is available from the publisher, and from your campus book store if your instructor has ordered it. It has many exercises that will help you. A more complete description of this workbook appears in the previous section of this preface, "To the Instructor."

Finally, we have a request to make. We very much want your specific suggestions on improving this book. It is difficult for us to use comments such as "This is a good book" or "This is a terrible book" in improving the next edition, but specific comments such as "Include more examples of how to write multiple-choice test items" or "Add a step-by-step description of how to calculate reliability for criterion-referenced measures" can be very helpful.

We would like to get your suggestions on the entire book, but *we are asking for your comments on only a single chapter*. Which chapter you comment on is your choice, but at the end of each chapter is a statement suggesting (by surname initial) which students we would invite to react to that chapter. This will assure us of getting suggestions for improving all 22 chapters. Of course, if you want to comment on a different chapter or on more than one, we will welcome all suggestions you can give us.

The Suggestion Sheet is printed at the back of the book and can be cut out and mailed in.

We hope you will find this book helpful not only in completing your present academic work but in your later career as well. Good luck!

Blaine R. Worthen
Karl R. White

SECTION ONE
Getting You Oriented

Many introductory texts in educational measurement and evaluation
plunge you immediately into the specifics of the field: definitions,
techniques, and the like. We choose rather to provide first a context for
such specifics. Section One contains information we feel is essential to
make the traditional content that follows more understandable and
meaningful. In Chapter 1 we acquaint you with the role and functions of
educational measurement and evaluation and the various uses to which
educational measures are put in today's schools. In Chapter 2 we
summarize the historical developments and trends in measurement and
evaluation that have led to how they are used in today's schools. In
Chapter 3 we examine several current measurement issues, including
concerns about test bias, the impact of legal decisions on the use of
educational measures, right-to-privacy issues, ethical implications of
testing, unethical practices that pollute test score results, the
controversy over minimum competency testing, the call to abolish
standardized testing (and contradictory demands for increased
standardized testing), and the movement to use testing to certify
classroom teachers.

Collectively, the information in these three chapters will help you
appreciate fully both the contributions and the challenges of
measurement in our schools.

CHAPTER 1

What Is Measurement and Why Study It?

Overview

Although educational measurement is a familiar activity in today's schools and universities, its functions and usefulness are not always well understood. To some educators, tests and other measures are very helpful—even essential—tools that support a host of important decisions about teaching, counseling, and placing students. To others, they are merely something to be tolerated, endured, or even criticized.

How you feel about measurement probably depends on how well you understand its role and potential utility in your own professional activities. Our purpose in this chapter is to help you expand that understanding by providing a context for the more specific material that will follow.

Objectives

Upon completing your study of this chapter, you should be able to

1. Discuss the importance of educational measurement, including the role it plays in today's educational systems.
2. List and describe various ways in which educational measures are used for making important decisions about various aspects of education.
3. Discuss the relative advantages and disadvantages of objective measurement data and subjective judgments in making educational decisions.

4. Describe one or more ways that you might use educational measurement to help you perform more effectively in your professional role.

THE ROLE OF MEASUREMENT IN EDUCATION

By now you have doubtlessly taken many educational tests, and have almost certainly formed an opinion about their usefulness. We invite you to put your opinion aside for just a moment while we review how widely tests are used and why you are not a stranger to them.

Most people who live in a nation with a well-developed educational system are familiar with various types of tests and examinations. School-age children and their parents in Miami, London, Winnipeg, and Seoul are all well acquainted with educational tests and concerned about test results. Further, testing is not confined to schools and universities but plays an important role in decisions that extend from preschool to job entry and sometimes beyond. Test results may determine who receives a scholarship or qualifies to attend a certain college, who gets hired for a decent job or receives a promotion at work. In fact, chances are that you presently attend a university or hold a job as the result, at least in part, of test scores. And you are not alone.

Despite widespread complaints and criticisms about testing, the use of tests is booming. Lasden (1985) noted a 25 to 43 percent increase in sales of tests over a two-year period for companies such as Science Research Associates and Psychological Services, Incorporated. Although we have no accurate account of how many standardized tests are administered each year, even conservative estimates are staggering. In the United States, for example, there are nearly 50 million kindergarten through high school students, most of whom take at least one standardized test each year. Since most achievement tests are multitest batteries, and since many students actually take several such tests during the course of a year, the number of individual standardized tests administered to American students could easily approach a *quarter billion* annually. When teacher-made tests are added to the total, even that estimate pales. One survey of Ohio teachers (Marso, 1985) found that the typical classroom teacher gives students nearly a hundred teacher-made tests during a school year. Extrapolated to teachers at large, that report would mean that approximately five billion teacher-made tests are administered annually to students in the United States alone.

In view of so much measurement of educational outcomes, it is astounding to realize that almost no time or resources are allocated to training educational practitioners or policy makers in sound methods of assessing student performance (Stiggens, 1991).

Do We Need So Much Measurement?

Those who support the broad use of tests argue that tests stimulate student effort, set performance expectations, and provide feedback on accomplishments. Tests, they assert, provide relevant information on the attainment of curricular goals and the effectiveness of new or revised educational programs. Supporters question how schools could adequately assess student learning or the utility of educational programs, processes, and products intended to bring that learning about without the aid of tests. As one official in the National Institute of Education put it, "States and localities will look to test results for confirmation of whether or not their reforms—reforms with substantial costs—have succeeded" (Selden, 1985, p. 16).

Public demand for evidence that teachers and schools are effectively educating students is increasing, and test scores are typically the kind of evidence the public finds most credible.[1] Given this trend, dependence on data from tests and other assessment devices is likely to increase rather than decrease in the years ahead.

States and localities are not unique in relying on tests to assess the status of educational systems. The National Commission on Excellence in Education (1983) outlined 13 general indicators of educational risk, 11 of which were based directly on educational test results.

Not everyone is happy to see tests carry as much clout as that accorded them by the National Commission. Many argue that tests do more harm than good. They point to bright students unable to demonstrate their learning on tests because of debilitating test anxiety and to problems of cultural, racial, or gender bias in tests. Critics complain that tests are artificial (and rather poor) substitutes for teachers' qualitative, professional judgments about student performance.

Our own position on testing is simple. We believe that tests and other assessment instruments are essential to the educational process, *but only to the extent that they are well designed and appropriately applied by qualified persons.*

It is not hard to defend the proposition that tests and other measurement instruments are valuable tools for educators. One need only examine the wide range of important decisions that depend on test data. For example, test results are pivotal in each of the following situations:

- Assessing student attainment of particular skills or knowledge as a basis for further instruction
- Classifying students into groups, curriculum tracks, and the like
- Selecting applicants for educational programs, jobs, or other opportunities where predicting future performance is important
- Deciding whether an individual has met some designated standard of competence
- Determining the effectiveness of particular teaching methods or curricula

Even from such an abbreviated list,[2] it should be apparent that measurement instruments are valuable tools. We find it difficult to conceive of effective teaching

---

[1] Which is not the same as saying that test scores are the most revealing or diagnostic; this point has been argued by advocates of alternative methods of assessing student performance, such as student profiles and portfolios, anecdotal records of student performance, and other devices included under the rubric of "alternative assessment" measures, which we discuss in Chapter 15.

[2] See Haladyna, Nolen, and Haas (1991) for a list of 29 uses of standardized tests.

or learning taking place in the schools without some structured, reliable way to measure student performance.

At the same time, we recognize that naive or ill-trained users can misuse or abuse even the best tools, and that improper use of good measurement instruments is commonplace. Even worse, poorly designed measures abound. One of our goals is to help you learn how to spot poorly designed instruments so you will avoid basing educational decisions on their possibly spurious results. Another goal is to provide you with the specific knowledge to use well-designed measures properly.

Subjective Judgment, Objective Testing, and Quantification

If one wave of a magic wand were to rid the earth of all tests, how would we accomplish the variety of tasks for which we now use tests and measurement data? We would rely, of course, on professional judgment. And what is so bad about professional judgment? At the risk of stating the obvious, the problem with professional judgment is that it is not always professional, and its judgments are not always sound. Educators are only human, and their judgments are colored by a variety of subtle influences, from the way a student looks to how a teacher is feeling.

Such judgments, when made without measurement data, are *subjective*—that is, personal and peculiar to that individual and likely to differ with judgments other individuals might make under the same circumstances. Conversely, measurement instruments attempt to produce *objective* judgments—meaning that most reasonable persons who are confronted with the available measurement data would score and interpret it in the same fashion. (Of course, two persons might still make subjective judgments about the same score, leading them to different conclusions.)

The choice between subjective and objective judgments should not be either/or. Personal perceptions are often insightful and may be the only way to assess certain valued educational outcomes—such as humaneness or justice—which current measures capture clumsily, if at all. Furthermore, sole reliance on measurement data is unwise, since no test score is perfectly accurate. Even shaky subjective judgments may be better than scores on measures that may be invalid or irrelevant to the decision at hand.

Combining objective measurement data with educators' professional judgments allows us the best of both worlds. Objective test data offer protection against the pressures, politics, and presuppositions that often result in weak, capricious judgments when subjectivity is left to carry the burden alone. And the teacher's subjective, commonsense awareness and knowledge are often vital in counterbalancing skewed or misleading test results. In our view, objective measurement data and less objective professional judgments are necessary partners in an effective educational assessment program.

Let us say a word about *quantification*, which underlies measurement and supports objectivity.[3] Some qualities seem to many educators to be simply unmeasurable—essentially qualitative rather than quantitative. One student seems

---

[3] In our discussion of quantification, we draw somewhat on a much earlier work by Ebel (1965).

kinder than another; Mary seems more sensitive than Bill to the feelings of others. Kindness and sensitivity are only examples of many qualities that are not easily quantified, at least not with present measures.

Other educators, however, argue that *all* important outcomes of education are measurable. To be important, the logic goes, an educational outcome must make a difference. If it does make a difference, then the basis for measurement exists (even though it may not be measurable with current tests or techniques). Most qualities of interest to educators are, therefore, potentially quantifiable. Indeed, were it not so, we would despair of being able to distinguish between higher and lower "quality" of performance on those dimensions.

We see this line of reasoning as generally but not absolutely true. We suggest that educators will continue to rely, in the foreseeable future, on qualitative judgments on dimensions such as kindness and justice. But this does not detract from the essential importance of using quantitative measurement wherever possible.

If you accept our conclusion that schools and teachers will be increasingly required to provide evidence of desired educational outcomes, then a second conclusion is inescapable: You are going to be even more involved with measurement in the future than teachers in the past have been. Perhaps your own role in educational measurement and evaluation will become clearer as we consider the various uses of educational measures in more detail.

VARIOUS USES OF EDUCATIONAL MEASURES

We mentioned earlier the wide range of uses that educators make of tests. But *educators* is a broad term. Who specifically employs tests and measures in educational systems? The *Standards for Educational and Psychological Tests* (American Psychological Association, American Educational Research Association, & National Council on Measurement in Education, 1974) defined a test user as "one who chooses tests, interprets scores, or makes decisions based on test scores . . . not necessarily the person who administers the test following standard instructions or who does routine scoring" (p. 58).[4]

In education, then, virtually everyone is a test user, including:

- Teachers—to determine students' progress in learning specific knowledge or skills.

---

[4] The American Psychological Association (APA), the American Educational Research Association (AERA), and the National Council on Measurement in Education (NCME) have collaborated on three sets of standards, published successively in 1966, 1974, and 1985. In 1985, AERA was listed as senior author of those standards, which will hereafter be referenced as AERA et al., while APA was listed as senior author for the 1966 and 1974 versions, referred to hereafter as APA et al. (1966) and APA et al. (1974). The 1966 volume is now of only historical interest. There are significant differences in the 1974 and 1985 versions of the *Standards* (which is how we will frequently refer to these volumes hereafter to avoid tedious referencing). While we feel the 1985 version is an important update, we still find much of use in the 1974 version. We shall designate by year whenever we refer to or quote from a particular version; "*Standards*," with no date designation will refer to the contribution of both the 1974 and 1985 volumes together.

- Students—to ascertain if they are learning what they are being asked to learn.
- Parents—to determine how well their children are doing in school.
- Principals—to determine how well their students are learning.
- School psychologists—to assess students' particular strengths and needs to guide prescription and treatment more effectively.
- School counselors—to guide students in choosing courses of study and careers, and in making personal adjustments.
- Lawmakers and policy makers—to set educational priorities and allocate resources.
- Research and evaluation directors—to collect data to extend general knowledge about educational processes or help evaluate the effectiveness of particular school programs, instructional products, and the like.
- News reporters—to report on the quality of schooling and other educational issues.
- Lawyers—to argue for or against the appropriateness and legality of particular educational practices (perhaps even testing itself).

So, educational tests and measures are employed by a wide range of people both in and out of education. But how competent are they in using the results obtained from tests and measures? Authors of the 1974 *Standards* suggest, "Users of educational and psychological tests in schools . . . and other places where educators and psychologists work should have had at least some formal training" (APA et al., 1974, p. 58). They define competence in test use as "a combination of knowledge of psychometric principles, knowledge of the problem situation in which the testing is to be done, technical skill, and some wisdom" (p. 6). Unfortunately, many test users lack formal training and do not meet this definition of competence. (We hope this book will provide you with the necessary knowledge and expertise so that you are not among them.)

How do all these people use tests? Again, the purposes are impressively wide ranging, but can be grouped into the following five categories based on the types of decisions that will be based on the test results.[5]

1. Direct instructional decisions
2. Instructional management decisions
3. Entry-exit decisions
4. Program, administrative and policy decisions
5. Decisions associated with expanding our knowledge base

---

[5] In developing these categories, we have relied on Findley (1963), the *Standards* (1974, 1985), Kubiszyn & Borich (1987), Thorndike & Hagen (1977), and Anderson, Stiggins, & Gordon (1980)—especially the latter two.

1. Direct Instructional Decisions

Observing, measuring, and drawing conclusions are ongoing activities in most classrooms. Teachers not only test students to see what they have learned, but they also observe the learning process. Raised eyebrows, glazed eyes, and slumped posture all send signals that teachers struggle to interpret correctly. One teacher observes how children use algorithms to solve math problems in order to plan the next instructional step. Another uses a test he designed himself to diagnose the learning problems of students who seem to be having difficulty. Commercial, text-linked tests help teachers determine when it is time to move to the next unit of content. *Snapshot tests* (''Would all of you who think the answer is 'Venus' raise your hands?'') provide a quick reading of how many students have internalized some bit of knowledge. Between grading periods, teachers evaluate students on everything from academic performance to manners. Indeed, measurement and evaluation are ever present in the classroom.

Let's take a closer look at four types of direct instructional decisions.

Immediate Instructional Decisions

Every teacher's day is filled with dozens of instructional dilemmas that must be resolved on the spot. Should I review this concept again, or do the students grasp it? Should I introduce exponents today or will they understand it better after we've spent more time on multiplication? As important as those decisions are, they are more pedagogy than measurement, since they are made without the aid of any formal assessment or measurement tools (although they often depend on *informal* assessment, as we will discuss later).

Grading Decisions

Here the teacher is also on familiar ground. Valid evaluation of what students have learned is impossible without some type of testing, whether it be individual interviews or a commercially prepared test. Most often, grades are based on teacher-made assessments, and grading will only be as good as the tests or other assessment devices used. Later, we will help you learn to construct and interpret your own classroom tests or alternative assessments and translate scores into grades or other performance indicators.

Diagnostic Decisions

Tests are probably used more often for diagnostic purposes than for any other. Teachers often base diagnostic decisions about the learning progress of students and classes on tests they have constructed themselves. Although school psychologists, special educators, and other specialists trained in the use of special standardized diagnostic measures are valuable resources, teachers face too many diagnostic decisions to rely entirely on help from others, and many small districts have few such specialists to which teachers can turn for help. It is critical, therefore, that teachers develop skill in test construction, and in using alternative assessment methods where appropriate.

Instructional Planning Decisions

Teacher-made tests play an important, if sometimes indirect, role in prompting better planning. Teachers *can* scatter classroom tests carelessly along a twisted, unplanned pedagogical pathway with little thought about how the tests relate to instruction; but in the process of developing classroom tests teachers usually are made to think carefully about their instructional goals and how to reach them. In short, teacher-made tests facilitate and support instructional planning decisions. As Nitko (1989) has demonstrated, tests that are integrated directly with instruction are the ideal.

2.   Instructional Management Decisions

Instructional management decisions, which have to do with placing students in situations where they are most likely to succeed, are typically made by school administrators, psychologists, counselors, or committees, rather than by individual teachers. Such decisions fall into either classification and placement decisions or counseling and guidance decisions.

Classification and Placement Decisions

Educators use tests as prime tools for placing individual students in particular groups, classes, or course sequences. A placement test used to sort tenth-grade students into remedial, standard, or honors English is a good example. Reading readiness tests used at the beginning of first grade for grouping in reading is another. Classification and placement tests are generally broader in coverage and are used far less frequently than diagnostic tests—usually only once or twice per year. Such tests are sometimes called *prescriptive*, because different scores suggest students should receive different treatments.

Standardized tests are often used for placement decisions, but should *never* be the sole basis for grouping students or deciding what instructional program a student will follow (Airasian, 1979). Supplemental judgments of teachers and specialists are vital.

Counseling and Guidance Decisions

Tests often play a pivotal role in guiding students in their career choices or planning future educational pursuits of programs of study. Students, their parents, and guidance counselors base decisions on tests that cover broad academic areas and tell the students where they stand in relation to other students. Academic test scores should never serve as the sole criterion, however. Guidance decisions, so important to a student's future, should include interest tests, personal adjustment inventories, and other affective measures well known to most guidance counselors.

3.   Entry-Exit Decisions

Educators depend heavily on tests to help them decide (1) who should enter particular educational institutions or programs of study and (2) who has completed the requirements to leave that program (honorably, that is). We will consider separately entry or *selection* decisions and exit or *certification* decisions.

Selection Decisions

Scores on the Scholastic Aptitude Test (SAT), the Graduate Record Examination (GRE), and other similar tests play an important role in admissions screening at many institutions, but even test producers caution against using test scores as the sole criterion in admission decisions, proposing that prior grades, recommendations, and interviews should be used as well. But because of the ease and speed with which scores can be examined and compared, tests have become increasingly important in college admissions. Moreover, test alternatives are suspect for a variety of reasons—high school grades because of differential grade inflation in different high schools; personal recommendations because of possible nonconfidentiality; and interviews because of interviewers' prejudices and the applicants' interview skills, which may have little to do with success in the programs (Ravitch, 1984).

Psychological screening tests administered by employers to job applicants are also examples of tests used in making selection decisions. Another example is found in tests used to help decide who "qualifies" for remedial programs.

It is sometimes difficult to distinguish between selection and placement, but the distinction is easier if you remember that

- In *placement* everyone gets placed—it is only a question of in which group or track, while
- In *selection* there is a limitation on who participates—some people will be selected and others rejected, not receiving placement in any other group or track in the relevant agency.

Measures used to help guide selection decisions are typically designed, administered, and interpreted by testing specialists.

Certification Decisions

Educators and agencies that control admission to various professions routinely *certify* whether acceptable minimum levels of skill or knowledge have been attained by students, or provide licenses that allow individuals to practice particular professions. High school diplomas, a Red Cross lifeguard certificate, and a license to practice law are all examples of credentialing decisions. A key characteristic of tests used for credentialing decisions is that the pass-fail criteria are standard for everyone taking the examination, whereas those who take a *selection* test like the GRE will find that different departments or colleges require different minimum scores.

As Smith and Hambleton (1990) make evident, tests used in credentialing decisions are among the most controversial and frequently challenged, no doubt because they affect individual lives so significantly. They cannot be simply filed and forgotten.

4. Program, Administrative, and Policy Decisions

Program, administrative, and policy decisions do not directly influence individuals, but rather affect educational programs, curricula, or systems. Three examples follow.

Program or Curriculum Decisions

Which of two computer-assisted writing programs is better for our school? Is our humanities curriculum producing the outcomes we desire? The answers to such questions are best found through program or curriculum evaluation, which depends on a variety of educational measures. (See Chapter 22 for details on setting up a good school evaluation system.) Unfortunately, existing measurement instruments—including standardized tests—are often unsuited for making judgments about specific local programs; therefore, new measures must be developed.

Administrative Decisions

Administrators at various levels scrutinize trends in achievement scores and other test data within the systems for which they have responsibility, and their decisions are often heavily influenced by these tests. They may ask, how effective is this system in preparing students academically? Have "career ladder" merit pay increases for teachers produced better student outcomes? Administrators keep an eye on scores yielded by standardized tests and any other relevant measures to help them answer such questions. This form of administrative monitoring or "quality control" is different from evaluation in that it focuses not on specific program or curriculum innovations, but rather looks for trends and patterns over time, drawing on the data for systemwide planning.

Policy Decisions

Legislators and other policy makers look to test results for information about educational progress and problems in their jurisdiction. In fact, tests have become the single most pervasive influence in many policy decisions—often being used as the primary basis for setting national and state educational priorities and allocating funds to schools. Tests can even set implicit instructional priorities—determining the curriculum—because teachers will stress and students will strive to learn that which they know will be tested. The dangers in policy makers' overdependence on test scores is described this way by Madaus (1985 b):

> For decades, we have warned test users *never* to use a single administration of a test to make important decisions about students. I see this tradition . . . eroding in the face of policy demands. Policymakers mandate situations where test scores are used to make crucial decisions about certification and placement. . . . I was trained in more cautious times, before policymakers discovered our tests and long before the rush to litigation. However, I still believe that we should not use test scores as necessary conditions for placement, certification, promotion, or credentialing, or in merit pay schemes. Test information can play an important part in such crucial decisions, but ultimately the decisions should be made by educators. (p. 7)

We agree heartily.

5. Decisions Associated with Expanding Our Knowledge Base

Educational measurement has supplied a rich array of tools for use in research, so essential to expanding our yet-limited knowledge base about educational processes. Beyond the scope of this book, educational research and the various types of measurement instruments and strategies it uses are discussed in a separate volume (Borg & Gall, 1989).

SUGGESTED READINGS

Anderson, B. L., Stiggins, R. J., & Gordon, D. W. (1980). *Educational testing facts and issues: A layperson's guide to testing in the schools*. Portland, OR: Northwest Regional Educational Laboratory and California State Department of Education.
    This booklet addresses the role of testing in today's public education system and presents a series of questions and answers that will be of particular interest to teachers, administrators, school board members, and others. An excellent overview is provided of test purposes, test users, and common types of tests.

Selden, R. W. (1985). Measuring excellence: The dual role of testing in reforming education. *Curriculum review, 25*(1), 14–32.
    This article provides perspective on the uses to which tests can be put to improve education, reasons for test use, problems stemming from misuse of tests, and ways misuses of tests can be avoided.

SELF-CHECK QUIZ

Choose the *best* answer for each question.

1. In comparison to the number of standardized tests administered during a typical school year, the number of teacher-made classroom tests administered during that same period is:
   a. much larger.
   b. slightly larger.
   c. about the same.
   d. slightly smaller.
   e. much smaller.

2. One relative advantage of subjective judgment over objective testing is that:
   a. different evaluators are more apt to draw the same conclusions.
   b. presuppositions and politics tend to play a smaller role.
   c. qualities that are not easily quantified are more readily assessed.

3. The authors believe that tests are essential to the educational process, but only to the extent that they are:
   a. prepared by the teacher most familiar with the students' abilities.
   b. standardized and certified by the National Commission on Education.
   c. well-designed and appropriately applied by qualified persons.

4. Which of the following is an example of using a test for placement purposes?
   a. Choosing students to participate in an after-school enrichment program based on their math test scores.
   b. Dividing a class into three reading-ability levels based on the students' reading test scores.
   c. Screening out college applicants due to their low Scholastic Aptitude Test scores.

5. Which of the following best describes the difference between placement decisions and selection decisions?
   a. Placement decisions allow all to participate in the program while selection decisions do not.
   b. Placement decisions are generally based on standardized test results while selection decisions are not.
   c. Placement decisions make diagnostic use of tests while selection decisions do not.
6. According to the 1974 *Standards for Educational and Psychological Tests*, a test user is defined as one who:
   a. administers and scores tests following standard instructions.
   b. chooses tests, interprets scores, or makes decisions based on scores.
   c. takes tests in order to be evaluated for mastery or achievement.
7. In recent years, the use of standardized tests in the United States has:
   a. increased substantially.
   b. stayed about the same.
   c. decreased substantially.
8. According to Madaus, decisions such as placement, certification, and promotion should ultimately be:
   a. based on test scores.
   b. left up to the individual organization.
   c. made by educators.
   d. mandated by policy makers.

SUGGESTION SHEET

If your last name starts with the letter *A*, please complete the Suggestion Sheet at the end of the book while this chapter is still fresh in your mind.

CHAPTER 2

How Did We Get Where We Are in Measurement?

Overview

The roles, functions, and uses of measurement did not spring full-blown onto the educational scene. Each has historical roots, and it is important to discuss some of the developments and trends that have led us to where we are.

We have organized this chapter into four major sections:

- Early "pre-scientific" uses of measurement
- Development of scientific measurement techniques: pre-1920
- Important trends and developments from 1920 to 1965 that have shaped today's use of educational measurement
- Recent developments and trends in educational measurement that provide the current context for measurement and evaluation in our schools

Objectives

Upon completing your study of this chapter, you should be able to

1. Describe important historical developments in measurement up to the mid-1960s, identifying the individuals, events, and forces that influenced and shaped those developments.
2. Describe major trends and developments in measurement that have occurred since the mid-1960s.

3. Discuss the importance of each development or trend you identified in Objective 2 and its implications for educational institutions.

EARLY "PRESCIENTIFIC" USES OF EDUCATIONAL MEASUREMENT

Ours is not the only generation to be well acquainted with measurement and evaluation. Various means of testing human performance are sprinkled throughout recorded history. In the Bible, for example, we find (in Judges 12:4–6) the first recorded instance of a short, oral examination devised by the Gileadite armies to detect vanquished Ephraimites who attempted to escape under assumed identities. Positioning themselves at the "passages of Jordan," the Gileadites refused passage to anyone unable to pronounce the word "shibboleth" correctly, knowing that Ephraimites mispronounced it as "Sibboleth." This inability to pronounce the *h* proved unfortunate for some 42,000 Ephraimites who failed to pass this single-question *final* examination and were summarily executed. Thankfully, most testing has been conducted for somewhat more educational purposes.

As early as 2000 B.C. Chinese officials used civil service examinations to measure proficiency of candidates for public office (DuBois, 1970) and, by the time of the Han Dynasty (206 B.C. to A.D. 220) this had grown into an elaborate series of written essay examinations. Hu (1984) explains that success in these written essay examinations was the only route to the status and enormous wealth that came to those in high public office. But only a tiny percentage of those who took these tests passed and became eligible for public appointment. Soon all manner of clever ways were conceived to beat the system, including cribbing, impersonation, and bribery of examiners. The state responded with preventive measures such as frisking the examinees for crib notes, patrolling during examinations, requiring proof of identity, and having examinations recopied before scoring so bribed examiners could not recognize the handwriting of their collaborators. Some of these stratagems and counter-stratagems have a familiar ring about them even today.

The ancient Greeks also used examinations as a part of the normal educational process. Socrates used oral questioning as an integral part of the teaching-learning process some four centuries before Christ. The effectiveness of this method resulted in its continued use as the primary mode of examination for many centuries. The recitation mode that persisted in many schools well into the 1900s is but a degenerate offspring of this early method of Socratic questioning. Of course, oral examinations have been a central part of university curricula since universities began and remain in use even today. But by the late 1800s, oral exams were giving way to written tests that provided the first real potential for laying a scientific foundation for educational measurement.[1]

---

[1] Even though the earlier Chinese civil service examinations were written, they were hardly scientific; the absence of objective standards and agreed-upon criteria resulted in passing scores being as much a result of luck, or the mood of the examiner, as of performance. Small wonder that fate was often blamed by those who failed the tests.

DEVELOPMENT OF EARLY SCIENTIFIC
MEASUREMENT TECHNIQUES: PRE-1920

The seeds of scientific educational measurement in the United States were sown in the last century.[2] From 1838 to 1850, Horace Mann used results of written tests to identify educational concerns in Massachusetts, simultaneously arguing persuasively for the superiority of written over oral examinations (Mann, 1845). In 1845, the Boston School Committee made the first use of printed tests for wide-scale assessment of student achievement. In 1847 the testing was discontinued because no use was made of the results (Travers, 1983).

Oral tests continued to be dominant for another half century, despite sporadic proposals for written examinations and objective scoring (Chadwick, 1864; White, 1886). And when written tests were used, most were essay examinations that depended on highly subjective scoring procedures.

In 1892, attention was galvanized on testing procedures by Joseph Rice, a physician turned educational reformer. In appraising American public education, Rice visited schools in 36 cities and talked with over a thousand teachers before issuing scathing indictments of school administrators as political hacks and teachers as incompetents who blindly led innocent students in singsong drill and rote repetition. Rice was not overly popular with many educators.

Turning his attack on the practice of rote spelling drills, Rice organized an ambitious assessment program carried out in large school systems throughout the United States. To document his claim that school time was inefficiently used, he developed and administered specially constructed tests, under *uniform* conditions—something largely ignored before then. This was perhaps the first (albeit crude) use of norm-referenced comparative testing. After administering his spelling tests to some 29,000 students, he found negligible differences in students' performance from one school to another, regardless of the amount of time spent on spelling instruction. Rice used these data to support his proposals for restructuring instruction (Rice, 1897a,b).

Meanwhile, several other movements were beginning to shape the future of educational measurement as calls for more scientific measurement began to mount. The first of these came from E. L. Thorndike, often referred to as the father of the educational testing movement because of his far-reaching work in both achievement and intelligence testing. His pioneer measurement textbook (Thorndike, 1904) gained support for the many standardized achievement tests and scales he and his students devised. Thorndike was enormously influential in persuading educators that it was worthwhile to employ precise measurement techniques to evaluate student learning. Largely because of Thorndike and his students, measurement technology flourished in the United States during the early twentieth century, and testing emerged as the primary means of evaluating schools. Standardized achievement tests were developed and used in a variety of subject areas, and by World War I, many large school systems had bureaus of

---

[2] See DuBois (1970), Travers (1983), and Haney (1984) for more extensive treatments of the history of educational measurement from the mid-1800s to the dates of their respective writing.

school research working on large-scale assessments of student achievement (Madaus, Airasian, & Kellaghan, 1980).

Based on Binet's earlier development of the first "intelligence" test, Terman's Stanford-Binet intelligence test, published in 1916, also had profound influence on measurement, paving the way for a barrage of individual and group mental ability tests. By 1918, individual and group tests were being developed for use in many educational and psychological decisions. Even the military accepted the notion that good decisions about individuals could be made only when objective test information was available. This belief also extended to psychologists' use of tests in screening job applicants. By the early 1900s, about 50 percent of federal jobs were awarded by civil service examinations, and tests began to appear for screening nongovernmental typists, clerical workers, and salespersons.

Meanwhile, objective testing (tests that depend on selected responses, such as multiple-choice items) was also getting a boost from a series of studies that found grading of written essay examinations highly arbitrary and unreliable (Meyer, 1908; Johnson, 1911; Starch, 1913). Startling variations in grades were found when the same person marked the same paper on different occasions, or when the same paper was scored by several different teachers. Such disturbing revelations seriously undermined the credibility of subjective scoring and grading practices then in use, creating an intellectual environment in which the objective testing proposals Thorndike and others were making could take root and grow.

TRENDS IN EDUCATIONAL MEASUREMENT: 1920 TO 1965

The 1920s saw increasingly widespread use of objective tests in public and private schools. Norm-referenced tests emerged as the new standard for measuring individual performance. In 1923, the *Stanford Achievement Tests* became the first published comprehensive achievement test battery. The New York Board of Regents examination appeared in 1927 and the Iowa tests in 1929. Commercialism in testing had come of age. Criticisms of the new objective tests were also launched during the 1920s by such luminaries as Walter Lippmann, the journalist, who decried psychologists' efforts to construct general tests of intelligence (Lippmann, 1922). During the 1930s, criticism continued amid growing concerns that narrowly focused tests might overemphasize particular types of content at the expense of other, more important outcomes. For example, critics of Dewey's progressive education philosophy maintained that students educated in those high schools would fare poorly in higher education programs when compared to students educated in conventional Carnegie-unit curricula. This controversy led to the landmark Eight Year Study, in which Ralph Tyler developed and used a wide variety of objective instruments to measure a wide range of educational outcomes in 30 high schools. The results (Smith & Tyler, 1942) showed how new objective assessment procedures could be developed to measure such important outcomes as personal adjustment, aesthetic sensitivity, critical thinking, and other higher-order mental processes.

By the mid-1930s, over half of the states in the United States had some form of statewide testing. More and more test publishers and other commercial groups turned their attention to the production and scoring of standardized tests, including IBM's introduction of machine scoring in 1935. Buros's test compilations grew from a relatively short bibliography of 44 pages in 1934 to over 400 pages (listing more than 4,000 available tests) in 1938 (Buros, 1938). In addition, teacher-made achievement tests mushroomed, forming a basis for most school grading systems.

During the 1940s and early 1950s, earlier measurement developments were consolidated and applied. The National Council on Measurement in Education (NCME) was formed specifically to provide a forum for improving educational measurement, and in 1947 the Educational Testing Service (ETS) was established and quickly became an influential force in educational testing. Psychologists and educators joined forces in the 1950s to develop standards intended to guide both test developers and test users, an effort that would continue to the present.

The 1950s and 1960s also saw numerous technical developments that influenced the quality of objective tests, including two influential taxonomies of possible educational objectives (Bloom, Engelhart, Furst, Hill, & Krathwohl, 1956; Krathwohl, Bloom, & Mazia, 1964), which have become indispensable reference tools for educators.

Despite these developments, popular criticisms of testing continued. Such works as *The Tyranny of Testing* (Hoffmann, 1962), *They Shall Not Pass* (Black, 1962), and *The Brain Watchers* (Gross, 1962), prompted the American Psychological Association (APA) and the United States Congress to give serious consideration to issues of test use. Although these popular criticisms did not topple the testing industry, they did contribute to increased sensitivity about privacy rights of examinees and to later laws aimed at the protection of human subjects in research and evaluation studies.

Finally, in 1965, the Elementary and Secondary Education Act (ESEA) mandated evaluation studies in thousands of school districts across the United States, especially in federally supported programs for education of children from low income families. The result was a huge influx of norm-referenced tests, chosen because of governmental support of a norm-referenced model for judging program effectiveness.

RECENT DEVELOPMENTS AND TRENDS IN EDUCATIONAL MEASUREMENT

Since the mid-1960s, most significant developments in educational measurement have been direct or indirect responses to taxpayers' concerns about whether public education is accomplishing what they expect of it. The increasing public outcry for educational accountability has caused policy makers and educators to rethink education's responsibilities and outcomes and ways of documenting them. Following are 10 recent trends that have helped reshape educational measurement and evaluation.

1. National Assessment of Educational Progress

Desire to increase educational achievement has fostered student testing programs at both federal and state levels. The first of these, the National Assessment of Educational Progress (NAEP), began in 1964 with an ambitious plan to assess annually the performance of U.S. students and young adults (ages 9, 13, 17, and 26 to 35) in ten subject areas (e.g., mathematics, writing, art) by administering exercises to a national sample drawn from virtually all geographic and socioeconomic sectors of U.S. society. The first NAEP data were collected in 1969.

Concerns about potential misuses of NAEP results at first caused substantial opposition among educators, but misuse was prevented by carefully controlled reporting that allowed only census-like comparisons on such dimensions as socioeconomic status, regions of the country, gender, and the like—and resistance crumbled. NAEP's acceptability among school administrators may have been due less to the value of the information it produced than to its avoidance of comparisons among states, districts, and individual schools.

The general approach used by NAEP provided a framework others would emulate. State departments of education soon began designing state assessment systems, and state legislatures began requiring school reports on student achievement in subjects like reading and mathematics. Most sta. es today conduct some type of statewide testing—often based on the NAEP design.

In recent years, however, NAEP's assessment plans, focus, and reporting have been modified significantly. Now known as "The Nation's Report Card," NAEP reports congressionally mandated surveys of educational achievement of American students in various curriculum areas. But far from its beginnings (when comparisons were purposefully precluded), NAEP has recently reported state-by-state comparisons of results of a voluntary eight-grade math assessment conducted with representative samples of public school students in 37 participating states (Mullis, Dossey, Owen, & Phillips, 1991). This "Trial State Assessment Program" is slated to include other subject areas at various grade levels. The probability looms large that—because of public pressure for comparative information on school effectiveness—states not choosing to participate in the first round or two may not have that option long.

2. The Accountability Movement

Despite results reported through NAEP and state assessment programs, the 1970s saw continued skepticism about the extent to which public investments in the schools were producing desired outcomes. Even the statewide testing results left many legislators troubled because they had no way to know which school districts were productive or unproductive, or whether some districts were frugal with the public purse while others returned too little for the taxpayers' investment.

Into this climate came those who proclaimed that greater accountability could reform education (Lessinger, 1970; Lessinger & Tyler, 1971). Not surprisingly, legislators liked the notion that school personnel should be held accountable for educating students.

Several state legislatures passed educational accountability laws that required each district to set educational goals, test to see how well those goals had been attained, and report results back to the lawmakers. So far, so good. But excess enthusiasm caused some state legislatures to go one step too far, ruling that *next* year's budget for each school district would depend on how well the district's test results demonstrated it had done in attaining the objectives it had set for itself *this* year. The more success in attaining objectives, the more money next year, and vice versa. (Never mind that struggling districts might well need more money to succeed, not less.)

Efforts to implement such flawed legislation were met by a storm of opposition. Fortunately, lawmakers recanted and this momentary flirtation with legislative insanity faded nearly as quickly as it had come upon the scene, leaving the concept of accountability (at least as defined by lawmakers) in general disrepute among most educators. But during its fleeting moment of glory, it spurred numerous efforts to match measurement instruments to local objectives. Although few legislatures today attempt to pass explicit accountability legislation, this movement left a legacy that influences countless other bits of educational legislation aimed at assuring that taxpayers' dollars are translated into acceptable levels of student achievement.

3. The Trend toward Criterion-referenced Measurement

Perhaps the most important outgrowth of the accountability movement, and one of the most popularized developments in measurement during the past twenty years, is the increasing use of criterion-referenced measurement.[3] The accountability movement had urged the use of specific educational objectives to determine how well the schools were performing. In support of such an objectives-based approach, Popham and others (Popham & Husek, 1969; Popham, 1978) argued that traditional norm-referenced tests (NRTs) were flawed for several reasons: (1) they failed to provide precise instructional targets; (2) they often produced unrecognized mismatches between what was taught and what was tested; and (3) they purposefully omitted important items that most examinees would answer correctly—thus ignoring the very information teachers thought most important. Although these charges were disputed by advocates of NRTs, they were persuasive to those already struggling to enforce better specification and testing of learning objectives. Soon, test publishers and several state education agencies began to shift away from NRTs and toward criterion-referenced tests (CRTs), and measurement experts (e.g., Haladyna & Roid, 1983) focused attention on how CRTs should be constructed. Even though the accountability movement had failed, it had infused new life into CRTs. Recently, agencies as powerful as the National Education Association have issued resolutions supporting CRTs as a viable alternative to or replacement for standardized NRTs. Many thoughtful measurement experts have consistently maintained, however, that the labels CRT and NRT

---

[3] Criterion-referenced measurement and norm-referenced measurement (to be introduced shortly) are defined and described more fully in Chapter 4.

merely distinguish different types of test score interpretations, not different types of tests. More will be said about this later.

4.   Trends in Scholastic Aptitude and Achievement Test Scores

Ever since standardized tests came into broad use, student test scores have been vigilantly scrutinized; the nation has kept its collective finger on the throbbing pulse of standardized test scores—and fretted when that pulse weakened.

Until the mid-1960s, test scores were generally increasing and all was well. Then in 1964, the national average score on the Scholastic Aptitude Test (SAT) slipped. A one-time fluke, most observers assumed. But they continued to fall every year for the next 15 years. Other tests of general aptitude showed the same unnerving downward trends between the mid 1960s and early 1980s, including the venerable American College Test (ACT) and GRE.

These remarkably consistent declines across aptitude tests were alarming, and they were echoed by trends in achievement test scores for the same period. Waters (1981) reported that composite achievement scores for all major achievement test batteries showed pervasive downward trends beginning with fifth grade. The declines were not trivial. For example, on the General Educational Development test (GED), 75 percent of the 1962 examinees passed (met minimum requirements to receive a high school equivalency credential), compared to only 60 percent of the examinees who passed in 1979.

One conclusion was inescapable. The average national performance on scholastic aptitude and achievement tests had slipped dramatically! In one government-supported publication, it was announced that

> This decline has been found in nearly all subjects and all regions of the country, and in almost all national testing programs, ranging from college entrance tests to elementary school achievement test batteries . . . . declines tend to be more pronounced through the high grade levels . . . . (Anderson et al., 1980, p. 11)

Alarms were sounded. Crimes had been committed against American youth. Searches were launched to find the guilty, to uncover any plausible culprits that might have contributed to such tragic backsliding. Presidential commissions were appointed to investigate potential causes of such slippage.

Critics of standardized tests were quick to propose that the problem lay with the tests themselves rather than with the educational system, arguing that standardized tests had no place in the schools. The testing industry responded that tests could hardly be faulted for examinees' inability to add two-digit numerals.

Amid the controversy, one perplexing fact was largely overlooked. Average scores on some tests had actually *increased* during this period of general test-score decline. But no one seemed to notice these countertrends, and drawing attention to them was little more effective than pointing out to frenzied sharks that the blood in the water is coming only from a small wound. Test scores had declined, and any gains seemed of small consequence in the context of concern that permeated American education in the late 1970s. Some explanation of the ''declining test scores phenomenon'' was essential, both for valid scientific reasons and as a political form of national face-saving. Volumes of explanations were published. Space does not permit our discussing the multiple factors—many outside of the schools control—that could have caused declines in test scores. For excellent summaries of the many hypotheses proposed as plausible explanations of this troubling phenomenon, readers are referred to fascinating analyses by Anderson et al. (1980), Austin and Garbar (1982), Haney (1984), and Turnbull (1985).

We probably will never know which of the many proposed explanations actually played a part in the test score slippage, for before researchers were able to arrive at any definitive conclusions, test scores simply stopped declining.

The test score decline ended as mysteriously as it had begun—slowing, steadying, and then gradually turning upward for most tests somewhere between 1979 and 1982. Since then, most national test scores made small but steady increases until the mid-1980s, after which they have flattened or see-sawed across the past few years.

Whatever the causes of the trends in national test scores, this much is certain: They have had profound effects on schools. Concerns over test declines have played a direct role in several significant educational developments:

- Educators' challenging the appropriateness of tests
- Minimum competency testing, viewed by proponents as necessary for putting rigor back into American education
- Increased attention to basic skills instruction in math, reading, and writing
- Litigation attacking the validity of using test scores for selection and promotion decisions

More will be said about the outcomes of the declining test scores in our discussion of current measurement issues in Chapter 3.

5. The Establishment of Minimum Competency Testing Programs

It is difficult to define *minimum competency testing* (MCT) precisely, since the term has come to be used so many different ways. We use "MCT" to refer to criterion-referenced, objective testing mandated by state or local governing bodies who have decided on minimum standards of competency they will accept for key educational pass-fail decisions about individual students (or teachers).

The MCT movement was triggered at least in part by the test score declines we discussed earlier. Indeed, many educators see proposals for installing minimum competency testing programs as little more than the cynical expression of continued lack of public confidence in American education. As Jaeger (1982) pointed out, "minimum competency achievement testing is primarily a political movement, not an educational movement. Such programs reflect the blind faith of state legislatures and state boards of education in their power to mandate—through law, regulation, or administrative action—some minimum level of educational success'' (p. 227).

Such beliefs resulted in a legislative stampede to develop MCT programs, especially during the late 1970s. Some form of MCT program now exists or is under consideration in almost every state in the United States, mandated by either the state legislature or the state education agency. In addition, many local school districts have initiated their own MCT programs, either voluntarily or as an alternative to an otherwise required state program (Jaeger, 1989). Amid the swirling debates about whether it is wise or technically sound to use tests in this way, MCT use continues to expand and many measurement experts devote their time to devising better and more unassailable MCT programs. MCT has become a pervasive and controversial national phenomenon. Given the direct use of their results in making important decisions about individuals, it is not surprising that the use of MCT has been repetitively challenged in U.S. courts. We shall discuss the controversy and legal issues surrounding MCT programs in Chapter 3.

6.   Renewed Calls for Reform in Educational Measurement

Renewed criticisms of testing occurred in the early 1970s, sparked by indications that some widely used standardized tests discriminate against racial or cultural minorities. The National Education Association voted for an immediate end to standardized testing in the schools, and Ralph Nader, the consumer advocate, leveled numerous charges against the ETS and the tests it had developed. During the 1980s, a growing body of literature on the effects of using standardized tests to make high-stakes decisions emerged. From these studies, many educators—and not a few measurement specialists—have concluded that such testing practices may be having serious negative effects on the education of America's youth (for reasons we will discuss in Chapter 3). Yet despite growing discontent in many sectors, "Support for using standardized tests to reform our public schools is mounting rapidly" (Darling-Hammond & Lieberman, 1992, p. B.1). Clearly the proper role of standardized tests in American schools will be a major issue in the 1990s. Whether or not critics ever derail standardized testing, the attention they have forced on issues of fairness in all testing has had far-reaching impact. (Much more will be said in Chapter 15 about criticisms of standardized tests and what research says about this topic.)

7.   Development of Professional Organizations
for Measurement Specialists

Three professional associations—APA, AERA, and NCME—have significantly contributed to the improvement of educational and psychological measures, particularly in producing sets of standards for educational and psychological testing. Of these three, only NCME was established specifically to further the advancement of sound measurement techniques in education. NCME is primarily concerned with such issues as test theory and development, test interpretation and use, test monitoring and control, test user education, and the social and political consequences of testing (Lennon, 1982). Collectively, these three organizations have contributed greatly to the improvement of educational measurement and evaluation.

8. Positions Taken by Professional Associations toward Measurement Issues

In addition to the direct contributions to measurement made by APA, AERA, and NCME, the attitudes and positions taken by other professional education associations have the potential of influencing their members and, thus, of influencing testing practices in the schools. The perspectives of several practitioner-oriented professional associations are captured in the following summary reported in *Educational Measurement: Issue and Practice* (1982):

- *National Education Association*—Voted in 1972 for an immediate moratorium on standardized testing, then softened its stance in 1982, warning against inappropriate use of such tests, while proposing use of carefully constructed CRTs as an alternative.
- *American Federation of Teachers* AFL-CIO—Opposed the elimination of standardized tests, while warning against misuses of such measures.
- *National Association of Elementary School Principals*—Attacked standardized testing vigorously in 1975 and again, in only slightly moderated tone, in 1982.
- *National Association of Secondary School Principals*—Refused to join other professional associations in attacking standardized tests, instead passing resolutions supporting *quality* standardized testing efforts.
- *American Association of School Administrators*—Adopted a moderate position recognizing the limits of any test while supporting efforts to assure that all tests are used correctly.
- *National School Boards Association*—Argued in favor of local attention to testing to assure that local control of education is maintained.
- *American Educational Research Association*—Passed a resolution encouraging careful consideration of the practice of measuring the success of schools by student scores on standardized tests.

Although the influence of association leaders and governing bodies on rank and file members is difficult to measure, these positions on testing, taken by organizations of professional educators, may well have had considerable impact on actual practice in the schools.

9. The Use of Competency Tests for Teacher Certification

The concept of testing teachers is not new. Examinations were developed to "certify" teachers for church-supported universities in medieval Europe. Several proposals have surfaced during this century endorsing the notion that teaching credentials should be awarded on the basis of test results, including the following:

- Selection of teacher education candidates on the basis of their scores on tests of intelligence, "teaching aptitude," subject matter competence, and knowledge of testing (late 1920s and early 1930s)
- Development and sale of early standardized admissions tests for teacher education programs (1920s and 1930s)
- Development and promotion of comprehensive teacher selection tests by the American Council on Education's Cooperative Test Service (1930s)—eventually resulting in the development of the National Teacher Examinations (late 1930s)[4]
- Implementation of state requirements that prospective teachers must pass competency tests to be certified or, in some cases, that experienced teachers must pass such a test for recertification (1940s to the present)

Underlying these developments were assumptions that (1) both schools and society would be well served if teacher competence could be assured; and (2) the best single assurance was having candidates for (or occupants of) teaching positions demonstrate their competence in basic literacy and "numeracy," knowledge of subject matter, and knowledge of professional principles pertinent to their practice. The move to teacher competency testing followed in the wake of reform efforts aimed at making U.S. schools more accountable, efficient, and effective. The public has shown great enthusiasm for the idea; a 1984 Gallup poll reported that 89 percent of those citizens polled favored competency testing for teachers (Martin, 1986). At the time of this writing, 28 states currently test or plan to test applicants for admission to teacher education programs, while 36 test or plan to test applicants for teacher certification. In addition, 3 states have experimented with rulings that experienced teachers must pass a test before they can be recertified, and several other states are considering such action.

These trends have not been enthusiastically viewed by many educators, and debates continue over the wisdom (and even the ancestry) of those who propose them. Legal challenges have been made regarding the use of competency tests for recertification of veteran teachers. In Chapter 3, we will examine in greater detail the professional dialogue and legal issues surrounding the use of teacher competency testing.

10. Calls for Alternative, "Authentic" Performance Measures

During the past decade, the perceived urgency of educational reform has resulted in inordinate weight being given to traditional, standardized tests as indicators of the "health" of our schools. Increasing pressure on educators to raise test scores has resulted in high-stakes tests, where lower scores held dire consequences not only for the student, but also for their teachers and administrators. Not surprisingly, school personnel began taking pains to prepare their students well—some-

---

[4] See Wilson (1985) for a historical summary of early uses of teacher tests and forces that led to the development of the National Teacher Examinations.

times too well—to take the high-stakes standardized tests. Soon the confidence educators could have in the results of these tests was seriously shaken.

In this context, known limitations of traditional multiple-choice tests were greatly magnified by their misuse. Those already critical of standardized tests responded by proposing the use of alternative assessment devices—nontraditional measures that depended on direct, "authentic" assessment of student performance on important learning tasks. The logic of this movement is simple. Since educators are concerned about aiming their instruction so that students will perform optimally when tested, why not use as "tests" the most essential performances that we desire students to accomplish, and then "teach to the test" without apology. In short, test the actual habits and capacities society views as essential, in the context of actual performances where those habits and capacities can be observed, rather then using tests whose items are proxies for such performances.

The results of such thinking are a variety of alternatives (to traditional tests) for assessing student learning. Long familiar assessment alternatives such as oral debates, typing tests, and writing samples mingle with less familiar alternatives such as student diaries, art portfolios, and science fairs. Much more will be said in Chapter 15 about the potential (and potential pitfalls) of these alternative forms of assessment. Suffice it to say here that no recent measurement trend has swept the field of education as quickly and aroused such sudden interest as have proposals to base student assessment more firmly on direct measures of student performance.

SUGGESTED READINGS

Anderson, B., & Pipho, C. (1984). State-mandated testing and the fate of local control. *Phi Delta Kappan*, *66*(3), 209–212.

This article provides a brief, but insightful, summary of new trends involving accountability programs, criterion-referenced testing, and minimum competency testing, along with consideration of how policy makers view and use testing.

Austin, G. R., & Garbar, H. (1982). *The rise and fall of national test scores*. New York, NY: Academic Press.

This edited book contains a series of chapters that provide scholarly treatment of the causes and implications of national aptitude and achievement test score trends. Many common misperceptions about test score trends are corrected in this volume.

DuBois, P. H. (1970). *A history of psychological testing*. Boston: Allyn & Bacon.

An excellent, comprehensive history of the uses, abuses, and development of psychological and educational tests. For the person who wishes extensive and interesting coverage of this topic.

Haney, W. (1984). Testing reasoning and reasoning about testing. *Review of Educational Research*, *54*(4), 597–654.

This review recounts in concise form the history of research and reasoning about mental testing and its role and influence in educational practice. Future areas of research regarding testing are also proposed.

SELF-CHECK QUIZ

1. What *major impact* did Joseph Rice's study of the effectiveness of spelling drills have on educational measurement?
   a. It asserted that criterion-referenced testing is preferable in classroom settings.
   b. It demonstrated that test anxiety can lower test scores significantly.
   c. It revealed that rote spelling drills could not be measured effectively.
   d. It showed the utility of objective testing and scoring procedures.

2. Who has been commonly referred to as the father of the educational testing movement?
   a. E. L. Thorndike
   b. Joseph Rice
   c. Ralph Tyler
   d. Lewis Terman

3. Which of the following trends in educational measurement belongs to the 1920–1965 era?
   a. Development and institutionalization of the National Assessment of Educational progress
   b. The accountability movement
   c. Increasing use of criterion-referenced testing
   d. Concern over declines in national aptitude and achievement test scores
   e. Establishment of minimum competency testing programs
   f. Rapid expansion and multiplication of commercial, standardized tests
   g. The use of competency tests for teacher certification

4. Which of the following best describes the national trend in scores obtained from standardized tests of general aptitude, such as the ACT, GRE, and SAT, during the period between 1965 and 1980?
   a. Downward score trends
   b. Rather flat score trends
   c. See-saw up-and-down score trends
   d. Upward score trends

5. The accountability concept is in general disrepute among most educators in part because
   a. it relies so heavily on criterion-referenced testing and so little on norm-referenced testing.
   b. it tends to hurt the successful school districts the most.
   c. some legislatures use it as a basis for setting school district budgets.
   d. the public is basically unwilling to support the concept.

6. Which professional organization opposed standardized testing so strongly that in 1972 it voted for an immediate moratorium on all such tests?
   a. American Association of School Administrators
   b. American Federation of Teachers
   c. National Association of Elementary School Principals
   d. National Association of Secondary School Principals
   e. National Education Association
   f. National School Boards Association

7. An important outgrowth of the accountability movement is the
   a. increasing use of criterion-referenced measurement.
   b. increasing use of norm-referenced measurement.
   c. balanced use of both criterion- and norm-referenced measurement.

8. In recent years, the use of minimum competency tests in America has
   a. decreased.
   b. increased.
   c. stayed about the same.

9. Which of the following professional associations was established specifically to further the advancement of sound measurement techniques in education?
   a. American Education Research Association
   b. American Evaluation Association
   c. American Psychological Association
   d. National Council for Measurement in Education
   e. Society for Measurement and Evaluation in Education

10. Who argued persuasively for the superiority of written examinations during a period when oral examinations were prevalent?
    a. E. L. Thorndike
    b. Horace Mann
    c. Joseph Rice
    d. Ralph Tyler

SUGGESTION SHEET

If your last name starts with the letter *B*, please complete the Suggestion Sheet at the end of the book while this chapter is still fresh in your mind.

CHAPTER 3

Coming to Grips with Current Social, Legal, and Ethical Issues in Measurement

Overview

What has triggered the well-publicized legal battles over testing, and what have the courts decided? What impact do ''truth-in-testing'' laws and other related legislation have on schools? Is there substance to claims that most tests are flawed by cultural or social bias? What ethical guidelines can schools follow to be certain they are using measurement instruments properly? What impact is minimum competency testing likely to have on our educational systems? What role—if any—should competency tests play in certifying and recertifying classroom teachers? These are some of the major questions we attempt to answer in this chapter.

We have organized this chapter into six major sections dealing, respectively, with concerns about bias in educational tests, and the legal and legislative efforts to remedy perceived biases; issues in minimum competency testing; right-to-privacy issues in using educational tests; concerns about test disclosure; ethical considerations and guidelines in testing, including problems with teaching to the test; and issues in using tests for teacher certification.

Objectives

Upon completing your study of this chapter, you should be able to

1. Define *test bias* and discuss how bias can affect test results for individuals and groups.
2. Identify concerns and cautions about cultural, social, and gender bias in tests and discuss to what extent each type of bias undermines current educational measures.
3. Describe what impact court decisions and legislative enactments that pertain to testing in the schools have had on educational testing.
4. Define *minimum competency testing*, and discuss legal and ethical issues in using such tests. List the criteria for a legally defensible minimum competency test.
5. Discuss the impact of truth-in-testing and right-to-privacy legislation on the use of educational tests.
6. Explain the ethical responsibilities of test users, including ethical problems associated with teaching to the test.
7. Explain the role and utility of standards for tests and test use.
8. Discuss unresolved issues in teacher competency testing, and identify steps necessary to resolve them.

SOCIAL AND LEGAL CONSIDERATIONS IN TESTING

Debates about testing have become a prominent part of the educational scene. But the disagreements do not end with intellectual jousting. They have flowed over into courtrooms, legislative assemblies, and the major channels and tributaries of dialogue about the social values associated with testing.

The day is long gone when measurement experts—or even the prestigious and powerful testing corporations—could ply their trade with legal or social impunity. Concern that tests be free of discrimination by reason of gender, race, color, religion, or national origin has prompted responses from professionals, such as the well known *Standards* (APA et al., 1974, AERA et al., 1985), for which much of the rationale is rooted in the social questions and civil rights pressures that emerged during the late 1960s and early 1970s. Those who make and use tests can no longer do so without regard to their impact on *every* individual and subgroup—including women, ethnic minorities, and children with disabilities. Scrutiny of testing by the legal system has become commonplace, and litigation over testing issues has proliferated to the point where it has occupied the attention of even prominent legal scholars (e.g., Bersoff, 1981a, 1981b). What can be measured in the schoolroom is increasingly being determined by what happens in the courtroom.

In this section, we consider several aspects of educational measurement that have become the focus of legal, ethical, and/or social concern. We examine particularly concerns about cultural, ethnic, linguistic, socioeconomic, and gender test bias in tests.

Test Bias and Discrimination Issues

Concerns about bias most often revolve around questions of whether tests discriminate against those whose cultural, linguistic, racial, economic, or social background differs from that of the majority. The possibility that many tests might have a gender bias, favoring males, has also become an increasing concern since the sixties.

But What Is Test Bias?

So far we have written as if everyone understands and agrees on what test bias is. That is not the case. To prove our point, try answering this multiple-choice item.

Does test bias refer to

- bias inherent in the test itself?
- bias created by inappropriate selection of a test?
- bias created by how a test is administered?
- bias in the way test results are used in making decisions?

The answer is yes.[1] Inappropriate test construction, selection, administration, or use can all bias test results. Many factors might bias the scores on a test, leading to many different definitions of test bias. For purposes of this chapter, we give only an example or two of the most common and obvious types of bias. (For a more complete discussion of test bias, see Cole and Moss, 1989).

A test is biased if one individual or group has an unfair advantage over another. An *unfair advantage* is one totally unrelated to what the test is designed to measure. For example, giving directions in English for a manual dexterity test might bias scores against Laotian bilingual students who are not fluent in English, resulting in the erroneous conclusion that Laotians have less manual dexterity than other students. Or, if the story-problem items on a mathematical placement test are loaded with words like *regatta, oarsman, opera, sonata, bassoon* or *pirouette*, then children from wealthy families may have an unfair advantage because they are much more familiar with the vocabulary. Since the test is supposed to measure math ability, not vocabulary, we say it is *biased in favor* of high socioeconomic children, or *biased against* middle and lower socioeconomic children.

Similarly, a test labeled as an *intelligence* test, but consisting solely of items that require knowledge of ghetto street slang is rather obviously measuring cultural (and possibly racial) background more than intelligence, as it has been commonly defined. For example, Williams's (1972) Black Intelligence Test for Cultural Homogeneity (BITCH) consists of 100 "street-slang" items selected because whites were found to score more poorly on them than African-Americans; this test was designed so that educated whites would perform poorly, (thus showing how other tests might be loaded with culture-specific items that disadvantage African-Americans).

---

[1] Don't accuse us of unfairness or giving you a trick question. We did not tell you there was only one correct answer. In a later chapter, we will talk more about the importance of giving good instructions.

In summary, any time that differences observed in test performance are caused by systematic factors you did not intend to measure (e.g., economic status), and such observed differences could result in systematic unfairness toward any group of examinees, the possibility of bias exists. Or stated more precisely, bias is present when a test score has a different meaning or implication for one subgroup of examinees than for another, thus resulting in the interpretation of a test score being more valid for one subgroup of test takers than another (Cole & Moss, 1989).

Let us examine briefly each of the specific areas in which test bias is a reoccurring concern.

Concerns about Cultural, Ethnic, and Linguistic Test Bias

Despite significant gains during the past 30 years toward providing equal educational opportunities for all children, we obviously have a long way to go. Inequality and unfairness are pervasive and pernicious specters that continue to haunt many ethnic, cultural, and/or linguistic minorities[2] and to penetrate school curricula, instructional materials, instruction, classroom management, school governance—and educational tests. Yet of all facets of schooling, testing is by far the most common target for those who complain of bias. Why? The reason is probably because educational and psychological test scores have become intertwined with prominent social and educational policies such as upward mobility, admission to higher education, or placement of individuals into special treatment programs (e.g., special education programs).

The *potential* for bias toward minority children exists in all kinds of measurement and evaluation—including teacher-made tests and grading, where it is more difficult to detect because of the subjectivity that is typically (though not necessarily) more prevalent. Yet standardized ability and achievement tests have borne the brunt of the criticisms alleging bias against minorities.

Many studies have shown that members of some minority groups tend to score lower on standardized ability tests than members of the white majority. In some studies the difference in average test scores has been unsettling, as Linn (1982) notes:

> a difference between average scores for white and black students of roughly one standard deviation is typical of a number of studies that have compared these two groups (e.g., Coleman et al., 1966).
>
> With differences of this magnitude it is obviously important to consider the possibility that the lower average test scores for the poor and for certain minority groups are attributable, in whole or part, to bias in the tests themselves. (p. 285)

Yet Linn's observation does not eliminate the opposite possibility that the tests are not biased, and thus the lower scores of minority students are true reflec-

---

[2] For simplicity, we will use the term *minority* hereafter to refer to those who differ from the dominant societal group in race, ethnicity, language, or culture; we recognize the overlap that frequently results because some individuals would simultaneously be classified as minorities in more than one of these areas.

tions of lower levels of performance. If the tests are not at fault, then only two explanations seem plausible: Either minorities have been denied cultural and educational opportunities to develop the skills and knowledge sampled by the tests, or else those minorities (considered as a *group*) are inherently less able in the areas tested.

This last explanation is at the root of much controversy. Although enshrined for centuries in racial bigotry, perceptions that minorities were *by nature* inferior have never been accorded much scientific respectability. In 1969, Jensen reviewed indirect evidence suggesting that differences in IQ and scholastic aptitude within white populations were partly attributable to genetic inheritance, and extrapolated to suggest that it was reasonable to hypothesize that "genetic factors are strongly implicated in the average Negro-white intelligence difference" (1969, p. 82). The suggestion that differences in the measured IQ scores of blacks[3] and whites were the product of genetic differences created a controversy that dominated the popular and professional periodicals for several years. Although Jensen's thesis has been largely discounted on scientific as well as societal bases (Light & Smith, 1969; Haney, 1984), over half of 877 measurement experts who responded to a 1984 survey on intelligence and aptitude testing still believed that genetic factors contributed to black-white differences in IQ scores (Snyderman & Rothman, 1987). So the controversy continues.

As Shepard (1980) observes:

> One reason that bias in mental testing is so volatile an issue is that it involves the specter of biological determinism, i.e., whether there is a large difference in intelligence (IQ) between black and white Americans which can be attributed largely to inherited differences. (p. 5)

What may have fueled the controversy most is the fact that minority students (especially African-American, Native-American, and Latin-American children) and economically disadvantaged white students have been classified in disproportionate numbers as educable mentally retarded (EMR) students and placed in special education programs (Reschly, 1981). Many of those affected have viewed these classifications and the referral-placement process as unfair, stigmatizing, and humiliating to individuals, and possibly racist. Since tests play such a pivotal role in these classifications, the possibility of test bias has led to legal challenges.

As early as 1954, of course, the landmark case of *Brown v. Board of Education of Topeka* (1954) established the right of minority children to equal educational opportunities. This vindication of the constitutional rights of minorities provided the foundation for subsequent legal challenges to educational inequality. A decade passed, however, before litigation began to focus seriously on the role that educational testing might play in assuring all children equal access to educational oppor-

---

[3] In this section and elsewhere in this chapter, we refer to African-Americans as blacks, and to children with disabilities as handicapped children, where those terms were used in the court case or historical controversy to which we refer; elsewhere we prefer the terms African-American and children with disabilities, unless using a direct quotation.

tunities. Racial minorities, objecting to their children being labeled as "retarded" and being removed from regular classrooms, have taken the testers to court. Space permits us to provide only a sketchy coverage of the litigation and out-of-court settlements concerning testing in the last 25 years, touching on only a few of the cases we believe to be most significant.[4]

Hobson v. Hansen *(1967)*

Legal opposition to educational and psychological tests really began in 1967, in a case before the District of Columbia federal court, in which minorities questioned the constitutionality of using group IQ and achievement measures in placing children in educational tracks, since black children were overrepresented in lower ability tracks (especially EMR classes) and white children were placed disproportionately in upper ability tracks (especially college preparatory classes). The court prohibited the use of these tests for the purposes of grouping, holding that the tests had been standardized on mostly white, middle-class populations and therefore yielded biased results when administered to minority children.

Diana v. California State Board of Education *(1970)*

Plaintiffs on behalf of nine Latin-American students charged that the children were inappropriately placed in EMR classrooms as a result of scores on IQ tests that assumed equality of examinees' linguistic and cultural backgrounds. When these students were permitted to take the test again in their primary language, there was an average increase of 15 IQ points. This case led to an out-of-court settlement stipulating that children from non-English-speaking homes would be tested in their native language, and to subsequent out-of-court settlements specifying that IQ tests used for special education placement must be (1) normed on culturally and linguistically relevant groups, and (2) contain no culturally unfair content (see Oakland & Laosa, 1977).

Larry P. v. Wilson Riles *(1979)*

One of the two most significant legal precedents related to IQ testing comes from this celebrated California class action suit, first filed in 1971 against the San Francisco Unified School District. Plaintiffs were parents of six black students who claimed their children had been wrongly placed in EMR classes because the standardized IQ tests used for placement were racially and culturally biased. After several years of injunctions and appeals, the case finally came to trial, and in 1979 the court rendered a decision in favor of the plaintiffs. Noting that disproportionate numbers of black students were placed in EMR classes (blacks constituted about 27 percent of the total student population, but over 60 percent of the EMR population), the court pointed out that

> there is less than one in a million chance that the overenrollment of black children and the underenrollment of nonblack children in the EMR classes in 1967–77

---

[4] For excellent in-depth reviews of this topic, see Anderson et al. (1980), Bersoff (1981a, 1981b), Lambert (1981), and Menacker and Morris (1985).

would have resulted under a color-blind system of placement. (Quoted in Anderson et al., 1980, p. 19)

Advocates of minority student rights rejoiced, while the State of California appealed the decision. In 1984, an appellate court upheld the court's decision. The issue was decided, but as Lambert (1981) so aptly states:

Psychology and psychological measurement were on trial in *Larry P. v. Wilson Riles*. The plaintiff and the judge chose to center attention on tests and attack them as the cause of the greater prevalence of retarded intellectual development among black children, rather than being concerned about the role of environmental factors in intellectual performance, the slow learning child's need for special educational assistance, or other remedies that would protect the rights of black children to equal educational opportunity while also insuring their rights to special education services as needed. (p. 944)

PASE (Parents in Action on Special Education) v. Hannon *(1980)*

Less than a year after the "Larry P." opinion in California, a very different decision was rendered on a similar case tried before a federal district court in Illinois. In this suit, filed in 1975 on behalf of black children placed in the Chicago public school's EMR classes, the court found in favor of the state. After examining each test item (something not done in the California case), the judge concluded that very few items on the tests were culturally biased and that the IQ tests did not discriminate against black children.

"Golden Rule" Lawsuits and Legislation

In 1976, the Golden Rule Insurance Company sued the Educational Testing Service (ETS) and the Illinois Department of Insurance, claiming that the ETS exam used to license insurance agents in Illinois discriminated against black candidates. After eight years of legal battling, an out-of-court settlement (*Golden Rule v. Washburn*, 1984) stipulated that items dealing with the *same content* would be compared according to the percentages of black and white examinees who answered correctly, and questions with the least difference would be given preference in developing future licensing tests. Lawmakers in California, New York, and Texas have proposed this "Golden Rule Principle" as a means of assuring fairness not only in licensure exams, but also in admission and placement tests used in educational institutions. The wisdom of such proposals has created sharp debates, however; the Summer 1987 issue of *Educational Measurement: Issues and Practice* was devoted entirely to pro and con debates about the usefulness of the "Golden Rule" strategy. In 1988 the APA, apparently convinced that the "Golden Rule" procedure is ineffective in detecting biased items and may actually undermine the reliability and validity of test scores, went on record as opposing this procedure as a model for anti-bias legislation in testing (Faggen, 1990).

Legal Restrictions on the Use of Achievement Tests

The fairness to minorities of various types of *achievement* tests has also been challenged in the courts. Fleming (1982) describes the impact of court-ordered desegregation on school districts' testing programs. In Cleveland, Ohio, for example, the court mandate in effect (*Reed v. Rhodes*, 1978) orders the schools to "insure that all tests, whether standardized, criterion-referenced, or *teacher-made,* are developed, administered, and scored in a nondiscriminatory manner" (*Reed v. Rhodes*, 1978, p. 74, emphasis added). The "long arm of the law" has reached into the classroom, making it imperative that teachers be prepared to defend the measurement instruments they create.

So Where Does All the Litigation Leave Us?

The litigation surrounding testing bias may have clouded as much as clarified murky issues. But some things are clear.

First, the court decisions have changed few minds; those who were critical of tests before the lawsuits were filed are still largely critical, and test proponents have not been much dissuaded, even by negative rulings.

Second, test makers have not been deaf to legal concerns, and efforts to standardize tests on representative norm groups have been launched by most publishers to counter charges that norms are based entirely on the performance of middle-class whites (Burrill & Wilson, 1980).

Third, test use has more often been the legal target than tests themselves—although both have been challenged.

Fourth, some types of tests (e.g., typing tests and other skill tests) have gone relatively unscathed, rarely being accused of bias.

Fifth, many common misunderstandings about test bias are evident in the court-orders and legislation. The assumption of the legislators and jurists in several previously cited examples seemed to be that differences in average group performance could be taken as *prima facie* evidence of bias. Not so, as Linn and Drasgow (1987) point out. Noting that this popular view of bias confuses the *measurement* of a behavior with the *cause* of that behavior, they acknowledge that differences in group performance on tests may reflect test bias, but argue that it is by no means evidence of such bias.

Sixth, "the jury is still out"—court orders aside, the research evidence is not conclusive about the extent to which bias toward minorities is a problem in educational tests. (See Linn, 1982 and Cole, 1981 for insightful summaries of this research.)

Concerns about Socioeconomic Bias in Tests

Many economically disadvantaged students are also racial or cultural minorities, but it is often difficult to separate poverty from minority status in examining test scores for possible socioeconomic bias. Perhaps that is why there has been little direct litigation focusing on economic or social bias.

It is clear that the poor—whether of minority status or not—perform less well on achievement and intelligence tests, on the average, than do their counterparts from more affluent homes. Is it possible that lower average test scores for the poor are attributable to bias in the tests? Of course it is possible. But whether it is *true* still eludes us. In a critique of the Educational Testing Service (ETS) sponsored by Ralph Nader and his associates (Nairn, 1980) asserted that (1) students' SAT scores are highly correlated with family income, and (2) tests are a major instrument in preserving the socioeconomic *status quo*. In response, the ETS (1980) (1) drew on White's (1976) data to show that family income relates no more closely to test scores of children (.25) than to grades given to those children (.24), and (2) challenged the thinking of those who would terminate testing because tests help disclose the negative effects of unequal resources and disparate learning opportunities among children of different classes.

Care should be taken not to attribute the biases in our society to the instruments that report their cumulative effects. In many respects our tests are only a mirror that reflect the educational results of cultural bias; shattering the mirror will not solve the problem.

Concerns about Gender Bias in Tests

Increased social conscience has led to a parallel increase in efforts to assure equality between the sexes in educational, vocational, and economic opportunities. As part of this effort, educational and psychological tests have been examined for possible bias against females. In 1989, for example, a federal court judge ordered New York State to stop awarding college scholarships based on SAT scores, saying the test is unfair to girls, since their SAT scores are significantly lower than males, while their grade-point averages were higher.

In general, females are found to do as well or better than males on educational tests—perhaps because females are superior in verbal ability or, as Waetjen (1977) suggests, because boys perform less well in stress-producing situations. Only in mathematics achievement do males seem to score higher, on the average, than females. It is not yet entirely clear whether such differences are attributable to innate gender differences (e.g., males possessing greater quantitative aptitude) or to cultural attitudes and societal expectations and stereotypes. (For interesting discussions of this topic, see Waetjen, 1977; and Plake, Ansorge, Parker, & Lowry, 1982.)

Our concern here, however, is not with innate gender differences—or even with societal attitudes and expectations. Instead, our interest lies in the question, Do cultural attitudes (or other factors) inject gender bias into educational tests? Although somewhat dated, the most comprehensive and thorough exploration of this topic is still that of Tittle and her associates (Tittle & Zytowski, 1978; Tittle, 1978) resulting in the following conclusions concerning sex bias in tests:

- Achievement tests are selectively biased against females in *language usage* (as evidenced by an imbalanced ratio of male to female noun and pronoun referents).
- Achievement tests are selectively biased against females in content (male characters are mentioned more often).
- Achievement tests reinforce and contain numerous sex-role stereotypes (e.g., male characters are portrayed in more active roles and in other stereotypical ways).

- Aptitude tests are frequently written and interpreted according to sex-role stereotypes.

- Occupational and career interest inventories often restrict individual choices for females. Their separate male and female scales and norms result in disproportionate counseling about career options.

- Educational tests are neither inherently fair nor biased to either gender; fairness is a result of careful test construction and wise policies concerning test selection and use.

- Local and state educational administrators, teachers, counselors, parents, and students have the authority and responsibility to assure that tests do not discriminate against females.

- Guidelines concerning the review, selection, use, and interpretation of tests are needed so policy makers and educators can prevent sex bias from entering into educational decisions.

Since Tittle carefully restricts her conclusions to the particular tests she examined, we suggest you peruse her original reports rather than generalizing these conclusions to all tests of those types.

ISSUES IN MINIMUM COMPETENCY TESTING

In Chapter 2, we noted that the minimum competency test (MCT) movement has been controversial from the outset, with debate focused on the issues of test utility and fairness. Proponents tout MCTs as essential to the quality (and accountability) of education and look to MCT programs "to provide (a) a new standard for the award of the high school diploma, (b) a guide for grade-to-grade promotion, and/ or (c) a means of identifying students in need of remedial instruction" (Haney, 1984, p. 629). Opponents argue that MCT programs are little more than inappropriate reactions of policy makers who mandate testing policies they feel will force schools to teach "basic competencies," thus achieving their goals of instructional "reform" indirectly and relatively simply. "Interestingly, the principal sanction associated with MCT programs—diploma denial or retention in grade—fell on the ill-served students rather than on the instructional system" (Benjes, Heubert & O'Brien, 1980, cited in Airasian and Madaus, 1983). Also, critics argue that MCT programs fail because the required *minimum* quickly becomes the *maximum*, thus lowering standards for all students.

Popham (1984a) has summarized some of the pro-MCT arguments, while Pullin (1982) has summarized the opposing views. Brickell (1978) and Perkins (1982) have provided very useful overviews of arguments in favor of and against MCTs. We have drawn on these authors in developing the list of perceived advantages and disadvantages of MCTs that appears in Table 3.1.

TABLE 3.1 Some Advantages and Disadvantages Claimed for Minimum Competency Testing

Advantages	Disadvantages
1. Restores confidence in schools and in the meaning of a high school diploma	1. Emphasis on easy-to-measure, basic results in narrow curriculum that includes only easily testable content
2. Sets meaningful criteria for grade promotion and diploma award	2. Results in "teaching the test"
3. Emphasizes products of schooling rather than process (e.g., seat time and course credits) in certifying student accomplishments	3. Concentrates on low-achieving students at the expense of better prepared ("average" and "gifted") students
4. Motivates and certifies student achievement of minimum competencies in basic skills in reading, writing, and math	4. Underestimates difficulty in reaching agreement on the nature and difficulty of minimum competencies; setting of standards may be arbitrary
5. Involves the school and community in defining educational standards	5. Loses commonality of what the high school diploma means when competency definition is left to local districts
6. Enables a school district to target resources toward a clear set of goals	6. Will stigmatize and label underachievers and adversely affect their future educational or career goals
7. Promotes better teaching, curriculum design, and course revision	7. May increase numbers of students who are retained or who drop out, depending on the minimum that is set
8. Promotes development of competencies relating to life after school	8. Places responsibility for failure solely on the student
9. Enables schools to identify and assist students lacking basic skills and needing remedial help	9. Student abilities, aptitudes, and backgrounds are too diverse to be accommodated by any single standard of performance
10. Provides information that enables the public to hold schools accountable for the educational process	10. Causes the disadvantaged to be even more disadvantaged by being singled out and labeled for failing to meet the standard
	11. Increases costs and record-keeping burdens for schools

Standard Setting

One of the thorniest problems faced by those who initiate MCT programs is how to set the standards—that is, how to determine the acceptable minimums. If competency-testing standards are set arbitrarily, obviously students might be unfairly declared incompetent (or competent, for that matter) on the basis of factors that have little or nothing to do with their abilities. Concern that such arbitrariness be avoided has led to the development of many proposed standard-setting procedures and a voluminous research literature on the results of applying these various standard-setting methods. Coverage of this topic is beyond the scope of this book, but teachers should be aware that minimum cutoffs should not be set arbitrarily, and that considerable work has been done that can help guide them should they ever be involved in setting standards for competency tests. For those who need further information, Jaeger (1989) provides an excellent summary of prior thinking about the best way to set standards and establish defensible cutoff scores.

Legal Challenges to MCTs

Because most MCT programs are imposed by external bodies without any accompanying curriculum or syllabus, many school districts' curriculum and instruction predictably are not well-matched with test content. As a result, many children fail, and the failure rate is greater for poor and minority students (Airasian & Madaus, 1983). This differential failure rate has led to a number of legal challenges to MCTs. Speaking of legal issues in competency testing, Anderson and her colleagues describe where MCT programs are most likely to "run afoul of the law":

> Minimum competency testing requirements that incorporate some sanction upon students for failing to pass the tests run the greatest risk of legal challenge. These legal challenges are most likely to be raised if competency testing programs touch on any of the following issues:
>
> • Potential for racial and linguistic discrimination
> • Adequacy of advance notice and phase-in periods prior to the initial use of the test as a graduation requirement
> • Psychometric validity or reliability of the tests
> • Match between the instructional program and the test
> • The degree to which remedial instruction may create or reinforce tracking (Anderson et al., 1980, pp. 23–24)

Failure to steer clear of these legal land mines has resulted in several lawsuits involving competency testing, of which we will briefly mention only a few representative examples.

Debra P. v. Turlington *(1981)*

This case, filed initially in 1978, had its roots two years earlier in Florida's 1976 legislation specifying that a functional literacy test be developed and used (along with other graduation requirements) to determine which Florida students should be awarded high school diplomas. Students would have three chances to pass the new "diploma test," which became known as the Florida Functional Literacy Test (FFLT). The FFLT was first administered in 1977, with two startling results: (1) 36 percent of the students failed and were thereby judged functionally illiterate and (2) while only 24 percent of the white students failed the FFLT, 77 percent of the black students failed. By 1979, the overall failure rate had dropped substantially but the racial imbalance was even worse. Based on the test results, 20 percent of Florida's black seniors and 2 percent of the state's white seniors were to be denied high school diplomas. A group of black students and their parents challenged the test on grounds that it was biased and discriminatory on the basis of race. After six years of legal battling, focused both on the FFLT's validity and possible bias against blacks, an Appeals Court ruled that the test was both technically adequate and free of racial or ethnic bias, and declared that Florida had the authority to deny diplomas to students unable to pass the FFLT. The most widely publicized litigation concerning MCTs had ended with apparent victory for the proposition that the use of MCTs to deny diplomas is legally permissible, at least under certain circumstances.

Anderson v. Banks (1982)

Another legal test of MCTs challenged Georgia's Tattnall County School District's use of the California Achievement Test (CAT) as a proficiency exam (with students required to score at least at the 9.0 level in reading and mathematics to receive a high school diploma) on the basis that it created racially unfair diploma sanctions. After examining the test content and the district's curriculum objectives and text materials, the court found that the CAT test was a fair test of the curriculum and could, as a proficiency exam, be used as a diploma requirement.

Bester v. Tuscaloosa City Board of Education (1984)

An Alabama school district's policy that elementary school students who fell below minimum reading levels required for their grade be retained rather than given "social promotions" triggered another challenge to MCTs. Implementation of this policy resulted in a retention rate for black students (24 percent) approximately four times that for white students (6 percent), and the plaintiffs argued that a district could not shift to a new minimum standard for reading if that shift resulted in blacks being retained more than whites. The court rejected this argument, holding that it was unreasonable to expect standards (and by implication, minimum test scores) to remain fixed at unacceptably low levels.

Board of Education v. Ambach (1981)

In this case, use of MCTs was challenged on grounds that withholding a handicapped student's diploma because of failure to pass a competency standard violated the student's constitutional rights. The courts disagreed, concluding that schools must provide quality educational services to all handicapped students, but could not be held accountable if such students were unable to reach desired educational goals, including graduation.

Brookhart v. Illinois State Board of Education (1983)

This suit, brought against the Peoria School Board, alleged that the district's MCT requirement violated the constitutional rights of handicapped students. The court ruled that altering MCT content or cutoff scores to accommodate students with mental disabilities would thwart the very purpose and meaning of the diploma requirement. An appeals court did rule, however, that the schools must administer the MCTs in a manner that would minimize the impact of students' physical impairments on their test performance, making whatever modifications in test format and environment were necessary to permit physically handicapped students to demonstrate their actual knowledge.

Summary of What the Courts Have Said about MCTs

So far, the major conclusions from court cases concerning MCTs have been these:

- Schools are not required to *guarantee* that a student achieves basic literacy (something that may be beyond the school's control).
- MCTs are *legally* permissible as long as they contain no racial bias and are fair tests of what is actually taught in schools.
- MCTs used for a decision (e.g., awarding diplomas) cannot be required to meet criteria not required of other tests that could influence the same decision (e.g., course tests).
- Schools need not prove that every child has been exposed to everything in the curriculum, but only that the schools' intent and effort was to provide such exposure.
- Schools can raise minimum standards where prior minimums can be shown to be unacceptably low.
- Schools can use MCTs in deciding whether to award diplomas to students with disabilities, and will not be held accountable if such students cannot meet educational goals (assuming appropriate services have been provided).
- MCTs must be administered to students with disabilities in such a way that physical impairment does not prevent students from demonstrating their actual knowledge.

Characteristics of Legally Defensible MCTs

Recent court cases have defined the characteristics of MCT programs that will withstand legal challenges. Madaus (1983) has listed the following characteristics:

1. Valid objectives describing skills that are truly basic competencies
2. A test that is a valid measure of those objectives
3. Evidence that the skills assessed are actually reflected in the curriculum and taught in the classrooms
4. Early assessment and identification of those needing remedial help
5. Provision of remedial help for all who require it
6. Sufficient advance notice and multiple opportunities to pass the competency test

Given our current societal climate, when so many disagreements end in litigation, testing programs as potentially volatile as MCT programs are likely to encounter further legal challenge. The issues surrounding MCTs will not be resolved soon. In the meantime, any educational agency contemplating the use of MCTs would be well advised to assure that their program meets the six criteria implicit in Madaus's list. Since we have not dealt here with the technical issues concerning MCTs (such as how to determine their validity) and will touch only lightly on such issues in Chapter 7, those who propose to use MCTs may wish to read Madaus's entire book and/or Berk's (1986) and Jaeger's (1989) excellent summaries of the status and potential of the MCT movement.

RIGHT-TO-PRIVACY ISSUES IN TESTING

In part to protect against invasion of privacy, governmental regulations have been established in the United States to ensure that individuals' rights—broadly understood to include not only rights to privacy, but also confidentiality and the need to obtain informed consent when such rights are waived—are protected whenever human behavior is measured.

With adults, privacy rights can be waived voluntarily through informed consent procedures. With children who are legal minors, however, the informed consent of parents (or legal guardians) to take a test is necessary if there could be any risk of psychological harm, embarrassment, or loss of privacy to the student. Routine classroom tests do not normally require such consent and educators have traditionally been trusted to exercise good judgment in making sure that tests administered to students are relevant and necessary to the educational goals being sought by the schools.

Sax (1989) makes some excellent suggestions on how not to invade students' privacy through thoughtless employment of dubious measurement devices. He suggests, for instance, that decisions concerning which tests should be required of students might best be made by a panel including (1) professionals familiar with testing and (2) concerned citizens. Such a panel could, for each test

- Assess how well the test would measure the school's objectives.
- Determine the risk of students' suffering embarrassment or damage from taking the test.
- Review the acceptability of the test in terms of community values.
- Gauge the potential benefits of using the test.
- Decide whether the test should be required of all students or only volunteers.
- Decide how confidentiality of test scores will be maintained.
- Determine whether the data are already available from existing sources, thus eliminating the need for the test.

Students must not be exploited. Wherever measurement instruments are used for any purpose except those of assisting students or reporting on their achievement, the purposes of using the instruments must be explained thoroughly to parents, along with an explanation of any potential risks, and an informed consent to test must be obtained from parents (or legal guardians).

TEST DISCLOSURE ISSUES IN TESTING

Critics feel that the testing industry and professionals who use its products are too secretive with test results, often withholding them even from examinees. Test disclosure was brought into sharp focus in the United States in 1974 with passage of the "Buckley Amendment" (officially the Family Education Rights and Privacy Act, or FERPA). This legislation directs those educational institutions receiving federal education funds to allow parents and eligible students access to all records pertaining directly to the student's school performance. The intent of FERPA was to bring student test scores and professional interpretations of those scores "out of the closet." In fact, however, this law seems to have had limited impact, possibly because it affects only federally funded education programs.

The concern that motivated the passage of FERPA re-emerged in the form of the so-called truth-in-testing proposals considered in the late 1970s in legislatures in several states, and even in the U.S. Congress. The legislative proposals related to truth-in-testing generally stemmed from a conviction that test disclosure was a matter of simple fairness—allowing examinees to review test results used to make important decisions about their future. Laws requiring test disclosure were eventually passed in both California and New York.

However, the proposals met with strong resistance, not only from within the testing industry but from some sectors of the education profession as well. The argument against test disclosure is very simple: "Secure" standardized tests are important (for reasons we discussed in Chapter 1), and if you disclose items on a secure test, replacement items will have to be written the next time the test is administered, resulting in increased costs and/or decreased item quality. Since developing good standardized test items is both time-consuming and expensive, everybody loses. Not everyone accepts this rationale, and the debate about test disclosure continues. We have summarized in Table 3.2 some of the more common arguments made by proponents and opponents of truth-in-testing legislation.

There has been *some* apparent softening of positions on both sides. Some test publishers (e.g., ETS and the College Board) have moved toward liberalizing release of questions and answers on certain tests. And when disclosure revealed scoring errors in some venerable tests (e.g., SAT and GRE), the testing industry not only admitted the errors, but also did what was feasible to correct them, sometimes rescoring tens of thousands of tests to correct one faulty item. (See Fiske, 1981a, 1981b, and Jacobson, 1981 for delightful accounts of media coverage of these events.) In late 1981, the ETS Board of Trustees passed a resolution that softened their earlier posture and allowed increased public access to test questions and answers (ETS, 1981). At the very least, dissemination of their resolution to test users and test critics could be viewed as bearing an olive branch to one's adversaries. Yet the truce has been uneasy. Even amid evidence of test makers' increased awareness of test takers' feelings about test disclosure, the public clamor about this issue seems to ebb and flow. Shimberg (1990) reports that New York legislators have attempted to extend their 1980 truth-in-testing law to certification and licensing tests, even though a federal court had ruled in January 1990 that the law was invalid. So, the issue of test disclosure remains unresolved.

TABLE 3.2 Common Arguments For and Against Truth-in-Testing Legislation[a]

Arguments FOR:	Arguments AGAINST:
1. Fairness requires that examinees be allowed to review corrected test results that will be used to make important decisions about their lives.	1. Test security ensures fairness, since all students take tests on an equal footing.
2. Information about limitations of tests (e.g., the margin or error surrounding any individual score, and imperfect validity of tests) should be provided to all examinees (or their parents or guardians).	2. Proponents of test disclosure legislation have failed to demonstrate its need; of several competing public interests at stake, their proposals address only one.
3. Test disclosure will promote greater accuracy and validity of tests.	3. Test disclosure would violate test security, invalidating tests for future use.
4. A commitment to consumer protection and sunshine laws should extend to an area as important as testing, in which secrecy should not be tolerated.	4. Test publishers and educational institutions already provide sufficient information and protection to examinees; analogies to consumer protection are misleading and inflammatory.
5. Test disclosure will reveal culturally biased questions and errors in scoring.	5. Secure tests are more fair and democratic than less objective alternatives that could permit various biases to influence decisions in ways that could work to the disadvantage of minorities and those with disabilities.
6. The testing industry should be accountable for the quality and consequences of their products, and test disclosure and public scrutiny is necessary to ensure such accountability.	6. The testing industry is already accountable (to the psychometric profession, the academic community, and to market demands).
7. Test disclosure would prevent racism and bias in college admissions, requiring all decisions, processes, and instruments to be open for inspection.	7. Test disclosure will lower test quality by shortening the time allowable for test development and by eventually exhausting the number of test questions that can be asked.
8. Test disclosure need not increase test development costs as much as opponents suggest.	8. Test disclosure would substantially raise test development costs (since new tests would have to be developed frequently). These costs would have to be passed along to users (schools and/or examinees).
9. Test security is not a serious issue. This problem could be eliminated if new measurement technologies were developed.	9. Test disclosure will provide no discernible cost benefits to individuals and society, since any benefits would be offset by increased costs.
10. Poor students would benefit since items now only available to expensive tutoring schools would be available to everyone.	10. Federal test disclosure legislation would constitute dangerous and possibly unconstitutional incursion into local control of education.

[a] This table is patterned after a similar table prepared by Anderson et al. (1980) and draws heavily from that work as well as from the thinking of Bersoff (1981b) and Haney (1981, 1984).

ETHICAL CONSIDERATIONS
IN USING EDUCATIONAL MEASURES

Many of the issues discussed in the previous sections are, implicitly or explicitly, *ethical* issues. Even if there were no legal constraints, the public welfare demands that all professionals who participate as partners in the educational enterprise behave ethically in relation to all aspects of educational measurement and evaluation. For most of us, potential test bias, invasion of privacy, and related issues are more ethical than legal concerns.

Testing ethics is the responsibility of two major groups: measurement professionals and test users.[5] Messick (1981) reminds his colleagues in the first group that "from the standpoint of scientific and professional responsibility in educational and psychological measurement, it seems clear that ethics, like character, begins at home" (p. 19). This sentiment has been echoed by other measurement professionals, who recognize their responsibility to protect the public's interests and have moved to ensure those interests through the development and adherence to standards and principles that guide measurement practice.

Ethical Responsibilities of Measurement Professionals

Although many proposed sets of ethical guidelines and standards apply to educational measurement, and many efforts have been made to assure that measurement professionals behave ethically, the following standards seem the most directly pertinent.[6]

Standards for Educational and Psychological Tests/Testing

Earlier we mentioned the *Standards* produced jointly by APA, AERA, and NCME over twenty years ago (APA et al., 1966) and revised twice to assure their relevance and currency (APA et al., 1974, & AERA et al., 1985). Long considered the bible (or at least the cardinal commandments) for test construction, use, and evaluation, these *Standards* were developed and approved by the three professional associations to which most measurement professionals belong. It may be overstating to say that all measurement professionals are guided by these *Standards* as they develop, refine, and critique educational measures; it is not an overstatement to say that they should be.

Standards for Educational Testing Methods

Two measurement specialists in Israel, desiring to broaden test standards beyond usual considerations of reliability and validity, proposed a set of 23 standards for judging the merit of alternative testing methods and organized them into four

---

[5] We recognize that these are not exclusive groups and that many measurement professionals also are *test users*, but we use the latter term here to denote those who disavow special expertise in measurement.

[6] For an excellent summary of the history and development of standards and other efforts to improve tests and testing practices, see Millman and Harrington (1982).

groups, dealing respectively with the utility, accuracy, feasibility, and fairness of tests (Nevo & Shohamy, 1984). These proposed standards can also provide useful guidance to measurement specialists.

ETS Standards for Quality and Fairness of Testing

In 1981, the Educational Testing Service (ETS) adopted a set of standards to assure quality and fairness of their tests and testing programs. Revised recently (ETS, 1987) the standards include principles, policies, and procedural guidelines of importance to test producers. Although intended primarily for use within ETS, these standards have heuristic value for any person seriously concerned with improving educational measurement through careful and ethical measurement practices.

Code of Fair Testing Practices in Education (1988)

In 1988, AERA, APA, NCME, the American Association for Counseling and Development, the Association for Measurement and Evaluation in Counseling and Development, and the American Speech-Language-Hearing Association formed a Joint Committee on Testing Practices whose charge was to produce this code. The purpose of the code is to clarify the obligations of professionals toward those who take educational tests used in admissions, educational diagnosis, student placement, and educational assessment. Instead of being concerned with teacher-made tests, the code is directed primarily at tests sold by commercial test publishers or used in large-scale assessment programs. The code depends on the *Standards* cited earlier, attempting to present a selected portion of those standards in a way that they can be understood by key stakeholders such as test takers and their parents or guardians.

Credentialing for Measurement Specialists

Adherence to all the previously mentioned sets of standards and guidelines is voluntary. There are no serious consequences (aside from possible litigation) for violating those standards.[7] As a result, there is no coherent, cohesive, and canonized code of ethics by which measurement specialists are bound. In view of this circumstance, it is a credit to the measurement community that serious ethical violations in testing are as rare as they are.

In other professional fields (e.g., law, medicine, and psychology), some form of credentialing—usually licensure or certification—has been used to create and enforce professional standards. Measurement specialists have also proposed increased regulation in their field (e.g., Madaus, 1985b; Millman & Harrington, 1982). Recently the National Council on Measurement in Education (NCME) studied the feasibility of developing and operating a credentialing system for educational measurement specialists. The study revealed a variety of problems that

---

[7] An exception to this statement exists if a psychologist violates any principle in the American Psychological Association's *Ethical Principles of Psychologists* (APA, 1981) concerning testing and other assessment devices. In that case, there is a clear-cut ethical violation that can, if judged of sufficient import, result in serious professional sanctions against the offender.

would render such credentialing difficult, if not impossible (Sanders, Hathaway, Johnson-Lewis, Madaus, & Worthen, 1987; Worthen, 1987). One of the more compelling difficulties is the fact that educators in a wide variety of roles use measurement in so many different ways and for so many different purposes that it would be a Herculean task just to define the term *measurement specialist* and to identify them all—let alone contemplate credentialing them. Thus, while credentialing for educational measurement specialists may seem desirable, no such effort is likely in the near future.

Ethical Responsibilities of Test Users

Ethical responsibilities weigh as heavily upon the professionals who administer or interpret measurement instruments as upon those who develop and publish them. Measurement experts (e.g., Sax, 1989) have outlined concerns about ethical and unethical conduct in testing. The authors of the *Standards* (APA et al., 1974, & AERA, et al., 1985) have developed nontechnical guidelines for test users—a *test user* being defined as " one who chooses tests, interprets scores, or makes decisions based on test scores. (People who do *only* routine administration or scoring of tests are not included in this definition, although test users often do both.)" (APA, 1974, p. 1, emphasis added). We draw on these sources in proposing the following guidelines for the use of standardized tests. Any educator who uses (or advises others in the use of) standardized tests *should*

1. Possess a general understanding of measurement principles.
2. Understand the limitations of tests and test interpretations.
3. Understand clearly the purposes for which a test is given and the probable consequences of scores resulting from it.
4. Be knowledgeable about the particular test used and its appropriate uses.
5. Receive (or arrange for others to receive) any training necessary to understand the test, its uses and limitations, and to administer, score, and interpret it.
6. Possess enough technical knowledge to be able to evaluate technical claims (e.g., validity or reliability claims) made in the test manual.
7. Know the procedures necessary to reduce or eliminate bias in test selection, administration, and interpretation.
8. Advise examinees in advance of testing of the fact that they will be tested and of the purposes and nature of the testing.
9. Keep all standardized test materials secure at all times so as not to invalidate present or future uses of the test.
10. Provide examinees with information about correct procedures for filling out answer sheets (the *mechanics,* not the *substance* of responding).
11. Proctor and monitor examinees during testing to ensure that no academic dishonesty occurs.
12. Keep test scores confidential (except in certain circumstances we will discuss later).

Educators who use tests should *not*

1. Threaten examinees with use of test results or otherwise heighten examinees' anxiety about the test.
2. Teach the specific content of an upcoming test to future examinees.
3. Provide copies of actual test questions to examinees in advance, either in instructional materials or any other form.
4. Use standardized test questions on locally constructed tests.
5. Administer alternate forms of a test as practice for examinees scheduled to be tested with another form of the same test.
6. Deviate in *any* way from standardized procedures for administering, scoring, or interpreting a test.
7. Give extra help or any verbal or visual clues to examinees during test administration (except when clarifying a test of which the user is the author).
8. Attempt to raise examinees' scores through coercion, bribery, or competition.

Looking beyond the use of standardized tests to the broader issue of teacher competence in all forms of student assessment, a committee representing three major professional associations for teachers and measurement specialists (American Federation of Teachers [AFT], National Council on Measurement in Education, & National Education Association, 1990) proposed that all teachers should be skilled in

1. Choosing assessment methods appropriate for instructional decisions.
2. Developing assessment methods appropriate for instructional decisions.
3. Administering, scoring, and interpreting the results of both externally produced and teacher-produced assessment methods.
4. Using assessment results when making decisions about individual students, planning teaching, developing curriculum, and school improvement.
5. Developing valid pupil grading procedures that use pupil assessment.
6. Communicating assessment results to students, parents, and other educators.
7. Recognizing unethical, illegal, and otherwise inappropriate assessment methods and uses of assessment information.

We attempt to cover all of these in this book.

Maintaining Confidentiality of Test Results

Earlier we discussed test disclosure, in which there may be legitimate needs for test results to be revealed to the *examinee*, or to others who can use such information to serve the examinee's interests. Here our concern is with the opposite case, where test results are *not* kept confidential, and students' test scores are divulged in ways that could be harmful. It is an essential ethical canon that strict confidentiality of test scores should be maintained, and failure to do so is not only a serious ethical violation but is also illegal, except under the following circumstances pointed out by Sax (1989):

1. If test results (e.g., in a psychological examination) reveal a "clear and immediate danger" to a student or to others, other professionals or authorities may be advised of that danger.
2. If sharing a student's test scores with other professionals would be of significant help *to the student*.
3. Where test results are intended for use in making professional decisions about individuals (e.g., promotion decisions), and are shared with appropriate professional personnel.
4. If a student waives the right to maintain confidentiality.

Ethical Problems Associated with Teaching to the Test

Popham (1987) popularized the term *high stakes testing* to describe test situations in which the results of testing (especially standardized achievement testing) were used in ways that could have severe negative consequences for students (e.g., retention in grade, denial of eligibility for extracurricular activities, failure to graduate from high school or gain entrance to post-secondary education), school districts (e.g., published reports by the media that lead to ranking of districts, reductions in budget, dissatisfaction by patrons), and/or teachers (e.g., reduced salary increments, requirements for in-service training). Based on surveys and interviews with public school teachers and administrators in all 50 states, Shepard (1990) concluded that 40 of the 50 state testing programs (or aggregation of local district test results) were in a high-stakes testing situation, not to mention sometimes intense, high-stakes pressure *within* many local districts.

In those situations where the results of standardized achievement testing are used to make important decisions, there is increasing concern that district administrators, teachers, and/or students might look for inappropriate ways to raise the test scores. The controversy over such practices was fueled by a 1987 report by a West Virginia physician, John J. Cannell, that showed that the vast majority of school districts in the United States were reporting standardized achievement scores above the 50th percentile.

As anyone with a modicum of statistical training knows, it's impossible for more than half the population to be above the 50th percentile. Consequently, Cannell's observation was quickly dubbed the "Lake Wobegon" phenomenon in honor of the mythical Minnesota town immortalized by Garrison Keillor (in the "Prairie Home Companion" radio series) as a place where "All the women are strong, all the men are good-looking, and all the children are above average."

One of the most frequent initial explanations of Cannell's observation was that the norms on which his findings were based were somewhat outdated, and the fact that achievement was rising would explain the apparently illogical finding that more than half the students were above the 50th percentile (e.g., Lenke & Keene, 1988; Williams, 1988). Cannell (1988, 1989) responded that the argument that achievement was rising was inconsistent with other indicators of educational progress. He suggested that instead of rising achievement, the finding was best explained by inaccurate initial norms, inappropriate "teaching to the test" (or to be less diplomatic, cheating), and collusion and misrepresentation by test publishers to make schools look good and thus sell more tests.

Cannell's writing and other rejoinders have generated a vigorous—and, in our opinion, healthy—debate over the role of standardized achievement testing in the school. That debate has highlighted the facts that (1) results from standardized achievement tests are frequently used inappropriately and that (2) some school personnel prepare students for taking tests in ways that are unethical, if not downright sleazy. Based on the currently available evidence, however, we do not believe that there has been any conscious effort or conspiracy on the part of publishing companies to make school districts look good and, by so doing, to increase sales of tests. Instead, we believe that the Lake Woebegone effect can be explained by a combination of the following four factors.

1. *Real gains in achievement have occurred since the time norms were calculated.* Although the gains in achievement are not nearly large enough to explain why the vast majority of school districts score above the 50th percentile, there is solid evidence that (1) achievement is improving nationally and that (2) few achievement tests' norms are kept very current. Thus, the simple fact that the norms are increasingly outdated, juxtaposed with a rising achievement score trend, means that real, but relatively modest achievement gains are partly responsible for the dramatically better "Lake Woebegone" performance compared to the norms (Linn, Graue, & Sanders, 1989; Koretz, 1988; Lenke & Keene, 1988).

2. *Norms for standardized achievement tests are not nationally representative.* It has been known for some time that even though test publishers attempt to obtain representative samples on which to calculate norms, a substantial number of school districts choose not to participate in such norming studies. Baglin (1981) showed that the reasons that determined which school districts do or do not participate would contribute to findings similar to Cannell's report (see also Phillips & Finn, 1988; Shepard, 1990).

3. *Schools districts' efforts to match their curriculum with the test being used give those districts unfair advantages in comparisons with the norms.* A test publishing company selects schools to be in their norming sample without any consideration of how closely the curriculum in that district matches the content of the test. Thus norms are based on a sample of schools, some of which match the test objectives closely and some of which do not. When a school district selects a particular test to use, however, they pay a great deal of attention to how well the test matches their curriculum. It should come as no surprise that their students' performance on that test (which was selected to closely match the curricula) would be higher than expected when compared to the norms.

4. *Inappropriate teaching to the test has yielded spuriously high test scores.* Standardized test items are expected to represent a sample of items from the domain of instructional objectives that have been taught during the year. If the curriculum is structured so that students are given an opportunity to practice the specific items that are on the test over and over again, you would expect them to do better on the test than someone who had not had an opportunity to practice

those specific items. The same would be true, though to a lesser degree, with very similar items. Such dubious procedures have been referred to as *test score pollution* by Haladyna, Nolen, and Haas (1991) because they make it difficult to interpret the meaning of scores from such students in relation to the norming sample.

We believe that each of the four factors discussed above is in part responsible for Cannell's finding that the vast majority of school districts report test scores above the national median. Although the severity of some of these problems could be reduced by technical means (e.g., more frequent norming of tests, or greater efforts to achieve nationally representative samples), teaching to the test—possibly the major contributor to the Lake Wobegon effect—is likely to remain with us as long as the results of standardized achievement tests are used to make high stakes decisions—unless human nature changes in the meantime, which we doubt.

But What Is Wrong with Teaching to the Test?

There's nothing wrong with testing the same material that is being taught. In fact, it makes eminently good sense to do so. No sensible teacher would ever think of giving her children a Spanish vocabulary test to determine how well they had mastered the German vocabulary words she had been teaching. Such phrases as "integration of testing and instruction" (Nitko, 1989), "instructional alignment" (Cohen & Hyman, 1991), and "measurement driven instruction" (Popham, 1987) are increasingly used to emphasize that testing and teaching should be closely related. Although we agree totally with the commonsense notion that there should be a clear link between teaching and testing, there is a point at which legitimate efforts to ensure correspondence between what is taught and what is tested on standardized achievement tests changes to inappropriate teaching to the test (frequently referred to as cheating). Not everyone agrees at what point the crossover from legitimate to illegitimate occurs. We can, however, define a number of points along that continuum and give you our recommendations.

The continuum along which we can link teaching and testing is summarized below (adapted from Haladyna, Nolen, & Haas, 1991; and Mehrens & Kaminski, 1989), with the most legitimate linkages of teaching and testing listed first, and decreasing in legitimacy thereafter.

1. Using specific instructional objectives to guide your teaching without knowing what objectives are covered by the particular standardized test used in your district
2. Motivating students to do their best on tests and teaching general test-taking skills (e.g., appropriate use of available time, deductive reasoning, familiarity with various testing formats, etc.)
3. Structuring the curriculum so it corresponds to the objectives included in the standardized test used in your district
4. Teaching the specific format and objectives used in the test as a major part of the instructional activities

5. Teaching the *specific* content of an upcoming test to future examinees, but without using the actual test items
6. Under the guise of instruction, using one parallel form of a test for students to "practice," prior to being examined with another parallel form of the same test
7. Having students "practice," using the same form of the standardized test, or providing copies of actual test questions to examinees in advance, whether in instructional materials or any other form

Virtually everyone would agree that appropriate high-quality instruction would include the first item in the above list. Most would also view the second as appropriate. There is less agreement, however, with respect to the third and fourth items. Most measurement experts agree that the last three items in the list constitute inappropriate teaching to the test—if not downright cheating. Surprisingly, however, such activities are not uncommon. Gonzalez (1985) found that over half the teachers interviewed in their study did not consider it cheating to have students practice on previous versions of the test currently used by the district. Almost a quarter thought it was acceptable for a teacher to teach students specific items from the standardized test if she happened to remember them from the last time the test was administered.

How much of an effect can teaching specific items from the test have? Actually, quite large. Shepard (1990) noted that for two of the most frequently used standardized achievement tests (the Stanford Achievement Test and the California Achievement Test), a third grader who scored at the median in reading, language, or mathematics would gain from two to seven percentile points by getting one additional item correct. Differences of that magnitude are likely to appear quite large when the local newspaper compares the results of two different schools.

Some people believe that the closer the alignment between what is taught and what is tested, the better the information will be about how well the students have mastered the intended content. People who take this position (e.g., Cohen & Hyman, 1991; Popham, 1987) see nothing wrong with having a one-to-one correspondence between the objectives and even the format of what is being taught and tested.

Others (e.g., Madaus, 1985a; Mehrens & Kaminski, 1989; Shepard, 1990) point out that in those situations where the test items are best thought of as representing a sample from a larger domain of skills, knowledge, and behaviors that are thought to be important for students to master, such close "instructional alignment" (i.e., a one-to-one correspondence of the objectives and format between what is taught and what is tested) will give a substantially inflated estimate of how well students have mastered the domain of material. To see why this is so, imagine that you have been asked to memorize a list of 100 Russian vocabulary words. At the time you begin studying, you are told that the test of how well you have mastered the assignment will be a multiple choice test of 10 of those 100 words and are given a copy of the items. Most of us would focus our attention (and consequently our learning) on those 10 words on the final mastery test. The remaining 90 words would likely receive short shrift, especially if time and energy for the assignment were limited.

Another potential problem with such close alignment between teaching and testing is that over time, the objectives of the standardized test may begin to define what teachers are willing to spend time teaching. As Shepard (1990) pointed out, "test-curriculum alignment is a reciprocal process . . . once the test is chosen that best fits the curriculum, the practiced curriculum is adjusted further in response to the test" (p. 18). For example, Hatch and Freeman (1988) found that 67percent of the kindergarten teachers in their sample implemented instructional practices that they thought were contrary to children's learning needs because they thought it would improve the children's scores on standardized achievement tests. Similarly, Darling and Wise (1985) found that many teachers stopped using essay tests in their classes because they had been told that the use of such tests during instruction would interfere with the students' performance on standardized multiple-choice tests.

Your position on how much teaching-testing alignment is "too much" should depend on your answers to two questions. First, do you believe that the objectives for a particular standardized test represent a *sample* or the *total universe* of what should be taught? Second, how much influence are you willing to grant to test publishing companies regarding the selection of objectives to be taught in your school?

We believe schools should provide students with broad coverage of important and meaningful content, as well as teaching them to generalize their learning to various other contexts and situations. Therefore, we believe that the objectives of any standardized test and the formats in which those objectives are measured should be viewed as a sample and not the universe. We also believe that educators should be allowed to thoughtfully establish their instructional objectives without undue concern about whether each particular objective is included on the standardized test used in their district.

Those beliefs lead us to a simple position. Even though teaching should be guided by clear instructional objectives and students should be taught general test-taking skills, it is entirely inappropriate to let teaching be substantially influenced by the objectives and item formats of a particular standardized test. It is even more inappropriate to use current or previous versions of the test as an "instructional tool." Of course, some colleagues disagree with our position (e.g., Cohen & Hyman, 1991; Popham, 1987) and we will doubtlessly continue to hear these issues debated even more vigorously as the consequences of doing well or poorly on standardized achievement tests becomes more apparent.

ISSUES IN USING TESTS FOR TEACHER CERTIFICATION

Tests have been used to evaluate teachers in a variety of indirect ways, such as the unfortunate and usually unfair use of achievement test scores of students to judge teachers' ability. Here we are concerned with competency tests administered directly to teachers or teacher candidates as a basis for making decisions about certification or recertification.

The Impetus for Teacher Competency Testing

Sandefur (1985) contends that the movement to test teachers' competency was spawned by increased use of minimum competency testing to assess students' basic skills. As the public saw significant proportions of school students failing such tests, it seemed logical to ask how much of the blame could be traced to incompetent teaching. Soon lawmakers, responding to public opinion, were mandating that prospective teachers (and in some cases veteran teachers) be tested to assure their competency. Attitudes toward preservice testing and in-service testing for teachers are somewhat different, however. The use of competency tests for preservice certification decisions has spread quickly and is now a requirement in a majority of the United States (Jaeger, 1990). Relatively little opposition has been posed to such tests, even among teacher organizations. This is not so for *re*certification tests, which have been vigorously opposed by most teachers and teacher organizations. Yet, legislators continue to ask why screening aimed at preventing those who are illiterate from entering teaching should not also be used to "weed out" illiterates who already hold teaching positions.

Such concerns led to legislative mandates in Arkansas, Georgia, and Texas to test the competency of practicing educators. In a fascinating account of Texas' development and use of such a test, Shepard and Kreitzer (1987) trace the economic and political circumstances that resulted in perhaps the most widely publicized case of its type. Pressure for a "teacher test" began in 1983, when Texas' Select Committee on Public Education began conducting surveys and taking testimony relative to its charge. The committee heard numerous horror stories about the "incompetence" of some practicing teachers:

> Apparently one teacher was said to have had difficulty explaining to her class why the weather was so different in Hawaii and in Alaska even though they were right next to each other (in the corner of the map). (Shepard & Kreitzer, 1987, p. 24)

Select Committee members also reported that teachers, arguing for pay raises, had sent them letters "that were peppered with bad grammar and misspelled words" (p. 24). Deeply concerned, the legislature mandated teacher testing to eliminate incompetent teachers. The result was the Texas Examination of Current Administrators and Teachers (TECAT), developed to assess minimum reading and writing skills. The TECAT was first administered to 202,000 Texas educators in 1986; the passing rate was high (96.7 percent), but 6,579 teachers failed. Of those, 4,704 signed up to be retested three months later, with 1,199 failing this second time.

How useful was the TECAT? Texas educators ended up about equally divided in opinion, with half of the teachers saying that the test had done what legislators intended by getting rid of the bad teachers, while proving the majority competent. The other half complained that all teachers had been made to seem less competent by humiliation, embarrassment, and slanted media coverage that made the test seem laughably easy.

Legislative enthusiasm for testing veteran teachers seems to have crested and may now be waning. Shepard and Kreitzer (1987) report that, when they began their study, "legislation to test practicing teachers was pending in two states and talked about in others. Today these actions are neither passed nor pending. We sense . . . that there is less enthusiasm to jump into teacher testing now than 18 months ago" (p. 31). Also, the TECAT has been ruled discriminatory by a federal agency and its use threatens Title VII litigation (Kuehn, Stallings, & Holland, 1990). So, for those in other states, the publicity surrounding the TECAT may yet serve to cause caution in their legislative assemblies.

On the national U.S. scene, the major teacher organizations (National Education Association [NEA] and AFT) both oppose testing of veteran teachers (Martin, 1986; Madaus & Pullin, 1987), although the AFT would soften its opposition if certain concessions were granted teachers who failed. The AFT has issued strong statements in favor of a national test for certifying prospective teachers, however (Shanker, 1985).

Types of Teacher Competency Tests in Use

Teacher competency tests can take varying forms, focusing on one or more of the following clusters (Conklin, 1985): (1) basic skills, (2) subject area knowledge, (3) professional knowledge and skills (pedagogical), and (4) on-the-job performance. Some states use only one of these types of measures, while others use some combination in their assessment of teacher competency. The National Teacher Examinations (NTE) attempt to assess all but on-the-job performance. Despite the breadth of the NTE, however, the chances of serious errors in judging teaching competence by any single test are doubtlessly greater than when multiple criteria and measures are used to judge teachers. This multifaceted approach is embodied in a promising current effort to develop a teacher assessment system predicated on the position that

> The ideal teaching assessment is unlikely to take the form of a single examination for which a candidate "sits" during a designated period, as is the case with the NTE and its state-level equivalents. (Shulman, 1987, p. 39)

The Pros and Cons of Teacher Competency Testing

Many educationists (e.g., Popham & Kirby, 1987) argue that assessment of teaching competence should not stop with *applicants* for teaching positions, but should also be required of *occupants* of such positions. And some teacher groups agree. For example, one of the strongest statements in favor of competency testing for prospective teachers originates with the AFT, America's largest teachers' union, which urges tough teacher exams coupled with high financial incentives for those who pass.

Not everyone is enamored with the idea of teacher competency tests, however. Conklin (1985) questions their use because there is no research evidence that passing such an exam is related to on-the-job success in teaching. The validity of teacher competency tests has also been challenged in the courts. Beginning in the early 1970s, a number of lawsuits charged that the NTE was being used to discriminate against minority teachers and teacher candidates.

The legal outcomes were mixed. In some (e.g., *Georgia Association of Educators v. Nix*, 1976), the court ruled that the NTE could not be used as a criterion for awarding teaching certificates. In others (e.g., *United States v. South Carolina*, 1977), the court dismissed the charge that state use of the NTE for teacher certification had racially discriminatory purposes.

Legal battles over the use of teacher competency tests will probably continue as long as such tests are used, and the issue of their validity remains unresolved. But experience suggests caution in basing teacher certification or recertification decisions solely on competency examinations. For those who want to pursue this topic in greater depth, we suggest reading Beckham (1986), Madaus and Pullin (1987), Shepard and Kreitzer (1987), and Carlson (1990).

Two points can be made here, however. First, teacher competency tests can measure basic verbal and numerical ability and subject matter knowledge very adequately. Second, while they are useful in assessing whether teachers possess essential verbal and intellectual abilities, teacher competency tests are not now (and possibly never will be) of much value in measuring teaching skills.

SUGGESTED READINGS

Cole, N. S., & Moss, P. A. (1989). Bias in test use. In R. L. Linn (Ed.), *Educational Measurement* (3rd ed.). London: Collier Macmillan.
    This is a very informative analysis of technical issues pertaining to test bias, especially as they relate to test validation, and some social consequences of using biased tests. Special attention is devoted to ways to detect and eliminate bias in educational and mental tests.

Bersoff, D. N. (1981). Testing and the law. *American Psychologist, 36*(10), 1047–1056.
    This article reviews court cases dealing with (a) cultural bias in educational tests, (b) the validity of employment tests, and (c) the disclosure of test materials. An excellent summary of legal interpretations of psychometric concepts.

Jaeger, R. M. (1989). Certification of student competence. In R. L. Linn (Ed.), *Educational Measurement* (3rd ed, pp. 485–514). London: Collier Macmillan.
    This chapter contains an excellent summary of issues pertaining to the MCT movement, including: (1) definitions of competency testing, (2) the breadth of efforts to use MCTs in the United States, including examples of two very different MCT programs, (3) various methods for setting standards and research evidence on their relative usefulness, (4) strategies for assuring students opportunities to learn the minimum competencies, (5) legal issues pertaining to MCTs, and (6) social and curricular consequences of competency testing.

Educational Measurement: Issues and Practices (1988), 7(4).
    This is a special issue devoted to Cannell's report that the vast majority of school districts in the United States have accomplished the impossible by reporting standardized achievement test scores above the median. Following the lead article by Cannell, representatives from the U.S. Department of Education and most major test publishing firms respond. The debate highlights some major issues about standardized achievement testing.

Berk, R. A. (1986). Minimum competency testing: status and potential. In B. S. Plake & J. C. Witt (Eds.), *The future of testing.* Hillsdale, NJ: Lawrence Erlbaum Associates.

This chapter contains a very comprehensive treatment of the origins, current status, and potential of the minimum competency testing movement. The discussion includes definitions, policy issues, technical specifications and issues, and critical issues that must be resolved if MCTs are to contribute positively to education.

Madaus, G. F. (Ed.) (1983). *The courts, validity, and minimum competency testing.* Boston: Kluwer-Nijhoff.

This book contains ten chapters that deal with the issue of how one might evaluate the match between the skills and knowledge measured by an MCT and a school district's curriculum and instruction. An additional chapter contains an excellent overview of the evaluation of the concept of content validity, especially pertaining to MCTs.

AERA, APA, & NCME (1985). *Standards for educational and psychological testing.* Washington, DC: American Psychological Association.

This is the most recent set of standards for educational and psychological testing, superseding the 1974 *Standards.* This booklet describes the purpose of the *Standards* and cautions that should be exercised in applying them. The volume lists and explains (1) technical standards for test construction and evaluation, (2) standards for test use, (3) standards for particular applications in testing minorities and those with disabilities, and (4) standards for administrative procedures.

Beckham, J. C. (1986). Objective testing to assess teacher competency: Emerging legal issues. In T. N. Jones & D. P. Semler (Eds.), *School Law Update 1986.* Topeka: National Organization on Legal Problems of Education.

This chapter provides a concise discussion of the legal challenges to teacher competency testing, the bases for those legal challenges, and the limitations and applications of the court rulings as they relate to testing teachers.

SELF-CHECK QUIZ

1. *Test bias* refers to
   a. the influence on scores of factors other than those the test is intended to measure.
   b. intentional efforts to bias the test against those with particular ethnic, cultural, linguistic, or gender characteristics.
   c. any kind of unfairness in administering a test.
   d. use of subjectivity rather than objectivity in scoring tests.
2. Which of the following is an example of test bias?
   a. Using specialists from one linguistic or cultural group to administer individual tests to pupils of the same linguistic or cultural group
   b. Using equal ratios of pronoun referents of both genders in a test
   c. Making placement decisions about minority children on the basis of a test standardized on white, middle-class children
   d. Assessment of actual on-the-job performance
3. Truth-in-testing proposals deal with
   a. disclosing test questions and answers to the public.
   b. efforts to prevent students from cheating on tests.
   c. notifying examinees in advance about the content of a test.
   d. the actual monetary cost of administering a testing program.
   e. the consequences of performing poorly on a test.

4. It is considered ethically *permissible* for teachers to
   a. use standardized test items in their own classroom tests, as long as credit is given.
   b. tutor students on the specific subject matter of an upcoming standardized test.
   c. explain to students the mechanics of taking a standardized test.
   d. excuse from testing students they know will do poorly on standardized tests.

5. What is the major purpose of having standards for tests and test use?
   a. To assure that tests are developed and used in an ethical and correct manner
   b. To guarantee that test scores will be accurate for all individuals
   c. To have criteria for use in credentialing measurement specialists
   d. To have standards that can guide court decisions in cases concerning (alleged) test misuse

6. Which type of assessment gives the best appraisal of teacher competency?
   a. Tests of basic skills (e.g., reading, writing, math)
   b. Tests of knowledge in subject-field teaching specializations
   c. Tests of professional knowledge and skills
   d. Assessment of actual on-the-job performance
   e. A multifaceted approach using several types of criteria and measures

7. Which of the following words included in a test of general academic aptitude is most apt to be considered biased against lower socioeconomic children?
   a. Airport
   b. Concerto
   c. Gravity
   d. Restaurant
   e. Weapon

8. *High stakes testing* refers to
   a. only using tests which have demonstrated reliability and validity.
   b. the unreasonable expense associated with purchasing standardized achievement tests.
   c. the motivation to perform well on standardized tests because results are used to make important decisions.
   d. the need to make sure that the objectives of a test are appropriately aligned with the instructional goals.

9. Which of the following may be concluded from recent court cases concerning minimum competency tests (MCTs)?
   a. MCTs may be used in deciding whether or not to award diplomas.
   b. MCTs used for making decisions must meet higher criteria than regular course tests.
   c. Schools are required to guarantee that a student achieve basic literacy.
   d. Schools will be held accountable if students with disabilities cannot meet educational goals.

10. Which of the following practices is considered ethical for test users?
    a. Administering alternate forms of a test as practice.
    b. Advising examinees in advance of the nature of the test.
    c. Promoting competition as a means of raising examinees' scores.
    d. Teaching the specific content of an upcoming test.
    e. Using standardized test questions on locally constructed tests.

SUGGESTION SHEET

If your last name starts with the letter *C*, please complete the Suggestion Sheet at the end of the book while this chapter is still fresh in your mind.

Beginning Your Excursion: An Overview of Basic Measurement Concepts and Principles

In this second section of our text, we attempt to accomplish four things. First, in Chapter 4, we provide more precise definitions of various types of measures and some of the basic concepts and principles pertaining to such measures. In Section One, we avoided dwelling much on terminology, definitions, and technical concepts, but we cannot maintain that posture here. You now need to understand some of the basic concepts and principles that underlie educational measurement and evaluation. If we were to consider your learning about measurement and evaluation as a voyage into strange waters that may appear to you uncharted and possibly difficult to navigate, then we would serve you poorly if we failed to provide you with all the charts and navigational aids possible, together with a simple but solid anchor or two for when you feel yourself drifting. Chapter 4 is intended to provide you with the basic navigational and survival aids you will require on your excursion. (And don't let the word *survival* scare you; you'll make it if you are just willing to keep paddling!)

Second, in Chapter 5, we help you learn to read, interpret, and understand test scores, introducing you to various types of test scores and the ways each should be interpreted. We also provide simple descriptions of some statistical concepts necessary for understanding test results.

Third, in Chapters 6 and 7, we review what makes an educational measure good or bad, trustworthy or treacherous. We outline characteristics of measures that discriminate between high and low quality measures, discussing and providing examples of a test's usefulness, validity, and reliability. We discuss how to make test results more objective and how to reduce errors in measurement. In Chapter 6 we focus on the important characteristic of reliability. In Chapter 7 we turn our attention to the vital characteristic of validity, and how it is affected by reliability. In both of these chapters we try to help you see what is necessary for an educational test to be considered really useful.

Finally, in Chapter 8, we discuss techniques for reducing errors that can readily creep into test scores if we are not vigilant in detecting and ejecting them. Dozens of extraneous factors—such as how the test is administered, or distractions in the testing environment, or students' guessing when they don't know an answer—can confound test results. Chapter 8 is intended to help you identify and be alert to such factors and enable you to take steps to reduce or eliminate their influence on tests for which you are responsible.

We know we just used a few terms that could set your alarm flags fluttering—words like *statistical concept*. But don't hoist them to the masthead just yet. Give us a chance to prove that we can guide you safely across the technical and conceptual shoals where so many practitioners have shipwrecked previously. It really is not a difficult voyage, and once through it, you'll be in the deep and calm waters where you can use the tools provided in these chapters to chart your own course and sail in whatever direction you please in using educational measurement and evaluation to help you ply your professional practice.

CHAPTER **4**

Getting Your Bearings:
Some Concepts
and Classifications
Basic to Measurement
and Evaluation

Overview

In the first three chapters we spoke often of *testing, measurement, assessment*, and *evaluation*. How are these terms similar? How do they differ? We have reached a point where answers to these questions are necessary for your understanding of later content. This chapter also provides more precise definitions and explanations of the types of tests we have referred to previously, such as *standardized tests* and *criterion-referenced measurement*, comparing and contrasting each of them with alternatives. Much of this chapter is devoted to imposing some order on the enormously varied and complex field of measurement. We examine several dimensions useful in classifying educational measures, providing categories and distinctions that you should know for each. Finally, we present a classification system that combines two of those dimensions, yielding a useful outline of the more common types of measurement instruments.

The chapter contains three major sections, dealing respectively with important definitions, distinctions, and terminology; examination of several dimensions for classifying measurement instruments; and presentation of a system we have found useful for classifying measures used in education.

Objectives

After completing your study of this chapter, you will be able to

1. Define and give an example of each of the following:

   - Test
   - Measurement
   - Assessment
   - Evaluation

   - Reliability
   - Validity
   - Objectivity

2. Discuss differences between norm-referenced measurement and criterion-referenced measurement and give the relative advantages and disadvantages and possible uses for each.

3. Discuss differences and similarities between standardized and teacher-made tests, and explain where each would be appropriate.

4. List at least eight dimensions useful for classifying educational measures.

5. Explain how teachers can use the outline of measurement instruments provided in this chapter to identify instruments useful in their classrooms.

DEFINITIONS, DISTINCTIONS, AND TERMINOLOGY

In our preceding chapters, such terms as *measurement, testing, evaluation, validity*, and *standardized* have not been made explicit. Now we must define them more clearly to enable you to understand later content.

Some Simple Definitions

First, let us define very simply three important measurement concepts: *validity, reliability* and *objectivity* (more will be said about these in Chapters 6 and 7). All three refer to characteristics of educational measurements. Since we have not yet differentiated between tests, measurement, and the like, we ask that you keep in mind a *test* as we define each of these three. The definitions would not be greatly altered if we were to speak of other, nontest types of measurement. The following definitions have been oversimplified for the sake of brevity and clarity.

Validity

Test scores are valid to the degree to which they accomplish the purpose for which they are being used. More precisely, the scores obtained from the test are valid to the degree that differences represent actual differences in the characteristic being measured. Validity is essential in educational measurement and evaluation. What self-respecting educator would be satisfied with a test that purported to measure mathematics problem-solving skills but cast the items in such difficult language structure and vocabulary that proficiency in English was more important in determining scores than proficiency in mathematics? If a test does not measure what it was designed to measure, the information it yields is useless.

Reliability

A test is reliable if it measures whatever it measures consistently. Reliability is a measure of how stable, dependable, trustworthy, and consistent a test is in measuring the same thing each time. Assume that you gave your students a history test yesterday and used the scores to rank the students from highest to lowest on "history knowledge." Then assume that today you gave it again to the same students and found that the rankings were completely reversed. The student who scored highest the first time scored lowest the next, and vice versa, right through the class. Given such inconsistent results, we would say that test was unreliable. A test has little value if the score it yields for Mary today is dramatically different from the score she would receive if she took it again tomorrow, under similar circumstances. Few educators would be enthusiastic over an academic aptitude test that showed Jerry with a score of 140 on Tuesday and 75 on Wednesday, while Jose's score jumped from 95 to 155.

Objectivity

A test is objective to the degree that two or more reasonable persons, given a scoring key and/or scoring criteria, would agree on how to score each item, thus agreeing on the number of points each examinee should receive for the total test. Objective scores are not affected by scorers' opinions or biases. Objectivity is, therefore, a function of scoring, but it entails more than interscorer agreement on individual items.

Care must go into the construction of the test, design of the scoring key or criteria, and procedures for seeing that everyone takes the test under the same conditions. All these factors help make objective scoring not only possible but meaningful. Matching, true-false, and multiple-choice items lend themselves to objective scoring, and most objective tests depend on such items. It is possible, however, although much more difficult, to devise administrative procedures and scoring keys that are so precise that even essay items can be scored very objectively (Page & Paulus, 1968).

The flip side of objectivity is, of course, *subjectivity*, the bane of measurement instruments. A test is subjective to the degree that scorers cannot agree on how to grade each item, resulting in different scorers assigning different numbers of points to the same item and arriving at different total scores for the same student. Subjectivity is the degree to which personal prejudice or bias can influence the test score; it is primarily a function of scoring. But the scoring is greatly affected by the nature of the test and the scoring key (or absence thereof). An essay test that allows extended answers and provides no criteria for use in scoring is a good example of a subjective test. A personality test that asks examinees to respond to ambiguous stimuli (e.g., paint blotches) and provides no scoring key would be the epitome of subjectivity—likely yielding as many psychoanalytical interpretations as there are psychoanalysts interpreting the scores.

Subjectivity in measurement should be avoided as energetically as objectivity should be pursued. One of our primary objectives is to help you increase objectivity and decrease subjectivity in the educational measures you use.

Distinguishing among Testing, Measurement, Assessment, and Evaluation

Measurement, testing, assessment, and *evaluation* are closely intertwined activities and functions that are not easily separable. Sometimes one is embedded within or grows from the other, and frequently several functions come into play within a single educational activity. Yet there are important distinctions among them that make it useful to separate them, and to sort out some terms that look similar and are frequently confused with measurement, testing, assessment, and evaluation.

Data Collection

Some measurement experts have broadly defined measurement as the collection, retention, and retrieval of information, or as the process by which data are gathered and made available. Such a broad definition is not very useful. Is the teacher who clips newspaper articles dealing with space shuttle flights and who makes his scrapbook available to students engaging in measurement? We think not. Although *most* data collection efforts in education depend on some form of measurement, many do not; taking attendance and counting the school's lunch money are not forms of measurement.

Measurement

Measurement is the process of making empirical observations of some attribute, characteristic, or phenomenon and translating those observations into quantifiable or categorical form according to clearly specified procedures or rules. The attribute, characteristic, or phenomenon measured could be a person, an event, or even an object, but we shall focus on measurement of human characteristics or of educational or social phenomena of interest to educators.

Measurement is usually quantitative and involves assigning numbers to the attribute measured according to explicit rules for doing so. Nonquantitative measurement is also possible. An example would be observing and categorizing different types of cooperation among students in problem-solving groups. While instances of behavior in a particular category might be quantified (e.g., counted), we would consider the act of observation and categorization as more typically a form of nonquantitative measurement, just so it followed clearly specified rules and procedures.

Educational measurement is broader than educational *testing*, for while measurement frequently employs tests, it may also employ observation instruments, use of checklists, and other methods that cannot precisely be construed as testing.

Testing

Testing is one form of measurement. A *test* is a set of tasks or questions presented to an examinee in a systematic procedure and used to elicit a sample of the examinee's behavior on the attribute or characteristic of interest. A test is a certain type of educational measure. It provides a *sample* of behavior from which we infer how well a student would have done if presented with *all* possible test questions pertaining to the area tested. Suppose we wanted to test a student's knowledge of multiplication facts for numbers from 0 to 12. Only a teacher with an obsessive-compulsive personality disorder would give a written test containing every possible fact appearing in those multiplication tables. The more economical approach would be to select a representative sample of facts, test the student on those, and infer from the score how well he had mastered the multiplication facts from 0 to 12. The inference could be wrong; whenever tests contain a sample of the possible test items, some measurement error can be expected. The student *could* happen to know all of the facts that appeared on the test and *not* know *any* of those that were omitted, but the probability of that happening is about as great as that of the Internal Revenue Service deciding that you overpaid on your annual tax return.

Although tests are most often formal measurements with written responses, they need not be. A simulation can be a type of performance test. Trainees in a Red Cross class may be asked to use CPR to revive an electronically monitored dummy; they fail the test if the flashing red light shows they would have ruptured a real person's spleen.

Test Item

A *test item,* put most simply, is a single question, exercise, or stimulus in a test. We suspect you've seen enough of these to know what we mean.

Assessment

The term *assessment* can be used to refer to either (1) assessment of the performance of individual students or (2) assessment of the performance of entire educational systems (e.g., a school district or state education system).

Assessment of Individual Performance.   Educators frequently speak of *student assessment*, sometimes referring to it as an *appraisal of learner outcomes*. Such terms denote an activity broad enough to encompass both measurement and testing. In short, assessment of individual performance is the process of collecting data to make decisions about pupils. Such assessment data may be in the form of familiar quantitative data or in the form of qualitative data typical of many of the increasingly popular nontraditional forms of assessment.

Assessment of System Performance.   We define *system assessment* as the use of specially constructed tests to determine the overall condition of an entire system (e.g., the public school system) or its major components. Examples of system assessment exist in the well known National Assessment of Educational Progress (NAEP) or the many state assessment programs that have spun off from it. Whereas testing typically seeks to compare individual student scores, system assessment disregards individual scores and concentrates on the whole system and/ or broad subgroups or cross-sections in the system (e.g., all second graders or all rural schools).[1] System assessment has historically avoided aggregating or reporting data in ways that would permit evaluative comparisons to be made between or among students, classrooms, schools, school districts, or state educational systems.

Accountability

Not itself a form of measurement, *accountability* consists of the legislative or administrative use of tests with the intent of holding schools and school personnel responsible for their expenditures of public funds. Tests used to compare school districts, individual schools, classrooms, school programs, and curricula serve as one basis for "accountability decisions." Use of minimum competency tests to certify teachers or award high school diplomas are also examples of tests used for accountability decisions, although the sanctions eventually fall upon those denied the diplomas or certificates, rather than upon the professional preparation programs that produced them.

Evaluation

At its most general level, *evaluation* is the determination of a thing's worth, value, or quality. In education, the term is used in two rather different senses, though both are in harmony with this general definition.

In the first sense, *educational evaluation* is the formal determination of the quality, effectiveness, or value of a program, product, project, process, goal, curriculum, or some other educational entity. Here the focus is on identifying standards for judging quality, collecting relevant information (often through measurement), and applying the standards to determine quality. We treat this type of evaluation explicitly in Chapter 22. Any reference to this broader type of evaluation prior to Chapter 22 will be referred to as *educational evaluation*, to distinguish it from evaluation of an individual's performance.

In the second—and more frequent—usage of evaluation, we focus on making qualitative judgments about an individual's performance. This is an integral part of good teaching—judging how well individual students have grasped the content and concepts presented. Sometimes the teacher makes *informal* judgments about students' learning or progress, but such intuitive (and typically subjective) "evaluations" should be buttressed by more objective evidence such as achievement or other types of tests. In this context, then, *evaluation of pupil performance* is the observation of pupil behavior and the interpretation and conversion of scores from tests or other measurement devices to provide judgments about the quality of the progress or performance of individual students. These judgments lead to decisions about how instruction can be improved, which students need remedial help or

---

[1] Womer (1973) and Anderson, Welch, & Harris (1982) provide more complete discussions of those differences between testing and assessment, and Millman (1978) has provided a useful discussion of particular types of assessment models.

advanced work, which students might benefit from referral to a school psychologist or counselor, and so on.

Evaluation of pupil performance requires that information yielded by the tests (or other measuring instrument) be converted to some type of qualitative indicator. This might be a verbal statement (e.g., "satisfactory," "needs improvement," or "unsatisfactory"), or a letter grade (A, B, C, D, or F) and is a way of expressing how good or bad the student's performance is in relation to the knowledge, skill, or attribute being judged. Such evaluation goes beyond simple measurement because explicit value judgments are being made about the performance that measurement has produced. Chapter 14 concerns the translation of measurements into qualitative judgments about pupil performance.

One way to think of the relationships among several of the above terms is to think of test items as leaves on the twigs of testing, which grow on the branches of measurement and assessment, which, in turn, grow on the limb of evaluation, which is part of the tree of instruction.[2]

MAPPING THE TERRAIN: CLASSIFICATION OF MEASUREMENT INSTRUMENTS

Every measurement book has its preferred way of classifying educational and psychological measures. As a result, there are dozens of alternative, sometimes conflicting lists of types of measurement instruments, leaving practitioners wondering which is the best way to categorize measurement devices. We believe it is largely a matter of preference and see merit in many different ways to classify measurement tools into types. In this section we present 13 dimensions useful for describing and classifying educational measures. We briefly describe each dimension and list categories or types of instruments, providing examples wherever they seem helpful.

By Discipline or Subject Area of the Content

Measurement instruments are frequently classified by discipline or subject area. For example, standardized achievement tests are often divided into mathematics tests, reading tests, and other commonly tested content areas (usually including those thought of as basic skills). Assessment programs (e.g., NAEP) frequently test students in a broader array of content areas, covering every common school subject from math and science to music and art. Usually categorizing by content area is analogous to categorizing by discipline, but sometimes a subject matter test cuts across several disciplines (e.g., a science test might include a sample of students' knowledge in biology, physics, and chemistry). Some test batteries cut across many disciplines and can only be classified as *omnibus* on this dimension.

---

[2] Although we have adapted and modified it, a similar simile was originally suggested to us by Lavisky (1975).

Test compendia and review volumes frequently use this dimension of discipline or subject area to classify measurement instruments.

By Psychological Constructs

Perhaps the most common way of classifying measures is by the psychological construct targeted for assessment: intelligence, aptitude, achievement, attitude, creativity, personal adjustment, and vocational interests are some examples. Most testing companies' catalogs and most measurement review volumes depend at least in part on this classification system. Such classification is directly dependent on the accuracy with which the psychological construct measured is identified and labeled. A test labeled as a "creativity" test will usually be so classified, even though it is really a thinly veiled test of intelligence or verbal ability. In using this dimension to classify instruments, remember, "A rose by any other name will smell as sweet."

By Specific Skills, Type of Knowledge, or Behaviors Measured

Another dimension for classifying measurement devices uses somewhat more specific operational distinctions. Tests may be classified as *verbal* or *nonverbal*, depending on whether they require reading, speaking, or writing (verbal) or working with numerals or pictures (nonverbal). Tests are also often categorized by particular types of skill or knowledge; a reading test might be further subdivided into tests of students' reading *vocabulary* and reading *comprehen*sion. This dimension more often ends up being used to describe characteristics of tests rather than to place them in categories in professional publications.

By Item Format

Although not all educational measures have *items* per se, most do, and these can also be categorized by their format. For example, we often speak of

- *Essay tests* (items elicit written essay responses).
- *Completion/short answer tests* (students are asked either to "fill in the blank" or provide short answers to direct questions).
- *Multiple-choice tests* (items on which students are forced to select from among multiple answers).
- *True-false tests* (students decide whether written statements are correct or incorrect).
- *Matching tests* (students are asked to correctly match terms or concepts).
- *Rating scales* (students are asked to rate particular aspects of schools or other educational entities).

Obviously these terms really pertain to *item* types, and one instrument may use items of all these types.

By the Type of Data Produced

Much has been said recently about the relative utility of collecting quantitative and qualitative data in attempting to answer educational questions (see, for example, Worthen & Sanders, 1987). We will not revisit the debate here or try to summarize the reasons why various individuals favor one or the other type of data. Indeed, we view both qualitative and quantitative methods of collecting data as useful, compatible, and complementary approaches, each contributing to educational measurement and evaluation when applied to appropriate purposes and questions. We simply note here that many writers tend to describe or categorize measurement devices as *quantitative* or *qualitative*, depending on the nature of the data they collect. We have no discomfort with that, just so the labels are not used disparagingly.

By the Purpose for Which They Are Used

Measurement instruments, especially tests, are frequently categorized by the purpose for which they are administered. There are *diagnostic* tests, *placement* tests, *admissions* tests, *job application* tests, *certification* tests, *licensure* examinations, and so on.

By How the Instrument Is Administered

The most common distinction on this dimension is between *individual* (or individually administered) tests and *group* tests. Many reputable intelligence tests are individual tests that require examiners to develop considerable expertise in test administration. Such tests are thus usually falling to the province of the school psychologist or counselor. Most achievement tests are group tests administered by teachers.

Educational measures containing identical items may be given different labels, depending on how the items are presented. In conducting a survey of parent opinions, for example, parents may be presented with the same questions in a questionnaire mailed to their home or during a personal interview with the school curriculum director. Despite identical questions, these two measures would be labeled differently because of differences in how questions are presented and in how parents respond (in writing versus orally).

By How the Instrument Is Scored

Earlier we differentiated between objectivity and subjectivity. This distinction provides one of the more common ways of classifying measurement instruments—as *objective* (those on which scorers would readily agree about what constitutes a correct response) and *subjective* (those on which two or more scorers might have considerable difficulty agreeing on a "correct" or "strong" response). This dimension tends to subsume the classification-by-item format, for that is a key element in determining objectivity. Multiple-choice, true-false, and matching item tests are usually objective whereas essay exams are more notoriously subjective.

By the Type of Performance Called For

Sometimes we want to measure *typical performance*, how a student usually performs when there are no unusual incentives, pressures, or motivators. Observation without the student's awareness would be viewed as a measure of typical performance. This is often referred to as a type of *naturalistic* observation or *unobtrusive* measure. Often we want to measure *maximum performance*, the very best the student is able to do when given whatever encouragement, inducement, incentives, or pressures (within reason) are necessary to motivate maximum effort. Most educational tests would fall into this category. Such distinctions remind us that many of our measures only determine the student's ability, not his disposition to use it in normal, nontest situations.

The common distinction between power tests and speed tests is also relevant here. *Speed tests* are those with strict time limits that require everyone to stop when time expires. Such tests usually have more items than most students can answer in the allotted time. *Power tests* are those with generous (or no) time limits; examinees are allowed to respond to each item, and the items are frequently arranged in order of increasing difficulty. Here the interest lies in what students are able to do, not how quickly they can do it. The chapter quizzes in this book are power tests.

By Ways of Recording Behavior

Another meaningful classification is based on how measurements of behavior are recorded. Measurement data can be recorded by

- *Mechanical devices* (e.g., tape recorders and electronic simulators).
- *Independent observers* (e.g., using rating scales or checklists).
- *Interviewers* (e.g., conducting telephone surveys).
- *Students' self-reports* (e.g., questionnaires and attitude scales).
- *Students' personal products* (e.g., tests and samples of work).
- *Unobtrusive instruments* (e.g., instruments of which the examinee is unaware, such as a hidden camera).

By the Types of Objectives Measured

Measures are often classified on the basis of the type of educational objectives they are intended to measure. Such classification mostly follows the well known categories of *cognitive*, *affective*, or *psychomotor* objectives that became popularized with the publication of influential taxonomies of educational objectives (Bloom et al., 1956; Krathwohl et al., 1964). Consequently, we often hear of cognitive tests (concerning thinking, knowing, and problem solving), affective measures (dealing with attitudes, values, interests and appreciation), and psycho-motor tests (concerning manual and motor skills).

By How the Score Is Interpreted

One of the most important ways to differentiate among types of tests is by how the scores are interpreted. Is a student's test score compared to some specified reference group of persons "like him," such as other students in his class or a nationwide sample of students at his grade level? Or is his performance judged only in terms of some absolute standard specified by his teacher (such as the percent of the test items answered correctly) without referencing the performance of others? We are not distinguishing here on the basis of how the tests are scored—objective tests versus subjective tests—but rather on the basis of the referent (e.g., explicit criteria, other students' scores) for *interpreting* the score. This leads to the common classification of achievement testing into norm-refer-enced and criterion-referenced measurement, between which we need to be able to differentiate clearly.

Norm-referenced versus Criterion-referenced Measurement

Some people classify testing instruments as being either norm-referenced tests (NRTs) or criterion-referenced tests (CRTs). They base this classification on the ideas of Glaser (1963), but the distinction he made was between two different ways of interpreting scores rather than between two different types of tests. When we interpret an individual's score by comparing it to the scores earned by other students in the class or in some norming group, we are making a *relative comparison*. Glaser referred to this way of interpreting test scores as *norm-referenced measure-ment*. On the other hand, when we interpret an individual's score by describing how well or to what extent a student can perform the tasks in some well-defined domain of valued tasks, we are making an *absolute comparison*. Glaser referred to this way of interpreting scores as *criterion-referenced measurement*. The norm referenced interpretation does not describe what Johnny can or cannot do, but only whether his performance is better or worse than the performance of his peers. The criterion-referenced interpretation provides descriptive information about Johnny's proficiency in performing the tasks, but provides no information about his relative standing in a referenced group. Thus, the fundamental distinction between criterion-referencing and norm-referencing is a matter of how the scores are interpreted rather than the type of testing instrument used.

Some test users and textbook authors continue to classify tests as either criterion-referenced or norm-referenced (e.g., Popham, 1990), but many measure-ment specialists contend that these labels are misleading when used to modify the word *test*. Scholars in this latter camp accept the distinction between criterion-referenced and norm-referenced measurement, but they prefer not to speak of criterion-referenced and norm-referenced tests because they claim that scores from any test can be interpreted either in a criterion-referenced manner or in a norm-referenced manner. We agree.[3] It is not always easy or useful to classify tests as being norm-referenced or criterion-referenced. But we also want to emphasize that tests designed to serve one of these purposes usually will not serve the other purpose equally well.

Tests used primarily for one of these purposes are generally designed and constructed differently than tests used primarily for the other purpose. Tests created as a basis for making norm-referenced interpretations generally include items from a very broad, vaguely defined domain, whereas tests designed to support criterion-referenced interpretations generally focus on a much more limited and more clearly defined domain. Furthermore, tests designed for criterion-referenced purposes usually include many more items per objective and such items are often sampled randomly from the domain they represent. Also different criteria are used in selecting acceptable items for these two different purposes. Items with maximum discrimination between high scoring and low scoring examinees are preferred for norm-referenced purposes, but this quality is not so important for tests designed for criterion-referenced purposes. Reliability is a very important characteristic for tests designed to serve either of these purposes, but reliability is defined and estimated differently for each of these purposes. The completed tests may be very similar in appearance because the same kinds of items are used in both, but the procedures in constructing them reflect the different purposes they are intended to serve. One should be suspicious of the claim made by some standardized test publishers today that their tests can be used for either purpose. Usually their tests will serve one purpose much better than the other, but sometimes such hybrids may not serve either purpose very well.

With that background drawn, let us try to define norm-referenced and criterion-referenced measurement simply and succinctly, and to comment briefly on some writers' use of two other related terms, *objectives-referenced* and *domain-referenced* measurement.

Norm-referenced Measurement. Put most simply, *norm-referenced measurement* tells us where a student stands in relation to other students. Put less simply, norm-referenced measurement determines how a given student's test score compares with the test scores of a group of other, presumably similar, students whose test scores collectively comprise the norm.[4] Norm-referenced measurement involves giving meaning to a test score for an individual (or the average score for a group) by comparing it against the scores of others taking the same test.

Criterion-referenced Measurement. *Criterion-referenced measurement* tells us how a student's test performance compares to some absolute standard or some set

---

[3] We beg indulgence when we lapse on occasion, in later chapters, into using the terms *criterion-referenced test* and *norm-referenced test*, both for convenience and because we are referring to terminology used by others. When used, remember the reference is actually to score interpretation, not to different types of tests.

[4] By *similar*, we refer to factors such as age, grade in school, sex, and socioeconomic background—obviously not ability or performance on that which is tested.

of meaningful tasks without comparison to the performance of others. Criterion-referenced measurement does not compare students with one another but rather against an absolute standard of proficiency. Such measures are often used to set a minimum level of mastery a student must attain in one unit of instruction before being allowed to proceed to the next. They usually involve instructionally relevant items and are typically used to determine whether students have mastered specific instructional content or to describe students' progress through well-defined curricula.

Objectives-referenced and Domain-referenced Measurement. Some writers have thought it useful to add two other types of score interpretations that do not depend on norms. *Objectives-referenced measurement* provides information about how well the student performs on test items measuring attainment of the specific instructional objectives for which the test was developed. Such measures contain test items selected to measure how well students have obtained specified (usually behavioral) objectives. Performance on items related to a particular objective are summarized into statements about how well the student (or group of students) has attained the objective.

   Domain-referenced measurement consists of a random sample of items drawn from a well-defined pool representative of all test items for a well-defined content area. Such measures provide scores that estimate how well a student (or group of students) is likely to perform on a set of similar items, drawn from the same domain. This approach to measurement depends upon a careful specification of the limits of the domain, a representative sampling of test items from the domain, and an estimation of the likelihood that individuals (or groups) will perform similarly on another sample of items drawn from the domain compared to how they performed on those on which they were tested.

   Actually, both objectives-referenced and domain-referenced measurement are merely variant forms of criterion-referenced measurement. We do not differentiate among them hereafter, except for the following example, which is included to help you distinguish among the various types of criterion-referenced measurement, as well as to distinguish them from norm-referenced measurement.

Time Out for an Illustration

To help you differentiate between norm-referenced measurement and various types of criterion-referenced measurement, imagine an eighth grade remedial English class taught by Lotta Smart. At the beginning of the year one of the students, Jimmy, was struggling—in part because of poor spelling. Lotta has given Jimmy some individual help and is amazed at the improvement he has shown. But just how well is he doing? Lotta wants to know, so she asks Seymour Childs, the school psychologist, to help her measure Jimmy's spelling ability in as many different ways as possible. Seymour recommends four different tests, each of which uses a different referent for interpreting the test scores.

NORM-REFERENCED

The Everytown School District has administered the *Herkijerk Spelling Test* in grades 4 to 8 each year for the past three years and has developed local norms, in the form of a distribution of test scores, for each grade level tested. Jimmy's test score is at the 85th percentile of the distribution of test scores for Everytown's eighth graders (the norm), so Lotta concludes he is now spelling better than 85 percent of his peers in the district.

CRITERION-REFERENCED

Lotta and Seymour decide that the minimum standard for good performance is getting at least 80 percent of the test items correct on the spelling test they have developed. Jimmy answers 82 percent of the items correctly. Lotta concludes Jimmy has met (actually exceeded) the criterion and is prepared to go on to more advanced subject matter.

OBJECTIVES-REFERENCED

In this variant of criterion-referenced measurement, Lotta lists her instructional objectives and Seymour helps her develop a test with multiple items to "get at" each spelling objective she has listed. Jimmy's test is scored to see how well he performs on items related to each objective. For example, historically Jimmy has had trouble in spelling words correctly that include diphthongs, but when Lotta looks at the 16 items that deal with diphthongs, she finds that Jimmy has answered twelve of them correctly. She informs Jimmy that he passed 75 percent of the test items written for the objective "To spell correctly words containing diphthongs."

DOMAIN-REFERENCED

In this approach to criterion-referenced measurement, Seymour teaches Lotta about content domains and together they develop a pool of 200 spelling items they believe cover the domain of basic eighth grade spelling. They randomly select twenty test items from that item pool and administer them to Jimmy. He spells 18 of the 20 words correctly. Lotta informs him that, based on this test, she estimates that if she tested him over and over again, each time drawing twenty items randomly from that same item pool, he would likely be able to spell about 18 (90 percent) of the spelling words correctly.

The Relative Utility of Criterion-referenced and Norm-referenced Measurement

Each of these approaches to achievement testing has utility for certain purposes, and also limitations. Each has attracted loyalists, and discussions about which is best have evoked much debate and more than a little acrimony. We shall not repeat or extend that debate here, for we are convinced that each type of test listed above is useful for given purposes, under appropriate circumstances, when used intelligently. While there is much to learn about the best way to test achievement in our schools, we know enough to suggest that the best achievement-testing system will probably use a combination of norm-referenced and criterion-referenced measurement to serve the various purposes needed in our schools.

(Categorizing Tests) by Who Constructs Them and How

The development of educational measures demands widely variable levels of knowledge and expertise. If a test is to be published, sold, or otherwise disseminated widely, it is usually the product of considerable work and measurement savvy. If it is to be used in a single classroom, less effort need be invested in its development, but fundamental principles of good measurement must be maintained.

Tests are often categorized by the manner in which they were constructed and the professional role normally performed by the test developer. The most common designations that fit (loosely) along this dimension are standardized tests, teacher-made tests, and experimental measures.

Standardized Tests

A *standardized test* is a set of tasks presented to individuals under similar (standard) conditions, designed to measure some particular aspect of those individuals' behavior (e.g., knowledge of particular content, skill in certain tasks, or certain personal attributes or characteristics) and allowing individuals' scores to be arrayed on a measurement scale for that behavior. To fulfill the above definition, tests must have a standard set of instructions that are followed each time the test is administered, must be scored to conform with specified objective scoring procedures, and must be interpretable in relation to information provided by the developer. Although most standardized tests are norm-referenced, increasing numbers of criterion-referenced standardized tests have appeared recently.

Standardized tests are typically constructed by measurement experts and usually go through several trials and revisions to improve their technical (psychometric) characteristics. For norm-referenced standardized tests, such tryouts also serve to develop the test norms. *Norms* are the statistical summary of performance on the test by those groups who took it during its development (standardization) period (or later, for *renorming*—updating the norms). Norms should ideally include the performance of all relevant types of students of various ages, grades, gender, race, culture, and geographic setting. Good norms usually require thousands of cases collected from broad national samples, divided into appropriate subsamples on these dimensions. They are usually expressed in percentile ranks, grade equivalent scores, deviation IQ, and the like. They allow an individual student's test score to be compared with scores of other students similar on relevant characteristics (e.g., sex and age).

One caution! Just because a measure has been standardized is no guarantee that it is any good. Some commercially marketed standardized tests are a monument either to the innocence (or greed) of the publisher or the gullibility of school practitioners, or both. Even good standardized tests can become obsolete as knowledge grows, social change shifts our priorities, and the composition of our population is altered. A test depending on 1960 norms might be viewed as suspect, given the different educational opportunities afforded to various ethnic, cultural, and geographic subgroups in recent decades.

Teacher-made Tests

Although millions of standardized tests are given each year, that number is eclipsed by the enormous number of teacher-made tests students take during the same period. In one study a sample of Ohio public school teachers reported that they administered (on the average) nearly 100 teacher-made tests during a school year (Marso, 1985). Unless you think Ohio teachers are especially "test happy," you can multiply the number of teachers in your school district, state, or country by 100, and then multiply the result by the average number of students in your classrooms to get a rough idea of one reason our forests in the Northwest are disappearing.

A teacher-made test is one constructed entirely by a teacher to test pupils in that teacher's classroom. Although some teacher-made tests are appalling, well-crafted teacher-made tests are the backbone of classroom measurement and evaluation. Where one finds high quality teaching, one is likely to find high quality teacher-made classroom tests also. Chapters 9 to 13 of this book are devoted to helping you learn how to improve your classroom tests and other measures you can construct and use in your own classroom. Although we believe well developed and properly used standardized tests are very useful, it does not follow that tests must be standardized to be useful. Nonstandardized tests are not only legitimate, but essential. Taking the time and resources required to standardize every needed educational measure would be impossible, as well as absurd.

Teacher-made tests come in many forms, not only on the dimensions noted earlier (e.g., speed vs. power, objective vs. subjective), but also on conditions for taking the test, such as open-book versus closed-book examinations, or in-class versus take-home examinations.

Experimental Measures

Not all educational measures are used for such practical purposes as classroom testing. Measurement is also central to most educational research, and many investigators depend upon it to collect data. Often an investigator can use an existing measure with good psychometric properties. But sometimes, if no existing measure is adequate to collect the needed research data, a new measure must be developed. Such a measure, an *experimental measure*, is one intended for research use only, and not intended for use in other applied settings.

There are considerable data available on the reliability and validity of some experimental measures—and some even provide preliminary norms. Thus, despite our cautions, there are applied situations when an experimental measure can be used. Remember that such situations are the exception, not the rule, and should only occur when (1) no standardized measure is available, (2) a well-developed experimental measure is available, (3) a measure of the construct is essential, and (4) test scores are applied with caution.

In any case, no experimental measure should be used prematurely by persons who may not understand its limitations and tentative nature. This point is so important as to be stressed in criteria for tests presented in both the 1975 and 1985 *Standards* (APA et al., 1974, and AERA et al., 1985).

An example may help. A few years ago, two of us were asked by the National Association for Advancement of Humane Education (NAAHE) to evaluate a humane education curriculum they had developed. We almost immediately encountered a problem. We could find no suitable measures of humaneness that were conceptually and psychometrically sound. After discussion, NAAHE agreed to delay the evaluation by one year while we developed, with their support, a battery of humaneness tests needed to measure children's concepts and attitudes related to humane education. During the next year we developed the following new instruments (Western Institute, 1982):

- Humane Education Concept Mastery Tests (grades K, 2, 4, and 6)
- Pupil Attitude Toward Humaneness Scale (primary and intermediate forms)
- Situational Test of Humane Responses (primary and intermediate forms)
- Attitude Transfer Scale (primary and intermediate forms)
- Parent and Teacher Humane Education Survey

We would wager a sizable bet that you have never heard of any of these instruments. Why not? Because we never intended that you would—at least not yet. We copyrighted those measures to retain control, and have refused to allow them to be used (except for experimental purposes) until we are certain they possess the validity, reliability, and objectivity we feel they should. Only then will we release them for general use. In the meantime, we are continuing to analyze the large amount of data from our last nationwide tryout of the tests to see what further refinements are necessary.

One Measure May Fit Several Classifications

The 13 ways we have outlined to classify measurement instruments are not independent. Indeed, one instrument may simultaneously be classified along several dimensions. For example, let's assume that an uninformed teacher, Les Wise, decides to use the *Music and Me* (M & M) test, a nationally normed music appreciation test, to assess his students' singing ability. We could classify that test on the 13 dimensions as follows:

1. By subject area of the content—a *music* test
2. By psychological construct—music *appreciation*
3. By specific behaviors measured—student's *understanding* of various types of music, *ability to discriminate* among types and qualities of music, and *demonstrating positive affect* toward music that is judged by music experts to be worthy of such regard
4. By item format—*multiple-choice* and *rating scale* responses (to audio stimuli)
5. By type of data produced—*quantitative* data (although those data reflect some qualitative judgments)
6. By the purpose for which the test is used—a test of *performance*, and here we see Les making a serious mistake, for a test of music appreciation is obviously a poor choice for measuring musical ability
7. By how the instrument is administered—*group administered* test
8. By how scored—*objective* test scoring
9. By type of performance called for—*typical performance* is what a music

appreciation test would measure (but Les is applying it in a setting where he should be measuring maximum performance)

10. By ways of recording behavior—*student personal product* (the knowledge items tested) and *student self-report* (the affective rating scales)
11. By types of objectives measured—it is hard to classify Les's example here, for although the test he selected gets at both cognitive and affective objectives, he seems unaware of the importance of having objectives, let alone of the necessity of matching measures to them
12. By who constructs them and how—*standardized* test
13. By how the score is interpreted—*norm-referenced* test

Many test collections or compendia use several of the above classifications simultaneously. For example, the *Tenth Mental Measurement Yearbook* (Conoley & Kramer, 1989) presents descriptions and critiques of measurement instruments under several classifications: psychological construct (e.g., personality), subject matter (e.g., mathematics), and specific behaviors measured (e.g., sensory-motor).

Now that we have reviewed with you several ways to classify measurement instruments, let us share one especially useful classification system that draws on some of the dimensions discussed above.

AN OUTLINE OF TYPES
OF EDUCATIONAL MEASUREMENT INSTRUMENTS

We have tried to emphasize that many different dimensions can be used to classify measurement instruments. Sometimes it is useful to classify a particular measure on all or most of the dimensions we have described, especially if it is to be used for an important measurement task. More often, though, it is useful to have a simple outline or classification system for use in thinking about educational measures. For example, in evaluating a school curriculum, data must be collected to answer a variety of evaluative questions, and it is useful to have an outline or some system to prompt thinking about alternative ways in which those data might be collected. It is for such uses that we provide the classification system outlined in this section.[5] Although we have attempted to make this a comprehensive outline, we recognize it is not possible for any one system to accommodate every measure comfortably. We also recognize that this outline builds on some of the dimensions we discussed earlier, while ignoring others, and that it treats as parallel some entities that could subsume one another. For example, we could have placed rating scales under questionnaires and also under several other major categories, but we wish only to provide an annotated outline useful in helping you think about measurement instruments.

---

[5] This set of categories draws somewhat on Furst (1958) and on discussions and lectures he gave while serving as mentor to one of the authors. We express our gratitude for his insights and influence on our thinking.

In addition to describing each category, we provide examples in those categories that may be unfamiliar to readers.[6] We do not discuss the major strengths and weaknesses of the measures in each category, but reserve that for later chapters where those instruments most useful to practitioners are described more fully.

I. DATA RECORDED BY AND COLLECTED DIRECTLY FROM INDIVIDUALS

The primary method of collecting information in most educational settings is to get it directly from students, teachers, administrators, and significant individuals in other categories. In many cases, the information is gathered through a simple self-report; a question is posed and the individual responds, using the format requested. Even more often, the data are collected from personal products the individual is asked to provide or that arise naturally from daily activities.

A. Self-reports

Here we include all measures used to elicit information about personal activities, attitudes, thoughts, feelings, and opinions directly from the one person who is in the best position to provide it (assuming self-awareness, memory, and honesty are all operating). Self-reports usually seek information about typical performance rather than maximum performance. Common types of self-report measurement devices are listed here.

1. Diaries or Anecdotal Accounts

Narrative accounts can provide excellent information on typical activities or reactions to particular events or circumstances to which the individual is exposed. Such measures can be rich and telling, but can also be barren, unless individuals are informed ahead of time about the types of content that will be most useful. They can also be difficult to analyze unless careful thought has been given in advance about how to extract and summarize data.

2. Checklists and Inventories

Checklists are often used to collect simple, straightforward data about everything from physical facilities to leisure time activities or inventories of personal preferences.

3. Rating Scales

Rating scales are similar to checklists, except they place responses along a continuum (e.g., ''Strongly Agree'' to ''Strongly Disagree'') instead of in unordered categories. In addition to the general strengths and weaknesses discussed for most self-report measures, rating scales are very adaptable, and they are quick and

---

[6] We have not attempted to develop items without psychometric flaws, but provide typical examples only to illustrate item or instrument format.

economical to administer and score. They often tell more about the person rating, however, than about what he is rating. Some students are very positive in nearly all their ratings, while others are very negative. More will be said in Chapter 12 about rating scales, their uses, and cautions concerning them.

4. *Questionnaires*

Too familiar to require description, questionnaires can use a wide variety of question formats, but all are typically of paper and pencil form.

5. *Interviews*

Although very familiar, interviews are challenging, requiring careful thought about how to follow up on questions, probe responses, and record and interpret those responses.

6. *Sociometric Measures*

Several methods have been developed for measuring social distance, social acceptability, and other perceptions of individuals in social settings. These include the *nominating* technique ("List your three best friends") and the *guess who* technique ("Guess who is pleasant and cooperative and attracts other people"). A simple visual summary of student responses is constructed to reflect within-class social structure and identify social isolates who may need special attention. Although considerable caution is advised in using sociometry, such devices can be informative if used appropriately.

7. *Projective Measures*

School psychologists and counselors trained in the use of projective tests can use them to provide potentially useful information about the individual. Most projective measures provide ambiguous stimuli (e.g., an inkblot) and ask individuals to describe what they see. Although projective techniques allow measurement of variables typically unavailable through other techniques, thus providing important clinical insights, they are dangerous in the hands of all but the most skilled clinicians. Even then, their uncertain validity and reliability and their highly subjective interpretation are disquieting to many measurement experts.

B.   Personal Products

Self-reports may be recorded either by the informant (e.g., a rating scale or questionnaire) or by the person administering the instrument (e.g., an interview). *Personal products*, as we use the term, are always recorded by the informant. They are distinguished from self-reports by the fact that they usually involve maximum performance (as opposed to the typical performance measured by most self-reports). The two most common types of personal product measures are tests and samples of work.

1. Tests

There are two general categories of tests: supplied-answer tests and selected-answer tests. As the names imply, these categories differ according to whether the student supplies the answer out of his own head, or selects the answer from among alternative answers provided.

a. Supplied-answer Tests. Essay, completion, short response, and problem-solving items are the most common types of items found on supplied-answer tests.

ESSAY ITEMS Essay items allow students to demonstrate, integrate, and synthesize their knowledge about a topic, but can be difficult to score objectively. They are also time-consuming to answer, thus limiting the sampling of content possible on a test consisting solely of essays.

COMPLETION ITEMS Completion items can typically be answered with a single word or a short, familiar phrase. They usually measure factual recall, and thus may encourage the testing of trivial content if used to the exclusion of other item types. If constructed carefully, they can be scored quite objectively. If items are poorly crafted, scoring is complicated by the fact that there may be more than one correct response. Consider this item: "The largest mammal that hibernates is _____." "A bear" may be the desired response, but it would be hard to fail a student for answering "brown," "sleeping," "found in Alaska," or even "hungry next spring."

SHORT-RESPONSE ITEMS Short-response items differ from completion items only in that they require somewhat longer responses—more than a word or pat phrase—but responses short enough to be readily scored. Students may answer with a word or a sentence, but should show understanding.

PROBLEM-SOLVING ITEMS Most common in mathematics or science areas, problem-solving items can test not only mastery in an area but—if carefully structured—can also perform a diagnostic function by revealing the actual mental processes a student uses to arrive at the answer. An example would be having students show all steps and computations in solving a math problem.

b. Selected-Answer Tests. The most common types of selected-answer test items are multiple-choice, true-false, ranking, and matching items. The first three are too familiar to require further comment. A matching item is one that supplies all the elements of the answer and asks the student to match or rearrange them (in correct sequence, for example).

2. Samples of Actual Work or Performance

Perhaps the best way of determining how well individuals can perform is to obtain an actual (nontest) sample of their best work or performance. Such products are common in our schools: term papers and written essays; completed pieces of art, computer programs, or musical scores; and samples of penmanship or drafting.

Furst summarizes well the advantages of this approach to measuring a person's ability:

> In a real sense, the product *is* the ultimate test of a person's ability. If he can produce a fine piece of work and do that consistently, then we must credit him with ability. The product of his efforts thus gives proof of his accomplishments. Furthermore, samples of work have analytic value in their own right. They may indicate strong and weak points in technique, and such personal habits as neatness, accuracy, style of expression, and methods of thinking. . . . Finally, those that can be filed or saved provide a valuable record for later interpretation . . . [thus giving] us a basis for judging progress in the learning of a skill or in the development of some other characteristic. (1958, p. 140)

Actual samples of work or performance are the best measure of ability or mastery in a host of areas. Yet often cost, time, or other factors make it infeasible to measure every important learning or behavior in this fashion. Were it practicable to collect actual samples of work in every area, tests and other more efficient measures would probably become obsolete.

II. DATA RECORDED BY AN INDEPENDENT OBSERVER

Turning from data recorded by the individuals about whom we are collecting the information, we consider data recorded by an independent observer. Such measurement approaches are of two major types: written accounts (such as an observer's written notes made while observing or after observing a teacher present a lesson) and observation forms (such as checklists or rating scales an observer may fill out during or shortly after the same lesson).

A.   Written Accounts

A written record is an uncomplicated, direct way of summarizing observable behaviors and events. Yet even a shorthand expert can seldom capture a complete account of all the verbal and nonverbal behavior going on in a classroom. Written accounts typically focus on particular types of behavior or specific events. Anecdotal records, containing either reports of critical incidents or running narratives are often the best that can be produced. Focusing on critical incidents can eliminate much "chaff" without losing the real kernels of important information. The temptation to add unwarranted interpretations to factual observations should be avoided.

B.   Observation Forms

Special recording forms can be prepared in advance to make observations simpler to record, more objective, and more focused. Such forms usually provide categories, scales, or lists of items that observers can check off, tally, or code on-site.

Recording forms not only save time, but help ensure consistency and thoroughness. They may incorporate rating scales, checklists and inventories, or observation schedules. One can also use a rating scale on which observers can judge degrees or levels of performance. Such interpretive observations require careful training of observers to assure accuracy and commonality in the way the scale is used.

III. OTHER DATA COLLECTION PROCEDURES

Three less frequently used but very useful means of collecting data depend on mechanical devices, unobtrusive methods, and existing sources.

A. Mechanical Devices

Some mechanical devices have been used to record student behaviors or performance: (e.g., audiotape recordings, videotape recordings, time-lapse photography). Furst summarizes nicely the usefulness of such devices:

> For many purposes, mechanical recording devices can replace the human observer. Not only that, they can very often improve upon him as well. In particular, they can minimize many of the errors that an observer is likely to make; they can "see" more than he can; they can "stay on the job" for long periods of time without impairing their efficiency. Their greatest limitations are their cost and the fact that they cannot make the sorts of judgments that a human observer can. (1958, p. 130)

They also may not really *measure*, thus requiring some human deduction or interpretive analysis. This limitation has been partly obviated, however, by computer collation of student responses in interactive computer-assisted instruction, where computers can be programmed to help with actual measurement, per se. Computer-generated repeatable testing (Dunkleberger & Heikkinen, 1982) and computer-adaptive testing (B. F. Green, 1983) are additional variations of the use of computers for direct measurement tasks.

B. Unobtrusive Measures

Unobtrusive measures are any measures that can be used to collect information about an individual or group without their awareness. Being unaware of the data collection, they cannot react to the instrument or to the act of measurement itself in ways that might alter or distort the data. Webb, Campbell, Schwartz, and Sechrest (1966) provide a comprehensive discussion of unobtrusive measures that cannot be duplicated or even summarized here. One example must suffice.

Assume we wanted to measure reading preferences of high school students. We could ask the students or their parents. We would learn much, but might be misled by those who felt the need to "improve the truth" by telling us that they savored Shakespeare, when in reality they devoured Mike Hammer. An alternate, unobtrusive way to gauge students' reading preferences would be to scan the shelves of the high school library for volumes that were dogeared, worn, and obviously well-used. While one might have some confidence in information gained in this way, possibilities for error obviously exist. Does a particularly worn volume signal that it is widely read or merely that it is read constantly by one student who has a fixation? Such are the potential perils of using indirect measures. Yet, used thoughtfully (and generally in combination with other measures) they can be useful.

C. Existing Information Resources or Repositories

Although more data collection than measurement, we mention this category to complete our set. The items listed below are useful sources of information, even though the instruments for collecting data are "hands and eyes."

1. Review of public documents (e.g., proposals, reports, and course outlines)
2. Review of institutional or group files (e.g., files of student records, fiscal resources, and minutes of meetings)
3. Review of personal files (e.g., correspondence files of individuals reviewed by permission of the correspondent)
4. Review of existing data bases (e.g., statewide testing program results)

SUGGESTED READINGS

Nitko, A. J. (1984). Defining criterion-referenced test. In R. A. Berk (Ed.), *A guide to criterion-referenced test construction* (pp. 8–28). Baltimore, MD: Johns Hopkins University Press.
This chapter clarifies the meaning of "criterion-referencing" and what it is and is not. The author provides a helpful framework for distinguishing among various kinds of criterion-referenced measurement and offers practitioners six guidelines for conceptualizing and using this measurement approach.

Worthen, B. R., & Sanders, J. R. (1987). *Educational evaluation: Alternative approaches and practical guidelines*. White Plains, NY: Longman.
This book provides a comprehensive treatment of all types of educational evaluation. Distinctions among student evaluation, program evaluation, assessment, measurement, and testing are provided in a context that is easy to grasp. A discussion of quantitative versus qualitative measurement should also prove helpful.

Furst, E. J. (1958). *Constructing evaluation instruments*. New York: David McKay.
This excellent old standard contains a straightforward and thoughtful discussion of educational measurement and evaluation. It includes coverage of such topics as determining what to measure, determining appropriate situations for measurement, recording and summarizing data, and constructing teacher-made classroom achievement tests.

Webb, E. J., Campbell, D. T., Schwartz, R. D., & Sechrest, L. (1966). *Unobtrusive measures: Nonreactive research in the social sciences*. Chicago: Rand McNally.

This is still the single best volume for understanding the potential (and perils) of unobtrusive measures. This book contains numerous examples of such measures that can be adapted for use in school settings.

SELF-CHECK QUIZ

1. The concern that a test accomplishes the purpose for which it was intended is primarily a concern of
   a. objectivity.
   b. subjectivity.
   c. validity.
   d. reliability.

   Match the following phrases with the terms in the second list (a–f) by placing the letter of each term in the blank to the left of the phrase that it *best* matches. You may use each option once, more than once, or not at all.

2. ____ Making empirical observations and translating them into quantifiable form according to specified rules

3. ____ Using specially constructed tests to determine the overall condition of a school system

4. ____ Presenting a set of tasks or questions to an examinee in a systematic manner so as to elicit responses from the examinee

5. ____ Using test scores to judge the quality or extent of individual pupils' achievement

6. ____ Formally determining the quality, effectiveness, or value of an educational program

   a. Accountability
   b. Assessment
   c. Testing
   d. Educational evaluation
   e. Evaluation of pupil performance
   f. Measurement

7. Which of the following is most useful for describing how a student's performance compares to that of other students?
   a. Norm-referenced measurement
   b. Criterion-referenced measurement
   c. Objectives-referenced measurement
   d. Domain-referenced measurement

8. If we classified tests into multiple-choice or essay tests we would be classifying them by
   a. item content.
   b. type of data produced.
   c. item format.
   d. recording procedures.

9. Which of the following is a weakness of self-report data?
   a. Dependence on an individual's memory or honesty
   b. Too costly to collect
   c. Inability of responders to record products of thought or thought processes themselves
   d. Frequent observer unreliability

10. Which of the following is an advantage of using written accounts rather than observation forms to record direct observation data?
   a. The critical incidents are easier to record.
   b. The observations are more focused.
   c. The results are more objective.

SUGGESTION SHEET

If your last name starts with the letter *D*, please complete the Suggestion Sheet at the end of the book while this chapter is still fresh in your mind.

CHAPTER 5

Learning to Read the Sign Posts: What Do Those Test Scores Really Mean?

Overview

Most of you are probably already more adept at using statistics than you think. Decisions you make every day about how far you drive your car between fill-ups, how you dress for the weather, where you invest your money, and who you think will win the World Series are all influenced and made easier by your use of statistics—consciously or subconsciously.

There are many different types of statistics, and some statistical procedures are very complex. But, for virtually everything you will need as a successful educator, Ludwig Meis van der Rohe's observation that "less is more" is as applicable to statistics as to architecture. This chapter will provide you with the basic tools needed to convert the raw materials of test scores and results to meaningful, useful summaries. Understanding all the techniques presented in this chapter requires only simple arithmetic, a hand calculator, a willingness to try, and an open mind. Much of the material will be new and you may need to review it several times. However, you will do just fine if you can count to a hundred, add, multiply, subtract, divide, and push the square root button on a calculator.

Objectives

Upon completing your study of this chapter, you should be able to

1. Develop a frequency distribution, given a set of scores.
2. Use a frequency distribution to summarize and interpret test scores.
3. Explain the importance of a normal curve in examining human behavior.
4. Give examples of how deviations from the normal curve can be useful in interpreting test scores.
5. Compare and contrast different measures of central tendency (i.e., mean, median, and mode).
6. Identify situations in which different measures of central tendency would be the most appropriate.
7. Explain why the concepts of standard deviation and range are important in interpreting test scores.
8. Explain why correlations are important in interpreting measurement and evaluation data.
9. Give examples of inappropriate uses of correlational data.
10. Explain how the concepts of correlation and causation are related.
11. Explain how measurement error affects the interpretation of test scores.
12. Describe the pros and cons of different methods of reporting test scores (e.g., raw scores, percentiles, standard scores).
13. Give an example of a situation in which each method of reporting test scores would be appropriate.
14. Recognize the benefits and dangers of using test profiles to describe students' performance.
15. Given a standardized test report, interpret the results for various audiences (e.g., school administrators, teachers, parents, students).

ACQUIRING THE BASIC TOOLS OF INTERPRETATION

The French philosopher Poincaire, once said, "Science is made up of facts as a house is with stones. But a collection of facts is no more a science, than a heap of stones is a house." So it is with test scores. A test administered to a class of 100 students sometimes produces only a heap of numbers which are neither useful nor understandable. As an educator, you are responsible for making sense of that heap of numbers. Fortunately, some simple tools can help.

Organizing Measurement and Evaluation Data

As an example, consider a hypothetical test designed to measure students' *test-wiseness*, that is the degree to which they are able to outsmart the test and obtain a good score even if they haven't learned the material. Shown below is an item from that test.

Who discovered how to pasteurize milk?
 a. Madame Pompadour   c. Louis Pasteur
 b. Marie Curie   d. Albert Einstein

A testwise student will recognize that *pasteurize* is merely an extension of the name *Pasteur* and will get the item correct.

Assume that a teacher administers this 20-item test to 120 students and obtains the scores shown in Table 5.1. The teacher now has a whole heap of data and a lot of questions. For example, she may want to know:

- What was the average score on the test?
- Are children in her class more or less testwise than other children their age?
- What percentage of her students got 80 percent or more of the questions correct?
- Which children have the most and fewest testwiseness skills?
- Are students' testwiseness skills affecting their performance in other subjects?
- How she can equalize the testwiseness skills of all her students?

Before such questions can be easily answered, the numbers have to be organized. By looking at the information in Table 5.1, you could eventually determine that

TABLE 5.1 List of Testwiseness Scores in Alphabetical Order of Children's Last Names

3	10	9	12	11	9
19	15	5	8	15	13
7	17	18	10	7	4
10	12	12	13	16	11
12	20	11	9	10	9
13	8	4	12	14	17
14	11	10	14	8	12
12	12	7	12	10	11
7	15	8	4	6	16
11	9	11	16	15	11
12	10	16	14	13	14
8	17	6	13	10	6
16	14	13	10	12	8
9	12	9	13	14	7
15	16	13	6	10	15
6	11	12	11	9	9
13	13	15	12	17	11
7	8	8	8	7	8
18	12	11	18	14	10
10	19	13	15	12	5

the low score was 3 and the high score was 20. But even such a simple task requires unnecessary time and effort. The need to quickly interpret and use test scores is what led to organizational techniques such as those shown in (a), (b), and (c) of Figure 5.1. Let's consider some of the advantages of each technique.

Frequency Distributions

The simplest organizational technique is a *frequency distribution*, such as that shown in (a) of Figure 5.1. To construct a frequency distribution by hand, list the possible scores in order, and then make a tally each time a particular score occurs. The resulting display shows the frequency with which scores are distributed across the possible range—hence the name, frequency distribution. It also reveals the highest and lowest scores, and the middle-most score, or *median*. In this case, the median can be found by counting up sixty scores from the bottom or down sixty scores from the top of the 120 scores. For the numbers in Table 5.1, the median score has a value of 11. It is also clear that about 80 percent of the class scored between 7 and 16.

Frequency Polygons

Similar information is provided in (b) of Figure 5.1, in what is known as a *frequency polygon*. Each of the possible scores on the test is represented along the horizontal axis. For each score, the height of the dot above the horizontal baseline corresponds to the frequency with which that score was obtained.

For example, two children obtained a score of 5. Hence, the dot directly above the 5 on the horizontal line (representing a score of 5), is parallel with the crosshatch corresponding to the number 2 on the vertical line. Frequency polygons are often used in computer programs to represent distributions of scores.

Histograms or Bar Graphs

Panel (c) in Figure 5.1 shows another way of representing the same information. In this display, values that fall within a certain range (e.g., all numbers between 6 and 8 inclusive) are shown in a bar whose height indicates the number of scores in that range. The resulting *histogram,* or *bar graph*, is particularly useful when the range of possible scores is large. In such cases, groups of scores can be combined so that the resulting graph becomes more readable. For example, the six scores between 3 and 5 inclusive are shown on the first bar on the left and the 35 scores between 12 and 14 inclusive are represented on the tallest bar.

Guidelines for Depicting Distributions of Scores

Figure 5.1 demonstrates again that a picture is worth a thousand words. As sets of data become large, it grows increasingly difficult to comprehend, organize, and extract meaning from numbers without tools such as these. Technically, a frequency polygon is preferred for depicting *continuous* data, (that is data that occur along some unbroken continuum, such as test scores. A histogram or bar graph is better for depicting discrete or noncontinuous data, such as types of

(a)

Frequency Distribution

Score	Tallies	# of Students with each score
1		
2		
3	I	1
4	III	3
5	II	2
6	ЖЕ	5
7	ЖЕ II	7
8	ЖЕ ЖЕ	10
9	ЖЕ IIII	9
10	ЖЕ ЖЕ II	12
11	ЖЕ ЖЕ II	12
12	ЖЕ ЖЕ ЖЕ I	16
13	ЖЕ ЖЕ I	11
14	ЖЕ III	8
15	ЖЕ III	8
16	ЖЕ I	6
17	IIII	4
18	III	3
19	II	2
20	I	1

(b)

Frequency Polygon

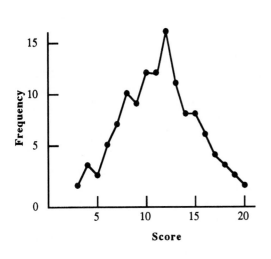

(c)

Histogram or Bar Graph

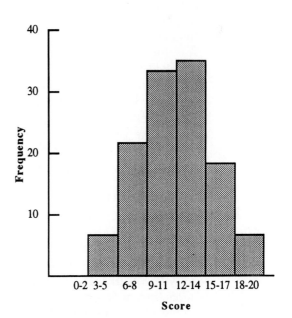

FIGURE 5.1 Different Ways of Representing Test Scores for 120 Children

automobile—Ford, Chevrolet, Volvo, Porsche, that cannot be ordered along a continuum. The most important consideration, however, is whether the display communicates effectively. If you are more comfortable using a histogram for test scores, use it. For the sake of clarity and consistency, the guidelines shown in Figure 5.2 are useful in constructing either frequency polygons or histograms.

APPLICATION PROBLEM #1

Listed below are 30 scores obtained on a test of biology terms for a ninth-grade science class. Construct a frequency distribution and frequency polygon for these scores.

71	75	64	71	66	70
67	68	66	69	71	67
72	66	71	67	69	69
69	70	70	68	68	68
69	68	67	68	72	68

The Normal Curve and Other Distributions

You may have already heard of the *normal curve*, which is often referred to as a *bell-shaped* distribution. Understanding the normal curve is fundamental to all that happens in statistics and measurement. Interestingly, many human characteristics (e.g., height, weight) are more or less distributed among the population according to a normal curve.

Figure 5.3 (p. 96) shows a theoretical normal curve—symmetrical and shaped much like a bell. Notice that it is very similar to the frequency polygon you just constructed, with the numbers along the horizontal axis representing scores, and the height of the curve at any point indicating the frequency with which a particular score occurred. The normal curve differs from the frequency polygon, however, in that the vertical axis is omitted and the points are connected with a smooth curve instead of straight lines. Nonetheless, you can gather much of the same information by looking at a smooth curve as at a frequency polygon. For example, from Figure 5.3 it is clear that the majority of the observations in this set of data fall between 85 and 115. The median of the distribution can be determined by identifying the point from which about half the scores rise above and half fall below (in this case, 100). Normal curves are used repeatedly in measurement and evaluation to provide a general sense of score distribution.

Although many human characteristics approximate a normal curve, there are very few mathematically perfect normal distributions. Because of these "departures from normality," most smooth curves you see will not look exactly like that in Figure 5.3. However, all smooth curves can be divided into two large categories: those that are *symmetrical*—that is, one half of the curve is a mirror image of the

1. The horizontal axis of the diagram should read from left to right, and the vertical axis should read from bottom to top. Each axis should have an appropriately descriptive label.

2. The horizontal axis is generally 1 1/2 to 2 times as long as the vertical axis.

3. Whenever possible, the zero point should appear on both the vertical and horizontal axes. If the zero point does not appear, or if there are breaks in the sequence of numbers on either axis, double slash marks should be used as shown below to indicate that some of the numbers have been omitted.

4. Graphs are easier to read if only a minimum number of calibration points on the vertical and horizontal axes are used.

5. Particularly important parts of the graph should be indicated with a numerical value on the graph itself using subordinate emphasis (e.g., the height of each bar, mean or median values of a frequency polygon, particularly salient points in the distribution such as cutoff points).

6. The ends of the frequency polygon line should be "tied" to the baseline, instead of being allowed to float free.

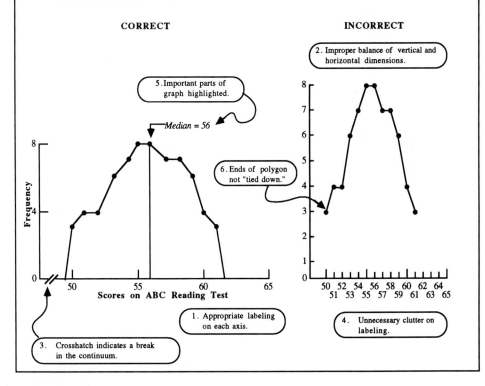

FIGURE 5.2 Guidelines for Constructing Frequency Polygons or Histograms

SOURCE: Adapted and extended from Kubiszym and Borich, 1987, p. 219.

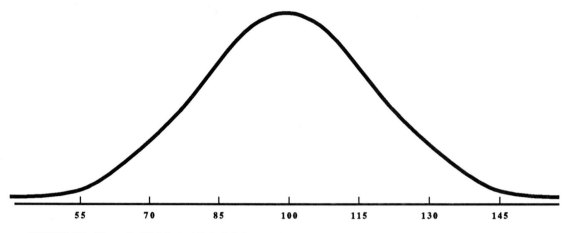

FIGURE 5.3   Normally Distributed Set of Data

other), and those that are *asymmetrical*—that is, one half of the curve is *not* a mirror image of the other. There is an infinite variety of curves in both categories. Examples (a), (b), and (c) in Figure 5.4 show distributions that are symmetrical, though not perfectly normal. These distributions are respectively too *peaked,* (that is, the points are scrunched together near the middle of the distribution); too flat; or the *tails,* the part of the distribution greater than about 120 and less than about 80, are too thick. Such departures from normality are relatively inconsequential for most applications.

For purposes of measurement and evaluation, two departures from normality are particularly important to understand: *bimodal distributions* and *skewed distributions*. Let us consider each.

Bimodal Distributions

To understand the term *bimodal,* which means two modes, we must define the concept of *mode*. The mode is the point within a distribution that occurs most frequently. Because frequency of occurrence is indicated by the height of the curve, the mode occurs at the highest part of the curve. Example (d) in Figure 5.4 shows a truly bimodal distribution because there are two distinct points that are higher than all the rest (these points occur at about 90 and 115). Although not truly bimodal, example (g) is often referred to as bimodal because it has two distinct humps—even though one is substantially lower than the other. Example (g) is referred to as a J-shaped distribution because the top part of the curve is shaped like a letter *J*. Because most human characteristics approximate a normal distribution, you should be cautious when you encounter a bimodal distribution. When such distributions occur, there is often a problem with how the variable has been defined or measured.

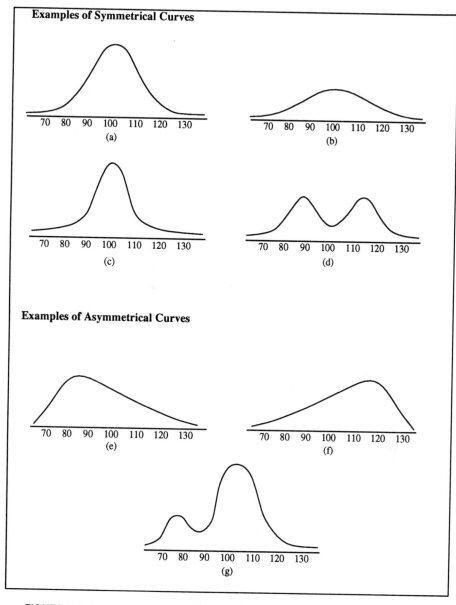

FIGURE 5.4 Examples of the Variety of Symmetrical and Asymmetrical Curves

Skewed Distributions

The most frequent way in which data "depart from normality" is when a distribution is *skewed*. A skewed distribution has the majority of the data points clustered at one end of the distribution. Distributions may be *positively skewed*, as in example (e) of Figure 5.4, where most of the scores are bunched toward the low end, or *negatively skewed*, as in example (f), where most of the scores are bunched toward the high/positive end and the tail points toward the low/negative end of the distribution.

Recognizing seriously skewed distributions is extremely important. For example, when a distribution is positively skewed, it shows that most of the group scored poorly (the majority of the scores are bunched toward the low end of the distribution), but a few students did very well (as indicated by the much lower height of the tail pointing in the positive direction). The question to ask is, Why? It may be that most students did poorly because the test was too difficult, many of the items were confusing, the content was not taught well, or there was not enough time allowed for the test. Tests that result in positively skewed distributions are said to have a *floor effect* because the majority of the scores are found at the *floor,* or the bottom of the distribution.

Notice that a positively skewed distribution does not tell you why most students did poorly on a test; instead it is a red flag that suggests a need for further analysis. In this sense, it is similar to the oil pressure light on your automobile. When the light comes on, it does not tell you exactly what is wrong with your car. But you do know that unless you take some corrective action, you may be faced with a very expensive repair bill.

A negatively skewed distribution provides a similar warning, with most of the students bunched at the top of the distribution, and only a few students in the tail pointing in a negative direction (often called a ceiling effect). This suggests that the test may have been too easy for most of the class or a copy of the answers may be circulating.

Norm-referenced tests that exhibit floor or ceiling effects are usually not an accurate measure of students' ability. A ceiling effect suggests there are students who would have done better had they not bumped into the ceiling. If more difficult items had been included, providing the more capable students with an opportunity to demonstrate their skills, some of them would have achieved even higher scores, spreading out the distribution. With most criterion-referenced tests, however, you should expect a ceiling effect if the content has been effectively taught. The presence of a floor effect suggests that the test does not differentiate between the average and the least capable students, since most of the students do poorly.

Measures of Central Tendency

Statisticians use the term *measures of central tendency* to refer to various kinds of averages. For most people, average connotes being in the middle. But there are different ways to be in the middle.

There are three commonly used measures of central tendency, and each has its advantages and disadvantages under different conditions. Each measure of central tendency is an effort to describe a set of scores when we must rely on one number to describe a whole set of numbers. After defining and giving an example of the various measures of central tendency—the *mean*, the *median,* and the *mode*—we will help you decide which measure to use in what situation.

TABLE 5.2 Examples of Mean, Median, and Mode

24	40	33
27	27	17
18	15	25

(a) Mean ($\overline{X}$) = (24 + 27 + 18 + 40 + 27 + 15 + 33 + 17 + 25) ÷ 9 = 25.11

(b) Median (Mdn) = middle score = 25: 15 17 18 24 25 27 27 34 40

(c) Mode = most frequent score = 27: 15 17 18 24 25 27 27 33 40

Definitions and Examples

Of the three measures of central tendency, the *mean* is the most frequently used. This is what most people have in mind when they refer to an *average* score. Whenever someone talks about a basketball player's scoring average or the average temperature for a particular time of year, she is probably referring to the mean. The mean is simply an arithmetic average: that is, the sum of all the scores, divided by the number of scores. The symbol most frequently used for the mean is $\overline{X}$. For example, consider the nine scores shown in Table 5.2. The mean of these nine scores is simply their sum (226), divided by the number of scores (9), which equals 25.11.

The *median* of a distribution is the value in the middle when all scores are rank ordered from lowest to highest, as shown in Table 5.2(b). It is easy to see that 25 is the score in the middle, or the median score. The symbol most often used for median is *Mdn*. The median of an even number of scores is halfway between the two scores that fall in the middle. The *mode* of a distribution is the score that occurs most frequently. As Table 5.2(c) shows, the mode of this distribution is 27, since it is the only score that occurs more than once. Some distributions have more than one mode.

Comparing the Mean, Median, and Mode

To better understand the important differences among these three commonly used measures, let's consider an example (admittedly somewhat exaggerated). The superintendent of Nowhere School District, who also serves as principal at the high school, has had virtually total control over the school for almost 40 years. Members of a newly elected school board are disturbed over reports of morale problems among the staff about salaries. After some quick computations, school board members are puzzled, noting that the salary account shows a total of $302,550 paid to the 11 persons employed by the district (a custodian, a secretary, eight teachers, and the superintendent). According to the board's calculations, that is an "average" of $27,505 for each employee; they believe this to be adequate and decide not to pursue the matter further.

Following further complaints, however, the board invites both the superintendent and the head of the teachers' union to attend their next meeting, where they become even more confused. The head of the teachers' union reports that the "average" salary is really $9,000, and the superintendent reports that the "average" salary is $16,800. The members of the board decide that someone is lying (not an infrequent accusation when statistical summaries are involved).

Based on what you know now about the different definitions of mean, median, and mode, can you see how the three different "averages" could all be correct?

The explanation is apparent when we look at Figure 5.5. Panel (a) shows the histogram presented to the board by the superintendent. Her statement that the average salary is $16,800 (the median salary as shown in panel (b) of Figure 5.4) seems consistent with the information represented in this histogram. Not wanting to make it too obvious that her salary is more than six times higher than anyone else's, the superintendent has shown it on the histogram as $20,000+.

Understandably, the head of the teachers' union showed the average (in this case, the mode) that would most likely result in a pay increase. The board was also correct in concluding that the average was $27,505, because that is the arithmetic mean of the money being paid for salaries.

All three averages are correct, but radically different. The high estimate is more than three times the size of the low estimate. How does one choose the most appropriate measure of central tendency?

FIGURE 5.5   A Dispute over "Average" Salaries in Nowhere School District

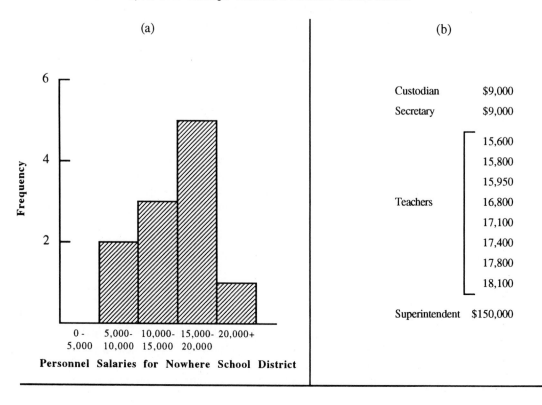

Selecting the Most Appropriate Measure of Central Tendency

Consider the frequency polygons shown in Figure 5.6. As seen in (a), when distributions are approximately normal, it makes no difference which measure of central tendency is used, because all three will have the same value. It is only when distributions are positively or negatively skewed, or have several unusually extreme values, that the mean, median, and mode will be substantially different.

In general, the mean is the most stable measure of central tendency. In other words, if you were to measure the same characteristic among a group of individuals on two different occasions, the two mean scores would differ less than the two medians or the two modes. Mean scores, however, are significantly influenced by extreme scores, or by *skewness*. As shown in Figure 5.6, a positively skewed distribution tends to pull the mean toward the positive end. A negatively skewed distribution pulls the mean toward the negative end.

Where we want to minimize the influence of extreme scores, the median provides the best indicator of central tendency. By *best* we mean that, if you have to use only one number to describe a distribution, the median will be the most accurate. Such situations arise frequently in education and the median should be more widely used than it is. For example, if a test is very easy, student's scores will cluster at the top of the distribution. In such cases, the median is a better indicator of average achievement than the mean.

The mode is appropriate where it is important to know which option "got the most votes." Where scores exist along a continuum or range, both the median and mean generally provide a better indication of the average.

FIGURE 5.6 Relative Position of Mean ($\overline{X}$), Median (Mdn), and Mode in Different Types of Distributions

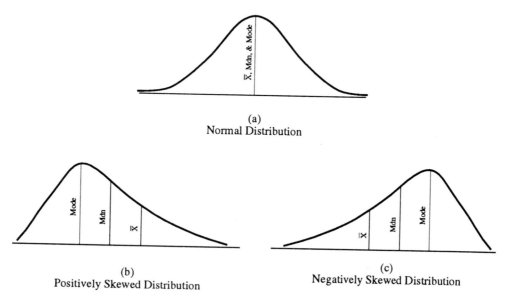

(a)
Normal Distribution

(b)
Positively Skewed Distribution

(c)
Negatively Skewed Distribution

As a final illustration of the differences among these three measures of central tendency, we repeat an anecdote given by two of our colleagues.

Five men sat together on a park bench. Two were vagrants, each with total worldly assets of 25 cents. The third was a workman whose bank account and other assets totaled $2000. The fourth man had $15,000 in various forms. The fifth was a millionaire with a net worth of $5 million. Therefore, the mode of the cash worth of the group was 25 cents. This figure describes two of the persons perfectly, but is grossly inaccurate for the other three. The median figure of $2000 does little justice to anyone except the workman. The mean, $1,003,400.10, is not very satisfactory even for the millionaire. If we *had* to choose one measure of central tendency, perhaps it would be the mode, which describes 40% of this group accurately. But if we were told that "the modal assets of 5 persons sitting on a park bench were 25 cents," we would be likely to conclude that the total assets of the group are approximately $1.25, which is more than 5 million dollars lower than the correct figure. Obviously, no measure of central tendency whatsoever is adequate for these "strange bench fellows," who simply do not tend centrally. (Hopkins & Stanley, 1981, pp. 32–33)

Obviously, even though measures of central tendency are very useful in describing most distributions, sometimes no measure of central tendency is appropriate. Often, it is best to report two or three different measures of central tendency. Or, if the number of data points is small, simply report all the data.

Measures of Dispersion

Although, a well-chosen measure of central tendency is informative, it generally does not tell us nearly enough. Consider two different schools. In School A, the above-grade-level readers are in one class, at-grade-level readers in a second, and below-grade-level readers in a third. In School B, every class has some above-, below-, and at-grade-level readers. Would the same instructional strategies be appropriate in both schools? Probably not. The need for different strategies is a function of the increased *variability* among students in classrooms in School B and the relatively homogeneous classroom groupings in School A.

To understand the importance of variability, consider Table 5.3. All four

TABLE 5.3 Examples of Distributions of Scores with Different Degrees of Variability

	Group W	Group X	Group Y	Group Z
	65	50	44	30
	40	35	32	30
	30	30	30	30
	20	25	28	30
	5	20	26	30
Mean =	32	32	32	30
Median =	30	30	30	30

groups have identical median scores, and three groups have identical mean scores. Yet the variability of scores across the groups is very different. Minimum and maximum scores range from 60 points in Group W to 30 points in Group X, 18 points in Group Y, and *no* difference in Group Z.

Whereas measures of central tendency provide information about a test's overall difficulty, measures of variability—often called measures of *dispersion*—provide information about differences among scores. In other words, measures of central tendency are points, whereas measures of dispersion describe distances. The larger the value of a measure of dispersion, the greater the variability or heterogeneity among the scores. The two most commonly used measures of dispersion are *range* and *standard deviation*.

Range

The easiest estimate of dispersion to compute is the *range,* which is simply the difference between the highest and the lowest scores. In Table 5.3, the range for group W is 60 (65 − 5 = 60), for Groups X, Y, and Z it is 30, 18, and 0, respectively.

While the range is easy to compute, it has one very serious deficiency: Because it is determined only by the two extreme scores, it can be dramatically altered by adding or dropping a single extreme score. Such instability makes the range almost useless as a basis of comparing dispersions across two or more groups.

Standard Deviation

The most widely used measure of dispersion is the *standard deviation,* which typically is symbolized by *s* or *SD*. The standard deviation for a group of scores provides a summary number that indicates in general how far each score is from the mean. Because all scores in a group contribute to the computation, standard deviations tend to be influenced less by extreme scores than the range. Because many hand calculators will compute the standard deviation of a set of scores, we will not explain the computational details. Instead we will focus on the interpretation of a standard deviation.

In every normal distribution, the standard deviation can be used to express the way scores vary or are dispersed about the mean. By definition, for all normal curves 34.13 percent of the scores fall in the segment of the curve that is between the mean and one standard deviation from the mean. Thus, as shown in Figure 5.7, 68.26 percent of the scores fall between −1.0 standard deviation and +1.0 standard deviation. Consider some specific examples. Most IQ tests are developed to have a mean of 100 and a standard deviation of 15. Hence, approximately 68 percent of the population have IQs between 85 and 115. Furthermore, fifth grade reading achievement has a mean score in Grade Equivalent Units (GE)[1] of 5.0 and 68 percent of children score between 2.6 and 7.4 GEs.

The concept of standard deviation vastly enhances what we know by examining a normal distribution. For example, knowing that the standard deviation on an IQ test is 15, we see that very few people can be expected to have IQs above 130,

---

[1] A detailed explanation of Grade Equivalent Units is given later in this chapter.

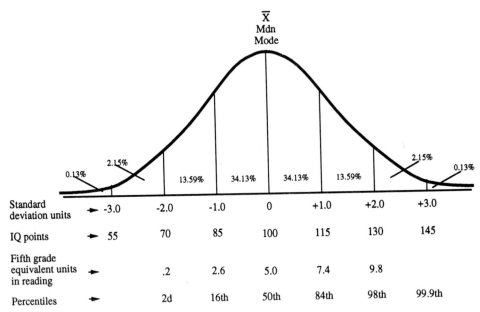

FIGURE 5.7 Percentage of Data Points and Example Scores Dispersed around the Mean in a Normal Distribution

or below 70. In other words, if the mean of the distribution of IQ scores is 100 and one standard deviation is equal to 15 points, 2 standard deviations will be 30 points. Thus, a score of 70 is two standard deviations below the mean. From Figure 5.7, you can see that only 2.28 percent of a normally distributed population is more than two standard deviations below the mean. Thus, about 2.28 percent of the population would be expected to have an IQ less than 70. The same reasoning applies to the percentage who would be expected to have IQs greater than 130, because the normal curve is symmetrical.

Since SD is an estimate of the average dispersion of each score around the mean, a distribution with a large standard deviation will contain scores that are more spread out, while a distribution with a small standard deviation will contain scores more closely clustered around the mean. To demonstrate, refer back to Table 5.3. The standard deviation for Group W is 22.5 while the standard deviation for Group Y is only 7.1.

Another important, frequently used concept is that of *percentile*. The point below which 50 percent of the scores fall is known as the 50th percentile of a distribution. In a normal distribution, the 50th percentile corresponds with the mean, median, and mode. In Figure 5.7, the 50th percentile of IQ scores is 100, meaning that half the persons tested will have scores over 100, and half will have scores below 100. Similarly, 75 percent of the scores fall below the 75th percentile, 90 percent of the scores fall below the 90th percentile, and so on. An IQ score of 115 (see Figure 5.7) is at the 84th percentile because 84 percent of the distribution falls below that point. An IQ of 70 is at approximately the 2d percentile because approximately 2 percent of the group (actually 2.28 percent) have IQs lower than 70. The concept of percentile is particularly important in educational measurement.

To understand why it is important to consider measures of dispersion and central tendency in interpreting test results, try the next application problem. This one is a bit challenging, so don't give up easily.

APPLICATION PROBLEM #2

Horatio is enrolled in a chemistry class with 50 students. He has received the following scores on the various assignments for the first half of the year. On which test or assignment did he do the best relative to the other members of the class? On which did he do the worst?

| | Possible Points | Class Scores | | | | Horatio's Scores | |
		Lowest	Highest	Mean	Standard Deviation	Actual Points	Percentage Correct
Homework assignment 1	50	22	48	35	5.0	30	60
Homework assignment 2	25	8	23	14	3.0	20	80
Homework assignment 3	75	48	75	60	6.0	66	83
Midterm	100	56	91	70	7.0	70	70
Semester exam	174	128	174	150	10.0	130	75

HINT: Class scores for each assignment or test are approximately normally distributed. Use what you have learned about standard deviations and normal curves to solve this problem.

The Correlation Coefficient: A Measure of Association

A clear understanding of the correlation coefficient can be invaluable in interpreting test scores and seeing how they relate to educational activities. Although you may use different words, you already use the concept of correlation frequently. Unfortunately, the concept of correlation is one of the most frequently abused concepts in educational evaluation and measurement.

So far, we have discussed only scores within a single distribution (e.g., the average salary for a group of people, or dispersion among reading test scores). Correlations describe how scores in one distribution relate to scores in another, or how one variable is related to, or associated with, another. Correlations help to answer questions like the following:

- Do people who are good at math have a greater than average musical ability?

- Is achievement lower in larger classes than in smaller classes?

- If you had good grades in high school, will you have good grades in college?

Assume the improbable case that people who are good at math have a less than average musical ability. If this were true, the two distributions of math ability and musical ability would look like those in Figure 5.8. Students' scores on a test of math ability and a measure of musical ability are approximately normally distributed. A correlation coefficient tells how accurately a student's position in the second distribution can be predicted given her position in the first. After giving some additional definitions and examples of correlation coefficients, we will provide guidelines for interpreting correlation coefficients. You will find that using correlation coefficients is a little like riding a bicycle—a handy skill, but tricky until you get the hang of it.

Definitions and Examples

Two variables are correlated if they are related or tend to "go together." For example, tall people tend to weigh more than short people. Hence, height and weight are correlated. Correlations can be either *positive*—high scores associated with high scores and low scores associated with low scores)—or negative—high scores on one variable associated with low scores on the other variable.

Correlations can also be computed for variables other than test scores. For example, some people believe that the size of an elementary school class (i.e., number of students) is correlated with, or associated with, teacher job satisfaction. According to this belief, if you examined 100 elementary school classes, you would find that the most satisfied teachers tended to be those teaching the smallest classes.

Some variables are not correlated at all. If you examined the number of the month in which students in a college math class were born with their grade point average (GPA) prior to taking that class, you would probably find no association. In other words, knowing the month in which a student was born would not allow you to predict her GPA any more accurately than if you did not know it.

We will not discuss the computational steps involved in calculating a correlation coefficient since we are most concerned that you be able to understand and interpret the meaning of a correlation coefficient. Furthermore many hand calculators provide the correlation coefficient if you enter the raw data. (For those interested, computation details can be found in most introductory statistics books.)

Correlation coefficients range from -1.0 to $+1.0$. The closer a correlation is to zero, the less you can use performance on one measure to predict performance on the other. Remember that a high correlation can be either a high negative or a high positive correlation. A correlation of -1.0 or $+1.0$ is sometimes referred to as perfect correlation because you can perfectly predict a person's performance on one variable by knowing her performance on the other.

What constitutes a high, moderate, or low correlation depends so much on the situation that only general guidelines can be given. High correlations are generally considered to have absolute values of .80 or higher. For example, two different forms of a well-constructed achievement test should correlate about .90. Moderate

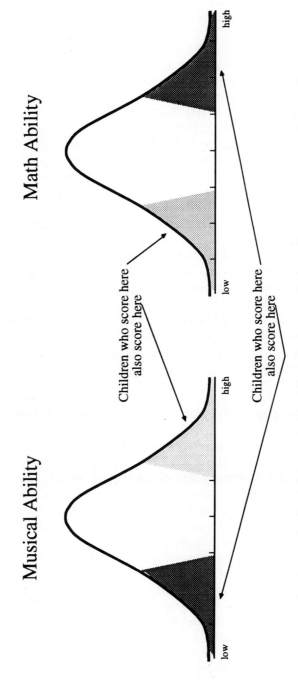

FIGURE 5.8 Conceptual Illustration of a Hypothetical Negative Correlation between Ability in Math and Ability in Music

correlations are in the range of .40 to .80—aptitude test scores generally correlate with later grades about .50. Low correlations are less than .40—the correlation between manual dexterity and scores on a test of reading comprehension are close to 0.0.

To better understand correlation coefficients, it is useful to examine what statisticians refer to as scatterplots or scattergrams. Figure 5.9 contains hypothetical scores on two variables for 20 students. The first score is the number of days absent during the semester and the second score is the number of correct answers on the final math test. Could you predict a child's math score any more accurately if you knew the number of days she was absent from school? By looking at the numbers in the top half of Figure 5.9, it is difficult to see a relationship. However, when the numbers are plotted on the scattergram in the lower part of Figure 5.9 (for now ignore the fact that part of the graph is shaded differently), it becomes clear that there is a tendency for students with fewer absences to score better on the test. The actual correlation coefficient (indicated by r) is $-.33$ for the twenty students. This fairly weak negative correlation indicates a tendency for people who have a *higher* rate of absenteeism to score *lower* on the math test.

Since you will be using scattergrams quite frequently, be sure you understand how this one was constructed. The dot associated with each person provides information on that person's absenteeism and math score. For example, John (whose dot is in the upper left-hand corner) was absent thirty days and scored 20 on the math test. This dot corresponds with the 30 on the vertical axis (number of days absent), and the 20 on the horizontal axis (score on math test). Each of the twenty scores is represented by a similar dot. The elliptical shape shown in Figure 5.9 is often used instead of dots to represent the approximate shape of the scattergram.

As you become more familiar with correlation coefficients, you will find that the shape of the plot of dots gives you an approximate idea of the magnitude of the correlation coefficient. If the correlation is perfect (i.e., 1.0 or -1.0), the scatterplot will be represented by a single line. If there is no correlation, the scatterplot will be a circle or rectangle. As the scatterplot changes from a circle to narrower and narrower ellipses (eventually becoming a single line), the corresponding correlation coefficient gets larger and larger, as shown in Figure 5.10 (p. 110). Once you become familiar with the approximate shapes of scatterplots associated with correlations of various magnitudes, you can judge the strength of an association at a glance.

Now, refer back to Figure 5.9 for a moment. A review of *all* the scores reveals a *tendency* for children who are absent more days to score lower on the test. However, there are some exceptions. Ellen, who obtained the highest score on the math test, was absent more days than anybody except for Brigham, John, Collette, and Hunter. To show how individual scores affect the magnitude of the correlation coefficient, we have calculated the correlation coefficient, means, and standard deviations on each variable for several subsets of the data in Figure 5.9 and summarized the information in Table 5.4 (p. 111).

If we consider only the ten scores inside the narrower ellipse, the correlation coefficient is $-.92$. This is consistent with our previous discussion suggesting that

Name	Number of Days Absent	Score on a Math Test	Name	Number of Days Absent	Score on a Math Test
John	30	20	Artemus	18	30
Susan	23	40	Harriette	12	30
Harold	15	18	Barbara	12	43
Oliver	8	50	Collette	27	44
Nancy	23	70	William	6	90
Juan	20	46	Chad	10	66
Marie	7	78	Ellen	24	100
Hunter	30	50	Karl	12	80
Sylvia	18	80	Allyson	15	70
Brigham	25	10	Brigette	22	60

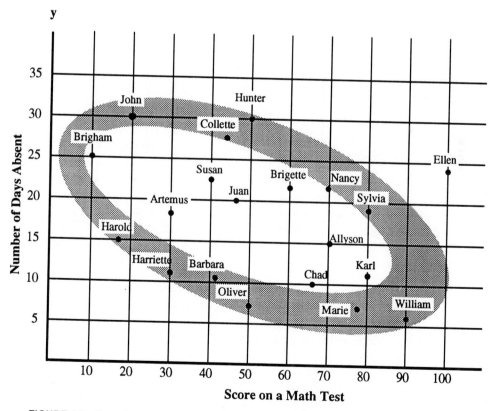

FIGURE 5.9 Hypothetical Distribution for Math Scores and Number of Days Absent for 20 Children

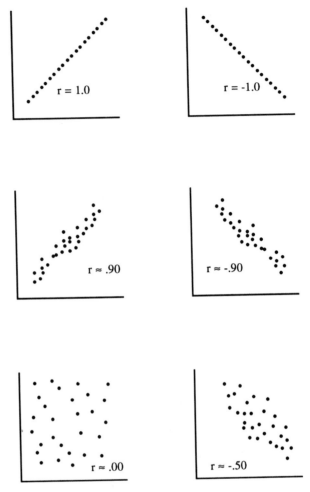

FIGURE 5.10 Examples of Scatterplots Associated with Correlations of Different Magnitudes (The symbol "≈" is used to indicate *approximately equal to.*)

the more closely the ellipse approximates a straight line, the higher the correlation. As the ellipse is broadened to include all students except for Ellen, the magnitude of the correlation changes to $r = -.46$.

Adding the single data point for Ellen further reduces the correlation coefficient ($r = -.33$). Clearly, *outliers* can have a considerable influence on the magnitude of a correlation coefficient when the total data set is relatively small. To demonstrate just how serious that impact can be, consider what happens if we were to add just two more data points to those already shown. Assume that Mike, who has not been absent at all, scores a 0 on the math test; and that Suzanne, who has been absent 50 days during the semester, scores 100 percent on the math test.

TABLE 5.4 Means, Standard Deviations, and Correlations for Different Subsets of the Data Shown in Figure 5.9

n = 10	n = 19	n = 20	n = 22
$r = -.92$	$r = -.46$	$r = -.33$	$r = +.19$
$\overline{X}_{absent} = 19.50$	$\overline{X}_{absent} = 17.53$	$\overline{X}_{absent} = 17.85$	$\overline{X}_{absent} = 18.50$
$SD_{absent} = 5.64$	$SD_{absent} = 7.60$	$SD_{absent} = 7.53$	$SD_{absent} = 10.74$
$\overline{X}_{math} = 51.60$	$\overline{X}_{math} = 51.30$	$\overline{X}_{math} = 53.75$	$\overline{X}_{math} = 53.41$
$SD_{math} = 21.56$	$SD_{math} = 23.37$	$SD_{math} = 25.22$	$SD_{math} = 28.54$
Ten Students in the Inner Ellipse	**19 Students in the Entire Ellipse**	**All Students**	**All Students with Addition of Mike and Suzanne**

Adding these two points to the scatterplot would change the correlation from $r = -.33$ to $r = +.19$. Adding two such points changes the interpretation substantially. Instead of *low* scores being associated with *high* absenteeism, *high* scores would be associated (albeit weakly) with *high* absenteeism.

The fact that adding or deleting a few points can have such a dramatic influence emphasizes the need to interpret correlation coefficients very carefully. In almost all decisions concerning correlation coefficients, it is worthwhile to examine a scatterplot to make sure that the correlation is not being unduly influenced by one or two aberrant scores.

Interpreting Correlation Coefficients

Since the concept of correlation is so widely used in education, it is important to point out a number of the cautions that you should keep in mind as you interpret correlation coefficients.

Causality. During the early twentieth century, there was a positive correlation between the number of storks' nests and the number of babies born in Northern European cities—cities with more storks' nests also had more babies. One might interpret this as evidence that storks do bring babies. There is at least one alternative explanation for the observed correlation. Storks apparently like to build nests on the chimneys of houses. As the number of houses increased, so did the number of babies. More houses meant more chimneys—hence more storks' nests. Thus, the number of storks' nests can be correlated with the number of babies without it necessarily being true that storks bring babies.

Similar examples of interpretational problems with correlational data are easy to find. For example, it would be poor logic to conclude that people who drive fire engines were arsonists just because there almost always seemed to be a fire engine at the scene of a fire shortly after it started. Similarly, you should not conclude that hospitals make people sick just because you find a higher percentage of sick people at a hospital than you do at other places. We hope you are beginning to see why it is so important to remember that *correlation does not necessarily mean causation.* Each of you would probably be well served if we borrowed some pedagogical techniques from the early twentieth century and required you to write that phrase on the blackboard 500 times. However, we doubt that we can convince you to do that, so we will settle for a plea to always be on guard against jumping to conclusions about a causal relationship based on correlational data.

APPLICATION PROBLEM #3

There is a correlation between the amount of education people obtain and their later income. This evidence is sometimes used to conclude that increased education will result in higher income. See if you can come up with a logical explanation for why a strong correlation exists between education and income, even if there is no causal link.

Although it is generally unwise to conclude there is a causal connection between two variables based on correlational data, it is not impossible. For example, based largely on correlational data, it is now well accepted that smoking causes lung cancer. However, before correlational data can be used as evidence for causality, it is important to consider the possibility that an observed correlation is present because of problems with *directionality* or *third variables*. To illustrate this concept, consider a hypothetical data set that shows a correlation of .78 between the amount of praise children receive and their scores on a measure of self-concept. Even though the correlation is substantial, there are at least four ways in which such a correlation could be obtained. Consider the information in Figure 5.11.

FIGURE 5.11 Alternative Models for Explaining the Observed Correlation between Rates of Praise and Self-esteem (arrows indicate direction of causal effect)

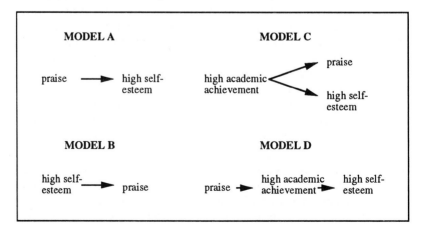

Model A indicates a true causal effect between praise and high self-esteem. However, before concluding that this model is most likely, we must first rule out the other three models. Model B suggests that children who have high self-esteem get more praise but that the children's high self-esteem causes the praise—not the reverse. In other words, there may be something about children with high self-esteem that elicits praise from teachers. This is what is referred to as a *directionality* problem.

Models C and D are both examples of *third variable problems*. In Model C, having high academic achievement results in more praise and also results in high self-esteem. However, there is no causal relationship between self-esteem and praise. It just so happens that they are both associated with a third variable (i.e., academic achievement). In Model D, praise is causally related to higher academic achievement, which in turn causes higher self-esteem. However, there is no direct causal link between praise and self-esteem.

Even though it is possible to draw conclusions about causality based on correlational data, the process is extremely complex and requires careful examination of alternatives. Before concluding that a correlation provides evidence for a causal link, one must first rule out all plausible third variable and directionality explanations.

Obviously, many situations consist of much more complex relationships involving a larger number of third variables, as well as complex interactions involving the set of variables. The process of ruling out alternative explanations is painstaking and time consuming. Being aware that such a process exists can help you avoid a common abuse of correlation data—namely, using such data to support erroneous conclusions about causality.

Curvilinearity.   All of the examples we have shown you so far are linear relationships. It is possible to have a very strong relationship between two variables even though the linear relationship is described by $r = 0.0$. For example, if the scatterplot depicting the relation between test anxiety and performance on standardized achievement tests looked like Figure 5.12, the correlation between the two variables would be close to $r = 0.0$. However, it would be possible to predict with considerable accuracy how someone would score on an achievement test if we knew her level of test anxiety. Those with no anxiety tend to do poorly, those with moderate anxiety do best, and those with high anxiety are so debilitated that they do poorly. (We emphasize that this is a hypothetical example. The relation between anxiety and test scores is discussed in Chapter 8.) That such *curvilinear* relationships exist means it is essential to examine scatterplots of data to make sure that the presence of a curvilinear relationship is not making it appear as if there is no association between two variables when, in fact, there is a very strong curvilinear relationship.

Restricted Range.   Before drawing conclusions about an observed correlation between two variables, it is important to know whether data are available across the entire spectrum of possible scores for each of the variables. Where the range of scores has been reduced through selection, absenteeism, or some other factor,

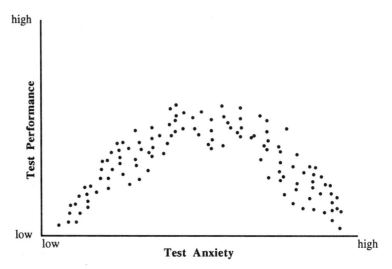

FIGURE 5.12 Hypothetical Scatterplot of Scores between Test Anxiety and Test Performance

it is possible to have a very low observed correlation even though the two variables would be substantially correlated if the total population of scores were available. For example, Figure 5.13 illustrates how a scatterplot between Graduate Record Examination (GRE) scores and performance in graduate school might look if all college students were required to take the GRE and all went to graduate school.

A fairly strong correlation (approximately $r = .70$) exists in Figure 5.13 when these assumptions are true. However, not all college students take the GRE and even fewer go to graduate school. Assume that the triangles in Figure 5.13 represent those students who take the GRE, while the circles represent those who do not. The magnitude of the correlation coefficient for that portion of the scatterplot represented by triangles is only .46. Furthermore, not all of those who take the GREs actually complete graduate school. Those who do are indicated on the scatterplot by the triangles in the shaded area. The magnitude of the correlation coefficient for this group is only .11. Is the data from the triangles in the shaded area a fair indication of how well scores on the GRE predict success in graduate school? Obviously not. Estimating the correlation between two variables in which data for one or both represent a very restricted range is clearly risky business.

Number of Cases.   You already know what can happen to the magnitude of the correlation coefficient when an *outlier* is introduced. (Remember Ellen, who was frequently absent but still outscored her peers on the math test?) The effect of such outliers is proportionately greater the smaller the data set. Consequently, correlations computed from small samples should be interpreted with caution. In situations with ten or fewer cases, correlations are often spuriously high or low.

To help decide whether correlation coefficients are meaningful, procedures have been developed that indicate whether the correlation coefficient is *statisti-*

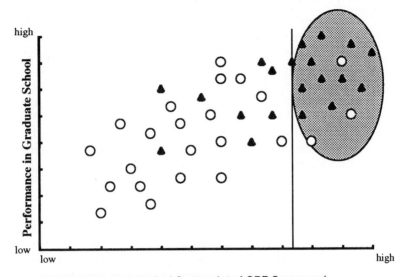

FIGURE 5.13 Hypothetical Scatterplot of GRE Scores and Performance in Graduate School for Students Who Do Not Take the GRE (○) and Those Who Do (▲)

cally significant. Statistical significance is used to decide how probable it is that correlations of similar magnitude would occur if random samples of comparable size were drawn from a larger population of scores in which the true correlation was zero.

A statistically significant correlation is not necessarily a practically *important* correlation. To be important, correlation coefficients should be both statistically significant and meaningfully large in terms of indicating the degree of relationship between the two variables under consideration. For example, it is not unlikely that there is a small, but statistically significant, correlation between month of birth and reading ability for all first grade children (suppose such a correlation were − .15). Such a correlation might occur because at such a young age, children born in January would be 12.5 percent older than children born in October, and the additional maturity would give the older child a slight edge. Even though the correlation is statistically significantly different from zero, it is not very important because it will disappear within a few years, and is not large enough to predict anything meaningful. Furthermore, it is very unlikely that the government would issue an edict to have all children born in January!

Magnitude of Correlation Coefficients.   There are no simple rules for deciding how large a correlation coefficient must be to be practically important. Larger correlation coefficients (either positive or negative) are indicative of a stronger association between two variables. However, it is inappropriate to interpret *r* as a percentage in the usual sense. When $r = 0.0$, there is no linear relationship between the two variables. But, if $r = .75$, there is not a 75 percent linear relationship. Furthermore, an increase of r from .20 to .30 does not indicate as much increase in the strength of the relationship as an increase in r from .70 to .80.

For nonstatisticians, the best guide to interpretation is previous experience. For example, it is not unusual for two well-constructed measures of discrete academic skills to correlate .85 to .95. Alternatively, a correlation of .65 to .75 is quite good between two affective measures such as self-concept and test anxiety. Mother-child IQs tend to correlate about .50, IQs of identical twins raised in the same home correlate about .90, and the correlation in the general population between physical strength and IQ is about .20.

Measurement Error

Imagine an IQ test that has been given to two people. Suzanne obtains a score of 108, and Laura obtains a score of 106. Who has the highest IQ? Perhaps Laura has a true IQ of 120 but was feeling ill when the test was given, or was not very motivated because she was thinking about the homecoming dance. It may well be that Laura's true IQ is substantially higher than Suzanne's true IQ, even though on this test it appears that Suzanne has a slight edge.

How do we decide how accurate the results of a test really are? Think about your own testing experience and all of the factors that influenced your performance on even the most "objective" tests. You can probably remember taking tests when you felt miserable, or the teacher asked exactly the six questions which you did not study, or there was a big game that night and you were worried about how you would perform. On such occasions you probably obtained a score that underestimated what you really knew.

But what about the other times? Have you ever taken a test when you just happened to make some lucky guesses, or you only studied a third of the material, but that was the material the teacher included on the exam.

Since we do not know what affected Suzanne or Laura, it is difficult to know who really has the highest IQ. But now we have raised a more general issue. Having admitted that no test yields a perfect score, and having pointed out a few of the infinite number of factors that can cause scores to be spuriously high or low, where does that leave us? Even though we cannot know exactly what a person's "true score" is, we can estimate a range, or what statisticians refer to as a *confidence interval*, which usually provides us with a sufficiently good estimate of the true score.

To illustrate these concepts, assume that IQ is a perfectly stable trait that is totally inherited and never changes throughout your life. Furthermore, imagine that your true IQ is 120, and that someone administers the same IQ test to you 1000 different times, but in such a way that there is no improvement from test to test as a result of the repeated administrations. Impossible you say? Well, it is in practice, but in theory, it could be done.

Obviously you would not get the same score every time the test was administered. Factors like those we mentioned above, as well as a host of other factors—such as the way in which the test was administered each time—means that

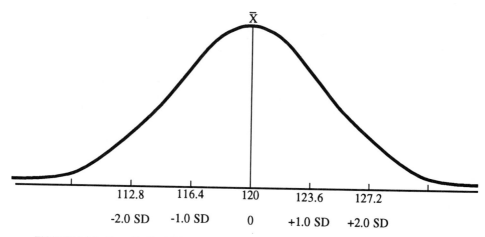

FIGURE 5.14 Hypothetical Distribution of Scores from 1,000 Administrations of the Same IQ Test to a Person with a "True" IQ of 120

the observed score on each administration of the IQ test would vary somewhat. A distribution of those test scores would look something like the distribution in Figure 5.14.

Confidence Intervals

Because your true IQ score is 120, it is not surprising that the distribution in Figure 5.14 has a mean of 120. This happens because for well-developed tests that are appropriately administered the variables that tend to elevate or depress your score are random variables (e.g., making a lucky guess, feeling sick, studying for just the right questions). In other words, on any given test administration, a factor that elevates your score is as likely as one that depresses it. Over a large number of administrations, these factors tend to balance, so that your average score is the same as your true score.

It is also apparent from the distribution in Figure 5.14 that most test administrations have some error, but how much? The concept of standard deviation can help us answer this question. Since the scores are normally distributed, we can use the standard deviation of the distribution, which equals 3.6, as an indicator of the amount of error[2]—or the degree to which scores are dispersed about the true score. You know that approximately 68 percent of the distribution falls within plus (+) or minus (−) one standard deviation from the mean. In other words, about 68 percent of this distribution will be between 116.4 and 123.6. This band of scores is referred to as a 68 percent *confidence interval*. Because 68 percent of our theoretical distribution of scores falls between 116.4 and 123.6, we can be fairly confident that the true score lies somewhere within this range. If we want to be more

---

[2] We have not told you how we calculated the value of 3.6. How the exact value of the standard deviation is computed is less important to our discussion than the concept of measurement error. Those interested in the computational details should refer to Magnussen (1967).

confident, we can move out two SDs from the mean on each side (112.8 to 127.2). This band contains about 95 percent of the scores in our theoretical distribution and is referred to as a 95 percent confidence interval.

Measurement experts use some specific terms to refer to these concepts. Your *observed score* is the score you obtain on each administration of the IQ test. Your *true score* is the theoretical true IQ, which in this case is 120. Your *error score* is the difference between the observed score and the true score for any specific administration of the test. The relationship between these three scores is *observed score = true score + error score*. Error scores can be either positive or negative depending on whether they elevate or depress the observed score from the theoretical true score.

Standard Error of Measurement

The distance of one standard deviation in our theoretical distribution of 1,000 administrations of the IQ test, shown in Figure 5.14, is referred to as the *standard error of measurement* (SEM). The standard error of measurement is useful because it provides a uniform way of estimating the degree of error in any given test.

The standard error of measurement is related to the concept of *test reliability*. Reliability is a measure of how consistently a test measures whatever it is intended to measure. If the test were perfectly reliable, the results of each test administration would be perfectly consistent, and every score in the distribution in Figure 5.14 would be the same. Thus, the standard error of measurement would be 0. The mathematical relationship between standard error of measurement (SEM) and reliability (r_{tt}) is

$$SEM = SD \sqrt{1 - r_{tt}}$$

The standard error of measurement is often more informative than the reliability coefficient (Williams & Zimmerman, 1984). This is because the standard error of measurement combines information about the standard deviation of the test as well as the reliability of the test. Hence, you can estimate whether a particular score is likely to be in error by 1 point or by 20 points.

Return for a moment to the IQ scores obtained by Suzanne (108) and Laura (106). Which person has the higher IQ? It is hard to say if you want to know the *true* IQ scores—which, of course, are the most interesting. It is easy to say that Suzanne's observed score is two points higher than Laura's. But, what if Laura had a particularly bad day, or Suzanne made a number of lucky guesses? Now that we know about the standard error of measurement (SEM), we can estimate the range in which each true score is likely to fall. Table 5.5 provides an easy reference to estimate how much error is likely in each person's score as a function of the test's standard deviation and reliability. Since Suzanne and Laura took an IQ test, we will estimate that the standard deviation is 16 points,[3] and the reliability

---

[3] Those of you with unusually good memories will recall that we told you earlier of an IQ test with a standard deviation of 15. Not all IQ tests have standard deviations that are exactly the same. Most IQ tests are developed to have a standard deviation of either 15 or 16, but a few have standard deviations as low as 12 or as high as 20.

TABLE 5.5 Standard Errors of Measurement for Various Combinations of Reliability and Standard Deviation

SD	Reliability Coefficient					
	.95	.90	.85	.80	.75	.70
30	6.7	9.5	11.6	13.4	15.0	16.4
28	6.3	8.9	10.8	12.5	14.0	15.3
26	5.8	8.2	10.1	11.6	13.0	14.2
24	5.4	7.6	9.3	10.7	12.0	13.1
22	4.9	7.0	8.5	9.8	11.0	12.0
20	4.5	6.3	7.7	8.9	10.0	11.0
18	4.0	5.7	7.0	8.0	9.0	9.9
16	3.6	5.1	6.2	7.2	8.0	8.8
14	3.1	4.4	5.4	6.3	7.0	7.7
12	2.7	3.8	4.6	5.4	6.0	6.6
10	2.2	3.2	3.9	4.5	5.0	5.5
8	1.8	2.5	3.1	3.6	4.0	4.4
6	1.3	1.9	2.3	2.7	3.0	3.3
4	.9	1.3	1.5	1.8	2.0	2.2
2	.4	.6	.8	.9	1.0	1.1

This table is based on the formula SE (Measurement) = $SD\sqrt{1 - r_{tt}}$, where SD is the standard deviation of the test scores and r_{tt} is the reliability coefficient. Reprinted from J. E. Doppelt, *How Accurate is a Test Score?* Test Service Bulletin, No. 50 (New York: Psychological Corporation).

is quite high (.95). As Table 5.5 shows, the resulting standard error of measurement is 3.6 (the same as the distribution in Figure 5.14). The means of the distributions for Suzanne and Laura would be 108 and 106, respectively. Consequently, we can estimate the range in which most scores for each of the girls will fall. For Suzanne, 68 percent of the scores will fall between 104.4 and 111.6. For Laura, 68 percent of the scores will fall between 102.4 and 109.6. Because the two confidence intervals overlap considerably, the girls' true IQ scores are probably not very different; in fact, there is a good chance that Laura's true IQ is higher than Suzanne's.

Knowing that any observed score is made up of the true score and the error score should make you more cautious about interpreting small differences between scores as meaningful. More important, if you have information about a test's standard deviation and reliability, you can accurately estimate how large an observed score difference must be before one can confidently conclude that the true scores are different.

INTERPRETING TEST SCORES AND DATA

One of the most frequently encountered types of data for educational purposes comes from standardized, norm-referenced tests. Consequently, a wide variety of methods for reporting and interpreting such scores have been developed. As we introduce you to the vocabulary and terminology associated with interpreting norm-referenced tests—stanines, normal curve equivalents, z-scores, objective mastery scores—you might think you have been time-warped into a foreign country with a strange language, but the underlying concepts are really quite simple. This section defines the various terms used to describe test scores and gives you some examples.

Norms

Knowing that the ten-year-old girl next door is 56-inches tall provides you with a fair amount of information about her height. You probably know some other ten-year-olds to whom you can make a comparison, so you can judge whether she is tall or short for her age. However, knowing that she scored 56 on her spelling test tells you almost nothing about her spelling ability. You do not know whether the words on the test were easy or hard, how many words were on the test, whether she had to write the words out or simply recognize the correctly spelled word from among three alternatives, or how well other children in the class did on the test.

Another reason that "56-inches tall" conveys so much more information than "a score of 56 on the spelling test," is that height is measured on a scale that has an absolute zero point, with equal units of measurement from one point of the scale to another. Because of this, it is possible to talk about someone being twice as tall as someone else. Also, the difference between 12 and 24 inches is exactly the same as the difference between 120 and 132 inches. The concept of "56-inches tall" is the same whether we are talking about the little girl next door, the Shetland pony at Grandpa's farm, or the chest of drawers in your bedroom.

The same rules do not apply to most educational measures because they do not have an absolute zero point. Someone who scores a zero on a spelling test probably does not have zero ability to spell. Furthermore, a person who can spell 10 of the 60 words correctly does not necessarily know how to spell *twice* as many words as a person who only spells 5.

Once again, the normal curve can help us with some of these interpretational problems. Let us return to the spelling score of the little girl next door. If she tells her father that she got a score of 56 on the spelling test, her father will probably ask questions about how that score relates to other variables: "Out of how many?" or "How did the other children in the class do?" We tend to ask the same kinds of questions, albeit subconsciously, about variables such as height and temperature. If I tell you that the girl next door is 56-inches tall, you have a *norm reference* group in mind—other children of about the same age. Thus, if I go on to say that the girl is only two years old, you immediately recognize that something is wrong with either my yardstick or the girl next door. The information about the girl's height becomes meaningful when compared to the heights of other girls in similar circumstances.

Norms for test scores are used in the same way. Knowing that Vicky can say the alphabet from A to Z has a very different meaning depending on whether Vicky is eighteen months old, six years old, or eighteen years old. In judging Vicky's knowledge and skill, you use your experience with other children of comparable ages to establish a norm reference in your mind. The norms for standardized tests serve exactly the same purpose, but are created in a more systematic way.

What Are the Characteristics of Good Norms?

Although norms can be useful, they can also be misleading. Learning that your daughter is the best speller in the class may seem good news until you discover she is also the only native speaker of English. Before you can be sure what a score on a norm-referenced test means, you need some information about how the norms were constructed.

Test norms are created by administering a test to a group of people whose scores are then used as a basis for comparison. Whether such norms are useful for your purposes depends on the characteristics of the people in the group. Several characteristics—*relevance, representativeness, currency, and comparability*—should be considered in judging the adequacy of norms.

Relevance.   To whom do you want to compare your test scores? Most standardized tests provide national norms—that is, scores from a nationally representative sample of students—but some also provide norms for different subgroups—boys versus girls, those in college preparatory tracks versus those in noncollege preparatory tracks. Many test scoring services also provide local norms, such as the scores for all of the students in your school or district who took the test. Whether the norms are relevant depends on the purpose for which you are using them.

For example, if you are counseling a student about whether to attend a large university, it would be more helpful to know that she was at the 15th percentile on math ability for national norms than it would be to know that she was at the 90th percentile for local norms. Such scores indicate that even though she is one of the best math students in her school, she really does very poorly when compared to a national sample of students with whom she would likely be competing at the university.

Representativeness.   Having norms that have been labeled in a way that sounds relevant for your purposes is not enough. You must know whether the students in that norm group are representative of a given population. For example, a norm group that consists of students in inner-city schools from Chicago, New York, and Los Angeles is clearly not representative of *all* students in the country, even if such a group is labeled as a national sample. In determining representativeness, the size of a sample is less important than the way it has been selected. For example, according to Hopkins, Stanley, and Hopkins (1990), most national opinion surveys are based on carefully selected samples of about 1,500 people—less than .001 percent of the population. Yet the results from these small samples are extremely accurate. The critical issue is whether the people included in the norm sample are really representative for your purposes. Good standardized tests provide demographic information about the norm sample to help you answer this question.

Currency.   How people score on a test changes over time. For example, the relative abilities of girls and boys in math has changed substantially over the past

30 years. Therefore, a math test that was normed in 1960 would not provide very useful information about the current performance of boys versus girls in your district.

Comparability. It is often important to compare the scores from two or more tests. Norms can be very useful for this purpose, provided that they are collected in approximately the same manner. Obviously, it is not very useful to know that a student scored at the 72nd percentile on Test A and the 50th percentile on Test B if the norming populations for the two tests are dramatically different. In cases where the norming procedures and samples are quite similar, you can make rough comparisons between the same types of scores obtained on different tests (e.g., percentiles on math computation). Such comparisons are only approximations and small differences should not be accorded too much importance.

Norms Are Not Standards

Because the term *norms* is frequently used in conjunction with *standardized* tests, there is a tendency to equate the terms *norms* and *standards.* Such confusion of terms is dangerously misleading. The word *standard* denotes a level of achievement that has been established as a goal for all students. *Norms,* on the other hand, are descriptions of typical performance for some comparison group. A standard is a description of what ought to be. A norm is a description of what is.

Sometimes, norms are used to establish standards. Someone might decide that all students in a particular school should be reading at the 75th percentile of the national norm-reference group. Whether or not this standard is appropriate depends on the values of the community, the historical performance of its students, and the goals of the school system. Remember, however, that standards and norms are never synonymous. The fact that the average school child in America watches several hours of television each day, which is the norm, does not mean that watching several hours of television daily should be an established standard.

Scores Yielded by Standardized Tests

The simplest type of test score is the student's raw score on the test. A *raw score* is one that has not yet been "cooked" in the cauldron of statistics. It is a simple tally. If the girl next door spells 56 words correctly on a spelling test of 100 words, her raw score is 56. Because raw scores are not very useful for interpreting standardized test results, a number of other scores have been developed.

Grade Equivalent Scores

Probably the most widely used score for reporting test results is the grade equivalent (GE) score. Unfortunately, it can often lead to serious misinterpretations. Grade equivalent scores are seductively simple and direct. A GE of 5.0 means the student's score was comparable to the average score of students in the norm-reference group at the beginning of the fifth grade. A GE score of 5.4 indicates that the student's score was comparable to the average score of students in the norm-reference group in the fourth month of the fifth grade.

Although it seems logical to report that a student's score in spelling is comparable to that of the average pupil in the fourth month of fifth grade, there are problems with accepting this statement too literally. Consider a student who is in the fourth grade, but obtains a GE score of 6.9 on a math test. Does this mean that she is capable of doing the math that students are typically taught during the ninth month of the sixth grade? Not necessarily. It does mean that her math skills are well above the average fourth grader. But, it would be inappropriate to assume that she is capable of doing math usually taught in the ninth month of the sixth grade. In fact it is unlikely that any sixth graders even took the version of the test on which the norms were based.

To understand how GE scores can be misleading, let's consider how they are created. To establish GE scores for a fourth grade test, the test is usually administered to a group of third, fourth, and fifth graders. Suppose the test is administered in September and the median raw scores are 46 (for third graders), 60 (for fourth graders) and 68 (for fifth graders). These median scores are used to establish the GE scores for 3.0, 4.0, and 5.0, respectively. As shown in Figure 5.15, GE scores between these points are obtained by process of *interpolation*, dividing the distance between established points in equal intervals, or *extrapolation*, extending the approximate line above and below the points for which data were obtained. Since there are ten months in the school year, the 14 points between 3.0 and 4.0 are divided into 10 equal units to calculate the GE for 3.1, 3.2, etc. Using the hypothetical data from Figure 5.15, the GE for 3.5 would be 53. Extrapolation after grade 5 and before grade 3 is done assuming similar rates of growth as those observed.

Both interpolation and extrapolation result in tenuous approximations at best. For example, interpolation makes the inaccurate assumption that there is a constant rate of growth during the year (Bernard, 1966; Conklin, Burstein, & Keesling, 1979). Although norms are usually based on tests also administered to students in one grade above and below the intended grade, caution should be used whenever scores have been extrapolated further.

Another peculiarity of GE scores is that the standard deviation gets larger as children get older. Consequently, a child who is one standard deviation below the mean of the Comprehensive Test of Basic Skills at the beginning of first grade will have a GE score of 0.7 (only .3 GE units below "normal"). If that child remains at one standard deviation below the mean at the beginning of the sixth grade, she will have a GE score of 3.9 (the discrepancy has increased to 2.1 GE units!). Although it appears that the student is losing ground, she is maintaining exactly the same position with respect to the reference group. Standard deviations on GE scores also differ between subtests of the same test. Therefore, it is impossible to say that a seventh grader who has a GE score of 6.8 on a reading test and only 6.1 on a math test is relatively better at reading than she is at math.

GE scores have other problems as well. Consider the following:

- Students who obtain the same GE score may have dramatically different skills. Because a test for fourth graders contains different types of items

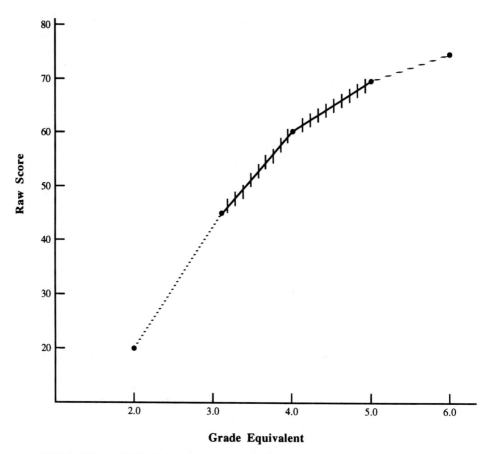

FIGURE 5.15   Hypothetical Data for Creating GE Scores for a Third Grade Test

than a test for ninth graders, an exceptionally good reader in grade 4 might obtain the same GE score as a very poor reader in grade 9.

- GE scores are meaningless when a subject is not taught across all grades. What does a chemistry GE score of 6.9 tell you if chemistry is not taught until ninth grade in that school?

- People often forget that half the students will always be below average. For example, if a reading test is administered at the beginning of the third grade, half the norm group must score at 3.0 or below. The fact that half the students are "below normal" is not as bad as it first sounds.

- When GE scores are extrapolated substantially above or below the grade for which the test was designed, even a single item can change a student's score by more than one year.

Despite the many problems associated with using GE scores, they remain one of the most popular ways of reporting standardized achievement test results. This is probably because many teachers, administrators, and parents mistakenly believe that GE scores are easy to interpret. We recommend that you avoid using GE scores. If they are used in your school and you need to explain them to parents, remember that they are only useful for providing a *very general* indicator of whether a student is performing well above, well below, or about at the level that would be expected for her grade in school.

Percentile Scores

A percentile score indicates the percentage of students who scored below a given point in the norm-reference group. Percentile scores are a substantial improvement over GE scores. Since the score is typically referenced only to students within a particular grade, there are no problems associated with comparing students across grades. Furthermore, percentile scores indicate exactly where the student stands with regard to other students in the group.

Percentile scores can be misinterpreted, however, as indicated by the following statements, all of which appear logical at first glance, but *all of which are false.*

1. *Between the beginning and the end of the year, Susan moves from the 50th to the 60th percentile, and Linda moves from the 89th to the 99th percentile. They have made equal progress.* As shown in Figure 5.16, the difference between the 50th and the 60th percentiles represents less than one-third of a standard deviation, while the difference between the 89th and the 99th percentiles represents almost two standard deviations. Clearly, percentiles do not represent equal interval units. In the middle of the distribution, where relatively large frequencies of scores occur, an increase of one or two points might be associated with a relatively large increase in percentile scores. For example, if 10 percent of the class got 70 out of the 100 spelling words correct, changing your score from 70 to 71 would put you in front of that 10 percent and increase your percentile score by 10 points. At the extremes of the distribution (where frequencies are quite small), a change of several points may not change your percentile score. For example, if the top two scores in the class on a math test are 117, and 110, a change in the second highest score from 110 to 115 will not change the percentile scores because the relative rankings are maintained.

2. *Mary Ellen scores at the 84th percentile, Nancy scores at the 98th percentile, and Diane scores at the 99.9 percentile. Although there is little difference between Diane and Nancy, there is a great deal of difference between Nancy and Mary Ellen.* From Figure 5.16 it is clear that Mary Ellen and Nancy are one standard deviation apart, as are Nancy and Diane. In this sense, the differences between Diane and Nancy and between Nancy and Mary Ellen are equal.

3. *It makes good sense for the state legislature to appropriate extra money for any district that can have at least 75 percent of its students scoring at or above the 50th percentile of the students in the district by the end of a three-year period.* Because percentiles indicate the relative standing of one student with respect to other students, it is impossible for 75 percent of the

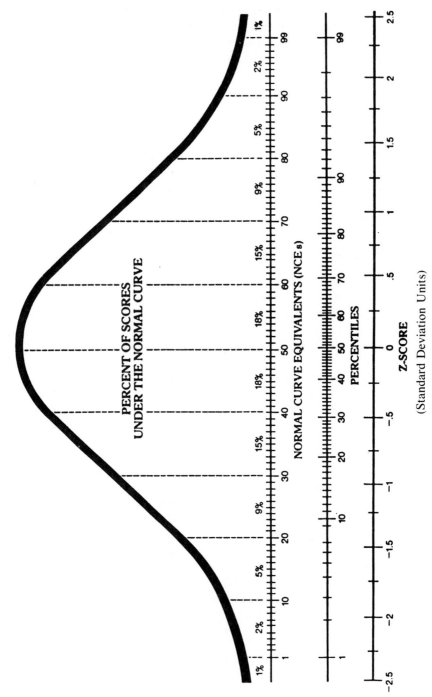

FIGURE 5.16 Relationship between Percentiles, Z-Scores, and Normal Curve Equivalents (NCEs)

district to score at or above the 50th percentile for the district. By definition, half the children must be above, half must be below the 50th percentile for the district. It is possible for 75 percent of the district to be above the 50th percentile for a national norm group.

4. *Students who score below the 25th percentile deserve a failing grade.* A score at the 25th percentile is about two-thirds of a standard deviation below the mean and is better than scores for 25 percent of the students in the class. A frequent mistake with percentiles is to interpret them as *percentage correct* instead of *percentiles*. In most cases, a score at the 25th percentile is quite respectable.

As long as you remember that percentile scores do not represent equal interval units, and that they should not be interpreted as "percent correct," they are a relatively good way of reporting standardized test scores. They are limited by the adequacy of the norm group to which they are referenced, yet they do provide an accurate way of estimating how well students have performed with regard to that norm group.

Z-Scores and Other Standard Scores

A z-score is the distance in standard deviation units between a particular score and the mean. For example, looking back at Figure 5.16, the 84th percentile has a z-score of 1.0, and the 16th percentile has a z-score of -1.0. A z-score of 1.5 is exactly one and a half standard deviations above the mean (at approximately the 93rd percentile) and a z-score of $-.25$ is one quarter of a standard deviation below the mean (at approximately the 39th percentile).

A z-score for any person on a particular test can be computed by subtracting the mean score on the test from the person's observed score and dividing by the standard deviation of the test.

$$z = \frac{score - test\ mean}{test\ SD}$$

For example, consider a test which has a mean of 65 and a standard deviation of 8. A person who scored 69 on that test would have a z-score of $+.50$ because (69 $-$ 65) $\div$ 8 $=$ .50. People who scored 62 and 51 would have z-scores of $-.375$ and -1.75 respectively.

Z-scores are very important because they form the basis for a number of other scores which are frequently reported. The standard score with which you are most familiar is probably the IQ score. For example, Wechsler's Intelligence Scale for Children–Revised (WISC-R) has a mean of 100 and a standard deviation of 15. A WISC-R score of 115 corresponds to a z-score of 1.0 because both scores are one standard deviation above the mean.

A z-score can be transformed to a standard score with any mean and standard deviation by multiplying the z-score by the standard deviation you would like, and adding to the result the number you want for the mean of your new standard score. For example, a popular standard score is a *T-score*, which has a mean of 50, and a standard deviation of 10. Any z-score can be transformed to a T-score as shown below.

$$T\text{-}score = (z\text{-}score \times 10) + 50$$

You are probably already familiar with a number of other standard scores which are derived using similar procedures. Examples include SAT (Scholastic Aptitude Test) and GRE (Graduate Record Examination) scores.

Normal Curve Equivalents

Normal curve equivalent (NCE) scores were created to capitalize on the advantages of percentile scores while avoiding (1) the disadvantages of dealing with unequal units at different points in the distribution and, (2) the confusion between percentiles and percentage correct. NCEs have a mean of 50 and a standard deviation of 21.06. As shown earlier in Figure 5.16, NCEs correspond with percentile scores at three points in the distribution, the 1st percentile, the 50th percentile, and the 99th percentile. At all points in between, NCEs have been spaced so that they are on equal interval units.

NCEs were created to provide an equal interval scale with essentially the same meaning across different tests. To the degree that norming populations and procedures are similar between two tests, this goal is accomplished. A student who scores at an NCE of 65 on the California Achievement Test would have an NCE of 65 on the Comprehensive Test of Basic Skills if the two tests were normed similarly and measure similar content. Tallmadge (1985), who was involved in the early development of the NCE score, claims that this is not an unreasonable assumption for most well-developed and widely used standardized achievement tests. Unfortunately, this logical assumption has not yet been supported with any objective evidence.

Stanines

Another popular type of standard score is the *stanine* (the word comes from a combination of *standard* and *nine*). Stanines are computed by dividing the normal distribution into nine equal units, each one-half standard deviation wide. The middle stanine straddles the median of the normal curve (one-quarter standard deviation distance on each side), with each succeeding stanine being one-half standard deviation in width. The proportion of the normal distribution falling in each stanine is shown in Table 5.6. The top 4 percent of the scores are assigned a stanine score of 9, the next 7 percent are assigned a stanine score of 8, and so on, until the bottom 4 percent of the scores are assigned a stanine score of 1.

The strengths of stanine scores are that they are easily computed, recorded, and manipulated arithmetically. Also, since each stanine represents a band of scores, there is less likelihood that too much importance will be attached to trivial differences between two students. For example, two students who score at the 45th and 55th percentiles, respectively, on a test would both receive a stanine of 5. Although there are 10 percentile points between the two students, a 10-percentile point difference in the middle of the distribution might easily represent only a one-point difference. The fact that both students receive the same stanine score offers some protection against overinterpreting this difference.

Such protection can be a double-edged sword, however. Having been taught that stanines help preclude attaching importance to trivial differences, some people assume that when there are differences between stanines, they must be important.

TABLE 5.6 Percentage of Normal Distribution
Contained in Each Stanine

Stanine	Percentage of Normal Distribution
9	4
8	7
7	12
6	17
5	20
4	17
3	12
2	7
1	4

Not necessarily. If a difference occurs on the borderline between two stanines, it may still be very small. For example, a student scoring at the 89th percentile would have a stanine of 8, while a student scoring at the 88th percentile would have a stanine of 7. This problem cannot be totally eradicated because there will always be "cutting points" between categories.

Because stanines are frequently reported, you should know how they are derived and interpreted. However, since they are no more understandable than percentiles, NCEs or standard scores, and offer relatively few advantages, you would generally be better off avoiding them and using one of the other standard scores.

Growth Scale Scores

A number of standardized achievement tests have developed standardized scores that extend across grade levels. It is important to realize that such scores can be used, in theory, to track a student's progress across grades. This makes growth scale scores different from most of the scores we have discussed, which are referenced to a particular grade and test level.

Profiles

Many standardized tests contain several subtests. For example, an achievement test battery often provides scores for reading, math, science, and so on. Frequently, they subdivide these general areas even further. A reading subtest might include scores for word attack, vocabulary, and comprehension. The purpose of reporting these scores separately is to identify areas in which a student or group of students has particular strengths or weaknesses. This type of analysis supposedly allows instruction to be targeted where it is most needed.

Information about subscale scores in related areas is presented in a *profile*. Many standardized test publishers automatically provide a profile of subtest scores

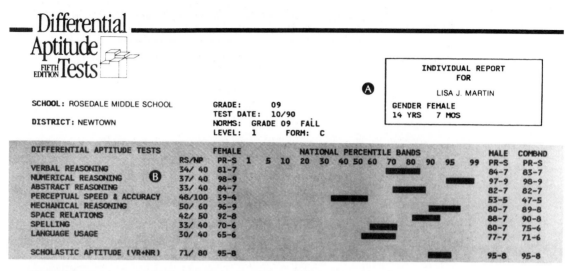

FIGURE 5.17 Example of a Profile from an Aptitude Test

for a particular battery. Figure 5.17 illustrates an example of a profile of scores for a student on the Differential Aptitude Tests. As can be seen, the student is above average on all areas except perceptual speed and accuracy. Her strongest scores are in numerical reasoning, followed closely by mechanical reasoning. Just how different are her scores, however?

As discussed earlier, every score contains some error. The "percentile bands" for each of the scores in the profile in Figure 5.17 provide a confidence interval around each score. For example, on perceptual speed and accuracy, this student scored at the 39th percentile of girls (see the number to the right of the subtest name). However, the dark band indicates the range of scores within which the true score probably lies. For perceptual speed and accuracy, this range is approximately between the 32nd percentile and the 59th percentile.

Notice that even though the observed score for perceptual speed and accuracy is at the 39th percentile for girls and the observed score for language usage is at the 65th percentile for girls, the confidence intervals overlap. Therefore, we should be cautious in concluding that this person's scores on perceptual speed and accuracy are higher than her scores on language usage. Profile scores that do not include some type of confidence interval can be easily misinterpreted (Brown, 1976, p. 199).

If you construct a profile for a test you have developed yourself, some type of confidence interval is equally important. While it may not be as precise as the confidence interval created for a standardized test, you can make a good approximation by computing the standard deviation of the scores in your class and looking in Table 5.5 for the standard error of measurement associated with the SD for your test and an estimated reliability. For locally developed tests that are carefully constructed, the reliability will generally be between .70 and .85. Add the standard error of measurement to, and subtract it from, each student's score to create the 68 percent confidence interval for that score.

Obviously, a profile does not make sense unless the scores for each subtest included on the profile are on the same scale. Therefore, if you are creating a profile for a test, you must make sure that each subtest has the same mean and standard deviation. One way of doing this is to convert the scores for each subtest to z-scores.

Profile analyses can be useful in pointing out those areas in which a particular student has the greatest need. Parents particularly like profile scores because they offer a better feeling for each child's strengths and weaknesses across the full spectrum of subjects. However, you need to be sure that parents do not overestimate the importance of small fluctuations in the profile.

Relationship among Types of Scores

It would be nice if there were one type of score suitable for all situations in interpreting the results of standardized tests. One reason so many different types of scores exist is that they serve different purposes and have different strengths and weaknesses. Now that you understand something about each of the specific types of scores, it is important to see how they relate to one another as shown in Figure 5.18. Until you become familiar with the different kinds, it is a good idea to keep a chart like this handy so you can get your bearings when you encounter a score you remember having seen before, but about which you have forgotten many details.

Reports for standardized achievement tests often contain various test scores, such as those shown in Figure 5.19 from the Comprehensive Test of Basic Skills. If we examine this report, it will provide a useful summary of several key points discussed in this chapter. Notice that the report provides percentiles that are referenced to the local group (all the children in the district who took this test), as well as to the national norm group (a nationally representative sample of students). Recall further that NCEs and percentiles are equivalent at three points on the scale (1, 50, and 99), but that NCEs are spaced at equal intervals across the remainder of the distribution. You can see this by looking at the language expression score and the language mechanics score. The language expression score is at the 51st NCE and the 51st national percentile. However, for the language mechanics score, there is quite a difference in the numbers for the NCE (64) and the national percentile score (74).

The report also provides information about a confidence interval around the national percentile. For example, on the word attack subtest, the obtained score was at the 55th national percentile, but the band of scores indicated by the Xs on the Individual Test Record is from approximately the 40th to the 65th percentile. Such a confidence interval provides some protection against overinterpreting small differences. Note that confidence intervals for some subtests are much wider than others, indicating that the standard error of measurement for those subtests is much larger.

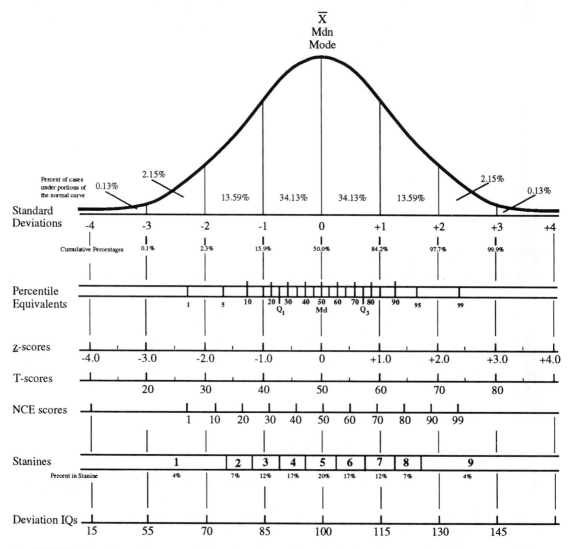

FIGURE 5.18 Illustration of the Relationship among Different Types of Standard Scores

The information indicated by the Xs is an example of how profile scores can be useful. For example, even though three of the four reading scales—vocabulary, comprehension, and total reading—are near the top of the national norm group (94th, 97th, and 99th percentiles, respectively), the word attack subscale is much lower (55th percentile). The importance of this difference is emphasized by the fact that the percentile bands do not overlap. This suggests a need for instructional emphasis on word attack skills, even though this child's vocabulary and comprehension are quite good.

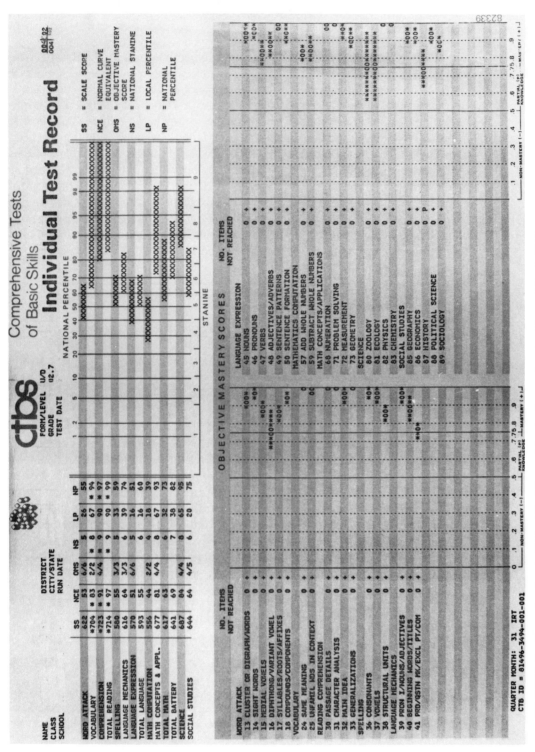

FIGURE 5.19 Example of an Individual Test Record for the Comprehensive Tests of Basic Skills

SOURCE: *CTBS Classroom Management Guide*. 1981, CTB/McGraw-Hill, Monterey, CA. Reprinted with permission of the publisher.

133

A new, but self-explanatory score—the objective mastery score—is introduced in this report. This is an example of an increasing trend among test publishers to combine the advantages of norm-referenced and criterion-referenced tests. Information at the top of Figure 5.19 is what has typically been thought of as norm-referenced test information. Information on the bottom half provides some specific information about the kinds of items passed or failed—what has traditionally been considered to be criterion-referenced test data. Even though the number of items used to assess any one skill area will not be as high in a norm-referenced test as in a criterion-referenced test, such scores may provide valuable information for instructional planning. For example, in looking at the word attack skills, we can see that this student has demonstrated mastery in all areas except diphthong/variant vowels. This information gives the child's teacher some direction about the specific type of word attack skills in which further work may be needed.

APPLICATION PROBLEM #4

For the report shown in Figure 5.19, the child's parents want to know why she is scoring at the 75th national percentile but only the 20th local percentile on social studies. How could she be doing so much worse on one than the other? What would you tell them?

Computer generated reports of standardized achievement tests represent a tremendously valuable but largely untapped resource for teachers. Too often, standardized achievement testing is a district program in which teachers have little interest or involvement. Properly used, however, standardized achievement tests can give teachers important instructional information. As you might guess from examining Figure 5.19, a number of different kinds of output can be requested. By becoming involved in decisions concerning the standardized achievement testing program in your district, you can help tailor the reports to make them more beneficial for you.

SUGGESTED READINGS

Angoff, W. H. (1982). Norms and scales. In H. E. Mitzel (Ed.), *Encyclopedia of Educational Research* (5th ed., pp. 1342–1355). New York: The Free Press.
This is a more technical discussion than that contained in this chapter about the advantages and disadvantages of different types of scores. Angoff discusses the characteristics of good norms and summarizes different techniques used for test score equating, including a brief discussion of item-response theory.

Hills, J. R. (1986). *All of Hills' handy hints*. Washington, DC: National Council on Measurement in Education.

In 1983 and 1984, John R. Hills published a series of six articles in *Educational Measurement: Issues and Practice* that provided entertaining and imaginative summaries of truths and fallacies in the interpretation of widely used test scores. The National Council on Measurement in Education assembled all six articles in this single booklet for wider distribution.

Hopkins, K. D., & Glass, G. V. (1978). *Basic statistics for the behavioral sciences.* Englewood Cliffs, NJ: Prentice-Hall.

This is an excellent introduction to the methods and rationale for computing the various descriptive statistics used in measurement and evaluation. A very readable book with many examples, anecdotes, and sample problems.

Seashore, H. G. (1980). *Methods of expressing test scores* (Test Service Notebook #148). New York: The Psychological Corporation.

This is a summary of how various standard and derived scores are related to each other and to the normal distribution. It contains an informative graphic depiction of the relationship among scores.

Tufte, E. R. (1983). *The visual display of quantitative information.* Cheshire, CT: Graphics Press.

For anyone interested in an in-depth discussion of the techniques used for displaying quantitative information such as was introduced in our discussion of histograms and frequency distributions, this book is a *must*! Both entertaining and informative, it contains hundreds of examples of well-established and innovative ways of depicting information.

SELF-CHECK QUIZ

Use the following illustration to answer questions 1–3.

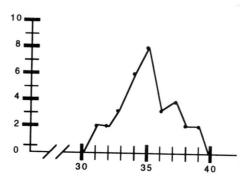

1. In the frequency distribution shown above, how many people obtained a score of 37?
   - a. 0
   - b. 4
   - c. 10
   - d. 35
   - e. 40

2. What is the range of scores shown in the distribution?
   - a. 6
   - b. 8
   - c. 10
   - d. 30
   - e. 40

3. What is the mode of the scores shown in the distribution?

a. 2   d. 35

b. 8   e. 40

c. 31

4. Which of the following would most likely be shaped like a normal distribution?

a. The distribution of measured height for players in the National Basketball Association

b. The distribution of expected scores on a criterion-referenced test of math for 1,000 second graders

c. The average speed of cars driven along a particular stretch of the interstate highway

d. The distribution of a set of IQ scores for 1,000 children

e. A histogram of scores for all those who pass a minimum competency test

5. A norm-referenced standardized math test has a mean of 67 and a standard deviation of 6.0. Approximately what percentage of a group of 1,000 respondents would you expect to score between 67 and 73?

a. 84 percent   d. 13 percent

b. 50 percent   e. 2 percent

c. 34 percent

6. The correlation between hours spent on homework and scores on the semester math test is +.73. Which of the following is the best interpretation of that observation?

a. Doing homework causes higher math scores.

b. Children who do more homework tend to get higher math scores.

c. There is very little association between doing homework and scores on the math test.

d. Doing homework has no effect on math scores.

e. Getting good math scores causes children to do more homework.

7. You are trying to decide whether a difference between scores of 117 and 115 on your American history final exam is an "important" difference. Which of the following is most relevant to your deliberation?

a. Standard deviation   d. Measures of central tendency

b. Normal curve equivalent   e. Standard error of measurement

c. Correlation

8. Which of the following standard scores was developed in part to prevent people from overemphasizing the importance of small differences between scores?

a. Percentiles   d. T-scores

b. Stanines   e. z-scores

c. Grade equivalents

9. For a group of fifth graders tested at the beginning of the school year, which of the following is most equivalent to a percentile score of 84?

a. A z-score of 1.0   d. A Normal Curve Equivalent score

b. A Grade Equivalent score of 5.0   of 50

c. A z-score of -1.0 e. A stanine score of 5

10. Which of the following ways of reporting standardized test scores is subject to the greatest amount of misinterpretation?

a. Normal curve equivalent scores   d. Profile scores with confidence

b. Percentile scores   intervals

c. Grade equivalent scores   e. Stanine scores

SUGGESTION SHEET

If your last name starts with the letter *E*, please complete the Suggestion Sheet at the end of the book while this chapter is still fresh in your mind.

ANSWERS TO APPLICATION PROBLEMS

#1

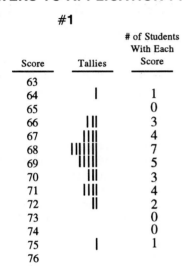

Score	Tallies	# of Students With Each Score
63		
64	I	1
65		0
66	III	3
67	IIII	4
68	IIIIIII	7
69	IIIII	5
70	III	3
71	IIII	4
72	II	2
73		0
74		0
75	I	1
76		

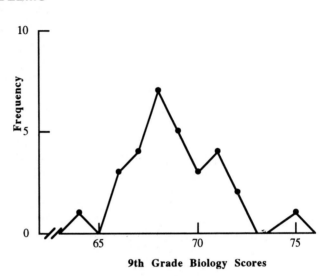

9th Grade Biology Scores

#2

Since the question asks how Horatio did in relation to the other class members, the key to finding the correct answer is to convert all of the scores to standard deviation units with respect to the class distribution of scores. Although it is not absolutely necessary, it is sometimes easier to do this by drawing a picture as shown below.

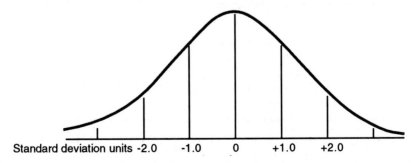

Standard deviation units -2.0   -1.0   0   +1.0   +2.0

With the normal curve as a reference, let us look at Horatio's scores using the relevant parts of the original table. We have added two important columns (standard deviation units, and percentile) and retained one irrelevant column (percentage correct) for illustrative purposes.

	Class Scores				Horatio's Scores	
	MEAN	STANDARD DEVIATION	POINTS	SD UNITS	PERCENTAGE CORRECT	PERCENTILE
Homework assignment #1	35	5.0	30	-1.0	60%	16th
Homework assignment #2	14	3.0	20	+2.0	80%	98th
Homework assignment #3	60	6.0	66	+1.0	83%	84th
Mid term	70	7.0	70	0	70%	50th
Semester exam	150	10.0	130	-2.0	75%	2nd

As can be seen from the above numbers, Horatio does better than 98 percent of the class on homework assignment 2. Thus, in relation to the rest of the class, this is his best performance, even though he obtained a higher percentage correct on homework assignment 3. His worst performance in relation to the rest of the class was on the semester exam. Even though he got 75 percent correct, he did better than only 2 percent of the class.

#3

Even if there were not a causal link between amount of education and amount of income, the presence of a positive correlation between the two variables could be explained in at least two ways. First, more affluent parents provide their children with the encouragement and financial support to continue their education. These parents also are able to pass on wealth to their children. Since a great deal of wealth is inherited, children of affluent parents will be wealthier than the children of nonaffluent parents regardless of education. It just so happens that because affluent parents tend to value and support education, their children usually receive more education.

A second explanation could be that the correlation is a result of a selection process rather than a causal link. For example, to finish high school and then college, students must be able to overcome increasingly complex obstacles and demonstrate the types of abilities that are associated with earning money (e.g., persistence, interpersonal skills, ambition). Although education does not enhance those qualities directly, the same qualities are required for completing increasingly higher levels of education and earning money later. Those who survive the hurdles of education are the same people who would earn more money regardless of whether they received more education.

#4

The national percentile indicates how well the student is doing with respect to a nationally representative sample of students in her grade. The local percentile indicates how well she is doing with respect to other students in her district. The fact that her local percentile is so much lower indicates that most students in her district are above the national average.

CHAPTER 6

Why Worry about Reliability? Reliable Measures Yield Trustworthy Scores

Overview

Every test—and every other measurement instrument used in schools—has imperfections. Those you develop for use in your classroom will be no exception. And even those developed by well-qualified psychometricians are flawed, some seriously. Hopefully that admission of our collective inability to produce the perfect measure will not discourage you any more than the fact that no teacher's informal appraisal of a student's attitude or ability is perfectly accurate should cause you to abandon those essential aspects of student assessment.

Educational measures do not need to be perfect to be useful. The critical question for any measure is simply *how imperfect is it?* In other words, is it good enough to be useful for the purposes for which you intend to use it? Or are its imperfections serious enough to cast doubt on the truthfulness of the story it tells about your students?

This chapter and the next help you answer such questions for instruments you develop and for others you may wish to use to assess your student's achievement, attitude, interests, or other traits discussed in later chapters. These two chapters collectively provide benchmarks against which you can judge the "truthfulness" of other assessment instruments used in district, state, or national testing or assessment programs.

In this chapter, we expand on the concept of reliability that we introduced briefly in Chapter 4. We show why the story told by a test is not credible if that story changes with each telling. We demonstrate that an instrument is not useful if it does not produce stable, consistent results if administered again to the same individual(s) under the same circumstances (assuming no intervening learning had occurred). We help you understand that no test can be telling the truth if it produces unstable or contradictory results with every use. We expand on the concept of measurement error introduced in Chapter 5 and show how you can ascertain from a student's test score how likely it is that the score is a good estimate of the student's real capability on the trait measured.

We also describe, using simple examples, several common ways of estimating reliability. Although you may not often (or perhaps ever) use some of these methods, we assume you will wish to be aware of them and their limitations when they are presented to support claims for a measure proposed for use in your school or classroom. We also suggest how to interpret these reliability estimates to help you decide when a test is sufficiently reliable.

Finally, we devote one section of the chapter to how you can increase the reliability of your classroom tests, and another to the particular problems of determining the reliability of criterion-referenced measures, an important issue with the increasing use of mastery tests.

In all this, we avoid all the statistical formulas and sophisticated psychometric concepts we can without leaving you ill-prepared to help in the important task of improving student assessment. But without exposure to the basic, technical concepts and terminology we do introduce, you will be unable to distinguish adequate from inadequate measures. A test manual's assertion that "This test was found to have a reliability coefficient of .62, using the Kuder-Richardson 20 method" is not helpful to those who are no more familiar with reliability coefficients than they are with Kuder and Richardson.

So bear with us—we think you will be surprised that the topic of reliability is not as complex as it sometimes seems, and surely not beyond the grasp of the typical classroom teacher.

Objectives

After studying this chapter, you should be able to

1. Explain why no measurement instrument can be considered a good measurement instrument unless it yields reliable scores.

2. Describe the relationship of reliability to true scores and to measurement error.

3. Distinguish between random and constant errors of measurement.

4. List and describe the advantages and disadvantages of five alternative approaches used to determine test reliability, and specify conditions under which each approach is appropriate.

5. Compute a reliability coefficient for one of the five alternative approaches and interpret reliability coefficients for all of the approaches.

6. Describe the effect of test length on reliability.

7. List four ways to increase the reliability of a set of test scores.

8. Estimate the reliability of criterion-referenced decisions.

RELIABILITY OF EDUCATIONAL MEASURES

Imagine that a high school student wishes to enter a police academy that requires candidates to be a minimum of six feet tall, and he asks you to measure him. Now imagine his frustration—and yours—if the only available measuring tape were made of rubber so pliable that it was impossible to pull it straight without stretching it. Your first measurement of five feet and six inches is discounted, since you know you are five feet nine inches and shorter than the student. Suspecting you may have stretched the tape, you relax a bit in taking a second measurement, and obtain a measurement of five feet eleven inches. Still concerned, you take a third measurement, dangling the tape limply, and record his height as six feet and one-eighth inch.

Of course, no sensible person would use a rubber measuring tape. But many educational and psychological measures are rather "elastic," being subject to fairly large measurement errors. They can yield one result on one occasion and quite a different result on another. Such instruments are unreliable, or inconsistent; and the more unreliable they are, the more untrustworthy they are.

Assume that you gave your students a vocabulary test yesterday and used the scores to rank the students from highest to lowest. Today you gave it again to the same students and found that the rankings were completely unrelated to the rankings obtained yesterday. Some students who were ranked very high yesterday also received high rankings today, but others who had high rankings yesterday received very low rankings today. Conversely, some students who were ranked quite low yesterday were ranked quite high today, while others who were ranked quite low yesterday were still ranked low today. Given such inconsistent results, we would say that the reliability of the scores obtained from the test was low (and thus the test and the scores it produces would be of little value).

In Chapter 4, we said a test is reliable if it measures whatever it measures consistently. The adage, "Consistency, thou art a jewel" applies as much to measurement as to temperament. In a sense, reliability is a measure of how well a test agrees with itself—how stable, dependable, trustworthy, and accurate it is in measuring the same thing with the same results each time.

Up to now we have taken a bit of literary license. We have sometimes written as if reliability refers to the measurement instrument itself. Not so. Technically reliability refers to the consistency of the *results* obtained with a particular instrument, not to the instrument itself. It is the reliability *of the test scores* obtained by using a test that is the criterion for evaluating the test. Not surprisingly, many practitioners and authors have adopted the shorthand of speaking of the test' reliability, a sin which can probably be forgiven as long as you understand this distinction, which should become more clear as we delve deeper into the concept of reliability.

Reliability, True Scores, and Measurement Error

Test scores (or any measurement results) are reliable to the extent that they reflect *true scores* (accurate assessments of the ability or performance being measured) rather than random *error* that is swept up by the instrument and incorporated in the test scores. For example, assume that you administer a math achievement test (with a score of 100 possible) to your class and that one of your students, Alfonso, receives a score of 75. That is his *obtained score*, the number of points an examinee receives on a test. But is that a good measure of Alfonso's math ability? That depends on a wide variety of things other than math ability that could have affected the score. Suppose Alfonso took the same test a week later and received a score of 66. Which obtained score do you believe to be the most accurate estimate of his math ability? To answer that question, you need to know more about several factors that might have introduced error into one or both of his scores. For example, might the fact that Jim kept poking him with a pencil during the second test affect his score? Could it make a difference if Alfonso had stayed up most of the night before taking the second test? Might the fact that a substitute teacher who scored the second test had trouble deciphering Alfonzo's handwriting be a factor? The answer to each of these questions is "Of course."

Anything that might cause a student to score higher or lower than his actual ability is called *measurement error*. There will nearly always be some error in every student's test score, for chance or random factors usually enter in to make the obtained score an underestimate or overestimate of the student's true score, which leads you to ask: How will I ever know what Alfonso's "true" score is—that score that would reflect his pure math ability, unadulterated by any random or chance sources of measurement error? You won't. We can never know a student's true score, because a true score is a hypothetical value, a score we believe exists, but can never measure. But it is possible to get a reasonable estimate. A student's *estimated true score* is the average of his obtained scores from repeated administrations of the same test under the same testing conditions, disregarding possible effects of the practice he would receive in taking that test.

Every obtained score may be viewed as consisting of two components: (1) the *true* score that reflects the student's ability or knowledge, and (2) an *error* component that reflects random variations in scores. We can portray this relationship as

$$\text{True score} + \text{Error} = \text{Obtained score}$$

Alternatively, we can think of it as

$$\text{Obtained score} - \text{True score} = \text{Error of measurement}$$

This discrepancy between the obtained and true score—measurement error—is very important in determining how much to trust a particular test score. Knowing how much measurement error exists in a particular test is crucial.[1] If we could state, unequivocally, that scores from a particular test contained *no* measurement error (a nearly impossible dream), we would know (from the above equations) that every student's obtained and true scores would be equal. Conversely, we would know that obtained scores on a test with a high measurement error would often differ greatly from the true scores—that is, they would usually be poor estimates. So, the less measurement error a test possesses, the more closely *obtained* scores estimate the unseen *true* scores.

Now you ask: How can I determine *how much* measurement error a test score includes? You only need to know two things: (1) the standard deviation of the scores obtained when you administer the test, and (2) the reliability of the test, which we will explain fully in this section.[2] Before explaining different ways to determine test reliability, we should say more about the variety of random or chance factors that can introduce measurement error, and thus lower reliability.

Random versus Systematic Error

To understand reliability it is helpful to distinguish between two different kinds of measurement errors: random errors and systematic errors. For example, suppose that a classroom of first graders were weighed on a set of incorrectly adjusted scales, resulting in a systematic, two-pound overestimate of each child's actual weight. The recorded weights would be incorrect by the same amount for all of the children. The error would be uniform and systematic. Since the size and direction of the error is the same for each child, it is called *systematic error*.

By definition, random errors are random; that is, the amount of error differs

---

[1] For any particular individual, the amount of measurement error may be large or small and the direction of the error may be positive or negative. Concern over measurement error is somewhat less critical when dealing with groups, however, since group scores would typically have a very low quantity of measurement error because measurement errors will always sum to zero (theoretically) across a set of scores, unless only absolute values are used.

[2] The amount of measurement error in an individual's test score is estimated by a statistic called the *standard error of measurement*. The standard error of measurement = (standard deviation) $\sqrt{1 - \text{test reliability}}$; i.e., $\text{SEM} = \text{SD} \sqrt{1 - r_{tt}}$. As we discussed in Chapter 5, you need not learn how to calculate the standard deviation by hand to use this formula, since any hand calculator with built-in statistical functions will allow you to obtain the standard deviation by inserting the raw test scores and "pressing a button."

unsystematically from one measurement to another. To extend the analogy used above, random errors would occur if some of the children's weights were underestimated, others' were overestimated, and the amount of error differed from child to child in an unsystematic manner. Since the size and direction of the error differs unpredictably from child to child, it is called *random error*.

Random errors cause the resulting measurements (or scores) to be inconsistent and undependable. Systematic errors lead to inaccurate measurements, but at least they are consistent and predictable. Both kinds of errors are of concern in testing situations: Random errors reduce the reliability of a set of test scores; systematic errors reduce the validity of the scores and interpretations based on those scores (as we discuss in Chapter 7).

The key to high reliability on a test is to reduce the influence of extraneous sources that introduce random error into the test scores. Although some of these factors may be beyond our control, we can still heighten our awareness of them and take their effects into account when interpreting test scores. Controlling all the factors that contribute measurement error to test scores may not be possible, but the more sources of random error we can eliminate, the more consistent the test results will be from one use to another. Consequently, the test scores will be more reliable.

ALTERNATIVE WAYS TO ESTIMATE RELIABILITY OF NORM-REFERENCED SCORE INTERPRETATIONS

There are several different ways to estimate the reliability of a test, and most depend on the concept of correlation explained in Chapter 5. Speaking generally, a correlation coefficient is a measure of relationship. Speaking specifically, in this context, a reliability (correlation) coefficient is the correlation of a test with itself. It is a special type of correlation used to determine the consistency of scores produced by a test. The higher the reliability coefficient, the safer one is in assuming that the obtained scores are dependable and free from random errors of measurement.

The various methods for estimating the reliability of a test are often labeled differently in measurement texts. We prefer the following simple labels that suggest the process used to arrive at the reliability estimate:

> *Test-Retest (Same Form) Method*: a correlation between scores from two administrations of the same test to the same students.
>
> *Parallel Form Method*: a correlation between scores of the same students on two or more "equivalent" forms of the same test.
>
> *Internal Consistency Reliability Estimates*: correlation or consistency among the items on a single test. Includes the
>> • Split-half method
>> • Kuder-Richardson method
>> • Cronbach's alpha method

TABLE 6.1 Common Labels for Each Method of Estimating Reliability

Method of Estimating Reliability[a]	Labels Used in This Text	Other Common Labels for This Approach
Correlation between scores on the same test, taken twice	Test-Retest Reliability	(1) Measures of Stability (2) Repetition Method
Correlation between scores on two or more forms of the same test	Parallel Form Reliability	*If administered together:* (1) Alternate Form (2) Equivalent Form (3) Measure of Equivalence *If administered at different times:* (1) Measure of Stability and Equivalence (2) Test-retest with Parallel Equivalent Forms
Correlation or consistency among the items on a single test	Internal Consistency Reliability • Split-half Method • Kuder-Richardson Method • Cronbach's Alpha Method	(1) Measures of Homogeneity (2) Measures of Inter-item Consistency

[a] This column depends on Sax (1980, p. 259).

In Table 6.1 we provide alternate labels sometimes used by others to denote each method we will describe.

In the remainder of this section, we will describe briefly each method of estimating reliability, where and when it might be useful, and limitations and cautions in its use. We will show how to calculate one type of reliability coefficient, and list steps one could take to calculate the other types. Examples and application problems are provided to solidify your understanding of each method. Finally, we will compare and contrast all these alternative methods in a summary intended to help you decide which method is best for which purposes. Before turning our attention to the first method of estimating reliability, we need to say a few words about how far we intend to go in teaching you how to calculate reliability coefficients, if only so you'll sleep easy tonight.

Procedures for Calculating Various Reliability Estimates

The correlation coefficient forms the basis for determining most reliability estimates. As noted in Chapter 5, you need not learn how to calculate correlation coefficients by hand, since many hand calculators have built-in statistical functions that enable you to obtain correlation coefficients for any two sets of test scores for the same individuals with little fuss at the touch of a single key, or nearly so. Since each hand calculator is different, it would be futile to try to explain here precisely how to enter the data into the calculator, but it is a relatively simple matter to follow the instruction manual for any hand calculator which includes

built-in statistical functions. Given the availability of such calculators to mos
educators, we see no point in devoting attention in this chapter to describing how
to calculate correlation coefficients by hand. Those without such a hand calculato
can turn to any good statistics textbook for instruction in computing the Pearson
Product-moment Correlation (or Pearson *r*), which is used to calculate most relia
bility coefficients we will discuss.

Many measurement texts also tell you to refer to a statistics text or a hand
calculator to compute your reliability coefficient, but they omit one critical detail
Precisely what do you do to obtain the test scores you will use in calculating the
coefficient? We answer that question for you in this chapter. For each type o
reliability we discuss, we list simple, straightforward steps you would take to
obtain the test scores that you will use in determining the reliability coefficient for
your test.

TEST-RETEST (SAME FORM) METHOD

This is one of the simplest ways to estimate a test's reliability, for it consists
merely of giving the same test twice to the same individuals and then determining
the correlation between the two sets of scores. Let us suppose, for example, tha
a teacher gives a group of eight students the identical 100-item "Little Marvel"
spelling test *twice* on consecutive days, with the following results:

	First Day	*Second Day*
Al	98	98
Alice	95	98
Bob	91	92
Barbara	83	87
Carl	83	85
Cathy	80	82
Dave	79	80
Donna	73	79
Mean =	85.3	87.6

By examining these scores, you can see two things:

1. Overall, scores increased slightly from the first day (mean = 85.3) to the
   second (mean = 87.6).
2. Individual student scores vary little from one day to the next; students'
   ranks on the first and second days are nearly identical.

We would probably all agree that this test measured spelling ability of these
students very consistently. The two sets of scores are highly correlated. In fact,
where a reliability coefficient of 1.00 would reflect a perfect correlation between

two sets of scores, in our example the test-retest correlation is .98, or nearly perfect.

Problems and Potential of Test-Retest Reliability

Before you conclude that the "Little Marvel" is the most reliable spelling test ever and rush out to purchase a five-year supply for your school, we need to point out a few problems with the test-retest method of estimating reliability, as well as some of its potential advantages.

The Major Disadvantage of Test-Retest Reliability

The most serious limitation of the test-retest approach is that it requires that the same test be administered to the same students on two different occasions. This may not be feasible in many classroom situations. Even when repeated administration is feasible, there are problems with determining the best interval between them.

Problems with Short Intervals between Tests

Test-retest reliability can be artificially increased if a test is repeated immediately or after only a short interval. This is because many students will recall their answers on the first test administration and respond identically to many items on the second (repeating any responses to an item will raise test-retest reliability, whether or not the answer is correct). This is often termed the *memory effect*. So the "nearly perfect" reliability of the "Little Marvel Spelling Test" may owe its magnitude more to consecutive-day testing than to any inherent qualities of the test. Test-retest reliability coefficients must be viewed with great skepticism when the interval between tests is short.

Problems with Long Intervals between Tests

On the other hand, a too-long interval between tests may also cause problems. Although memory of the test may have faded sufficiently that students are not automatically repeating answers, new learning may occur before the second testing. For example, suppose test-retest reliability of an oral Spanish test is being estimated. The longer the interval between tests, the greater the likelihood that students' oral ability in Spanish will have increased—even without formal instruction. Incidental learning from new Spanish neighbors or self-initiated study of a sibling's language tapes are only some of the ways students could acquire skill outside the classroom. The more scores change from test to retest because of *real* changes in the attribute tested, the lower the reliability coefficient. Thus, long intervals between testing invite unknown student growth or change; and an apparently low reliability may simply reflect the impact of incidental learning and have little to do with the consistency of the test itself.

What Is the Correct Time Interval?

Unfortunately there is no pat answer to this important question. Generally, the shorter the time between testings, the higher the test-retest reliability. On most tests of rapidly changing traits such as achievement, probably the best answer that can be given is a few days to a few weeks, depending on the nature of the test. Students who are being retested seem less likely to recall answers to routine and familiar items than to novel items. For this reason, tests of multiplication facts might tolerate a shorter test-retest interval than a problem solving or creativity test, where even an interval of several weeks might not erase recall of specific responses. For tests of intelligence or other traits that are more stable, test-retest intervals up to one year or more may not be unreasonable. For very unstable traits, such as moods that can be expected to fluctuate, the test-retest method of estimating reliability should be avoided altogether, for this method assumes that the trait remains constant during the interval over which retesting occurs.

Potential Advantages of Test-Retest Reliability

Assuming that an appropriate testing interval can be found, test-retest reliability does have some advantages. First, because the same test is given twice, no random error can be attributed to different items being selected for use in different forms of the test. Second, it avoids the difficult and time-consuming task of constructing alternative forms deserving of the label *parallel*. Third, although it has other drawbacks, same-day test-retesting controls random errors introduced by students' day-to-day variations. Fourth, test-retest reliability is simple to calculate. Fifth, it is appropriate for use with timed (speeded) tests. Because the test-retest reliability estimate assesses the extent to which the scores on the same test are stable across test administrations, this reliability estimate is often called the *index of stability*.

Major Uses of Test-Retest Reliability

With an appropriate interval, test-retest reliability may be used when: (1) Teachers are giving tests with time limits (speed tests); (2) no parallel form of the test is available or possible to construct; and (3) content is routine or familiar enough that "memorable" content will not exacerbate the problems of recall from the first test. Despite various advantages, however, test-retest reliabilities are perhaps less useful than other reliability estimates we will consider next.

Calculating a Test-Retest Reliability Coefficient

The step-by-step procedure for estimating test-retest reliability of a test is as follows:

Step 1. Determine the appropriate interval between test and retest.

Step 2. Administer the test (Time 1).

Step 3. Score the Time 1 test.

Step 4. After the selected interval, administer the same test again to the same students—that is, retest (Time 2).

Step 5. Score the Time 2 test.

Step 6. Correlate the two sets of scores. Use a hand calculator or a formula for the Pearson r from any statistics book, with the n in the formula being the number of students for whom test and retest scores are obtained.

The procedure for estimating test-retest reliabilities would be the same regardless of the time interval between the test and retest, except that Steps 3 and 4 would be reversed if the tests were administered immediately after one another, allowing no time for scoring between test and retest.

PARALLEL-FORM METHOD

It is often desirable to have one or more alternate, equivalent forms of the same test. Suppose a student misses his regularly scheduled examination, and the teacher is concerned that conversations with classmates about specific test items may give that student an unfair advantage if he is administered the same test. This concern is eliminated if an equivalent form of the test can be administered under conditions as nearly equivalent as possible.

The question, however, is whether or not the two forms are truly equivalent. To determine this, it is important to do three things: (1) Analyze the content of each form; (2) determine whether the average score obtained by the same group of students on each form is the same; and (3) examine the correlation between the two tests. To determine the correlation, administer the two tests to the same students within a short time period. The short interval eliminates day-to-day variations in individuals, but memory of the first test should not affect student performance on the second test since the two forms would contain different (although similar) items. Interestingly, the procedure for ascertaining the equivalence of the two forms also can be used to estimate the reliability of either test. Once there are two alternate or parallel forms of a test, the correlation between scores on the two provides a basis for estimating the reliability of either test.

The critical issue in developing equivalent test forms is to have the two tests similar in content, form, and difficulty without having them so similar that they include the same items or those that are nearly the same (e.g., 2×3 and 3×2). Inclusion of such items will result in a spuriously high correlation between the two tests, with a consequent overestimate of test reliability. Conversely, if the test items are too dissimilar, the reliability will be spuriously low. This problem underscores the difficulty of creating alternate forms that are truly equivalent. It is difficult to develop one good test, let alone two. Thus, the parallel form of computing reliability is most often used for standardized psychological and educational achievement tests, where concern for test security makes this approach necessary.

Because of the difficulty of constructing parallel test forms, most classroom teachers will be unlikely to use this method. But test publishers should provide data on how nearly equivalent their parallel forms are, and teachers should consider such data carefully in determining when one form might appropriately be substituted for another.

With or Without an Interval?

Parallel-form reliability may be calculated with or without an interval of elapsed time between administration of the two forms of the test. When there is little or no interval between test administrations, this reliability index is often termed the *coefficient of equivalence*, thus differentiating it from the *coefficient of stability* that results from the simple test-retest method. When the two parallel test forms are administered with a significant interval between them, however, it becomes a type of test-retest with parallel forms and is sometimes referred to as the *coefficient of stability and equivalence*. Test specialists differ in what they see as the optimal interval to be used between parallel forms, with some opting for no interval (thus reducing errors due to day-to-day variations within individuals), and others favoring sufficient time to reduce or eliminate the effects of fatigue, memory, or practice on test scores. The parallel-form method of estimating reliability is generally considered superior to the simple test-retest method, largely because it reduces the possibility that individuals' memory can spuriously inflate the reliability estimate. Simple memory is not the only issue, however. If the time between administrations is short, scores on the second test may be inflated for some students because of familiarity with the content area or practice with the types of items. When the two tests are relatively far apart, however, this memory or practice effect seems significantly less. Transfer or practice effects can also be reduced or eliminated if half the students receive Form A followed by Form B, with the sequence reversed for the other half.

Problems and Potential Advantages of Parallel-form Reliability

Like test-retest reliability, parallel-form reliability has its own particular advantages, disadvantages, and uses.

Problems with Parallel-form Reliability Estimates

No two forms of a test are ever *perfectly* parallel. Test items will vary in the extent to which they measure the same objectives adequately. The more test items differ across forms, the greater the unreliability. Further, the necessity of developing two equivalent tests is a serious disadvantage. Like the test-retest method, parallel-form reliability estimates require two test administrations, possibly creating student boredom, fatigue, or low motivation. In addition, administration or scoring methods are likely to differ, at least slightly, from test to test. Because of these factors, parallel-form reliabilities are also likely to be lower than test-retest reliabilities. The most serious limitation of the parallel-form method is that it requires two alternative, but equivalent versions of the same test. Constructing a parallel form is time consuming and difficult; therefore this procedure may not be practical for most classroom teachers.

Advantages of Parallel-form Reliability

This method has one distinct advantage over the test-retest method: It can largely eliminate the effects of memory and practice. Like the test-retest method, it can be used with timed tests. When parallel forms are administered at different times, the resulting *index of stability and equivalence* is perhaps the most stringent estimate of reliability.

Major Uses of Parallel-form Reliability

This method is primarily used to help establish the equivalence of parallel forms. Although teachers will seldom use this method directly, they must be familiar with it so as to understand and interpret parallel-form reliability estimates reported for standardized achievement and psychological tests. Care must be taken in interpreting parallel-form reliability coefficients, since they are likely to yield lower estimates of reliability than does the test-retest method. Also, reliability for parallel forms administered at different times will tend to be lower than test-retest reliabilities, or reliabilities for parallel forms administered at the same time. Because this reliability method controls more potential sources of error, it is likely to be the more believable, albeit conservative, estimate of reliability.

Calculating a Parallel-form Reliability Coefficient

The step-by-step procedure for estimating parallel-form reliability of a test is as follows. It would be the same whether the second form were administered concurrently (immediately after the first) or after a time interval.

Step 1. Administer Form 1 of the test.
Step 2. Administer Form 2 of the test to the same students.
Step 3. Score both Forms 1 and 2.
Step 4. Correlate the two sets of scores by obtaining the Pearson *r*, as you did earlier for the test-retest reliability coefficient.

INTERNAL CONSISTENCY RELIABILITY ESTIMATES

A major drawback of both test-retest and parallel-form reliability is that both require two test administrations. For teacher-made tests, methods of estimating reliability that require only a single test administration are more feasible. Such methods are typically referred to as *measures of internal consistency or homogeneity,* since they are based on estimates of how well a test is correlated with itself (for example, how well two halves of a test are correlated). We shall discuss three useful measures of internal consistency: the split-half method, the Kuder-Richardson method, and Cronbach's alpha method for estimating reliability from a single test administration.

SPLIT-HALF METHOD FOR ESTIMATING RELIABILITY

In a split-half procedure the total set of items is divided into halves, and scores on the halves are correlated to obtain an estimate of the test's reliability. For this method to work, however, the test must be divided into two comparable halves that are approximations of two parallel forms (although each is only one-half the length of the total test).

When test items are sequenced in the order of their difficulty (e.g., easy items first as warm-up, difficult items later), one cannot simply divide the test into first and last halves, for obvious reasons. In this case, the odd-even split (items 1, 3, 5, 7, versus items 2, 4, 6, 8, etc.), is generally used to create two half-length tests. When using an odd-even split, it is important to keep groups of items that deal with a single problem intact, since scores on such clusters of items are obviously not independent and cannot be split between test halves. If item difficulty is random—that is, items do *not* become increasingly difficult through the test—then the division of a test into first and last halves is appropriate. Whichever method is used, the key is to create two halves that are comparable in both content and difficulty.

Before we can discuss the split-half method further, we must take time to discuss briefly the relationship between reliability and test length.

Reliability and Test Length

Generally, the longer a test is, the more reliable it is. The more items there are in a test, the less likelihood there is that answering any one item differently in two test administrations will significantly reduce the reliability coefficient. (Of course, this assumes all items measure the same thing.) Suppose a teacher administers a 10-item vocabulary test to his students, splits the test into two 5-item halves, scores those halves, and obtains a correlation between the scores. The resulting correlation is the reliability of each *half* of the test, rather than reliability of the test *as a whole*. To obtain the reliability of the total 10-item test, a statistical correction must be made by using a formula known as the Spearman-Brown Prophecy formula, by which the reliability of the total test, R, can be inferred from the correlation of the two halves, r, as follows:

$$R = \frac{2r}{(1 + r)} \qquad \text{(Formula 6.1)}$$

Since reliability is affected by test length and, generally speaking, the longer a test, the higher its reliability, it is necessary to correct the reliability coefficients obtained from one-half of a test. The Spearman-Brown Prophecy formula is intended to correct the underestimate when reliability is calculated on half-tests, giving an approximate estimate of what the reliability of the test would be had it not been artificially shortened into halves. The Spearman-Brown Prophecy formula, given in Formula 6.1, can be stated verbally as

$$\text{Reliability of the Whole Test} = \frac{2 \times \text{Uncorrected Split-half Reliability}}{1 + \text{Uncorrected Split-half Reliability}}.$$

Problems and Potential Advantages of Split-half Reliability Estimates

Now we must consider the major advantages, disadvantages, and uses of split-half reliability coefficients.

Advantages of the Split-half Method

The major advantage of the split-half method is that it requires only one test administration and thus avoids any effects of practice, memory, or differential test administration or scoring.

Major Disadvantages of Split-half Reliability Estimates

A major premise of split-half reliability is that both halves of the test are parallel and equivalent. But perhaps the items actually differ enough so that the two halves can not really be considered equivalent. Most important, split-half reliability estimates should not be used with a pure *speeded test*, which is defined as a test that consists of such easy items that few students miss any item they attempt, but has so many items that very few students can finish the entire test. This is in contrast to *power tests*, where the difficulty of items may vary from easy to very difficult, and time limits either do not exist or are sufficiently generous that most students can attempt most items.

On speeded tests, the split-half reliability (i.e., the correlation between odd and even items) will always be spuriously high. Consider a speeded test of very easy items in which virtually all students finish only half the test. For items in the second half the correlation would be perfect because everybody misses all the items. Thus the split-half reliability (the correlation between odd and even items on the entire test) gives a higher estimate of test reliability than the actual reliability because of the perfect correlation between items on the second half of the test. Since most classroom tests combine elements of a speeded test and a power test, the split-half reliability estimate will be artificially inflated in proportion to the degree that time limits prevent students from completing the test. When speed is an element of a classroom test, it is wise for the teacher to use a second, supplemental reliability estimate (e.g., the test-retest or parallel form).

Major Uses of Split-half Reliability Estimates

The primary use for the split-half method is for tests developed locally by classroom teachers or university professors. Here, dependence on a single test and elimination of memory or practice effects are important considerations. The split-half method should not be used when time limits are imposed on the test, however.

Calculating a Split-half Reliability Coefficient

The step-by-step method for estimating the reliability, or internal consistency, of a test by the split-half method is as follows:

Step 1. Determine how the test is to be divided (e.g., odd-even items, which we will assume is the case for this example).

Step 2. Add all the scores of *odd-numbered* items for each student (e.g., items 1, 3, 5, 7, etc.) to obtain that student's total score for that half of the test. Separately, add the scores of the *even-numbered* items for each student (e.g., items 2, 4, 6, 8, etc.).

Step 3. Treat the separate totals for odd and even items as separate tests for each student, creating two scores for each student, and thus two sets of test scores for your class.

Step 4. Compute a Pearson r to determine the correlation between these two "tests" (half-tests, actually), using the same procedure as outlined earlier for test-retest and parallel-form reliability.

Step 5. Apply the Spearman-Brown Prophecy formula to correct the split-half reliability estimate, thus obtaining the reliability estimate of the whole test.

KUDER-RICHARDSON RELIABILITY ESTIMATES

One difficulty with the split-halves method of estimating reliability is that different reliability estimates would result from subdividing the total set of test items differently. The correlation of the odd and even items, for example, may be very different from the correlation between the first and second halves of the test. Several formulas developed by Kuder and Richardson (1937) provide internal consistency estimates but avoid the problem of deciding how a test should be split into halves. Like the split-half method, Kuder-Richardson reliabilities are determined from a single test administration. With this method, however, the test is not actually split or scored in halves. Rather, the Kuder-Richardson method provides an estimate of what the average reliability would be if *all possible ways* of splitting the test into halves were used. Thankfully, this estimate is obtained by relatively simple statistics and not by the tedious (if not infeasible) task of actually calculating all possible split halves. There is no need to use the Spearman-Brown Prophecy formula in the Kuder-Richardson method to correct for shortened test length, because the test is not actually split into halves for scoring.

Of the several formulas Kuder and Richardson developed for this purpose, the most highly regarded is the Kuder-Richardson formula 20 (KR_{20}), which has very satisfactory psychometric properties. It can be difficult to compute, however, and therefore would be useful to the typical classroom teacher only if provided in the output from computer analysis of test scores. Conversely, the most simple Kuder-Richardson formula to calculate is their formula 21 (KR_{21}). The formula for this reliability estimate (which requires only knowledge of the number of items in a test, the mean, and standard deviation of the raw test scores) is

$$KR_{21} = \frac{(k \times \text{standard deviation}^2) - [\text{mean} \times (k - \text{mean})]}{(k - 1) \times \text{standard deviation}^2} \quad \text{(Formula 6.2)}$$

where k represents the number of items in the test. Because of its simplicity, this is the one reliability estimate we will show you how to calculate in this chapter. But first . . .

Problems and Potential Advantages of Kuder-Richardson Reliability Estimates

Before showing you how to calculate the KR_{21}, we will discuss some of its uses and limitations of which you should be aware.

Major Disadvantages of Kuder-Richardson Reliability Estimates

Like the split-half method, the Kuder-Richardson method of estimating reliability is appropriate only for power tests and should not be used with speeded tests. When the Kuder-Richardson (or any internal consistency) reliability method is used on speeded tests, the resulting "estimate of reliability" would be artificially inflated. Thus, since most classroom or standardized achievement tests possess elements of speeded tests (time limits, and some relatively homogeneous easy items), estimates of internal consistency reliability using this method will be somewhat inflated, sometimes requiring an additional estimate of reliability that is not affected by time limits. Second, KR_{20} and KR_{21} can be used only if all items on the test measure a single concept. For example, this method of estimating reliability would be appropriate for use on a test of multiplication facts, but not a broader mathematics test covering multiplication, division of fractions, and problem solving. If test items do not all measure the same trait or ability, the reliability coefficient is lowered. Third, the KR_{21} is very conservative and (with the exception of speeded tests) often tends to underestimate actual reliability. Fourth, the KR_{20} and KR_{21} can only be used when test items are scored dichotomously (i.e., either right or wrong). Fifth, KR_{21} assumes all items have the same difficulty level. To the extent that this assumption is violated, KR_{21} will seriously underestimate KR_{20}.

Potential Advantages of KR_{21} Reliability

Unlike the split-half method of determining reliability from one single test administration, the Kuder-Richardson method is not affected by the particular way in which the test is "split" into halves. In a split-half method, the reliability is in part a function of how the test is split; a fluke in splitting the test may result in a misleading reliability estimate. With the Kuder-Richardson method, however, the estimate is the average of the correlations between *all possible* split halves, so there's no need to worry over how best to split the test. Second, the KR_{21} is very simple to compute. Third, it requires only a single test administration and is free from memory and practice effects. Finally, since the test is not actually split, there is no need to use the Spearman-Brown formula for correcting the reliability estimate.

Major Uses of Kuder-Richardson Reliability

This is perhaps the most useful reliability estimate available when classroom tests are not speeded. It is very useful when only one test administration is feasible. Remember, however, that it should be used only when the entire test is focused on measuring a single construct or concept or a set of closely related objectives, and all items are scored dichotomously.

Calculating a Kuder-Richardson 21 Reliability Estimate

Here is a step-by-step method for estimating the reliability, or internal consistency, of a test by the Kuder-Richardson 21 formula:

Step 1. Count the number of items in the test (we'll designate that as "k").

Step 2. Calculate the *mean* of the test scores (see Chapter 5 for a discussion of how to compute the mean).

Step 3. Calculate the *standard deviation* of the test scores (see Chapter 5 here also).

Step 4. Calculate the Kuder-Richardson 21 reliability estimate, using Formula 6.2.

Suppose, for example, that we have a 100-item social studies test with a mean score of 80 and a standard deviation of 5. The KR_{21} reliability estimate for this test would be calculated as follows, using Formula 6.2:

$$\frac{(100 \times 25) - (80 \times (100-80))}{(100 - 1) \times 25} = \frac{2500 - (80 \times 20)}{99 \times 25} = \frac{2500 - 1600}{2475} = \frac{900}{2475} = .36$$

The KR_{21} estimate of internal consistency for this test is .36, suggesting that the test items are only moderately related to one another. Even though KR_{21} may underestimate reliability, achievement tests with KR_{21} reliability estimates this low are likely to be of little practical value.

CRONBACH'S ALPHA METHOD FOR ESTIMATING RELIABILITY

The Kuder-Richardson reliability estimates we have discussed can be used only with tests containing dichotomously scored items. Where such scoring is possible, then the previous methods for estimating reliability are appropriate. On many instruments, however, dichotomous scoring is not possible.

For example, assume that a teacher wishes to administer a 40-item attitude scale, with some items calling for dichotomous yes-no responses and others asking respondents to indicate their attitudes along a seven-item scale. Since these latter scales cannot be scored dichotomously, but answers must be weighted depending on where respondents place themselves on the scale, the previous methods of estimating reliability are not applicable. Fortunately, Cronbach (1951) developed an approach he termed *coefficient alpha*, which will work in this case.

Cronbach's coefficient alpha is another way of estimating the homogeneity or internal consistency of the scores obtained from a single administration of a single test. Cronbach's formula is algebraically equivalent to KR_{20} and produces the same results within rounding error. Coefficient alpha is a generalization of the Kuder-Richardson formulas that is not limited to tests that include only dichotomous items. It can be used with essay questions and other types of items where partial-credit scoring is possible. Like the Kuder-Richardson formulas, coefficient alpha does not depend on any single correlation but rather on the average intercorrelation among all items. This makes it computationally complex, but this difficulty is offset by two factors:

1. Computer programs to calculate coefficient alpha are readily available, thus allowing its use without computational difficulty, and

2. The logical and conceptual properties of alpha are important, since it can be thought of as the expected correlation between a particular test and a hypothetical alternative form of the same length, even though that alternative has never been constructed.

Problems and Potential Advantages of Cronbach's Alpha Method

Again, it is important to weigh several considerations in determining when—or whether—to use this reliability estimate.

Major Disadvantages of Estimating Reliability with Cronbach's Alpha

If computer programs are not available, the computational difficulty of Cronbach's alpha makes it nearly prohibitive for most classroom uses. Also, it should not be used with speeded tests or with tests that measure more than one concept or objective, unless they are closely related.

Potential Advantages of Cronbach's Alpha

Cronbach's alpha is applicable to more types of tests than any other method of estimating reliability. It requires only a single test administration; thus memory and practice tests do not influence this approach. It is a very general reliability coefficient, which can provide reliability information about any type of homogeneous scale or test (i.e., one where all items measure the same concept), regardless of whether item scoring is dichotomous or weighted.

Major Uses of Cronbach's Alpha

Cronbach's alpha is a good choice for any nonspeeded test consisting of items all designed to measure the same characteristics, and it can be used for instruments with either dichotomous or weighted scoring. It is the only commonly available computer-calculated reliability estimate for tests whose items are not scored dichotomously. Therefore, it is frequently used on attitude and rating scales and other instruments where interest is measured in gradations of response. Once these responses have been weighted, reliability can then be estimated by this method.

COMPARISON OF METHODS FOR ESTIMATING RELIABILITY: A SUMMARY

To help you recall what we have said about the various methods for estimating reliability, we have summarized the most salient points in Table 6.2.

TABLE 6.2 Comparisons among Six Methods of Estimating Reliability

Comparison	Test-retest Reliability	Parallel Form Reliability	Internal Consistency Reliability		
			Split-half	Kuder-Richardson Methods	Cronbach's Alpha
Method used to establish reliability	Correlation between scores on same test, taken twice	Correlation between scores on two or more forms of the same test, taken at different times	Correlation between scores on two halves of the same test	Estimates the average reliability found by correlating all possible split-halves (without actually doing so)	
Purpose	To determine how stable test scores remain over time	To determine either (1) how equivalent two forms of the test are (if administered together), or (2) how stable and equivalent they are over time (if an interval between Form 1 and 2)	To determine the homogeneity of dichotomously scored items within a test	To determine the homogeneity of dichotomously scored items within a test	To determine the monogeneity of multichotomously scored items within a test
Administration of the measure	Twice	Twice either (1) in close succession or (2) with an interval between testing	Once	Once	
Sources of error controlled	Individual day-to-day variation (if interval between testing). Speed of work. Memory effect (if interval between testing)	Task sample. Speed of work. Memory effect (unless interval is short)	Practice or memory effect (variation in administration or scoring)	Practice or memory effect (variation in administration or scoring)	

Sources of error uncontrolled	Memory effect (if interval is short). Task sample. Variations in administration or scoring	Individual day-to-day variation. Variations in administration and/or scoring. Differences in item content	Individual day-to-day variation. Speed of work. Differences in item contents if split-halves are not equivalent	Individual day-to-day variation. Speed of work	Individual day-to-day variation. Speed of work
Major advantages	Easy to calculate. Works with speeded tests	Easy to calculate. Theoretically better than test-retest or internal consistency measures. With interval between tests, yields stringent reliability estimates	Requires only one test administration. Works well with power tests	Requires only one test administration. KR_{21} is very simple to calculate. KR_{20} is a good estimate of equivalence when time interval is short	Requires only one test administration. Provides reliability estimates with nondichotomous item scoring
Major disadvantages	Requires two administrations of test. Examinee may recall item responses from test-retest, inflating reliability coefficient	Requires two administrations of test. Requires construction of two test forms with interval, likely to have lowest reliability coefficient and all sources of error of test-retest and parallel forms can operate	Useless with speeded tests. Requires use of Spearman-Brown Prophecy formula for correction. Items that do not measure same trait or ability as others lower realiability coefficient	Useless with speeded tests. Items that do not measure same trait or ability as others lower reliability coefficient. KR_{21} is usually a conservative estimate (perhaps an underestimate)	Useless with speeded tests. Items that do not measure same trait or ability as others lower reliability coefficient. Computationally difficult without a computer program
Primary use:	When only one test form is available and a reasonable interval exists	To establish equivalence of two forms and, with interval, to establish both stability *and* equivalence	When only one test administration is possible and items can be split into two equivalent halves		When only one test administration is possible and deciding how to split the test into halves is difficult

---

APPLICATION PROBLEM #1

You have two history tests. Test A is a 50-item multiple-choice test. Test B is a 30-item test that contains 15 dichotomously scored true-false items and 15 questions with multiple responses, each of which is weighted, with from 1 to 3 points for each item. Test A has a possible total score of 50; Test B has a possible total score of 60.

1. Would KR_{21} be an appropriate method for estimating the reliability of Test A? Of Test B? Why?
2. Would Cronbach's alpha be an appropriate method for estimating the reliability of Test A? Of Test B? Why?
3. If both KR_{21} and coefficient alpha are appropriate for one or both of those tests, which would you use, and why?

USE AND INTERPRETATION OF RELIABILITY ESTIMATES

No reliability coefficient is completely accurate. Some methods will overestimate the actual reliability of a particular measure, while others will underestimate its reliability.

Given that reliability estimates always include some error, can we still make intelligent use of those estimates? Yes, but keep in mind that each of the reliability coefficients discussed previously generally range from 0 to +1.0.[3] These are correlation coefficients (or estimates of them) and are so interpreted. The closer the reliability coefficient is to 1.0, the more reliable the scores. For example, a parallel-form reliability coefficient of 0 would suggest that the scores on the two forms are completely unrelated—the reliability was nil—while a coefficient of 1.0 would indicate they were perfectly correlated, and thus their scores were perfectly reliable. Here are some *general* guidelines for interpreting reliability coefficients.

1. *Test scores used for decisions about an individual student require a much higher degree of reliability than those used for making decisions about groups of students.* When teacher-made tests are used in critical decisions about individual students (e.g., passing a course), they should possess reliability coefficients of .80 or higher. By contrast, coefficients as low as .50 are acceptable if the tests are used to make decisions about groups (e.g., determining when to move a class on to the next curriculum unit).

   The need for higher reliability with tests used to make individual decisions is obvious if you remember that the higher the reliability, the less error

---

[3] The only exceptions are measures of internal consistency, which mathematically can be negative if many items have negative intercorrelations; if that occurs, you clearly do not have a homogeneous test.

associated with test scores. When averaged across all students, measurement error tends to balance out; there will be as many positive errors of measurement as negative errors. Thus, across a group of scores, measurement error will generally not bias the results. Given a test with low reliability, however, an individual student's observed score may be substantially higher or lower than his true score.

Although practical considerations may occasionally force teachers or others to use tests with reliability coefficients below desired limits, they can at least interpret resulting scores with great caution and in combination with other information if they are aware that the test results they are using are less dependable than desired.

2. *Higher reliability coefficients are essential if decisions on which test scores are based have important, lasting consequences that cannot be reversed or disconfirmed by other sources of information.* Some decisions about individual students have long-term, perhaps permanent consequences. In this case, very stringent standards for reliability (coefficients of at least .90) should be set as minimums.

3. *Lower reliability coefficients are tolerable for tests used in decisions that are of less consequence, are reversible, have only temporary impact, and can be confirmed by other sources of information.* When decisions are of less importance, we can afford to be less confident in making them. In such cases, reliability coefficients need not be as high, even for decisions about individuals.

4. *Reliability coefficients for standardized tests should be .90 or higher.* This is so for two reasons. First, since the norm groups on which standardized tests' reliabilities are calculated are usually very heterogeneous, their actual reliability in (typically) more homogeneous classes will be somewhat lower. Second, critical decisions about individual students—placement, for instance—may be made on the basis of standardized tests, and unreliable tests are an intolerable basis for such decisions.

5. *Lower reliability coefficients may be acceptable if the test is handicapped by factors or circumstances that would tend to lower its reliability, whereas higher coefficients may be judged inadequate if the test is advantaged by factors or circumstances that automatically enhance reliability.* Any limits on "acceptable" levels of reliability are necessarily arbitrary, for coefficients can be influenced by so many factors.

Relative Reliability Coefficients Produced by Varying Methods

The various methods for estimating reliability tend to produce reliability coefficients that are roughly similar, but of differing magnitude. Thus, it is difficult to interpret "how high" a particular reliability coefficient really is unless you know what method was used to produce it. Although there are many factors that cause variations beyond those shown below, generally the sizes of the reliability coefficient produced by each method of estimating reliability follow the patterns described below.

1. *Test-retest method*. This method typically produces *high* coefficients, perhaps highest of any method relative to the actual reliability of the test, if the interval between test administrations is short. As the interval between tests increases, the coefficients typically decrease to *moderate* levels.
2. *Split-half method*. Next to test-retest without interval, this method typically produces the highest reliability coefficients, and generally are *high*. Coefficients for speeded tests should be disregarded as spuriously high, however.
3. *Parallel form method*. If there is no interval between test administrations, coefficients produced by this method are typically somewhat lower than those produced by the test-retest method, but they still tend to range upward from *moderate* to *high*. If there is an interval between administering the two forms, however, reliability coefficients produced by this method are usually *moderate,* and lower than for any of the previously listed methods. Thus, a lower reliability coefficient produced by this method may actually indicate higher *true* reliability than a higher coefficient produced by a less stringent method. As the interval between tests increases the coefficients typically are reduced (but that may still be acceptable given the stringency of this method).
4. *Kuder-Richardson and Cronbach's alpha method*. Reliability coefficients produced by these methods are typically *lower* than for the other methods just listed[4] and tend to *underestimate* the actual reliability of the measure. They set a lower bound for what the reliability might be. Coefficients for speeded tests produced by these methods should be disregarded as spuriously high.

The varying sizes of reliability coefficients resulting from the different methods listed above are a direct result of the sources of error controlled and uncontrolled by each method, as summarized in Table 6.2. One cannot decide whether a particular reliability coefficient is satisfactory without knowing the method by which it was calculated. Smaller reliability coefficients produced by more stringent methods (e.g., the parallel form method with a time interval or the KR_{21}) might actually reflect more acceptable reliability than larger reliabilities reported for the split-half or immediate test-retest method.

APPLICATION PROBLEM #2

You administer a *Math Anxiety Scale* at the beginning of the school year. One month later, you administer the scale again to the same group of students. Given the following data, what is the test-retest reliability coefficient of the *Math Anxiety Scale*?[5]

---

[4] The exception is often the parallel form method with an intervening time interval, which may be lower.

[5] We suggest you calculate this coefficient, if possible. If not, look up the actual coefficient in the "Answers to Application Problems" at the end of the chapter before responding to the final question. These suggestions apply to Application Problems #3 through #5 as well.

	Test Score	Retest Score		Test Score	Retest Score
Lynn	18	20	Marty	13	14
Larry	15	18	Nanci	16	18
Meg	17	17	Norman	14	12

Based on this reliability estimate, are you satisfied with the reliability of this test?

APPLICATION PROBLEM #3

From a pool of 300 items that test knowledge of American history, you have drawn 100 to make a classroom test. A colleague uses your 300-item pool to devise another 100-item American history test so both of you can have alternative, equivalent forms for use at the beginning and end of your history units. You have examined the two tests and judged their content to be equivalent. Four of your students volunteer to take your exam and the new exam (on the same day) so that you and your colleague can examine the equivalence of the two tests. Their scores are as shown below.

	Form 1 (Yours)	Form 2 (Your Colleague's)
Sandra	89	76
Sam	97	82
Tamara	93	90
Tom	89	84

Calculate the means of the students' performance on the two test forms. What would you conclude about equivalence of the forms from those means? What is the parallel-form reliability coefficient for the two forms of this test? How would you interpret such a reliability estimate?

APPLICATION PROBLEM #4

You would like to find out the internal consistency of your new social studies exam. You decide that the fastest way to do so is to score odd items versus even items. The following data results:

	Correct responses on	
	Odd Items	Even Items
Vicki	42	43
Vern	41	43
Wendy	44	45
William	44	42

What is the correlation between scores on the odd-numbered and even-numbered items? What is the estimated reliability of your whole exam? How would you interpret such a reliability estimate?

APPLICATION PROBLEM #5

You have just computed scores for a 100-item, end-of-term math test which will be important in determining final math grades for your class. The mean of the test is 50 and the standard deviation is 6. What would the test's index of internal consistency be, using the KR_{21} method? Does that estimate convince you that the test is reliable enough for your purposes?

APPLICATION PROBLEM #6

You are choosing between two speeded mathematics tests, both of which appear suitable for your purposes. The manual for Test X reports it possesses a split-half reliability of .98, whereas the manual for Test Y reports it possesses a test-retest reliability of .65, across a six-week interval. Which test should you choose as most reliable, and why? What types of decisions could you justify making with such a reliability coefficient?

HOW TO INCREASE THE RELIABILITY OF A TEST

You may recall our earlier guideline for interpreting reliability estimates: "Lower reliability coefficients may be acceptable if the test is handicapped by factors or circumstances that would tend to lower its reliability, whereas higher coefficients may be judged inadequate if the test is advantaged by factors or circumstances that automatically enhance its reliability." We will say a bit more about this guideline.

Several conditions can directly affect the reliability coefficients resulting from methods presented in this chapter. Several of these are under the control of the teacher or administrator giving the test, and understanding how these factors work not only allows for more intelligent interpretation of reliability coefficients, but also helps users in constructing more reliable classroom tests. Generally speaking, test reliability can be increased if one attends carefully to (1) consistency in scoring, (2) group variability (the spread of scores in the group tested), (3) the difficulty level of the test, and (4) test length.

1. Reliability of Scoring

Reliable scoring occurs when (1) different scorers agree with one another as they score the same test items, or (2) a single scorer assigns the same scores to the same test, if scored on different occasions. The first of these is called *interscorer reliability*, while the second is called *intrascorer reliability*. In both cases, the greater the agreement, the greater the reliability. Without reliability in scoring, the testing procedure is likely to be unreliable. In fact, the reliability of scoring limits test reliability, since the reliability of a test can be no greater than the reliability (agreement) among scorers. This is one reason that objectivity has been stressed throughout this book: Objectively scored items will yield high interscorer agreement or reliability, and thus will increase reliability of the test scores.

For example, if interscorer reliability on an essay test is only .55, the reliability of that test can be no higher than .55 and will almost certainly be lower, since other sources of error will also enter in. For this reason, it is essential that scoring of essay items be made as objective as possible by developing adequate scoring systems that clearly specify points to be awarded to certain aspects of different essay responses. Increasing scorer reliability can substantially increase test reliability.

Most so-called objective test items (e.g., multiple choice, true false, matching, and completion) do not suffer from much scorer unreliability.

2.   Group Variability

Reliability also depends on the amount of nonextraneous variability, or true variance, of scores within the group tested. All other things being equal, the greater the variability in the true scores, the higher the reliability estimate. If variability is small, and most students score at nearly the same levels, even small changes in individual scores from one testing to another can significantly shift the relative position of a student within the group. It follows logically that when scores are spread across a broader range, small changes in individual scores tend to have much less impact on a student's relative position within the group. Since reliability is higher when students remain in the same relative position from one test to another, greater variability tends to enhance reliability.

The range of scores in turn depends, to some extent, on how heterogeneous the examinees are in the trait being tested. If the group to which the test is administered has a restricted range of ability (e.g., a remedial class, or an honors class), reliabilities are likely to be less than if that same test were administered to a regular classroom where students tend to differ more widely in ability levels.

Similarly, if tests are administered across grade levels, the group variability will be high enough that reliability estimates are likely to be substantially higher than if the same test were used at a single grade level. Similarly, the reliability of a test administered to all students in a particular grade is likely to be higher than if the same test were administered to a single class at that grade level.

If one wished to increase the reliability coefficient of a test, then it should be apparent that the test should be administered to a group with the maximum variability that is appropriate (i.e., a group no more diverse than subsequent groups with which the test would normally be used). Conversely, administering tests to students with restricted ranges in ability will reduce the obtained reliability coefficient, even though the actual reliability of the test has not changed.

3. Difficulty Level of the Test

Tests that are too easy result in clusters of scores close together at the top end of the scale. This restricted spread of scores lowers the reliability coefficient because, as noted earlier, when scores tend to cluster together, even small changes in scores between tests can produce major shifts in rankings.

Similarly, very difficult tests cause scores to cluster at the bottom end of the scale—again lowering the reliability coefficient. Very difficult tests also encourage guessing; this introduces random error, thus lowering reliability still further. Easy tests are somewhat more reliable than difficult tests, but neither are as reliable as tests that are sufficiently moderate in difficulty to allow greater variability of scores. It follows, therefore, that one way to increase test reliability is to make sure that the difficulty level is appropriate for the students tested.

4. Number and Quality of Test Items

In general, the more items on a test, the higher the reliability. A longer test permits the variability of scores (i.e., group variability) to increase, thus leading to increased stability in student rankings across test administrations. Further, longer tests provide students with a better opportunity to show their true knowledge of content, whereas shorter tests increase the probability of their attaining high (or low) scores simply because of the selection of the small number of items included in the test. A student may get lucky and guess correctly all three items on a 3-item test, but he is highly unlikely to guess all items correctly on a 24-item test.

Simply lengthening the test won't guarantee higher reliability, however. If reliability is to be increased, the new items that are added must measure the same characteristic as the original items and must be similar in quality. Adding items that are unrelated in terms of what they measure or items that are ambiguous, vague, or otherwise poorly constructed is likely to lower reliability even though they lengthen the test. In short, one should follow the guidelines for writing good test items presented in Chapters 9 and 10.

One additional caution. Since test reliability and test length generally go hand in hand, unusually high reliabilities for relatively short tests may signal that something is amiss (Wainer, 1986).

RELIABILITY AND THE STANDARD ERROR OF MEASUREMENT

We have devoted substantial space to helping you understand reliability coefficients. Why? Because they are an essential criterion in comparing tests to determine their fallibility and are, within interpretive limits, comparable from test to test. But as we have noted, the reliability coefficient is a group statistic that depends on the variability of scores in the group tested. Its utility—indeed its purpose—is to estimate the reliability of all scores yielded by a test (hence the common misnomer of the *reliability of a test*, rather than the correct referent *the reliability of scores produced by that test*).

If one wishes to interpret an *individual* score, however, reliability coefficients are much less directly useful than a closely related statistic discussed in Chapter 5, the *standard error of measurement (SEM)*, which is an estimate of the reliability of the score obtained by an individual student. Since test scores always include some measurement error, the score that a student obtains from a test is only an approximation of the student's true level of achievement. The smaller the standard error, the more accurate the approximation.

The score obtained by a student is *not* a fixed, unvarying measure of that student's achievement. If the student were to take the test again, he would likely obtain a score that is somewhat higher or lower than the first score. Similarly, if he took the test repeatedly, his obtained scores would vary. Some would be higher than his true achievement level and some would be lower, but the average of the obtained scores would provide the best estimate of his true score.

Because of this expected variation in the scores that each student is likely to obtain, it is best to report each student's achievement as a band or interval along the scale of possible scores rather than as a single point. This band provides limits within which the individual's true score is most likely to be located. It also emphasizes that an obtained score is only an estimate of the student's true level of achievement. The upper limit of the band for a particular student's true score can be determined by adding two SEMs to the person's obtained score. The lower limit can be determined by subtracting two SEMs from the obtained score.[6]

The practice of reporting and interpreting scores in terms of such bands or intervals helps to guard against the tendency to interpret small differences in the obtained scores of two students as representing differences in their actual achievement levels. If the bands for two students overlap, we should assume that the observed differences are due to measurement error and that the actual level of achievement for the two students does not differ.

In reality, a student rarely takes the test more than once. But it is possible to ask the question of how similar a student's scores would likely be from one testing time to another if the student were to take the test several times. If there were a large amount of variation in the student's scores, we would tend to distrust the results. The SEM provides an answer to the question of how many raw score points an individual's obtained score is likely to vary.

In summary, the SEM is relatively independent of the group tested, is expressed in the same units of measurement as the original test scale, and can be used to construct *confidence intervals* around an individual student's score. Even though the SEM is not comparable from test to test, it is an extremely useful tool in interpreting scores of individual students.

THE RELIABILITY OF CRITERION-REFERENCED MEASURES

The reliability coefficients described previously in this chapter were developed for use in estimating the consistency of scores obtained from tests designed to be used in making norm-referenced interpretations. Some scholars (e.g., Popham &

---

[6] See the discussion of *confidence intervals* in Chapter 5.

Husek, 1969) have argued that these traditional procedures should not be used to compute the reliability of criterion-referenced measures because the size of these coefficients is unduly influenced by the amount of variation in the scores. They argue that scores obtained from tests designed for criterion-referenced purposes generally have less variance (i.e., the scores are not as spread out) than scores obtained from norm-referenced tests. The logic is simple. Those methods are designed for use with norm-referenced measurement and are workable only when there is at least a reasonable amount of variability in test scores. Whereas norm-referenced measures are designed to emphasize differences among individuals, criterion-referenced measures are not. Indeed, teachers might well expect all students to score relatively high on mastery tests. When teaching has been effective, variability among students' scores is not necessarily desirable, and mastery test scores could be expected to bunch together near the top of the scale. This bunching reduces variability and lowers the computed correlation coefficient. In such cases, the use of classical reliability methods with mastery tests and criterion-referenced measures is likely to yield coefficients that seriously underestimate the tests' true reliability.

Not all measurement specialists have been persuaded by this reasoning, but enough have been that several different procedures specifically designed for estimating the reliability of criterion-referenced measurements have subsequently been proposed. Most of these procedures are beyond the scope of this text, but some are conceptually simple and reasonably easy to compute. We will describe one of the simpler coefficients here.[7]

One use of criterion-referenced measurement is to classify examinees into categories based on their performance on a test. For instance, students in a mastery learning program are often tested at the end of each instructional unit and classified as having "mastered" or "not mastered" that particular unit. Similarly, many states require that prospective lawyers, medical doctors, and teachers be tested to determine whether they are "qualified" or "not qualified" to practice their profession.

Because of measurement error, examinees sometimes receive test scores that overestimate or underestimate their actual status. Consequently, students are sometimes misclassified. So are prospective teachers, lawyers, or other persons taking a professional license or certification test. If the test scores are very unreliable, a person who "passed" a test may be classified as "failing" if he were tested on another occasion on another form of the test. Of course, the reverse could also be true. Because of the importance of minimizing misclassification, whenever test scores are used as a basis for making classification decisions, it is important to be concerned about the reliability of those decisions.

Reliability of Classification Decisions

If a student takes an equivalent form of the test, will he be classified in the same category? Or will he be classified in the same category if he takes the same test over on another occasion? These questions focus on the dependability of the

---

[7] Interested readers can learn about other coefficients by studying Berk (1984).

classification decisions. To the degree that classification decisions are consistent across alternative forms of a test or across two separate administrations of the same test, we can have confidence in the reliability of those decisions. The importance of addressing reliability issues of this type is emphasized in the most recent edition of the *Standards for Educational and Psychological Testing* (AERA et al., 1985).

Table 6.3 provides a useful way of analyzing the consistency of classification decisions. The four cells in this table represent the four kinds of consistency or inconsistency that can occur when students are cross-classified on the basis of two test scores. The cell designated by the letter *a* represents the number of students who were categorized as "masters" on both tests. The cell labeled *d* represents the number of students who were classified as "nonmasters" on both tests. The cells labeled *b* and *d* represent the two possible types of classification errors.

To illustrate how this summary table can be used to analyze classification consistency, suppose that we have administered two alternate forms of a 10-item test to 20 students and that we want to determine to what degree the mastery classifications on the two versions of the test were consistent. Assume that the standard used to distinguish between masters and nonmasters on this test has been set at 70 percent. This means that a student who earns a score that equals or exceeds 7 is classified as a "master" and a student whose score is 6 or less is classified as a "nonmaster." Table 6.4 shows the scores earned by 20 students on each form of this test. The fourth column in this table indicates the mastery category in which each student would be classified as a result of that student's score on Form A. Similarly, the fifth column lists the master/nonmastery classification determined by each student's score on Form B. Inconsistent classifications occur when students who are classified as "masters" on Form A are subsequently classified as "nonmasters" on Form B and vice versa. Consistent classifications occur when students are classified either as "masters" or "nonmasters" on the basis of both tests.

The *proportion of agreement* (usually symbolized by p_A) is a single number that summarizes the consistency of mastery/nonmastery classifications (or any other dichotomous decision such as pass/fail, certified/noncertified, etc.). This

TABLE 6.3 Summary Table for Analyzing the Consistency of Mastery/Nonmastery Classifications

	Form B		
	Mastery	Nonmastery	
Form A Mastery	*a* Consistent "Masters"	*b* Inconsistent Decisions	$a + b$
Nonmastery	*c* Inconsistent Decisions	*d* Consistent "Nonmasters"	$c + d$
	$a + c$	$b + d$	N

TABLE 6.4 Raw Scores and Classification Decisions for 20 Students on Two Different Forms of a Mastery Test

Student	Raw Score		Classification Decisions		Cell in Summary Table
	Form A	Form B	Form A	Form B	
1	7	9	Master	Master	a
2	5	6	Nonmaster	Nonmaster	d
3	10	9	Master	Master	a
4	7	10	Master	Master	a
5	7	6	Master	Nonmaster	b
6	6	5	Nonmaster	Nonmaster	d
7	9	7	Master	Master	a
8	8	8	Master	Master	a
9	5	7	Nonmaster	Master	c
10	6	9	Nonmaster	Master	c
11	7	7	Master	Master	a
12	7	8	Master	Master	a
13	5	4	Nonmaster	Nonmaster	d
14	6	7	Nonmaster	Master	c
15	10	8	Master	Master	a
16	9	7	Master	Master	a
17	8	7	Master	Master	a
18	8	10	Master	Master	a
19	9	8	Master	Master	a
20	5	5	Nonmaster	Nonmaster	d

statistic represents the proportion of students who are consistently classified as "masters," plus the proportion who are consistently classified as "nonmasters." The mathematical formula for this agreement coefficient can be expressed as follows, where a equals the number of persons classified as masters on both forms of the test, d equals the number classified as nonmasters on both forms, and N represents the total number of students tested (see Table 6.3).

$$p_A = \frac{a + d}{N} \qquad \text{(Formula 6.5)}$$

The maximum possible value of p_A equals 1.0 (or 100 percent when multiplied by 100). This value can occur only when all of the students tested were classified constantly on both forms of the test. For the data shown in Table 6.4 and summarized in Table 6.5, p_A equals .80. The meaning of this statistic is simple and direct. It means that 80 percent of the students were classified in the same categories on both tests. Since 80 percent were consistently classified, only 20 percent $(1 - p_A)$ were inconsistently classified.

TABLE 6.5   Summary of Data in Table 6.4

Form B

$$p_A = \frac{a + d}{N} = \frac{12 + 4}{20} = \frac{16}{20} = .80$$

For Those Who Want to Dig Deeper

Since p_A is likely to be inflated by some classifications that happen to be consistent just by chance, its minimum value is likely to be larger than zero. To correct for the proportion of chance agreement that is likely to occur, some measurement specialists recommend using Cohan's Kappa (coefficient κ) in lieu of p_A. However, Kappa has some serious limitations when used by itself as a chance-corrected index of agreement (Berk, 1984). If Kappa is used, it should be used *in addition* to p_A rather than in place of it (Crocker & Algina, 1986). For the sake of brevity and simplicity, we have chosen not to present and explain the formula for computing Kappa in this book. However, the formula is readily available in Crocker and Algina (1986) or Berk (1984).

Neither p_A nor Kappa are difficult to understand or compute, but they can be time consuming and laborious. Subkoviak (1988) has provided tables that can be used to obtain reasonably accurate approximations of both p_A and Kappa without all the computational time and effort.

The procedure for assessing the degree of agreement presented here requires scores from two different forms of a test. Instead of using an alternate form of the test, it is possible to administer the same test twice on a test-retest basis and then compute the proportion of agreement using the procedure presented above. Subkoviak (1988) has also proposed a split-half procedure for estimating decision consistency based on a single administration of a single test.

SUGGESTED READINGS

American Psychological Association, American Educational Research Association, & National Council on Measurement in Education. (1974). *Standards for educational and psychological tests*. Washington, DC: American Psychology Association.
    Although there is a later (1985) set of standards for educational and psychological testing published by the same three organizations, and excellent in its own right, this one has the advantage of expository sections on validity and reliability lacking in the later version.

Various approaches to test validation and to estimation of test reliability are described in very lucid fashion, and standards for evaluating the validity and reliability of tests are provided along with useful examples. If your library does not have this out-of-print volume, it appears in its entirety in *Tests In Print* (Buros, 1974), which appears in the references to this text.

Berk, R. A. (1988). Criterion-referenced tests. In J. P. Keeves (Ed.). *Educational research methodology, and measurement: An international handbook* (pp. 365–370). Oxford, England: Pergamon Press.

A brief overview of essential characteristics of criterion-referenced tests (mastery and domain-referenced), their dissimilarities to norm-referenced tests, and issues pertaining to their reliability and validity.

Berk, R. A. (1984). Selecting the index of reliability. In R. A. Berk (Ed.), *A guide to criterion-referenced test construction* (pp. 231–266). Baltimore, MD: Johns Hopkins University Press.

Berk describes the various indexes that have been proposed for estimating the reliability of criterion-referenced measurements and provides guidelines for deciding which one to use in a given testing situation.

Livingston, S. A. (1988). Reliability of test results. In J. P. Keeves (Ed.). *Educational research methodology, and measurement: An international handbook* (pp. 386–392). Oxford, England: Pergamon Press.

This is a nontechnical summary of the relationship between various sources of measurement error and the alternative types of reliability estimates. It includes a useful procedure for calculating interrater reliability, a topic we have not discussed directly in this chapter.

SELF-CHECK QUIZ

1. One advantage of using the split-half method for estimating reliability is that
   a. memory and practice effects are avoided.
   b. only two test administrations are required.
   c. the halves of the test need not be parallel.
   d. this method is appropriate for use with speeded tests.

2. The Spearman-Brown prophecy formula is used to
   a. correct for chance errors of not completing a speeded test on time.
   b. estimate the reliability of a test, had the test not been split in halves.
   c. give a rough estimate of validity, given any reliability coefficient.
   d. predict test-retest reliability from a coefficient of internal consistency.

3. Cronbach's alpha coefficient should be used instead of KR_{21} to estimate reliability when
   a. a speeded test has been administered.
   b. KR_{21} is too difficult to compute.
   c. some of the test items cannot be scored dichotomously.
   d. two parallel test forms have been administered.

4. Administering a test to students with high variability in ability levels tends to
   a. increase the reliability of the scores.
   b. decrease the reliability of the scores.
   c. not effect the reliability of the scores.
   d. increase the standard error of measurement.

5. Classical methods for estimating reliability can provide misleading results when applied to criterion-referenced measures (CRMs) because CRMs often
   a. are shorter.
   b. are speeded tests.
   c. have a lower standard error of measurement.
   d. have less variance.

6. Which of the following is an example of constant measurement error?
   a. Adding 5 points to each student's score to make the maximum possible score 100 instead of 95
   b. Computing test scores using a key that has one of the test items miskeyed
   c. Having a tough grader always score the boys' essays and a lenient grader score the girls' essays
   d. Including on every test an extra-credit item worth 5 points that only the faster students have time to complete

7. Which of the following techniques can be used to estimate internal consistency reliability?
   a. Parallel forms method *with* an intervening time interval
   b. Parallel forms method *without* an intervening time interval
   c. Split-half method
   d. Test-retest method

8. Which of the following statements best describes the general relationship between test length and the reliability of test scores?
   a. The longer the test, the more reliable the scores.
   b. The shorter the test, the more reliable the scores.
   c. Test length has little to do with test score reliability.

9. KR$_{21}$ can be appropriately used to estimate the reliability of a test
   a. containing items that measure a single concept.
   b. that begins with very easy items and ends with very difficult items.
   c. that most of the students will not have enough time to finish.
   d. where up to 5 points may be earned on each item.

10. It is tolerable to accept lower reliability coefficients for tests used in decisions that
    a. affect groups rather than individuals.
    b. are difficult to reverse or disconfirm.
    c. are important to students but not to parents.
    d. have lasting consequence.

SUGGESTION SHEET

If your last name starts with the letter *F*, please complete the Suggestion Sheet at the end of this book while this chapter is still fresh in your mind.

ANSWERS TO APPLICATION PROBLEMS

#1

1. Since Test A is dichotomously scored, KR$_{21}$ can be used because it is appropriate with dichotomously scored items. Conversely, it is not appropriate for Test B, since KR$_{21}$ cannot be used with weighted-item scores.

2. Cronbach's alpha would be appropriate for estimating the reliability of both Tests A and B, since it can be used either with dichotomous or weighted scoring.

3. Both KR_{21} and Cronbach's alpha are appropriate for Test A, which is scored dichotomously. Unless a convenient computer program were available to calculate the alpha coefficient, we would use KR_{21} because it is easier to compute. For Test B, Cronbach's alpha is the only appropriate choice.

#2

If you used a hand calculator with statistical functions correctly on the data given in this application problem, you will have obtained a test-retest reliability coefficient of .82. It is difficult to decide how seriously to take this reliability estimate which, if taken at face value, suggests the test is highly reliable. A possible concern is whether a one-month interval is sufficient so that memory does not artificially inflate the reliability estimate. Depending on how the anxiety-test items are posed, memory could be a problem, but we feel one month would typically be long enough to cease worrying much on this score. Further, math anxiety can be rather specific, being influenced by particular events (e.g., a student with little math anxiety before a critical exam may feel very different two days later after learning he failed that exam). We feel that a .82 test-retest reliability reflects a test that probably is acceptably reliable for purposes proposed in this example.

#3

You should have obtained a mean for Form 1 of 92; and for Form 2, 83, and a parallel-form reliability coefficient of .30. Apparently the content of the two forms is not as equivalent as you judged it was. Form 1 appears to be considerably easier than Form 2. The low parallel form reliability coefficient for these two forms confirms the fact that these two test forms are not really very parallel at all. Given the evidence from this coefficient and the test means, you might re-examine whatever procedure led you to conclude that the two forms contained equivalent content. Apparently, the items selected from the pool were not well selected to test parallel history knowledge.

#4

You should have obtained a split-half reliability coefficient (correlation between the students' responses on the odd and even items) of .22. The estimated reliability of your whole exam is .36, which you could find by applying the Spearman-Brown Prophesy formula. There is only a slight correlation between the odd- and even-numbered items on this test or, in other words, the test appears to possess relatively low internal consistency, which means that the items apparently are measuring different things.

#5

Using the KR_{21} formula, the reliability is:

$$\frac{(100 \times 36) - (50 \times (100-50))}{(100 - 1) \times 36} = \frac{3600 - (50 \times 50)}{99 \times 36} = \frac{3600 - 2500}{3564} = \frac{1100}{3564} = .31$$

We would suggest you avoid placing much weight on this math test in determining grades. Its reliability suggests that student scores may well fluctuate on retesting, even though their ability might remain relatively constant. However, if the individual items are not reasonably similar in difficulty level, .31 may be an underestimate of the value you would obtain by using KR_{20}.

#6

Since the split-half method produces spuriously high reliability coefficients with speeded tests, the apparently high coefficient of .98 for Test X should be disregarded. Although a test-retest reliability of .65 is not outstanding, even across a six-week interval, it is the better choice here and probably acceptable if decisions are to be made only about groups, or if decisions about individual students will not be of lasting, irreversible, and critical importance.

CHAPTER 7

Why Worry about Validity? Valid Measures Permit Accurate Conclusions

Overview

In Chapter 6, we noted that every measurement instrument has imperfections, whether a teacher-made test, an interest scale administered by a school counselor, or a standardized achievement test developed by a large testing corporation. But as we noted there, tests do not have to be perfect to be useful. The critical issue for any test is *how imperfect* it is. Tests differ enormously—from excellent instruments that are directly relevant and technically sound (though still imperfect) to those that are so poorly conceived and designed that no informed test administrator would choose to use them.

If some tests are that bad, how do they survive? If Darwin's "survival of the fittest" theory pertained to measurement instruments, wouldn't the poor tests simply die out as better tests proved to be superior? Sometimes, but not as often as one might hope. Some horrid, but hardy commercial tests survive from one decade to the next—despite evidence that they are so deeply flawed they should be banned for school use. And many classroom or locally developed tests are never evaluated against any objective standards to see whether they are at all useful in providing the information for which they were intended.

Why are inadequate measurement instruments so often tolerated in our schools? There are two reasons. First, dependable information about quality is (unfortunately) lacking for many tests. Second, even when such information exists, many school practitioners are untrained in the technical concepts and terminology necessary to understand what it means. But Chapter 6 and this chapter are intended to change all that. In them we provide you with the tools you need to determine whether a test or other measurement instrument is adequate for your purposes. Chapter 6 should have provided you with the knowledge and skill to determine whether scores yielded by any measurement instrument you use are reliable enough to fulfill your purposes. But reliability, alone, is not enough to judge any instrument to be useful, even if its reliability is very high. To use a well-worn phrase: Reliability is "necessary but not sufficient" to categorize any measure as adequate without also knowing something about the *validity* of the scores produced by that measure. Put simply, test scores must be both sufficiently reliable and valid to be useful. While reliability allows us to ascertain whether test scores are consistent and stable, it does not tell us whether the scores are accurate. A test may reliably (i.e., consistently) yield test scores that tell the same story every time that test is used, but the story may still be false. The even greater concern is, do those test scores accurately reflect reality? Are inferences and conclusions you draw from those scores valid—that is, do they tell the truth?

In this chapter we explain why validity is the cornerstone of good measurement, and we describe in some detail the major approaches educators and psychologists have found useful to establish validity. We warn of factors that can reduce validity if you are not vigilant, and we explain how to improve validity coefficients and how to interpret them. We briefly discuss some controversies about how to measure the validity of criterion-referenced measures.

Finally, we discuss at greater length how both reliability and validity determine the usability and usefulness of any educational measure.

Once again, we avoid burdening you with the more sophisticated concepts and formulas that may be of interest to the psychometrician, but we do give you a few simple and straightforward tools you can use to establish validity when you use a test or other measure. You should exit this chapter as well armed as any practitioner need be to judge the adequacy of either home-grown tests or commercial instruments.

Objectives

1. Discuss why validity is an essential concern in every use of a measurement instrument.

2. Differentiate among three major approaches used to establish validity.

3. Identify where and when each of these three approaches would be of primary concern.

4. Interpret validity coefficients, describing what they mean and where they would be useful.

5. List three factors that decrease the validity of scores obtained from a particular instrument, and explain how to counteract them.

6. Explain how reliability and validity relate to each other and to other psychometric characteristics in determining a test's usefulness.

VALIDITY: THE CORNERSTONE OF GOOD MEASUREMENTS

"How valid is it?" looms as the most important question one can ask about any educational measure. In Chapter 4 we defined validity as the degree to which a test measures that which it is intended to measure or, more accurately, accomplishes the purpose for which it is intended. From such a definition, it should be apparent that validity is essential in educational measurement and evaluation. Whatever other merits a test may have, it is useless if it does not measure what the user is intending to measure.

Validity is not, however, a property of the instrument itself. Rather, it is an indication of the extent to which the interpretation of test *results* for a particular group of students are appropriate for a given purpose. Therefore, validity indicates how well a test measures what it is supposed to measure and if it is free from the influence of extraneous factors.

Validity is meaningful only as it pertains to the *particular* use for which the test results are intended. Therefore, one should not speak of a test as *valid* or *invalid* in general; rather, test scores can be spoken of as valid or invalid with reference to the specific purpose and use for which the test was intended, and the accuracy and appropriateness of the interpretations and decisions made from the resulting scores. Scores from a particular test may be highly valid for one purpose with one population of examinees and totally invalid if used for another purpose or with a different set of examinees.

Validity is concerned with the accuracy of the inferences or interpretations a user draws from the test scores. The test score earned by a student provides information about that individual's performance on the set of problems or tasks that make up the test. The information provided by a student's score is used as a basis for making inferences about that student. The inferences may be about how this student's performance compares to the performance of other students, or about how this student would perform on other similar tasks or problems. In either case, there is an assumption that the scores accurately reflect the trait they are intended to measure, and that differences in the scores obtained by various students represent differences in the degree to which they possess or lack that trait.

However, sometimes the scores obtained from a test do not provide adequate grounds for the kinds of inferences the test user wishes to be able to make. For example, consider the following cases.

Case 1. A second grade teacher developed a test intended for use in assessing students' proficiency in subtracting one two-digit number from another. The test consisted of 10 problems similar to the following:

$$\begin{array}{ccccc} 78 & 54 & 27 & 69 & 95 \\ -35 & -41 & -16 & -57 & -83 \end{array}$$

The teacher wanted to be able to infer that students who obtained high scores on this test were proficient in performing two-digit subtraction and that students who obtained low scores lacked this proficiency. However, none of the problems included in the test involved the regrouping and renaming operation (sometimes called *borrowing*). Hence, the sample of problems that made up the test was not representative of all important aspects of the task about which the user wanted to make inferences. Students who could perform successfully on problems that did not require regrouping would likely obtain high scores, but these scores would not provide sufficient evidence to warrant the conclusion that they could perform successfully on problems requiring regrouping and renaming.

Case 2. The science specialists in a State Department of Education prepared a 60-question, multiple-choice test to assess fifth graders' understanding of the basic concepts and principles in the science curriculum taught in that state. The specialists assumed that students who obtained high scores would understand the science concepts and principles and that students who obtained low scores would not understand these ideas. However, many of the questions were written at a level that required reading skills and vocabulary that were too advanced for most of the fifth graders. Since they could not understand the questions, many students earned scores that reflected their reading ability and underestimated their knowledge and understanding of science. Thus the scores were contaminated by influences that go beyond the pure measurement of science knowledge. The meaning of the scores was distorted because they contained excess information that is irrelevant to the trait the test was intended to measure.

In both of these cases, the validity of inferences or interpretations based on the scores would be questionable.

An Integrated Concept of Validity

Since the early 1900s, textbook authors have referred to validity as if it were a characteristic of the text or the instrument from which measurements were obtained. In the last two decades, this traditional view has been replaced by the view that validity is a characteristic of the scores and the inferences and interpretations based on those scores, rather than an intrinsic property of the instrument itself. The 1985 *Standards for Educational and Psychological Testing* emphasizes this point: "The inferences regarding specific uses of a test are validated, not the test itself" (AERA et al., p.9).

The quality of the test and the tasks that make up the test certainly have an important influence on the validity of the score-based inferences, but several other factors also influence the validity of the scores and inferences based on the scores. These additional factors include (1) the nature of the group tested, (2) the conditions under which the test is administered, (3) the scoring criteria and procedures used, and (4) how the scores are used.

For example, a kindergarten readiness test may lead to highly valid influences when used to distinguish between children who are well prepared to begin kindergarten and children who are not, but the same test would likely provide less valid scores if used to predict which college seniors will succeed in graduate school. The validity of scores from this test will vary greatly when used in these two different ways, not because the instrument has changed, but because of differences in the nature of the examinees and in the purpose for which the instrument was used. Even if this test were administered twice to the same group of kindergartners, however, the validity of the scores would likely vary unless the test were administered under similar conditions each time, using the same scoring procedures and criteria.

The most important question that can be asked of a set of test scores is: How valid are they for the particular purpose for which they are being used? Posing this question is a way of asking to what extent the scores measure what they are intended to measure, all of what they are intended to measure, and only that which they are intended to measure (Thorndike, Cunningham, Thorndike, & Hagen, 1991). However, this multi-faceted question is much easier to ask than it is to answer. Validity is not self-evident. It must be demonstrated. As Sax has so aptly stated, "Validity is not established by declaration but by evidence" (1989, p. 292).

Establishing validity is a cumulative process that is ongoing. It is not completed once and for all in a single effort. The process involves building a case including several different kinds of evidence. The three most commonly collected types of validity evidence include (1) content-related evidence, (2) criterion-related evidence, and (3) construct-related evidence. No one of these forms of evidence is sufficient by itself. A much stronger case is presented by accumulating evidence from each of the three categories and showing that these different types of evidence lead to a similar conclusion. Hence, validity is a matter of degree. It is not a simple either-or, all-or-none question of *valid* versus *invalid*. It is an attribute that exists along a continuum, from high to low, in varying degrees. It is inferred, or judged from existing evidence, not measured or calculated directly.

The traditional approach to validity classified it into three different types: (1) content validity, (2) criterion validity, and (3) construct validity. But these are not separate, independent *types* of validity, but rather different *categories of evidence* that are each necessary and cumulative. One danger of conceptualizing these three types of evidence as separate kinds of validity is the tendency to think, for example, that questions about content validity are the only validity issues that need to be considered when dealing with achievement tests; that questions about criterion-related validity are the only important concerns when dealing with tests used for selection purposes; and that questions related to construct validity are important only when working with a test intended to assess some psychological construct such as creativity, anxiety, or readiness. But validity, properly conceived, is a single, unitary concept that includes each of the three categories of evidence and recognizes that each type of evidence is necessary and important when attempting to validate the meaning of inferences and interpretations from test scores. This integrated view of validity is described in the most recent version of the *Standards for Educational and Psychological Testing* (AERA et al., 1985). However, many of these ideas had surfaced previously in the writings of several influential scholars. Currently, Messick's (1989) treatment of validity is probably the best and most comprehensive explanation of this topic.

APPROACHES TO ESTABLISHING VALIDITY

The process by which a test developer or test user collects evidence to support the types of inferences that are to be made from test scores is called *validation*. The goals of this process are to gather evidence that supports the particular kinds of inferences and interpretations the test was intended to serve and that discredits other plausible interpretations. In the following sections, we discuss the three types of evidence needed to achieve these goals.

Content Validation

Content validation refers to the extent to which the content of a test's items represents the entire body of content (often called the *content universe* or *domain*) to be measured. Although it is most commonly assessed for achievement tests or other tests of skill or knowledge, it is also possible to judge the content validity of a personality inventory, aptitude test, intelligence test, or attitude measure. With these latter measures, however, establishing content validity is somewhat more difficult, since it is not always easy to recognize whether particular test items measure personality, aptitude, or attitude.

The basic issue in content validation is *representativeness*. In other words, how adequately does the content of the test represent the entire body of content to which the test user intends to generalize? Since the responses to a test are only a sample of a student's behavior, the validity of any inferences about that student depends upon the representativeness of that sample.

In this context, the word *content* refers to both the subject-matter topics (e.g., math or reading) included in the test and the cognitive processes that examinees are expected to apply to the subject matter. The processes to be sampled may include recalling, classifying, comparing, predicting, analyzing, inferring, evaluating, interpreting information, or applying a principle to a specific problem situation. The domain of interest is not merely a subject-matter domain, therefore, but a behavioral domain (Anastasi, 1988). Hence, in collecting evidence of content validity, it is necessary to determine what kinds of mental operations are elicited by the problems presented in the test, as well as what subject-matter topics have been included or excluded.

Ideally, a test should sample *all* important aspects of the content domain. No important parts of the domain should be underrepresented or excluded. Similarly, no aspects of the domain should be overrepresented. Overrepresentation of one aspect of a content domain usually occurs at the expense of underrepresenting some other important aspect. For example, a high school teacher who devotes 80 percent or more of the problems in a test to assessing students' ability to recall factual information will most likely fail to adequately assess higher order processes such as predicting, analyzing, and applying.

In practice it is difficult to accurately determine what cognitive processes are elicited by the various problems in a test. However, any serious attempts to collect content validity evidence should include a detailed analysis of the nature of the tasks presented in the various test items and whether the items actually function as intended. A test that purportedly measures science process skills may actually assess only the students' knowledge of science vocabulary.

Gronlund and Linn (1990) emphasize the need to judge whether the problems or items in a test function as intended. If some students are able to answer an item correctly because of a clue in the item rather than because of their knowledge or ability, then the item is malfunctioning. Similarly, if some knowledgeable students miss an item because it is vaguely worded or contains inappropriate vocabulary, the item is not functioning as intended. In either case, the cognitive task the student actually performs is not the intended task. Therefore, the validity of the scores will be decreased. After all, "It is the [actual] tasks presented by the items that really define what the test measures" (Thorndike et al., 1991, p. 126).

In summary, the two basic questions that need to be addressed in content validation are these.

1. To what degree does the test include a representative sample of all important parts of the behavioral domain?
2. To what extent is the test free from the influence of irrelevant variables that would threaten the validity of inferences based on the observed scores.

Collecting Content Validation Evidence

Evidence of content validity is a matter of judgment. Collecting this evidence involves comparing the items in a test with the objectives they are intended to assess and then making an informed judgment about the degree to which the subject matter covered by each item and the cognitive process it elicits match the process and topic specified in the corresponding objective. To the extent that the items are congruent with the objectives they are intended to assess, inferences based on scores from the test will have content validity.

Teachers generally have to judge how well the items in their tests match their objectives, but they may want to ask one or more colleagues (even some of their students) to assist in making these judgments. To avoid making undue demands on their colleagues' time, a teacher may wish to personally rate the congruence of her test items with the corresponding objectives, and then ask colleagues to rate only those items about which she has the most serious reservations. Teachers who take this process seriously will almost always produce more defensible tests.

Content validation is especially important for teacher-made tests and will usually be the primary type of validity evidence teachers can provide. It is especially pertinent when teachers have specified their instructional objectives, since it then reflects the extent to which the test matches or measures those objectives.

Tests that produce content valid scores generally do not occur by accident. They result from careful planning and thoughtful development efforts. Evidence of content validity for a teacher-made test can be strengthened by adhering to the following steps.

Step 1: Describe and specify as clearly as possible the domain of behaviors to be measured. In educational tests, this would typically require analysis of curriculum guidelines, courses of study, syllabi, textbooks, and other items that reflect the intent of those who have designed the instructional experience. This is to ensure that all the content that students are expected to learn is included.

Step 2: Analyze the domain of behavior outlined in Step 1 and subcategorize it into more specific topics, subject-matter areas, or clusters of instructional objectives. For example, if we were to test how well you have learned and can apply the content of this section on validity, we might decide to subdivide the content into the following categories: "face validity", content validation, criterion-related validation, and construct validation. We also may decide that we have three categories of objectives with which we are concerned: knowledge, understanding, and application.

Step 3: Draw up a set of test specifications that shows not only the content areas or topics to be covered during the instructional processes, or objectives to be tested, but also the relative emphasis to be placed on each. Using our previous example, we could develop a set of specifications in a two-way matrix as a blueprint for our test, shown in an uncompleted form in Figure 7.1. Predictive validation and face validation will be defined in upcoming sections.

Step 4: Decide how many questions to include in the test. Remember previous discussions of reliability and test length, and also practical considerations such as examinee fatigue.

Step 5: Determine how many items will need to be developed in each cell of the matrix to make sure there is representative coverage of all content areas and categories of instructional objectives.

Step 6: Construct or select test items appropriate for each cell.

Step 7: Enlist another teacher or a content expert to construct a second set of items, using the same matrix of specifications or, if that's infeasible, review your items. Reviewing similarities and differences between the two sets, or reviewing the critique, will help identify unwitting biases you might bring to the item-writing task, as well as strengthen the final set of test items that are selected.

Using steps such as these and thinking about validity *before* a test is constructed goes far toward ensuring that a classroom test will have high content validity. Increasing content validity *after* test items are written may involve extensive item revision or rewriting.

Criterion-related Validation

Criterion-related evidence of validity refers to the extent to which one can infer from an individual's score on a test how well she will perform some other external task or activity that is supposedly measured by the test in question. This external

Categories of Instructional Objectives

		Knowledge	Understanding	Application
	Desired Emphasis	20%	50%	30%
"Face Validity"	10%			
Content Validation	20%			
Construct Validation	30%			
Criterion-related Validation	40%			

FIGURE 7.1 Sample Test Blueprint

task or activity that is to be predicted is called the *criterion*.[1] Ideally, the criterion should be some socially-valued, behavioral variable that cannot be directly measured by a test, such as successful on-the-job performance as an employee, or grade point average for the first year in college. However, performance on a different but already existing test is often used as a surrogate measure of the criterion of interest. The degree to which scores on the test being validated predict successful performance on the criterion is determined by (1) administering the test in question to a representative group of individuals for whom scores on the criterion can be obtained, and (2) then computing a correlation coefficient summarizing the degree to which the two sets of scores are related. The resulting correlation coefficient is called a *validity coefficient*. External criteria are of two types: criterion measures taken at approximately the same time as the test is administered, or criterion measures taken significantly later (e.g., after several months or years). Correlation with the former produces concurrent evidence of validity; correlation with the latter yields predictive evidence of validity.

Predictive Evidence of Validity

Predictive validity refers to how well a measure predicts or estimates *future* performance on some valued criterion other than the test itself. For example, one may wish to use a test score to predict how well the examinee will do in college or on the

---

[1] Note that *criterion* has an entirely different meaning in this context than when referring to criterion-referenced measurement; do not confuse the two.

job—or even on a later (different) test. Predictive validity is especially important in selection and placement decisions (e.g., college entrance exams or employment tests).

To determine predictive validity, it is important to identify a satisfactory future criterion that can be measured successfully. Then obtaining the predictive validity coefficient is simply a matter of following the steps outlined below.

Step	*Example*
1. Administer and score the test you will use for the prediction.	1. College Entrance Exam (CEE)
2. Wait an appropriate period of time.	2. Allow examinees to attend two years of college.
3. Measure the external criterion on which you are attempting to predict performance.	3. Obtain the grade point average (GPA) for examineees.
4. Correlate the scores on the predictor test with measurements on the external criterion.	4. Correlate CEE scores with examinees' GPAs.
5. Interpret the resulting validity coefficient.	5. Interpret the correlation of CEE and GPA scores.

A high predictive validity coefficient indicates that a test is a good predictor of the criterion because both measure the same trait(s). A low coefficient indicates that the test does *not* measure the same trait(s) as that reflected in the later criterion, thus making it a poor predictor of relevant future performance.

Predictive validity is very important for standardized achievement and aptitude tests, and educators should require evidence that such tests are good predictors of later outcomes they value before expending time and resources to administer such tests. Predictive validity is seldom established for teacher-made tests, although doing so would be both feasible and informative.

Concurrent Evidence of Validity

Sometimes educators or psychologists are interested in validating a new test by seeing how well it correlates with an existing test (or some other criterion) that is generally considered an accurate indicator. Concurrent validity is frequently used to establish that a new test (possibly a teacher-made test) is an acceptable substitute for a more expensive measure.

For example, assume that the personnel officer of a large corporation wants to screen out job candidates who are inflexible, but finds the highly regarded Test of Flexibility (TOF)—the criterion—too expensive and time-consuming because it requires individual administration. The corporation may fund development of a shorter, group-administered Flexible Attitude Scale (FAS), and then administer both FAS and TOF to the same examinees, concurrently, to see if they correlate highly. If they do, then FAS could be considered a valid test, based on concurrent criterion-related evidence, because it measures the same trait as that of the widely accepted TOF.

The steps for determining concurrent validity are the same as those outlined previously for predictive validity, except Step 2 is eliminated since the two measures are taken concurrently.

Validity and Reliability of the Criterion

In both predictive and concurrent validation, it is essential that the validity and reliability of the criterion be well established. A criterion will not be useful if it is unstable or invalid. Trying to predict performance on an unreliable and invalid criterion is like trying to hit a moving target that constantly changes size and shape. Whether an adolescent does or does not have a criminal record is readily determined, for instance. Similarly, a grade point average of 3.0 is a clear target. But a concept like "success in life" is nebulous, subjective, and hard to define in a way on which everyone can agree. We cannot say whether a test is a good measure or a good predictor unless we know precisely what it is we are measuring or predicting.

Construct Validation

Words like *assertiveness, giftedness,* and *hyperactivity* refer to abstract ideas that humans construct in their minds to help them explain observed patterns or differences in the behavior of themselves or other people. Intelligence, self-esteem, aggressiveness, and achievement motivation are also examples of such abstractions. So are concepts like creativity, critical thinking ability, reading comprehension, mathematical reasoning ability, and scholastic aptitude. Some of these constructs come to us from scholarly disciplines such as psychology or sociology. Other examples such as shyness, curiosity, hypocrisy, and procrastination are informal constructs that are part of our ordinary language and everyday culture. Nevertheless, all of these example are constructs. A *construct* is an unobservable, postulated attribute of individuals created in our minds to help explain or theorize about human behavior. Since constructs do not exist outside of the human mind, they are not directly measurable.

According to Cronbach (1984), the word *construct* is a noun that is derived from the verb *to construe.* He claims that "a construct is a way of construing—organizing—what has been observed" (p. 133). Observant parents use constructs as they attempt to describe similarities or differences in the behavior of children. Teachers and other professional educators often use constructs in their attempts to account for behavioral patterns they observe in students (or one another). Sportscasters, journalists, political scientists, economists, and medical doctors all create and use constructs. In fact, thoughtful observers of human behavior in all disciplines and all walks of life develop and use constructs to explain human behavior. One can hardly read the daily newspaper, watch the TV news, or watch a hockey game without encountering several different examples of constructs. Some commonly used constructs are only vaguely defined, while others are more clear-cut.

Many different tests have been created in recent years that purport to measure different constructs used by educators. Supposedly, the Whimpleton Reading Readiness Test measures children's readiness to learn how to read, and the Syracuse Mathematics Anxiety Test provides accurate measures of students' anxiety about learning mathematics. However, just because the title of a test suggests that it measures a certain construct does not mean that scores from that test are valid, dependable measures of that construct. Remember, validity is established by evidence, not by declaration. Responsible test users are skeptical of test titles and expect additional evidence that the test actually measures the construct it purports to measure, and not something else.

Construct validation is the process of collecting evidence to support the assertion that a test measures the construct claimed by the test developer. This process involves accumulating empirical data from several sources and building a logical case to support the conclusion that scores from the test *do* measure what they are supposed to measure and that they *do not* measure other extraneous factors. Evidence of content validity and evidence of criterion-related validity are both used in this process. In that sense, content validation and criterion-related validation become part of construct validation.

For example, suppose that one wanted to validate scores from a new test that supposedly measured creativity. A good place to begin would be to define the domain of tasks, abilities, attitudes, habits, or mind sets that are ascribed to creativity. One would then want to determine to what extent the items that make up the test are representative of all important aspects of this domain. The next step would be to determine how well scores from this new test are correlated with other measures and variables—to which they would be expected to be related—based on existing theories of related constructs such as flexibility, independence, and divergent thinking. Then one would check to determine whether scores from this new measure of creativity are relatively uncorrelated with other distinctive and theoretically unrelated constructs such as verbal intelligence. Logical inferences, drawn from empirical data, would be used to determine whether the test faithfully measured creativity rather than other constructs.

Construct validity can seldom be inferred from a single empirical study or from one logical analysis of a measure. Rather, judgments of construct validity must be based upon an accumulation of evidence indicating that the test measures the construct it is intended to measure. Construct differs from content validity in that the *content* to be measured in the latter (e.g., Civil War history) is typically known and agreed upon, whereas the *construct* to be measured (e.g., intelligence) is typically hypothesized and can only be inferred from other, observable behaviors.

Construct validity is most relevant during the development and piloting of a test and is more often important for standardized measures of various hypothetical constructs than it is for teacher-made tests of achievement.

Validity Depends on Both Logical and Empirical Approaches

The kinds of validity evidence discussed so far can be sorted into two general approaches: logical or rational approaches (content validity) and empirical or statistical approaches (predictive and concurrent criterion-related validities). Con-

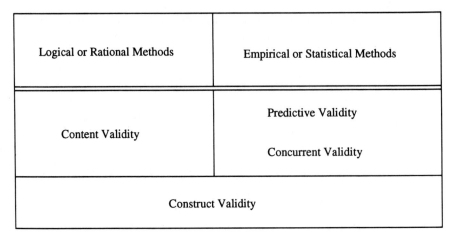

FIGURE 7.2 Processes Used in Collecting Different Types of Validity Evidence

struct validation bridges both categories, drawing on logical and statistical bases alike for its evidence. Figure 7.2 portrays these relationships graphically.

"Face Validity"

"Face validity," often discounted as the mere appearance of validity, refers to the degree to which a measurement instrument appears to measure that which it is intended to measure. A test might be viewed as having "face validity,"[2] for example, if its title and items appear (to those who administer and/or take the test) to be relevant and to measure what is intended.

Admittedly, matters of appearance are usually less important than matters of substance, in measurement at least. The psychometrician ought never to aspire to the art of the magician, of dealing in illusions. Clearly, face validity alone is not sufficient evidence that a test possesses genuine validity. It is not comparable to the kinds of validity evidence we have discussed previously, and cannot replace them, for it is truly only the appearance of validity.

While the appearance of validity is less important than true validity, it is not unimportant. In some cases, lack of face validity also suggests a lack of true validity. Imagine that a test were entitled Test of General Mathematical Reasoning Ability, but an inspection revealed that *all* of its items were numerically expressed multiplication facts (e.g., 3 × 3 = 9), and there were *no* story problems or problem-solving items of any type. Similarly, the expectations raised by a test titled Universal Sixth-Grade Spelling Test would be dashed when closer examination showed that it contained only lists of correctly and incorrectly spelled Latin verbs. Both of these tests could be rejected as invalid *on their face*—unless, of course, you really wanted to measure only multiplication facts or knowledge of how Latin verbs are spelled.

In other cases, an instrument might actually measure what we want to measure, but have little face validity—that is, not *appear* to measure it. So what? Isn't

---

[2] We shall hereafter drop the quotations used so far for emphasis.

what it measures more important than what it *appears* to measure? Yes, but in our opinion (and that of Nevo, 1985 and Anastasi, 1988), low face validity can be lethal to a test for several practical reasons. Those who choose tests do not always understand technical discussions of validity and, consequently, tests that appear valid are more likely to be used than those that appear invalid, regardless of their actual validity. Anastasi makes this point well:

> Face validity pertains to whether the test "looks valid" to the examinees who take it, the administrative personnel who decide on its use, and other technically untrained observers. Fundamentally, the question of face validity concerns rapport and public relations. Although common usage of the term validity in this connection may make for confusion, face validity itself is a desirable feature of tests. . . . Certainly if test content appears irrelevant, inappropriate, silly, or childish, the result will be poor cooperation, regardless of the actual validity of the test. Especially in adult testing, it is not sufficient for a test to be objectively valid. It also needs face validity to function effectively in practical situations. (1988, p. 144)

Thus, ignoring face validity can be risky in view of the many practical realities that exist in the educational setting.

Face validity by itself, however, is never a sufficient criterion in choosing educational measures. Too often teachers or administrators trust titles or appearance, only to find that a test labeled as a test of creativity turns out to be a measure of vocabulary, or verbal fluency, and nothing else. Good choices depend on thorough knowledge of genuine, objective, evidence of validity.

It should be apparent that although both content validity and face validity depend on rational processes (as opposed to empirical methods), they are quite different. Where face validity requires only that the measure *appear* valid, content validity depends on a verified match between the content of the instruction and the content of the test. Face validity should never be accepted as a substitute for validity based on evidence.

APPLICATION PROBLEM #1

Assume we wish to construct a 100-item test of the content and objectives outlined in Figure 7.1. How many test items would you propose for each cell?

Factors That Can Reduce Validity

Gronlund and Linn (1990) suggest several categories of factors that can adversely affect the validity of test scores, including

1. *Factors in the test itself,* such as (a) vague directions, (b) irrelevant items, (c) poorly constructed items with inappropriate difficulty or reading level, (d) items that contain clues to the correct answer, and (e) too few or improperly sequenced items.
2. *Factors in test administration and scoring,* such as (a) insufficient time to

complete the test, (b) undetected cheating, (c) inappropriate help or coaching, and (d) unreliable item scoring.

3. *Factors affecting pupil responses,* such as (a) high level of fear or anxiety about taking the test, (b) a tendency to rush through the test with more concern for speed than accuracy, (c) a persistent tendency to guess when uncertain about the correct answer.

The list might easily be extended, but this should suffice to make our point that anything that can introduce error into test scores will have an adverse effect on a test's validity. In addition, some specific considerations influence validity coefficients, as outlined below for those who want to learn more.

Interpreting—and Improving—Validity Coefficients

Content, construct, and face validity do not yield statistical validity coefficients, and therefore cannot be interpreted in as precise and universally understood terms as can the criterion-related validities—predictive and concurrent. But even where the latter approaches to validity produce validity coefficients, interpretation must be done carefully.

For Those Who Want to Dig Deeper

The following guidelines should help in interpreting validity coefficients.

1. *Predictive validity coefficients will typically be lower than concurrent validity coefficients.* This is so because the chances are higher that the former will be affected by changes in behavior of the individual during the period between the predictor test and the later criterion measure. The longer the time interval, the lower the predictive validity coefficient might be expected to be. Following are some very rough guidelines for acceptable levels for validity coefficients:

	Predictive Validity	*Concurrent Validity*
Very acceptable	.65–1.00	.85–1.00
Minimally acceptable	.55–.65	.75–.85
Unacceptable	<.55	<.75

2. *The size of a predictive validity coefficient will vary in relation to the reliabilities of both the criterion and the predictor.* As for all measures, both predictors and criteria are fallible to some degree and thus subject to errors of measurement. To the extent such errors operate, the measurements of the predictor and/or criterion are unreliable, thus lowering the correlation coefficient. When this happens, the coefficient will underestimate the correlation that *would* exist between the true scores if no error were present. Fortunately, this (theoretical) correlation can be estimated by use of the following formula:

$$\frac{\text{Obtained validity coefficient}}{\sqrt{\text{Criterion reliability}}} = \text{Corrected validity coefficient} \quad \text{(Formula 7.1)}$$

To illustrate the effect of using unreliable criteria to validate predictors, solve the following problem.

APPLICATION PROBLEM #2

Assume you develop a measure of mechanical aptitude and correlate it with the American Mechanical Aptitude Test (AMAT), a standardized measure, and obtain a validity coefficient of .60. Assume that the reliability of the AMAT is .90. What would the corrected concurrent validity coefficient be if the AMAT contained *no* measurement error?

Similar corrections can be calculated to find what the corrected validity coefficient would be if both the predictor and criterion were perfectly reliable, using the following formula:

$$\frac{\text{Obtained validity coefficient}}{\sqrt{\text{Predictor reliability} \times \text{criterion reliability}}} = \text{Corrected validity coefficient} \quad \text{(Formula 7.2)}$$

3. *Validity coefficients derived from scores of homogeneous groups will be lower than those from scores of heterogeneous groups.* The rationale here is identical to that outlined earlier of the effect of group variability on reliability coefficients. One practical implication is that anything that lowers variability will lower validity coefficients. For example, if those who score low on a particular test of academic aptitude elect not to go to college, information on the criterion (success in college) can only be available for a more homogeneous group, possibly leading to an incorrect inference that the test is a poor predictor.

4. *Increasing the length of the predictor test will slightly increase predictive validity.* Added test items would need to be comparable in quality to existing test items in order for predictive validity to increase. Also, the increases in predictive validity are relatively modest, even if test length is doubled or trebled, raising questions as to whether this is a cost-effective or practical way to increase predictive validity.

VALIDITY OF CRITERION-REFERENCED MEASURES

Almost all scholars in educational and psychological measurement agree that concerns about validity are just as important in the context of criterion-referenced measurement as in the context of norm-referenced measurement. However, scholars have been divided in their answers to questions about what kind of validity evidence should be gathered and what procedures should be used to collect it. Some scholars (e.g., Popham & Husek, 1969) have emphasized that validity approaches that depend upon the use of correlation coefficients are not very useful in the context of criterion-referenced measurement because of the limited variation often obtained in scores from these tests. Scholars in this camp have traditionally emphasized the need to conduct content validation studies, but they have downplayed the need for criterion-related validation and construct validation. Other scholars (e.g., Linn, 1979) have taken a different point of view. They agree that evidence of content validity is particularly important in the context of criterion-referenced measurement, but they also emphasize the importance of collecting evidence of criterion-related validity and construct validity.

The long standing debate between these two camps has been influenced by publication of the latest version of the *Standards for Educational and Psychological Testing* (AERA et al., 1985) that refines the definition of validity to be a unitary concept and places increased emphasis on the idea that construct evidence of validity encompasses both content validity and criterion-related validity. Consequently, in recent years there has been increased emphasis on the need for collecting evidence of both criterion-related validity and construct validity in addition to evidence of content validity. Because of this view, measurement experts are increasingly taking the stance that validity of criterion-referenced interpretations is no different than for validity of any other type of interpretation.

THE ROLE OF RELIABILITY AND VALIDITY IN DETERMINING A MEASURE'S USEFULNESS

Now we will discuss how reliability and validity interrelate and combine to determine the utility of any educational measure.

Reliability is a necessary precursor to validity. One can hardly conclude that a test is measuring what it is supposed to, if it measures something different every time. Conversely, scores from a test *can* be reliable without being valid, measuring the wrong thing every time, but doing so with marvelous consistency. So even though reliability is necessary, it is not sufficient. Test scores can lack validity even though they are highly reliable. In other words, they can be free from random errors of measurement, but still reflect the effects of constant (systematic) errors. In order for the testing procedure and the resulting scores to have validity, the scores must be relatively free from both random errors and constant (systematic) errors.

Validity, Usability, and Usefulness

It is not enough for a test to be valid; it must also be usable. Tests that are too expensive, too time-consuming, or too technically sophisticated for intended users to interpret are simply not usable, however impressive their validity coefficients may be. Cangelosi provides a clear illustration:

> one-to-one conferencing between a trained teacher and a student is often one of the more valid means for measuring how well the student achieved a learning objective. However, if a teacher has 30 students in a class and only 5 hours a week scheduled with that class, then a more expedient (and probably less valid) means

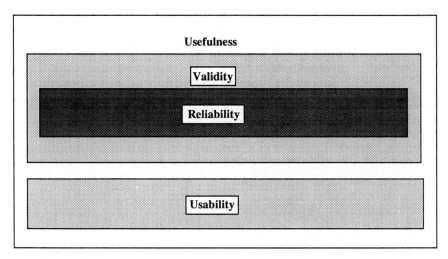

FIGURE 7.3 Components of Usefulness

SOURCE: Reprinted with permission from Cangelosi, J. S. (1982). *Measurement and Evaluation: An Inductive Approach for Teachers.* Dubuque, IA: W. C. Brown.

must be considered. The conferences may be rejected, not on validity grounds, but because of low usability. Expense, time, strain on students, and a myriad of other considerations affect measurements' usability. (1982, p. 59)

A *usable* measure is not necessarily *useful,* however. An instrument that is quick, cheap, and simple to use, score, and interpret is still useless if it is not valid. A measure must be both valid *and* usable to practitioners, and both concerns must be kept in mind when such measures are designed or selected. In fact, usefulness is the ultimate criterion educators should apply in choosing or developing every measure that will be used in our schools.

The relationships among validity, usability, and usefulness are illustrated in Figure 7.3.

SUGGESTED READINGS

Messick, S. (1989). Validity. In R. L. Linn (Ed.), *Educational measurement* (3rd ed., pp. 13–103). New York: American Council on Education and Macmillan.

Messick traces the historical evolution of the concept of validity and how various evidences of validity have been categorized. He explains the various types of validity evidence we have used in this text but goes beyond them to present a philosophically based argument that alters traditional conceptions of validity and presents validation as a unitary conception. This chapter is an excellent resource for those who wish to pursue this topic further and to stretch to assimilate exciting, new thinking in the field of measurement.

Zeller, R. A. (1988). Validity. In J. P. Keeves (Ed.), *Educational research methodology, and measurement: An international handbook* (pp. 322–330). Oxford, England: Pergamon Press.

This is a very useful summary of the various approaches to test validation, including practical examples that illustrate the similarities and differences among those approaches.

SELF-CHECK QUIZ

1. Which type of validity evidence depends upon both rational *and* statistical approaches?
   a. Construct validity
   b. Content validity
   c. Concurrent validity
   d. Predictive validity

2. Which type of validity evidence is most likely to be of concern to the classroom teacher attempting to improve a test of Civil War history?
   a. Face validity
   b. Content validity
   c. Construct validity
   d. Concurrent validity
   e. Predictive validity

3. It is possible for a test to be
   a. valid, but not reliable.
   b. useful, but not valid.
   c. reliable, but not valid.
   d. useful, but not reliable.

4. Which type of validity evidence should be used to determine how well a measure estimates future performance on some valued criterion?
   a. Construct validity
   b. Content validity
   c. Concurrent validity
   d. Predictive validity

5. Which type of validity evidence is usually the primary type provided by teachers for teacher-made tests?
   a. Construct validity
   b. Content validity
   c. Criterion validity

6. Content validity evidence provides information about
   a. how well the scores from the test measure what they are supposed to measure without measuring other extraneous factors.
   b. the degree to which the test problems are representative of the domain of tasks and topics about which the user wants to make inferences.
   c. the extent to which the user can infer from the test scores how well the examinees will perform on some other valued measure.

7. Which type of validity evidence is frequently used to establish that a new test is an acceptable substitute for a widely accepted test?
   a. Construct validity
   b. Content validity
   c. Concurrent validity
   d. Predictive validity

8. A nebulous external criterion, such as humaneness, is a useful measure for determining
   a. concurrent validity but not predictive validity.
   b. predictive validity but not concurrent validity.
   c. both concurrent and predictive validity.
   d. neither concurrent nor predictive validity.

9. The current concept of validity states that validity is a characteristic of
   a. the administration of the test.
   b. the domain which the test is supposed to sample.
   c. each individual item on the test.
   d. interpretations based on the test scores.
   e. the test itself.

10. When estimating construct validity, it is important to
   a. use evidence of content validity but not criterion-related validity.
   b. use evidence of criterion-related validity but not content validity.
   c. use evidence of both content validity and criterion-related validity.
   d. avoid using evidence of either content validity or criterion-related validity.

SUGGESTION SHEET

If your last name starts with the letter *G*, please complete the Suggestion Sheet at the end of this book while this chapter is still fresh in your mind.

ANSWERS TO APPLICATION PROBLEMS

#1

The blueprint for your test might look like that illustrated below:

Categories of Instructional Objectives

	Desired Emphasis	Knowledge 20%	Understanding 50%	Application 30%	Total Items
"Face Validity"	10%	2	5	3	10
Content Validation	20%	4	10	6	20
Construct Validation	30%	6	15	9	30
Criterion-related Validation	40%	8	20	12	40
Total Items		20	50	30	100

A Completed Test Blueprint

#2

$$\frac{.60}{\sqrt{.90}} = \frac{.60}{.9487} = .63.$$

This is the corrected concurrent validity coefficient, if the AMAT was free of any measurement error.

CHAPTER 8

Cutting Down Test Score Pollution: Reducing the Influence of Extraneous Factors

Overview

Chapters 6 and 7 emphasized the importance of making sure that a test is measuring what it was designed to measure—that it is a *valid* test. Unfortunately, many people think of validity as a characteristic inherent within the test. However, validity depends on how a test is administered, the purpose for which it is interpreted, the particular students with whom it is used (and how they behave on that particular day), and the setting in which it is given. People sometimes forget that many other sources of error may render a test that is perfectly good for one purpose, quite ill-suited for another.

No one would use a math test to measure a student's self-concept. Other sources of error, however, are not so apparent. This chapter outlines the most frequently encountered *extraneous variables* that can affect a respondent's score on a particular test, and thereby reduce the validity. Extraneous variables are those characteristics, occurrences, or behavior patterns that can result in an apparently valid test becoming an inaccurate measure of what it was designed to measure.

In the same way that industrial waste pollutes air or water, we say that extraneous variables cause test score pollution; they introduce foreign matter into what should be a pure measure of some trait, knowledge, or proficiency. This chapter summarizes the factors that "pollute" the meaning of test scores (e.g., a student's motivation and test-taking skills, or inappropriate test administration practices) and suggests some procedures to minimize the effect of test score pollution. The major extraneous factors that can inappropriately influence performance on cognitive tests are summarized first. Next, the extraneous factors that can inappropriately influence performance on affective measures are outlined. Finally, suggestions are given for ways to reduce the impact of extraneous factors.

Objectives

Upon completing your study of this chapter, you should be able to

1. Explain how the validity of a cognitive or affective measure can be affected by extraneous variables.
2. Describe extraneous factors that affect cognitive test scores, including test taking skills, testwiseness, response sets, anxiety and motivation, administration factors, coaching and practice, and test bias.
3. Explain procedures and techniques that can be used to prevent or minimize the influence of extraneous variables on cognitive tests.
4. Provide definitions and examples of extraneous factors that influence the scores on affective measures, including social desirability response set, faking, problems of interpretation, self-deception/lack of insight, and acquiescence response set.
5. Explain procedures and techniques that can be used to prevent or minimize the influence of extraneous variables on affective measures.
6. Given a specific measurement situation, identify the extraneous variables most likely to be present.

A TASTE OF TEST SCORE POLLUTION

Let us begin by having you experience the effects of test score pollution. Imagine you have just arrived for a job interview. You are sitting in a room with seven other applicants. A sour-looking bureaucrat arrives, passes out sheets of paper similar to Figure 8.1 (do not turn to it yet), and quickly reads the instructions in the section below in a disinterested monotone. Please read these instructions quickly once *as if you are listening to the bureaucrat read them to you*, then turn the page and complete the task *without looking back* at the instructions.

INSTRUCTIONS FOR TEST ON PAGE 200

You will now take the test designed to make a determination as to whether you will be allowed to proceed to the next step of the interview process. It is a very difficult test and most of you will fail it, so attend carefully. Fill in the space below the correct answer. Any other marks on the paper will disqualify you from further consideration.

Which one of the alternatives I am about to mention would be the cheapest to buy? Listen carefully and I will explain to you what they cost. The hyperbola costs more than the trapezoid, the trapezoid costs the same as the asterisk and the asterisk costs more than the ampersand. Mark the cheapest one (wait 3 seconds). STOP! Put your pencils down. Turn your paper over.

(Turn now to Figure 8.1 and indicate your answer in 3 seconds or less; then return to this page and continue reading.)

Imagine your reaction had you been waiting in that room with the seven other applicants. You would probably have been frustrated to learn that you might not even be interviewed if you did not do well on a test that you were not expecting. Having had no time to prepare, you probably would have become confused because the directions were read so quickly. The monotone voice and obvious disinterest of the examiner would not help. The directions were more complicated than necessary, and some of the vocabulary may have been unfamiliar. Read the directions again and you will see that the test item is designed to assess your understanding of the concepts of "greater than" and "less than," but the examples used are unnecessarily complex.

Think about the influence a test administrator has in this situation. Had the same instructions been presented differently, it would have been much easier for you to show your understanding of the concepts being tested. For example, you were asked to fill in the space *below* the correct answer, but there is no space below the asterisk because the test (Figure 8.1) is printed upside down. Furthermore, the "space" where you were expected to mark your answer is different (and consequently confusing) from what you have seen on most tests.

There are some test-taking strategies that could be employed in figuring out the correct answer. If you had an idea of what to expect, had a piece of scratch paper, and knew all of the vocabulary, you could have quickly figured out that the ampersand is the cheapest item. However, in our experience in doing workshops on test administration, we find that many people stop listening after they hear the word *hyperbola*.

For most people, this test is an experience in frustration, rather than a measure of the concepts of "greater than" and "less than". Our goal was for you to experience in this safe situation some of the factors that can influence test scores in real life. It may surprise you to learn that this item is taken from a second-grade standardized achievement test. The only differences are that the instructions were made more complex and the symbols were changed from teddy bear, football, truck, and doll. Obviously, many factors that are unrelated to mastery of learning outcomes can affect test performance.

EXTRANEOUS FACTORS THAT CAN INFLUENCE PERFORMANCE ON COGNITIVE TESTS

Cognitive tests are designed to measure how well respondents have mastered specific learning outcomes or to what degree they possess particular traits or characteristics. The validity of a test for a particular purpose (i.e., how well it does what it purports to do) depends on many factors.

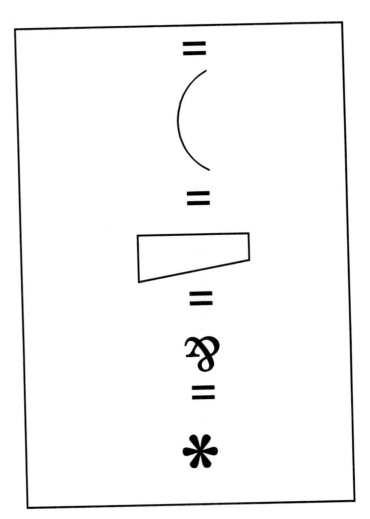

FIGURE 8.1 Test for Job Interview

Of course, validity is influenced by how well individual items are written. However, as you have just experienced, many other variables can affect scores on a test. In this section, we discuss seven such variables.

1. *Test-taking skills.* Mastery of certain skills (e.g., appropriate allocation of time, deductive reasoning, and guessing strategies) allows respondents to more fully demonstrate mastery of test objectives.
2. *Testwiseness.* The ability to use clues in the test to obtain a higher score than deserved is referred to as testwiseness. We distinguish between test-taking skills—which allow the respondent to demonstrate the full extent of her knowledge—and testwiseness, which enables a respondent to appear as if she knows more than she really does.

3. *Response sets.* Test takers exhibit certain styles or preferences in the way they respond to tests (e.g., some people work very quickly, others slowly). Unless tests have been carefully constructed, these styles, referred to by Cronbach (1946) as *response sets*, cause people of equal ability to earn different scores.

4. *Anxiety and motivation.* Performance may be impaired by excessive anxiety or inadequate motivation.

5. *Administrative factors.* The way in which a test is administered (e.g., the extent to which cheating is allowed or the clarity of instructions) can dramatically affect scores.

6. *Coaching and practice.* Coaching (e.g., special practice sessions) can substantially affect test scores.

7. *Test bias.* The degree to which a test is biased (i.e., constructed in a way that some people have an unfair advantage over others) may cause some people to do more poorly than others.

Test-taking Skills

Taking tests requires certain skills and behaviors generally not acquired unless specifically taught or learned through extensive practice. If students are unskilled at the types of behaviors required during test taking, their scores will be lower than they deserve to be.

Selecting the "Best" Answer

In many tests students are asked to select the "best" answer. If students have not been taught to think this way about test items, they may have mastered the content being tested and still select an incorrect answer. For example, Taylor, White, Bush, and Friedman (1982) interviewed children who had answered standardized achievement test items incorrectly to determine *why* they had selected the wrong answer. Examples of two items, with the student's explanation in italics are shown in Figure 8.2. Unfortunately, a student may understand the concept and still give an incorrect answer. For example, on the right side of Figure 8.2, the respondent understood that since the cactus and flower were still growing, they would have continued need for water, whereas the cabbage head would only need water one time during washing. Someone with better test-taking skills would have realized that even though the answer was technically correct, "cabbage" was not the desired answer.

Responding on Machine-scorable Forms

On some tests, students record their answers on machine-scorable forms which are very different from the instructional materials with which they are familiar. When the answer format is confusing or distracting, students may miss items they would otherwise get correct. Some experts (e.g., Noll, Scannel, & Craig, 1979) even suggest that separate answer sheets should never be used by students below the fourth grade.

Other special skills are associated with marking machine-scorable answer

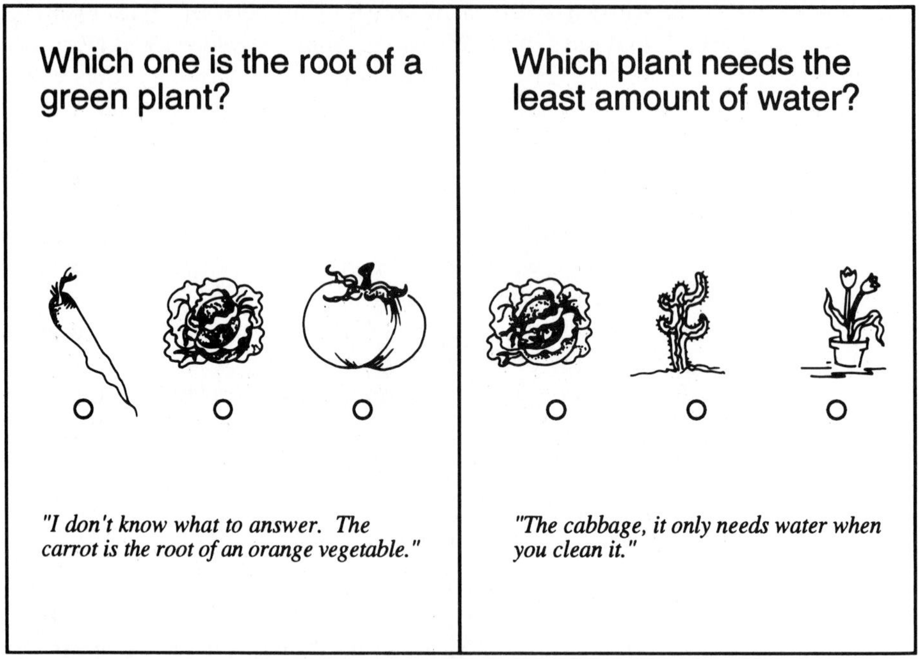

Which one is the root of a green plant?

"I don't know what to answer. The carrot is the root of an orange vegetable."

Which plant needs the least amount of water?

"The cabbage, it only needs water when you clean it."

FIGURE 8.2   Examples of Actual Standardized Test Items Where Content Has Been Mastered, But the "Best" Answer Has Been Misunderstood. Italicized Portion Indicates Explanations for Giving the Wrong Answer

SOURCE: Taylor et al., 1982.

sheets. For example, if the "bubble" is not filled in enough, it will not be scored by the optical scanning machine. Many people do not realize, however, that only one-third of the bubble needs to be darkened. Some students spend so much time carefully filling in the bubble as completely as possible, they do not have time to finish the test. Such false precision can be detrimental.

Working in Highly Structured Settings with Specialized Directions and Rules

During a test, students may be asked to respond to unusual directions given in a highly structured and often unfamiliar situation. Not surprisingly, such directions are sometimes misunderstood, and students have difficulty demonstrating what they know. Consider the following item taken from a standardized achievement test:

Directions:

Read the first word; now read the words next to it. Find the word that can be added to the first word that makes ANOTHER word. Fill in the space that goes with the answer you choose.

1. Air   land   port   road   wing

                     0   0   0   0

The correct answer, of course, is *port,* because *air* and *port* form the single word *airport.* However, a third grade student who has never been exposed to this type of item might have good mastery of compound words and still be confused about how to respond.

Students may also be confused by the setting in which the test is administered. For example, during testing students are generally seated in straight rows with desks that are not touching. They frequently cannot have directions repeated, cannot obtain assistance from their teacher, and are not free to move about the room. In some ways, standardized testing requires behavior that is exactly opposite from that for which students are usually rewarded. This reversal can be disorienting, and can interfere with performance.

Performing under Time Limits

In most educational settings we want students to understand exactly what is expected of them, and to have adequate time to complete a task as well as they can. Some test taking is different. For example, in most standardized tests directions are given only once, and there is a specified amount of time to perform the task. Students not accustomed to performing in such settings may become flustered and not perform well.

Following Advice to Guess

Consider the following excerpt from the instructions for a commercially available standardized achievement test:

> There may be some items that you cannot do. If you are not sure of an answer, choose the answer you think is right or skip that item and go to the next one.

This instruction is advising students to guess if they do not know the right answer. Similar directions are contained in most standardized achievement tests, and were a part of the procedures during the norming process. Students will substantially improve their scores if they can eliminate one or more obviously wrong answers and make their best guess from among the remaining alternatives. Appropriate guessing is a valuable test-taking skill, and the results of tests where students systematically eliminate options, and guess appropriately are more indicative of a student's true ability. Because they are often discouraged from guessing during regular instruction, however, some students hesitate to do so during a test.

A Test-taking Skills Summary

Taking tests in ways that demonstrate true level of mastery is a skill that must be learned. Unless students have mastered test-taking skills, their scores will probably not be a valid indicator of what the test purports to measure. Lack of such skills can be exhibited in many ways, but in general, a student with poor test-taking skills will:

- Read too quickly
- Miss important words
- Jump to conclusions
- Make random guesses
- Be confused by different answer formats
- Have difficulty adjusting to the structured setting of a test
- Not understand the concept of "best answer"

A student who has good test-taking skills has learned to:

- Underline important words (where permissible)
- Analyze items systematically
- Guess (after eliminating unreasonable options)
- Pace herself during the test
- Skip difficult items and return if time permits
- Make sure she understands all directions

One way to recognize test-taking skills in your students is to be familiar with the tests you administer and analyze the skills *you* would need to be successful. Then make sure you have taught those skills to students before administering the test.

APPLICATION PROBLEM #1

A first-year teacher comes to you for some advice about testing. It seems that she has several students who race through tests, do not appear to be carefully considering possible options to items, and then disrupt the rest of the class because they are finished early and have nothing to do. What advice would you give her?

Testwiseness

It is important to differentiate between test-taking skills and testwiseness. The concept of testwiseness has been discussed extensively for over forty years (see Evans, 1984; Millman, Bishop, & Ebel, 1965; and Thorndike, 1951). Millman and his colleagues defined testwiseness as, "a subject's capacity to utilize the characteristics and formats of the test and/or the test-taking situation to receive a high score (1965, p. 707)." The testwise student will frequently

- Identify common elements between the stem and any of the options. (Remember the example with *pasteurized* and Louis *Pasteur* in Chapter 5.)

- Recognize and use clues from grammatical construction, such as subject-verb agreement.
- Learn the test constructor's tendency to use certain response positions more—or less—frequently, for example a tendency for option *c* to be the correct answer on multiple-choice tests.
- Select the longest option in the absence of any knowledge about a multiple-choice item.
- Avoid options that use such absolutes as *never* and *always*.
- Use clues from one item to answer another item.

Figure 8.3 gives several examples of items in which testwiseness will lead the student to the correct option even without any knowledge of the content being tested. As you can see, a testwise student can use many extraneous clues to obtain a higher score than she deserves.

The primary difference between test-taking skill and testwiseness is that the former allows the respondent to demonstrate her true level of knowledge, while the latter allows her to take advantage of extraneous clues to obtain a score higher than she deserves. Test-taking skills increase the validity of a test because they allow the test to more precisely measure what it is designed to measure. In contrast, testwiseness reduces test validity, because a student's score may reflect factors other than those the test is designed to measure (Messick, 1982).[1]

To what degree is testwiseness a problem, and how can it be corrected? The literature is not clear. Numerous researchers have claimed success in teaching testwiseness skills (e.g., Bajtelsmit, 1977; McMorris, Brown, Snyder, & Pruzek, 1972; Moore, Schutz, & Baker, 1966); others have been unsuccessful (e.g., Board & Whitney, 1977; Dolly & Williams, 1983); and some suggest that before students can profitably apply testwiseness skills, they must first possess knowledge about the content area being measured by the questions (Rogers & Bateson, 1991). In an extensive review of the literature on testwiseness, Scruggs, White, and Bennion (1986) concluded that training in testwiseness has little, if any, effect on achievement test scores of most students, even though it has substantial effect on measures of testwiseness and some effect on reducing test anxiety.

How often are poorly constructed items a factor? Tests that are not carefully developed often have such problems (Gullickson & Ellwein, 1985; Stiggins, Conklin, & Bridgeford, 1986). However, for standardized achievement tests, it is probably not a serious problem. While earlier studies (Metfessel & Sax, 1958) found that standardized tests contained many problems that would allow testwise respondents to use extraneous clues in raising their scores, Messick (1982) concluded in a later analysis that testwiseness was "rarely [a] demonstrable problem with professionally developed tests." The change may be due to the attention that testwiseness has received in recent years.

---

[1] It is important to note that it is impossible for a testwise student to take unfair advantage of a test unless inappropriate clues are present. The best way to avoid the effects of testwiseness is to only use well-written tests.

ITEM	EXPLANATION OF TESTWISENESS CLUE
The muscular system is made up of: ○ a) bones *(16.7%)* ○ b) muscles *(75.0%)* ○ c) fatty tissue *(4.2%)* ○ d) blood vessels *(4.2%)*	The words "muscular" in the stem, and "muscles" in the option are obviously related.
The stretch of land between two mountains is called a: ○ a) hill *(16.7%)* ○ b) river *(12.5%)* ○ c) mound *(12.5%)* ○ d) valley *(58.3%)*	If the answer refers to land "between two mountains," then it cannot be a hill or a mound since those are similar to mountains. A river is not a stretch of land. So without knowing the word *valley*, the student can select the correct answer by a process of elimination.
The number of miles from the earth to the moon is less than: ○ a) 225,000 *(16.7%)* ○ b) 240,000 *(12.5%)* ○ c) 245,000 *(12.5%)* ○ d) 250,000 *(58.3%)*	Since the question asks for a distance which is "less than," the largest number has to be technically correct, even if it isn't what the item writer intended.
The Susan B. Anthony dollar honors: ○ a) one of our founding fathers *(29.2%)* ○ b) a leader of the suffragette movement *(16.7%)* ○ c) a famous baseball player *(16.7%)* ○ d) the husband of Betsy Ross *(37.5%)*	Susan is a woman's name, and three of the options obviously refer to men. Therefore, without even knowing what "suffragette" means, a testwise person would see that it's the only answer left.
Dwight Eisenhower: ○ a) was a general during World War II *(57.1%)* ○ b) astronaut *(19.0%)* ○ c) of Russia *(9.5%)* ○ d) in the United States *(14.3%)*	Only option (a) fits grammatically with this stem.

NOTE: Numbers in parentheses indicate the percentage of over 700 second and third grade students who selected each option in a project conducted by White et al., 1982. As can be seen, all of the options are attractive choices for some students.

FIGURE 8.3 Examples of Items That Can Be Answered Using Testwiseness Clues Even If Student Has No Knowledge of the Content

Response Sets

Suppose you had a student who, when she did not know the correct answer, always selected the "true" option. She would do better than she deserved on tests constructed by a teacher who tended to write items that were true, and not as well as she deserved on tests written by a teacher who tended to write false items.

Such behavior is referred to as a *response set*. Response sets are tendencies to respond in consistent ways on tests and may be related to the types of options chosen, the speed with which work is done, or the probability of guessing when the correct answer is not known. The existence of response sets has been recognized and researched for almost fifty years. Three types of response sets are most relevant to our purposes here: (1) the speed versus accuracy response set, (2) the gambling response set, and (3) response sets related to item construction.

The Speed versus Accuracy Response Set

Some people work very quickly, writing down the first answer that comes to mind when they take a multiple-choice test. Other people ponder the pros and cons of each option and move deliberately from item to item. What is the relationship between ability and the speed with which a person completes test items?

Suppose Suzanne can do math problems faster than Linda. Does that mean that Suzanne knows how to do math *better* than Linda? Is Linda's slower pace attributable to less knowledge of math, a personality factor that results in her working more deliberately, or the way in which instruction has been delivered? If a test is supposed to be a test of math ability, it would be misleading if personality or response style factors affected test scores.

The importance of this response set is indicated by the fact that many standardized tests have time limits that prevent some students from finishing (Boag & Neild, 1962; Kahn 1968). Consequently, students who work quickly have an unfair advantage over those who are more deliberate. If slowness in completing a test is caused by lack of knowledge, then the lower score is justified; but if the slowness merely reflects extra care, then the lower score is an inadequate measure.

Some tests measure educational objectives for which speed is important (e.g., typing). A speed component makes sense for such tests, but all other tests should be constructed so that the vast majority of well-motivated students are able to complete them. Obviously, it is impossible to control for stragglers who refuse to focus their attention, but, if a test is constructed so that all conscientious students have enough time, that test is more likely to measure what it was designed to measure.[2]

A great deal of research shows that the correlation between measured ability and the rate at which tests are completed is very low (e.g., Ebel 1954; Hopkins, 1964; Tate, 1948). Even when item content is made extremely easy so that lack of knowledge should not be a factor, research reveals that some respondents will

---

[2] Tests in which part of the objective is to see how quickly students can complete the items are referred to by psychometricians as *speeded* tests. Tests where mastery of the learning objective is the only important criterion are referred to as *power* tests. Most educational tests should be designed as power tests to reduce the irrelevant influence of speed.

work much slower than others (e.g., Bennett & Doppelt, 1956). These findings reinforce the notion that the speed with which items are completed is partly a personality factor rather than a reflection of knowledge and skill.

Since most tests for classroom use are achievement tests, teachers should be sure that, wherever possible, speed of completion is not a factor. Of course, on standardized achievement tests with prescribed time limits, the amount of time cannot be changed. In such cases, you should make sure that the students understand the time limits and know how to pace themselves so that they have adequate time to complete the test.

The Gambling or Guessing Response Set

Some people are risk takers, others are not. In taking multiple-choice or true-false tests, some people are more willing to guess when they are not sure of an answer, while others are more likely to leave the response blank. To understand the effect of such behavior, referred to as the *gambling response set*, consider two students—Harriette, who is a gambler, and Emily, who is not. Assume that both students know the answers to exactly half the questions on a 100-item true-false test. Harriette guesses on every item she does not know, while Emily omits them. Harriette gets 75 percent correct, while Emily gets 50 percent correct. Even though both students "know" exactly the same amount, their scores are radically different.

The gambling response set would not be a problem if everyone were equally likely to guess, but individuals differ markedly and these differences are consistent over time (Slakter, 1969). Further, such differences are unrelated to ability (Crocker & Benson, 1976). A number of scoring techniques have been developed, however, to correct for the effects of such differences in scores.

Scoring Procedures to Correct for Effects of Guessing. The most frequently used formula to adjust scores for the effects of guessing is:

$$S = R - \frac{W}{N - 1}$$

Where S = the respondent's score corrected for guessing

R = the number of right responses marked by the respondent

W = the number of wrong responses, not including omitted items

N = the number of options for each item which are equally

likely to be chosen if the respondent guesses blindly.

The preceding formula is viewed by some as negative because it appears to punish students for guessing. An alternative formula (Traub, Hambleton, & Singh, 1968) supposedly has a better psychological effect on students because it "rewards" them for omitting items that they do not know. This formula is

$$S = R + \frac{O}{N}$$

Where S and R and N are defined as before and O = the number of omitted items. Even though the two formulas will yield scores that differ in average value and variability, they will correlate perfectly. Hence, the effects will be exactly the same. To demonstrate the effects of each formula, consider the results for Harriette and Emily shown in Table 8.1.

The correction based on number of wrong responses has the advantage of being logically more understandable, since it is closer to the hypothetical true score. The lack of logic with the correction score based on omitted items is demonstrated by the fact that a person who omitted all 100 items on this true-false test would still receive a score of 50. Nevertheless, with respect to students' relative ranking, the results are identical.

Other techniques proposed to correct for guessing include elimination scoring, answer until correct methods, and confidence scoring. We will not discuss these techniques here, however, because the evidence concerning their efficacy suggests that they are not sufficiently useful to warrant the increased complexity of procedures and extra testing time required. Until further evidence appears, we do not propose them for classroom use.

Summary of Research on Corrections for Guessing.   At first glance it seems logical that correction for guessing would improve test validity. Before reaching such a conclusion consider the following considerations from past research.

- *Not everyone is equally likely to guess.* Correction-for-guessing formulas assume that everyone is equally likely to guess. This is clearly untrue. In fact, Wood (1976) concluded that even directions designed to discourage guessing affected students differentially, with less able students paying less attention to such directions than more able students.
- *There are very few instances of totally "blind" guessing.* Correction-for-

TABLE 8.1   Scores for a Gambler and Nongambler under Different Assumptions about Correcting for Guessing

	Harriette the Gambler	Emily the Nongambler
True knowledge of 100 T-F items.	50	50
Score on test where Harriette guesses for 50 items she does not know; Emily omits 50 items she does not know.	75	50
Score corrected for guessing based on wrong responses.	50 [75 − (25 ÷ 1) = 50]	50 [50 − (0 ÷ 1) = 50]
Score corrected for guessing based on omitted items.	75 [75 + (0 ÷ 2) = 75]	75 [50 + (50 ÷ 2) = 75]

guessing formulas assume that each response on a multiple-choice test is equally likely to be chosen. Because respondents possess partial knowledge about most items, there are very few instances of totally "blind" guessing. Several research studies have documented that guessing improves scores over pure chance, even on items for which students claim absolutely no knowledge (Cross & Frary, 1977). As Cureton (1971) notes, if a respondent has a hunch, she will do well to play it, because hunches are often right.

- *The probability of obtaining a reasonably good score on a cognitive test as a result of guessing is extremely small.* As Hopkins, Stanley, and Hopkins (1990) point out, 68 percent of the students taking a 100-item true-false test about which they had absolutely no knowledge would score between 45 and 55, and 98 percent of the students would score between 40 and 60. Only about one respondent in 1,000 would score 65 or higher by chance alone, and the chances of getting 75 or more of the 100 items correct is less than one in three million.

- *Corrected scores rank students in the same order as uncorrected scores.* Depending on the number of items omitted, corrected scores can be either slightly more reliable and valid, or slightly less reliable and valid (Ebel, 1979), but the differences are usually trivial. The correlation between corrected and uncorrected scores is generally in the high .90s, and the relative ranking of students is virtually identical. Thus, for norm-referenced applications, corrections for guessing offer few advantages. For criterion-referenced applications, the corrected score may be closer to the true score *if* the correction formula is based on number of wrong answers, but the instructor will not know which of the objectives were achieved by guessing and which were achieved through knowledge.

- *Corrections for guessing do not eliminate the effects of chance.* Some people believe that corrections for guessing will eliminate the effects of luck. Unfortunately, corrections for guessing have no bearing on the probabilities of guessing correctly. Whenever students guess, some will be luckier than others and those odds are controlled purely by the mathematics of probability.

In most cases, there is little to be gained by the application of corrections for guessing. Unless some students omit many items and others omit very few, the ranking of students' corrected scores will be the same as their uncorrected scores. All students should be encouraged to guess when they are not sure of the answer. This is similar to the instructions given in virtually all standardized achievement tests, and it would be well to follow this advice in locally developed tests.

APPLICATION PROBLEM #2

Imagine you have prepared a 40-item multiple choice test with five options per question. Listed below are scores for three students in your class. Indicate what corrected scores would be for (1) a correction based on wrong answers, and (2) a correction based on omitted questions.

Student Name	Number of Correct Answers	Number of Wrong Answers	Number of Omissions	Corrected Scores Based on	
				Wrong Answers	*Omissions*
Diana	30	10	0		
Susan	30	5	5		
Vicky	30	0	10		

Response Sets Related to Item Construction

Some people behave predictably in the way they write test items and some are predictable about the way they respond to items. To the degree that these styles of item writing and item responding correspond or conflict, test scores might be higher or lower than they deserve to be. Consider several examples.

- *The Acquiescence Set*: Respondents are more likely to select the option designated as "true" when they are uncertain (e.g., Gustav, 1963). Some instructors have a tendency to include more true than false items on their tests (e.g., Metfessel & Sax 1958). In those cases where there is a match, students will receive undeserved credit.

- *The Positional Preference Set*: Metfessel and Sax (1958) found that many standardized achievement tests have fewer than expected correct answers for the initial and final options of multiple-choice tests. Guilford (1965) concluded that, "When examinees are ignorant of an answer to an item, their habits of taking tests are such that they do not choose among the alternatives entirely at random" (p. 490). Thus, students may receive undeserved credit when their style of responding matches the style of the person who wrote the items. More recent research (e.g., Ace & Dawis, 1973; Jessell & Sullins, 1975) has found little, if any, effect of a positional preference set, so the problem may be more apparent than real.

- *The Option Length Set*: Several researchers (Dolly & Williams, 1983; Evans, 1984) have found a tendency for the longest option on multiple-choice tests to be the correct option more often than expected, and a tendency for some test takers to choose the longest option more frequently when they do not know the answer.

All of the response sets associated with item construction can be neutralized by good item construction. The option length set can easily be offset by inserting several long, incorrect options. The acquiescence set can be neutralized by making sure that there are an equal number of true and false answers. The positional preference set can be counteracted by making sure that correct answers in a multiple-choice test appear in each position (e.g., *a, b, c,* and *d*) an equal number of times in random order.

Anxiety and Motivation

We will use *motivation* to describe students' desire to perform as best they can. *Anxiety* will be used to describe students' feelings of uneasiness, or even fear of testing situations. Motivation and anxiety can both influence test performance and it is worthwhile to examine briefly how each operates, and how they interact.

The Impact of Motivation on Test Performance

An interesting example of how motivation affects test scores appeared in the Washington Post (see Figure 8.4). From this article, it is clear that a test will not accurately reflect what students know unless they are motivated to do their best. Ideally, respondents will be motivated to succeed in test situations because they understand how the test score will affect them. However, motivation has been shown to differ substantially among various ethnic and socioeconomic groups (Anastasi, 1958).

The effects of differential motivation have been examined extensively. For example, Taylor (1981) identified eighteen studies in which various rewards (e.g., money, candy, praise) were used to enhance students' motivation to do well on tests. Taylor found that highly motivated students performed substantially higher on standardized tests than poorly motivated students (for examples of this research see Clingman & Fowler, 1976; Maller & Zubin, 1932; Sweet & Ringness, 1971; Taylor & White, 1982; Weiss, 1980).

The Impact of Anxiety on Test Performance

Students who become *overly* motivated to do well on a test may become anxious. Dozens of research studies have examined the relationship between anxiety and test performance (see Sarason, 1980, and Tobias, 1984, for reviews of this research). Although some have found moderately large negative correlations (e.g., Hill, 1984), most of this research is consistent in showing a small negative correlation between anxiety and performance on cognitive tests. The specific nature of the relationship between anxiety and test performance is still the subject of ongoing debate.

According to some, test anxiety interferes with the student's ability to recall information learned previously (Hill & Wigfield, 1984; Wine, 1971). A conflicting explanation suggests that students who experience high test anxiety are those with deficient study or test-taking skills (Culler & Holahan, 1980; Kirkland & Hollandsworth, 1979). In fact, Kirkland and Hollandsworth (1980, p. 438) suggest that the concept of *test anxiety* should be replaced with the phrase *ineffective test taking*.

Unfortunately, research has not yet been able to pinpoint whether test anxiety depresses test scores, or whether inadequate test-taking skills result in poor performance on tests—which in turn generates high anxiety. Several experiments have been done to manipulate levels of anxiety in an effort to see how it affects test scores. Thus far, the evidence has failed to support the hypothesis that experimentally induced anxiety depresses test scores. It is clear that students who suffer high test anxiety tend to have poorer study habits and test-taking skills than other

Students Flunk Test
To Score a Point

By Katharine Macdonald
Special to The Washington Post

LOS ANGELES, April 2--You might say that the speed bumps in the parking lot at Chico High School cost $66,000. And they weren't even installed by a Defense Department contractor. In fact, it wasn't putting them in that was so expensive--it was not taking them out. That and a couple of other things. But the story is getting ahead of itself.

Chico is a small town some 90 miles north of Sacramento, where this story began more than a year ago. It was in Sacramento that the state legislature passed a package of education reforms, one of which was the California Assessment Program (CAP).

CAP is an incentive (the word "incentive" is the key) program that grants $66,000 to any state high school that annually tests 93 percent of its graduating seniors in reading, written expression, mathematics and spelling, and shows an improvement in each year's scores.

Now to Chico, and the part about incentive. It shows how smart the kids at Chico High are, even if most of them did score somewhere in the moron percentile on the CAP test.

The seniors at Chico knew about the $66,000 the school would get if they did well on the test. They also knew that if they didn't do well on the test, it would not affect their own grades or college admissions.

So, in the words of school superintendent Robert Jeffries, "They offered to negotiate."

According to principal Roger Williams, the four "ringleaders" have good academic records. This was the deal they offered: We take your test, we do well. We earn you $66,000. For our efforts we want some things. We want the speed bumps taken out of the parking lot. We want to smoke on campus. And we want a senior class trip to Santa Cruz.

What's a school to do? They said "no," of course. And then took some precautions. Before forwarding the CAP tests to the state, Chico High pulled the tests taken by the four student ringleaders. Maybe they didn't know about the leaflets the four had circulated on campus, urging all 333 seniors to fail the test.

Two weeks ago, Chico High School got the test results. It had dropped from the top third of the state's high schools to the bottom third. The overall percentile ranking had dropped from 70 percent to somewhere in the teens. In one subject category, Chico High's scores had plummeted from 73 percent to 2 percent. Suddenly, Chico High was $66,000 poorer.

Principal Williams said the four ringleaders were "reprimanded" last week after the scores were revealed but that they reacted with "indifference."

Some might think these high school seniors selfish and inflexible, with petty demands. But Kevin Turcotte, the reporter for the Chico Enterprise-Record who first reported the story, says it is not true that the students demanded the speed bumps be removed from the parking lot--just lowered.

FIGURE 8.4 An Example of How Motivation Can Affect Test Scores

SOURCE: Katherine MacDonald, "Students Flunk Test to Score a Point." *The Washington Post*, April 3, 1985, p. D4. Copyright © Katherine MacDonald.

students. Unfortunately, anxiety reduction techniques seldom improve test performance. Culler and Holahan concluded that research tended "to contradict the
common stereotype of the highly anxious student who knows the subject matter
but 'freezes up' at test time" (1980, p. 18). There are studies which show that test
scores can be improved by changing variables that are logically related to lower
levels of anxiety (e.g., Hill, 1984), but these studies do not demonstrate a causal
link between test scores and feelings of anxiety. More definitive research is needed
before we can know just how anxiety and test performance are related. Meanwhile,
regardless of how anxiety affects test scores, we do not want to create unnecessary
anxiety in our students. The fact that motivation and anxiety are closely linked,
coupled with the fact that highly motivated students do better on tests, suggests
that tests should be administered in such a way that students know that tests are
important, and are motivated to do their best without experiencing undue anxiety.

Administrative Factors

A more complete discussion on the proper procedures for administering tests was
given in Chapter 11. From that material it is clear that improper test administration
is a frequently encountered extraneous variable that can pollute test scores.

Examiner Effects

A great deal of research has examined the relationship between administrator
characteristics and test performance. Some people have claimed that performance
on cognitive tests is maximized if the race of the examiner and race of the student
are the same (e.g., Abramson, 1969), but others disagree (Graziano, Varca, &
Levy, 1982). It does appear that having the test administered by an examiner with
whom students feel comfortable often results in substantially higher test scores
(Fuchs & Fuchs, 1986).

In most classroom testing situations, the race of the examiner is not easily
changed, but there are many ways in which the administrator can establish rapport
and make sure that students know what is expected and feel comfortable with the
environment. Many other variables related to examiners have been investigated
relatively infrequently, and more research is needed. For the time being, we suggest making sure that the test is administered by someone with whom the students
feel comfortable, concentrating on clarity of directions, the enthusiasm displayed,
and the procedures used to monitor and support students during the test.

Advance Notice

Some educators argue that it is preferable to announce tests well in advance so
that students will be motivated to study. They point out that unannounced quizzes
and tests often increase student anxiety. Available research suggests, however,
that advance notice has no real impact on test performance. It does appear, however, that students who are given unannounced quizzes are more anxious and
dissatisfied with the course. Since there is no evidence that unannounced quizzes
improve performance, it seems reasonable to provide students with as much advance notice about testing as possible.

Disturbances and Interruptions

Disturbances and interruptions during test taking should be minimized. This suggestion is based largely on logic, since research has not demonstrated a significant effect attributable to minor disturbances and interruptions during test taking (e.g., Super, Braasch, & Shay, 1947; Ingle & de Amico, 1969). Nonetheless, minimizing disturbances and interruptions seems only common sense.

Cheating

Most tests are designed to measure what individual students know, not how well they use their neighbors or other sources of information during the test. Unfortunately, cheating appears quite widespread. Zastrow (1970) found a 40 percent incidence of cheating among graduate students, and Cornehlsen (1965) found that almost half of high school students felt that cheating was justified when it meant the difference between success and failure. Valid testing requires that opportunities for cheating be minimized, and that testing situations be appropriately controlled through conscientious monitoring and appropriate disciplinary action when cheating is discovered.

Changing Answers

A frequent misconception about testing is that students will obtain higher scores if they mark answers to multiple-choice tests based on their first impression, resisting the urge to change answers after further reflection. Research has demonstrated that this is absolutely incorrect. Although the effect of changing answers is relatively small (Mueller & Shwedel, 1975), there are consistent benefits across all types of tests (Smith, White, and Coop, 1979). Consequently, students should be encouraged to change an answer if, on reflection, they believe another answer is better.

Coaching and Practice

Aptitude tests, such as the SAT (Scholastic Aptitude Test) or the ACT (American College Test) are used extensively by colleges and universities to help make admission decisions. Recently, there has been considerable controversy about the degree to which such test scores can be raised by coaching and practice. Slack and Porter (1980) claimed that since the results of the SAT could be increased substantially by coaching programs, the results were obviously not a measure of aptitude and should not be used in admission decisions.

Such conclusions stand in stark contrast to beliefs long held by the testing community. For example, the trustees of the College Board who are responsible for the SAT stated in 1968, "The evidence so far leads us to conclude that intensive drill for the SAT . . . is at best likely to yield insignificant increases in scores" (College Entrance Examination Board, p. 8). A review conducted by researchers at the Educational Testing Service (Messick & Jungeblut, 1981) concluded that most studies on the effects of coaching for the SAT were methodologically flawed, but that when the best evidence was considered, the coaching time required to boost average test scores more than 20 or 30 points (on a 200- to 800-point scale) approached that of full-time schooling, and that students' time could be spent more productively in school rather than being coached.

One problem with drawing conclusions about the effects of coaching is that the term may refer to any of at least three different types of experiences.

1. Formalized coaching classes that provide opportunities for students to practice items similar to those on the test as well as offering instruction about strategies for taking the test.

2. Test familiarization booklets, which are completed independently and provide information similar to that offered in coaching clinics but in an independent study format.

3. Controlled practice, wherein students complete parallel or identical forms of the tests in order to improve their scores.[3]

Furthermore, much of the research has been conducted by persons with a vested interest in the outcome—either those who have developed and who administer the aptitude tests, or those who operate commercially available coaching clinics. Payne concluded that "it is very difficult to prepare a student for a particular secure test if training involves primarily the examination of old test items. If, however, coaching involves a more elaborate and broadly-based educational experience whereby academic skills are, in fact, taught, the likelihood of increasing test scores is improved" (1982). Pike (1978) claimed that short coaching programs (one to six hours) resulted in gains of about 10 points on the SAT (.10 standard deviations), whereas intermediate length programs (fifty hours) resulted in gains of 20 to 25 points on the SAT. Alderman and Powers (1980) report average gains of only 8 points as a result of a secondary school course designed to improve SAT verbal scores. Such findings fall far short of the results claimed by commercially available coaching clinics (Conroy, 1987; Sesnowitz, Bernhardt, & Knain, 1982), but there is not sufficient evidence to support either position.

In their review of 23 different studies of the effects of practice on aptitude tests (mostly IQ tests), Kulik, Kulik, and Bangert (1984) found gains of .25 of a standard deviation for a single-practice trial on an alternate form of the measure, and gains up to .67 of a standard deviation resulting from five or six practice sessions on parallel forms. The degree to which these results can be applied to SAT/ACT types of tests is unclear.

The existing research does not invite definitive conclusions about the results of coaching. Much of it suffers from serious methodological flaws, and the better research has not been conducted with the more comprehensive coaching classes. For the time being, we believe that the summary offered by Payne in the *Encyclopedia of Educational Research* still holds.

> The crucial question here is not whether one can increase the scores, but whether the increase (1) is worth the time and financial investment, and (2) helps the student

---

[3] It is interesting to note that Educational Testing Service (ETS) recently won a lawsuit against a coaching firm for using current ETS test items as a part of controlled practice.

perform better in college. The response to both parts of the question is negative. Students might better spend their time being educated rather than coached. (1982, p. 1198)

Coaching may have significant effects for some students, but it is unlikely to dramatically change scores for most, as noted by the College Entrance Examination Board.

The Board also believes that instruction in test-taking skills may be helpful to *some* students. Such instruction is designed to ensure that students know what the test is about and how it is structured, how to make the most efficient use of time limits, how to "attack" the different kinds of questions, and when an "educated" guess using partial knowledge is sensible. Students with such skills and knowledge about test-taking are able to perform to the best of their ability. (1979, p.7)

In recent years, some school districts have begun using another type of "practice" for standardized achievement tests which may contribute to inflated and invalid test scores. Specifically, a number of commercially produced packages are now available that are ostensibly designed to teach students test-taking skills (see Mehrens & Kaminski, 1989, for a review of several of these packages). Unfortunately, the material in some of these packages is so similar to what is in the standardized achievement test for which they were designed that "it is equivalent to giving the parallel form of the test as a practice test and explaining all the answer choices to students" (Shepard, 1990, p. 19). If one wishes to draw conclusions about how much students know about a broader domain of material based on the sample of test items, the use of such "practice" material is clearly inappropriate.

Test Bias

A test is biased if "individuals from different groups who are equally able, do not have equal probabilities of success" (Anderson et al., 1980, p. 16). In Chapter 3, we introduced three different types of bias that should be considered in the construction, administration, and interpretation of tests: (1) cultural, ethnic, and linguistic test bias—in which examinees are at a disadvantage if they belong to some minority group such as Latin Americans, African Americans, or Native Americans; (2) socioeconomic bias—in which examinees are disadvantaged if they are poor; and (3) gender bias—in which either males or females are at a disadvantage.

If a test is biased, an extraneous influence is affecting the scores of one group of respondents, but not the other. Clearly, bias is a potential extraneous influence on any cognitive test. For example, if the instructions for a mathematics test include vocabulary and language that would likely be misunderstood by children from rural agricultural settings, then the test is biased against those children. Such bias would be reflected in the fact that rural children, regardless of actual math ability, would tend to receive lower scores in general than nonrural children. It is important to note, however, that the fact that one group does worse than another, does not *in itself* indicate test bias. Bias exists only if the groups are known to be *equally able*. This point has been widely misunderstood by representatives of various minority groups in recent years who have argued that test score differences between groups are sufficient to demonstrate that tests are discriminatory.[4]

Bias may be exhibited in many ways, some of them quite subtle. For example, valid test scores depend on respondents being motivated to do their best. Chapman and Hill (1971) found that some cultural groups are inherently more motivated to take tests than others. Children from groups with low levels of motivation are unlikely to perform as well as those from highly motivated groups even given equal ability.

It is important to recognize and eliminate test bias for at least two reasons. First, bias in the way tests are constructed and presented may encourage inappropriate societal norms and expectations. If the illustrations in tests always depict doctors and lawyers as males, and nurses and secretaries as females, children may assume that these roles are gender related. Second, if the instructions or items used in the test are less comprehensible to one group, that group may not perform well on the test, yet their lower performance may have nothing to do with mastery of test content.

It is clear from existing research that, although the size of the differences vary, economically disadvantaged and minority group members do obtain lower average scores on many different kinds of tests. The more important question, however, is whether members from different groups who are *equally able* have an equal probability of success. As summarized by Oakland and Parmelee, "a considerable body of literature currently exists that does not substantiate a claim of cultural bias against ethnic minority children with regard to the use of well-constructed, adequately standardized intelligence and aptitude tests" (1985, p. 717). Reynolds (1981) also concluded that cognitive tests "measure the same construct with equivalent accuracy for African Americans, whites, Latin Americans, and other native-born American ethnic minorities for both genders." Additionally, based on an extensive analysis of psychometric characteristics, predictive validity, factor analyses, and item bias characteristics, Reschly (1980) could find no evidence that professionally developed standardized tests are biased.

Jensen summarized an extremely important point about bias in mental testing when he said "by and large, current standardized tests of general mental ability and scholastic achievement, as well as many vocational aptitude tests, are not biased with respect to any native born, English speaking minority groups in the United States. . . . The fact that tests are not biased, however, does not guarantee that they will be used properly or wisely. Tests can be abused in the ways that they are used. Indeed it is much easier to find fault with the *uses* of tests than with the tests themselves" (1980, p. 715, emphasis original).

Although virtually everyone agrees that tests can be and often are misused, not everyone believes that professionally developed standardized tests are un-

---

[4] See the Summer 1987 issue of *Educational Measurement: Issues and Practice* for a thorough discussion of both sides of this issue.

biased (e.g., Harris, 1980). Whether tests are biased is not the type of question that will be resolved by research alone. It is inextricably related to issues of equity, social fairness, and opportunity, and the debate is likely to continue for a long time.

What does this mean for locally developed tests? First, it suggests that it is possible to avoid test bias of the type that allows people of equal ability to obtain different scores. How well bias is avoided depends on the item writer. Often, bias is another label for many of the extraneous variables discussed above (e.g., testwiseness or anxiety). If such extraneous variables affect members of one group more than those of another group, the test is biased. Recognizing that extraneous variables may affect members of various groups differently provides another checkpoint to consider in reviewing tests.

EXTRANEOUS FACTORS THAT CAN INFLUENCE
THE RESULTS OF AFFECTIVE MEASURES

Until now we have focused on the extraneous variables that can pollute the interpretation of cognitive tests. Generally, when we think about assessment we think about such cognitive variables. But without attention to the social or affective variables (e.g., self-concept, friendship patterns, attitudes, values, and learning styles), instruction will be much less effective, and cognitive goals less readily attained.

To understand why the assessment of affective variables is important, consider the conclusions reached by Stiggins and his colleagues about how differently children from different cultures and ethnic backgrounds learn:

> Among Native American children, for example, direct questioning will commonly evoke silence, whether or not the child knows the answer, since assertive demonstration of knowledge is not seemly in the Indian home. . . . Black children also tend to respond to known-answer questions with silence, especially in test-like situations. . . . Hawaiian children tend to interrupt each other, co-creating narrative, a pattern that appears to some teachers as off-task and disruptive. (1986, p.11)

Personality, interactional style, motivation, and self-concept all contribute to or interfere with teaching and learning. Therefore, the assessment and incorporation of affective variables into decisions about teaching and learning is very important.

Most cognitive tests have one correct answer. However, the "correct" answer to items on affective measures such as self-concept or perceptions of school climate is whatever the respondent feels, perceives, or believes about a particular situation, activity, or behavior. Most affective measures are self-report measures, so information can only be collected about those things that respondents are able and willing to share. Consequently, there are myriad ways in which extraneous variables can affect or distort the results of such measures.

Many extraneous variables that influence scores on affective measures are similar to those we discussed in the previous section (e.g., anxiety and motivation, administrative factors, and test bias), and will not be repeated here. However, we need to describe several additional extraneous variables that are particularly problematic for affective measures.

Social Desirability

Just as with cognitive measures, some people have a tendency to respond on affective measures in predictable ways that are somewhat independent of the content of the question. One of the most frequently observed response sets with affective measures is referred to as the *social desirability* response set. Social desirability refers to the fact that some respondents will respond to items in a way they believe would be most socially appropriate, regardless of their true feelings. Suppose you lived in a town where a task force had just completed an effective campaign about the dangers associated with latch-key children, and the local PTA president wished to interview you. Suppose you were asked to respond to the following item:

If both parents are employed, it is appropriate for them to expect their six-year-old child to take care of herself when she comes home from school.

0 Strongly   0 Agree   0 Undecided   0 Disagree   0 Strongly
   Agree   Disagree

Regardless of your true feelings, you might be tempted to answer *Strongly Disagree,* given the social atmosphere in which the item was administered. If people give socially desirable answers instead of indicating how they really feel, the questionnaire will be of little value.

One of the earliest suggestions to counter the social desirability response set was made by Edwards (1957a), who developed a social desirability scale that could be embedded in whatever questionnaire was being used to assess the degree to which social desirability was affecting the respondent's answers. A number of similar scales have been proposed, the most popular being the Marlowe-Crowne Social-Desirability Scale, which has items such as the following:

0   I always try to practice what I preach.
0   I never hesitate to go out of my way to help someone in trouble.
0   I am always courteous, even to people who are disagreeable.

Obviously, most people are somewhat inconsistent in their everyday behaviors. Consequently, if a person answers *Strongly Agree* to each of these items, there is a good probability that a social desirability response set is operating. The rationale behind such measures is that if those people can be identified for whom social desirability is affecting their responses, their results can be adjusted, analyzed separately, or discarded.

Another approach is to attempt to prevent the social desirability response set from occurring in the first place by using a *forced choice* item format. This requires respondents to choose between two alternatives that are designed to be equally acceptable, as in this example:

Is it better to contribute money to

_____ The United Way
_____ A college or university of your choice

Here both options are socially desirable—so the respondent must rely on what she really believes to make a choice. Forced choice items, either positive or negative, are used widely in professionally developed affective measures. Because they are more difficult to develop and interpret than other types of items, they are less well suited to locally developed measures.

Another way to minimize the influence of social desirability is to assure respondents' anonymity, create a rapport with them, and convince them that the results of the questionnaire are important and will be more beneficial if responses are honest. In some cases, anonymity is difficult to achieve, but where it is possible, it appears that it can contribute substantially to reducing the social desirability response set.

For example, we have asked you to give us your perceptions about this book to help us improve future editions. Those perceptions are being collected in a way that your anonymity is assured. Consequently, we hope that you will be completely honest in your feedback. Telling us that the book is interesting, engaging, contains all the essential content, and has changed your life for the better will make us feel good—but it will do little to improve the practice of educational measurement and evaluation—unless, of course, those are your true feelings.

Application Problem #3

The PTA president has asked you to review a questionnaire about school climate to be administered to the sixth and seventh grades. You notice that students are required to provide their names and ask why. The president says that she wants students' names so she can see whether boys and girls, or sixth and seventh graders, feel differently. She thinks that students are accustomed to providing their names on tests so this will seem familiar to them. What is your advice about whether to ask for names?

Faking

Anastasi (1988, p. 456) noted, "As long as a subject has sufficient education to enable him to answer a personality inventory . . . he probably has the ability to alter his score appreciably in the desired direction." Because affective measures do not have one correct answer, subjects can easily fake responses to achieve desired results. For example, someone who does not want to serve on a jury might try to convince the judge that she has a preconceived bias about the defendant's guilt. Or a person interviewing for a job might lie about her work habits, initiative, and past experience. Faking occurs. How likely it is on a particular measure depends on the perceived benefits, how easy it is to do, and the willingness of the respondent to distort the truth.

As with the social desirability response set, techniques for dealing with faking have centered on either detecting its presence or attempting to prevent it. A number of standardized measures, such as the Minnesota Multi-Phasic Personality Inventory and the Kuder Occupational Interests Surveys, have special subtests, often referred to as *lie scales*, designed to detect the faker. In some cases, scores on the lie scale are used to adjust the obtained score. Unfortunately, adjustments based on lie scales are difficult and are not usually appropriate for locally developed measures.

There are alternatives, though. One is to disguise the purpose of the assessment. A questionnaire designed to investigate honesty might ask the respondent to check the number of books she had read from a list of alleged best-sellers. If the list contained several fictitious titles, which the respondent checked, there would be some doubt about her honesty. Such an approach is only applicable in certain very specific types of assessments. Even then, its practical and ethical problems should be carefully considered.

The most frequent approach to reducing faking is to convince the respondents that a truthful response is important and will not have negative effects for them personally. A guarantee of anonymity also helps. Sometimes it is possible to avoid self-report measures if respondents might be motivated to lie or try to look good. For example, instead of asking people how many traffic tickets they received during the last 12 months, it might be possible to obtain the same information from city records.

Item Omission

Leaving items blank is a frequent problem with affective measures. Hattie (1983) pointed out that such omissions may be the result of fatigue, confusion about what was being requested, or hesitancy about disclosing information. When data are missing, one might just as well not have administered the item in the first place. Here are some suggestions for increasing the probability of complete data.

- Keep assessment measures short to avoid fatigue.
- Pilot test measures to make sure they are understandable.
- Convince respondents that the information will be used appropriately.
- Protect confidences—especially where sensitive information is involved.

Problems of Interpretation

Many affective measures ask people to respond on a continuum like one of these:

Always	Usually	Sometimes	Occasionally	Never

Strongly Agree	Agree	Uncertain	Disagree	Strongly Disagree

Unfortunately, people do not interpret such words consistently. Almost fifty years ago Simpson (1944) pointed out that when asked to interpret the word *frequently*, 25 percent said it applied only to events that occurred more than 80 percent of the time, and another 25 percent said it applied to events that occurred more than 40 percent of the time. Similar discrepancies have been noted more recently by Sudman and Bradburn (1982).

Problems also exist with interpreting questions. Take the question, "Do you like school?" How much does someone have to like school to answer yes? We cannot say. A response of "yes" may mean, "Yes! It's the best thing in my life!," while another means, "Well, yes, it's tolerable." Furthermore, one respondent may be rating recess, and another may be rating math. Better item construction reduces this problem, but, it is impossible to eliminate all ambiguity with affective items.

Self-deception and Lack of Insight

Results of affective measures can only be as good as the *willingness* and *ability* of respondents to provide information. In some situations respondents might be unwilling or simply unable to provide accurate information. Very few people have totally accurate perceptions of themselves or of others. Sometimes, cultural or environmental experiences prevent someone from honestly and accurately responding to certain types of items. Or lack of insight may stem from inadequate knowledge. For example, if we asked seventh grade boys to indicate a career they would pursue, an unrealistically high number might indicate professional athletics because of their perceptions about the prestige, earning power, and probabilities of success portrayed for athletes in the media.

The Acquiescence Response Set

The tendency to agree with affective items which ask for an agree/disagree response is referred to as the *acquiescence response set*. People constructing affective measures are frequently advised to mix positively and negatively worded items to avoid the possibility that respondents will answer all items one way. Although such advice is logical, some researchers have concluded that this is not as much of a problem as has been suggested (Schriesheim & Hill, 1981). However, since it is easy to balance positive and negative items, balancing is probably wise. It is even more important to make sure items are carefully worded and respondents are motivated to provide accurate information.

GENERAL STRATEGIES FOR REDUCING
THE IMPACT OF EXTRANEOUS FACTORS

Figure 8.5 summarizes the sources of cognitive test score pollution we have discussed and the possible remedies for each; figure 8.6 provides a similar checklist for affective tests. While there are no magic solutions, test score pollution can be

Checked?	Source	Possible Remedies
	Test-taking Skills	Make sure respondents are familiar with testing format, procedures, and expectations of the test. Don't overinvest in test-taking training, however.
	Testwiseness Skills	Carefully constructed items will minimize or eliminate the effects of testwiseness skills. See specific suggestions for item construction in Chapters 9 and 10.
	Response Sets: *Speed vs. Accuracy*	All tests should be power tests instead of speeded tests unless speed of response is an essential characteristic of what is being measured (as in typing).
	Gambling Response Set	Instruct and encourage all respondents to answer <u>*every*</u> question based on their best guess. Correction formulas and complicated scoring procedures are generally not worth the effort.
	Item Construction Response Sets	Double-check items to make sure that no systematic patterns of correct answers exist (e.g., more true than false, first option or longest option correct more often than chance).
	Anxiety and Motivation	Explain importance of testing information, establish rapport, provide a comfortable testing situation, and make sure respondents know what to expect and have had experience with similar tests. Provide special attention to students with particularly high anxiety, or refer them for specialized help.
	Administration Factors	Know the test and prepare specifically for proper administration. As a test administrator, your job is to make sure students know exactly what is expected, are motivated to do their best, and have an appropriate working environment. See Chapter 11 for more detailed procedures.
	Coaching and Practice	Used primarily in conjunction with aptitude tests for secondary age students and older, coaching and practice is primarily useful for reducing anxiety and increasing self-confidence. Available evidence does not support the value of intensive courses for the purpose of increasing individual scores or enhancing test validity.
	Test Bias	Watch for students who, because of cultural, ethnic, or gender-based differences, may experience difficulty in understanding vocabulary/instructions, being motivated or responding to items; then make individual adjustments as necessary.

FIGURE 8.5 Sources and Possible Remedies of Cognitive Test Score Pollution

Checked?	Source	Possible Remedies
	Social Desirability Response Set	Forced-choice items and embedded social desirability scales are useful for professionally developed measures, but not usually for locally developed measures. Do your best to establish rapport and communicate the importance of answering honestly. Preserve anonymity when possible.
	Faking	Forced-choice items and embedded lie scales are useful for professionally developed measures, but not usually for locally developed measures. Do your best to establish rapport and communicate the importance of answering honestly. Preserve anonymity when possible.
	Problems of Interpretation	Define words and phrases that are ambiguous, use concrete examples where possible, and pilot test measures to identify sources of confusion and ambiguity.
	Self-deception/Lack of Insight	Since self-report measures are limited by the ability of respondents to report, not much can be done about this extraneous influence except to recognize that it exists and to consider it as a part of interpretation.
	Acquiescence Response Set	Although commonly considered a potential problem with self-report measures, available evidences does not support its seriousness. Balancing positively and negatively worded items is easy to do, however, and should correct any problems that do exist.
	Test-taking Skills[a]	Make sure respondents are familiar with testing format, procedures, and expectations of the test. Don't overinvest in test-taking training.
	Speed vs. Accuracy Response Set[a]	All tests should be power tests instead of speeded tests unless speed is an essential characteristic of what is being measured.
	Anxiety and Motivation[a]	Explain importance of testing information, establish rapport, provide a comfortable testing situation, and make sure respondents know what to expect and have had experience with similar tests. Provide special attention and assistance to students with particularly high anxiety.
	Administration Factors[a]	Know the test and prepare specifically for proper administration. As a test administrator, your job is to make sure students know exactly what is expected, are motivated to do their best, and have an appropriate working environment. See Chapter 11 for more detailed procedures.
	Test Bias[a]	Watch for students who, because of cultural, ethnic, or gender-based differences may experience difficulty in understanding vocabulary/instructions, being motivated, or responding to items; then make individual adjustments as necessary.

FIGURE 8.6 Sources and Possible Remedies of Affective Test Score Pollution

[a] Although primarily a problem with cognitive tests, these sources of test score pollution can also affect results on affective tests.

minimized through careful test construction, appropriate preparation of students, and correct test administration practices. Use this checklist frequently to remind yourself of extraneous factors that can influence test scores, and to plan strategies for remediation. As you can see, some sources of test score pollution are the same for affective or cognitive tests (see the last five sources listed in Figure 8.6).

Although it is important to teach basic test-taking skills to all students, it is possible to overinvest in such training. In their analysis of test-taking skills research, Scruggs and his colleagues concluded:

> Should schools pursue training in test-taking skills? Hopefully, the results of this analysis will temper some of the unfounded enthusiasm in support of training children in test-taking skills. However, it would be unwise to conclude that training is unwarranted or detrimental. Although the effects of such training are small, the investment is also relatively small, and there is tentative evidence that for particular groups of children, training in test-taking skills can have substantial effects. (1986, p. 79)

Rather than embark on a whole new curriculum of teaching test-taking skills to children, we agree with Matter and Ligon that "Preparation for standardized testing should not be an isolated part of school-wide activities, but instead should be incorporated into a year-long plan" (1984, p. 2). The incorporation of such activities should be sensible and not ignore the primary goals of schooling. For example, we decry the types of activities reported by Madaus:

> Testifying at the 1981 National Institute of Education hearing on Minimum Competency Testing, . . . [the] principal of a public school in Manhattan said that reading instruction in New York City closely resembles practice in taking tests in reading. In typical reading classes, students read commercially prepared materials made up of dozens of short paragraphs about which they then answer questions. The materials they use are designed to look exactly like the tests they will take in the spring . . . when synonyms and antonyms were dropped from a test on word comprehension, teachers promptly dropped the commercially prepared materials that stressed them. (1985a, p. 616)

If we as educators are to succeed in eliminating extraneous variables that pollute test scores, we must remember that test scores are a tool and not an end in themselves. To the degree that we keep tests in the proper perspective, and develop, administer, and interpret them in ways that minimize distortion, they can be an extremely valuable tool. Once they become an end in themselves, efforts to eliminate extraneous variables are likely to be futile.

SUGGESTED READINGS

Cole, N. S. (1981). Bias in testing. *American Psychologist, 36*, 1067–1077.
    Briefly summarizes the massive literature on bias in testing as a basis for arguing that the discussion of bias should extend beyond the psychometrics of selection, prediction, and

validity to issues about fairness in the selection process and whether tests are being used appropriately. Concludes that research on test bias has not provided answers to important social policy questions that must be decided regardless of whether tests are involved.

Dobbin, J. E. (1984). *How to take a test*. Princeton, NJ: Educational Testing Service.

Published by one of the largest developers and distributors of tests in the world, this booklet is designed to help its readers take all kinds of tests with more confidence and a greater probability of success. Written primarily for high school-aged and older students, the booklet gives advice about all aspects of test-taking from preparation, to test-taking strategies, to interpreting scores.

Jensen, A. R. (1980). *Bias in Mental Testing*. New York: The Free Press.

A comprehensive presentation of the evidence in support of the position that standardized tests of aptitude and achievement are not biased with respect to minority groups. Although the arguments presented herein are not accepted by all people, this book is *must* reading for anyone who wants to consider both sides of the arguments about bias in testing.

Messick S., & Jungeblut, A. (1981). Time and method in coaching for the SAT. *Psychological Bulletin*, *89*, 191–216.

A comprehensive review of the research on the effects of coaching for the Scholastic Aptitude Test. Although available data is fragmentary and fraught with methodological problems, the authors conclude that the best available evidence suggests that coaching is of limited utility for most people.

Paulman, R. G., & Kennelly, K. J. (1984). Test anxiety and ineffective test-taking: Different names, same construct? *Journal of Educational Psychology*, *76*, 279–288.

Following a brief review of the research literature on test anxiety, the authors describe a study designed to determine whether test anxiety is any different from ineffective test taking skills. This is a readable and interesting example of how research can be used to help answer very complex questions about cognitive behavior.

SELF-CHECK QUIZ

For each of the following items, select the one best answer.

1. The presence of testwiseness skills inflates scores primarily on
    a. standardized achievement tests.
    b. poorly constructed tests.
    c. diagnostic tests designed to identify discrepancies between aptitude and achievement.
    d. tests with time limits.

2. The social desirability response set refers to the
    a. need to protect test takers' right to privacy.
    b. difficulty of gathering information about sensitive topics.
    c. fact that most people score near the middle of the distribution on cognitive tests.
    d. tendency of people to give answers consistent with societal expectations.

3. According to current research, test bias
    a. is a problem with children before but not after the sixth grade.
    b. is so serious that test scores should never be used to compare children from different ethnic groups.
    c. has ceased to be a problem because of computerized scoring.
    d. is not a serious problem with most professionally developed standardized tests.

4. Students who change answers on multiple-choice achievement tests
   a. will, on the average, increase their scores.
   b. are not following good test-taking practices.
   c. probably suffer from unusually high anxiety about tests.
   d. are exhibiting the acquiescence response set.

5. Which of the following conclusions is best supported by research on the practice of correcting scores for guessing?
   a. The corrected scores generally rank the students in a different order than the uncorrected scores.
   b. Most guessing is "blind" or random guessing.
   c. Some students are more likely to guess than others.
   d. The corrected scores eliminate the effects of chance.

6. If students have mastered the material being tested, the way in which a standardized test is administered
   a. can still have a substantial effect on test scores.
   b. has little if any effect on test scores.
   c. is important only for children younger than third grade.
   d. is not important for tests of math and science because the content is so concrete.

7. Which of the following is most useful in minimizing faking on locally developed affective measures?
   a. Embedding a lie scale and adjusting scores
   b. Using all forced-choice items
   c. Have respondents complete the measure anonymously
   d. Rewarding respondents (e.g., with money, privileges, candy) if they answer honestly

8. A good way to reduce the effects of the acquiescence response set in affective measures is by
   a. convincing respondents that the information will be used appropriately.
   b. keeping assessment measures short to avoid fatigue.
   c. mixing positively and negatively worded items in a balanced manner.
   d. pilot testing measures to make sure they are understandable.
   e. protecting confidences, especially where sensitive information is involved.

9. Coaching for standardized aptitude tests such as the SAT and ACT
   a. has seriously impaired the validity of these tests.
   b. is primarily effective for minority group students.
   c. improves the predictive validity of the tests.
   d. generally has only minor effects on scores.

10. Teaching children test-taking skills for standardized achievement tests
    a. is beneficial only if it is done the day before the test.
    b. often interferes with students' ability to demonstrate what they know.
    c. is contrary to standardized testing procedures.
    d. is a good idea no matter when it is done.

SUGGESTION SHEET

If your name starts with the letter *H*, please complete the suggestion sheet at the end of the book while this chapter is still fresh in your mind.

ANSWERS TO APPLICATION PROBLEMS

#1

Except where prohibited on standardized tests, time limits should be established so that everyone who tries has time to complete all items. Some people tend to complete tests quickly, others are slow. This is referred to as the speed versus accuracy response set. The speed with which someone finishes the test is generally unrelated to test scores, but it is important that respondents take time to read and consider every option. If students complete the test early they should be encouraged to review their answers and change those where they think a different answer would be better. If there is still time they should be monitored so they do not disturb other students. Instruction before the next test for the class on how to pace themselves during the test may be helpful.

#2

We will use the information given in Application Problem #2 with the formula below:

Formula for correction based on wrong answers $S = R - \dfrac{W}{N-1}$

Formula for correction based on omitted items $S = R + \dfrac{0}{N}$

The computations from these formulas result in the following scores:

Student Name	Number of Correct Answers	Number of Wrong Answers	Number of Omissions	Corrected Scores Based on Wrong Answers	Omissions
Diana	30	10	0	27½	30
Susan	30	5	5	28¾	31
Vicky	30	0	10	30	32

As shown, the rank order of corrected scores is the same for either formula. However, the rank order of either corrected score is different from the uncorrected scores because the number of items omitted by each student is substantially different. It is important to remember that correction formulas are usually not worth the bother unless some students omit a substantial number of items.

#3

On this type of a questionnaire there will be a tendency for students to give the answers they think teachers and administrators want to hear. Particularly if respondents are identified by name, there may be personal benefit to giving answers that teachers want. Therefore, it makes more sense to make responses anonymous and make sure that students understand the purpose of the questionnaire. Also, make sure the students are convinced their concerns will be carefully considered and appropriate action taken. To see if boys and girls or sixth and seventh graders respond differently you can include several demographic items on the questionnaire in a way that does not threaten anonymity.

SECTION THREE

Constructing New Measures: Learning to Use a Blueprint

As we suggested in Section One, there is great wisdom in using available measures—*if* such measures will serve your needs satisfactorily. However, sometimes existing measures just won't work. And while it is important not to waste time recreating the wheel, it is even more important not to use wheels designed for someone else's vehicle. In this section, we suggest ways of knowing when you are better off developing your own measures. We also cover ways of ensuring high quality in the measures you develop and using locally developed measures effectively to assess student performance. In addition, we provide some practical guidance for creating test items of various kinds.

Chapters 9 and 10 cover the why, when, and how of building your own achievement measures, including specific steps, ways of using a test blueprint, and ways of writing various types of achievement test items—among them, multiple choice, true-false, matching, short-answer, and essay items.

Chapter 11 extends this topic by describing procedures for assembling and administering tests effectively. We also discuss how you can evaluate and improve your own achievement tests by use of simple item analyses procedures.

Chapter 12 provides practical suggestions for how to develop instruments useful in collecting descriptive information. Specifically, we discuss the uses of questionnaires, interview schedules, observation scales, and other rating scales. This chapter covers ways of constructing and using those instruments, warns of some problems you might encounter along the way, and suggests ways to resolve those problems.

Chapter 13 directs your attention to measures of attitudes, interests, and values—indices of how students feel about school and about a multitude of other things. We include these kinds of measures in this section (rather than the following one in which other various kinds of existing measures are described), because attitude measures are often developed locally. We show how the most common type of attitude scale is developed, provide examples of some typical attitude measures, and indicate how to judge the acceptability of such instruments. Vocational and other interest measures are similarly discussed.

Chapter 14 teaches you how to translate achievement test scores into grades or other statements of student performance while maintaining both the utility and equity of your grading system. This chapter also examines several purposes of grading, and examines the pros and cons of different grading systems.

Collectively, the information in these six chapters will help you become more comfortable and more competent in constructing and using the results of your own "home grown" educational measures.

CHAPTER 9

Constructing Your Own Achievement Tests— Deciding When and How to Do So

Overview

Have you ever taken a class where you thought the tests were poorly constructed, confusing, misleading, or trivial? Probably so. You may even have been responsible for constructing a few tests, and perhaps have wondered if the same criticisms could be leveled against them.

Many locally developed, classroom achievement tests are poor (Stiggins & Bridgeford, 1985), but they do not have to be. The techniques and principles that result in good tests are straightforward and easy to learn. Sadly, few teachers receive sufficient instruction or practice in item writing or test construction (Gulliksen, 1986; Stiggins, 1991) even though teachers spend substantial time constructing their own tests. Indeed, Herman and Dorr-Bremme (1982) concluded that as many as three-quarters of the assessments used in classrooms are developed by teachers. With such heavy dependence on teacher-made tests in making important day-to-day decisions about students, it is essential that teachers and other practitioners know *when* to develop their own classroom achievement measures and *how* to do so. This chapter and the next are provided to help teachers understand the why, when, and how of constructing local classroom achievement tests.

In this chapter we discuss why locally developed achievement tests are so frequently used, even though so many commercially marketed tests are available. We explain how commercial tests and locally developed tests can complement and enhance each other's value. The steps that should be followed in planning an achievement test are summarized and specific guidelines and examples are given to assure that the plans will result in a high quality test that will fulfill the purpose for which you developed it.

In Chapter 10, we turn our attention to specific steps for constructing the actual test items.

Objectives

Upon completing your study of this chapter, you will be able to

1. Describe situations in which it would be better to construct your own achievement test rather than using a commercially available test.
2. Explain the pros and cons of four different ways of adapting commercially available achievement tests for local needs.
3. Identify situations in which adaptations of commercially available achievement tests would be inappropriate.
4. Explain why it is important to clarify your instructional objectives before developing a test.
5. Give examples of instructional objectives that are overly narrow or broad.
6. Identify items representing different levels on a taxonomy of educational objectives.
7. Explain why most tests should include items from several different levels.
8. Demonstrate how a test blueprint can be used to guide the construction of a valid test.

WHY CONSTRUCT YOUR OWN ACHIEVEMENT TESTS?

Hundreds of standardized achievement tests are now commercially available. Constructed by teams of professional test developers to be consistent with the results of comprehensive analyses of the most widely used curricula, the items contained in the best standardized achievement tests are meticulously pilot-tested and repeatedly revised so that only the best items are included in the final version. Computerized scoring is capable of furnishing dozens of different reports that provide information about the objectives achieved, diagnosis of the areas in which a student is having difficulty, descriptions of a performance in relation to national and local norms, and various learning objectives. The variety and number of commercially available tests is almost overwhelming, and the quality and appeal of the best of these tests is excellent and getting better as a function of competition among test publishers.

You may ask: Why do teachers ever need to develop their own achievement tests? Surely if there are so many commercially available tests, there is probably a good one for every need, so why not let the experts develop the tests, while teachers do the teaching? There are at least six reasons why locally developed achievement tests continue to be an extremely important part of effective teaching.

1. *Relevancy:* Because commercially available tests must appeal to a broad market, they focus on the objectives and content that are most frequently present in typical schools. Locally developed achievement tests are designed and constructed by the classroom teacher, and can be tailored to the specific needs and situations in that classroom. Who knows better than the teacher the relative importance of the different concepts taught? Even the format of items in locally developed tests can be tailored to the specific classroom. At first, questions may be asked in the format used during instruction, so as not to confuse students. Later, new formats might be introduced to see how well students can generalize to other situations the information they have learned.

2. *Frequency of Administration:* Most commercially available achievement tests are designed to be given either at the beginning or end of the school year as a measure of students' overall achievement. They frequently require several hours or even days to administer. Because scoring and reporting options for such tests have been substantially improved over the last decade, the results can be very useful in diagnosing learning problems, providing information to students and parents, and helping administrators make decisions. However, teachers need information about student progress, weaknesses, and areas of mastery on a weekly or even daily basis—once or twice a year is not enough. Locally developed tests can provide current information on student performance as often as teachers care to create and administer them. Further, a local test can cover as much or as little of the curriculum as desired.

3. *Timeliness of Information:* The variety and quality of scoring and reporting formats in commercially available tests is one of their major strengths, but it is also one of the reasons that locally developed tests can be so valuable. Most commercially available tests require at least six weeks to provide the computer-generated scoring and reporting. Teachers often need information much more quickly. For example, a teacher does not want to proceed to the next unit until he is sure that most of the class has mastered the information in the previous unit. Giving a quiz on Friday afternoon can provide the information he needs to plan his instruction on Monday. Furthermore, even in a relatively short quiz, he can include more items per objective than would be available on many specific topics in most standardized achievement tests.

4. *Identification of Learner Needs:* Good teachers do not present material students have already mastered, or that is so far above their current level of

understanding that it would be confusing. Effective instruction requires knowing whether some students can go through the material at an accelerated pace while others need to go slower. Pre-instruction assessment can provide this information, but it must happen weekly or even daily to be useful. Locally developed tests can provide such information when the teacher most needs it.

5. ***Consistency with Local and State Curricula:*** Commercially available tests are designed to be consistent with the most frequently used curricula objectives and goals across the country because they need to have wide appeal. But the process of developing a *good* standardized achievement test requires several years, and the curriculum in a particular school can change dramatically in the meantime. At a single meeting the local school board may decide that the school needs a much stronger emphasis on science than it had previously. Standardized achievement tests cannot respond quickly to shifts in priorities. Furthermore, since the selection of any standardized achievement test is usually a lengthy process, committees of teachers and administrators will not want to repeat the process every year just to accommodate changing priorities. Locally developed tests can be more responsive.

6. ***More Detailed Information:*** Most standardized achievement tests provide breadth of coverage, but not depth. Where a locally developed test can have half a dozen items on a single learning objective, a standardized achievement test may have only one. Additional items can provide information about what students have mastered and what they still need to learn.

ADAPTING COMMERCIALLY AVAILABLE TESTS FOR LOCAL NEEDS

Finding an appropriate test for your needs is not necessarily a decision between purchasing an existing test or developing your own. It is also possible to adapt commercially available tests to make them more appropriate for your local needs. Discussed below are the following two different approaches:

- Customizing the scoring of standardized achievement tests
- Using existing collections of test items (often called *item banks*)

Customizing Standardized Achievement Test Scoring

When selecting a standardized achievement test, a committee usually tries to match the test objectives with the local curriculum objectives. No matter how carefully this is done, however, the match is never perfect. For example, assume that the test selected for the sixth grade measures beginning algebra skills. If the district does not teach beginning algebra skills until the seventh grade, students' test scores will be lower when compared to the national norms than they would have been had algebra been taught in sixth grade.

Because of this, some school districts use the information reported by the publisher to develop a customized report that indicates how well students did on only those items that measure objectives taught by the district (see Wilson & Hiscox, 1984, for a more detailed discussion of one way of doing this). The process requires a fair amount of work, but is conceptually quite simple.

1. Review test items to determine which ones measure objectives explicitly taught in your district. Be careful to look at the specific items and not just at the objectives listed by the publisher. Objectives are often stated in such broad terms that a match with the general objective does *not* ensure a match with individual items.
2. Include only the district objectives that are covered by at least three items. This ensures a more reliable estimate of how well students in the district have mastered that objective.
3. Using the publisher's scoring reports, develop a form on which you can indicate for each objective the average percentage of students who correctly answered the items which measure that objective.
4. Use the results for those objectives taught by your school to calculate the percentage correct for each objective and for each subtest. Subtest scores will be based only on those items that measure objectives that are taught within the district.

Customizing scoring procedures will generally be possible only for relatively large school districts. It can be valuable, but you should remember that such a procedure is only useful to determine how well students have mastered the objectives taught within the district. Furthermore, information on the reliability and validity of the original test may no longer be applicable because some of the items will have been dropped. Unless the test has been drastically shortened, the reliability of the test will probably be similar to the original, but the validity of using scores from the customized test for specific purposes is an unknown.

It's also important to emphasize that many people, including us, believe it is useful to know how students do on related material that has *not* been taught. As D. R. Green points out:

> If the students have learned fundamental skills and knowledge and understand it, they will be able to answer many questions dealing with material not directly taught . . . Since all the specifics can never be taught . . . this development is highly desirable and tests . . . should try to assess it. This can only be done by having items that ask about content not directly taught. (1983, p. 6, emphasis in original)

Using Previously Developed Item Banks

Over the years, a number of people have developed collections of individual test items referenced to particular instructional objectives. These item banks, which can be purchased or sometimes obtained at no charge, contain hundreds of items that teachers can use to assemble a customized test. Since the items are already written, test construction is rapid and efficient. The best item banks are carefully documented and referenced to specific learning objectives. For descriptions of item banks maintained by universities, private organizations, and state agencies, see Naccarato (1988).

Item banks should be used cautiously, however, for they will never be able to do all the things that are possible with teacher-made tests. For example, most of them only have two or three items per objective. In addition, many test bank items have never been tried out as part of an actual test, and, although they look good, they may not be free from technical defects and may not be as good a match for a particular objective as items you would develop yourself. Item banks can save time and help generate new ideas if used thoughtfully. Like many shortcuts, however, they can be counterproductive if used indiscriminately.

Never Borrow Items from Standardized Tests

Although it may be tempting, *never* borrow items from commercially marketed achievement tests. Such items are protected by copyright and their unauthorized use is against the law. Furthermore, since they were designed to be used as a part of a total test, they may function very differently when embedded in another test. Standardized tests are not like test banks from which you can pick and choose, and should not be used in this way.

CONSTRUCTING AND USING LOCAL ACHIEVEMENT TESTS

It has been observed that "linking testing and instruction is a fundamental and enduring concern in educational practice" (Burstein, 1983, p. 99). Anyone who has spent much time in classrooms knows that testing in some form consumes a major part of every teacher's effort. This effort is only justified if testing actually contributes to effective student learning. As pointed out by Nitko (1989), the failure to appropriately link testing and teaching will often lead to situations where: (1) students' motivation for learning is reduced; (2) incorrect information is given about students' learning progress and difficulties; (3) critical decisions about promotion may be made unfairly; and (4) incorrect decisions may be reached about instructional effectiveness.

Research indicates that most classroom testing involves locally developed achievement tests. In a survey of high school teachers, Salmon-Cox (1981) found that 44 percent relied primarily on their own tests in making evaluative decisions about students' achievement, 33 percent depended primarily on classroom interactions with the students, 21 percent relied primarily on homework, and only 2 percent relied primarily on standardized achievement test scores. (See Kellaghan, Madaus, & Airasian, 1982; Stiggins & Bridgeford, 1985; and Yeh, 1978 for similar conclusions.)

By emphasizing the importance of locally developed achievement tests, we do not mean to deemphasize the importance of standardized achievement tests. As Stiggins, Conklin, and Bridgeford point out:

> Politically, [standardized testing] has given educational measurement a visible role in documenting the effectiveness of schools in our society. The coin of the realm in determining the value of schools is clearly the standardized test score. . . . [However, standardized testing] represents only a small fraction of the assessments that takes place in schools and that influence the quality of schooling and student learning. Unfortunately, due to the narrow scope of measurement research, we know little about the nature, role, or quality of the preponderance of school assessment: that developed and used by teachers in the classroom. (1986, p. 6)

In planning, developing, and applying the results of local tests, each of the eight steps shown in Figure 9.1 is important. To organize your thinking for the rest of this chapter, we also have provided brief narrative descriptions of how each step relates to the planning, development, and application process. (We show the specific steps within each of these more general processes here, but delay discussion of the specific steps for test development and application, respectively, until Chapters 10 and 11. All three stages of the testing process—planning, development, and application—are interrelated, and each can be thought of as one leg in a three-legged stool. Together they provide a sturdy foundation for student learning. If any one of the legs is removed, the stool collapses. For example, a teacher who ignores planning and proceeds immediately to developing test items

FIGURE 9.1 Steps in Using Locally Developed Achievement Tests to Contribute to More Effective Student Learning

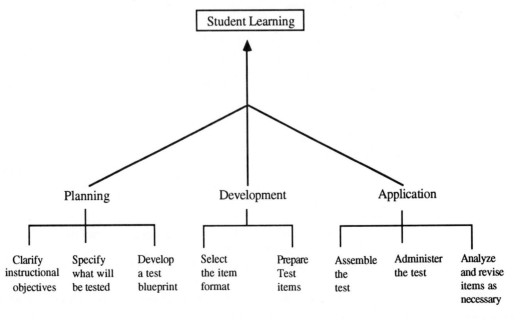

runs the risk of omitting important instructional content from the test. Similarly, the teacher who spends a great deal of time planning and developing test items, without paying attention to the appropriate procedures for assembling and administering the test, may find that the test is not particularly useful.

In the remainder of this chapter, we discuss the steps involved in test planning. Chapter 10 discusses test development and Chapter 11 addresses the issues associated with assembling, administering, scoring, reporting, and improving your test.

Planning Steps

Step 1: *Clarify instructional objectives.* The most important step in developing a classroom test is to decide what you want students to learn. Include all of the objectives you think important, regardless of how difficult you may think it is to develop a test item for any particular objective. Keep in mind that broad, general objectives are of little value in helping you develop test items.

Step 2: *Specify what will be tested.* Any given objective can be tested at many different levels. You must decide whether you are testing a student's ability to recall facts or apply principles; whether the test is being used to diagnose potential difficulties, demonstrate mastery, or motivate students; and how difficult test items should be.

Step 3: *Develop a test blueprint.* When a contractor builds a house, he usually follows a blueprint to make sure that he does not forget important components. Developing a test is similar. Having decided which objectives are most important and the specifics of what will be tested, you must develop a plan to guide the construction of the test so that the final product will be successful.

Development Steps

Step 1: *Select the item format.* Items can be written in many different forms, including true-false, multiple choice, matching, and essay. The format selected depends on your objectives and the time available for testing and scoring.

Step 2: *Prepare test items.* Writing test items should only happen after the preliminary decisions noted above. In addition to the content mastery, other skills are necessary to write good items.

Application Steps

Step 1: *Assemble the test.* Just as the individual components of a house have to be assembled in specific ways if the house is to be attractive and structurally sound, test items, no matter how well they are written, need to be assembled appropriately if they are to be useful.

Step 2: *Administer the test.* As pointed out in Chapter 8, the way in which a test is administered can have a dramatic impact on whether it achieves its intended purpose.

Step 3: *Analyze and revise items.* Once the test has been given, teachers need to examine the results to make instructional decisions, and to decide whether the test needs to be revised to function more effectively.

STEPS IN PLANNING ACHIEVEMENT TESTS

Each step in the planning process is essential if the test is to be successful. In the remainder of this chapter, we consider the specifics of each major step in this process.

Step 1: Clarifying Instructional Objectives

What is taught in the classroom should affect what is tested. No teacher would think of asking students to define a list of German vocabulary words in an algebra class. But in many, less obvious instances, the content of the test is not consistent with the content of the class.

The first step in developing an achievement test should be to systematically examine the course content and decide what is most important for students to learn. Indeed, an important fringe benefit of testing is that it helps to operationally define the instructional objectives for the class. Defining instructional objectives is easier said than done, however. One problem is achieving the appropriate level of specificity as shown by an excellent example taken from Hopkins, Stanley, and Hopkins (1990) and reproduced in Figure 9.2. As indicated in the figure, it is appropriate to want a student to achieve his personal goals and fulfill his obligations to society. This objective is so broad, however, that it is almost useless in designing test items. An almost infinite number of items could be used to measure the various components of such a broad objective—and it would be very difficult to say when it had been addressed adequately. If instructional objectives are too specific, however (note the objectives at the end of the list in Figure 9.2), the teacher is likely to spend an inordinate amount of time writing instructional objectives—probably to the exclusion of some instruction.

How broad is *too* broad? What is the right degree of specificity? It is impossible to define the appropriate level of specificity for every situation. However, we suggest that instructional objectives similar to those in the middle of the list in Figure 9.2 are generally the most appropriate. Such objectives provide teachers and students with a clear set of expectations, but still provide opportunities for students to demonstrate that they can generalize, or apply the skill in a broader context.

Another frequent mistake in preparing instructional objectives is to include only those that are easily measured by paper and pencil tests. This tendency leads to tests which are trivial and irrelevant, as A. Lawrence Lowell pointed out almost 70 years ago:

> The popular impression . . . is that a student whose primary object is a high grade devotes himself . . . to memorizing small, and comparatively unimportant, points in a course, and thereby makes a better showing than a classmate with . . . a larger real command of the subject. . . . As the examination questions are often made

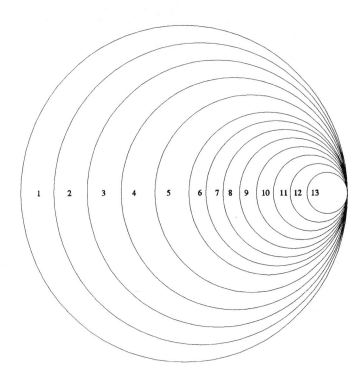

1. The student will be able to achieve personal goals and fulfil his or her obligations to society

2. The student will be able to demonstrate functional literacy.

3. The student will be able to perform mathematical operations.

4. The student will be able to perform simple addition, subtraction, multiplications, and divisional operations.

5. The student will be able to perform simple addition operations.

6. The student will be able to add any two single-digit numbers.

7. The student will be able to add 3 and 2.

8. The student will be able to add 3 objects and 2 objects.

9. The student will be able to add 3 apples and 2 apples.

10. The student will be able to add 3 apples and 2 apples when words (not objects) are used.

11. The student will be able to add 3 apples and 2 apples when words are present in writing.

12. The student will be able to add 3 apples and 2 apples 90% of the time, when the problem is posed in written form.

13. The student will be able to add 3 apples and 2 apples 90% of the time when the problem is phrased, "If you had 3 apples and I gave you 2 more, how many would have have?"

FIGURE 9.2 A Graphic Illustration of the Various Levels of Specificity in Statements

SOURCE: From Kenneth D. Hopkins, Julian C. Stanley, and B. R. Hopkins, *Educational and Psychological Measurement and Evaluation*. Seventh Edition. Copyright © 1990. Reprinted with permission of Allyn and Bacon.

out and marked this result may, and does, occur. But if all examinations were so conducted as to be an accurate and complete measure of the education the course is intended to give, . . . then there would be no reason why the student should not work for marks, and good reason why he should. To chide a tennis player for training himself with a view to winning a match, instead of acquiring skill in the game, would be absurd because the two things are the same. . . . If marks are not an adequate measure of what the course is intended to impart, then the examination is defective. If examinations were perfect the results would command universal respect, and high grades would be a more general object of ambition. (As cited in Frederiksen, 1984, p. 193)

Of course, tests influence how students spend their time studying and how teachers spend their time teaching. Students naturally use test content to decide how they should allocate their study time. Consequently, the most easily tested instructional objectives sometimes become those on which both students and teachers focus most of their efforts.

Unfortunately, many of the most important educational objectives are difficult to teach or test. Unless such objectives are explicitly included in the planning, there is a danger that they will be excluded from testing and eventually lost as a part of instruction. This must not happen. Important instructional objectives must not be deemphasized because they are difficult to test. All important instructional objectives should be listed as the first step in developing a valid achievement test.

To clarify instructional objectives, write down what you want students to be able to do as a result of your instruction. Using the middle of the list in Figure 9.2 as a guide, select an appropriate level of specificity. Remember that if you make instructional objectives too specific, you will not have time to develop both objectives and items. If you make them too broad, you will find that they are neither very useful nor readily measurable. In either case, you will quit using them. The best criterion for whether instructional objectives are at an appropriate level of specificity is whether you find them valuable in teaching and in developing tests.

Instructional objectives should also be reconsidered periodically, for two reasons. First, instructional goals may change because of changes in administrative policy, societal shifts, or information from students' performance or parent conferences. Second, it is easier to test for how well students have achieved some instructional objectives than others. Unless you are careful, there will be a natural tendency to gradually increase the emphasis on objectives that are easy to test and exclude those that are difficult.

The value of systematically and frequently evaluating instructional objectives is supported by research. For example, Boersma (1967) found that teachers who regularly evaluated the learning objectives for their class were judged by independent experts to be better teachers.

Step 2: Specifying What You Want to Test

Once you have established your instructional objectives, you must determine what type of behavior you want students to exhibit, the purpose of the test, and the difficulty of test items. We will discuss each in the following sections.

Using a Taxonomy of Educational Objectives
to Select the Behaviors to Be Exhibited on a Test

Suppose you want students to learn about the election of John F. Kennedy to the presidency of the United States. What best describes what they should be able to do when the instruction is completed?

- Recognize Kennedy's name from a list of names as being a president of the United States.
- Recall Kennedy's name as being a president of the United States.
- Describe the variables and conditions that resulted in the election of Kennedy.
- Compare and contrast the attributes of Kennedy with some of his rivals and explain why Kennedy was selected.
- Judge whether the variables and attributes that led to Kennedy's election will likely be significant factors in the next presidential election.

Each of the preceding behaviors is relevant to the election of John F. Kennedy as President, but each would require very different types of instruction. The first two require only recognition or recall of facts, while the last one requires that the student apply knowledge about Kennedy's circumstances and make a judgment as to the probable outcome.

One of the most frequent criticisms of educational tests is that they focus primarily on rote memorization and recall of facts, although everyone agrees that education should teach higher order thinking skills such as comprehension, analysis, and evaluation. This criticism applies to professionally developed standardized tests as well as teacher-made tests. For example, Bowman and Peng (1972) asked five experts to rate the items on the Graduate Record Examination (GRE) as to whether they were primarily a measure of memory, comprehension, analytic thinking, or evaluation. The consensus was that 70 percent of the items required only memory, 15 percent measured comprehension, 12 percent required analytic thinking, and only 3 percent involved evaluation. The predominance of memory or knowledge type items on tests is particularly unfortunate in view of research suggesting that when students have mastered items that measure higher order skills such as analysis and evaluation, they are more likely to retain the information than if they have only mastered items that measure knowledge (Nungester & Duchastel, 1982; Gay, 1980; and Frederiksen, 1984).

Classification systems, referred to as taxonomies have been developed for categorizing the level of cognitive skill needed to answer test questions. The oldest, best known, and most widely used taxonomy was developed by Bloom and

TABLE 9.1   A Summary of Bloom's Taxonomy of Educational Objectives for Cognitive Domain

1. Knowledge	Requires recall or recognition of facts, procedures, rules, or events	Most Common
2. Comprehension	Requires reformulation, restatement, translation, or interpretation of what has been taught or identification of relationships.	↑
3. Application	Requires use of information in a setting or context other than where it was learned.	
4. Analysis	Requires recognition of logical errors, comparison of components, or differentiation between components.	
5. Synthesis	Requires production of something original, solution to an unfamiliar problem, or combination of parts in an unusual way.	
6. Evaluation	Requires formation of judgments about the worth or value of ideas, products, or procedures that have a specific purpose.	↓ Least Common

SOURCE: Bloom, Englehart, Furst, Hill, & Krathwohl, 1956.

his colleagues and consists of the six levels shown in Table 9.1 Other taxonomies have been suggested (see Ebel, 1956, for an example), but Bloom's is by far the most popular. The levels are presumed to be hierarchical, with knowledge representing the lowest level of learning, and evaluation the highest.

Although six levels can be defined, it is sometimes difficult in practice to differentiate among them. For example, consider the following item.[1]

> Two preschool children are playing together. Child A refuses to share his toys with child B even when he is told that child B has no toys of his own. Which of the following explains the behavior of child A?
>
> _____ a. Child A has not had sufficient opportunities to interact with other children.
>
> _____ b. Child A has previously lent toys to the children and they have not been returned.
>
> _____ c. Child A is emotionally immature and stubborn.
>
> _____ d. Child A is intellectually unable to take the role of another person.

Because the taxonomy is presumed to be hierarchical, the item obviously requires a certain level of knowledge about child development and comprehension of that knowledge. However, experts would likely disagree about the level of Bloom's taxonomy that best describes the item. A case could be made for the item being primarily one of application (using information in a context other than where it

---

[1] Adapted from Sybil Carlson, _Creative Classroom Testing._ 1985, Educational Testing Service, Princeton, NJ. Adapted with permission of the publisher.

was learned), analysis (differentiation among components), or evaluation (forming judgments about value of specific procedures).

Although the taxonomy is helpful in developing items that measure different levels of learning, the difficulty in differentiating between and among some of the levels has resulted in many people recommending the use of fewer levels—perhaps dividing the taxonomy into a dichotomy, with knowledge being the lowest level and everything else (comprehension, application, analysis, synthesis, and evaluation) representing higher order cognitive skills. Others suggest that three levels be used: (1) knowledge, (2) comprehension and application, and (3) analysis, synthesis, and evaluation. We prefer to use three levels of the taxonomy and give examples below of test items written at each of the three levels.

Example of an Item Measuring Factual Knowledge
The president of the United States during World War II was

    a. Franklin Roosevelt
    b. Harry Truman
    c. Dwight Eisenhower
    d. Woodrow Wilson
    e. Warren Harding

The answer to this item (Franklin Roosevelt) requires only recall of facts. The student does not have to interpret, translate, apply, analyze, or evaluate any information. There is nothing wrong with having some items on a test that require only knowledge. Although it is not the total aim of education, the acquisition of factual knowledge is a legitimate and necessary goal. In fact, without an adequate knowledge base, it is impossible to acquire higher level cognitive skills. Most tests should include some knowledge-based items, otherwise, it is hard to know whether a student is having trouble with higher level items because of an inadequate knowledge base or because of other difficulties.

Example of an Item Measuring Comprehension and Application
Below, you are given a complete sentence which you must rephrase in a way that retains the original meaning. After you have rephrased the sentence according to the directions, select the choice that contains the phrase included in your revised sentence. Your rephrased sentence must be grammatically correct and natural in phrasing and construction.[2]

Sentence: John, shy as he was of girls, still managed to marry one of the most desirable of them.

Directions: At the beginning of the sentence, substitute *John's shyness* for *John, shy*. Your rewritten sentence will contain which of the following phrases:

---

[2] Adapted from *Multiple Choice Questions: A Close Look*. 1963, Educational Testing Service, Princeton, NJ.

a: . . . him being married to . . .
b: . . . him from marrying . . .
c: . . . was himself married to . . .
d: . . . him to have married . . .

Each of the phrases in the above item could be used to develop a sentence, but only one of them provides a sentence that uses the phrase "John's shyness" and is still grammatically correct, natural in phrasing and construction, and retains the meaning of the original sentence. Listed below are sentences that could have been constructed using each option.

a. John's shyness with girls did not stop *him being married to* the most desirable of them.
b. John's shyness with girls did not prevent *him from marrying* one of the most desirable of them.
c. John's shyness with girls did not keep him single; he *was himself married to* one of the most desirable of them.
d. John's shyness with girls was not a reason for *him to have married* the most desirable of them.

The correct answer is option *b*. The other answers are either grammatically incorrect (option *a*), or change the meaning of the original sentence (options *c* and *d*). To get the correct answer, the student must use grammatical rules learned elsewhere and reformulate the original sentence.

Example of an Item Measuring Analysis, Synthesis, and Evaluation
The shading on the map in Figure 9.3 is used to indicate

a.   population density
b.   percentage of labor force in agriculture
c.   per capita income
d.   death rate per 1,000

Population density (option *a*) is a good choice because the darkest shading is in India, Eastern China, much of Europe, the Nile Valley, and the northeastern part of the United States. Percentage of total labor force in agriculture (option *b*) would be an attractive alternative except for the dark shading in the northeastern United States and much of Europe. Per capita income (option *c*) would be an attractive choice if one looked only at the United States and Europe, but it certainly would not apply to India and the Nile River area. Option *d* is not plausible because the death rate per 1,000 of population would probably be high in India and in China but low in the United States and Europe. Recognizing that population density is the only logical option requires analysis and synthesis of information and then evaluation of which option fits the available information.

It is not easy to write objective test items that test higher order thinking skills. As Green points out:

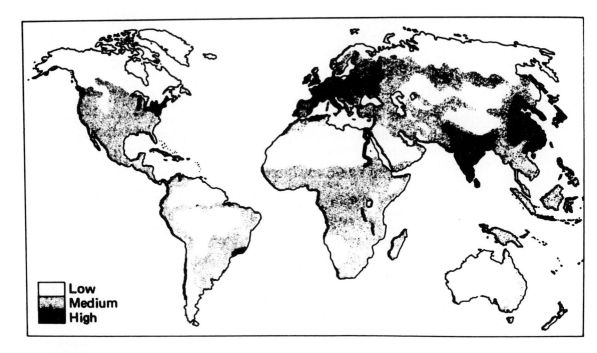

FIGURE 9.3

SOURCE: Adapted from *Multiple Choice Questions: A Close Look.* 1963, Educational Testing Service, Princeton, NJ.

> Critics of multiple choice items claim that only surface facts can be tested in this way, not deep understanding. Professional testers disagree; items probing understanding are possible, but they are certainly difficult to devise. (1981, p. 1003)

Difficulty notwithstanding, it is possible and important to include test items that require comprehension, application, analysis, synthesis, and evaluation. A taxonomy such as Bloom's can help you remember the different types of thinking skills students should master. This reminder is useful for preparing instructional materials and for testing what has been taught.

APPLICATION PROBLEM #1

Consider the following item.

Who was President during the most substantial escalation of U.S. military forces in the Vietnam War?

a. Dwight Eisenhower
b. John F. Kennedy
c. Lyndon B. Johnson
d. Richard Nixon

At what level is this item in Bloom's taxonomy?

Write an item that tests a higher level cognitive skill concerning the President's involvement in the escalation of U.S. military forces in Vietnam.

Specifying the Purpose of the Test

The types of items included on a test will depend in large part on the test's purpose. A test given at the beginning of an instructional unit to determine what students already know and what remains to be taught should look very different from a test designed to motivate students to study. It is important to distinguish among the following five different types of tests.

1. *Pre-instructional assessments*. Before beginning an instructional unit with an unfamiliar group of students, it is useful to know what skills they have already mastered. Items for such a test should cover a broad range, focus on basic content within that range, and not attempt to make fine discriminations. Such tests usually focus primarily on knowledge and comprehension, rather than higher order cognitive skills.

2. *Interim mastery tests*. Before moving from one instructional unit to another, you should know whether students have mastered the critical concepts in the previous unit. Because such interim mastery tests can be given frequently, the level of detail assessed in individual items can be quite specific. Items should sample all levels of cognitive objectives in the proportion you have decided is important for final course outcomes.

3. *Mastery tests*. At prespecified times during the year (e.g., end of semester, end of year) you will need information for such things as assigning grades, deciding on promotion, or selecting students for special programs. Because such tests are administered infrequently, they carry disproportionate importance and scores on such tests often have long term implications. Thus, it is particularly important for items on such tests to be thoroughly tested and validated.

4. *Diagnostic tests*. Similar in purpose to a pre-instructional assessment, a diagnostic test is designed to discover where and why students are having difficulty learning material. However, a diagnostic test tries to discover what kinds of mistakes students are making in addition to whether they have mastered particular content. The construction of such tests is much more complicated than a pre-instructional assessment.

5. *Tests to motivate students*. Research shows that students who know they will be tested frequently spend more time studying and demonstrate greater mastery of the material. Complete coverage of the material being presented is not necessary on such tests as long as students do not know what material will be included. Such tests are usually quite brief and often focus on factual knowledge, since complete mastery of the material is not yet expected.

Although a test can serve more than one of these five purposes, multipurpose testing makes item development much more difficult. In most cases, it is best if the purpose of the test is limited to only one of those described above. How difficult you choose to make items, the number of items you include on a test, and the types of behaviors tested all depend on the purpose of the test. Therefore, it is important to keep these categories of tests in mind as you study the guidelines for writing test items in Chapter 10.

Deciding How Difficult Test Items Should Be

Items about a particular instructional objective can be written at a wide range of difficulty. For example, consider the following objective:

> When presented with an appropriate problem, the student will be able to add two single-digit numbers with at least 90 percent accuracy.

It is difficult to imagine a reasonable educational objective that is any more specific. Yet even with such an objective, items can be written at many different levels of difficulty. Note the difference in difficulty of the following three items:

$$5 + 3 =$$
$$5 + \_ = 8$$

Henry has 5 apples and John has 3 more apples than Henry. How many apples does John have?

There is no formula for deciding how difficult items should be. Your experience as a teacher, and your judgment about what you think students should be able to do as a result of instruction, are the best guides in deciding about item difficulty.

Sometimes you will write an item that, once used, is easier or more difficult than you anticipated. If the item is too difficult, you must consider how the instruction related to that item was delivered. Was it sufficient? Was it clear? Depending on your answer, you may need to revise the item or your future instruction.

Step 3: Developing a Test Blueprint

When students complain that a test is unfair, what are they really saying? Often they are complaining that the test's emphasis was inappropriate (e.g., "We spent three weeks discussing market analysis techniques and the test did not have a single question about that!"); or the level of cognitive skill required to answer questions was inappropriate (e.g., "I thought there was more to this class than memorizing facts!"). The use of a test blueprint can help avoid such problems.

What Is a Test Blueprint?

Think for a moment about an engineer building a bridge or a contractor building a house. Without a comprehensive and detailed set of plans, it would be almost impossible to know how much concrete will be needed, whether structural reinforcing will be needed at a particular point, and whether the client will be able to afford the project. Throughout the building process, blueprints are used to make sure that everything is done in the proper order, at the right level of detail, and with the correct components. No competent contractor would ever dream of building a house without a blueprint.

As illustrated by the following scenario, constructing an achievement test is also complex.

> Samuel had studied hard all semester and thought he had learned the material in his American History course. He was sick and missed the last class period before the final exam, but was not too concerned because the teacher had announced that they would only be discussing the events of the last 10 years during the last class period and only a few pages of the textbook were devoted to recent events. The night before the test, Samuel reviewed the major periods and events in American History (e.g., the colonial period, the westward expansion, the Civil War, the Prohibition era, the Korean and Vietnam Wars). Although there was a dizzying amount of information, he felt confident as he arrived at class to take the test. Imagine his feelings (frustration, anger, despair?) when he saw the following test:
>
> *American History—Final Examination*
> Instructions: Because you've been such a good class, I want to reward you with an easy final exam. All of the questions come from our discussion last Friday and I think you'll find them relatively easy. Good luck.
>
> 1. Who was Reagan's first Secretary of State?
> 2. On what date was Reagan's first summit with Gorbachev?
> 3. During Reagan's administration, the national debt rose from $ _____ to $ _____.
> 4. In what incident were the most American military personnel lost during Reagan's term?
> 5. Discuss the most important disagreements Reagan had with Congress during his two terms.

Although the preceding example is exaggerated to make a point, it is, unfortunately, grounded in the real-life experiences of many students. Such tests lack content validity because they are not a fair representation of what was taught. But there is no reason for this to happen. In the same way that a blueprint helps a contractor, a test blueprint helps teachers be sure that: 1) the content covered on the test is consistent with the content covered during instruction, and 2) that the level of cognitive skill that students need to answer questions on the test is consistent with what is intended.

Table 9.2 shows a sample test blueprint that could be used for the material in Chapters 9 and 10. The left-hand column lists major content areas while the top of the table is divided into three levels of cognitive skill based on Bloom's Taxonomy. Not all parts of the chapter receive equal emphasis on the test and the emphasis is not necessarily proportional to the number of pages devoted to that topic in the chapter. Instead, the number of items reflects our judgment about what is most important.

TABLE 9.2 An Example of a Test Blueprint for a Textbook Chapter Entitled, "Constructing Your Own Achievement Tests—Why, When, and How"

Content Area	Knowledge	Comprehension and Application	Analysis, Synthesis, and Evaluation	Total
Why construct your own achievement test?	2	2	1	5
Adapting commercially available tests for local needs	1	1		2
Clarifying objectives and developing a test blueprint	2	2	1	5
Specifying content to be tested and selecting item format	1		1	2
How to write items:				
Multiple Choice	2	4	4	10
Essay	3	4	3	10
Other	2	2	2	6
Total	13	15	12	40

From the information in Table 9.2, you can tell that the instruction about how to write items is the most important (that category contains 65 percent of all questions and 70 percent of the questions that tap higher cognitive skills). Also, although knowledge of content is obviously important (e.g., every category has at least one knowledge level item), higher-order cognitive skills are *more* important; 68 percent of the items measure higher-order skills. Finally, notice that the categories in the left-hand column resemble, but are not identical to the topical listings for this chapter. Some topics have been combined. The test blueprint should be a flexible tool the teacher can use and adapt as necessary in making sure that the most important points are emphasized in both teaching and testing. (See the differing responses of two teachers in Table 9.3.)

How Is a Test Blueprint Developed?

Ideally, the development of a test blueprint begins long before the test is administered. Early development is important because the blueprint guides teaching as well as testing. The first step in developing a blueprint is to write down all the course objectives. When objectives are developed by the state or district, they may need to be modified for your particular situation, teaching style, or desired emphasis. The next step is to develop a preliminary blueprint listing course content areas down the left-hand column and the levels of Bloom's taxonomy across the top.[3]

Next, think about the proposed learning activities for the course as you decide how many items you need for each cell of the matrix. How much time will students

---

[3] We usually divide Bloom's Taxonomy into three levels as we did in Table 9.2. You may want to use six levels or some other taxonomy. What is important is that you use the blueprint to help you decide whether you are covering all of the desired areas in teaching and testing.

TABLE 9.3 Relative Emphasis of Two Different Teachers for the Content Taught in This Chapter

Emphasis of Teacher 1

Content Area	Knowledge	Comprehension and Application	Analysis, Synthesis, and Evaluation	Total
Why construct your own achievement test?	10	5	0	15
Adapting commercially available tests for local needs	5	0	0	5
Clarifying objectives and developing a test blueprint	10	5		15
Specifying content to be tested and selecting item format	5	0	0	5
How to write items:				
Multiple Choice	20	5	0	25
Essay	20	5	0	25
Other	5	5	0	10
Total	75	25		100

Emphasis of Teacher 2

Content Area	Knowledge	Comprehension and Application	Analysis, Synthesis, and Evaluation	Total
Why construct your own achievement test?	5	3	2	10
Adapting commercially available tests for local needs	10	5	5	20
Clarifying objectives and developing a test blueprint	2	2	0	4
Specifying content to be tested and selecting item format	2	0	3	5
How to write items:				
Multiple Choice	2	10	10	22
Essay	2	10	10	22
Other	2	10	5	17
Total	25	40	35	100

spend in discussion groups, doing homework, doing library research and writing papers, listening to lectures, reading, going on field trips, and so forth? Will these learning activities provide students with opportunities to master all the content at the cognitive level of mastery that you think is important? Are there activities that will contribute to learning outcomes that are not listed on your preliminary blueprint?

You may decide that in certain areas you only want students to remember facts, while in others it is critical that they develop skills in analysis, synthesis, and evaluation. Some extremely important concepts may require very little time to teach, while other less important concepts require a great deal of time. A useful technique to ensure that each activity receives the appropriate emphasis is to assign a total of 100 points to the various cells in your matrix. Using the blueprint presented in Table 9.2, Table 9.3 shows the relative allocations for two different teachers. As you can see, Teacher 1 emphasizes acquisition of knowledge and believes that information about "Adapting commercially available tests for local needs" is much less important than does Teacher 2.

The blueprint does not indicate which teacher is correct—that depends on a myriad of factors such as local priorities, the characteristics of students, and where the course fits in the total curriculum. But the blueprint, once established, gives clear direction to what concepts should be taught and tested. The numbers in each cell of the matrix indicate the percentage of test items to be used. For example, a 50-item test written by Teacher 2 should have one item that assesses knowledge of how to write multiple choice questions and five analysis/synthesis/evaluation items about how to write essay questions.

Particularly for older students, it is best to develop the test blueprint at the beginning of your course, and distribute it to the students so that they will understand the relative emphasis on various content and cognitive skills. This knowledge gives students a better idea about how to allocate their study time. Students who are familiar with the blueprint can also provide valuable feedback about whether your instruction is consistent with your testing plan. Of course, you can change your test blueprint during the course if your priorities shift, as long as you keep students informed.

SUGGESTED READINGS

Bloom, B. S., Hastings, J. T., & Madaus, G. F. (1971). *Handbook on formative and summative evaluation of student learning*. New York: McGraw-Hill.

This book is a comprehensive discussion of techniques and procedures for evaluating student learning. Written for classroom teachers, it contains sections on the use of educational objectives, summative and formative evaluation techniques, and evaluation of cognitive and affective objectives. The final section contains 11 chapters written by experts in their respective fields about how to evaluate learning in different content areas. Each chapter contains many excellent examples of items.

Salvia, J., & Hughes, C. (1990). *Curriculum-based assessment: Testing what is taught*. New York: Macmillan.

This is an introductory book for teachers who have little, if any, experience in curriculum-based assessment. The book provides practical guidelines for assessing students' learning in classroom contexts. The first four chapters focus on issues related to planning tests and other assessment procedures.

Popham, W. J. (1990). *Modern educational measurement* (2d ed.). Englewood Cliffs, NJ: Prentice-Hall.

The chapter on planning in most how-to-do-it books on test construction do not distinguish between the type of planning needed when developing norm-referenced measures and the planning necessary when constructing criterion-referenced measures. Popham's Chapter 9 "Specifying What a Test Should Measure," presents practical suggestions for teachers on how to plan both kinds of measures.

Tinkelman, S. N. (1971). Planning the objective test. In R. L. Thorndike (Ed.), *Educational measurement* (2d ed., pp. 46–80). Washington, DC: American Council on Education.

This chapter is a classic treatment of the issues and procedures involved in planning a test including (1) clarifying the purpose of the test, (2) developing the test specifications, and (3) deciding what kinds of items to use, how many items of each kind, and how difficult the items should be.

Popham, W. J. (1984). Specifying the domain of content or behaviors. In R. A. Berk (Ed.), *A guide to criterion-referenced test construction* (pp. 29–48). Baltimore, MD: Johns Hopkins University Press.

The traditional table of specifications that is so useful in planning norm-referenced measures has limited utility in developing specifications for criterion-referenced measures. Popham illustrates several alternative approaches for specifying a "well-defined domain" to serve as a basis for making criterion-referenced interpretations.

Millman, J., & Greene, J. (1989). The specification and development of tests of achievement and ability. In R. L. Linn (Ed.), *Educational measurement* (3d ed., pp. 335–366). New York: Macmillan.

This chapter is a technically sound treatment of the problems and issues involved in planning a test, but it is written primarily for professional test constructors rather than for classroom teachers.

SELF-CHECK QUIZ

1. As compared to commercially available achievement tests, locally developed achievement tests are usually
   a. more reliable since they are constructed by someone who better understands the needs of local students.
   b. more consistent with the learning objectives emphasized by the teacher who developed the test.
   c. used for making end-of-year decisions, rather than providing interim feedback.
   d. more superficial in terms of the material tested.

2. "Borrowing" items from a commercially available standardized achievement test to use with items you have written yourself on a locally developed test is
   a. appropriate if the learning objectives for both sets of items are similar.
   b. appropriate if you do not plan to administer the commercially available test to the same students.
   c. inappropriate unless you have directly taught the skills measured by those items.
   d. inappropriate in all cases.

3. Regarding the level of cognitive skill measured, a common problem is that items from most locally developed achievements tests
   a. measure skills that are too complex given the maturity of the students.
   b. confuse the need to measure affective and cognitive skills.
   c. focus too much on lower level cognitive skills.
   d. focus too much on comprehension and not enough on synthesis.

4. According to Bloom's taxonomy, which of the following is the highest level cognitive skill?
   a. Application
   b. Comprehension
   c. Evaluation
   d. Self-actualization

5. A test blueprint contributes most to increasing the test's
   a. content validity.
   b. construct validity.
   c. reliability.
   d. ease and accuracy of scoring.

6. A test *item bank* is
   a. a file of test questions compiled by an individual teacher from various sources over a period of time.
   b. a file of test questions submitted by different teachers in a school from which each contributing teacher can select relevant questions when creating a test.
   c. a set of model questions accompanied by a series of item-writing rules that teachers can use to generate additional test items of their own.
   d. a file of previously used tests that a teacher can modify or select from when creating new tests.
   e. a collection of test items, classified by objective, from which a teacher can select when making a test.

7. One acceptable way to tailor a published, standardized test to better fit the needs of a local school district is to
   a. request customized score reports that summarize students' performance only on the objectives taught by the local district.
   b. identify all items that are not taught in the local curriculum and instruct students to skip these items when they take the test.
   c. prepare a shortened version of the test that includes only items referring to objectives that are taught in the local curriculum.
   d. edit the items in the test so that each item better reflects the objectives taught in the local curriculum.

8. When one is working with objectives or test items, Bloom's taxonomy is a useful tool for _____.
   a. classifying·
   b. defining
   c. developing
   d. evaluating

9. Which is the highest level in Bloom's taxonomy that would be used extensively in creating a new idea or product?
   a. Analysis
   b. Application
   c. Comprehension
   d. Knowledge
   e. Synthesis

10. If the rows in a test blueprint represent the different topics or subjects to be tested, what do the columns represent?
   a. The various kinds of item formats to be used in test items
   b. The different levels of cognitive skills to be tested
   c. The chapters, readings, or other source documents to be covered
   d. The kinds of scoring procedures to be used
   e. The different purposes for which scores from the test will be used

SUGGESTION SHEET

If your name starts with the letters *I* or *J*, please complete the suggestion sheet at the end of the book while this chapter is still fresh in your mind.

ANSWER TO APPLICATION PROBLEM

#1

As currently written, the item is measuring the knowledge level of Bloom's taxonomy. One example, among many possibilities, of a higher level item related to the same issues is the following:

The most difficult aspect for President Lyndon Johnson in ordering a substantial increase in the U.S. military forces in Vietnam was the fact that
a. he was philosophically opposed to all war.
b. he was afraid that the backlash in voter sentiment would cost the Democrats the majority edge in Congress.
c. he knew that escalation would require massive amounts of money that he wanted to spend on domestic programs instead.
d. Vietnam had been an important ally in the U.S. war effort against the Japanese during World War Ii.

To answer this item, the student must relate the substantial increase in the U.S. military forces to historical circumstances. He must also be able to evaluate the validity of various factors and relate those to Johnson's order to increase the number of personnel and resources committed to the Vietnam War. Although both *b* and *c* are true, *c* is the best answer.

CHAPTER 10

Steps in Developing Good Items for Your Achievement Tests

Overview

Classroom teachers (including college professors) spend months, if not years, of their careers developing, administering, scoring, and interpreting the results of classroom tests. Essay tests, mathematical problem-solving quizzes, and various types of teacher-made, multiple-choice and true-false tests are a part of schooling very familiar to teacher and student alike. Classroom testing—using locally developed tests—occupies a substantial portion of the total time teachers and students spend together, far more than the amount of time students spend taking standardized tests of all varieties. It seems safe to say that classroom tests, collectively, have far more impact on a student's educational development than do all the standardized tests that he may be required to take.

If classroom tests are that important, then a crucial question is: Are they of adequate quality to fulfill the purposes for which they are used? Unfortunately, too often the answer is no. Little has changed since Ebel reported that "The view that classroom tests . . . could be, and ought to be, much better than they often are is shared by most school teachers and college professors" (1965, p. 2).

If teachers believe classroom tests should be better than they are, then why not get about the business of improving them, rather than lamenting their inadequacies? Don't teachers care about the quality of the assessment tools they use? Don't they care that poor student assessment can impede their students' learning? Of course they do—the occasional misanthrope aside—but caring is not enough. As Stiggens (1991) has pointed out, through no fault of their own, most teachers are not well prepared to plan and develop good student assessment instruments. Few universities devote enough of their teacher preparation curriculum to student assessment. The predictable result is teacher discomfort with the entire business of classroom testing.

Writing good test items and designing other useful student assessments is both an art and a science. Good classroom tests depend in part on the teacher's creativity in presenting items in ways that student responses elicit relevant, meaningful student performance. Yet much of the task of developing good classroom tests depends more on the "science" of good item writing—mastery of the fundamentals of item writing, including principles and rules that can be readily communicated and learned. Helping you understand such fundamentals is the purpose of this chapter. In it we remind you of several major types of test item formats and explain their advantages and disadvantages. We provide you with guidelines and examples to help you write good test items in each format. And we provide you with ample practice to give you confidence that you can develop good classroom measures that will serve you and your students well.

Objectives

Upon completing your study of this chapter, you will be able to

1. Explain the advantages and disadvantages of the major types of item formats typically used in locally developed tests.
2. Select the most appropriate item format for testing any particular instructional objective.
3. Write high-quality test items for each of the following types: true-false, multiple choice, matching, completing, and essay.
4. Use the guidelines presented in this chapter to review and identify flaws in items written by others.
5. Score responses to essay questions in a way that is objective, valid, and replicable.

STEPS IN DEVELOPING AN ACHIEVEMENT TEST

The conceptual work in the three steps described in Chapter 9 lays the necessary foundation for writing test items. In this chapter we describe two major steps: (1) how to select an appropriate item format, and (2) how to write good test items.

Step 1: Selecting an Item Format

Although there are dozens of item formats, most are some variation of the following five basic types:

1. *True-false*. A statement is presented and the respondent decides whether it is correct (true) or incorrect (false).
2. *Multiple choice*. A phrase, question, or example is presented followed by two or more options. The respondent is asked to select the option that provides the best answer or completes the phrase most accurately.
3. *Matching*. Two lists are provided (e.g., names and dates, people and places). The respondent is asked to select from the first list an item that best matches each item in the other list.
4. *Completion or short answer*. A statement with one or more blanks or a question is presented. The respondent is asked to complete the statement by providing missing information or to supply brief information.
5. *Essay*. The respondent is asked to write a paragraph or more responding to an idea or answering a question.

Fleming and Chambers (1983) point out that teachers use short-answer questions most often in locally developed tests, use more matching items than multiple choice or true-false items, and generally avoid the use of essay questions. Unfortunately, they also note that most items (almost 80 percent) focus primarily on acquisition of knowledge instead of comprehension and application, or analysis, synthesis, and evaluation.

The advantages and disadvantages of each type of item format are summarized in Table 10.1. Some people like to categorize items as objective (true-false, multiple choice, and matching) or subjective (short-answer or essay items). Sometimes items are also categorized as recognition items (true-false, multiple choice, and matching) or recall items (short-answer or essay). Such distinctions have important limitations. For example, essay questions can be scored very objectively and multiple choice questions can require much more than recognition of the correct fact or name. The format selected for any particular test depends on the time available for testing and scoring, your personal preferences, and the type of information being tested.

It is important to emphasize that every type of item can be written in a way that tests higher level cognitive skills as well as recall of knowledge. But for this to happen, the person developing the test must spend time learning and practicing the skills of item writing. As Hopkins, Stanley, and Hopkins point out, "Test construction is in one sense more of an art than a science, but this 'art form' can be dramatically improved with special instruction and systematic practice and feedback" (1990, p. 166).

Step 2: Preparing Test Items

Many entire books have been devoted to writing test items. We make no pretense of being able to provide such detail on one topic here, given the comprehensive scope of this book. But we can—and do—provide, in the remainder of this chap-

TABLE 10.1   Advantages and Disadvantages of Commonly Used Types of Achievement Test Items

Type of Item	Advantages	Disadvantages
True-False	Many items can be administered in a relatively short time. Moderately easy to write and easily scored	Limited primarily to testing knowledge of information. Easy to guess correctly on many items, even if material has not been mastered
Multiple Choice	Can be used to assess broad range of content in a brief period. Skillfully written items can measure higher order cognitive skills. Can be scored quickly	Difficult and time consuming to write good items. Possible to assess higher order cognitive skills, but most items assess only knowledge. Some correct answers can be guesses
Matching	Items can be written quickly. A broad range of content can be assessed. Scoring can be done efficiently	Higher order cognitive skills are difficult to assess
Short Answer or Completion	Many can be administered in a brief amount of time. Relatively efficient to score. Moderately easy to write items	Difficult to identify defensible criteria for correct answers. Limited to questions that can be answered or completed in very few words
Essay	Can be used to measure higher order cognitive skills. Easy to write questions. Difficult for respondent to get correct answer by guessing	Time consuming to administer and score. Difficult to identify reliable criteria for scoring. Only a limited range of content can be sampled during any one testing period

SOURCE: Based on Dwyer, 1982.

ter, a variety of aids intended to help you write high quality items of whichever format you may have selected.

Of course, guidelines alone are not enough. There is no substitute for practice and experience if you are to become really proficient.

Although the guidelines appear simple and straightforward, it is surprising how frequently such guidelines are ignored. As you write items, use the following suggestions as a checklist to examine each item. As you become more proficient, you will find that the guidelines tend to become second nature.

In the sections that follow, we will provide guidelines for each of the item formats we have presented. But first, we will give some general suggestions that apply to any type of item.

GENERAL GUIDELINES THAT APPLY TO SEVERAL ITEM FORMATS

You will find the following nine general guidelines applicable for most items you will write.

1. *Test for important ideas, information, and skills—not trivial detail.* Sometimes it is easier to write questions about specific details (e.g., What was the name of the ship on which Charles Darwin was sailing when he wrote *The Origin of Species*?). But, is that really the information you want to test? Knowledge about some specific facts is important if students are to master higher level cognitive skills. But, in developing any kind of test item, teachers must continually ask themselves what knowledge, abilities, and skills are of the most worth. However, just because something requires the skills of evaluation, synthesis, and application does not mean that it is worth including on a test.

2. *Write items as simply as possible, making sure that students know exactly what information is being requested.* Irrelevant details, grammatically or logically sloppy construction, unnecessarily sophisticated vocabulary, and bias can all contribute to confusion. Often the item writer has such a clear idea of what he wants to test that he does not realize how confusing an item may be for respondents. Consider the following two items, designed to determine whether the student knows when the U.S. Constitution was written.

Poor: The United States Constitution was written in _____.

Better: The United States Constitution was written in the year _____.

The poor example has dozens of "correct" answers (e.g., longhand, English, order to guarantee basic freedoms), most of which have nothing to do with knowing when the Constitution was written.

3. *Make items appropriate for the age and ability level of respondents.* An advantage of locally developed achievement tests is that they can be tailored to fit the skill levels of the students. Questions must be written so that the format is not a source of irrelevant distraction, vocabulary is familiar, and the task is consistent with students' ability and preparation. For example, first grade students should not be asked to write essays regarding the four basic food groups, even though they may be expected to have mastered such information. Because the writing skills of most first graders are not yet well developed, many would probably appear not to know information that they had really mastered. We are not suggesting that tests for young children should focus only on rote memorization. They should not. But you should make sure that the test format and vocabulary allow students to show what they really know.

4. *Make sure that objectively scored items have only one correct or best answer.* Consider the following items:

T F   Larger cities have higher crime rates than smaller cities.

Match the item in list A that goes best with the item in list B.

List A
1. Dwight Eisenhower
2. Ulysses S. Grant
3. Douglas McArthur

List B
A. President of the United States
B. World War II general
C. Civil War general

A leading cause of heart attacks is

  a) cholesterol.
  b) lack of exercise.
  c) high blood pressure.
  d) being overweight.

The correct answer to each of these examples is not easily determined. It may be true that larger cities generally have higher crime rates than smaller cities, but it is relatively easy to find exceptions. The second question probably expected answers that Dwight Eisenhower was president of the United States, Douglas McArthur was a World War II general, and Ulysses S. Grant was a Civil War general. The way the item is now written, however, it would be correct to say that Dwight Eisenhower was a World War II general and that Ulysses S. Grant was a president of the United States. In the multiple-choice item concerning a leading cause of heart attacks, any one of the answers could be considered correct. Even if the item had stated, "*The* leading cause of heart attacks . . . ," different experts might have different opinions about which answer is the best answer.

5. *Avoid using interrelated items*. Sometimes knowing the answer to one item is necessary to answer subsequent items. This gives undue weight to the first item in a sequence. If the first item is missed, all will be missed regardless of whether the student knows the material. There are times, of course, when you will want to use the same stimulus material (e.g., a paragraph of information, a graph, or a picture) for a number of different questions. There is nothing wrong with this practice as long as getting the correct answer to one question is not dependent on getting the correct answer to a previous question.

6. *Avoid irrelevant clues and "give-away questions."* Test writers sometimes include unintentional clues in the items they write. Some examples are common elements in the stem and the correct option, a tendency to use certain response positions more or less frequently, and subject-verb agreement between the stem and the correct option. Although no one does this on purpose, it is surprising how frequently it happens.

7. *Avoid using direct quotations from the text*. Writing good test items is time consuming and difficult. To save time, some people use direct quotations from the text in true-false, completion, and multiple-choice items. This practice is usually inappropriate. Taken out of context, such quotations are often ambiguous or confusing. Furthermore, this practice may encourage students to focus on memorization and recognition rather than on understanding the subject matter.

8. *Have someone else review all of your items*. It is extremely valuable to have a colleague review the items you have written. Find someone whose judgment you trust and offer to exchange item reviewing responsibilities with them. Often, those who develop items make obvious mistakes that a less involved person will notice quickly.

9. *Avoid trick questions*. One of the surest ways to make students cynical about tests is to use trick questions that confuse trivial detail and major issues. Consider the following example.

> T   F   John L. Kennedy was the youngest person to serve as President
>   of the United States.

The item is technically false because President Kennedy's middle initial was *F*,
not *L*. It is true, however, that John F. Kennedy was the youngest person to serve
as President of the United States. Even if the student recognizes the incorrect
middle initial, he does not know whether the initial was incorrectly typed, or
whether the test developer was really concerned about the student's knowing
President Kennedy's middle initial. The student should not be required to figure
out the test developer's motives (or typing skills) in answering questions.

GUIDELINES FOR WRITING TRUE-FALSE ITEMS

True-false items were once the most popular form of testing. However, one rarely
finds a true-false item on current standardized achievement tests. The declining
use of true-false items is probably attributable to beliefs that such items test only
trivial information, are often ambiguous, encourage rote learning, expose students
to erroneous ideas that might be accepted as truth, and are too susceptible to high
scores through guessing. Although there is an element of truth in such criticisms,
properly written true-false items can be used efficiently to obtain information
about students' mastery of essential knowledge. However, good true-false items
are not easy to develop and should not be the only, or even predominant, means
of testing.

The format for writing true-false items is seductively simple. A statement is
given and the respondent is asked to mark whether that statement is *true* or *false*.
A variety of variations have been attempted, most of them designed to minimize
any potential advantages of guessing. For example, some people have advocated
that students be instructed to correct false items by crossing out the word or phrase
that makes it false and writing in a word or phrase that makes the statement
correct. Others have suggested the use of correction for chance formulas. Still
others have suggested confidence scoring procedures in which the respondent
indicates how confident he is about a particular answer, and items are weighted
differentially depending on how confident the respondent is for that item. In our
opinion, these procedures add unnecessary complexity with little, if any, gain
in the value of the information provided. Until more research demonstrates the
superiority of such techniques, we believe that the standard, true-false item is still
the best. Following are five useful guidelines for writing true-false items:

1. *Ask questions about single ideas; avoid double-barreled questions.* Consider the following true-false item.

> T   F   Because of the massive amounts of financial assistance from the
>   United States, Israel maintains one of the largest military forces
>   in the world.

Interpreting a response to such questions is difficult because the statement
has two parts. It is true that Israel maintains one of the world's largest military

forces compared to its population. However, they would probably maintain a similar military force even if they did not receive financial aid from the United States. Thus, one part of the sentence is true, the other is false. A better true-false item would be the following.

T F   The United States provides very little financial aid to Israel.

2. *Avoid negative wording in false statements*. Consider the following item:

T F   The United States Constitution does not require the Secretary of
         State to be confirmed by the Senate.

Even if someone knew that the Secretary of State must be confirmed by the Senate, it is confusing to figure out whether the double negative results in a true or false answer. In most cases, it is better to be simple and direct. The preceding statement could be better phrased:

T F   The United States Constitution requires the Secretary of State to
         be confirmed by the Senate.

3. *There should be approximately the same number of true and false items, they should appear in a random order, and true items should be about the same length as false items*. If a particular teacher writes more true than false items, the testwise student would always mark true for items about which he was unsure. The best way to combat the negative consequences of such testwise behavior is to eliminate as many clues as possible through careful review of items and careful structuring of tests.

4. *Avoid statements that require complex construction or caveats*. Complex sentence construction and qualifications may turn test items into a measure of a student's reasoning ability, vocabulary, or reading comprehension rather than a measure of content knowledge. Where complex construction or qualifiers seem necessary, it is generally better to break the item up into two or more simple items that are a direct test of the information you think is important.

5. *Avoid the use of superlatives, and such words as* all, never, *and* always. Every test item should have one—and only one—correct answer. In an effort to make true-false questions clearly true or clearly false, test writers sometimes use words such as *usually* or *generally* in conjunction with items that are true, and words such as *always*, *none*, or *never* in conjunction with items that are false. Testwise students quickly learn that their chances for a high score are improved if they mark items true that use words such as *usually* and *sometimes* and mark items false that use words such as *never* and *always*. Superlatives can also cause problems. Consider the following item.

T F   Willie Mays was the greatest baseball player who ever lived.

Although some people might believe the statement to be true, others would have their own nominations for the greatest baseball player of all time. The more clear-cut the answers to true-false questions, the better those questions will generally be.

GUIDELINES FOR WRITING MULTIPLE-CHOICE ITEMS

Because they are versatile, easily scored, and useful in measuring a wide variety of learning outcomes, multiple-choice items are frequently used. A multiple-choice item consists of a statement or question, which we will refer to as the *stem*, followed by a number of possible responses, which we will refer to as *options*, *distractors*, or *alternatives*. One (or more) of the options is the correct or best response.

Although multiple-choice items are often criticized for measuring only recall, well-designed multiple-choice items can do much more. Consider the following two items[1] taken from a booklet on multiple-choice questions published by Educational Testing Service (1963):

> The concept of the plasma membrane as a simple sieve-like structure is inadequate to explain the
>
> a.   passage of gases involved in respiration into and out of the cell.
> b.   passage of simple organic molecules such as glucose into the cell.
> c.   failure of protein molecules to pass through the membrane.
> d.   inability of the cell to use starch without prior digestion.
> e.   ability of the cell to admit selectively some inorganic ions while excluding others.

To answer this question correctly, a student must understand how a plasma membrane functions, and he must evaluate and synthesize that knowledge with information about glucose, protein, starch, gases, and inorganic ions. The student who has mastered the material will realize that comparing a plasma membrane to a sieve may be adequate to explain why it allows very small molecules (such as gases and glucose) to pass through the membrane and rejects larger molecules (such as protein and starch). However, this explanation does not account for the ability of the plasma membrane to selectively admit some inorganic ions while excluding others. Thus, *e* is the only possible correct answer.

> *Directions*: The sentence below has blank spaces, each blank indicating that a word has been omitted. Beneath the sentence are five lettered sets of words. You are to choose the one set of words which, when inserted in the sentence, best fits in with the meaning of the sentence as a whole.
>
> From the first, the Islanders, despite an outward _____, did what they could to _____ the ruthless occupying power.

---

[1] Adapted from *Multiple Choice Questions: A Close Look*. 1963, Educational Testing Service, Princeton, NJ.

a. harmony . . . assist
b. enmity . . . embarrass
c. rebellion . . . foil
d. resistance . . . destroy
e. acquiescence . . . thwart

To answer this question, the student must recall definitions of words and must also apply that knowledge in a novel setting by selecting the pair of words that creates the appropriate contrast and fits the context. Options *a, b, c,* and *d* can be eliminated because, the word *despite* implies that the Islanders acted outwardly in one way while trying to do just the opposite in practice. For example, if the Islanders displayed an outward *harmony,* to *assist* the ruthless occupying power would probably create additional harmony. Similar arguments can be advanced for *enmity* and *embarrass, rebellion* and *foil, resistance* and *destroy.* Only option *e* implies two opposing actions.

The guidelines for writing multiple-choice items were aptly, but unfortunately, summarized by Nitko as follows: "Elder item writers pass down to novices lists of rules and suggestions which they and their item-writing forefathers have learned through the process of applied art, empirical study, and practical experience" (1984, p. 201). In an effort to systematize these item-writing "rules and suggestions," Haladyna and Downing recently compiled a taxonomy of 43 multiple-choice item-writing rules "based on a consensus of 46 authoritative references representing the field of educational measurement from as early as 1935 . . ." (1989a, p. 38). In a companion article based on an analysis of 96 empirical studies, they examined the degree to which those 43 rules were supported by credible research (Haladyna & Downing, 1989b).

The results of their analyses demonstrated that many of the rules that have been "passed down by our item-writing forefathers" have not been investigated empirically. For those rules where substantial research has been done, the results are not always clear-cut, and according to Haladyna and Downing (1989b), the vast majority of rules have not been sufficiently investigated.

Until more research is completed, it seems best to rely on the wisdom of measurement experts to write effective multiple-choice items. In what follows, we have used the taxonomy suggested by Haladyna and Downing (1989a), combined with our analysis of existing research, the "wisdom of our item-writing forefathers," and our own experience to outline a list of simple, but useful, rules for writing multiple-choice items. The following nine guidelines will help you write good quality multiple-choice items.

1. *Options should portray a single concept that appears plausible to students who have not mastered the material.* A multiple-choice item consists of a stem and a number of options or distractors. The purpose of a distractor is to "distract" away from the correct answer those students who have not mastered the concept. This is very different from tricking the student with trivial details. In other words, options should be constructed so they seem plausible to someone who has not learned the material. Consider the following multiple choice question:

The purpose of the Lewis and Clark expedition was to

   a. explore and map much of the western United States.
   b. explore Central America to locate a site for the Panama Canal.
   c. provide assistance to forces friendly to the U.S. during the Spanish American War.
   d. survey the area that was later acquired from France as the Louisiana Purchase.

Option *a* is the best answer, but each of the other options are plausible for a student who has some knowledge but has not thoroughly mastered the concept. A student who remembers that the Lewis and Clark expedition had something to do with exploration and mapping might select options *b* or *d*. The term *expedition* in the stem might suggest military involvement to some students, making option *c* a good choice. Good options do not trick students who have mastered the concept into selecting an incorrect answer. Rather they separate those students who have mastered the concept from those whose knowledge is limited.

Good distractors also prevent students with limited knowledge about the concept from obtaining correct answers through testwiseness. Consider the following item:

The largest city in the United States is

   a. New York, New York.
   b. Pocatello, Idaho.
   c. Gridley, California.
   d. Columbia, Maryland.

A student would have to know very little about the relative size of cities in the United States to get this answer correct. New York would be the most likely guess for an uninformed student based solely on the fact that he had never heard of the other three cities.

The creation of plausible distractors is one of the most difficult parts of writing good multiple-choice items, but the results are worth the time spent. The best distractors help the teacher understand what incorrect perceptions students have. Here are some suggestions to help you in creating good distractors.

- Base distractors on the most frequent errors made by students in homework assignments or class discussions related to that concept.
- Use words in the options that are associated with words in the stem (e.g., explorer—exploration).
- Use concepts from the instructional material that have similar vocabulary or were used in the same context as the correct answer.
- Use distractors that are similar in content or form to the correct answer (e.g., if the correct answer is the name of a place, have all distractors be places instead of using names of people and other facts).

• Make the distractors similar to the correct answer in terms of complexity, sentence structure, and length.

2. *Most multiple-choice items should have three to five options*. Experts disagree about the ideal number of options in a multiple-choice test (see Haladyna & Downing, 1989b, for a review of this literature). Some argue that the more options you have, the more variability the test will have and hence, the greater its reliability (Noll, Scannel, & Craig, 1979). Others argue that a three-option test discriminates just as well, is just as reliable, and is easier to construct because the test developer only has to devise two plausible distractors (Grier, 1975).

Although it is logical that tests having more options will be more discriminating and hence, more reliable, the *quality* of distractors is much more important than the *number* of distractors. What is important is to create plausible distractors that provide information about the kinds of misconceptions students are most likely to have.

3. *Words that need to be repeated in each option should be included in the stem*. Consider the following examples.

Poor: Test reliability

    a.   can be improved by making items more difficult.
    b.   can be improved by shortening the test.
    c.   can be improved by changing the test from a power test to a speeded test.
    d.   can be improved by increasing the number of items on the test.

Better: Test reliability can be improved by

    a.   using items with lower point-biserial correlations.
    b.   decreasing the number of items on the test.
    c.   changing from a power test to a speeded test.
    d.   increasing the number of items on the test.

4. *Use* none of the above *and* all of the above *sparingly*. Where absolute standards of correctness are clear (e.g., in arithmetic or spelling), *none of the above* may be a plausible or even correct response. In most cases, however, *none of the above* and *all of the above* tend to be overused placeholders, not serious and plausible distractors. Such phrases are often included because the test developer had trouble thinking of one more plausible alternative. Testwise students can improve their odds of getting the right answer just by eliminating such options.

5. *Generally, the stem of an item should be meaningful without having to read all the options*. Compare the stems in these two versions of an item:

Poor: The President of the United States

    a.   is chosen by the electoral college.
    b.   can serve a maximum of two four-year terms.

    c.   must be at least 45 years of age.
    d.   can be impeached only for felony offenses.

Better: The President of the United States is chosen by the

    a.   electoral college.
    b.   members of the Senate.
    c.   members of the House of Representatives.
    d.   people directly.

In the first example, the student knows only that the question has something to do with the President of the United States. Only by identifying the correct answer can he determine that the item writer wanted to test students' knowledge about the election process. The second example still tests the critical information but it is easier for students to read and understand and still contains plausible distractors.

6. *Avoid window dressing.* The item stem should be as concise, straightforward, and simple as possible. Some item writers provide elaborate explanations in an effort to make the item clearer. In reality, such window dressing often introduces ambiguity, and increases the amount of information the student must process to understand the question. Consider the following example:

Although many different people worked on the concept of a telephone, and several made discoveries that were key to its later development, the person who is credited with the invention of the telephone is

    a.   Alexander Graham Bell.
    b.   Benjamin Franklin.
    c.   Guglielmo Marconi.
    d.   Thomas Edison.

If the purpose of the item is to determine whether the student knows who is credited with the invention of the telephone, it is irrelevant that many different people worked on it and several others made discoveries that were key to its later development.

7. *Options should usually come at the end of the statement.* Although there are exceptions to this rule, items are usually easier to understand if they are phrased so the answer is a conclusion to an incomplete statement or the answer to a question. Consider the following two examples.

Poor: The city of _____ is the capital of California.

    a.   Los Angeles
    b.   San Francisco
    c.   Sacramento
    d.   San Diego

Better: The capital of California is _____.

    a.   Los Angeles
    b.   San Francisco
    c.   Sacramento
    d.   San Diego

8. *The correct option should be about the same length as distractors and should occur randomly.* Inexperienced item writers tend to word the correct option with more precision and make it longer than other distractors. They also tend to have the correct option appear as the first or last option more frequently. A test-wise student will notice such patterns and will have an unfair advantage, even if he has not mastered the material.

9. *Each item should have only one correct or best answer.* This seems obvious enough, but it is one rule that is frequently violated. Consider the following example:

Choose the man who does not belong in this group.

    a.   Ulysses S. Grant
    b.   Dwight D. Eisenhower
    c.   Adolph Hitler
    d.   Charles de Gaulle

The student who recognized that Eisenhower, Hitler, and de Gaulle were all leaders of countries during World War II might select Grant. Another student who recognized that Grant, Eisenhower, and de Gaulle were all military generals might select Hitler. Thus, there are at least two different correct answers based on different interpretations of the item. The best way to identify items with ambiguous answers is to have someone else review and answer your items without having access to your scoring key. Often, they will identify a correct answer that is different from the one you have selected.

APPLICATION PROBLEM #1

You are asked to review a test for a fellow teacher that contains the following multiple-choice question. What suggestions would you make for improvement?

Which of the following animals does not belong with the others?

    a. Elephant
    b. Crocodile
    c. Beaver
    d. Lion

GUIDELINES FOR WRITING MATCHING EXERCISES

A matching exercise generally consists of two columns of information. The respondent is supposed to indicate which option in the second column best matches each item in the first column. A matching exercise is really a series of individual items. Matching exercises are most frequently used to measure knowledge of events, dates, persons, and other such matters involving simple relationships. A typical matching item looks like the following:

> *Directions:* A number of inventions are listed on the left. The right-hand column contains names of inventors. Place the letter corresponding to the inventor in the space before the invention he made. Not all names of inventors will be used.

Inventions		*Inventors*	
_____ 1.	telephone	a.	Eli Whitney
_____ 2.	phonograph	b.	Robert Fulton
_____ 3.	cotton gin	c.	Alexander Bell
_____ 4.	steam boat	d.	Guglielmo Marconi
		e.	Thomas Edison
		f.	Cyrus McCormick

Constructing good matching exercises is relatively fast, but must be done carefully. The following six guidelines are useful in constructing good matching items.

1. *Lists to be matched should be relatively homogeneous.* When the items in each list are homogeneous, students are less likely to guess the correct answer unless they have mastered the information. For example, if the item given above had also included authors and books, athletes and sports, and explorers and discoveries, a student with superficial knowledge of the content area would be able to eliminate some of the possible answers and increase the likelihood of obtaining a high score.

2. *Directions for matching exercises should indicate the way to mark answers, the basis on which matching is to be done, and the number of times each option can be used.* The directions given in the previous example are a good model. Because matching exercises can be arranged in many different ways, it is very important to have explicit instructions. The most frequently omitted instruction is whether options can be matched with more than one item. Sometimes it is good to allow an option to be used more than once. In the following example, the list of items (List A) contains names of animals and the terms in the list of options (List B) can be used multiple times.

List A				*List B*	
_____ 1.	Ostrich	_____ 5.	Hyena	a.	Mammal
_____ 2.	Boa constrictor	_____ 6.	Rattlesnake	b.	Reptile
_____ 3.	Elephant	_____ 7.	Eagle	c.	Bird
_____ 4.	Crocodile	_____ 8.	Goose		

3. *Avoid matching exercises in which all items are used and each option is used once and only once.* If there are exactly the same number of options as items and each option is to be used once, the student can often get one or more answers correct by a process of elimination. A much better approach is to have several more plausible options than there are items. Look again at the matching exercise at the beginning of this section. Notice that while Cyrus McCormick and Guglielmo Marconi were famous inventors, they were not responsible for any of the inventions listed. Thus, a student who only knew three of the answers could not use a process of elimination to obtain the correct fourth answer.

4. *Make sure all options are plausible.* Unfortunately, some matching items look like the following:

> *Directions:* Listed below are the names of sports teams and famous athletes. Put the letter associated with the correct sports figure in front of the team for whom he played.

Sport Teams	*Athletes*
_____ 1. Green Bay Packers	a. Bart Starr
_____ 2. San Francisco Giants	b. Nancy Lopez
_____ 3. Boston Celtics	c. Willie Mays
	d. Larry Bird

A student who deduces that Nancy Lopez is female will know that she is not a plausible response for any of the sports teams listed.

5. *Matching exercises should generally be limited to no more than ten items.* With long lists of items, students have to spend a lot of time reading and organizing information before responding to the question. Such lists can be confusing and put too much emphasis on one particular content area. The best matching exercises contain only four to six items.

6. *Place all items and options on the same page.* Tests are sometimes arranged so that students are required to flip pages back and forth to see all the options and items. This is unnecessarily confusing and should be avoided.

GUIDELINES FOR WRITING COMPLETION OR SHORT-ANSWER ITEMS

Completion or short-answer items consist of a question that can be answered with a word or short phrase, or a statement having one or more omitted words, which the student is supposed to complete. For example

> A person nominated by the president to serve as the secretary of state must be confirmed by the _____.

The popularity of short-answer or completion questions is probably tied to the ease of construction and scoring and the fact that a relatively large number of questions can be asked in a limited amount of space. The same general guidelines listed earlier for development of any achievement items also apply here. In addition, the following four guidelines will help you develop effective completion or short-answer questions.

1. *Questions should be stated in such a way that only a specific and unique word or phrase can be the correct answer.* This is probably the most difficult part of writing good completion items. Consider the following question.

The capital city of the United States is _____.

The desired answer to this question was probably Washington, D.C. But a teacher might have a difficult time defending his correct answer to a student who

---

APPLICATION PROBLEM #2

A fellow teacher asks you to review a test that contains the following matching exercise.

Directions: Match the items below.

_____ 1. The Capital of the United States immediately following the Revolutionary War

_____ 2. A naval hero of the Revolutionary War

_____ 3. A French military officer who assisted Washington during the Revolutionary War

_____ 4. Site of the Constitutional Convention of 1787

_____ 5. Location of the first fighting of the Revolutionary War

_____ 6. Site of the final major battle of the Revolutionary War

_____ 7. The founder of Rhode Island

_____ 8. Settled the Colony of Jamestown

_____ 9. A traitor to the American cause during the Revolution

_____ 10. The country from whom the United States purchased the Louisiana Territory

a. Pilgrims
b. France
c. Yorktown
d. Roger Williams
e. Philadelphia
f. Marquis de Lafayette
g. Benedict Arnold
h. New York
i. John Paul Jones
j. Lexington

What suggestions would you make for improvement?

---

had written *large, where the president of the United States lives, pretty, in a temperate climate*, or any one of hundreds of other answers. To preclude having several appropriate answers be aware of such possibilities as you develop items, then have your items reviewed and answered by another teacher who is familiar with the subject matter.

2. *Omit only significant words from a statement to be completed.* Consider a completion item based on the following sentence:

> The executive, legislative, and judicial branches constitute a system of checks and balances for the United States government.

A better question that would test significant concepts is the following:

> The system of checks and balances for the United States government consists of the branches of executive, _____, and _____.

3. *Completion items should contain enough clues so that a person who has mastered the material can tell precisely what is being asked.* Consider the following item:

> The _____ River divides the states of _____ and _____.

Obviously there are dozens of different correct answers to the preceding question. If, however, the sentence were phrased as followed, the only possible answer is California.

> The Colorado River divides the states of Arizona and _____.

4. *For problems requiring numerical answers, specify the degree of precision required.* Consider the following examples.

> *Poor:* The size of Canada is approximately _____.
> *Better:* The size of Canada (within 100,000 square miles) is _____.

The actual area of Canada is 3,851,809 square miles. To avoid arguing about whether 6,000,000 square miles is correct, specify the required degree of accuracy.

GUIDELINES FOR WRITING AND SCORING ESSAY QUESTIONS

Essay questions are easier to construct than other kinds of test items—particularly if you want to test higher level cognitive skills. Essay questions also provide an opportunity for the student to demonstrate his ability to express written thoughts clearly, concisely, and correctly—an important skill not easily measured by the other kinds of test items we have discussed. Many people also believe that students prepare more thoroughly if they think essay questions will be asked. Here are two examples of essay items.

> Give two examples that demonstrate the differences between fiscal policy and monetary policy.

> Compare and contrast the social conditions, prevailing political thought, and economic conditions in the North and the South just prior to the outbreak of the Civil War.

Although essay questions are used frequently and vigorously defended by many, they have also been the object of much criticism. In fact, one of the most frequently cited examples of early educational research was a study by Starch and Elliot (1912, 1913b) that showed that when different teachers were asked to independently score the same "typical examination paper" in English and history, the results ranged from nearly perfect to a very low failure. In another early study, Eells (1930) found that when a teacher scored the same paper several months apart, the results were dramatically different.

Essay questions are also criticized because it takes a relatively long time for students to respond to them, fewer instructional objectives can be addressed during the same testing time, and they are time consuming to score. Such issues have prompted a great deal of controversy about the use of essay questions and emphasize the need to write essay questions carefully and score them in ways that avoid such problems. None of these problems is significant enough, however, to preclude the use of essay questions on tests.

In fact, although we are sure that the debate about whether or not to use essay questions will continue, we are just as sure that essay questions will continue to be widely used by teachers. Essay items appear to be simple to write, and it is this apparent simplicity that results in many of the problems noted above. The following eleven guidelines will help in writing good essay items.

1. *Restrict the use of essay questions to those learning outcomes that are difficult to measure with true-false, multiple-choice, matching, or completion items.* Never use essay questions simply to measure knowledge of facts. Even though it is difficult, it is possible to write fixed response items that measure higher level cognitive skills. In comparison, it is relatively easy to write essay questions that do this. Consider the following examples:

> *Poor item:* Public Law 99–457 is designed to encourage states to provide early intervention services to all children with handicaps. States who choose not to participate in P.L.99–457 will experience certain sanctions from the federal government. List those sanctions.

> *Better item:* Public Law 99–457 is designed to encourage states to provide early intervention services to all children with handicaps. States who choose not to participate in P.L.99–457 will

experience certain sanctions. Identify at least three sanctions that were considered but not included in the law. Discuss why you believe Congress selected the particular sanctions they did. Describe how effective you believe the sanctions will be in motivating states to participate.

The first question asks students to recall the sanctions included in the law. The second requires students not only to recall information but to present judgments about the worth or value of that information, and to predict how states will respond.

2. *Make sure that essay questions are appropriately focused and that students know exactly what is expected of them.* Sometimes essay questions are so general that it is difficult for students to know how to respond. Consider the following two questions.

Poor: Discuss the migration habits of birds.

Better: State two hypotheses about why birds migrate South in the fall. Summarize the evidence supporting each hypothesis and defend one you believe is most accurate.

With the poorly worded question, the student has a great deal of latitude about what to write and may completely miss the intent of the question. In fact, a testwise student may claim to have "misunderstood" the intent of the question and write a limited response based on those aspects of the question that are most familiar. It is also very difficult to score responses to questions that are as broadly worded as the poor example.

3. *Give students some guidelines as to time limits and amount of information expected.* Directions can be *too* specific and unnecessarily restrictive (e.g., make your answer 300 words long). Yet, students deserve and need some guidance regarding your expectations. Suggesting that students spend *about* 10 to 15 minutes or write *approximately* one page establishes some useful parameters that will help them know the level of detail you expect. The best way to estimate how much time or space is needed is to write out what you believe to be an appropriate response to the question before you give the test. Remember that students will require half again as much or more time because they do not know exactly what is wanted and have not mastered the material as well as you have. Generally, you do not want essay tests to be speeded tests. Instead, you want students to have time to organize and present their thoughts concisely and logically. It is usually wise to be somewhat generous in estimating time limits.

4. *Several items with a relatively narrow focus are generally better than one broad item.* One of the difficulties with essay questions is achieving sufficient sampling of the domain of instructional objectives. When broad essay questions are written, this disadvantage is accentuated. A better approach is to write multiple, more narrowly-focused essay questions that still require that the student demonstrate higher level cognitive skills but that assess mastery of a greater number of instructional objectives.

5. *Avoid the use of optional essay items.* Generally, students' scores will be compared either directly or indirectly. Such comparisons are only fair if all students respond to the same questions. Although it may reduce students' anxiety to have optional questions, it certainly decreases the validity of using scores to make comparisons, and there is no evidence that it increases the validity of the test for other purposes.

6. *Before giving the test, develop a list of the main points that should be included in each answer and develop a scoring system.* If true-false, multiple-choice, matching, and completion items have been written correctly, almost anybody who is careful can score the items. However, there is not just one correct answer to an essay question. Consequently, scoring is time consuming and difficult and must be done carefully. To be fair and accurate it is essential to prepare a scoring key that specifies the major points to be included, and the amount of credit to be assigned for each major point. This scoring outline should be developed *before* the test is administered so that you can make sure students have been taught what is expected in the answer, and you can give students some indication of how detailed each answer needs to be.

7. *Before scoring essays, review the material students were expected to learn.* You will be much more familiar with the content being tested than will students and in most cases, you will have enriched your knowledge with information from outside sources. Unless you are careful, you may be expecting students to use information from experiences or readings to which they have not been exposed. A quick review of course material and lectures will remind you how the course looks from their perspective and reduce the odds you will hold them accountable for material to which they have not been exposed.

8. *Inform students how you will deal with factors that are independent from the learning outcome being measured.* Variables such as the quality of handwriting, correctness of grammar, organization, and the use of interesting examples may influence the evaluation of essay questions—whether we intend them to or not. If those variables are reflected in the learning outcomes for the course, then they should be accorded some value in the scoring system. If they are not, they must not be allowed to influence scores. In any case, students should be informed prior to the time they take the test precisely which factors will influence their scores.

9. *Score essay questions without knowing which students produced which responses.* Unfortunately, a teacher may give more credit than is deserved to an answer because he believes the student really has mastered the learning outcome and simply did not demonstrate it in that particular response. Even when teachers are committed to not allowing previous performance to affect their scoring, there is a powerful subconscious influence that is difficult to avoid. The best way to skirt this source of bias is not to know which students wrote which responses. If you are so familiar with students' handwriting that their identity cannot be concealed, the best you can do is to make a conscious effort to eliminate any such bias from your scoring.

10. *Score all students responses to one item before scoring responses to another item.* Suppose you are scoring a test which contains five essay questions

for 25 students. One of the most difficult tasks in scoring essay questions is to keep the same standards as you score each paper. An average answer often receives a higher score if it follows a poor answer than if it follows an excellent one. One way to minimize such shifting of standards is to score all the answers to the first question, shuffle the papers, and score all the answers to the second question, and so on. This way, any bias associated with the order of scoring is balanced among students. Moreover, you only have to focus on one response at a time.

11. *Questions that ask students to draw a judgment or take a position should be evaluated based on the strength of their arguments, not on whether they agree with your position.* Because essay questions are often used to test higher order cognitive skills, students are frequently asked to evaluate information, make judgments, or defend a particular position. Some teachers have difficulty evaluating essays on the strength of the students' argument as opposed to whether the student agrees with their position. You should be aware of this potential source of bias and make sure that your scoring criteria are based on the *strength of the arguments presented.*

IN SUMMARY

Given all the guidelines and techniques for test development, not to mention the pros and cons of different types of test items, it is sometimes easy to forget the most important fact about testing. Namely, testing is only worthwhile if it contributes to better teaching and improved learning. To conclude this chapter, we share Frederiksen's perceptive thoughts on the powerful effect that the type of testing can have on learning.

> During World War II, . . . we conducted validity studies of the tests used in assigning recruits to naval training schools. One of our findings was that the best tests for predicting grades in gunner's mate schools were verbal and reading-comprehension tests, which didn't make much sense, in view of what gunner's mates are supposed to do. . . .
>
> Later, . . . we found that the lecture-demonstration method of teaching was used. The students studied the technical manuals, and . . . examinations [were] . . . based on the lectures and manuals. The items dealt with such topics as muzzle velocity and the function of the breech block locking bolt. Since the job for which these students were being trained was to maintain, adjust, and repair the guns aboard a warship, it seemed more reasonable to use performance tests. Accordingly, we developed a set of tests that required students to perform such tasks as . . . removing and replacing the extractor plunger on a 5/38'' antiaircraft gun. The instructors complained that the tests were too hard. They were right. Few of the students could perform the tasks, even with liberal time allowances. . . .
>
> The performance tests were nevertheless given at the end of each unit of training. . . . New students soon got word as to what the new tests were like, and they began practicing the assembly and disassembly of guns. . . . The instructors also got the point. They moved out the classroom chairs and the lecture podium and brought in more guns and gun mounts. The upshot was that students spent most

of their time practicing the skills required in repairing and adjusting guns. The tests soon became too easy. The validity coefficients changed too: the verbal and reading test validities dropped, and the mechanical aptitude and mechanical knowledge tests became the best bets for predicting grades in gunner's mate school.

Note that no attempt was made to change the curriculum or teacher behavior. The dramatic changes in achievement came about solely through a change in the tests. The moral is clear: It is possible to influence teaching and learning by changing the tests of achievement. (1984, p. 201)

SUGGESTED READINGS

Coffman, W. E. (1971). *Essay examinations*. In R. L. Thorndike (Ed.), *Educational measurement* (2d ed. pp. 271–302). Washington, DC: American Council on Education.

A comprehensive review and analysis of the research supporting and opposing the use of essay test questions. Although much of the research is now dated, more recent research is generally consistent with the conclusions of this article, which remains one of the best summaries of the issues.

Educational Testing Service. (1963). *Multiple choice questions: A close look*. Princeton, NJ: Educational Testing Service.

Although published almost 30 years ago, this short booklet is still one of the best examples available to show that multiple-choice test items can be used to measure higher level cognitive skills. Examples of such test items, along with item analysis data, and explanations of why particular distractors were chosen are used to illustrate the potential of good multiple-choice test items. This booklet is entertaining and valuable reading.

Educational Testing Service. (1985). *Creative classroom testing: 10 designs for assessment and instruction*. Princeton, NJ: Educational Testing Service.

In response to the frequently voiced perception that locally developed tests rely too much on essay, true-false, and multiple-choice test formats, ETS commissioned a committee of teachers to assemble examples of high-quality test items that use other formats. The resulting handbook describes a variety of different types of test items (illustrated with numerous examples) and outlines ways to practice the writing of such items. It is a thoughtfully prepared and stimulating book.

Gronlund, N. E. (1988). *How to construct achievement tests* (4th ed.). Englewood Cliffs, NJ: Prentice-Hall.

A much more detailed discussion than we have had space to present of the techniques for developing achievement test items. Many variations of the basic types of items are discussed. Numerous examples are included and the measurement of higher level cognitive outcomes is emphasized.

Roid, G. H., & Haladyna, T. M. (1982). *A technology for test item writing*. New York: Academic Press.

Many people believe that writing good test items is more an art than a science. The authors of this book believe otherwise. In this book, they offer extensive guidelines on how to systematically approach the writing of test items. The book provides a different and interesting perspective on how to write test items.

Osterlind, S. J. (1989). *Constructing test items*. Boston: Kluwer Academic.

The author intended this book to be the definitive reference on how to plan, design, and write high-quality test items. The book focuses on three main concerns: (1) the characteristics and functions of test items, (2) prescriptive rules for writing test items including editorial and stylistic guidelines, and (3) methods for assessing the quality of test items. The book also includes a compendium of other issues and concerns related to generating items.

SELF-CHECK QUIZ

1. Having a colleague review all of your test items used in assigning final grades is
   a. required by federal legislation, but is often not enforced.
   b. good for multiple-choice items, but usually not beneficial for others.
   c. usually not worth the time and effort if you've had a good measurement class.
   d. one of the best ways to improve your skill and ensure good items.

2. A *double-barreled* question refers to a
   a. true-false question that consists of two components, each of which could be true or false.
   b. true-false question in which the student marks and corrects the part that makes it false.
   c. multiple choice question that has two correct answers.
   d. matching question that includes two different types of relationships.

3. A multiple-choice item that contains unnecessary detail, elaboration, or clarification in the stem, is said to have
   a. distractors.
   b. window dressing.
   c. response bias.
   d. an obscure premise.

4. In scoring the responses to essay questions it is best to
   a. assign scores without knowing whose paper it is.
   b. assign scores based on your initial impression after reading the paper.
   c. use Bloom's taxonomy as a guide.
   d. refer back to your test blueprint to establish reference points.

5. Matching exercises are *usually* best for measuring
   a. relational synthesis.
   b. evaluation.
   c. application.
   d. knowledge.

6. One of the main limitations of using essay questions is that
   a. only a limited range of the course content can be sampled in a given testing period.
   b. students with partial knowledge are likely to guess the correct answer.
   c. only a narrow range of lower level objectives can be tested.
   d. writing good questions is more difficult and time consuming compared to other types of questions.

7. Which of the following best complies with the guidelines for writing completion test items?
   a. The Civil War started in _____.
   b. When did the Civil War begin? _____.
   c. The beginning of the Civil War was _____ .
   d. In what year did the Civil War begin? _____.

8. When writing true-false items, it is important to avoid using words such as *usually, sometimes, always,* and *never* because the presence of one of these words
   a. decreases the reliability of scores obtained from the test.
   b. provides a clue to the correct answer.
   c. makes the statement ambiguous.
   d. tends to penalize poor readers.

9. What is the most difficult task involved in constructing good multiple-choice questions?
   a. Wording the stem so that it presents a clear, meaningful problem.
   b. Creating distractors that are clearly incorrect, but plausible.
   c. Writing an answer that is clearly and unambiguously correct.
   d. Ensuring that the position of the correct answer varies randomly from item to item.

10. When writing options for multiple-choice questions, the best practice is to
    a. always include at least four options even if some of them are not very plausible.
    b. include only options that are plausible even if this means using only three alternatives.
    c. use *None of the above* or *All of the above* as options if necessary.
    d. avoid wasting time worrying about the number of alternatives included.

SUGGESTION SHEET

If your name starts with the letter *K*, please complete the suggestion sheet at the end of the book while this chapter is still fresh in your mind.

ANSWERS TO APPLICATION PROBLEMS

#1

The item asks which animal does not belong with the others. Unfortunately, there are a number of correct answers to this question, depending on what strategy is used to organize the information. One correct answer would be *c*, using the rationale that the beaver is not indigenous to Africa as are all the others. Another correct answer would be *d*, using the rationale that the lion is the only animal that is not comfortable spending substantial amounts of time in the water. Another correct answer would be *b*, using the rationale that the crocodile is the only animal listed that is not a mammal. The item would be better if the stem were more specific. For example, "Which of the following animals is not a mammal?"

#2

There are a number of problems with this matching exercise. First, the exercise is too long. Second even if you want to use such a heterogeneous group of items, the directions could be made much clearer. More appropriate directions would read something like the following:

> *Directions:* Two columns of information are listed below. Place the letter corresponding to the appropriate person or place from the list on the right in front of the number that matches from the list on the left. Each person or place can be used only once.

Of course, the exercise is more heterogeneous than we would recommend for a single matching exercise. Four of the options are names of cities, one is a country, four are names of persons, and one is a plural noun. There are also several clues that would enable a student to get some credit even if he had not mastered the material. For example, only one item calls for the name of a country and there is only one country listed in the options. Only four items need to be matched with the names of persons. Without too much difficulty, the student can make some pretty good guesses at these items. For example, item 3 is probably a French name. Of the four possible names (*d, f, g,* and *i*), only Marquis de Lafayette sounds French. Item 9 is a "give-away" because most people associate Benedict Arnold with being a traitor even if they've never studied American History. Thus, the student has a 50-50 chance on the remaining two names. Item 8 is the only item that calls for a plural ("they") and so option *a* is another giveaway. If you look carefully, you can see a number of other clues a testwise student could use to get a good score on this item without having mastered the material.

The Process of Becoming an Expert Tester: Assembly, Administration, and Analysis

Overview

We have never met a perfect tester. In fact, there are very few expert testers, but the secret to becoming better is twofold. First, remember that testing consists of more than writing technically correct items. Second, use your experience and the information available from past tests to improve your skills as a test developer and administrator.

This chapter summarizes a process and teaches you the skills you will need to improve your ability as an educational tester. Having mastered the skills of writing technically correct items (Chapters 9 and 10), you are now ready to master the skills that separate the professionals from the also-rans.

The purpose of testing is to produce accurate information about students' knowledge, skills, and attitudes. But even the best items can yield misleading or inaccurate information if the test is inappropriately assembled or administered. By analyzing the results of items you write, you can continually improve their quality. This chapter describes a cyclical process, consisting of assembly—administration—analysis, which can be used to substantially improve the quality and usefulness of information produced by tests.

Objectives

Upon completing your study of this chapter, you should be able to

1. Describe the advantages in and procedures for maintaining a file of test items.
2. Summarize the issues that should be considered in reviewing test items.
3. Explain how individual items should be arranged and formatted for a test.
4. Describe the key elements of good test directions.
5. Explain how to make testing a positive and productive experience for students.
6. Explain the pros and cons of different scoring techniques.
7. Explain how to discuss test results with students.
8. Explain the benefits and dangers of using item analysis procedures.
9. Demonstrate an item analysis procedure that can be used with teacher-made, norm-referenced tests.
10. Demonstrate an item analysis procedure that can be used with teacher-made, criterion-referenced tests.

ASSEMBLING THE TEST

Most tests you give will be ones you have written. If you think about tests like Christmas presents, commercially available tests come preassembled, but teacher-made tests have to be assembled before they are given. Unfortunately, like the exhausted parent on Christmas Eve trying to assemble the bicycle from "easy to read" instructions, teachers often leave test assembly to the last minute when they are exhausted and not likely to do their best work.

The process of assembling a good test can be broken into four steps:

1. Collecting or developing test items.
2. Reviewing test items.
3. Formatting the test.
4. Preparing directions for the test.

If you purchase a standardized test, these steps have already been completed. But, for the tests you develop, you will have to do all these steps yourself.

COURSE __History__   **UNIT**__ Revolutionary War__

OBJECTIVE _____

_____

ITEM

Who was the most influential in convincing the French to assist the Americans during the Revolutionary War with England?

    a) **George Washington**
    b) **Marquis de Lafayette**
 *c) **Benjamin Franklin**
    d) **Benedict Arnold**
    e) **Count de Rochambeau**

Date of last revision: *November 1991*

FIGURE 11.1   Example of Test Item Card

Collecting Test Items

Some teachers write test items a few hours before administering the test. The dangers (as well as the unnecessary stress) of this approach are obvious. A better procedure is to regularly develop item cards such as the one shown in Figure 11.1. Such cards can be prepared as you prepare lesson plans, or at the end of each teaching session. By developing items as you teach on a day-to-day basis, it is easier to create items for those aspects of instruction that you consider most important.

A collection of such cards is referred to as a *test item file*. Such a file gives greater flexibility and will lead to more effective tests. For example, you will always teach more material than you can include in a test. If you have already prepared items for all your lesson concepts, you can select a representative sample, or items to emphasize particular concepts. A pool of items also allows you to develop parallel forms of a test so that you can give students practice or make-up tests. Practice tests give students an opportunity to become familiar with the test-taking format so that their test performance will show what they know, instead of how well they have mastered the format and procedures.

A test item file also increases test security because you will have many more items than will be administered on any single test. Thus, you can use different items each time, making it impossible for students to cheat by obtaining a copy of a previous test. A test item file also contributes to the development of technically adequate items. If you have a pool of items from which to choose, you can afford to discard or rework items that exhibit weaknesses based on analyses of prior use.

Finally, an item file can help focus your teaching. Usually you will want to be teaching content that can be measured by a test item. Having a test item file provides a convenient way of double checking the importance of material included in your lesson plans. If there are not items in your test file for the information being taught, you should usually either create items, or reevaluate the amount of time spent teaching that concept. Obviously, there are some important concepts for which it is difficult, if not impossible, to create a test item. But the majority of information covered should be testable as well as teachable.

Reviewing Test Items

One major advantage of a test item file is that you will have time to review and refine items before using them. You can even have other people review the items to see whether the test results are likely to provide useful information. No matter how carefully items have been written, some will inevitably have weaknesses. For example, there may be verbal clues to the correct answer in the item stem. An item may be too difficult or may contain distractors that are implausible. Sometimes a second correct answer will mistakenly be included in a multiple-choice item. Your test writing skills will improve substantially if you set items aside for a few days after writing them, and then review them from the vantage point of the test taker.

As you review items, remember that each should provide information about how well students have mastered the content you are teaching. The following questions may help in refining the items you have written.

Is the item format appropriate for what you want to test? The item should require that students exhibit the type of behavior you wanted them to learn. For example, identifying the correct definition among a group of possible alternatives is very different from providing the correct definition when no alternatives are presented. In the former case, a multiple-choice item would be appropriate; but in the latter, a short-answer format would be better.

Is the intent of the item clear and unambiguous? Whether a student answers an item correctly should always be a function of how well she has mastered the content, not whether she understands the question. For example, items should have no awkward sentence construction, double-barreled questions, inappropriate vocabulary, or ambiguous intent. Reviewing items some time after writing them will help you identify problems you may have missed as the item was written.

Is the item straightforward and concise? Some item writers include extra material in the introduction of an item, as if to justify the content being tested, or perhaps in an effort to make the item more interesting. Such information may distract students from what is being tested and give an advantage to better readers. In most cases, items should be as concise as possible. Information not contributing directly to the skill being tested should be eliminated.

Is the item written at the appropriate level of difficulty? The difficulty level for criterion-referenced or mastery tests should be very different than for norm-referenced tests. In a mastery test, you want to know whether all students have mastered the minimum competencies. If instruction has been successful, you would expect all students to get most items correct. For a norm-referenced test, you want items that will "spread out" the members of the class, creating a continuum where there is a direct relationship between how well students have mastered the material and how many items they answer correctly. Ideally, with a norm-referenced test, about 50 percent of the class would answer any given item correctly.

Does the item have a "best" answer? Most items that are testing students' knowledge of factual material have unambiguous correct answers (e.g., 11 + 14 always equals 25). However, those items that ask students to provide the *best* answer or make the *most appropriate* interpretation can be problematic unless the distractors are carefully worded.

Is the item free from bias? All items should be written in language that is acceptable, nonoffensive, and equally understandable to different groups of people. Stereotypes (e.g., men consistently in executive roles, minorities in subservient roles, or women in homemaking roles) should be avoided.

Is the item free from irrelevant clues? Some items contain clues that allow a person to get the correct answer without having mastered the content. Such technical errors are often apparent only after an item has been set aside for a while.

Until now, the review process has focused on individual items. Even if you had perfect individual items, however, combining them into a test can create problems unless you pay attention to the following issues.

Is the group of items representative of the course content? Although it is usually impossible, because of time, to test all the material you have taught, make sure that items included on the test are *representative* of the material covered. In a course on American history, for instance, you would not want all the items to be based on the post–World War II era. Referencing items to course objectives, or to a test blueprint, helps to assess representativeness.

Do the items adequately cover the material taught? Coverage goes beyond representativeness by asking whether items provide the information necessary to make desired interpretations. For example, consider a test on American history that contains one item from each of the following periods:

- Prior to and including the Revolutionary War
- Between the Revolutionary War and the Civil War
- Between the Civil War and World War I
- After World War I

Such a test could be said to be representative of American history in that each period is equally represented by items. Nonetheless, it probably does not provide enough information about any single period to allow meaningful interpretations. While the number of items needed to make such interpretations will vary depending on the purpose of the instruction and the age of students, adequate coverage of each period will usually require more than a single item.

Is the group of items free from unnecessary overlap and duplication? Unnecessary duplication occurs when you have a number of items testing the same objective, but no items testing other equally important objectives.

Are items independent? Sometimes the stem of one item provides an unnecessary clue to the answer of another. Other times, items are written so that the correct answer can only be known if previous items have been answered correctly. In most cases, items should be independent.

Is the time required to answer the items appropriate? Balancing the need for greater coverage or more in-depth information with appropriate expectations for students' endurance and concentration is always difficult. You are in the best position to estimate your students' attention span and the length of time they can work at full capacity. Gauge the length of the test for the attention span of the lower third of the class rather than for the best students. In this way, students' ability to remain on task is less likely to play a role in their performance.

APPLICATION PROBLEM #1

Assume you are a seventh grade biology teacher. A friend who is teaching seventh grade biology in another school asks you to review her midterm examination because she knows you have been taking this class. Describe briefly the issues you would consider in reviewing her test.

Formatting the Test

Imagine you have all the components necessary to assemble a computer laid out on the table in front of you. Even though each component has been engineered to exact specifications, you could not produce a functioning computer by putting all the components into a bag and rattling them around for a while. Similarly, items haphazardly tossed together will not produce a coherent or effective test. Having developed, reviewed, and fine-tuned test items, it is important to assemble them correctly. The following guidelines will help.

Items with similar formats should be grouped together. A test will be more understandable if all the true-false items are grouped together, all the matching items are grouped together, and so on. Grouping similar items has several advantages. First, fewer sets of directions are required. Second, students can answer more items in the same amount of time since they do not have to switch gears continually. Third, scoring—particularly handscoring—is facilitated. And, fourth, there is less chance that students will be confused by alternating formats.

Proceed from the easiest to the most difficult items. How frustrating it must be for a student who is already apprehensive to discover she is unable to answer the first five questions. Many measurement experts believe that putting a few items that everyone can answer at the beginning of the test gives students confidence and allows them to better demonstrate what they really know (Sax & Cromak, 1966; Towle & Merrill, 1975). Although the position is logical, the empirical evidence is inconclusive (Hambleton & Traub, 1974; Klosner & Gellman, 1973). Nevertheless, in the absence of contrary evidence, it is probably best to arrange items from easiest to hardest.

Make the test as readable as possible. Tests that are neatly typed with clear illustrations and uncrowded spacing seem less threatening and difficult. Be sure that each item is distinct from the others. Diagrams or drawings should be accurately portrayed and placed above the stem of the item so that students do not lose track of what is being asked. Keep the stem of the item and the options on the same page so that students do not miss information or have to flip back and forth to answer questions.

Avoid predictable response patterns. Answers should not follow a predictable pattern: T F T F T F, or, C D B A C D B A. Rather, answers should be arranged in an unpredictable or random pattern. That way, students will not waste time trying to figure out the pattern, but will focus on answering the questions.

Preparing Directions for the Test

The teacher who spends a lot of time carefully developing test items and assembling them into a representative test only to throw directions together at the last minute is like the expedition leader who carefully assembles her equipment, engages in weeks of physical conditioning, and then sets off for her destination without a map.

Clear, concise, understandable test directions are essential if a test is to accomplish its purpose. It is particularly important that the directions be understood by *all* students taking the test—especially those who have difficulty reading or using standard English. It is often worthwhile to read directions aloud to the students. Directions should also always be written, even if given orally, because written directions provide a source of information for students to refer to during the test. Test directions should also explain what the student is to do, how to do it, where to record the answers, and how the information will be used. The following guidelines can assist you in preparing test directions.

Provide a specific set of directions for each different type of item format. Although general directions are useful, each group of items with a similar format should have directions explaining how answers are to be recorded, what to do about guessing, and how many points each item is worth.

Explain the basis for scoring. Directions should indicate whether partial credit will be given; whether points will be subtracted for lack of neatness, grammatical errors, or spelling mistakes; and whether students are expected to show their work.

Specify the amount of available time. In addition to noting how much time students have for the entire test, indicate the approximate time expected for each section so students can pace themselves. Such guidelines also help students know how much detail is expected. It is usually better to provide too much time than to make time limits so restrictive that some cannot finish.

Even though directions are written, make sure every student understands what is expected. Because you want to know how well students have mastered the content being tested, instead of how well they can understand the directions, it is important to make sure they understand what is expected. Written directions should be sufficiently detailed so that a student can understand exactly what is expected without having it discussed orally. However, for those students who have difficulty processing written information, it is important to discuss the test directions.

It is often useful to try out your directions with other teachers or with pupils of about the same age and ability level as your own before an actual test. Having others read through the directions and explain which parts are unclear or confusing can save substantial time during the test administration. A particularly useful technique is to ask reviewers to explain in their own words what they think is required on the test. Figure 11.2 is a checklist that you can use to help you assemble a good test.

FIGURE 11.2   A Checklist to Use in Assembling Items into a Useful Test

TEST ASSEMBLY CHECKLIST

_____ 1. Are items clear, concise, and free from jargon or unnecessarily difficult vocabulary?

_____ 2. Do items avoid sexual or racial bias?

_____ 3. Has someone else reviewed the items?

_____ 4. Has the answer key been checked?

_____ 5. Are items grouped according to type or format?

_____ 6. Are items arranged from easiest to most difficult?

_____ 7. Are items appropriately spaced?

_____ 8. Are item stems, options, and support material (e.g., diagrams) appropriately arranged?

_____ 9. Is the answer sequence random?

_____ 10. Are items representative of the material taught?

_____ 11. Can the test be completed in a reasonable time?

_____ 12. Have directions been checked for clarity?

_____ 13. Has someone else proofread the final copy for errors?

_____ 14. Is a space provided for students to write their names?

APPLICATION PROBLEM #2

The following directions are for a true-false test in a fifth grade social studies class.

Directions:

Listed below are 30 questions. For each question, circle whether you think the answer is True (T) or False (F).

What else should be included?

ADMINISTERING THE TEST

Although there are some differences, the general principles of test administration apply both to commercially available and teacher-made tests. Whether the test is a norm-referenced, criterion-referenced, applied performance, or a weekly quiz, there are certain principles that will make results more valid and usable. (Not to mention the fact that proper test administration will reduce students' anxiety).

It is important to remember that all classroom activities, including testing, should be positive experiences that result in productive outcomes. Students should leave the test feeling good about themselves and the work they have accomplished. Furthermore, the test should produce valid information about how well students have mastered the goals of instruction, and should contribute to more effective future instruction.

All tests should give students a fair opportunity to demonstrate their mastery of whatever is being measured. Therefore, the test-taking environment should be structured so that factors other than students' mastery of learning outcomes are minimized. If we are giving a chemistry test, we want the student's score to reflect her knowledge of chemistry, not her test-taking ability, her mood, or her ability to ignore distracting influences during testing.

Test taking will be a positive and productive experience for both students and teachers if we create a situation in which

1. Students have mastered appropriate test-taking skills.
2. Students are motivated to try their best.
3. Appropriate test administration procedures are used.

Here are some guidelines to help you in creating such an environment.

Be positive! Threatening students with tests if they misbehave, or with negative consequences if they fail a test, will convince them that tests are punishments rather than educational tools. Testing is already a traumatic experience for some students. Teachers can reduce the anxiety associated with testing by approaching it as a normal, important part of the educational experience and by demonstrating throughout the year that test results will be used to improve instruction. It is also important to convince students that they will be valued regardless of their test scores.

Make sure the physical space is appropriate. Tests should be administered in a physical setting which is familiar, and comfortable, whether it is an end-of-year standardized achievement test, or a regularly scheduled Wednesday quiz. A simple way to reduce unnecessary distractions is to close the classroom door and hang a sign on the outside that says, "Do Not Disturb—Testing." Check the seating arrangement. Students should not feel tempted to look at others' papers or be distracted every time someone needs to sharpen a pencil or leave the room. Having an aide assist with testing is highly desirable. Because most standardized achievement tests use aides during norming, you should particularly try to use an aide during standardized achievement testing.

Motivate students to do their best. Balance your efforts at reducing test anxiety with communicating a need for students to do their best. Research has demonstrated that highly motivated students do substantially better on standardized achievement and aptitude tests than similar, unmotivated students (Taylor & White, 1982). One of the most effective ways to reduce anxiety and increase motivation is to honestly convey to students the valuable contribution that testing makes to improving the teaching/learning process. Students who understand the reasons for testing are likely to do much better.

Avoid making statements that suggest that test results do not matter or that testing is unimportant. Imagine how students will respond if the teacher announces a test by saying:

> "I know you would rather be doing other things today and so would I. Unfortunately, the school board is requiring us to take this stupid test. You probably won't know a lot of the answers, and I don't really care how you do because I don't use the results anyway. But, I will get in trouble if I don't give you the test, so let's just get through it as best we can."

Know the test. If you have developed the test yourself, you will already be familiar with the content and format. With standardized achievement tests, however, becoming familiar with the test requires extra effort. One of the best ways to become familiar with a test is to take it yourself. Admittedly, this is time consuming, but you are likely to find it time well spent. Afterward, you will have a much better idea how results can be useful in teaching, and you will understand how students might become confused or frustrated by various items.

Make sure students understand what they are to do. Standardized achievement tests often require that students do things that are outside their regular routine. Without careful preparation, such tests may measure students' test-taking skills rather than their knowledge of content or skill in applying that knowledge. For example, standardized achievement tests require students to answer questions in formats that may be unfamiliar, to understand vocabulary that they may not have heard before, and to work more independently than usual. Since these expectations are not a part of most day-to-day classroom environments, some students may have difficulty demonstrating their knowledge of the content being tested.

Consider the results of a study conducted by White and Carcelli (1982). Second grade students were tested on exactly the same arithmetic items presented in eight different formats from popular standardized achievement tests. As Figure 11.3 shows, students' scores ranged from 26 percent correct to 81 percent correct.

Similar examples abound. The best way to make sure students understand what they are to do is to administer a *practice test* that is similar in format and content to the actual test. Almost all widely used standardized achievement tests provide practice tests and base their norms on test administrations that gave practice tests. Such practice tests tend to reduce students' anxiety by giving them a chance to become familiar with format and procedures. Students who are less anxious are in a better position to demonstrate what they really know—thus increasing the value of test results.

Your responsibility to make sure students understand what is being asked of them does not end with the practice test. During test administration, you may clarify directions as long as such clarification is not expressly prohibited by the standardized instructions. Most directions for standardized achievement tests allow students to ask questions after the directions have been given. However, most students are reluctant to pose questions. An alert teacher will watch for students who seem confused and make sure they understand what is expected before commencing the test.

Equalize advantages. Some students are better test takers than others. Do what you can to equalize test taking skills. For example, you might instruct students when it is best to guess at answers they do not know, and remind them about the general test taking strategies such as checking answers if they finish early, and skipping over difficult items and coming back to them later. Never give hints to students about the correct answers. Make sure all students understand rules about time limits, marking answer sheets, and clarifying directions. Keep the amount of time between breaks appropriate for those students with less endurance or shorter attention spans. A general guideline for the maximum amount of testing between breaks is given below.

Grade	*Amount of Testing Time*
K–3	30 minutes
4–6	60 minutes
7–12	90 minutes

Monitor the test administration. Most of us have seen teachers who pass out tests and then grade papers or read while students work. The fact that the tests have been distributed does not mean that the teacher can take a break. Indeed, this is one of the most important times if the students are to be able to demonstrate what they really know. The teacher is responsible for minimizing distractions, preventing cheating, and keeping students on task. Circulating about the room and establishing eye-to-eye contact or prompting a student whose attention is beginning to wander are ways of keeping students on task.

Cheating is more of a problem. As DeCecco noted:

> Failure to prevent cheating may have serious deleterious effects on student achievement: 1) when cheating occurs with impunity, honest achievement goes

TYPE OF FORMAT	RESULTS Percentage Correct on 12 Items
FORMAT #1: Wide Range Achievement Test Level I "Jack had six marbles. He found two more. How many did he have?" Oral response.	43%
FORMAT #2: Stanford Achievement Test Level II Form A "Read the problem to yourself and then mark under your answer." $2 + \square = 8$ 11 6 5 N 0 0 0 0	39%
FORMAT #3: Stanford Achievement Test 2 26 8 5 N +6 0 0 0 0	74%

FORMAT #4: SRA Achievement Series   Level C   Form 1
 	
"Work the problem, then fill in the space in front of the right answer."
 	
[2
  +6]   8   4   26   12
           0   0   0   0
	81%

FORMAT #5: Iowa Test of Basic Skills Level 7 Form 7 "What is two added to six? What is two plus six? Mark your answer in the row with the bird." 🕊 7 8 10 N 0 0 0 0	78%
FORMAT #6: Iowa Test of Basic Skills $6 + 2 =$ 12 8 9 N 0 0 0 0	67%
FORMAT #7: Key Math "These are addition problems. You may use a pencil if you wish." 6 + 2	72%
FORMAT #8: Key Math "Tell me about the number that goes in the box." $6 + \square = 8$	26%

FIGURE 11.3 Percentage Correct for 12 Arithmetic Items Answered by Students Using Different Formats

SOURCE: White and Carcelli, 1982.

unrecognized or punished and reduces student motivation to achieve; 2) there is no way to assess validly or reliably what the student has or has not learned; and, 3) ingenuity in devising ways to cheat becomes more important than attainment of the instructional objectives. (1968, p.640)

Recognized problems with cheating have led to such countermeasures as alternate seating arrangements or parallel testing forms, but research has shown that such techniques are not particularly effective (Houston, 1976). What's more, they're often impractical. Where there is good student-teacher rapport, and students are convinced that tests are helpful rather than punishing, cheating is less of a problem. An alert teacher who carefully monitors test administration with the intent of helping students do their best seems to be the best deterrent to cheating.

Documenting threats to test validity. No amount of preparation can totally remove the influence of unexpected events that impact on the validity of a particular test for a specific student. If Rachael is not feeling well the day of a test it does not matter that she has good test taking skills, feels positive about tests in general, and is motivated to do her best. She still won't perform well.

Such threats to test validity are less a problem for interpreting the results of locally developed tests since they are given more frequently, and substandard performance on any single test will be balanced by more typical performance on others. Since standardized achievement tests are given infrequently, however, you should be particularly alert for incidences that may explain a lower than deserved score for a particular student.

Although you will usually not have the luxury of re-administering a standardized achievement test for students who do poorly, it is important to note factors that may have contributed to their subpar performance. Such information can help you interpret test results and make better instructional decisions. One way of doing this is by using the "Teacher Index to Valid Test Performance" (Taylor, White, Bush, & Friedman, 1982). An example of what this index might look like when completed for a typical third grade class during standardized achievement testing is shown in Figure 11.4.

Standards for Test Administration

Problems caused by poor test administration have prompted a number of organizations to develop standards and guidelines to govern testing. One particularly clear set of standards was developed by three major professional organizations: Standards from that document that are most relevant for testing in schools are given below.

Standard 15.1   In typical applications, test administrators should follow carefully the standardized procedures for administration and scoring specified by the test publisher. Specifications regarding instructions to test takers, time limits, the form of item presentation or response, and test materials or equipment should be strictly observed.

Standard 15.2   The testing environment should be one of reasonable comfort

TEACHER INDEX TO VALID TEST PERFORMANCE

Student Name	lost place, confused	left blanks	poor attention	finished early	talking	cheating (?)	left room	Comments
John Albania				✓				
Frank Savage								
Harriet Rosenbaum								
Tom Braddock			✓					typical lack of attention, needs help before next test.
Liza Melmed								
Gary Barnett							✓	
Chuck Harris				✓				
Chris Henkle								
Nadine Olson				✓				
Marcia Golonca								
Katie Smith								
Monica Thomas	✓							not sure she knew what was expected on matching exercises.
Cheryl Nilson								
Reed Rowland	✓	✓		✓	?			didn't appear to feel well, may have been copying from Mark.
Mark Armstrom								
Brad Illich								
Maria Gonzales				✓				finished unusually early, which is not like her.
Carl Englestrom								
Harold Nordica								
Sophia Zimmerman				✓				
Vicky Roshle				✓				

April 18, 1992   SAT - Word Attack
Date of Test   Name of Test

FIGURE 11.4 An Example of a Completed "Teacher Index to Valid Test Performance" for a Standardized Achievement Test

and with minimal distractions. Testing materials should be readable and understandable. . . .

Standard 15.3   Reasonable efforts should be made to assure the validity of test scores by eliminating opportunities for test takers to attain scores by fraudulent means. . . .

Standard 15.4   In school situations not involving admissions . . ., any modification of standard test administration procedures or scoring should be described in the testing reports with appropriate cautions regarding the possible effects of such modifications on validity. . . .

Standard 15.7   Test users should protect the security of test materials. (AERA et al., 1985, p. 83–84)

Another important test administration issue is the competence of those who administer the tests. Some tests should only be administered by those who have had extensive training and experience in using those precise instruments, whereas other tests can be administered with basic instructions and limited orientation.

Although there are exceptions, the degree of competence generally required to administer various types of tests is outlined below.

Type of Test	*Necessary Qualifications*
Projective tests (e.g., Rorschach)	Extensive training and experience in administering these instruments, and in the underlying psychometric theory
Personality tests	
Individual intelligence tests (e.g., WISC-R)	
Aptitude tests	Knowledge of the principles of testing including some acquaintance with its technical and statistical aspects
Interest and inventory tests	
Attitude tests	
Teacher-made tests	
Standardized achievement tests	Orientation to the testing procedures and familiarity with content of the test manual

We do not hold with the prevalent view that classroom teachers are not competent to use educational tests (although we do agree that some test administrations require special competence, as noted above). The words of McCall echo to us from a half a century ago.

> Many years ago, certain specialists sought to secure a monopoly of the privilege of using standard tests by trying to persuade educators to regard the tests as possessing certain mystic properties. A few of us with Promethean tendencies set about taking these sacred cows away from the gods and giving them to mortals. Can teachers be entrusted with tests? If not, then teachers ought not to be trusted with 90% of their present functions. We now entrust them with the far more difficult task of teaching reading, creating concepts, and building ideals. Let us not strain at a gnat when we have swallowed fifty elephants. (1936, p. 3)

We share McCall's viewpoint. Teachers can and should be taught to use tests well.

SCORING TESTS

When students hand in their tests, their work is done, but yours is just beginning. How will you score the tests? There are many different techniques, each offering its own advantages and disadvantages. The best technique depends on the type of test, the ages and abilities of the students, and the resources available. During your own experience taking tests, you were probably exposed to most scoring techniques, but did not pay much attention, since you were more concerned about your score than the process used to produce it. To get an idea of the issues you are facing now, try your hand at the following true-false quiz.

T. F   1.   Separate answer sheets are always preferred for objective tests because they provide a more accurate measure of what the student really knows.

T F   2. By weighting items differentially, you can substantially improve the precision and validity of a test.

T F   3. Computerized scoring services should not be trusted because of the errors made by optical scanning equipment.

T F   4. Before submitting tests to a publisher's scoring service, you should not make or erase any marks on the separate answer sheet that accompanies the test.

T F   5. Once tests have been corrected and handed back, it is acceptable to give credit for an alternative answer.

T F   6. It is always inappropriate to consider factors other than the content being tested such as neatness, spelling, or grammar.

T F   7. Discussing specific items on the tests with students too soon after the test has been completed often results in unnecessary anxiety and frustration.

Scoring a test is not just a matter of marking answers and adding up numbers. Issues such as those in the preceding quiz (incidentally, all the answers except 5 are *false*) emphasize the need to be informed about different approaches to scoring. We will focus on objective tests since they constitute the majority of the tests you will be administering and scoring. (In Chapters 9 and 10, we discussed ways to improve the scoring of essay tests.) With objective tests, you have two basic choices: handscoring and machine scoring.

Handscoring

Because scoring objective tests is essentially a clerical task, many educators do not devote as much attention to it as they should. Unfortunately there are many opportunities to make mistakes. For example, Phillips and Weathers (1958) found mistakes in almost 30 percent of approximately 5,000 Stanford Achievement Tests scored by teachers as a part of their regular administration. Goodwin (1966) found similar results when the tests were scored by clerks.

A number of techniques have been developed to increase the efficiency and reduce the errors in scoring tests. One is to prepare an answer key on a strip of paper that you can lay over the student's paper alongside the answers. This enables you to score rapidly. But, rather than just marking the incorrect responses, it's a good idea to mark every item—perhaps by using a "√" for correct answers, and an "X" for incorrect answers.

Another method is to use a stencil the same size as the response sheet with holes punched out to note the location of the correct answers. This stencil, often referred to as a *scoring template*, can be laid over the top of the student's test form, and a mark made in each hole where no student answer is present. Before using such a key, you should scan the answer sheets to identify any questions for which more than one alternative was selected.

A third method is to have the test questions recorded on a page attached to a carbon page. When the student writes answers on the top page, the mark automatically transfers to the second page—which is sealed so the student cannot see it. The second page is constructed in such a way that correct answers will automatically appear inside a box, while incorrect answers will be outside the box. The number of marks appearing in the boxes indicates the total score.

If separate answer sheets are used, students must be familiar with the format and process necessary to complete them. Always administer a practice test using the same type of answer sheet. Research suggests that separate answer sheets should not be used with children at the second grade or under (Cashen & Ramseyer, 1969; Ramseyer & Cashen, 1971; Gaffney & Maguire, 1971); older children, however, can use them quite successfully.

Before giving the test, develop an answer key even if you wrote the questions yourself. This may sound obvious, yet many people have been embarrassed by skipping this step, then discovering that some questions had multiple correct answers.

If you handscore tests, you will likely be doing the scoring yourself. However, if you have clerical assistants, remember that they will probably not be as motivated as you, and consequently may not be as careful. Make sure that clerical assistants have been thoroughly trained and have had an opportunity to score practice tests before doing the actual tests. You should also have about 10 percent of the tests rescored during each scoring session to check error rates. If you discover that an unacceptable number of errors are being made, you should rescore all the tests. Having scorers initial each test is useful since they are more likely to be careful if they know that mistakes can be traced to them.

Although a great deal has been written about weighting test items differentially, there is no evidence that this results in more reliable scores, (e.g., Echternacht, 1976; Hakstian & Kansup, 1975; Raffeld, 1975). Differential weighting does make scoring more complex and introduces more opportunity for error.

Should students be given credit for partial knowledge of test content? This is a difficult question. One way of giving partial credit is to have students indicate how confident they are of each response. But while this method has received a great deal of interest among psychometricians, there is little evidence to suggest that it makes scores more reliable. Furthermore, it introduces another variable of complexity—which can result in other errors. Our advice at present is that weighting systems and confidence scoring procedures are not worth the extra effort.

There is nothing wrong with having such variables as neatness, spelling, grammar, or completeness of computations considered in scoring. However, it is essential to inform students well before the test if such variables are to be included.

Machine Scoring

Given proper preparations, machine scoring can be very efficient and accurate. Although machine scoring (a combination of an optical scanner and a computer) is most common for commercially available tests, many larger school systems have test scoring machines for locally developed tests as well. The general guidelines are the same.

First, make sure that students are familiar with the format and the procedures for providing answers. This is especially critical if a separate answer sheet is used. Give a practice test prior to the actual test so there will not be unnecessary anxiety or confusion. Second, after students have finished the test, check the answer sheets to make sure they have been filled out completely. Darken any answers that have been filled in too lightly (otherwise the optical scanning machine may miss them) and erase any stray marks or marginal notes the student has made. If such marks are not erased, the optical scanner may count them as intended responses. When multiple answers are marked where a single answer was requested, they will generally be marked incorrect but check to see how your program does it.

DISCUSSING TEST RESULTS WITH STUDENTS

Think about your own experience taking tests. When you did well, you felt the test was fair, and felt good about yourself and the teacher. What about those times when you did not do so well? You were probably frustrated and may have thought that the test was unfair. Those feelings emphasize the need, clearly supported by research, for discussing test results with students (Anderson, Kulhavy, & Andre, 1971; Wexley & Thornton, 1972). Such discussion not only gives them an opportunity to "let off steam," but often results in substantially improved test items and a valuable learning experience for them.

Here are a few guidelines about handling such a debriefing. First, debrief as soon after testing as feasible when impressions are still fresh. You will occasionally discover items that are subject to misinterpretation. Discuss such discoveries before handing tests back to students. Let students know that you are receptive to ideas about improving the test. But remember that students are more likely to listen if they do not yet have tests in their hands and are not thinking about their grades.

After you have returned the tests, listen to students' reactions. The purpose of such discussion is to improve the tests and help students learn. As they raise issues about specific items, let them know that you will not be changing any scores until you have considered those issues. Ask them to write brief notes about any items they would like reconsidered. Remember that students are likely to be more emotionally involved in their grades than you are. Throughout these discussions, be as nondefensive as possible. Remember that attacks on the unfairness of a test are not necessarily attacks on you personally.

If you do decide to make changes, make sure students know such changes will apply to all students, not just those who raised objections. Also, ask students to double check the arithmetic to make sure there are no clerical errors. Although students' feedback about the test can be useful, remember that the items they dislike the most are not necessarily bad. Student feedback should, therefore, be considered in conjunction with the results of analyses discussed in the next section.

Another important reason for discussing the test is to discover misconceptions students have about the content you have been teaching. Discussion after testing can help clarify instructional objectives and suggest how misunderstandings arose. Armed with such insights, you may find better ways to present the content.

ANALYZING TEST ITEMS

When you discuss test results with students you will always be reminded that there is no such thing as a perfect test. Frank Baker summarized it well in the *Encyclopedia of Educational Research* when he said:

> But even when [the best techniques of item writing] are employed by a skilled item writer, the resulting items are an enigma. It is not possible to evaluate an item as "good," or "bad" by inspection alone. The content covered may be appropriate, the distractors plausible, and the vocabulary at the level of the target population of the examinees, yet the item may be "bad" in some sense. (1982. p. 959)

Sounds hopeless, doesn't it? If bad items creep in like air pollution and higher taxes, what can a teacher do? Some teachers conclude that the "bad items" are the ones about which students complain the loudest. Not necessarily. This section provides some simple but powerful tools to assist you in improving the quality of test items. The tools we describe here are based on classical test theory and have been used by test developers for over fifty years.[1] Unfortunately, they are not used as frequently as they should be by classroom teachers. In the remainder of this chapter, we describe some simple step-by-step procedures for doing item analyses with norm-referenced and criterion-referenced tests.

Overview of Item Analysis Procedures

Before getting into specifics, let's look at the forest instead of the individual trees. The use of item analysis procedures with a norm-referenced test assumes that individuals possess knowledge or ability (e.g., spelling ability, knowledge of history, musical aptitude) to varying degrees. Given a group of test items representative of that knowledge or skill, we expect people with more skill to do better on individual items than those with less skill. Thus, there should be a positive correlation between success on any given item and total test score. Items that are nega-

---

[1] Since the early 1980s, many professional test developers have begun using item analysis techniques based on item response theory (also referred to as *latent trait theory*). Although most psychometricians agree that item response theory offers significant advantages to classical test theory (Crocker & Algina, 1986; Hambleton & Cook, 1977; Lord, 1980), it has not been as widely used because of its mathematical and computational complexity and the requirement of large sample sizes for analyses. With the wider availability of computers and appropriate software, item response theory has gained popularity. However, for most classroom applications, using item response theory is like using a helicopter instead of a step ladder to climb up on your roof. Either one will get the job done, but the helicopter requires a much greater investment of time, money, and training. For most classroom applications, item analysis techniques based on classical test theory are more than adequate and will lead to the same conclusion with dramatically smaller investments.

tively correlated with the total test score are viewed with suspicion. For example, if students who do well on the remainder of the test consistently miss a particular item, we should question whether that item is measuring something different, is miskeyed, ambiguous, or misleading.

Item analysis procedures provide a systematic method to examine items and determine whether students are answering them in suspicious ways. Item analysis results should never be the final word. Instead, item analyses provide clues for use in conjunction with the teacher's professional judgment by answering such questions as:

- What percentage of people pass or fail a particular item?
- Were some options never selected or always selected?
- Were there items on which high scorers did poorly, or low scorers did well?
- Were there items that appear to be generally misunderstood, responded to randomly, or miskeyed?

In other words, item analyses tell you whether individual items functioned as you intended. Item analyses also offer the following fringe benefits.

Better Class Discussions of Test Results

Although group discussion of test results can be an effective instructional technique, you do not want to spend time discussing items that most students already understand. The results of item analyses can help you focus on those concepts that students find difficult.

Better Focus for Reviews and Remediation

Item analysis will help you identify areas requiring review and remediation. For example, you may discover that a substantial part of the class does not understand subtraction items that require borrowing.

Assistance in Becoming a Better Teacher

The results of item analysis help reveal which teaching strategies were most effective allowing you to emphasize them in the future. You can also identify curriculum areas that are consistently too simple or too difficult to learn given current teaching techniques.

Improved Test Development Skills

Examining item analysis results will make you a better test constructor. You will become increasingly sensitive to such nagging problems as ambiguity, ineffective distractors, and poor wording. You will also learn to construct items that assess application and interpretation as well as knowledge.

The benefits of item analysis have been documented by research. For example, in a study with university faculty, Blessum concluded that the use of item analyses "resulted in an improvement, not only in the quality and fairness of each individual examination, but also in the technical and educational quality of successive tests'' (1969, p. 5). Given the substantial benefits associated with consistent use of item analysis data, more teachers should make the practice a part of their teaching repertoire.

A Step-by-Step Item Analysis Procedure for Classroom Use

Whether you are using a computer program or doing it by hand, the basic concepts of item analysis are the same. Because not all teachers have access to a computer item analysis program, we will describe a technique that is simple enough to be used without a computer, but accurate and complete enough to yield useful information. If you have a computer item analysis program, the rationale and principles summarized here can be applied just as well to the results of that program.

Assume we have an American history class of 32 students. We are analyzing a 50-item test on the American Revolutionary War. To gather the information we need, we will be comparing the results of the 10 highest scoring students with those of the 10 lowest scoring students. Why do we select the 10 highest and lowest scoring students? Kelley (1939) claimed that item analyses would be most accurate if based on the top and bottom 27 percent of the class, Henrysson (1971) recommended the upper and lower 33 percent, and D'Agostino and Cureton (1975) recommended the upper and lower 21 percent. For most applications, it does not matter which of these percentages you use. Using the top and bottom ten students (25 percent to 40 percent of typical classrooms) makes the arithmetic easier and has minimal impact on results. We will also give you the general formula so you can use the procedure with larger groups, but, if you are doing item analyses for much larger groups of students (e.g., 150 or more), you may wish to use one of the many computer programs available.

A simple but accurate item analysis can be accomplished using steps we will illustrate with one of the multiple-choice items from our hypothetical American history test on the Revolutionary War. The same procedure is applicable for any item format (e.g., true-false, multiple choice, matching, or short answer/completion) for which there is a right and a wrong answer.

Assume you have just given the test to the 32 pupils in your class. You will conduct your item analysis using the steps that are listed below and then discussed in detail in what follows.

1. After scoring the papers, rank order them from highest to lowest scores.
2. Put the ten papers with the highest scores in one pile and the ten papers with the lowest scores in another. Set aside the remaining papers since they will not be used in the analysis.
3. For each test item, count the number of students in the high-scoring group who selected each alternative. Do the same for the students in the low-scoring group, and record this information as shown in Figure 11.5.
4. For each item, compute the *difficulty level,* that is the percentage of the 20 students you are using in the analysis who got the item correct.

Number of students in high- and low-scoring groups who selected each option (n = 10 per group)		1. **Who was the most influential in convincing the French to assist the Americans during the Revolutionary War with England?**
High Scorers	**Low Scorers**	
0	1	a) George Washington
1	4	b) Marquis de Lafayette
8	2	* c) Benjamin Franklin
0	0	d) Benedict Arnold
1	1	e) Count de Rochambeau

FIGURE 11.5   An Example of Item Analyses Results for an American History Test Item

5. For each item, compute the *discrimination index,* that is, how well each option distinguishes between high scores and low scores.
6. Evaluate the *efficiency* of each of the options.

Let's go through each of these steps. The first three consist of collecting and tabulating data necessary for the analyses. Clerical help can do this tabulation as long as you supervise it closely to ensure accuracy. As Figure 11.5 shows, none of the students in the high-scoring group selected George Washington as the correct answer, and only one of the students in the low-scoring group did so. The correct answer (Benjamin Franklin), was selected by eight students in the high-scoring group, and only two students in the low-scoring group. Students in the low-scoring group opted most frequently for the French names (Marquis de Lafayette and Count de Rochambeau). Nobody selected Benedict Arnold.

The information in Figure 11.5 should begin to give you a feeling for the value of item analysis. About half the class got the item correct (ten of the twenty students included in the analysis), with most of the students in the high-scoring group getting the right answer, and most of the students in the low-scoring group selecting one of the incorrect options. Although this is the way you would expect it to be, think how important it would be to identify items where this was not so. If most students in the high-scoring group selected incorrect options, you would question whether the item was functioning as intended. That is exactly the purpose of item analysis—to reveal items to which students are responding in suspicious ways. Steps 4, 5, and 6, of the item analysis procedure provide a systematic way of identifying suspicious items. Let's discuss those steps now.

Computing Item Difficulty Level

The *difficulty level* of an item is the percentage of students who respond correctly to it. In cases where the calculation is based on ten students in the high-scoring group and ten students in the low-scoring group,[2] this will be the sum total of

---

[2] If you are doing an item analysis for a much larger class, we suggest taking the upper and lower 25 percent of the class and using the same approach. The formula would then be the number of students

correct answers in the high- and low-scoring groups divided by 20. In our example, this translates to 8 plus 2 divided by 20, or 50 percent.

Items in norm-referenced tests should have levels of difficulty in the 20 to 80 percent range so that scores will be spread out along a continuum of content mastery. If almost no one or almost everyone answers an item correctly, very little information is gained to spread students along this imaginary continuum. (Note that this rank ordering is very different from the purpose of criterion-referenced tests.) In our example, 50 percent of the class answered the item correctly. This assumes, of course, that the 12 students in the middle of the class scored about the same as students in the upper and lower groups. You could get a somewhat more precise estimate of the difficulty level for each item by including in your calculation the answers of this middle group, but experience has demonstrated that the small gain in precision rarely justifies the extra work.

Using 10 students from the upper and lower groups (wherever that is a reasonably close approximation of 25 percent of the total class) greatly simplifies your calculations. You should generally be able to compute the percentage in your head. For example: Add together the number of students in the upper and lower groups who got the item correct ($8 + 2 = 10$), divide by two ($10 \div 2 = 5$), move the decimal one space to the right (50), and add a percentage sign (50%). You will soon be able to rapidly calculate the difficulty level of each item just by looking at the tabulated data. The item difficulty in our example is 50 percent, which is ideal. Ideal difficulty level, however, does not necessarily imply an ideal item.

Computing the Discrimination Index

The *discrimination index* of each item tells how well that item distinguishes between students who did well on the total test and those who did poorly. The discrimination index is computed by subtracting the number of students who got the item right in the low-scoring group from the number of students who got the item right in the high-scoring group, and dividing the answer by the size of each group. For the illustrative item in Figure 11.5, the discrimination index is: $8 - 2 \div 10 = .60$.

The index of discrimination can range from -1.0 to $+1.0$. Hopkins, Stanley, and Hopkins (1990, p. 274) suggest the following guidelines for interpreting the discrimination index.

Discrimination Index	Item Evaluation
.40 and up	Very good item
.30 to .39	Good item
.20 to .29	Reasonably good item
.10 to .19	Marginal item, usually subject to improvement
Below .10	Poor item, to be rejected or revised

---

who got the item right in the high-scoring 25 percent, plus the number of students who got the item right in the low-scoring 25 percent, divided by the number of students in the high-scoring group plus the number of students in the low-scoring group. For example, if you have 60 students in your class: 25 percent of $60 = 15$. The formula would be the number of the high-scoring 15 who got the item right plus the number of the low-scoring 15 who got the item right divided by 30.

A positive index of discrimination suggests that getting that particular item right correlates positively with higher total test scores. A negative index of discrimination suggests that students who get that item right generally score lower on the test than students who get the item wrong. Assuming that each item is measuring a part of the content covered by the total test, it is worrisome if success on an individual item is not positively correlated with success on the total test.

If you base your item analysis on 10 students in the upper and lower groups, the index of discrimination can be computed very quickly. Subtract the number in the lower group who got the item right from the number in the higher group who got it right (in our example: $8 - 2 = 6$), move the decimal point one space to the left (.6), and add a zero (.60).

The same formula would apply when more than 10 students are used in the upper and lower scoring groups, but could not be worked out as quickly. Teachers are more likely to use item analysis procedures if they are simple. Hence, we recommend using the highest and lowest scoring 10 students for any class of 25 to 40 students.

A more precise way of conveying information about an item is to compute the discrimination index for each option. Instead of saying that the discrimination index for the item in Figure 11.5 was $+.60$, we would say that Option a has an index of $-.10$, Option b an index of $-.30$, Option c an index of $+.60$, Option d an index of $.00$, and Option e an index of $-.20$. Based on these results, the item performs exactly as we would hope. The correct answer has a high positive discrimination index, and all of the incorrect answers, or distractors, have discrimination indices which are negative or zero. The option with the largest negative index is also the option most frequently selected by low scorers in relation to high scorers. This suggests a misconception on the part of some students that should be addressed during instruction.

Evaluating the Effectiveness of Distractors

In good multiple-choice or matching tests, students are given a number of alternatives from which to choose. A good test offers distractors to the correct answer that are plausible, but incorrect. If you want a multiple-choice item that has five options, but no one selects 2 of the 5 options, you really have a 3-option instead of a 5-option item. Distractors should be worded so that you not only know which students are missing which items, but, so you can make a good guess as to why. In the illustrative item in Figure 11.5, George Washington and Benedict Arnold were probably included as options because they were prominent figures in the American Revolution. The Marquis de Lafayette and Count de Rochambeau were probably included because they were Frenchmen associated with the Revolution and the item stem mentions France.

Evaluating the effectiveness of distractors requires noting how many students in the high- and low-scoring groups selected each option. In tests taken by relatively large groups of students, the best items will be those where *each* option is selected by at least a few students. Low scoring students should select incorrect options more frequently. In our example, it might be possible to improve the item by replacing the Benedict Arnold option. However, one must be cautious about doing this based on only one test administration. One advantage of systematic item analysis over time is that decisions about refinement can be based on larger groups of students.

Recording Item Analysis Data

Earlier, we suggested that you begin a test item file on five- by eight-inch cards, and we pointed out how such a file can substantially improve test effectiveness. Each time you use an item from your file, you should conduct an item analysis. A convenient place to record the results is on the reverse side of your test item card, as shown in Figure 11.6. (Note that the information shown in Figure 11.6 would be on the back of the card shown in Figure 11.1.) As Figure 11.6 shows, the results of item analyses taken over time can provide important insights about item quality. First, we see that this particular item functions fairly consistently across years. Second, minor problems that appear to be present in one year (the fact that Benedict Arnold wasn't chosen at all in 1990) disappear in subsequent years. This is not an uncommon occurrence and suggests that we should not be too hasty about making major changes based on single test administrations. Particularly with small sample sizes (e.g., 25 to 40 students), sampling fluctuation is expected. Therefore, minor problems in an otherwise good item are probably best overlooked until a second administration.

FIGURE 11.6 Example of How to Record Results of Item Analyses on Reverse of Cards in Test Item File

ITEM ANALYSIS DATA

Response to Each Option

Dates Used	# of Students Tested		A	B	C*	D	E	Omit	Difficulty Level	Discrimination Index
1-21-90	27	upper 10	0	1	8	0	1		.50	.60
		lower 10	1	4	2	0	3			
1-19-91	31	upper 10	1	8	6	0	3		.45	.30
		lower 10	2	3	3	1	1			
1-22-92	29	upper 10	1	0	8	0	1		.60	.40
		lower 10	1	1	4	2	2			
		upper 10								
		lower 10								
		upper 10								
		lower 10								

Using Item Analysis for Revision and Improvement

The primary purpose for doing item analyses is to improve the way a specific item functions. The results of item analyses should be used as a guide, not as criteria to follow blindly. In conjunction with your experience and professional judgment, item analyses can be invaluable in enhancing the information provided by items. Consider the five items shown in Figure 11.7 in which the clerk who scored the test computed and wrote the difficulty level and the index of discrimination for each option in the left-hand margin of a copy of the test.

Item 17 has a difficulty level of .95. Ten students out of ten in the high-scoring group and nine out of ten in the low-scoring group answered it correctly. If the test were being used for norm-referenced purposes, this item would not be particularly useful to retain. It may be that all the students knew the answer prior to the instruction (in which case we hope the teacher did not spend too much instructional time on this objective), or perhaps the distractors were too easy. If you were convinced that students did not know the information prior to the instructional unit, you could attempt to revise the item by using other distractors. For example, Canada, France, Spain, and Holland might be good distractors since all were involved in colonizing North America.

The final decision about whether to revise an item or simply drop it depends on the purpose of the test, the teacher's assessment of students' knowledge at the beginning of the unit, and the amount of instructional time that is devoted to the concept. The results of item analysis suggest a need for a closer look, but they should not be followed slavishly or replace the teacher's judgment.

In item 18 we see a different problem. High scoring students chose options *b* (industrialized states versus agricultural states) and *c* (states with large populations versus states with small populations) with about the same frequency. This suggests some ambiguity about the answer, or the way the information was presented. In reality, experts would have a very difficult time agreeing on whether *b* or *c* was the better answer. The difficulty level of the item is also borderline. Together these results suggest that the item should probably be revised. One revision would be to change option *b* to read, "Cotton producing states versus tobacco producing states." This might attract students who remembered vaguely that the dispute had something to do with agriculture, but did not clearly understand that the dispute was between agricultural and manufacturing states rather than two types of agricultural states. The goal of distractors is to attract those students who have misconceptions or limited understanding, not to seduce students into selecting "tricky" answers.

Item 19 is one we have already seen. It has close to ideal difficulty level, a very good discrimination index, and all of the options except *d* function very well. We could replace option *d* with something more attractive. However, given the small sample size, differences in frequency of selection for options *a* and *d* may easily be a chance occurrence. Even when the item statistics are nearly perfect—as here—it is not necessarily a perfect item. Only the teacher can decide whether an item is testing content that is relevant and important. However, item

AMERICAN HISTORY MIDTERM (continued)

Difficulty Level	High vs. Low Group Scores	Discrimination Index	
			17. In the American Revolutionary War, the thirteen colonies were fighting against:
	10 - 9	+.10	* (a) England
.95	0 - 0	0	(b) Argentina
	0 - 1	-.10	(c) Kenya
	0 - 0	0	(d) Finland
(too easy)	0 - 0	0	(e) Japan
			18. During the Constitutional Convention of 1787, there were major disagreements between:
	0 -3	-.20	(a) Those wanting to reunite with England versus those wanting to remain independent
.20	5 - 1	+.40	(b) Industrialized states versus agricultural states
	4 - 0	+.40	* (c) States with large populations versus states with small populations
	0 - 3	-.30	(d) Rich states versus poor states
(ambiguous)	1 - 3	-.20	(e) Northern states versus southern states
			19. Who was the most influential in convincing the French to assist the Americans during the Revolutionary War with England?
	0 - 1	-.10	(a) George Washington
	1 - 4	-.30	(b) Marquis de Lafayette
.50	8 - 2	+.60	* (c) Benjamin Franklin
	0 - 0	.00	(d) Benedict Arnold
(good item)	1 - 3	-.20	(e) Count de Rochambeau
			20. In what way did the American Revolution affect econmic conditions of Europe?
	3 - 1	+.20	(a) Economic conditions in Europe were depressed as a result of the expenses associated with the war
.15	1 - 2	-.10	* (b) European countries were less able to use their respective colonies primarily for economic gains
	2 - 2	.00	(c) Economic chaos resulted because European peasants wanted the same freedoms gained by American colonies
(too difficult, random response)	2 - 2	.00	(d) European monarchs drastically cut taxes to avoid domestic unrest
	2 - 3	-.10	(e) The American Revolution fueled economic expansion in most European countries
			21. Which of the following was the most important contributor to starting the Revolutionary War?
	1 - 3	-.20	(a) Taxes paid by the colonies to England were extremely high
	1 - 0	+.10	(b) England eliminated all of the local legislatures and assemblies in the colonies
.25	0 - 1	-.10	(c) The British were not providing the colonies with sufficient military protection
(good item, but miskeyed)	7 - 2	+.50	(d) The colonies were upset about what they perceived to be taxation without representation
	1 - 4	-.30	* (e) The British tried to impose the Church of England as the official state religion for the colonies

FIGURE 11.7 Illustration of How Item Analyses Results Can Be Used for Revising and Improving Items

statistics provide a context in which to make such a decision and point out where unexpected factors are affecting the way it functions.

Item 20 obviously has problems. Not only is the difficulty lower than we like (.15), but the discrimination index for the correct answer is negative and the responses to distractors appear to be almost random (about the same number of people in both the high- and the low-scoring groups chose each of the distractors). This suggests that the item is too difficult, the content was not adequately covered, or the differences between right and wrong options are so subtle that students cannot differentiate. Again, the teacher must decide whether the objective measured by the item is important enough to justify revision. If so, substantial revision is necessary. The options appear to be clearly worded and logically distinct, which suggests that the problem may have been with the instruction.

The item analysis results for item 21 indicate an embarrassing, but not infrequent, problem. Option *e* was keyed as correct. If this were true, the item would have a difficulty level of .25 and a discrimination index of − .30 for the correct answer. Such item statistics suggest that it ought to be dropped or substantially revised. However, on closer examination, it becomes apparent that the item was miskeyed. Option *d* is really the correct answer. If the item were keyed correctly, it is nearly perfect based on item statistics. The difficulty level is .45, and the discrimination index + .50. Although a miskeyed item is an embarrassing mistake, it is easily corrected.

In summary, the items shown in Figure 11.7 demonstrate how item analysis data can be used to identify items that are too easy, too difficult, ambiguous, or miskeyed. Remember, however, that *item analysis statistics only provide guidance, and should never replace teacher judgment.*

Cautions about Interpreting the Results of Item Analyses

The results of item analyses can provide important insights, but criteria for labeling items as good or bad should not be rigid. *There is no substitute for teacher judgment.* Following are some cautions to keep in mind as you interpret item analysis data.

A good discrimination index does not necessarily indicate a valid item. The *sine qua non* of testing is that the test is measuring what it is expected to measure. In interpreting item discrimination statistics we implicitly use the total test as a criterion to validate each individual item. This is not a bad assumption where content is relatively homogeneous (e.g., the ability to add two-digit numbers). However, where the content is heterogeneous, item discrimination indices may be low because a person is able to master one part of the content but not another. If your test content is quite heterogeneous, you should expect that discrimination indices will be somewhat lower.

Low indices of discrimination do not necessarily indicate defective items. When the index of discrimination is low, check the item for ambiguity, inadvertent clues, inappropriate level of difficulty, and other technical defects. If none are found, and you believe that the item is measuring an important concept, it should probably be retained. Remember that difficulty level also contributes to the index of discrimination. Items at the 50 percent difficulty level have maximum potential of discrimination. As we move away from this optimum difficulty level (e.g., as items become easier or more difficult), the maximum index of discrimination goes down. For example, Hopkins, Stanley, and Hopkins (1990) point out that the maximum discrimination index for an item that is at a .10 or .90 level of difficulty is only .20. At times, you will want to retain items in the test that are relatively easy or difficult because they measure content you believe is important.

Sampling fluctuation is not uncommon in item analysis data from small samples. The results of item analysis data are so concrete that it is easy to be misled into believing that they represent "real truth." Our discussions about sampling error in Chapter 5 should make you cautious about accepting such statistics too literally. The results of item analyses for the same test will vary from one group to another, depending on total class performance, the students' educational background, and the instructional techniques used. When statistics are based on 10 students in each group, the answers of two or three can have a dramatic effect on results. The smaller the number of students in an analysis, the greater the potential for sampling error (Pyrczak, 1973). Thus, for most classroom applications, item analysis results should only be used for guidance.

APPLICATION PROBLEM #3

An item analysis of a ninth grade American history test given to a class of 35 students yields the following information. Compute the difficulty levels and discrimination indices and explain what suggestions you would make based on the data.

Number of students in high- and low-scoring groups who selected each item (n = 10 per group)

During the Civil War, Congress enacted the first national draft law. Which political party supported the draft?

High Scorers	Low Scorers	
6	3	*a. Republicans
4	7	b. Democrats
0	0	c. Secessionists
0	0	d. Whigs
0	0	e. Abolitionists

Item Analysis Procedures with Criterion-referenced Tests

Criterion-referenced tests (also referred to as mastery tests) and norm-referenced tests serve different purposes. Since criterion-referenced tests are designed to indicate how well students have mastered prespecified objectives—instead of where their scores fall on a continuum of mastery—the interpretation of item analysis data for criterion-referenced tests is quite different. The process of tabulating results is similar, but the data are used in different ways. As we shall see, indices of discrimination and difficulty are less meaningful, but an analysis of item scores and selected options still provides useful information.

Item Difficulty

With norm-referenced tests, the ideal difficulty level is .50. With criterion-referenced tests, the ideal difficulty depends on the teacher's expectations. If it is a learning outcome that you expect *all* students to achieve, then the ideal difficulty level would be 1.0.[3] When you cover objectives you do not expect all students to master, the ideal difficulty might be .50 to .70.

For criterion-referenced tests, items are not revised to achieve a level of difficulty that will maximize the potential for discrimination. The standard formula for item difficulty referred to earlier can be computed for criterion-referenced items, but should not be interpreted in the same way. Most criterion-referenced items have very high levels of difficulty (.80 or higher) if the instruction has been effective.

Index of Discrimination

Discriminating between high and low achievers is also not the goal for criterion-referenced tests. Some of the best criterion-referenced items will have zero indices of discrimination (e.g., if all students in the class answered an item correctly). For norm-referenced tests, such items would probably be eliminated or revised because they do not provide information useful in ranking students along a continuum of mastery. On criterion-referenced tests, such items provide evidence that instructional objectives have been achieved.

Effectiveness of Distractors

Although you expect a higher percentage of students to answer a criterion-referenced item correctly, the quality of distractors is still important. Distractors should still let you know which misconceptions are causing students to answer incorrectly. Examining the frequency with which each distractor is selected can help you understand where confusion exists and what parts of instruction need emphasis.

Analysis of Criterion-referenced Items

If a criterion-referenced test is used as both a pre- and a post-test, it is useful to portray the results in a format similar to that shown in Figure 11.8, which shows the results for 10 students for the first four items of a criterion-referenced test. The key question in evaluating a criterion-referenced test is: To what extent do the test items measure the effects of instruction? Indicating whether students got

---

[3] Remember that the term *difficulty level* means exactly the opposite of what you might expect. An item with a difficulty level of .80 is answered correctly by 80 percent of the respondents. Some writers have suggested that the term be changed to *item ease*, (see Gronlund, 1985, p. 247), but the suggestion, although logical, has not gained broad acceptance.

Student Names	Item #1		Item #2		Item #3		Item #4	
	Pre	Post	Pre	Post	Pre	Post	Pre	Post
Harold S.	-	+	+	+	+	-	-	-
Suzanne R.	-	+	-	+	+	+	-	+
Manuel G.	-	+	+	+	-	-	+	-
Eliza K.	-	+	+	+	+	-	-	-
Tom B.	+	+	+	+	+	+	-	+
Karl A.	-	+	+	+	-	-	-	-
Linda H.	-	+	+	-	+	-	+	-
Allyson W.	-	-	+	+	+	-	-	-
Lewis A.	-	+	-	+	+	+	-	-
Matt T.	-	-	+	+	+	-	-	-
Percentage Correct	10%	80%	80%	90%	80%	30%	20%	20%
Sensitivity to Instructional Effects (S)	.70		.10		-.50		.00	

FIGURE 11.8 Portraying the Results of Criterion-referenced Tests

an item incorrect (represented by a minus) or correct (represented by a plus) yields a useful visual representation.

For example, item 1 is a very good test item for a criterion-referenced test. Only one person got the item correct prior to instruction, and eight out of ten got it correct after instruction. This indicates that the instruction was effective, and that the item was able to measure its impact.

Item 2 was either too easy for both the pre- and post-test or the instruction was misdirected. About the same number of students (the majority of the class) got the item correct before and after instruction.

Item 3 indicates a relatively rare situation in which many more students got the item correct prior to instruction than following instruction. Such a situation could be caused by a badly written or confusing item, or if instruction was so poorly delivered that it confused students.

Item 4 is either too difficult, or is based on content not covered by instruction, since a small number of students scored correctly before and after instruction. This response might also occur if the item were acceptable but the instruction was poor.

As with norm-referenced tests, item analyses of criterion-referenced tests require professional judgment. Specific response patterns may reflect characteristics of the item, or of the instruction. In most cases, both item and instructional characteristics interact to produce the results, and teachers are best qualified to interpret data for their particular situations.

In interpreting the results of criterion-referenced tests, a measure of *sensitivity to instructional effects* is sometimes used (Haladyna & Roid, 1981). This index is a good way of summarizing the kind of information shown in Figure 11.8. Sensitivity to instructional effects (indicated by *S*) is obtained by subtracting the number of pupils who got the item right *before instruction* from the number who got the number right *after instruction* and dividing the result by the total number of pupils who tried it both times. For example, in item 1, eight students got the item right after instruction, and one student got it right before instruction. Ten students tried it both times; therefore,

$$S = (8 - 1) \div 10 = .70$$

The index of sensitivity to instructional effects for the other items in Figure 11.8 is computed in the same way. As can be seen, S is interpreted much like the discrimination index in that larger numbers indicate better items. Based on that criterion, the best item in Figure 11.8 is item 1. Analysis of the other items suggests either poor item construction or ineffective instruction.

Keeping a record of how items on criterion-referenced tests function is just as important as keeping records of items on norm-referenced tests. The same record-keeping system on the backs of cards in the item file can be used. The information recorded in that file should be reviewed periodically, especially right after each test administration, to help you improve instruction and test development skills.

SUGGESTED READINGS

Clemens, W. V. (1971). *Test Administration*. In R. L. Thorndike, (Ed.), *Educational Measurement* (2d ed., pp. 188–201). Washington, DC: American Council on Education.

An excellent discussion of the issues to be considered as a part of test administration procedures. Issues are discussed from the perspective of the test author, the administrator, and the examinee. Many specific suggestions are given for improving test administrations.

Crocker, L., & Algina, J. (1986). *Introduction to Classical and Modern Test Theory*. New York: Holt, Rinehart & Winston.

A detailed explanation of the theoretical basis underlying most aptitude, achievement, and affective measures. This book provides excellent discussions of criterion-referenced test development, item response theory, generalizability theory, and psychometric methods for investigating bias in test items.

Henrysson, S. (1971). Gathering, analyzing, and using data on test items.
In R. L. Thorndike (Ed.), *Educational Measurement* (2d ed., pp. 130–159). Washington,
DC: American Council on Education.

Provides a more technical and comprehensive discussion of various item analysis techniques than we've presented. Particularly good for those who want a better understanding of the statistical and theoretical foundation for item analyses.

SELF-CHECK QUIZ

1. Which of the following practices do the authors recommend teachers use as a basis for constructing classroom tests?
   a. Construct a completely new test each time consisting of original items not previously used.
   b. Create a few exceptionally good tests and use them repeatedly without alteration.
   c. Develop a file consisting of possible items that can be used to create several versions of a test.
   d. Maintain a collection of previously used tests from which new tests can be created by selective cutting and pasting.

2. According to test development experts, if the items in a test vary in difficulty level, in what order should the items be arranged?
   a. The easiest items should be concentrated near the end of the test.
   b. The easiest items should be located at the beginning of the test.
   c. The easy and difficult items should be alternated throughout the test.
   d. The order of the items is not an important concern.

3. When reviewing test items prior to use, it is important to ensure that
   a. a few of the items contain clues to help the less able students.
   b. each item has an unambiguous correct answer.
   c. interesting material is used to introduce each item.
   d. the item has not been used in a previous year's test.

4. First grade children who are taking standardized achievement tests should be given a break from testing every
   a. 15 minutes.
   b. 30 minutes.
   c. 60 minutes.
   d. 90 minutes.

5. Proper administration of most standardized achievement tests
   a. prohibits any elaboration or clarification of the instructions.
   b. requires that the test be given only by a licensed psychologist.
   c. can only be done with groups of 25 or fewer students.
   d. should be done using an assistant as well as a test administrator.

6. The "Teacher Index to Valid Test Performance" is an instrument used to
   a. calculate the ratio of each student's actual score to his expected score.
   b. compare the average class score with various national norms.
   c. determine the degree to which the test matches the curriculum.
   d. document unusual occurrences during the administration of a test.

7. Separate answer sheets that are submitted for machine scoring
   a. should have stray marks erased and light answers darkened before scoring.
   b. should be turned in *exactly* as the student marked them.
   c. need to be rechecked after scoring since errors frequently occur.
   d. should not be used with children younger than sixth grade.

8. A discrimination index lower than .20 indicates that the item
   a. is appropriate for norm-referenced tests but not for criterion-referenced tests.
   b. will generally be answered correctly by students who score low on the test.
   c. should be examined for possible clues, ambiguity, or other defects.
   d. is too difficult to use on most norm-referenced tests.

9. Which of the following scoring practices is recommended by the authors?
   a. Adjusting students' scores to correct for guessing.
   b. Having students indicate how sure they are of each answer.
   c. Using a scoring template.
   d. Weighing the items differentially.

10. For a norm-referenced test, good items generally have a difficulty level that is
    a. as close to 0.00 as possible.
    b. between .10 and .25.
    c. between .25 and .75.
    d. between .75 and .90.
    e. as close to 1.00 as possible.

SUGGESTION SHEET

If your last name starts with the letter *L*, please complete the Suggestion Sheet at the end of the book while this chapter is still fresh in your mind.

ANSWERS TO APPLICATION PROBLEMS

#1

Whether the items on the test require students to exhibit the type of behavior that the teacher had in mind can only be decided by the person who is teaching the class. However, as a biology teacher yourself, you should be able to provide valuable opinions about whether what is being asked is clear and unambiguous, and whether each item has a single correct answer. You could indicate any items that are too wordy, and items that, based on your experience, appear to be too difficult or too easy. You could identify items you think contain bias or that have irrelevant clues to the correct answer. You cannot provide a definitive judgment about whether the items are representative of all the material covered in the course or whether adequate coverage of the most important concepts is provided since your friend may teach the course somewhat differently than you do, but you can certainly make suggestions in each of those areas for your friend to think about as she finalizes the test.

#2

The directions are good as far as they go, but more information is needed. It would be good to note that each item is worth 1 point, that students will have 15 minutes to complete the test, and that if they are not sure of the correct answer they should make their best guess, continue on to other items, and then come back if they have time. Rather than just writing the directions at the top of the sheet, it would be useful to read the directions aloud with the students and make sure that they all understand exactly what they are supposed to do. By the fifth grade, students will probably be familiar with true-false tests, but you may have some students in your class who have recently immigrated to the United States or who may have other difficulties. It would be worth spending time with them individually to make sure they know what is expected.

#3

Difficulty level for the item is .45 and the discrimination index for the item is .30. If you want to compute discrimination indices for each option, it would be .30 for option *a*, − .30 for option *b*, and 0.0 for options *c, d,* and *e*. Based on this information, it appears that the item is quite successful in discriminating between high scorers and low scorers, but little is gained by having a 5-option question instead of just a 2-option question since no one chose options *c, d,* and *e*. This may be because students realize that only two major political parties (i.e., Republicans and Democrats) were active at the time. If the intent of including an item like this is to learn more about how well students understood the politics surrounding the national draft law, you may want to reword the question. As it is now worded, they may be answering based on their knowledge that there were only two major political parties at the time without knowing much about the national draft law.

CHAPTER 12

Constructing and Using Descriptive Measures: Questionnaires, Interviews, Observations, and Rating Scales

Overview

Many questions related to education call for descriptive information that cannot be collected by existing tests. In this chapter we discuss four methods of collecting descriptive information: questionnaires, interviews, observations, and rating scales. Questionnaires are a relatively low-cost method for collecting specific information such as years of teaching experience and teacher/child ratios. Interviews are useful for collecting more complex and sensitive information such as teachers' perceptions about school climate and parents' ideas about school discipline. Interviews permit clarifications by the interviewee and probing for more detailed answers by the interviewer, whereas questionnaires do not.

Direct systematic observations in various educational settings can provide valuable information about variables such as students' involvement in school work and effective teaching methods. Finally, we discuss rating scales since these measures are widely employed in education. We will examine some of the problems in using rating scales, and make some suggestions about developing and using these measures more effectively.

Objectives

Upon completing your study of this chapter, you should be able to

1. Briefly describe three methods of gathering descriptive data and list at least one advantage of each.
2. Explain how open-form questionnaire items can be used to develop closed-form items.
3. Describe two situations in which open-form questionnaire items would provide more useful data than closed-form items.
4. Describe rules you should follow in constructing questionnaire items.
5. Briefly describe procedures for analyzing questionnaires.
6. Define and discuss the use of structured, semistructured, and unstructured interviews.
7. Describe guidelines for constructing an interview schedule and conducting interviews.
8. Discuss some of the questions that can be answered by pilot testing the interview schedule and procedures.
9. Describe the advantage of using systematic observation to study the classroom.
10. Describe four methods of recording observational data and give an example of an appropriate educational question for each method.
11. Discuss some of the issues to be considered when pilot testing an observational schedule and procedure.
12. Briefly describe the steps necessary to train observers.
13. Explain some of the problems and errors often encountered when using rating scales.
14. List rules that should be observed in developing rating scales.

COLLECTING DESCRIPTIVE DATA

Educators often need to collect descriptive data for the following types of activities:

1. Surveys in which information is collected about various aspects of a school system, such as administrative procedures, curriculum, and the experience of teachers
2. School census conducted to predict future enrollment and related educational needs
3. Parent-teacher interviews to gather data about student problems

4. Questionnaires to gather information from students about extracurricular activities
5. Observation of teachers who have been especially successful in teaching reading to bilingual children
6. Interviews with students about the causes of low morale in the school

The tools most often used to collect descriptive information are questionnaires, interviews, observations, and rating scales. All of these techniques must be carefully planned and controlled so that the data will be *standardized, objective,* and *quantifiable*. Obtaining standardized information requires that the same procedures be used to collect the same data from all individuals. Furthermore, it is desirable to use procedures that are as objective as circumstances permit. Finally, descriptive information about individuals is usually combined so that averages, frequencies and other descriptive statistics may be used to interpret the data. However, the data must be quantifiable, (i.e., convertible to a numerical format) if these tools are to be employed.

Questionnaires, interviews, rating scales, and observations are often used to collect information about attitudes and behavior patterns that the individual may be reluctant to divulge. It is much easier to collect accurate descriptive data on relatively less personal variables such as years of teaching experience and students' extracurricular activities, than on highly personal variables such as teacher morale and students' use of drugs. Collecting sensitive data is difficult and requires considerable training and experience. In some cases it can stir up a hornet's nest of controversy in the community. For this reason, you should carefully lay the groundwork in the school and community before collecting data on controversial topics. For other affective variables, such as study attitudes, we recommend the use of existing affective measures such as those discussed in Chapter 13 whenever possible. However, a teacher who is interested in collecting descriptive data that is unique to the local situation often cannot find relevant measures. In such instances, the techniques described in this chapter should prove helpful.

QUESTIONNAIRES

Questionnaires are frequently used to collect information about current educational issues. Following are a few recent questionnaire studies that can provide insight into the variety of problems addressed using this questionnaire.

Borg, W. R., Worthen, B. W., & Valcarce, R. W. (1986). Teachers' perceptions of the importance of educational measurement. *Journal of Experimental Education, 55*(1), 9-14.[1]

Brubaker, D. L., & Simon, L. H. (1987). How do principals view themselves, others? *NASSP Bulletin, 77*(495), 72–78.

---

[1] This questionnaire study was conducted to determine which areas of educational measurement teachers considered most important—and which, therefore, should be included in this book.

Martin, D. S. et al. (1987). Curriculum development: Who is involved and how? *Educational Leadership*, *44*(4), 40–48.

Thibodeau, G. P., & Cebelius, L. S. (1987). Self perceptions of special educators toward teaching mathematics. *School Science and Mathematics*, *87*(2), 136–143.

In most cases, questionnaires are aimed at collecting very specific descriptive data; thus, it is rarely possible to use a questionnaire developed in earlier research. Usually, it is better to develop your own questionnaire, tailored to the local situation.

Framing Questionnaire Objectives

To develop a questionnaire, start with a broad objective such as "To determine the vocational goals of 10th grade students in the Riverside School District." Then, translate this broad objective into multiple specific objectives, each of which might become the basis for a question. The wording of each question depends on the interests of the questionnaire designer. For example, a committee developing a vocational counseling program might ask:

1. What persons have substantially influenced the student's vocational choice?
2. How committed are students to their vocational choices?
3. How accurate are students' perceptions of the academic preparation needed to achieve their vocational goals?
4. How realistic are students' vocational goals given other information—such as grades in relevant subjects, aptitude test scores, and vocational interest test scores?

Many other specific questions might be relevant to a survey of student vocational goals. It is usually best to start with more questions than you will eventually need and evaluate each possible question to determine which ones will yield the most useful data.

Constructing Questionnaire Items

The next step is to write prototype questionnaire items to obtain information about each objective. Constructing questionnaire items is not as simple as it may appear, and as a result, many questionnaires in education are poorly written. Poorly written items usually produce incomplete, inaccurate, or biased responses, resulting in data that may be useless, or even worse, may lead to erroneous conclusions and bad decisions.

Questionnaires are best for gathering concrete data such as the number of different schools a student has attended, his place of birth, or the names and ages of his siblings. However, questionnaires can also be used to collect more abstract information, such as a student's educational plans, parents' perceptions of school discipline, or teachers' evaluations of faculty meetings. As the information sought becomes more abstract, respondents must make more inferences and judgments, and the task of constructing good questionnaire items becomes more difficult.

Several books covering the construction of questionnaire items in depth (see Suggested Readings) are well worth consulting if you plan to construct a questionnaire that deals with complex issues. However, if your informational needs are straightforward, the following rules will get you started.

Rule 1: Relate Items to Objectives

It is easy to get "carried away" when writing questionnaire items, adding things that are interesting but are not relevant to your goals. Before you include a question, you should be able to specify why each question is asked, how the information from the question is related to your objectives, and how the results will be quantified and analyzed.

Rule 2: Use Closed-form Items

In most cases, you should construct closed-form (e.g., multiple-choice) items, rather than open-form (e.g., essay) items. Closed-form items require less time and effort on the part of the respondent and are much easier for the investigator to quantify and analyze. As the time and effort required to answer your questions increases, more people will refuse to answer.

Although closed-form questions are usually preferable, there are some situations where open-form items should be used—when you cannot anticipate possible answers, for instance. Suppose your school was planning to start an English program for bilingual students and you wanted to learn what specific kinds of English instruction parents favored. If you were unable to predict their responses, you could start by asking a small group of parents a series of essay questions. Their responses could be categorized and the results used to frame plausible closed-form alternatives for use in the revised questionnaire.

APPLICATION PROBLEM #1

This is a problem for your class.

1. Each class member should respond to the following open-form item: "Suppose you are teaching in a seventh grade classroom. John Bogus, the class clown, makes several silly remarks each period that disrupt the class. Briefly describe how you would stop this behavior." The objective of this item is to learn what strategies teachers use to deal with disruptive behavior in their classrooms.
2. Collect the responses from each person and categorize similar responses.
3. For each category write a single brief description.

4. Construct a closed-form item using the brief descriptions as alternate responses.

Open-form items are useful when you suspect that closed-form items may limit or cue the kinds of responses obtained. For example, in the closed-form question developed in Application Problem 1, (see the answer on page 347) some of the alternatives could suggest a classroom management technique that a teacher had not considered. In this case, a teacher might check this alternative even though he would never have thought of it if he had not been cued by the closed-form item.

Open-form questions at the end of a questionnaire also allow respondents to provide any additional information they believe is pertinent, but that was not elicited by your closed-form items. The final item might be: If we have forgotten to ask something or if you have any additional comments, please provide that information here.

Rule 3: Include an "Other" Choice

When writing closed-form questionnaire items where some unexpected responses might occur, it is useful to include an "other" choice for respondents to write answers that do not fit any of the alternatives. By providing this opening, you may elicit new ideas or unconventional approaches that would not otherwise be obtained.

Rule 4: Strive for Clarity

It is important that questions have the same meaning for all respondents. The clarity of items can be increased by observing the following guidelines:

a. Use short, simple sentences. Long complex questions are more difficult to understand and often lead to misinterpretations.
b. Avoid words such as *several, many, most,* and *usually.* These words have no precise meaning and will be interpreted differently by different respondents (Belson, 1981).
c. Avoid negative items; some respondents overlook the negative word, thus giving answers that are actually opposite their real opinion.
d. Avoid technical terms and jargon. Use the simplest language that clearly conveys your meaning.

Rule 5: Avoid Biased or Leading Questions

Respondents who are given hints may tend to give the answer you are seeking. Also, emotional or value-laden words can bias responses. A question such as "Do you support segregating students by ability?" is likely to receive a large number of negative responses because of the word *segregating*, which arouses negative feelings in many people. In contrast, "Should students be grouped by ability so that instruction can be matched to individual students' needs?" is biased in the opposite direction since it includes the concept of meeting individual student needs—a popular idea among educators.

Another way in which closed-form items are sometimes biased is demonstrated by the following item.

> How important is it for the public schools to teach basic American values to elementary pupils?
>
>   a. This is the *most important* thing that is taught.
>   b. It is *extremely important* to teach these values.
>   c. These values are *very important*.
>   d. These values are *more important* than most other subjects.
>   e. These values are *less important* than the basic skills.

Notice that four of the five choices are positive. Such an item increases the probability that respondents will select one of the favorable choices.

Leading questions also tend to slant responses in one direction or another. For example, compare the following items:

- In view of the many persons killed each year by handguns, do you believe owning these guns should be illegal?

- Since the police in many areas are unable to protect citizens from violent crime, should law-abiding citizens be permitted to own handguns for self-protection as guaranteed by the constitution?

Both these items attempt to lead the respondent. To learn what people really believe, write items in neutral terms and avoid value-laden language.

APPLICATION PROBLEM #2

1. Write a closed-form item that is biased in favor of teaching evolution in the public schools.
2. Write a closed-form item that is biased against teaching evolution in the public schools.
3. Write a closed-form item that is neutral on the question of teaching evolution in the public schools.

Frame all three items so they can be answered *yes, undecided,* or *no.*

Questionnaire Format

When an individual receives a questionnaire he must decide whether or not to complete it. The appearance of the questionnaire contributes to that decision. Therefore, you should give considerable attention to your questionnaire's appearance and format.

The following guidelines for questionnaire format based on the research of Berdie and Anderson (1974) and Heberlein and Baumgartner (1978) should be considered carefully.

1. Make the questionnaire attractive. Consider using colored ink or colored paper.
2. Organize and lay out questions so it is as easy to complete as possible.
3. Number the items and pages.
4. Put the name and address of the person to whom the form should be returned at the beginning and end of the questionnaire even if a self-addressed envelope is included.
5. Include brief, clear instructions, printed in bold type.
6. Use examples before any items that might be confusing.
7. Organize the questionnaire in some logical sequence. For example, group together related items or those that use the same response options.
8. Begin with a few interesting, nonthreatening items and do not put important items at the end of a long questionnaire.
9. If questions of a sensitive or potentially threatening nature are asked, make the response anonymous if possible.
10. Avoid using the words *questionnaire* or *checklist*. Many people are prejudiced against these words.
11. Include enough information for items to be meaningful to the respondent. Items that are interesting and clearly relevant to the study will increase response rate.
12. Longer questionnaires tend to reduce response rate, so the questionnaire should be as short as you can make it and still cover the objectives of the study.

Pilot Testing the Questionnaire

Always pilot test your questionnaire to increase clarity and correct other deficiencies before sending it out to respondents. To pilot test, administer the questionnaire to a small sample of individuals similar to the group you plan to survey. For example, if you wanted to survey all parents of fifth grade pupils in your school, you could pilot test your questionnaire with 20 to 30 parents of fifth grade pupils from another school that serves a similar neighborhood. A useful approach is to administer the pilot questionnaire as an interview to identify items that are not clear.

Once results from the pilot test have been collected, carefully check responses to each item for indications that respondents did not understand or did not have the information necessary to answer. Read all comments and suggestions for improvement. Finally, tabulate the results using the same procedures you plan to employ with the final version. At this point, you should ask whether the questionnaire produced the information you needed. Based on the information you have collected, revise the questionnaire.

Analysis of Questionnaire Data

Very simple analysis procedures are sufficient for most questionnaires. Described below are basic strategies for analysis of different types of questionnaire items.

Analysis of Closed-form Items

To analyze closed-form items such as multiple-choice, the simplest approach is to tally the number of respondents selecting each option for a given item, then convert these frequencies into percentages, which can be reported in a table.[2] If answers to items are on a logical continuum, it is useful to compute mean or median scores for single items, clusters of related items, or all items on the questionnaire. For example, given a multiple-choice item dealing with the use of punishment, a numerical value could be assigned to each answer based on the severity of the punishment advocated by that choice. For categorical variables, namely, those where the different responses to a multiple-choice item have no quantitative meaning, analysis is usually limited to simple frequency counts. For example, consider an item asking the individual to check the choice that indicates his racial or ethnic origin. Although these various choices could be assigned numbers, the numbers would have no quantitative meaning. Thus, it would be meaningless to combine the responses of all respondents to this item and compute a mean or a median.

When a questionnaire is administered to respondents from different populations—such as parents, teachers, and students—comparisons are often made between the responses of the different groups. For example, suppose you administered a questionnaire to gather information on the fairness of graduation requirements at your school. You would probably want to analyze parent, student, and teacher responses separately. One way of depicting the data to make interpretation easier is shown in Table 12.1. Each entry in Table 12.1 indicates the number of individuals in a particular respondent group who selected a given option of a multiple-choice item. Thus 16 percent of teachers, 5 percent of parents and 39 percent of students selected option *a* of the multiple-choice item. By inspecting Table 12.1, you can see that teachers, parents, and students responded differently

---

[2] Statistical techniques referred to in this section are usually covered in the first course in statistics. We will not deal with statistical computation here, but would suggest you consult an introductory statistics text, when you want to employ any of the statistical techniques mentioned.

TABLE 12.1 Responses to a Questionnaire Item Arranged for Analysis

Respondent Groups	Multiple Choices[a]				
	a	*b*	*c*	*d*	*e*
Teachers (n = 30)	16%	27%	37%	12%	8%
Parents (n = 554)	5%	15%	25%	40%	15%
Students (n = 397)	39%	31%	15%	8%	7%

[a] Table entries give the percentage of people in each group who chose each alternative

to this item. Most teachers selected option *c*, most parents preferred *d*, and most students preferred *a*.

Analysis of Open-form Items

The principal problem in analyzing responses to open-form items is to meaningfully categorize responses and assign numerical values to the categories of responses. Suppose you use an essay item that asks students to describe the study methods used in preparing for a science test. The first step is to scan the responses and set up categories into which most of the responses can be classified. These categories might be nominal, in which a number is arbitrarily assigned to each particular study strategy. Or, the categories might have quantitative significance; that is, you might rate each response on a scale of one to five, indicating the overall effectiveness of the study methods cited. Having set up a system to categorize responses, you could then assign numerical values to each type of response. Then you would need to read all responses again and categorize them according to your system.

Categorizing student responses is a time-consuming task, especially if a questionnaire has been administered to a large number of persons. Unless you classify open-form responses into categories, however, it is virtually impossible to draw any overall conclusions from the data. Once you have categorized responses, you can conduct the same types of analyses you might perform with closed-form items.

INTERVIEWS

Interviews are frequently more effective than questionnaires for gathering data about sensitive and complex questions. An interviewer can probe for details and clarifications, and thereby gain insights that rarely emerge from a questionnaire. For example, if you used a questionnaire to determine why students were dropping out of high school, most dropouts would likely give brief, socially acceptable responses. A skillful interviewer would be more likely to discover each individual's *real* reasons for dropping out—and would thus emerge with far more useful information.

However, interviews are not without problems. For example, interviews are much more costly than questionnaires because large amounts of time must be devoted to training interviewers and conducting interviews. Also, interviews are generally much less objective than questionnaires. Interviewers must decide what questions to ask and what responses to record. Not all interviewers will make the same decisions about such things, and thus the data tend to be somewhat subjective. An interviewer may, for example, record information that supports his preconceived notions while failing to record information that contradicts them.

Specifying Interview Objectives

The process for defining objectives is essentially the same for an interview as for a questionnaire. The first step is to specify a broad objective that can then be translated into specific questions. Since interviews often explore more complex educational questions than questionnaires, it may be more difficult to frame your objectives in precise terms. However, it is better to aim for as much precision as the broad objective of your interview permits.

Developing an Interview Schedule

An interview schedule, or guide, helps to increase objectivity and focus the interview on the designated issues. Figure 12.1 illustrates a brief interview schedule designed to obtain parents' perceptions of teacher contributions during parent-

FIGURE 12.1 Sample Interview Schedule

* After each question, space would be provided to write down parents' answers. On this sample, space for answers has been omitted.

Fill in before parent arrives: Parent's name _____

Student's name _____ Date of Int. _____ Date of P-T conf _____

> Opening Remarks (**Do not read this.** Instead memorize and rehearse until you are at ease. You need not use the exact words but should cover all underlined concepts.)
>
> > "Come in Mrs. _____ and take a seat. We want to **thank you** for volunteering to share your ideas with us. As you know, we are interviewing parents who were here for **parent-teacher conferences** last week. The purpose of the interview is to find out how we can **make our parent-teacher conferences more useful to parents.** Since you had conferences with several of your child's teachers, we want your **overall impressions.** **You need not name individual teachers** in your comments. Your comments will be kept **strictly confidential.** We plan to combine all parents' comments and focus our inservice training program on the areas that need improvement."

1. Shall we get started? First, did teachers give you specific information on **(student's name)** academic progress? Were there things you wanted to know that teachers didn't cover?* (Probe as necessary)

2. Did the teachers tell you how _____ was getting along with other students? (Probe as necessary)

3. (Ask only if academic or social problems were discussed) Did the teachers suggest things you could do to help _____ with these academic or social adjustment problems? (Probe as necessary)

4. Did teachers ask for your suggestions on how to work with _____ in the classroom? (Probe as necessary)

5. What suggestions can you give us that would make the conferences more useful to you? (Probe as necessary)

_____

teacher conferences. The specific objectives of this interview are to obtain information on the following questions:

1. Did teachers provide appropriate information on students' academic progress?
2. Did the teachers provide appropriate information on students' social adjustment?
3. Did teachers suggest what parents could do to enhance students' academic progress or social adjustment?
4. Did teachers ask for parents' suggestions?
5. What suggestions did parents have for making conferences more useful?

The typical interview guide contains space for the name of the respondent and other demographic data such as sex and age. Questions based on the specific interview objectives are then listed, each with space for the individual's response to be recorded. Probing or clarification questions are often included as well. Based on the level of structure provided in the interview schedule, interviews can be classified into three categories.

Unstructured Interviews

In an unstructured interview, the interviewer is guided only by the broad objective of the interview. There is usually no interview schedule and the interviewer follows whatever line of questioning he feels will accomplish the interview's goal. This approach is widely used in such areas as clinical psychology, where it is often difficult to establish specific objectives or anticipate the most useful questions. Unstructured interviews are also useful when educators are confronted with a new or ill-defined problem. An open structure leaves the interviewer free to follow leads and look for patterns that are difficult to anticipate. Keep in mind that results from unstructured interviews are hard to summarize if different questions are asked in each interview.

Fully Structured Interviews

Fully structured interviews maximize objectivity by allowing the interviewer very little latitude. Such interviews consist primarily of closed-form items. The interviewer asks each question exactly as written on the interview schedule and records the response. Few, if any, probing or follow-up questions are asked. If follow-up questions are included, they tend to be tightly structured. The same rules discussed for questionnaire items apply to constructing a fully structured interview schedule. In fact, the fully structured interview is much like a questionnaire administered orally. However, a higher percentage of respondents cooperate in interview studies than in questionnaire studies. It is difficult, for instance, to skip over certain items when the interviewer is asking questions and recording responses. Fully structured interviews are not widely used in education, however, because similar information can often be collected by questionnaire at a much lower cost.

Semistructured Interviews

For most educational information gathering, the semistructured interview is most useful. In this form, the interview schedule lists questions that relate to all the specific objectives identified by the investigator. Most questions for such interviews are open-form, which greatly reduces the chances of leading respondents. The schedule often includes supplementary questions that may be asked if an individual's initial response is inadequate or incomplete. Some degree of branching is often provided, so that if the respondent gives an answer that fits into category A, the interviewer asks follow-up question X. A category B answer is followed by question Y, and so on. The semi-structured interview provides much of the flexibility of the unstructured approach while achieving more objectivity and consistency that make responses easier to quantify and analyze.

Guidelines for Constructing an Interview Schedule and Conducting the Interview

Most rules for constructing questionnaire items also apply to constructing interview schedules. However, since most questionnaire items are closed-form and some interview items are open-form, the following rules are also appropriate:

1. Prepare an introduction the interviewer can use to open the interview—for example, a greeting, a description of the broad objective of the interview, information on how interview results will be used, and assurances that the respondents' remarks will be kept confidential.
2. Keep the number of questions to a minimum. The more you ask of the respondent, the harder it is to maintain rapport and motivation.
3. Do whatever you can to maintain a neutral interview. Never hint, by your remarks, facial expression, tone of voice, or other cues what response you want.
4. Always treat respondents respectfully.
5. Design the interview schedule so it is easy to complete and the results are easy to collate and analyze.
6. Keep in mind that open-form questions accompanied by an introduction to the topic usually produce more information and more accurate information than short closed-form questions (Sudman & Bradburn, 1982).
7. Structure the guide so that the writing demands on the interviewer are not excessive.
8. Train the interviewers. The amount of training and practice needed by each interviewer is determined by the experience of the interviewers, the complexity of the procedures, and the sensitivity of questions asked. The best way to determine when the training is sufficient is to observe the interviewer at intervals during training until he reaches an acceptable level of performance.
9. Pilot test the interview. This is by far the most important step in developing both the interview procedure and the interview guide.

Pilot Testing the Interview

Because interviews are somewhat subjective, it is important to try out both the procedures and the schedule before starting to collect information. The first step in pilot testing is to select a small group of individuals who are similar to those who will later be interviewed. Usually 10 to 20 interviews are necessary to try out procedures and make necessary revisions. In conducting the pilot test you should consider the following questions:

- Are there any words in the interview schedule your subjects do not understand?
- Are any other communication problems evident? For example, if the interviewer and subjects come from different socioeconomic or ethnic backgrounds, they may have difficulty understanding each other.
- Does the interview schedule allow responses to be recorded quickly and with minimal effort?
- How long does it take to conduct the interview? Can sufficient time be scheduled?
- Do the questions produce the information you need? Are there any questions respondents cannot answer? Are there any questions you do not need?
- Were respondents motivated to cooperate with the interviewer? If not, what steps can be taken to increase their motivation?
- Does the interviewer's opening statement adequately describe the purpose of the interview? Does it put respondents at ease?

In addition to improving the interview schedule and procedures, the pilot test gives the interviewer a chance to practice and improve his technique. If you plan to train interviewers, you should observe them and offer feedback on their performance. Tape-recorded training and pilot test interviews may help identify flaws in the interview schedule or procedures that would otherwise go overlooked. By listening to the tape, an interviewer can take a more objective view of his handling of the questions, often noticing strengths and weaknesses that were less obvious to him while he was interviewing.

Analysis of Interview Data

For interviews with open-form questions, the first steps in preparing data for analysis are to define categories of responses for each item, assign numerical values to different response levels, and score the interview schedule. Tentative response categories are usually set up during the pilot test. Because some new responses will likely occur during the regular interviews, these categories will usually need to be revised as the interviews proceed. Once all responses have been read and assigned numerical values, the analysis itself can employ the same statistical procedures used to analyze questionnaire data.

SYSTEMATIC OBSERVATION

Direct, systematic observation of teacher or student behavior is one of the most effective tools for improving teaching. In recent years, educators and educational researchers have become increasingly aware of the advantages of direct, systematic observation in the classroom. In a recent study by McKellar (1986), observers recorded 13 specific peer tutor behaviors and seven specific tutee behaviors. Each behavior was correlated with performance on a test of the material being learned to determine which behaviors were related to better achievement. The most frequent tutor behavior (over 60 percent of the time) was reading information to the tutee from the study guide. There was virtually *no relationship* between this behavior and achievement. Alternatively, elaborating on the information being learned and rephrasing it in the tutor's own words were both closely related to achievement, although they occurred less frequently.

Findings such as these have clear relevance for the teacher who wants to use peer tutors. It is unlikely such information could have been gathered using questionnaires or interviews. Although direct systematic observation can be time-consuming and expensive, it often yields valuable information that is impossible to collect in any other way.

Observational Procedures

Good observational procedures have the following characteristics:

1. They involve direct observation of participants in educational settings and the simultaneous collection of the desired information.
2. Specific objectives are identified to be achieved by the observation.
3. The behavior to be observed is defined in operational terms.
4. A structured format is used to record the relevant behavior.
5. The observation focuses on specific observable behavior instead of general or abstract characteristics. For example, motivation or enthusiasm cannot be observed directly and must be inferred from the behavior that is observed.
6. Observers are trained so they can reliably identify and record the targeted behavior.

Observational Objectives

The process of developing objectives for an observational study is essentially the same as for a questionnaire or interview. A broad goal is stated, then translated into a set of specific objectives or questions upon which the observations will focus. However, the kinds of objectives that can best be achieved by observation are different from those best achieved by self-report techniques. Observation is best to use when we are interested in what people actually do (i.e., their *observable* behavior), instead of ideas, interests, and perceptions.

Observation Schedules

Many observation schedules already exist. Some, like Flanders' system (1970), have been used in literally hundreds of observational studies and much is known about them. Most, however, have not been used widely and cannot be considered standardized in the sense that most published achievement test batteries are standardized. Sources of information about these schedules are listed in the Suggested Readings for this chapter.

There are several advantages to using an available observation schedule instead of developing your own. The main advantage is that you will save a great deal of work. Also, if your needs are met by a schedule that has been extensively tested, it is likely to be technically superior to a schedule you might develop.

To help you understand the nature of such systems, look at the Flanders 10-category system of interaction analysis in Table 12.2 and read the category descriptions. Although this system is quite old, it has been used frequently and is a good example of a well-developed system. Seven of the categories used by Flanders are used to classify teacher talk, two are used to classify pupil talk, and the last category is used to record short periods of silence or confusion. The observer uses tally marks for each three-second interval to indicate who is speaking and what category is applicable.

The main problem with using existing observation schedules is finding one that measures the specific behavior in which you are interested. For example, if you were interested in the specific *kinds of praise* used by teachers, the Flanders 10-category system would not be appropriate since all praise, regardless of type, is recorded in category 2.

Developing an Observation Schedule

Suppose you wanted to determine how much time students in your class were on task with their schoolwork. First, you would decide what kind of observable student behavior would indicate that the student was on task, and what behavior would indicate he was off task.

One of the authors recently conducted observations in this area using the schedule in Figure 12.2. Study it for a minute before proceeding. Before starting, the observer enters his name, the date, the teacher's name, and the time at the top of the form. He then enters the content of the lesson, the pupil's name, and the type of instruction. The eight types of instruction are listed at the bottom of the form. He observes the first pupil for two minutes and records what the pupil is doing every five seconds. Only four categories of pupil behavior are recorded: Involved in class work *(I)*, off task *(O)*, mildly disruptive *(M)* and seriously disruptive *(S)*.

If the pupil is off task during the majority of the first five seconds, the observer puts a slash through the first *O*, if involved for the majority of the next five seconds, the observer puts a slash through the second *I* and so on. The observer records the pupil's behavior twenty-four times during two minutes, making a slash through one of the four symbols *(I, O, M, S)* for every five seconds. He then observes the

TABLE 12.2 Flanders' Interaction Analysis Categories (FIAC)

Teacher Talk	Response	1. *Accepts feeling.* Accepts and clarifies an attitude or the feeling tone of a pupil in a nonthreatening manner. Feelings may be positive or negative. Predicting and recalling feelings are included. 2. *Praises or encourages.* Praises or encourages pupil action or behavior. Jokes that release tension, but not at the expense of another individual; nodding head, or saying "Um hm?" or "Go on" are included. 3. *Accepts or uses ideas of pupils.* Clarifying, building, or developing ideas suggested by a pupil. Teacher extensions of pupil ideas are included but as the teacher brings more of his own ideas into play, shift to category 5.
	Initiation	4. *Asks questions.* Asking a question about content or procedure, based on teacher ideas, with the intent that a pupil will answer. 5. *Lecturing.* Giving facts or opinions about content or procedures; expressing his own ideas, giving his own explanation, or citing an authority other than a pupil. 6. *Giving directions.* Directions, commands, or orders to which a pupil is expected to comply. 7. *Criticizing or justifying authority.* Statements intended to change pupil behavior from nonacceptable to acceptable pattern; bawling someone out; stating why the teacher is doing what he is doing; extreme self-reference.
Pupil Talk	Response	8. *Pupil-talk—response.* Talk by pupils in response to teacher. Teacher initiates the contact or solicits pupil statement or structures the situation. Freedom to express own ideas is limited.
	Initiation	9. *Pupil-talk—initiation.* Talk by pupils which they initiate. Expressing own ideas; initiating a new topic; freedom to develop opinions and a line of thought, like asking thoughtful questions; going beyond the existing structure.
Silence		10. *Silence or confusion.* Pauses, short period of silence and periods of confusion in which communication cannot be understood by the observer.

SOURCE: Flanders, N. A. *Analyzing Teaching Behavior.* Copyright ®1970, by Addison-Wesley Publishing Co. Reproduced with permission of the author.

next pupil for two minutes. Changes in lesson content and type of instruction are made in left-hand columns as they occur. The behavior of 10 pupils can be recorded on this form during a 20-minute period.

Using such a system we can get objective answers to important questions like the following:

1. During the total school day, for what percentage of time is the average student involved in class work?
2. Which students are off task more than 50 percent of the time?
3. What is the average percent of time students are involved in their class work for different content areas?
4. What type of instruction results in the highest level of pupil involvement?

Observer _____ Date _____ Teacher _____ AM PM _____

_____ _____ _____ _____ _____ _____ _____ _____ _____ _____

		Totals

1. Lesson content: _____
   _____
   Pupil _____ Instruction Type _____

```
I I I I I I I I I I I I I I I I I I I I I I I I I    _____
O O O O O O O O O O O O O O O O O O O O O O O O O    _____
M M M M M M M M M M M M M M M M M M M M M M M M M    _____
S S S S S S S S S S S S S S S S S S S S S S S S S    _____
```

2. Lesson content: _____
   _____
   Pupil _____ Instruction Type _____

```
I I I I I I I I I I I I I I I I I I I I I I I I I    _____
O O O O O O O O O O O O O O O O O O O O O O O O O    _____
M M M M M M M M M M M M M M M M M M M M M M M M M    _____
S S S S S S S S S S S S S S S S S S S S S S S S S    _____
```

3. Lesson content: _____
   _____
   Pupil _____ Instruction Type _____

```
I I I I I I I I I I I I I I I I I I I I I I I I I    _____
O O O O O O O O O O O O O O O O O O O O O O O O O    _____
M M M M M M M M M M M M M M M M M M M M M M M M M    _____
S S S S S S S S S S S S S S S S S S S S S S S S S    _____
```

4. Lesson content: _____
   _____
   Pupil _____ Instruction Type _____

```
I I I I I I I I I I I I I I I I I I I I I I I I I    _____
O O O O O O O O O O O O O O O O O O O O O O O O O    _____
M M M M M M M M M M M M M M M M M M M M M M M M M    _____
S S S S S S S S S S S S S S S S S S S S S S S S S    _____
```

5. Lesson content: _____
   _____
   Pupil _____ Instruction Type _____

```
I I I I I I I I I I I I I I I I I I I I I I I I I    _____
O O O O O O O O O O O O O O O O O O O O O O O O O    _____
M M M M M M M M M M M M M M M M M M M M M M M M M    _____
S S S S S S S S S S S S S S S S S S S S S S S S S    _____
```

6. Lesson content: _____
   _____
   Pupil _____ Instruction Type _____

```
I I I I I I I I I I I I I I I I I I I I I I I I I    _____
O O O O O O O O O O O O O O O O O O O O O O O O O    _____
M M M M M M M M M M M M M M M M M M M M M M M M M    _____
S S S S S S S S S S S S S S S S S S S S S S S S S    _____
```

7. Lesson content: _____
   _____
   Pupil _____ Instruction Type _____

```
I I I I I I I I I I I I I I I I I I I I I I I I I    _____
O O O O O O O O O O O O O O O O O O O O O O O O O    _____
M M M M M M M M M M M M M M M M M M M M M M M M M    _____
S S S S S S S S S S S S S S S S S S S S S S S S S    _____
```

8. Lesson content: _____
   _____
   Pupil _____ Instruction Type _____

```
I I I I I I I I I I I I I I I I I I I I I I I I I    _____
O O O O O O O O O O O O O O O O O O O O O O O O O    _____
M M M M M M M M M M M M M M M M M M M M M M M M M    _____
S S S S S S S S S S S S S S S S S S S S S S S S S    _____
```

9. Lesson content: _____
   _____
   Pupil _____ Instruction Type _____

```
I I I I I I I I I I I I I I I I I I I I I I I I I    _____
O O O O O O O O O O O O O O O O O O O O O O O O O    _____
M M M M M M M M M M M M M M M M M M M M M M M M M    _____
S S S S S S S S S S S S S S S S S S S S S S S S S    _____
```

10. Lesson content: _____
    _____
    Pupil _____ Instruction Type _____

```
I I I I I I I I I I I I I I I I I I I I I I I I I    _____
O O O O O O O O O O O O O O O O O O O O O O O O O    _____
M M M M M M M M M M M M M M M M M M M M M M M M M    _____
S S S S S S S S S S S S S S S S S S S S S S S S S    _____
```

1. Large-group
2. Small-group recitation
3. Individual help or tutoring

4. Seatwork-teacher circulates
5. Seatwork-teacher attends
6. Seatwork-teacher does not attend

7. Noninstructional Activity
8. Lecture

FIGURE 12.2 Classroom Management Observation Schedule

Methods of Recording Observational Data

There are a number of different methods for recording observation data: (1) duration recording, (2) frequency-count recording, (3) interval recording, and (4) continuous recording. Let's consider each.

Duration Recording

In duration recording, the observer watches for one or more specific behaviors and records the amount of time that each behavior occurs. For example, suppose you are interested in the amount of time that teachers in your school talk during instruction. Because time devoted to teacher talk reduces the opportunity for student participation, this kind of observational data can be very useful in letting teachers know whether their behavior during class discussions facilitates student performance.

In using duration recording to collect such data, the observer could use a stopwatch to record the number of seconds consumed by each teacher remark. Then, the total discussion time would be recorded. The time used by the teacher could then be summed and divided by the total discussion time to determine the percent of discussion time the teacher was talking.

Duration recording can be used to observe more than one behavior, provided the behaviors being observed will not occur simultaneously. For example, teacher talk in the preceding example could be divided into several categories:

1. Questions
2. Responses to student remarks or questions
3. Content remark not in response to a student
4. Classroom management remarks
5. Other teacher remarks

Frequency-count Recording

In this method the specific behaviors to be observed are listed on the observation schedule and the observer enters a tally mark each time one of the target behaviors occurs. For example, suppose you want to determine the amount of praise used by each teacher in your school. Since most praise statements are very short, recording their frequency might be more useful than recording their duration. An observation schedule such as that in Figure 12.3 could be used to record frequencies of different kinds of praise.

The difficulty of making frequency-count recordings of observed behavior depends on the number of behaviors being observed, the frequency with which each occurs, and the ease with which behaviors can be classified. When most of the behaviors to be observed are easy to classify and occur at a low frequency, observers can be trained to reliably identify and tally 20 or more different behaviors during a single observation. When more than one target behavior can occur at the same time, frequency-count recording is more reliable than duration recording.

Teacher	Observer	Subject Being Taught	Date

a. Starting time: ___ ___ ___
    hr. min. sec.

b. Ending time: ___ ___ ___
    hr. min. sec.

c. Each time the teacher makes a praise remark, cross out a number in the appropriate category:

    1. General praise--academic: Total: _____

       1 2 3 4 5 6 7 8 9 10 11 12 13 14 15 16 17 18 19 20 21 22 23 24 25

    2. Specific praise--academic: Total: _____

       1 2 3 4 5 6 7 8 9 10 11 12 13 14 15 16 17 18 19 20 21 22 23 24 25

    3. General praise--nonacademic: Total: _____

       1 2 3 4 5 6 7 8 9 10 11 12 13 14 15 16 17 18 19 20 21 22 23 24 25

    4. Specific praise--nonacademic: Total: _____

       1 2 3 4 5 6 7 8 9 10 11 12 13 14 15 16 17 18 19 20 21 22 23 24 25

d. Total discussion time in minutes: _____

e. Praise per minute: General praise--academic $\dfrac{c_1}{d}$ =

                     Specific praise--academic $\dfrac{c_2}{d}$ =

                     General praise--nonacademic $\dfrac{c_3}{d}$ =

                     Specific praise--nonacademic $\dfrac{c_4}{d}$ =

Total praise per minute: $\dfrac{c_1 + c_2 + c_3 + c_4}{d}$

FIGURE 12.3 Sample Observation Schedule for Frequency-Count Recording

Interval Recording

Using this method, the observer checks the target subject at regular intervals and records his behavior during that interval. In the observation schedule described earlier (see Figure 12.2), the observation interval was five seconds. The observer had a portable tape recorder that beeped in his ear every five seconds. At each beep the observer recorded the behavior of the student being observed. Every two minutes, a longer beep redirected his attention to the next student. Thus, during a period of two minutes, a student was observed 24 times for five seconds each.

Continuous Recording

In this method, the observer attempts to record all relevant behavior of the subject during the period of observation. This method is used most often when the investigator does not know what specific behaviors are relevant to his objective. For example, suppose you want to identify teaching techniques that relate to higher student achievement in algebra. You have identified 10 algebra teachers in your school district whose students consistently make the highest scores on standardized achievement tests. You could use continuous observation to identify what methods these teachers are using. In this case, the observer would attempt to record all teacher behavior that seemed to relate to effective teaching of algebra. After the observations were completed, the observer would try to identify patterns of behavior (i.e., specific teaching methods) that might account for the higher student achievement.

Continuous observation is more difficult than other procedures for recording observational data, and should only be used when other methods cannot be applied. Because the observer cannot usually record everything that happens, he must constantly make decisions and choices. This tends to make the method highly subjective.

Level of Inference

In developing an observation schedule, it is important to remember the level of inference required of the observer. It is much easier for the observer to accurately record the number of times a teacher smiles than it is to rate the amount of ''warmth'' the teacher displays in interactions with students. A *low-inference behavior* is one where the observer does not have to use much judgment to interpret what is observed. To rate a teacher on warmth, the observer must use his own judgment. What is *warm* to one observer may seem neutral or even negative to another. Thus, exhibiting warmth is a *high-inference behavior*.

High-inference variables such as warmth, dedication to teaching, creative imagination, or enthusiasm are much more difficult for the observer to evaluate than are low-inference behaviors such as use of praise, giving specific examples, or using pictures to illustrate points in a lesson. The frequency and/or duration of low-inference behavior is usually recorded as it occurs. For high-inference categories, the observer usually rates the subject on a quality scale at the end of the observation period. Low-inference behavior deals with specific events; high inference ratings usually deal with overall impressions.

Admittedly, many important educational questions can only be explored by attempting to evaluate high-inference data. But conclusions based on such data should be drawn with extreme care. There are many advantages to making direct observations of low-inference behavior, and this approach should be used whenever possible.

Developing Operational Definitions

The most difficult task involved in making an observation schedule is developing operational definitions of each behavior to be observed. To produce reliable information, the observer must be able to recognize each behavior when it occurs and discriminate between the target behavior and similar, but different, behaviors. The best way to develop clear operational definitions is to write a tentative definition and then use it in conducting a few hours of observation.

As the observation progresses, you will usually see some relevant behaviors that cannot be classified by your tentative definition. You should record such behaviors, and then revise your definition so that each of these behaviors can be classified. During this preliminary observation you should also note examples and nonexamples of each behavior included in your schedule. These should be added to the operational definitions since they help to clarify exactly what the definition means.

Pilot Testing

Once you are satisfied with your operational definitions, you should do a pilot test of the observational system. This pilot test provides an additional check of the operational definitions and gives you an opportunity to check the procedural details and analysis strategies for the study.

The following questions should be considered during the pilot test:

a. Do any newly observed behaviors require further revision or elaboration of the operational definitions?

b. How much observation time is needed to obtain a stable indication of the behaviors you are observing? Obtaining a stable measure of low-frequency behaviors (e.g., the number of serious student discipline problems) requires a longer period of time than measuring a high-frequency behavior.

c. Can the data be recorded quickly and easily onto the observation schedule? Is the format easy to follow? Is enough space provided? Can the data be combined easily to obtain desired totals and subtotals?

d. How do the subjects respond to the observation? If they are distracted by the observation, they are less likely to behave naturally, and your results will be biased. One approach to reduce such problems is to spend several hours in the observational setting before beginning to collect data. Another strategy is to place yourself where you can easily see the subjects but they cannot easily see you.

e. Can the observer keep up with what is going on? Is he being asked to observe more behavioral categories than is feasible?

f. Can behaviors be observed reliably? This can be checked by having two observers independently observe the same subjects during the same time period and the results compared.

Training the Observers

The first step in training observers is to have them study the operational definitions of the behaviors they are to observe and to become familiar with the schedule they will use. To classify an observed behavior quickly and accurately, the observers must be *very familiar* with these materials. It is usually advisable to test the observers after they have studied the definitions and schedule to assure they have mastered this material before proceeding.

It is often a good idea to show the observers brief videotapes that illustrate the behaviors they will observe. For example, if you wanted observers to note teachers' listening behaviors during class discussions, you might use a videotape illustrating such behavior—with some variations so that observers learn what to look for and how to recognize it. Have the trainees observe the tape and record the behaviors on the observation schedule. Then replay the tape, stopping whenever a target behavior occurs. Check how each observer classified the behavior, and explain what the correct classification should have been and why.

Repeat this procedure until the observers agree on their classifications. If fairly simple behaviors are being studied, observer agreement as high as 95 percent can be reached quite rapidly. For more complex behaviors, you may decide to be satisfied with a lower rate of agreement. Take time to discuss questions that may arise, since further clarification of the definitions and improvements in the observational schedule can only enhance the reliability of your results.

If observations are to be done for an extended period, observers should be given refresher training sessions at two-week intervals. During these sessions, they can discuss any difficulties they have encountered classifying target behaviors. They should also observe another videotape to recheck interobserver agreement. If refresher sessions are not held, observers gradually (and usually subconsciously) change the definitions they are using to identify the target behaviors. This is called *observer drift* and if left uncorrected, it progressively undermines reliability.

RATING SCALES

Rating scales are widely used in education, although there are serious questions about their reliability and validity. Many require the observer to recall the previous behavior of the subject and to evaluate him on various characteristics based on this recall. Such scales are used to rate concrete observable variables such as neatness, as well as complex abstract traits such as integrity.

The retrospection of the person doing the evaluation, based upon an unknown amount of contact over an extended period of time, is likely to be biased in a number of ways. For example, recent behavior is usually more easily recalled and may be given disproportionate weight. We also tend to remember unusual behavior better than ordinary behavior. Despite such problems, however, rating scales, anecdotal records, and behavioral checklists continue to be used widely.

Some Problems with Rating Scales

Perhaps the most common format for rating scales is a five-point scale such as that shown in Figure 12.4, item *a*. This item asks the rater to make a qualitative judgement—how good—rather than a quantitative judgment—how much or how

a. Rate the teacher's use of verbal student reinforcement on the following scale (circle one):

_____

Excellent   Good   Average   Weak   Poor

b. Rate the teacher's use of verbal student reinforcement by placing an X on the following scale:

_____

Excellent   Good   Average   Weak   Poor

c. Rate the teacher's use of verbal student reinforcement by checking the most appropriate level on the following scale:

_____ 1.   Excellent--The teacher makes reinforcement remarks for most correct student actions or responses. Undesirable student behavior is never reinforced by teacher attention.

_____ 2.   Average--The teacher makes reinforcement remarks for some correct student actions or responses. Undesirable student behavior is occasionally reinforced by teacher attention.

_____ 3.   Poor--The teacher almost never makes reinforcement remarks. Attention is often given to undesirable student behavior.

FIGURE 12.4   Rating Scale Formats

often. Unfortunately, it is impossible to determine exactly what qualitative terms such as *excellent* mean to the raters. If several raters are involved, there are probably different standards being used to decide what rating to give each individual. If each subject is rated by several raters, a composite rating may be obtained by summing the numerical values assigned across raters and then computing an average.

A common error in constructing rating scales is to use too many levels. For rating low-inference behavior that is easily observed, as many as seven levels may be used successfully. However, for high-inference traits most raters cannot reliably discriminate among more than three levels. When in doubt, use fewer levels rather than more.

When a scale such as that in Figure 12.4 item *a* is used, some raters may decide that some individuals are really *between* two points on the scale. To deal with this problem, a format such as that shown in Figure 12.4 *b* may be used. This permits the rater to place a mark at any point. Then a transparent overlay with five divisions is placed over the rating by the scorer to assign a numerical value to the rating. Or the distance from one end of the line can be measured and recorded to provide a continuous score, but this creates an illusion of precision in rating that does not exist.

As a rule, more accurate ratings will be obtained by supplying definitions for each level, as illustrated in Figure 12.4 *c*. However, the rater may be unable to accurately apply these definitions unless he uses the rating scale along with observations of the teacher. Notice in Figure 12.4 *c* that the words *most, some,* and *almost never* are used at the three levels. These words are, of course, just as ambiguous as *excellent, average,* and *poor.* If we substituted *more than half* for *most,* the definition would be a bit more precise. But without making a systematic observation of the teacher, it is unlikely that the rater would recall whether the teacher used reinforcement more or less than half of the time. On the other hand, if a systematic observation were made, the observer could actually count the teacher's reinforcing remarks, and the rating scale would be unnecessary.

Other problems arise when we attempt to collect accurate data with rating scales. People are often asked to rate other individuals on characteristics that they have had little or no opportunity to observe. For example, principals have been asked to evaluate teachers on such characteristics as integrity, dedication to teaching, and love of children. Principals rarely see teachers in situations where a characteristic like integrity can be observed. Unfortunately, rating scales often deal with traits that cannot be observed directly. In such cases it is left up to the rater to decide what they mean. In addition, raters are often not motivated to give the ratings the time and thought needed. If the rater regards the evaluation as a disagreeable chore to be gotten out of the way as quickly as possible, the results may be meaningless or even misleading.

One dilemma often encountered in obtaining ratings is that the people who are best qualified to make the ratings are often unwilling to do so because of friendship, emotional attachments, or identification with the person being rated. The ideal rater would usually be someone who had observed the individual a great deal but who had no strong feelings—positive or negative—about the individual. Such people are usually not available. So, the typical rater is likely to be someone who has observed the individuals being rated but whose observations are distorted by an unknown combination of likes and dislikes.

Rating Errors

As a result of the problems involved in using rating scales, the following errors are often made by raters:

1. *Error of Central Tendency:* If a rater is unsure of the correct rating for a given individual, or if he has limited information on which to base his ratings, he is likely to rate near the center of the scale.
2. *Error of Leniency:* Some raters rate nearly everyone near the top of the scale. This usually reflects a reluctance to give anyone a "bad" rating. The error of leniency, like the error of central tendency, may also indicate an effort to avoid making the unpleasant decisions that are a part of many rating procedures.
3. *Halo Effect:* This error occurs when the rater allows his general opinion of the subject (either positive or negative) to influence his ratings of other unrelated characteristics. Often the halo effect simply reflects a universal tendency to overrate people whom we like and underrate people whom we do not like.

Rules for Developing Rating Scales

In spite of their many limitations, rating scales are used widely because they are much easier and less costly to do than systematic observation or interviews. In some cases, ratings have been useful in exploring some important educational problems such as teacher enthusiasm. Although precise operational definitions of enthusiasm have rarely been provided, raters seem able to reliably rate teachers on this characteristic.

Listed below are some guidelines to help you develop better rating scales.

1. Whenever possible, ask for ratings of specific observable behavior rather than ambiguous traits or characteristics.
2. Always define the characteristics being rated as precisely as you can and give examples.
3. Only ask raters to provide information about variables they have had an opportunity to observe.
4. Whenever possible, provide a description for each level of the trait to be rated rather than relying on a single qualitative term such as *excellent, good*, or *unsatisfactory*.
5. Try to communicate the importance of the rating to the raters so they will be motivated to do a careful job.
6. If possible, have the ratings done under supervision. This allows you to explain their purpose, answer questions, and motivate raters to do their best.
7. Use as few rating levels as you can to collect the data you need. It is rarely advisable to use more than five.
8. Use rating scales only when systematic observations or interviews cannot be used.

SUGGESTED READINGS

Bakeman, R., & Gottman, J. M. (1986). *Observing Interaction: An introduction to sequential analysis.* New York: Cambridge University Press.

The authors' main theme is that the collection of sequential data in observational studies permits educators to study many questions that cannot be studied with typical methods of observation. Most of the topics in the book, such as developing a coding scheme, recording behavioral sequences, and assessing observer agreement, are relevant to any study that employs systematic observation. A good source for students or teachers who plan to conduct an observational study.

Berdie, D. R., & Anderson, J. F. (1974). *Questionnaires: Design and use.* Metuchen, NJ: Scarecrow Press.

This short book is filled with useful information on designing and carrying out a questionnaire study. The sections on item construction and procedures to stimulate responses are especially valuable. The appendices contain four sample questionnaires, follow-up letters, and a case history of a questionnaire study. Finally, an extensive and very useful annotated bibliography is provided.

Borich, G. D., & Madden, S. K. (1977). *Evaluating classroom instruction: A sourcebook of instruments*. Reading, MA: Addison-Wesley.

This book reviews a large number of instruments that can be used to evaluate teacher and pupil behavior. Many are observation forms. Most of the information needed to select an instrument is provided.

Evertson, C. M., & Green, J. L. (1986). Observation as Inquiry and Method. In M. C. Wittrock (Ed.), *Handbook of research on teaching* (3d ed.). New York: Macmillan.

This excellent chapter is recommended to anyone considering an observational study. After a brief historical orientation, the authors explore the observation process. Four broad systems of recording observational data are then discussed in detail. The authors are especially skillful in using tables to summarize and figures to illustrate important processes. A very extensive reference list is included.

Frey, J. H. (1983). *Survey research by telephone*. Beverly Hills, CA: Sage Publications.

This book gives an excellent comparison of the advantages and disadvantages of mailed questionnaires, face-to-face interviews, and telephone interviews. Design of the interview guide and administration of a telephone survey are also discussed. The section on computer-assisted telephone interviewing (CATI) will be especially useful to those planning this type of survey.

Simon, A., & Boyer, E. G. (1974). *Mirrors for behavior III: An anthology of observation instruments*. Wyncote, PA: Communications Materials Center.

The original anthology was published in 1967 in six volumes and covers 26 observation instruments. Volumes 7 through 14, published in 1970, cover 53 additional instruments. Two supplemental volumes to the 1970 edition covered an additional 12 observation systems. This 1974 anthology provides an extensive coverage of instruments related to education. Brief abstracts are provided that help the teacher or administrator locate instruments that may meet his needs. These are followed by a more detailed treatment of each system, which briefly describes the system on eight dimensions and also defines the categories of behavior observed.

Sudman, S., & Bradburn, N. M. (1982). *Asking questions: A practical guide to questionnaire design*. San Francisco: Jossey-Bass.

The authors have a very strong background of research and experience in survey research. The result is an extremely practical guide to writing questions for use in structured questionnaires and interview guides. Chapters focus on framing threatening and nonthreatening questions, knowledge questions and attitude questions. Most chapters start with a checklist of main points, followed by many examples. This book should be required reading for anyone planning to conduct either a questionnaire or an interview project.

Tolar, A. (Ed.). (1985). *Effective interviewing*. Springfield, IL: Charles Thomas.

Each chapter discusses a different type of interview. Most of the types described can be employed in education such as the behavioral interview, the oral history interview, and the research interview. Should be checked by students planning an interview study.

SELF-CHECK QUIZ

1. Generally, the most efficient method for collecting specific concrete information about educational questions is the
   a. questionnaire.
   b. interview.
   c. systematic observation.
   d. rating scale.

2. One good reason for using open-form items in questionnaires is because
   a. they are easier to score than other types of questionnaires.
   b. respondents are less likely to feel threatened about providing sensitive information.
   c. responses can be used to develop multiple-choice items for use in future questionnaires.
   d. they restrict the respondent to the specific information wanted by the investigator.

3. In designing your questionnaire, to which of the following rules should you adhere?
   a. Ask your most important questions at the end of the questionnaire.
   b. End the questionnaire with a few interesting and nonthreatening items to avoid fatigue.
   c. Avoid using the words *questionnaire* or *checklist* on your form.
   d. Arrange your items in random sequence.

4. When the school administrator is confronted with a new and ill-defined problem where it is not possible to write specific objectives, what form of interview is most appropriate?
   a. Client-centered interview
   b. Fully structured interview with no probing
   c. Semi-structured interview with no branching
   d. Unstructured interview with no interview schedule

5. Which of the following is an important guideline to follow in developing an interview schedule?
   a. Ask at least two questions for each objective to establish reliability.
   b. Keep the number of questions to a minimum.
   c. Only use closed-form questions to simplify analysis.
   d. Ensure that the interviewer takes a position on each objective to avoid confusion.

6. When you need descriptive information related to student behavior in the classroom, the best method is usually to
   a. develop a detailed questionnaire to be completed by both students and teachers.
   b. develop a quality scale using three- or five-point ratings.
   c. interview students on their classroom behavior.
   d. conduct systematic observations in the classroom.

7. Suppose you are interested in teachers' use of short, general, praise statements during recitation lessons. What type of observation recording would probably be best?
   a. Duration recording using a stop watch
   b. Frequency-count recording
   c. Interval recording, using ten-second intervals
   d. Continuous recording

8. In using rating scales, a common error is for the rater to allow his general opinion of the person being rated to influence his ratings on specific characteristics. This error is called the
   a. halo effect.   c. leniency error.
   b. central tendency error.   d. Hawthorne effect.

9. Which of the following rules should be observed in developing a rating scale?
   a. Use at least a seven-point rating to ensure accuracy.
   b. Use rating scales instead of systematic observation whenever possible.
   c. When possible, ask for ratings of specific observable behavior rather than general characteristics.
   d. Design the scale so that most ratings fall in the top two rating levels on each characteristic rated.

10. One problem that must be faced when you choose to use systematic observation to learn about effective teaching methods is
   a. the time and expense involved in training observers.
   b. the necessity of relying on the observers' memory.
   c. the difficulty of actually allowing the observer to be present in the classroom.
   d. high susceptibility to the error of leniency.

SUGGESTION SHEET

If your last name starts with the letter *M*, please complete the suggestion sheet at the end of the book while this chapter is still fresh in your mind.

ANSWERS TO APPLICATION PROBLEMS

#1

Many multiple-choice items could be developed for this objective. The following is an example of one such item:

Suppose you are teaching in a seventh grade classroom. John Bogus, the class clown, makes several silly remarks each period that disrupt the class. Which of the following strategies would you use to stop this behavior?

   a. Talk with him after school and explain why he must stop.
   b. Send him to the principal's office.
   c. Set up an agreement with him that gives him a reward for each fifteen minutes that he does not disturb the class.
   d. Make him stand out in the hall for five minutes each time he disrupts the class.
   e. Sharply tell him to be quiet each time he makes a silly remark.
   f. Other (briefly describe):

#2

Many different answers could be correct for this problem. The following is one example:

   1. Since evolution is a proven scientific fact, do you favor teaching this important concept in the public schools?
   2. Since the theory of evolution is in total conflict with creation as described in the Holy Bible, do you oppose teaching this theory in the public schools?
   3. Should the theory of evolution be taught in the public schools?

CHAPTER 13

Getting in Touch with Students' Feelings: Measuring Attitudes and Interests

Overview

In this chapter, we examine the measurement of two related constructs—attitudes and interests—both of which have an important impact on education. In our first section, we briefly discuss why formal measurement of attitudes, interests, and other affective variables is not common in our schools. In the second section, we introduce the measurement of attitudes, beginning by considering what attitudes are and how they influence our lives. We divide attitudes into the three separate components of belief, feeling, and behavior and examine how each is related to the measurement of attitudes. In our third section, we show how teachers and other educators can construct tailored attitude scales for their own use in the classroom or in research or evaluation studies. In the fourth section, we describe several commercially available attitude measures that are of possible interest to teachers and discuss the validity and reliability of such measures. Finally, we briefly examine the measurement of *interests*, which typically reflect activities that people like or dislike. We narrow the broad area to focus on students' academic and vocational interests, and briefly describe a few widely used instruments designed to assess such interests.

Objectives

Upon completing your study of this chapter, you should be able to

1. Define attitude and describe the three components of attitude.

2. Describe how attitudes influence the way people deal with problems and adjust to their environment.

3. Explain why most attitude measures focus on beliefs and feelings rather than on behavior.

4. Describe the steps you would take to develop (1) a Likert attitude scale, and (2) a *semantic differential scale* for use in your classroom.

5. List and briefly describe, at least one commercially available attitude measure appropriate for measuring each of the following: (a) attitude toward school, (b) attitude toward curriculum, and (c) attitude toward study methods and habits.

6. Describe methods that can be used to estimate the reliability of an attitude scale, and explain why attitude scales usually have lower reliability than standardized achievement tests.

7. Define interests and distinguish between interests and attitudes.

8. List and briefly describe one measure of academic interest and one measure of vocational interest.

MEASURING AFFECTIVE OUTCOMES

Most tests employed in the schools, such as achievement tests, diagnostic tests, and scholastic aptitude measures, are cognitive. In contrast to cognitive tests, which measure some form of knowledge, many tests measure noncognitive variables such as attitudes, interests, and values.

Many public school objectives are concerned with affective outcomes, such as social relationships, achievement motivation, and attitudes toward school; and there appears to be an increasing emphasis by researchers upon noncognitive objectives. However, although teachers often notice developing interests and attitudes among their students, their perceptions are almost entirely subjective. Few schools make any systematic effort to collect evidence of student growth in the achievement of affective objectives. One reason for this is that affective objectives are somewhat more difficult to measure than cognitive outcomes. Also, although there are many affective measures available, they tend to be less valid and reliable than cognitive measures.

Another problem with the measurement of affective objectives is that they are often stated in such abstract and general terms that it is difficult to decide specifically what outcomes should be measured to determine the degree to which the objective has been achieved. To illustrate this point, Krathwohl and his associates cite a typical affective objective: *The student should become interested in good books.* This objective can be interpreted in several ways.

The student should be able to distinguish between good books and not-so-good books.

The student should want to know more about what makes a book good.

The student should read an increasing number of books which experts classify as good.

The student should express a desire to read more good books.

The student should purchase good books for his personal library. (Krathwohl, et al. 1964, p. 22)

Each of these interpretations suggests a different measure, making the process complex and difficult. Finally, schools tend not to measure affective objectives because they do so little to promote their achievement. While individual educators may aspire and strive to create positive attitudes in students, a review of curriculum guides reveals few specific strategies for achieving such outcomes. Despite the absence of good measurement strategies, however, affective outcomes are often just as important as cognitive outcomes. In this chapter we will discuss two important affective variables, attitudes and interests, and learn how they can be measured.

THE INFLUENCE OF ATTITUDES ON BEHAVIOR

Personality theorists believe that attitudes perform a number of functions for the individual. First, attitudes tend to simplify (indeed, *over*simplify) many of the problems that people encounter in their environment. An individual with a given attitude tends to react toward the attitude object in terms of it being either good or bad. It is much easier to react to all members of a minority group as being bad than it is to consider and analyze all the individuals in the group and recognize that each one is different.

Many psychologists believe that attitudes are related to the maintenance of a favorable self-concept. Attitudes such as the feeling that we are members of a group that is better than other groups tend to bolster the individual's self-esteem.

Attitudes also help the individual find acceptance within his environment. He frequently chooses friends who have similar attitudes. His attitudes gain him acceptance with these individuals, and they tend to support and encourage him to maintain his attitudes. Thus, in effect, such groups tend to reward their members with social acceptance, and a feeling of belonging. Such reinforcement generally fosters consistency between attitudes and behavior. For example, assume an Alaskan fisherman has a negative attitude toward Japanese fishermen who ply the Alaskan waters. If this attitude is prevalent in his community, if it has resulted in abusive behaviors such as cutting the nets of their Japanese competitors, and if his friends praise him for joining in this behavior, then his behavior will likely become consistent with his attitude. But if federal marshals come to Alaska and start arresting people who abuse Japanese fishermen, his behavior may quickly change, even though his attitude may persist.

So far we have talked as if we all share a common understanding of what attitudes are. Such is not the case. Moreover, we cannot measure anything effectively unless we know what it is. And in the case of attitudes, a good definition is a bit tricky to pin down.

What sort of evidence leads us to say "John has a poor attitude toward school"? Is it what John says? What he does? How he appears to us? Since we cannot measure something we cannot define, psychologists have tried hard to capture this elusive concept. As a result, there are now nearly as many definitions of the term *attitude* as there are scientists who have studied it. Our definition, which draws from several sources (e.g., Allport, 1935; Triandis, 1971; Anderson, 1988), is: An *attitude* is an enduring system of beliefs and feelings about an object, situation, or institution that influences the individual's perceptions and behavior toward that object, situation, or institution.

Attitudes are directed toward an attitude object; people have either favorable or unfavorable attitudes toward other people or things. Triandis (1971) points out that attitudes have a cognitive component, an affective component, and a behavioral component. By *cognitive component* he means that the individual has certain concepts (ideas or beliefs) about the attitude object. These concepts may or may not be supported by any factual information, but they nevertheless represent the beliefs of the individual. For example, a person who has a negative attitude toward lawyers may believe that they are deceptive and untrustworthy. Such beliefs may have little or no factual basis, but still form an important component of the individual's attitude.

Attitudes also typically involve *feelings* about the attitude object; there is an emotional or affective component that is separate from the cognitive component. An individual who has strong feelings for or against an attitude object will frequently continue to display such feelings even if his beliefs about it are shown to be false.

The third component of attitude, which Triandis (1971) calls "predisposition to action," suggests that the individual's attitude influences his behavior toward the attitude object. For example, the beliefs and feelings of racial bigots are what prompt their unacceptable behavior toward racial minorities.

To summarize:

Cognitive Component → beliefs about the attitude object

Affective Component → feelings about the attitude object

Behavioral Component → behavior toward the attitude object

To illustrate these three components, consider a child who has a negative attitude toward school. The cognitive component of his attitude would be reflected in his belief that school is a waste of time. The affective component could involve feelings of resentment toward the teacher and the school administration for forcing him to waste his time by attending school, and the behavioral component could be reflected in his refusing to do homework, truancy, defying the teacher, and displaying acts of aggression against students, teachers, and school property.

In general, the cognitive, affective, and behavioral components of an attitude are consistent; that is, what the individual *believes, feels*, and *does* with regard to an attitude object are consistent. However, this general rule does not apply in all cases. Witness one classic study in the 1930s, where motel and restaurant operators were sent a questionnaire asking whether they would admit Chinese people to their establishments. A large percentage (92 percent) of the respondents indicated they would not. However, when a Chinese couple visited 66 motels and 184 restaurants, they were refused service only once (LaPiere, 1936).

One reason for inconsistencies between beliefs, feelings, and behavior is that an individual's behavior toward an attitude object is closely related to the norms of behavior; that is, what other people think he should or should not do. Remember our example of attitudes toward Japanese fishermen? Similarly, an individual who is prejudiced against Vietnamese refugees would probably have the same beliefs and feelings regardless of the setting in which he finds himself. However, his behavior would likely be influenced greatly by that setting. If he were in a setting where verbal or physical aggression against a Vietnamese refugee would be accepted or encouraged, such behavior might occur. However, in another setting where such behavior would be rejected or punished, there is much less likelihood that such aggression would occur. Triandis (1971) makes this point by suggesting that attitudes involve what people think about, feel about, and how they would like to behave toward an attitude object.

Probably another reason for the discrepancy often found between beliefs, feelings, and behavior lies in our very different ways of measuring attitudes. When we measure an individual's attitude by using an attitude scale, we usually obtain information about an entire class of people, such as African Americans, movie stars, welfare recipients, and so on. However, when we measure the same individual's attitude by observing his behavior, our observation focuses on his behavior toward a particular person who may not fit the stereotype he holds for people in that class.

CONSTRUCTING ATTITUDE MEASURES

Classroom teachers and other educators will often find it very useful to measure attitudes. After all, one societal function of education is to help students develop healthy attitudes, and measuring changes in attitude across time is necessary to determine the extent to which that is occurring. Also, you may find it easier to motivate and challenge students to do their best if attitude measurement has helped you identify those whose negative attitudes are impeding their progress in school or in personal or social development. In addition, it is frequently useful to know how students' attitudes toward particular subjects, activities, or teachers affect their academic achievement, so that strategies can be implemented to ameliorate the negative effects of such attitudes.

Frequently, you can find an existing attitude measure that will suit your needs, for there are many in the sources discussed later in Chapter 16 (and we will describe and discuss several such measures later in this chapter). But often you will find that no existing measure really fits the bill. In such cases, you may wish to develop your own instrument to use with students or others whose attitudes are important for you to understand. Before teaching you particular techniques for developing attitude scales, however, it is important to present some general considerations you need to keep in mind.

Measuring the Various Components of Attitude

You will recall that attitudes include a cognitive, affective, and behavioral component. In other words, attitudes are concerned with (1) the individual's beliefs, ideas, or knowledge about the attitude object, (2) his feelings or emotions about the attitude object, and (3) his behavior or performance with regard to the attitude object. The ideal attitude measure would provide a means of measuring all these components. But they are not all equally easy to measure. Let's see why.

Direct Observation of Behavior

Many psychologists regard the behavioral component of attitude to be the most important. Yet some attitude research has shown that looking only at behavior may not give us an accurate estimate of an individual's attitude, since how he will behave depends to a great extent on the setting in which his behavior occurs. For example, if you observed a sixth grader being persistently belligerent toward teachers who give him directions, you may well conclude he has a negative attitude toward adult authority figures. But if you had occasion to observe him enthusiastically following the directions of his scoutmaster or angelically conforming to the requests of a Sunday School teacher, you may realize that his schoolroom behavior may reflect something other than a generalized negative attitude toward adult authority. Therefore, although an individual's behavior may tell us a great deal about his attitude toward a particular attitude object, observing a few samples of behavior may not give us a very accurate estimate of his general beliefs and feelings about it. If we want to estimate his overall attitude toward a given group or class of individuals very accurately, it would probably be necessary to observe his behavior over a fairly long period and in a variety of different situations. This would give us a broader representative sampling of his behavior, but such extended observation of behavior quickly becomes an expensive and time-consuming way to measure attitudes. In fact, nearly endless observation would be needed to become fully confident about an individual's attitudes.

If direct observations are conducted in an unobtrusive or nonreactive fashion, the subject may not even know that he is being observed, and even if he does, he may have little or no knowledge of what kind of information the observer is collecting. This reduces the chances that the subject will fake a response by answering a verbal or written question in what he perceives as a socially acceptable way. Advantageous as this is, it is usually more than offset by the prohibitive time and cost needed to observe an individual's behavior long enough and in a wide enough variety of settings to estimate his attitude accurately. Consequently, most attitude measures involve efforts to determine beliefs and feelings rather than using direct observations of behavior.

Measuring Beliefs and Feelings

Because behavioral observations are time consuming and expensive, the usual procedure for measuring attitudes focuses on the cognitive and affective components rather than the behavioral component. For example, instead of observing students' behavior toward an attitude object, we ask them specific questions about it and infer their attitudes from their answers. This approach, which typically uses questionnaires wherein respondents are asked to respond to attitude scales, is much easier and less expensive than making direct observations of behavior. In many instances, this is the only feasible way to collect attitude data that would be too costly to obtain otherwise. Another important advantage of this approach is that it can elicit information about a person's private feelings and beliefs that would not be accessible by any other means.

Written attitude scales have three limitations, however, that are shared with any other measurement techniques that collect *self-report information*. First, we are assuming that our respondents know what their attitudes are, which requires more self-awareness than some people possess. Second, we must assume that they are willing to reveal their attitudes on the questionnaire or to the interviewer, something that requires a high degree of honesty and personal security. Third, we assume that they remember prior events accurately. These assumptions may not be true.

When using attitude scales we must keep in mind that such measures generally contain items or questions that are highly *reactive*. When we ask a reactive question, the respondent can determine a question's purpose from reading it and can structure his response to fit the impression he wants to make. This problem (which is an example of the second limitation listed above) can be largely offset by allowing individuals to respond anonymously to written attitude scales whenever there is reason to believe they may be sufficiently threatened by the questions to allow dishonesty and deception to creep into their responses. Thus use of written attitude scales is perhaps the most widely used—and most useful—means educators have for assessing attitudes of students and other important groups.

Methods for Developing Attitude Measures

There are a number of different methods of developing instruments to measure the beliefs and feelings of individuals concerning a given attitude object. Before describing any particular method, it may be useful to ask why we need formalized, written instruments to ascertain what attitudes are held by certain individuals or groups. Why not just ask people how they feel about the attitude object? The answer lies partly in our earlier discussion of how individuals may not always reveal their true feelings when confronted with a question or situation, especially where they cannot respond anonymously. And anonymity is obviously sacrificed when questions are posed directly—in person—to the respondent. Even if the respondent is permitted to answer anonymously in writing, it is difficult to know how to interpret or aggregate narrative descriptions of one's attitudes. Variations in language facility and the frames of reference of the respondents make it extremely difficult to summarize or score such "attitude essays" without injecting the scorer's personal attitudes and biases. This does not mean that narrative descriptions of attitudes are useless, but only that they are not objective, and earlier we underscored the importance of objectivity if our measures are to provide us with information that can be interpreted and judged by scientific standards. In short, objective information about attitudes will not be obtained simply by asking individuals how they feel or what they believe about a certain entity. Instead, it is preferable to use either appropriate, commercially available, objective measures, or objective tailored measures you can develop yourself, using methods described hereafter.

Methods That Use Adjectives

One objective method of measuring attitudes involves presenting individuals with a series of scales anchored at the end by evaluative, bipolar adjectives, and asking them to mark each scale according to how they feel about one single attitude object. For example, attitudes toward mathematics could be measured by having students mark for each scale in Table 13.1 the position that best reflected their true feelings. Each response would be weighted, with the midpoint of each scale neutral (as shown in parentheses in Table 13.1), and responses summed across scales to produce a total "attitude score." Such scales, termed semantic differential scales or bipolar adjective scales, are versatile and appealing because of their apparent simplicity. They are frequently criticized, however, on grounds that the scales depend on unwarranted assumptions about (1) true bipolarity of the paired adjectives, and (2) integrity of the midpoint as truly neutral. While resolution of the debate is beyond the scope of this book, we believe this method is potentially useful for practicing educators. We bypass further attention to it here, however, in order to devote more space to methods for constructing a Likert scale, which we see as the most useful attitude measure for the classroom. Those who wish to learn more about how to use the semantic differential can find a full explanation in Osgood's classic description of this technique (Osgood, Suci, & Tannenbaum, 1957).

TABLE 13.1 A Semantic Differential Scale Assessing Attitudes toward Mathematics*

	Mathematics					
sweet	(+2)	(+1)	(0)	(−1)	(−2)	sour
very sad	(−2)	(−1)	(0)	(+1)	(+2)	very happy
nice	(+2)	(+1)	(0)	(−1)	(−2)	awful
good	(+2)	(+1)	(0)	(−1)	(−2)	bad
ugly	(−2)	(−1)	(0)	(+1)	(+2)	beautiful
relaxed	(+2)	(+1)	(0)	(−1)	(−2)	tense
useful	(+2)	(+1)	(0)	(−1)	(−2)	useless

* Numerals shown in parentheses are weights for scoring responses and are not included on the actual scales, which would have only five blanks for each pair of adjectives.

Methods That Use Statements

The most common objective method of measuring attitudes is to provide individuals with a series of statements and ask them to react to each statement in the list by marking some graduated scale according to their actual feelings about the content of the statement. The three most frequently used scales are Likert scales, Guttman scales, and Thurstone scales (each of which is named after their originator). Of the three, only Likert scales will be discussed in this text, for the other two are much more difficult to construct and use.[1]

Steps in Developing a Likert Scale

Well over a half century ago, Likert (1932) proposed a relatively simple way to measure attitudes that has come to be called both the *Summated Rating Scale* and, not surprisingly, the *Likert scale*. By far the most widely used type of attitude scale, the Likert scale consists of a series of written statements that all relate to attitudes toward a single object (e.g., "my teacher"). A response scale is provided for each statement, and each respondent is asked to indicate on the scale the extent to which they endorse the statement. Typically, the scale response options reflect varying degrees of agreement, from "strongly agree" to "strongly disagree." The following is a typical statement and response scale used to measure attitudes toward "my teacher."

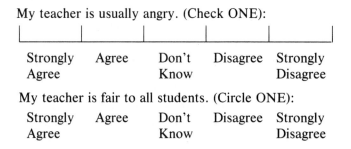

My teacher is usually angry. (Check ONE):

| Strongly | Agree | Don't | Disagree | Strongly |
| Agree | | Know | | Disagree |

My teacher is fair to all students. (Circle ONE):

| Strongly | Agree | Don't | Disagree | Strongly |
| Agree | | Know | | Disagree |

This approach to measuring attitudes does not require that an actual, visual scale be drawn. For example, a "scale" depending only on words would serve as well.

The two illustrations above reflect two types of statements that appear on Likert scales. The first is an unfavorable statement, whose endorsement (i.e., agreement with the statement) indicates a *negative* attitude toward the attitude object ("my teacher," in this case). The second is a favorable statement, whose endorsement indicates a *positive* attitude. A well-developed Likert scale should contain approximately the same number of favorable and unfavorable statements.

Likert's original scales (except for early experimental versions he found unsuitable) contained five response options ranging from strongly agree to strongly

---

[1] Students interested in learning more about constructing and using different kinds of attitude scales, including Guttman and Thurstone scales, should consult the suggested readings at the end of this chapter.

disagree. Subsequently, a great variety of modified Likert scales have appeared (sometimes referred to as "Likert-type" scales). These scales have included two-point or three-point scales (e.g., agree—disagree, or agree—undecided—disagree) typically intended for younger or less well-educated respondents thought to be incapable of making finer discriminations. Scales with up to seven response options are commonly used with older or better educated respondents. More response options—up to a reasonable limit of perhaps seven options—permit finer discriminations and increase scale reliability (for reasons we will discuss shortly). The following is a typical seven-option scale:

Agree Strongly	Agree Moderately	Agree Slightly	Uncertain	Disagree Slightly	Disagree Moderately	Disagree Strongly

Various labels can be used for the middle option, including: *don't know, not sure, uncertain, undecided, ?,* and many more. The choice seems to be a matter of preference.

Often, even-numbered response options are used (e.g., four or six options) when it is thought that respondents may tend to use the neutral middle option to avoid making a real choice. Thus respondents are forced to choose between options that reflect varying degrees of positive or negative attitudes toward the object. A six-point scale, for example, could be identical to the seven-point scale just described, with the middle option omitted.

Also, the format of the scale can vary widely, including those shown earlier where a check mark is placed on the scale (above the selected option) and those where the words denoting the selected option are circled. Another frequently used format has respondents circle numerals that form the scale. The numerals may all be labeled, as in example A below, or only the ends of the scales may be anchored, as in example B (which is a very common scale that departs somewhat more from Likert's approach and has some resemblance to individual semantic differential scales). These scales have the advantage of direct scoring without having to translate the responses into quantitative form.

Example A:
My teacher is polite when speaking to the class. (Circle ONE)

Strongly Agree	Agree	Undecided	Disagree	Strongly Disagree
1	2	3	4	5

Example B:
My teacher makes my school days unpleasant. (Circle ONE)

Strongly Disagree						Strongly Agree
1	2	3	4	5	6	7

Perhaps the most commonly used scale, however, is the five-point scale presented in a format where the five choices are abbreviated response options. This scale has the advantage of allowing the respondent to have each response option on the scale itself, while still being a parsimonious and convenient format. Example C shows such a scale.

Example C:

Circle the ONE option for each statement below that best describes your agreement or disagreement with each statement.

1. My teacher treats some students better than others.

Strongly Agree	Agree	Undecided	Disagree	Strongly Disagree
SA	A	U	D	SD

2. My teacher makes it fun to learn.

SA	A	U	D	SD

The sequence of the response options (i.e., which end is labeled with "strongly agree") is arbitrary, just so the assignment of scores to responses is done in a way that establishes whether high or low scores connote positive or negative attitudes (as we will discuss shortly).

Against this backdrop of a general introduction to Likert scales, we can now list and describe the steps necessary to develop a Likert scale for use in your classroom or school.

Step 1: Identify Diverse Beliefs and Feelings about the Attitude Object

Before actually putting pen to paper, you may want to examine three other sources of relevant statements that express a variety of both favorable and unfavorable *beliefs* and *feelings* about the attitude object. The first is to peruse collections of attitude instruments (see the sources outlined in Chapter 16) to identify existing instruments that have been developed to assess attitudes toward the same or a similar attitude object. You may find one that suits your needs well, but more often you will find several that are close to the target but none that hit the bullseye. In such cases, you may find some "attitude statements" that you can use as a heuristic to help you generate your own original ideas.

The second source is to listen to oral statements or browse through written opinions (e.g., articles, books, or even letters to the editor in the newspaper) of those who hold strong views (either favorable or unfavorable) toward the attitude object. For example, toward teacher professionalism, you might find useful statements scattered through written statements on the topic from teachers' professional associations, in books or journal articles on the topic (including those critical of education), or in the newspaper's editorial pages when teacher strikes or other relevant controversial issues are newsworthy. You also might get some very useful statements from sitting in at open PTA meetings, school faculty meetings, and the like.

The third way to generate relevant statements is to ask your target group (e.g., your students) to write about the attitude object (e.g., how I feel about working on computers). Good statements for your attitude scale can often be found in the resulting essays.

Step 2: Write Statements for Your Scale

Drawing on the sources listed in step 1, you now need to compose statements that reflect different degrees of acceptance or rejection of the attitude object. To do this, your statements will need to range from very favorable to very unfavorable, and should be written in a form that permits the respondent to agree or disagree with the statement.

The best suggestions we have found for writing statements for inclusion on attitude scales are from Edwards' classic list which are as follows:

a. Avoid statements that refer to the past rather than the present.
b. Avoid statements that are factual or capable of being interpreted as factual.
c. Avoid statements that may be interpreted in more than one way.
d. Avoid statements that are irrelevant to the psychological object under consideration.
e. Avoid statements that are likely to be endorsed by almost everyone or almost no one.
f. Select statements that are believed to cover the entire range of the affective scale of interest.
g. Keep the language of the statements simple, clear, and direct.
h. Statements should be short, rarely exceeding 20 words.
i. Each statement should contain only one complete thought.
j. Statements containing universals such as *all, always, none*, and *never* often introduce ambiguity and should be avoided.
k. Words such as *only, just, merely*, and others of a similar nature should be used with care and moderation in writing statements.
l. Whenever possible, statements should be in the form of simple sentences rather than in the form of compound or complex sentences.
m. Avoid the use of words that may not be understood by those who are to be given the scale.
n. Avoid the use of double negatives (1957b, pp. 13–14).

Step 3: Classifying the Statements to Identify Those That are Most Clearly Favorable and Most Clearly Unfavorable

In writing the statements for your scale, you know which ones *you* intend to be favorable or unfavorable, but there is no guarantee that your target audience will interpret them the same way. Therefore, it is useful to obtain the opinions of a sample of respondents drawn from your target group, to act as judges. These individuals can be presented with a list of all the statements you have written, in a form that allows them to record their rating of each statement as favorable, unfavorable, or neither. Or you could add *very* favorable and *very* unfavorable to their rating, using a form like this:

	Do You Think This Statement Is (Check ONE)				
Statement	*Very Favorable*	*Favorable*	*Neither Favorable nor Unfavorable*	*Unfavorable*	*Very Unfavorable*
1. Politicians are corrupt.					
2. The world is better off because of politicians.					

Whether you use a three- or five-point rating, it is important to have a neutral, "neither" category. Any statements that are classified as neutral by many of your judges should be eliminated. The best statements for the first version of your scale will usually be those that are classified by most of your judges as belonging in one of the outer "bipolar" extreme categories. Once you have selected the statements, you are ready to develop an initial pilot version of your attitude scale.

Step 4: Develop a Pilot Version of Your Attitude Scale

Make up a prototype scale in which the selected positive and negative statements are placed in a random order, with each statement followed by a five-point Likert scale (or whatever adaptation you prefer) on which the respondents can indicate their level of agreement with the statement. The prototype scale should contain an approximately equal number of positive and negative statements. You usually need at least twice as many items on the prototype as you want in the final form of the scale, since many items will be found to be unsatisfactory when the prototype is tried out.

Appropriate directions must be added at this point, telling respondents how to mark the response options so as to show their feeling about each statement. Respondents should also be told that there are no right or wrong answers. The purpose of the scale can also be stated if the explanation does not result in bias by causing some attitudes to seem more "socially desirable" than others.

Step 5: Administer and Score the Pilot Version of the Scale

Administer the prototype form to a sample of respondents who are drawn from the population that you wish to study. For example, a Likert scale intended for use with all high school freshmen in the school district would be administered to a sample of 50 to 100 freshmen. If you are developing a scale for use only in your own classroom, you should try it out in one or two classes taught by colleagues.

Compute the score of each person in the tryout sample using the following weighting system. For positively-worded items (those favorable to the attitude object), assign a score of 1 to a *strongly disagree,* 2 for *disagree,* 3 for *undecided,* 4 for *agree,* and 5 for *strongly agree.* For negative items, (those unfavorable to the attitude object), items are scored in reverse (i.e., a score of 1 for *strongly agree,* and 5 for *strongly disagree.* On a Likert scale, the person's total score equals the sum of the numeral weights of the individual responses that he circles or checks (which is why Likert scales are sometimes referred to as summated scales). Figure 13.1 illustrates how a respondent's completed prototype scale items would be scored (the numerical scoring key weights and the labeling of items as positive or negative would not appear on the actual prototype).

The responses marked on Figure 13.1 would be scored by adding up the respective numerical weights $(1 + 1 + 2 + 1 + 1 + 2 = 8)$ and dividing by the number of items (6) to obtain a *mean attitude score* $(8 \div 6 = 1.33)$. Since a 3 on this scale would be considered as reflecting a neutral attitude, scores below 3 would be considered negative, while scores above 3 would be considered positive. Our respondent's score of 1.33 on issues related to pet care reflects an attitude that is sufficiently negative that it would be of real concern to the Humane Society.

Humane Attitude toward Pets Scale

Reflects positive or negative attitude	Statements	Strongly Agree	Agree	Undecided	Disagree	Strongly Disagree
(+)	1. People should choose only pets that can adapt well to a human environment.	SA (5)	A (4)	U (3)	D (2)	(SD) (1)
(+)	2. I would be willing to confront a neighbor who was mistreating their pet.	SA (5)	A (4)	U (3)	D (2)	(SD) (1)
(-)	3. It is better to abandon a pet than to bring it to an animal shelter to be killed.	SA (1)	(A) (2)	U (3)	D (4)	SD (5)
(-)	4. Pet cats can usually take care of themselves when a family goes on vacation.	(SA) (1)	A (2)	U (3)	D (4)	SD (5)
(+)	5. I approve of using spaying or neutering if such operations are necessary to control pet overpopulation.	SA (5)	A (4)	U (3)	D (2)	(SD) (1)
(-)	6. If I couldn't take my dog with me on vacation, it would be kinder to let it run loose than to leave it in a boarding kennel.	SA (1)	(A) (2)	U (3)	D (4)	SD (5)

FIGURE 13.1 Example of Scoring Prototype Attitude Scale Items

Two cautions: First, it should be apparent that mislabeling of positive or negative statements or inadvertent reversals in the numerical weights will yield confusing or spurious results. Of course, one could arbitrarily define low numerical values as indicative of positive attitudes and higher values as reflective of negative attitudes. But the usual convention is to construct your scale so that positive attitudes are shown by higher scores and negative values by lower scores.

Second, many persons choose to use the *total score*—the undivided sum, which is 8 in Figure 13.1—rather than averaging to obtain a mean attitude score. There is no problem with that approach if one is only working with scores on that one scale (and they are the easiest score to use in revising your scale, as we will describe shortly). Total attitude scores cannot be compared across scales, obviously, since they depend on the number of items in the scale.

Step 6: Delete Items That Perform Poorly

Even though you had judges help you rate the statements that went into your prototype scale, those statements will not all work equally well. You can usually spot the poorer items by the following very simple *item analysis technique.* First, place your respondents completed prototype attitude measures in order, by total score. Select those papers with the highest total scores (the highest 25 or 30 percent would be a good sample), and then choose the same number of papers with the lowest total scores.

Second, compute the average numerical score attained on each item by those in your high-scoring respondents and by those in your low-scoring group. The items that discriminate the best would be those with the greatest difference between these mean scores for the two groups. For example, the maximum discrimination between the upper and lower groups would be obtained if all of the persons in the upper (positive) group strongly agreed with the statement given in the item and all members of the lower (negative) group strongly disagreed with that statement.

Third, select half of the total number of items you want in your scale from positive items that most clearly differentiate between the individuals obtaining the highest and the lowest total scores, and an equal number of discriminating negative items.

A more precise way to decide which items should be eliminated is to compute correlations between the total scale score and responses to each statement. Any statement whose correlation with the total score is not significant is jettisoned from the scale, thus creating a type of internal consistency we shall discuss more fully later in connection with reliability of attitude scales. Using this procedure produces a traditional Likert scale, while the more informal approach described earlier results in a "Likert-type" scale. Either is usable, depending on the purpose for constructing the scale and the nature of decision that will flow from it.

Whichever approach you use, do not skip the item analysis step, because until it is carried out you have no way of knowing which items most clearly differentiate individuals with different attitudes.

Step 7: Revise the Scale into a Final Form

Once you have selected the items that best differentiate between individuals with different attitudes toward the attitude object, put them into the final form of your attitude scale. When deciding on the order of items, here are a few practical suggestions.

- The first statement (and possibly the second) should not be so controversial as to risk offending the respondent.
- Controversial statements should not be lumped all together in the scale.
- General statements should precede more specific statements on the same topic.
- Statements should be sequenced so that there is a logical flow between and within topics, if such logic (or its absence) would be evident.
- Insofar as possible after the above suggestions have been followed, randomly mix the positive and negative items. If all of the positive items are listed first, followed by all the negative items, there is a danger that individuals will develop a *response set*.[2] By placing the items in random order, it is impossible for the respondent to predict whether the next item

---

[2] You will recall that response sets—the tendency to mark the same level of disagreement or agreement for all items—were discussed in Chapter 8.

will be positive or negative. Therefore he must read the item in order to decide what level of agreement he will indicate.

Advantages and Disadvantages of Likert Scales

Some of the most important advantages and disadvantages of Likert scales are as follows:

Advantages

- Easy to construct (relative to other attitude scales)
- Easily administered
- Scoring is easy and objective, whether manual template or computer is used
- Can be adapted to measure most any attitude
- Allows collection of attitude data that may be infeasible to collect any other way
- Results in reliable measurement of attitude if scales are constructed properly
- Can be used to measure both intensity and direction of attitude

Disadvantages

- Depends on respondents' honesty and/or security in revealing true feelings
- Although easier to construct than other attitude scales, developing a good Likert scale still involves a considerable amount of effort
- Difficulty in disguising purpose of scale often allows respondents to "fake" by giving only responses they consider to be socially acceptable
- Different response patterns can produce the same total or mean score. For example, a person who marked a neutral 3 on each item would receive the same mean or total score as another person who marked 1 on half the items and 5 on the other half, but the blasé feelings of the first scarcely resembles the strong but inconsistent sentiments of the other

APPLICATION PROBLEM #1

Based on what you have learned about Likert scales so far, identify all errors or weaknesses you can find in the following attitude scale:

Attitude toward Educational Measurement Text

1. After sex education, this is the most   SA   A   U   D   SD
fascinating subject I've ever
studied.

2. Hanging is too good for the guys who wrote this book.	SA	A	U	D	SD
3. There are many things in this book that are worth knowing.	SA	A	U	D	SD
4. This book is far better than most books used in education courses.	SA	A	U	D	SD
5. I've learned many things about tests that will help me as a teacher.	SA	A	U	D	SD
6. Educational measurement should definitely be included in the teacher education program.	SA	A	U	D	SD
7. College preparation is important.	SA	A	U	D	SD
8. The language in this book never obfuscates the point being made and the examples seldom are not useful to illustrate the point either.	SA	A	U	D	SD
9. This book was relevant.	SA	A	U	D	SD
10. I would rather see the authors go on welfare than have them write another book I had to read.	SA	A	U	D	SD

Reliability of Attitude Scales

Several of the methods for calculating test reliability described in Chapter 6 can be used to determine the reliability of attitude measures. When only a single form of the attitude measure is available, internal consistency (as estimated by the split-half method or Cronbach's alpha) is usually used. For those few commercially-published attitude measures for which more than one form has been developed, alternate form reliability, which produces a coefficient of equivalence, is often used. Since most attitudes are fairly stable over time, the test-retest method that yields a coefficient of stability is also appropriate.

The reliability coefficients obtained for attitude scales are typically lower than those obtained for cognitive measures such as achievement tests. This is partially due to the fact that reliability is determined to a large extent by length of the measure, and the average attitude scale has fewer items than the average achievement test. Also, affective measures in general deal with more complex and less-well understood constructs than cognitive measures and this probably contributes to their lower reliability. However, the most commonly used commercial Likert scales often have reliability coefficients above .80 and occasionally report reliabilities above .90. According to Anderson (1988), internal consistency estimates for well-developed attitude scales of 20 items can approach .90, and similarly high-reliability estimates are found for stability coefficients over periods as long as five weeks.

If your purpose in using an attitude scale is to obtain an overall estimate of the attitudes of students in your classroom, reliabilities of .70 or higher would be sufficient. However, if you wish to use the scale results to help give you insights into the attitudes of individual students, you should select attitude scales with high reliabilities, and as a rule, you should not use scales with reliability coefficients below .85 for individual diagnosis or interpretation.

As with other measures, reliability and length (i.e., the number of items) are positively correlated. This is true not only of the number of statements involved in the scale, but also of the number of response options for each statement. For example, using seven-point response options increases the number of total response opportunities respondents have, which is analogous to increasing the number of dichotomously scored items on a typical achievement test. The resultant increase in reliability should be apparent (if not, refer back to our discussion of this point in Chapter 6). Similarly, using only a three-point response option depresses the reliability estimate for the scale. Of course, it would make little sense to use nine-point response options (or more) if respondents could no longer discriminate meaningfully among points on the scale; sacrificing validity in an effort to increase reliability would be a poor tradeoff.

Validity of Attitude Scales

The validity of attitude scales is difficult to establish. Some attitude-scale developers attempt to establish content validity by having "experts" independently inspect the scale items and report their judgments on the validity of each item. If such judgments are consistent across raters, you may conclude that this provides some evidence of content validity.

Concurrent validity is perhaps the most widely reported type of validity for attitude scales. This is determined by computing correlation coefficients between scores on the measure being validated and a criterion measure obtained from the same subjects at about the same time. For example, an attitude scale that purports to measure student attitudes toward teachers could be validated by observing the frequency of positive and negative behavior of different students toward their teacher and then correlating their attitude scale scores with a composite score representing their classroom behavior toward the teacher.

As a rule, concurrent validity coefficients of this sort range between .20 and .50. Higher levels cannot be expected for two reasons. First, validity coefficients are lowered because of the fact that neither the scale score nor the criterion score is perfectly reliable. Second, many of the criterion measures used in computing concurrent validity only measure a small part of the individual's overall attitude toward the attitude object. You will recall that construct validity is concerned with the degree to which a measure is related to or based upon a theory or theoretical construct. Few developers of attitude scales address the question of construct validity (Gardner, 1975). When construct validity is addressed by attitude-scale developers, expert opinion is usually used to judge the degree to which the scale is based upon its underlying theoretical construct.

TYPICAL ATTITUDE MEASURES

We have taken a rather close look at attitudes and attitude scale construction because virtually all public school teachers and administrators are convinced that obtaining good student attitudes toward learning is one of the schools most important educational objectives. This is supported by research that typically finds significant positive relationships between scales measuring attitudes toward school subjects and cognitive measures such as achievement tests (Steinkamp & Maehr, 1984). A number of attitude scales are available that measure various aspects of students' attitudes toward school, teachers and peers, specific school subjects, vocations, and study habits. There are other attitudinal areas that are also important in the school environment. These include attitudes regarding race, alienation, achievement motivation, and level of aspiration. Such measures can give you insight into your students' attitudes, which in turn can help you improve the classroom learning environment.

Let us now look briefly at a few examples of commercially published attitude measures that are readily available. But first, we should note that such measures are not very plentiful. However, a great many attitude measures have been developed for research projects or are available from the Educational Testing Service (ETS) test collection. Fifteen ETS bibliographies deal with attitudes toward school or with attitudes of interest to educators. In the test collection bibliography entitled "Attitudes Toward School and School Adjustment, Grades 7–12 and Above," there are more than 140 attitude measures listed. All measures listed in the test collection bibliographies are available from the developer, the publisher, or from ETS. If you are interested in using attitude scales in your classroom, it is advisable to purchase copies of the test collection bibliographies that are most closely related to your interests.[3]

Measures of Attitude toward School, Teachers, and Specific School Subjects

We will limit our discussion to two commonly used attitude measures.

The Attitude to School Questionnaire (ASQ)

The ASQ is a 15-item scale designed to measure school-related attitudes of children in kindergarten through second grade (Strickland, 1970). On this test, children view a cartoon depicting a school situation while a narration is read to them. The children are asked to express their feelings about the situation by circling a happy, neutral, or unhappy face (this is a variation of Likert scaling often used with young children). There are two forms of the test—one for girls and one for boys. Each test item is printed on colored paper. Five different colors are used so that the teacher can see at a glance if children are responding to the correct pictures during

---

[3] A list of available bibliographies is given in Chapter 16.

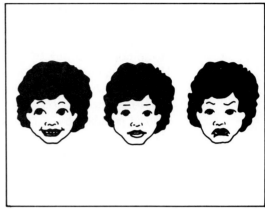

FIGURE 13.2 Sample Item from the Attitude to School Questionnaire.

the test. A typical item from this test is shown in Figure 13.2. As the child looks at the picture, the test administrator says, ''Now look at the blue page. It is time for school to begin. Show how you feel about this. Circle the face like your face.''

Factor analysis based on various revisions of this measure has revealed three factors: school, schoolwork, and school personnel.[4] The current version of the ASQ was developed based on these factor analyses. Correlations among the three ASQ factors range from .44 to .67 (Strickland, Hoepfner, & Klein, 1976). It has been suggested that these relatively high intercorrelations indicate that attitude toward school is a unidimensional trait for young children. Thus, the ASQ is designed to produce only one score that indicates the child's overall attitude toward school. Percentile norms for boys and girls based on about 10,000 cases per grade level are provided in the test manual.[5] Reliability data were computed for approximately 10,000 children at kindergarten, first grade, and second grade. The internal consistency reliabilities were .81 for kindergarten, .78 for first grade, and .76 for second grade.

The Quality of School Life Scale (QSL)

The QSL contains 27 items in true-false, multiple-choice, and Likert scale format, and provides scores on three subscales. The Satisfaction With School subscale is concerned with students' general reactions to school. The Commitment to Classwork subscale deals with students' reactions to classwork. The Reactions to Teachers subscale examines responses to instruction and personal interactions with teachers. You will notice that the three subscales on this measure correspond closely with the factors that emerged in the factor analysis of the Attitude to School Questionnaire (ASQ).

---

[4] Factor analysis is a statistical procedure that determines which test items are related, the degree of the relationships, and the probable construct (i.e., factor) that is being measured by each set of items.

[5] This test may be obtained from Monitor, P.O. Box 2337, Hollywood, CA, 90028.

This scale may be group administered within a time frame of about 20 minutes. The authors indicate that most students in grades 4 through 12 can read and interpret the items without difficulty. They provide information on the characteristics of the norming group by grade level and show comparisons of the sample with U.S. populations. Therefore, it is possible for users to compare the students in their local school districts with those tested in the norming group. Such comparison is important if users are to know the degree to which the norms are relevant to local populations.

Reliability coefficients for this scale are reported as ranging from .86 to .89 (Epstein & McPartland, 1976). Estimates of concurrent validity were obtained by comparing QSL scores to scores on a large number of criterion measures concerned with school activities, school evaluations, family experiences, personality measures, and student aspirations. Information on concurrent and construct validity are both provided in the test manual.

In summary, the QSL is somewhat more rigorously developed than most school attitude scales and deserves careful consideration for use in local schools.[6]

Measures of Attitudes toward Curriculum

A number of attitude scales focus on specific subject areas. In Chapter 16, for instance, there are separate ETS bibliographies for attitudes toward mathematics and attitudes toward reading. These are by far the best source for these measures.

Here are brief descriptions of two attitude scales in this area.

The ME Scales

This set of very brief scales is intended for use in the elementary grades. The primary version provides scores for attitudes toward school, reading, math, physical education, art, and music. The intermediate version covers the same subjects plus social studies and science. Each scale is based on the students' responses to five items. For each item, the child responds on a three-point rating scale consisting of drawings of a happy, neutral, and sad face. The child circles the face that best represents his response to the item. For example, to assess a student's attitude toward mathematics, a scale item (Figure 13.3) is used. Responses are scaled 0, 1, and 2 for each of the five items, giving a score range from 0 to 10 on each scale. Reliability coefficients for each of the scales range from .61 to .89. The lower reliabilities were obtained for the school and the reading scales. Omitting the school and reading scales, the median reliability is .84, which is very good for scales containing only five items. A factor analysis of the scales indicates that the items in each scale fit under the construct for that scale. This provides some evidence of construct validity.[7]

---

[6] Readers who are interested in learning more about this scale and about research on the quality of school life should see Epstein (1981).

[7] See Haladyna, T., & Thomas, G. (1979a & b) for more information on these scales. A copy of the ME scale and manual may be obtained by writing Dr. Tom Haladyna, Arizona State University-West, 2636 West Montebello, Phoenix, AZ 85017.

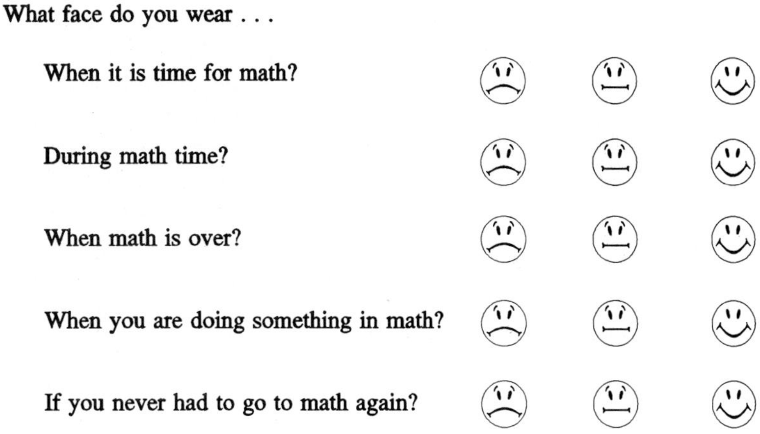

What face do you wear . . .
When it is time for math?
During math time?
When math is over?
When you are doing something in math?
If you never had to go to math again?

FIGURE 13.3 A Scale Item to Assess Student's Attitude toward Mathematics

Survey of School Attitudes (SSA)

This measure is designed to appraise students' attitudes toward four major curricular areas: reading and language arts, mathematics, science, and social studies. The primary level of the instrument is designed for use in grades 1 through 3 and the intermediate level for students in grades 4 through 8. Two comparable forms of the measure (A and B) are available at each level. The format of the scales at the two levels is very similar. At each level the students respond to each drawing by marking one of the three faces. At the primary level the administrator reads the text that accompanies each picture. For example in Figure 13.4, for Picture 7 the administrator says, "Here you see a boy looking at the stars. Fill in the face to tell if you like to learn about the stars."

Reliability coefficients are reported in the test manual for two measures of

7. Studying about the stars
LIKE
Not Sure or Don't Care
DISLIKE

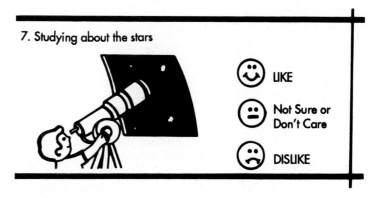

FIGURE 13.4 Sample Item from the Survey of School Attitudes, Intermediate Form A

internal consistency, the split-half and coefficient alpha. Split-half reliabilities for the primary level range from .80 to .91. Reliabilities for the intermediate form are at .80 or higher for all grade levels for which data have been collected (Hogan, 1975). Alpha reliabilities are very similar, although they tend to average two or three points lower. Reliability coefficients at this level are good for estimating overall class attitudes and are satisfactory for individual diagnosis, when the instruments are valid and used in conjunction with other evidence.

Some evidence of construct validity, based upon factor analyses, is presented in the manual.

The SSA appears to be a carefully developed measure that can give the teacher useful information about a student's attitude toward the four subject areas covered.

Measures of Study Attitudes

A number of self-report inventories can be used to give the teacher or counselor insight into student performance. Many of these instruments deal with both study methods and study attitudes and typically provide subscores for each of these areas. They can be used by teachers for several purposes, such as (1) identifying students with poor study habits or attitudes; (2) helping diagnose the problems of students having academic difficulties; and (3) providing a basis for helping such students improve their study habits and attitudes. We will briefly describe two measures of this type that have been widely used in the public schools over a number of years.

Survey of Study Habits and Attitudes (SSHA)

Two very similar forms of this measure are available, one for use with college freshmen and the other for use at grades 7–12. The SSHA has been widely used not only in the public schools but also in research. We will limit our description to the secondary school measure (Form H).

This instrument, which contains 100 items, takes the form of a modified Likert scale. Scores are provided on four basic scales: *delay avoidance* (student promptness in completing academic assignments); *work methods* (efficient work and study procedures); *teacher approval* (attitudes toward teachers); and *educational acceptance* (perceptions of educational objectives and practices). A *study habits score* is obtained by combining the first two of these subscores and a *study attitude score* is obtained by combining the remaining two subscores. An overall score, *study orientation,* is the sum of all four subscores.

The test manual reports test-retest reliability above .90 for the four subscales of Form H and .95 for the SSHA total score. Several concurrent validity coefficients are reported in the test manual, with an overall average of .49. Norms are provided for each of the four basic scales plus subscale combinations.

This test is easy to administer and score. Most students complete it in less than 35 minutes. It may be handscored, or scored by using optically scanned answer sheets.

The SSHA is a carefully developed measure with high reliability and satisfactory validity that can be useful to teachers in identifying students with poor study habits or study attitudes and in diagnosing their specific deficiencies.

Study Attitudes and Methods Survey (SAMS)

This instrument is a modified Likert scale that can be administered to high school students in 50 to 55 minutes. Factor analysis has yielded six dimensions for which scores may be obtained: academic interest, academic drive, study methods, study anxiety, manipulation, and alienation toward authority (Michael, Michael, & Zimmerman, 1980). These subscores are somewhat different than those obtained on the SSHA. Both high school and college norms are provided for each of these six dimensions. Split-half reliability coefficients for the six subscales range from .83 to .90. Some limited evidence related to construct, predictive, and concurrent validity is presented in the test manual. Correlations between high school grades and the various SAMS scales are generally low. When SAMS scales were correlated with biology grades, coefficients ranged from .05 to .33.

This measure reports lower reliabilities and less validity evidence than the SSHA. Generally, validity is higher for the first three scales (academic interest, academic drive, and study methods) than for the three remaining scales (anxiety, manipulation, and alienation). SAMS scales would be useful in situations where the teacher is particularly interested in some of the subscores that are not available on the SSHA.

MEASURING INTEREST

Interests appear to be closely related to attitudes. You will recall that attitudes have three dimensions: belief, feeling, and behavior. Based upon these dimensions, individuals either *accept* or *reject* the attitude object. Interests seem to involve the same three dimensions. Based on their beliefs and feelings about a class of activities, individuals engage to a greater or lesser degree in these activities. While attitudes lead to acceptance or rejection of the attitude object, interests lead the individual to *like, be indifferent to,* or *dislike* engagement in a set of activities. For example, a high school student who is *interested* in aviation may read books on that subject, take private pilot lessons, build model airplanes, aspire to a career related to aviation, and engage in other activities related to this area of interest. This student would also reveal a positive attitude toward aviation if he were administered an attitude scale on this subject.

At best, distinctions among the family of affective constructs that include attitudes and interests is not clear enough for us to reliably distinguish among them in all cases. We need a better understanding of how interests develop and change, and how they differ from attitudes and values (Davis, 1980). However, in spite of our limited understanding of the nature of interests, they can be measured reliably and information from interest inventories can be very useful in helping teachers understand their students and assist students in making better educational and occupational decisions.

Techniques for Measuring Interests

Interests can be measured by the same methods that are used to measure attitudes. Observation of behavior related to the interest being studied, interviews, and ratings by people who know the person in question have all been used to measure interests. However, most research on interests and virtually all the interest measures available have employed the self-report questionnaire.

The research on interests has been concerned with the development of valid measures of vocational interests. One outcome of this emphasis on applied research has been several carefully developed and validated vocational interest measures that are extensively used in the public schools as aids in vocational counseling.

There are also a few measures that are concerned with students' educational or academic interests, and these can be of use to teachers and counselors in helping students choose classes and other school activities in harmony with their interests. For example, over fifty measures of academic interest are listed in the ETS Test Collection Bibliography. Most of them measure interest in different curriculum categories at the secondary or college level. Many include subscores dealing with both academic interests and academic attitudes, again illustrating the rather fuzzy line differentiating these constructs. A few attempt to measure the school-related interests of elementary students. These measures have not undergone the extensive validity studies conducted on the best vocational interest inventories, however, and they sometimes appear nearly indistinguishable from them. Therefore, we will limit our focus to inventories of vocational interests relevant to school.

Measures of Vocational Interest

Several excellent measures of vocational interest have emerged that are now extensively used in vocational counseling, primarily at the secondary level.[8] Here we describe very briefly some of the measures that have resulted from the important work by Strong and Kuder and their associates.

Strong-Campbell Interest Inventory (SCII)

The SCII is the latest revision of the Strong Vocational Interest Blank, which was first published in 1927. This measure has been widely used in vocational counseling at the high school level—and counselors often share students' scores with teachers. As with most vocational interest measures, the SCII compares the students' interests with the interests of people who are successfully employed in a wide variety of occupations.

This measure can be scored for 264 different scales including: six general occupational themes such as "realistic," "artistic," and "social"; 23 basic interest scales in such areas as "agricultural," "mechanical activities," and "social service"; 207 specific occupational scales such as "art teacher," "dental assistant," and "secretary"; two special scales designed to measure introversion-

---

[8] For an overview of occupational measures, see Grisafe (1979).

extraversion and degree of comfort in an academic environment; and 26 administrative indices that help identify invalid or unusual profiles. This instrument has probably undergone as much careful research and development as any other educational measure.

Test-retest reliability over a two-week period is .90 or higher for most of the SCII scales, indicating a highly reliable measure. The median test-retest reliability of the occupational scales over a three-year period is .87, demonstrating the stability of these interests over time.

Many studies of the concurrent and predictive validity of this measure have been conducted. Most of the occupational scales discriminate effectively between people in different occupations and are reasonably accurate in predicting an individual's later occupational choice.

The Kuder Interest Inventories

The first of these inventories was published in 1939 and it has undergone several revisions. Currently two measures are in general use.

The Kuder Occupational Interest Survey Form DD (Revised). This instrument compares student interests with those of satisfied workers in 126 specific occupational groups. It is widely used for occupational counseling in high schools. Median test-retest reliability is about .90 over a two-week period, and .82 over a three-year period. Predictive validity studies have shown over half of sampled examinees to later be in occupations suggested by interpretations of their inventories.

Kuder E General Interest Survey. This measure, which can be used for students in grades 6 to 12, covers 10 vocational areas such as outdoor, mechanical, and artistic. These are somewhat similar to the general occupational themes covered in the SCII. Median test-retest reliability coefficients (over a six-week interval) are about .82 for grades 6 to 8 and .87 for grades 9 to 12. Internal consistency coefficients (KR_{20}) are similar to the test-retest reliabilities.

SUGGESTED READINGS

Aiken, L. W. (1980). Attitude measurement and research. *New Directions for Testing and Measurement, 7,* 1–24.

This article provides a brief but informative review of the current status of attitude measurement. The major approaches as well as several less well known techniques for measuring attitudes are described. Reliability and validity of attitude measures are discussed. Several theories of attitude development and change are briefly reviewed, and an extensive list of references is provided.

Anderson, L. W. (1988). Attitudes and their measurement. In J. P. Keeves (Ed.), *Educational Research, Methodology, and Measurement: An International Handbook* (pp. 421–426). Oxford, England: Pergamon Press.

Although only a few pages in length, this article contains a superb overview of attitude measurement, including a discussion of: (1) definitions of attitude; (2) alternative conceptual approaches to attitude measurement; (3) similarities and differences among Likert, Guttman, Thurstone, and semantic differential scales; (4) specific steps and processes involved in using each of these scales, and (5) how attitude measures are interpreted. Companion entries by the author in this same volume provide more detail about specific types of attitude scales.

Henerson, M. E., Morris, L. L., & Fitz-Gibbon, C. T. (1978). *How to measure attitudes.* Beverly Hills, CA: Sage.

This small book gives considerable attention to methods of attitude measurement other than the usual self-report scales. Such methods as interviews, surveys, using written accounts such as journals and diaries, observations and sociometric techniques are all discussed briefly. Major attention is also given to developing your own attitude measures. This is a practical and readable ''how to do it'' book with many examples and illustrations.

Mueller, D. J. (1986). *Measuring social attitudes.* New York: Teachers College Press.

Each of the major methods of attitude scale construction is discussed. Steps are clearly described and examples are given. Procedures for determining reliability and validity are described. Methods of attitude measurement are briefly discussed. This is a very useful handbook that covers the essentials in a bit over 100 pages.

SELF-CHECK QUIZ

1. The most widely used method of measuring attitudes is by
   a. carefully controlling direct observation.
   b. asking an individual's associates to rate attitudes of the individual in question.
   c. using self-report attitude scales.
   d. by using nonreactive measures—such as asking the individual to write an essay about the attitude object.

2. The main limitation of direct observation as a method of measuring attitude is that
   a. it is much too reactive.
   b. the individual's behavior toward the attitude object is much more general than his feelings and beliefs.
   c. it is difficult and costly to observe a broad representative sample of an individual's behavior.
   d. there is a lack of evidence to show a relationship between attitudes and behavior.

3. One characteristic of a Likert attitude scale is that the
   a. individual indicates his level of agreement with statements related to the attitude object.
   b. individual cannot determine what is being measured from the content of the items.
   c. scale takes the form of an essay in which the student tells about feelings and beliefs.
   d. individual's responses are selected from bipolar adjectives.

4. Which of the following statements best describes a semantic differential scale?
   a. It consists of semantic statements that form differential response options.
   b. It is a five-point scale anchored by the terms ''strongly agree'' and ''strongly disagree'' on either end.
   c. It resembles a bipolar adjective scale, but it has more than two adjectives per scale item.
   d. It uses opposing adjectives to form response scales.

5. Which of the following suggestions is good advice to follow when writing statements for a Likert scale?
    a. Ensure that statements can be interpreted in only one way.
    b. Include some statements that are likely to be endorsed by everyone.
    c. Phrase statements in past tense rather than present tense.
    d. Use statements that are factual.

6. Statements written for inclusion on attitude scales should
    a. use double negatives sparingly.
    b. use the past tense unless collecting attitudes about future entities.
    c. be agreed upon by almost everyone in the target group.
    d. avoid statements that are factual.

7. In Likert scales, controversial statements should
    a. be avoided whenever possible.
    b. precede specific statements on the same topic.
    c. be distributed throughout the scale but should not appear too early.
    d. be randomly distributed so that they have an equal chance of appearing anywhere on the scale.

8. Reliability of scores obtained from attitude scales will normally be *increased* by
    a. decreasing the number of items and increasing the number of response options.
    b. decreasing both the number of items and the number of response options.
    c. increasing the number of items and decreasing the number of response options.
    d. increasing both the number of items and the number of response options.

9. A serious limitation of the use of Likert scales is that
    a. a satisfactory scale takes several years to develop.
    b. the scale measures the direction but not the intensity of the attitude.
    c. the usefulness of the scale depends on the truthfulness of the respondents.
    d. scoring is time-consuming and susceptible to scorer bias.

10. The greatest amount of research and test development in the area of interests has been concerned with
    a. social interests.
    b. vocational interests.
    c. academic and school-related interests.
    d. interests related to personality and person-to-person interactions.

SUGGESTION SHEET

If your last name starts with the letter *N*, please complete the Suggestion Sheet at the end of the book while this chapter is fresh in your mind.

ANSWER TO APPLICATION PROBLEM

#1

You should have identified *at least* the following errors or weaknesses:

1. The attitude object ("educational measurement text") is ambiguous. Did you assume it was this text? From the information given, there is no way to tell.

2. No instructions are given. Do you circle one response for each statement, cross out all the options you don't like, or just what do you do?

3. No response option key is provided. Did you assume "SA" meant "strongly agree" rather than "somewhat appropriate?"

4. The first item is likely to offend many respondents (in fact, we think it's in poor taste), and the second one is nearly as bad. Never put sensitive or offensive statements at the beginning, or you may receive an incomplete response.

5. Statements 1, 5, 6, and 7 do not really pertain to the text, which is supposedly the object of this attitude scale, but rather (except for 7) to the topic of educational measurement. Statement 7 has strayed completely off the target.

6. The number of positive statements (8) far outnumbers the negative statements (only 2 and 10). Does that imbalance hint that we might have (unconsciously, of course) biased the statements a bit?

7. Statement 8 violates good practice in several ways: (a) the statement is overly long, complex, and ambiguous; (b) it contains a double-barrelled thought, being really two statements smashed together; (c) it includes a double negative; (d) the use of *never* is wrong; and (e) the unnecessary use of "obfuscate" obfuscates the statement.

8. The past tense in item 9 is troubling. Even if the book *was* relevant, is it *now*? And to whom and for what is it relevant? Ambiguity strikes again.

9. The scale is poorly spaced, with inadequate vertical space between items. The scale would be better if one vertical space were added between each item.

And there are probably other sins in our example that we did not notice. Maybe hanging *is* too good for the guys who wrote this book.

CHAPTER **14**

Picking the Right Yardstick: Assigning Grades and Reporting Student Performance

Overview

Grades are ubiquitous at all levels of education from preschool through the university, but the appropriate use of grades is not as straightforward and simple as many people assume. As Scriven noted, "Like so many other everyday practices, grading has often seemed too humble to merit the attention of high-powered test and measurement people. My feeling is, that it is far more important and in more need of help than anything else they work on" (1970, p. 14). Scriven is not alone in thinking that grading practices need a lot of work. In fact, many people have advocated that grades be abolished altogether.

This chapter describes how grades contribute to effective educational practices. After historical overview of grading practices, the purposes and functions of grading are described. Next, the pros and cons of various types of grading systems and some of the most frequent problems with grades are discussed. Finally, we provide guidelines for using grades effectively and fairly.

Objectives

Upon completing your study of this chapter, you should be able to

1. Explain the purposes for which grades are typically used.

2. Identify other sources of information that should be used to supplement grades.

3. Describe the way grading has changed throughout this century.

4. Give examples of how grades can be appropriately used by students, parents, teachers, administrators, employers, and other schools.

5. Compare and contrast different types of grading systems.

6. Discuss why alternatives for traditional grading are not more widely used.

7. Summarize the most frequent objections to grades and indicate which objections have the most merit.

8. Explain how well grades can be used to predict future success.

9. Describe how to develop an effective grading system.

10. Explain why parent conferences should be an important part of any grading system.

11. Summarize the variables that contribute to effective parent conferences.

HISTORY AND BACKGROUND

Grades of some type have always been used to report students' performance. The importance of grades is underscored by the fact that references to grades have become an important part of how we describe activities in many other areas of our lives. Without realizing that they are borrowing from education, people refer to such things as Grade-A eggs and Triple A Bonds. When the U.S. Secretary of Education described the current status of education as deserving a ''B−'' everybody knew exactly what he meant. Or did they? At least on a general level, people know that a B− is a long way from excellence and somewhat above mediocrity. But using a B− to describe something as complex as the American educational system leaves a lot unsaid.

Which brings us face-to-face with both the advantages and disadvantages of grades. Grades are a way of summarizing complex information about a student's performance in a particular area. Reducing that information to a single number or letter makes it more manageable, comparable, and recordable. But the resulting advantages are achieved at some cost. Because they are summative and general in nature, grades can never tell the whole story. Critics have argued that grading is misleading, superficial, unreliable, discriminatory, and generally disruptive (e.g., Kirschenbaum, Simon, & Napier, 1971).

Some people believe that grading is an inevitable part of education (Geisinger, 1982); some see it as valuable (e.g., Moynihan, 1971), and others see it as damaging for students and uninformative for parents (e.g., Glasser, 1969). Almost everyone agrees that grading is a difficult and time-consuming process. By the end of a given year, most school teachers will have spent several hundred hours grading and collecting the information necessary to determine grades. As noted by Hopkins, Stanley, and Hopkins:

> Converting scores and performance into grades, is at best a rather arbitrary process, which is further complicated by public relations problems in reporting to parents. Frequently, these difficulties produce double-talking teachers and confused students and parents. (1990, p. 319)

So much time and effort has been spent debating the pros and cons of various grading systems, one would think that substantial progress would have been made over the last several decades. Unfortunately, the issues being debated in the 1920s and 1930s are still being debated today. Let's look briefly at how grading practices have evolved over the years.

Prior to the early 1900s, teachers had total authority for judging a student's performance, and in most cases, parents respected that authority and had little interest in being kept informed. At about the turn of the century, objective tests began gaining popularity. The desire to be more objective in all aspects of education led to the development of systematic grading systems. According to Cureton (1971), the most frequently used grading system assigned each student a percentage between 0 and 100 to indicate the percentage of the material that the student had learned. After this system became well established, studies by Johnson (1911) and Starch and Elliot (1912, 1913a) demonstrated the subjectivity and arbitrariness of such grading even in areas such as arithmetic. Findings such as these led to the first published proposals for the abolition of grading (Dadourian, 1925) and such suggestions are still made periodically (e.g., Anderson, 1966; Glasser, 1969).

In the 1930s and early 1940s, most educational institutions switched from percentage grades to letter grades. This shift was accompanied by the development of the so-called progressive education movement with its emphasis on the need for freedom and democracy in the classroom and the child's need for support and encouragement. Widespread support for this progressive philosophy spurred criticism of the competition associated with grading and a growing belief that grades encourage students to pursue overly narrow objectives.

By the 1950s, the progressive education movement had begun to wane and people were arguing that grading needed to be more consistent with educational objectives (Smith & Dobbin, 1960). By the 1960s and early 1970s, concern over the quality of education led to increased emphasis on "basic education," and there were renewed calls for more formal evaluations of student progress and more rigorous standards for attainment. Concerns about the rigor associated with grading became even more pronounced in the late 1970s and 1980s as a function of the educational accountability movement, minimum competency testing, and grade inflation.

The history of grading is like a roller coaster riding the rails of prevailing educational trends. At one point, grades are seen as a threat to personal freedom and individuality. Then, before we have come to terms with that perspective, we're swept along by demands for increased rigor and accountability. It is easy to point out problems with grading practices. Yet, many people continue to believe that grading is an essential part of schooling (Gronlund & Linn, 1990). Many of the arguments we hear today are not new; but, amidst the furor, it is easy to lose sight of the purposes for grading. Before discussing different types of grading systems, therefore, let's clarify exactly what grades are supposed to accomplish.

PURPOSES AND FUNCTIONS OF GRADING

The primary purpose of grades is to condense a large amount of information into a very concise summary uncluttered by detail. To communicate information concisely and efficiently to a variety of audiences who will use that information for different purposes, grades must be limited in scope. Other methods are available for giving a more detailed and comprehensive description of a student's performance in any particular area. Take a hypothetical biology student, for example. As Feldmesser points out, grades were never designed to indicate to that student

> that his lab work was weak while his grasp of abstract concepts was strong, that he was high on understanding of cell-structure but low on understanding of ecological relationships and middling on understanding of reproductive systems. He [needs] to know what it all adds up to—whether, all things considered, he did "well" or "poorly" . . . (1971, pp. 2–3)

By emphasizing that grades serve a limited purpose, we are not suggesting that other forms of information and feedback (e.g., test scores, written comments on tests and papers, verbal discussions with teachers and other students) are not valuable. However, grades cannot serve all those purposes. When we recognize the limited, but valuable purpose grades are designed to meet, many of the criticisms are less compelling.

Whenever we summarize information about a student's academic performance into one letter or number, important detail is necessarily ignored. Did the student receive a low grade because she did not try, did not improve, or had limited aptitude? Was her low performance in math because of low performance in *all* areas, or was she average in fractions and story problems but dismal in decimals? The purpose of a grade is to communicate general performance, not to detail how or why that particular judgment was made.

Grades are used to communicate important information to a number of diverse audiences, each of whom uses that information for different purposes. These audiences include:

Students
Parents
Teachers and counselors
Administrators
Other schools
Employers

Let's consider the ways in which grades are used by each of these audiences.

Students

Research and common sense suggests that knowledge of past performance will improve subsequent learning. The type of information students need to enhance learning can be divided into short-term and long-term needs. In the short term, students need answers to questions like these.

Why did I get a B instead of an A on this composition?

Should I spend my time this weekend studying fractions or decimals?

Of the fifteen objectives in this chapter, which ones have I mastered?

In the long term, students need answers to questions like these.

Should I sign up for Algebra I or Intermediate Math next year?

How does my reading ability compare to other students in the class?

What are my chances of being admitted to law school?

Helping students make decisions in both areas is important. Grades are most useful, however, for making long-term decisions, because they cannot reflect the level of detail needed for short-term decisions. Such detailed information should be given in daily feedback through verbal reports, written comments on tests and papers, and class interactions.

Many educators believe that appropriate grading can motivate students to perform better. Clark (1969) found that graduate students performed better in situations where they competed for grades. However, Goldberg (1965) found no difference in the achievement level of students who were accustomed to strict or lenient grading practices. Becker, Geer, and Hughes (1968) contended that grading was actually counterproductive because it motivated students to work for an acceptable grade rather than to learn for the sake of learning. Unfortunately, there is not sufficient research to resolve this debate. Whatever you believe about the role of grades in motivating students, it is important to remember that motivational techniques affect students differently. Some students are motivated most by supportive encouragement, others through mild chastisement, and others through fear of negative consequences. Thus, any motivational benefit associated with grades will be different depending on the student.

Some people argue that grades help prepare students for life (e.g., Warren, 1971) because after they finish school, they will seldom be judged by their performance on written tests, homework assignments, or term papers. However, the kinds of judgments made in life are quite similar to the overall judgments made in assigning grades. For instance, overall judgments are used to decide whether someone receives a salary increase, continues on the job, or is promoted.

Regardless of how grades are used, it is vital that they be as accurate as possible. Unfortunately, according to LaBenne and Greene (1969), some teachers knowingly give some students better grades than they deserve because the teachers feel sorry for them or think they have done their best. Even though this is done with the best intentions, students cannot benefit from inaccurate feedback.

Parents

The grades written on a report card are often the only information many parents receive about their child's academic performance. Although this information can be useful, it is not sufficient if we want parents to be active participants in their children's education. A good reporting program for parents supplements grades with regular written information, parent conferences, summaries of standardized achievement test scores, and telephone calls or notes to suggest how parents can support the school program.

If they understand the purpose of grades, and if grades are supplemented with other information, parents can become effective partners in the educational process. Grades alone, however, will not be enough. Knowing that a child has received a C in reading will not be as helpful as knowing the specific problems she is having, and receiving some suggestions about how reading can be supported at home.

Teachers and Counselors

Grading has two types of benefits for teachers and counselors. First, in the process of determining the grade and analyzing information from many different sources, a teacher must set priorities, evaluate patterns and exceptions, and compare students' performance to her own expectations. This summarization process often gives her new insights about students' learning styles and needs, or reveals alternative instructional strategies she might not have considered. Second, previous grades provide a foundation for teachers to collect additional information that can guide instructional decisions for that student. It is important to emphasize that grades are only a beginning and should lead to consideration of such information as diagnostic test scores, observations of the child's interaction with other students, homework, and discussions with parents.

Administrators

Administrators often use grades in making decisions about promotion, awarding academic honors, selecting students for participation in extracurricular activities, awarding scholarships, or determining the value of a particular program. Depending on how they are used, grades can yield very good information for administrative decisions, or they can be totally inappropriate. For example, if Ms. Sampson knows that the success of her new American history course will be judged by comparing this year's students' grades with last year's students' grades, she might allow that knowledge to influence her grading practices. If so, grades would be a very poor measure of success.

Are grades a good source of information for administrative decisions? That depends on the decision. Done appropriately, grades can be quite useful in determining students' eligibility for extracurricular activities or in awarding academic honors (e.g., deciding who will be listed on the school's honor roll). While grades provide a broad-based indicator of a student's academic performance, they are clearly subject to somewhat subjective criteria. They are not a good measure, therefore, in cases where very detailed information is required, or where the people assigning grades are in a position to benefit or be damaged by the outcome of the decision.

Use by Other Schools

High school grades are frequently used in deciding which students should be admitted to a particular college; similarly, undergraduate grades are used in decisions about admission to graduate school. Jencks and Riesman (1968) argue that such a practice is discriminatory because students who do not perform well in high school, are denied the opportunity for further education, which is the only way they can improve their performance. Alternatively, Glazer (1970) contends that grades provide an objective measure by which students from minority backgrounds can demonstrate their ability to succeed in college. Even though this argument remains unresolved, it is generally recognized that earlier grades are one of the best predictors of later grades (Lavin, 1965; Willingham, 1974; and Geisinger, 1982). This emphasizes the importance of assigning grades accurately since they may be used later to make important decisions.

Employers

Grades are sometimes considered by employers in making hiring decisions. Warren (1971) points out that prestigious law firms routinely hire only those students who graduate near the top of their classes. Employers may use such information without understanding the process by which grades are assigned, or the limited information grades provide. Indeed, there is substantial evidence that college grades have very little relationship to occupational success (Hoyt, 1970; O'Leary, 1980). This is not surprising when we recognize that grades are a very general indicator of academic mastery, while success on the job consists of many attributes besides technical skill (e.g., personality, motivation, willingness to work hard, and just plain luck).

TYPES OF GRADING SYSTEMS

One of the earliest documented grading systems is described by Kunder and Porwoll (1977). A report card issued in 1851 for a student at the Tuscarora Academy in Pennsylvania read as follows:

> Behaviour tolerably good; tolerably studious; in Arithmetic, 2; in English Grammar, 2; in Algebra, 3; in all other exercises respectable. Recited 445 [Bible] verses, and lost but little time by absence.

More than a century later, report cards in a neighboring district in Pennsylvania had become substantially more complex, as shown in Figure 14.1. Notice how this report card provides information separately for academic achievement, effort, and social development. Also note how a four-point grading system is used instead of the more traditional five-point system. As we continue, you will see that there is an almost infinite number of ways in which grades can be reported.

All grading systems can be classified with respect to two variables: 1) the type of comparison used in assigning grades; and, 2) the type of symbol used to represent that grade. In what follows, we will explore the most frequently used types of grading systems to familiarize you with various options. In most cases, classroom teachers decide what type of comparison to use, and the school or institution decides on the symbol to be used for reporting. Thus, it is possible that the type of comparison would differ from teacher to teacher in the same school, even though grades are reported using the same symbol.

Type of Comparison Used in Assigning Grades

All grading systems consider how well a particular student has done in comparison to some standard. The five most frequently used standards are

Other students

Absolute standards

Aptitude

Improvement

Effort

Let's look at each of these standards next.

Using Other Students as a Basis of Comparison

A teacher who *grades on the curve* uses other students in the same class as the standard for comparisons. A certain percentage of the class will be assigned A's, a certain percentage B's, and so on. The grade assigned to any given student depends on how her classmates perform. Grading on the curve was suggested more than 75 years ago by Meyer (1908), and became popular during the 1920s and 1930s. According to Cureton (1971) the most common method uses 1.5 standard deviations or more above the mean for A's (about 7 percent), .5 to 1.5 standard deviations above the mean for B's (about 24 percent), .5 standard deviation above the mean to .5 standard deviation below the mean for C's (about 38 percent), .5 standard deviations below the mean to 1.5 standard deviations below the mean for D's (about 24 percent), and more than 1.5 standard deviations below the mean for F's (about 7 percent).

In most classroom applications, grading on a curve should not be used because the type of grade a student receives depends more on the other students in the class than on how well the student has mastered the material. If it is used at all, grading on the curve should only be used where the class is relatively large and it

JUNIATA VALLEY SCHOOLS
(Alexandria, Pennsylvania)   Team _____

Student _____

Year in School: K   1   2   3   4   5   6   7

SUBJECT DEVELOPMENT

Marking Key: A = Excellent; B = Good; C = Fair
                      D = Having Difficulty

Reading	Instructional Level				
	Gains Skills Needed to Read				
	Learns and Uses Sounds				
	Reads Well Orally				
	Understands What Is Read				
	Shows Interest and Makes Effort				
Language	Communicates Well Orally				
	Communicates Well in Writing				
	Shows Interest and Makes Effort				
Spelling	Spells Correctly in Written Work				
	Masters Assigned Lists				
	Shows Interest and Makes Effort				
Handwriting	Prints Legibly (manuscript)				
	Writes Legibly (cursive)				
	Shows Interest and Makes Effort				
Mathematics	Understands Number Concepts				
	Masters Number Facts and Skills				
	Solves Word Problems				
	Shows Interest and Makes Effort				
Social Studies	Understands Main Ideas				
	Shows Interest and Makes Effort				
Science	Understands Main Ideas				
	Shows Interest and Makes Effort				
Music	Learns Concepts and Skills				
	Shows Interest and Makes Effort				
Art	Learns Concepts and Skills				
	Shows Interest and Makes Effort				

Phys. Ed.	Learns Concepts and Skills				
	Shows Interest and Makes Effort				
Library	Learns Concepts and Skills				
	Shows Interest and Checks Out Books				
DAYS ABSENT					

Unmarked spaces indicate that these items are not
applicable at this time.

SUBJECT DEVELOPMENT

Marking Key: S = Satisfactory   N = Needs Improvement

Works Neatly				
Works Quietly				
Finishes Work on Time				
Follows Directions				
Listens Well				
Obeys Cheerfully				
Works and Plays Well with Others				
Tries to be Courteous				
Tries to keep the School Clean and Attractive				

TEACHER COMMENTS

_____
_____
_____
_____
_____
_____
_____

FIGURE 14.1   Example of a Report Card from Alexandria, Pennsylvania

SOURCE: Kunder and Porwell, *Reporting Pupil Progress: Policies, Procedures and Systems.* 1977, Educational
Research Services, Inc., Arlington, VA. Reprinted with permission of the publisher.

is not unreasonable to assume that the students represent the full range of ability on whatever subject is being graded. There are many instances where this assumption is not met. For example, Hopkins, Stanley, and Hopkins (1990) describe how, to help their husbands succeed in college, wives of World War II veterans enrolled in courses in which their husbands were enrolled and did little or no work. The wives received the predetermined number of F's and D's, assuring their husbands a grade of C or better.

Comparison to an Absolute Standard

This method of grading, sometimes referred to as *mastery grading*, compares the performance of each student to the material the instructor wants mastered, using a percentage grade. According to this system, a grade of 87 percent indicates that the student has mastered 87 percent of the material. Percentage grades are not as precise as they may appear at first. For example, a person may score 90 percent on a test either because the test is very easy, or because she has mastered the material. Given the same content, a teacher might construct an easy test on which students scored 95 percent, or a more difficult test on which the class average was only 60 percent.

The so-called absolute standard is also based indirectly on an implicit comparison of present students with previous students. In other words, the standard is established based on the teacher's perception about what previous children have been able to master when taught the same content. Unfortunately, this fact is often ignored when people argue that children should be measured against performance standards, not against each other. Grading compared to an absolute standard is particularly difficult to use in subject areas that are not well defined (e.g., the development of critical thinking skills) and easier in well-defined areas (e.g., mastery of spelling words).

Achievement Compared to Aptitude

Some educators believe that grades should rest on a comparison of performance to aptitude. Given the same level of achievement, a student with relatively low aptitude would receive a better grade than a student with greater aptitude. Although this approach is logically appealing, it must be considered in light of how difficult it is to measure aptitude. Our best measures of aptitude are relatively crude approximations and are only possible using standardized aptitude tests that are not routinely administered in many places. Further, this approach assumes that aptitude is unchanging, which is probably untrue. Finally, Thorndike (1969) demonstrated that teachers often overestimate or underestimate how well students should do based on aptitude scores. Interestingly, Geisinger and Rabinowitz (1979) found that relatively few university faculty members assigned grades based on aptitude, but Geisinger, Wilson, and Naumann (1980), and Terwilliger (1966) found, respectively, that a substantial number of community college faculty and over 50 percent of high school teachers employed this method. In most cases, this approach to assigning grades is potentially misleading.

Improvement as a Basis for Comparison

Some teachers assign grades according to how much improvement a student demonstrates. A student who begins a class knowing very little in the subject area but learns a moderate amount would get a better grade than a student who begins a class knowing almost everything and learns only a little. Students in such classes usually learn quickly that they need only to "play dumb" at the beginning of the course in order to receive a high grade. In addition, most people interpret grades as an indication of proficiency. If grades are used as an indicator of improvement, it is extremely important to make that clear to people who use the grades. Improvement is certainly important, but where grades are designed to serve as an overall indicator of students' level of academic mastery, degree of improvement is irrelevant.

Using Effort as the Basis for Grades

Some educators argue that those students who try the hardest should receive the best grades. Grades assigned in this way no longer describe the degree to which the student has mastered the material. Instead, they provide information about how hard the student tries. Although information about effort may be very useful, it is important to keep the information presented by grades as clear-cut as possible. Some schools have solved this problem by assigning one grade for academic achievement, and a separate grade for effort. Such grades must be reported separately and their meaning made clear. Problems arise when grades become a hodge-podge of different variables such as achievement and effort.

Contract Grading

In a relatively recent approach, referred to as *contract grading*, an absolute standard is used, but the standard varies from student to student (Hassencahl, 1979). In the tradition of legal contracts, the grade desired by the student, the learning goals that will be demonstrated, and the procedures for measuring goal attainment are specified. There is mutual agreement about the "contract," and if the student completes her part of the contract, she receives the grade specified. Although there is evidence that learning contracts can be an effective pedagogical tool (Christen, 1976), others argue that because the *quantity* of work is easier to describe than the *quality*, the work often deteriorates (Kirschenbaum et al., 1971). This type of grading encourages individualized learning, but it is questionable whether it provides a more accurate measure of that learning. Because it is individualized, it definitely provides a different type of information than do traditional grades (a fact that should be made clear to reporting audiences). Consequently it must be viewed cautiously as a replacement for grades.

Type of Symbol Used

Individual teachers usually decide what kind of comparison will be used to assign grades, but the school or institution usually decides what symbol will be used in reporting grades. The two most common grading systems, letter grades and percentage grades, have been supplemented in recent years by pass/fail grades,

TABLE 14.1   Elementary and Secondary School Percentage of Teachers Who Reported Using Different Grading Systems

Method of Reporting	Percent Elementary Teachers	Percent Secondary Teachers
Letter grades (e.g., A, B, C, D, F)	72	83
Parent-teacher conferences	60	20
Written description of performance	24	10
Number grades (e.g., 1, 2, 3, 4, 5)	10	9
Percentage grades	2	10
Pass-fail reports	8	3

SOURCE: Adapted from Gronlund (1985, p. 441)

narrative reports, and parent conferences. Gronlund (1985) reports the frequency with which different types of grading symbols are used, based on a nationwide survey (see Table 14.1). Letter grades, A, B, C, D, and F, and number grades, 1, 2, 3, 4, 5—which are really just a parallel way of reporting letter grades—account for over 80 percent of the grading in the elementary schools, and over 90 percent of the grading in secondary schools. Similar results have been reported in other studies (e.g., Kunder & Porwoll, 1977).

Letter Grades

The most widely used grading system is based on letters that portray a student's position on a scale ranging from excellent to failing performance, as shown in Table 14.2. The exact percentages and descriptive statements associated with each *letter grade* vary from teacher to teacher and school to school. In most cases, a grade of F indicates failing performance. Other letters may also take on special significance. For instance, an A may be used to select students for the honor role, or D's may indicate passing performance that does not count toward graduation. The ease with which tests, homework assignments, class presentations, and written papers can be scored on a numerical basis and then converted to a letter grade with roughly similar meaning probably accounts for the widespread use of such a system.

TABLE 14.2   Example of Percentage Grades Typically Associated with Different Letter Grades

Letter Grade	Numbered Grade	Typical Percentage Grade	Typical Description
A	4.0	90–100	Excellent
B	3.0	80–89	Above Average
C	2.0	70–79	Average
D	1.0	60–69	Below Average
F	0	Below 60	Failing

Many teachers or schools add pluses and minuses to the letters to further discriminate among students. Letter grades are also frequently converted to a *grade point average (GPA)*. To compute a GPA, the numerical value associated with the grade in each course is multiplied by the number of credit hours assigned to that course. These products are then summed over all courses taken and the sum is divided by the total number of credit hours.

Percentage Grading

Up until the early 1920s, *percentage grading* was the most popular system for reporting students' achievement (Smith & Dobbin, 1960). In this system, each student is assigned a number between 0 and 100, with the number supposedly reflecting the percentage of material the student has mastered. Concern over the accuracy with which teachers could differentiate between small increments on the scale led to its decline in the 1920s and 1930s.

Pass/Fail Grading

In the early 1960s, many colleges and some high schools introduced a *pass/fail* option for grading. The following rationale was offered:

- Since grades are unimportant outside the academic world, it is inappropriate to emphasize them in school.
- Concern about getting good grades prevents students from taking courses from which they would benefit.
- Pressure to get high grades interferes with learning for the sake of learning and encourages cheating and poor study habits, such as cramming just before a test.

Although there is some merit to each of these concerns, most schools have not found pass/fail grading to be a viable solution. For example, Gold, Reilly, Silberman, and Lehr (1971) found that student achievement declines when pass/fail grading is used, and Rossman (1970) reported that graduate and professional schools were less likely to accept applicants who had numerous pass/fail courses. Ebel (1979) suggests that pass/fail grading reduces motivation and leaves students with an incomplete or inaccurate record of their achievement.

> Most of us want to be valued as persons. Most of us don't particularly want to be evaluated, but we can't enjoy the first without enduring the second. The weakness of a pass/fail grading is that by doing a poor job of evaluating, it keeps us from doing a good one of valuing. (1979, p. 244)

Parent Conferences

Recognizing that one of the primary purposes of grades is to communicate information to parents, many schools supplement grades with systematic parent conferences. As a substitute for grading, parent conferences are not very effective, but, as a way of supplementing the limited information contained in grades and enlisting the support of parents in their children's education, parent conferences can be extremely valuable.

Parent conferences provide two-way communication between parents and teachers. Instead of just receiving a general summary of how their child is doing, parents can ask questions about the school's programs, tell the teacher about the child's out-of-school activities that may help in planning instruction, and learn about activities they can provide at home to improve the child's educational achievement. Such conferences also provide a good opportunity to clarify and interpret the student's most recent standardized test scores, which are sometimes difficult for parents to understand. The disadvantage of parent conferences is that they take a great deal of time and skill on the part of the teacher, and many parents are unwilling or unable to participate.

The effectiveness of parent conferences is enhanced if a structured guide, such as that shown in Figure 14.2, is used. Such a guide helps ensure that important topics are not missed, and documents what occurs during the conference. Completing the form during the conference and giving a copy to the parents is also an effective way of involving the parents in their child's education. Written documentation of past conferences can also help the teacher prepare for future meetings.

Narrative Reports

Some people advocate the use of narrative reports as an alternative to symbols used in traditional grading (Bellanca & Kirschenbaum, 1976; Burba, 1976). A narrative report can provide a qualitative description of a student's accomplishments, learning style, and strengths and weaknesses, and can also offer suggestions for improvement. Like a letter of recommendation, the narrative should include information about *how* the student learns as well as *how much* she has learned.

Although word processing technology makes such an alternative to grading more feasible, narrative reporting of each student's performance is still a very large undertaking for teachers. Furthermore, even if such reports were more understandable for parents, it is doubtful they could be used effectively by administrators and admissions offices because of the amount of paperwork that would be generated. Finally, according to Geisinger (1982), narratives have a tendency to focus on students' personalities rather than their mastery of academic material. Consequently, narrative reports have limited appeal as an alternative to traditional grading practices. If the logistics of generating such reports can be dealt with successfully, however, narrative reports could be a useful supplement to grades, particularly for parents.

Objections to Grades

Grades have often been attacked, and there have been frequent suggestions that they should be abolished. In fact, it has been said that a grade is an inadequate report of a biased and inaccurate judgment of the extent to which a student has attained an undefined level of mastery of an unknown proportion of unspecified material.

PARENT CONFERENCE GUIDE

——————————— ——————————— ——————————— ———————————
(Student)   (Parent)   (Teacher)   (Date)

ACADEMIC ACHIEVEMENT

Discuss: ___ past performance (class participation, homework, overall grades)

   ___ recent standardized test scores

   ___ future plans

Reading ————————————————————————————————————

English ————————————————————————————————————

Handwriting ————————————————————————————————

Social Studies ————————————————————————————————

Math ————————————————————————————————————

Science ————————————————————————————————————

Music ————————————————————————————————————

Art ————————————————————————————————————

Physical Education ————————————————————————————

PERSONAL GROWTH

Discuss: ___ level of functioning

   ___ suggestions for school or home effort

Respects rights of others ————————————————————————

Attitude towards school ————————————————————————

Works up to potential ————————————————————————

Follows directions ————————————————————————————

Tries Hard ————————————————————————————————

Uses time well ————————————————————————————

Gets along with others ————————————————————————

HEALTH

Discuss: ___ any concern or problems

Vision/Hearing ————————————————————————————

Health Habits (grooming, eating, etc.) ————————————————

General Health ————————————————————————————

Attendance ————————————————————————————————

SUGGESTIONS AND ACTION PLANS FOR SCHOOL OR HOME

——

——

——

FIGURE 14.2 An Example of a Form That Could Be Used as a Guide and Reporting Mechanism for Parent Conferences

Calls for the elimination of grading usually cite some combination of the following issues.

The fact that grades are not comparable from school to school, or even from instructor to instructor, means they are inaccurate. There is some truth to this statement. Carter (1952) found that boys tended to receive lower grades than girls of equal achievement. Hadley (1954) found that teachers gave higher marks to students they liked than to students of equal achievement who they liked less. Baird and Feister (1972) found that the average grade at most colleges was the same whether the average student at the college was scoring at the 95th percentile or the 5th percentile of ability. Palmer (1962) noted that some instructors used grades as rewards or punishments, independent of how well students were mastering learning outcomes. These findings demonstrate that grades can be misused. The solution is not to abolish grades, but to teach people to use them more appropriately. After all, unless we abolish *all* forms of student evaluation, these same problems would continue.

Grades cause feelings of anxiety and failure among less able students. Glasser states "The school practice that most produces failure in students is grading" (1969, p. 59). Such reasoning is like saying that we increase the national debt by measuring and reporting it. It is unfortunate that some students do not succeed in school, but there is no evidence that they would perform any better if their performance were not measured and reported. Most people are aware of failure, even when it's not explicitly reported. Any first grader knows which reading group she is in, and whether or not she is one of the better readers in her group. Obviously, it is possible to inappropriately ridicule and draw attention to someone's failure, but such inappropriate behavior does not happen as a result of assigning grades.

The assignment of grades leads to a reliance on extrinsic motivation and excess competitiveness. Although frequently claimed, there is little evidence that this is true. In fact, Gold and his colleagues (1971) found that achievement and learning actually declined when students took courses on a pass/fail basis. Similarly, Vasta and Sarmiento (1979) found that when liberal grading practices are implemented, achievement declines. As Ebel points out, "There is nothing wrong with encouraging students to work for high marks, if the marks are valid measures of achievement" (1965, p. 440).

Grades encourage students to cheat. This is like saying that money is bad because it encourages people to steal. If we eliminated all forms of evaluation, students might be less tempted to cheat, but it is also probable that they would learn less. Also, it is doubtful that students would be less likely to cheat with any other form of evaluation than they are with grades.

Grades are an ineffective way of communicating among teachers, students, and parents. If grades are the only means of communication, this objection is certainly true. Nothing about grades suggests that they should be used to the exclusion of other forms of communication. As a concise overall indicator of students' performance, grades are remarkably effective. However, any reporting system based on a single technique will be less effective than one based on several complementary methods.

Grades fail to measure some of the most important educational objectives. Sometimes grades are only used to communicate information about the attainment of cognitive objectives, but there is nothing that says that grades could not be used in a similar way to report students' performance in affective areas. It is clear that some teachers do not use grades appropriately, and fail to report students' performance on important educational outcomes. This failing is not a problem of grading itself, but of the evaluation procedures selected by the teacher. The solution, therefore, is not to abolish grading, but to improve the process by which we identify activities and outcomes to be evaluated.

Because of grade inflation, the information contained in grades is no longer meaningful. Between the mid 1960s and the early 1970s, GPAs based on a four-point letter grade system increased an average of about half a letter grade, even though there was no apparent increase in students' achievement. The most probable causes of grade inflation include (1) changes in grading policies—including the more frequent use of pass/fail grades (Geisinger, 1979); (2) a shift from norm-referenced grading to individualized, noncomparative policies (Geisinger, 1980); (3) increased use of student ratings in teacher evaluation procedures, accompanied by the desire of faculty to receive high student ratings (Longstreth, 1979); and, (4) competition for a declining student population (Longstreth, 1979).

Some have suggested that grade inflation has reduced the value of grades because (1) grades are no longer an incentive, (2) academic honors have less meaning, and (3) grades are less useful for making admissions decisions. However, Warren (1979) found no basis for these complaints. Although it is clear that grade inflation has occurred, we believe that the inflationary period is over. The inflation that has already occurred has undoubtedly skewed the distributions in a somewhat more negative direction. However, there is still enough variation in grades to distinguish between good and poor students, so that fears about grades having become meaningless are unfounded.

Most objections about grading arise because of inappropriate evaluation procedures, or a failure to recognize that grades are not intended to provide a detailed, comprehensive, individualized report of students' progress. Although any grading system is imperfect, some method of evaluating and reporting student performance is desired by virtually all teachers, parents, and administrators. As one part of the reporting mechanism, grades have endured the test of time. Until a better alternative is found, we should continue to use grades as effectively as possible.

APPLICATION PROBLEM #1

A teacher in your school believes that assigning end-of-quarter grades encourages cheating, and interferes with the love of learning that students should be developing. She claims that good teachers do not need to use grades to motivate students, and advocates changing all courses to a pass/fail system. Imagine you are the school principal. How would you respond?

How Well Do Grades Predict Future Success?

Many people believe that grades are valuable because they predict future performance. Yet we have just pointed out that different teachers might assign different grades to the same students, that grades are often contaminated by personality and stylistic differences, that different teachers use different standards of comparison, and that average grades have tended to drift upward over the last several years. Given all these problems, is it possible that grades *can* be effective predictors of future performance?

In a word, yes. Although the criticisms are valid to some degree, they are not as serious as many people assume. For example, Fricke (1975) and Werts, Linn, and Jorekog (1978) found that grades were remarkably consistent over the four years of college; and Hicklin (1962) found a correlation of .73 between grades received by students at grades 9 and 12. Grades correlate in the .70 range with student scores on standardized achievement tests (Nell, 1963), and a number of studies (e.g., Lavin, 1965; Lutz & Richards, 1967) have found that high school grades are even better predictors of college grades than are standardized achievement and aptitude tests.

All of this suggests that even though they are frequently maligned, and are sometimes used inappropriately, grades *are* good predictors of future success. Too frequently grades have been used as a convenient scapegoat for the ills of education. But, remembering the limited purposes they are designed to serve and the difficulty people have had in suggesting a feasible alternative, grades are a remarkably useful tool that should not be eliminated.

GUIDELINES FOR ASSIGNING GRADES

Grades provide a concise summary of student performance. By definition, any kind of summary leaves out some important information and grades are no exception. Almost always, therefore, grades should be supplemented with other information.

For example, if a new reading teacher is designing a reading program for Loretta, she might first look at Loretta's grades from the previous year, but she should not stop at this point. The fact that Loretta received a C− in reading indicates that she was experiencing some difficulties, but further information using standardized tests, diagnostic tests, observation, and perhaps discussions with Loretta's previous teacher should all be used to design an appropriate reading program. Previous grades provide a useful starting point, but they cannot tell the whole story.

Similarly, if Ms. Barclay wants to know why her daughter, Kirsten, does not enjoy school, she should not look to the grades on Kirsten's report card for a complete answer. The fact that Kirsten's grades have slipped from a B+ average the previous year to mostly C's and D's during the current year may well have prompted Ms. Barclay's concern. But a review of Kirsten's grades will not reveal whether her daughter's negative attitude is causing a decline in performance, or whether the decline itself is causing her to view school negatively. A parent-teacher conference, a visit to the school, discussions with other parents, and perhaps a discussion with Kirsten should all be used in trying to understand the shift in Kirsten's attitude and grades.

The value of grades is not that they are perfect for any single information need, but rather that they provide useful information for so many different situations and audiences. Like the proverbial jackknife, grades are useful in a great many different situations—although probably not ideal for any one. Therefore, grades are best used in combination with other sources of information such as:

- Results from standardized achievement and aptitude tests
- Written reports (including periodic newsletters, notes on homework, or notes written to individual parents)
- Diagnostic tests
- Parent conferences

Because we have previously discussed standardized achievement, aptitude, and diagnostic tests, we will not repeat that information here. With regard to written evaluations, there are an almost infinite number of ways to provide useful information to parents, administrators, and other teachers. Some parents may need a personal letter, admissions officers frequently want letters of recommendation in addition to transcripts of grades, and employers may want the results of applied performance tests. All are part of an effective reporting system. Our focus here, however, is primarily on grades. Additionally, because we think parent conferences are an essential part of explaining a student's performance, we will also give some suggestions about holding effective parent conferences.

Developing and Reporting Grades

Developing and operating an effective grading system requires substantial time and effort. In most cases, it is best to develop the general framework for grading at the district or institutional level to avoid unnecessary duplication of effort. However, no system will be entirely appropriate for every school in the district, or even for every classroom in a school. Individual teachers or schools should be able to modify and adapt any grading system to their specific needs. The following suggestions should help.

Those who need information from grades (e.g., teachers, administrators, parents, and students) should have a voice in designing the system. It is unfortunate when a grading system is imposed from the top down so that those who consume the information have little say in how it is structured. A committee approach in which major audiences can help design a grading system that is responsive to their needs is more effective, and heightens the probability that information from the system will be used. Student input is particularly important for older students since feedback to them is one of the primary purposes of grading.

A grading/reporting system should be consistent with the purposes it is de-

signed to serve. If all consumers of grades understand the limited information grades provide, they can design other types of information that should be used to supplement grades. Clearly, a system would be structured differently in a district that viewed grades as the primary means of communicating with parents than in a district that wanted grades primarily to serve the informational needs of students.

A single grade should not mix information about academic performance with information about other areas of concern such as citizenship, effort, improvement, work habits, and attitude. Grades can be used effectively for reporting different types of information if separate (and usually somewhat different) systems are used to report academic achievement and performance in areas such as work habits or attitude. Grades in academic areas should be a pure measure of academic achievement with separate grades or marks being given for performance in other areas.

The objectives most important to the school should be addressed by grades. Time limitations and other practical constraints make it impossible to use grades for measuring performance in all areas of interest. It is important to prioritize educational objectives and make sure that top-priority objectives are addressed first. As a part of the grading system, the committee should consider what type of performance or behavior will serve as sufficient, observable indicators that important objectives have been achieved.

Grading systems must achieve a balance between detail and practicality. All audiences want information that is as comprehensive as possible. The need for detail must, however, be weighed against the amount of time available to collect information and prepare understandable reports for pupils, parents, employers, and school personnel. The need to maintain an archive of reports in school records should also be considered.

Information on which grading is based should be collected as systematically, accurately, and objectively as possible. When grades are assigned on the basis of irrelevant or trivial achievements, or when they are contaminated by personality or other unrelated factors, they lose their meaning. The highest grades must go to those students who best master the relevant educational objectives.

The grading system should provide ample opportunity for parent conferences and discussion. The importance of parent conferences cannot be overemphasized. Although grades provide useful information, they should be a starting point for discussions that can substantially enhance the parent-school partnership by helping both sides discover the reasons behind the grades.

Student/teacher interaction should be a normal part of grading. Opportunities for students and teachers to discuss the meaning of grades, the way in which grades are assigned, and steps the student can take to improve grades should be a normal part of the grading process. Too often, such discussions are undertaken in the spirit of protest, and then only as a last resort, when a student feels that she has been graded unfairly. When students are angry and teachers defensive, the probability of a reasonable or useful discussion is minimal.

The weight associated with different components should be consistent with their perceived importance. Grades combine information about students' performance on tests, homework, everyday class work and so on. This means teachers have a great deal of flexibility in combining information to derive a final grade indicating overall mastery of course objectives. Generally, it is better to have homework play a relatively minor role in the summary because it is usually an opportunity for students to practice skills rather than an opportunity to demonstrate mastery. Other kinds of information, such as tests, demonstrations, and observable in-class performance, should be weighted in proportion to how important you think they are in demonstrating mastery.

Where possible, the basis for comparison should be the same within a given school. Grades can be assigned by comparing a student's performance to that of other students in the class, to some absolute standard, or to each individual's potential, as defined by that individual's aptitude, effort, or improvement. In most cases, some combination of comparison to peers and an absolute standard is best. It is generally better if each teacher within a given school uses approximately the same basis of comparison so as to avoid confusion among students as they move from class to class.

The criteria and process for assigning grades should be clear to all stakeholders. Because grades are a summary of so much information, it is often useful to attach to the grade report a brief summary of the procedures and criteria so that different audiences will understand exactly how the grades were determined. Students themselves need to know in advance how grades will be computed so they can allocate their efforts accordingly. Nothing is more frustrating to students than to be graded differently from what they expected.

The preceding suggestions can reduce, but never eliminate, all of the problems of grading—many of which can result from imperfect implementation. Nonetheless, it is illogical to conclude that because grading systems are not perfect, they should be abandoned. As Moynihan observes:

> One of the achievements of democracy . . . is the system of grading and sorting individuals so that young persons of talent born to modest or lowly circumstances can be recognized for their worth. (Similarly, it provides a means for young persons of social status to demonstrate that they have inherited brains as well as money, as it were.) I have not the least doubt that this system is crude, that it is often cruel, and that it measures only a limited number of things. Yet it measures valid things, by and large. To do away with such systems of accreditation may seem like an egalitarian act, but in fact it would be just the opposite. We would be back to a world in which social connections and privilege count for much more than any of us, I believe, would like. (1971, p. 4)

Suggestions for Holding Effective Parent Conferences

Parent conferences are not a good substitute for grades, but they are an essential supplement to grading. Whenever possible, parent conferences should be used to explain how the student is performing in school and to enlist the parents' support in helping their child learn most effectively. Unfortunately, much useful information lies buried in school cabinets where parents never see it. Parent conferences provide an opportunity and an excuse for retrieving this information and discussing it in ways that can benefit students, parents, and teachers.

Some educators avoid presenting much of the available data on child performance because they believe parents will misinterpret the information, or they mistakenly believe that education is the domain of professional educators, and parents have only a minor role to play. While it is true that information must be presented carefully and skillfully, following adequate preparation, there is no reason to presume that parents are incapable of understanding well presented information, or that conferences will not be beneficial. The following guidelines for effective parent conferences are based on suggestions made by Gronlund and Linn (1990), Hopkins, Stanley, and Hopkins (1990), and Bailard and Strang (1964).

Do's of Parent Conferences
1. Review the student's school records before the conference and organize the information you want to present to the parents.
2. Collect samples of the student's work that are indicative of her typical performance.
3. Use a structured outline such as the one shown in Figure 14.2 to guide the discussion and record information.
4. Hold the conference in a comfortable, informal setting in which you will not be interrupted.
5. Use language that will be understandable to parents without talking down to them.
6. Treat parents as equal partners in the home-school relationship. Be willing to listen and encourage two-way communication.
7. Be honest, but fair, about describing the student's strengths.
8. Describe areas needing improvement in a positive and tactful manner.
9. Accept appropriate responsibility for any problems the student is having.
10. Work with the parents to identify solutions, but be cautious about giving advice related to parenting or home activities.
11. Conclude the conference with a summary of the discussion, and check to see if the parents agree with your summary.
12. Use a checklist to give parents a copy of the written summary to take home.

Don'ts of Parent Conferences
1. Don't argue with parents or blame them for problems the child is having in school.
2. Don't compare their child with other students.
3. Don't make derogatory remarks about other students, teachers, administrators, or school practices.
4. Don't interrupt the parents.
5. Don't betray confidences.
6. Don't do all of the talking.
7. Don't ask parents questions that might be embarrassing.
8. Don't make excuses for any mistakes you may have made.

Conducting effective parent conferences requires practice, sensitivity, and a willingness to keep trying. It is unrealistic to expect your first parent conference to be completely successful. By following these guidelines, however, and being committed to the concept of using parent conferences to enhance the partnership between home and schools, you can become much more effective and students will be the major beneficiaries.

APPLICATION PROBLEM #2

Imagine that a friend comes to you with a concern about the parent conferences required in the spring each year. She complains that, as a teacher, she finds the conferences time-consuming and unenjoyable, that parents frequently get upset with her when their child is performing below average, and that most parents do not understand much of the information that is presented. She wants to enlist your support in asking the principal to discontinue the practice of required parent conferences. How would you respond?

SUGGESTED READINGS

Geisinger, K. F. (1982). Marking systems. In H. E. Mitzel (Ed.), *Encyclopedia of Educational Research* (5th ed., pp. 1139–1149).

A well-referenced summary of grading and marking practices in American education. Discusses the purposes of grading, different types of marking systems, and the psychometric quality of grades. Also provides several references to topics of current interest in grading.

Kunder, L. H., & Porwoll, P. J. (1977). *Reporting pupil progress: Policies, Procedures, and Systems*. Arlington, VA: Educational Research Service.

Based on a national survey of school systems, this 115-page booklet contains an excellent summary of grading practices and gives many examples of the forms and materials used to report information to students and parents. The numerous examples are an excellent sourcebook of ideas for anyone considering a revision of an existing grading and reporting system.

Selden, S. (1982). Promotion policy. In H. E. Mitzel (Ed.), *Encyclopedia of Educational Research* (5th ed., pp. 1467–1474). New York: The Free Press.

Grades are frequently used to make decisions about promotion/retention. This chapter reviews research on the effects of nonpromotion. It suggests that as competency-based education becomes more widespread we may need to reconsider the use of grades in such decisions.

Terwilliger, J. S. (1966). Self-reported marking practices and policies in public secondary schools. *National Association of Secondary School Principals Bulletin, 50*, 5–37.

A more detailed discussion than we have been able to provide in this chapter of practices and procedures for assigning grades to students and of reporting information to parents. Includes examples of how to summarize and differentially weight information from various tests and assignments to calculate grades.

Vasta, R., & Sarmiento, R. F. (1979). Liberal grading improves evaluations but not performance. *Journal of Educational Psychiatry*, *71*, 207–221.

An interesting example of how experimental research designs can be used to investigate the effects of different grading practices. The study found that liberal grading practices resulted in higher student ratings of the course, but did not affect students' study habits, attendance, or achievement.

SELF-CHECK QUIZ

For each of the following, select the *one* best answer.

1. The most frequently used system of grading in elementary schools is
   a. contract grades.
   b. letter grades.
   c. pass-fail reports
   d. percentage grades.

2. A single grade should present information about
   a. achievement alone.
   b. effort and achievement.
   c. improvement and achievement.
   d. potential and achievement.

3. When compared to students in classes in which traditional grading procedures are used, students in classes with pass/fail grading tend to
   a. learn more.
   b. learn less.
   c. learn the same.
   d. learn higher level skills better.

4. Grades in high school and college are least predictive of
   a. future grades from the same teacher.
   b. scores on standardized achievement tests.
   c. success on the job after graduation.
   d. future grades in subsequent years.

5. In the 1930s and early 1940s, most educational institutions switched from
   a. letter grades to percentage grades.
   b. pass-fail grades to letter grades.
   c. pass-fail grades to percentage grades.
   d. percentage grades to letter grades.

6. The best way to use parent conferences is as
   a. an alternative to standard grading procedures.
   b. a means of dealing with the parents who disagree with a grade.
   c. a supplement to standard grading procedures.
   d. a way of dealing with the students who are having difficulty.

7. The assignment of grades to indicate the proportion of material the student has mastered is referred to as
   a. percentage grading.
   b. grading on the curve.
   c. contract grading.
   d. validity-referenced grading.

8. As an alternative to traditional grading, narrative reports tend to
   a. be more ambiguous to parents.
   b. be more predictive of later success.
   c. focus more on the student's personality.
   d. help high-achieving students and harm low-achieving students.

9. Which of the following objections to grades is well-supported by evidence?
   a. Grade inflation has made grades meaningless.
   b. Grades are often not comparable from school to school.
   c. Grades hinder communication among teachers, students, and parents.
   d. Students would perform better if they were not graded.

10. Which of the following factors is a probable cause of grade inflation?
    a. A decrease in the use of pass/fail grades and an increase in the use of letter grades
    b. A decrease in the use of student ratings in teacher evaluation procedures
    c. A shift from norm-referenced grading to noncomparative grading procedures
    d. An increase of student achievement due to improvements in education

SUGGESTION SHEET

If your last name starts with the letter *O*, please complete the Suggestion Sheet at the end of the book while this chapter is still fresh in your mind.

ANSWERS TO APPLICATION PROBLEMS

#1

Before responding to the teacher, talk a few minutes about why she feels the way she does, and what kind of experience she has had with alternative grading systems. If she is concerned about grades not being useful, she probably has had some negative experiences with grades. Depending on how she responds, you would want to include at least the following points in your discussion.

1. Although there is evidence that grading systems are sometimes implemented inappropriately, students do need some feedback about how well they are learning the intended material. A pass/fail system provides some information about that, but probably not enough.

2. Many other people besides students depend on information contained in grades (e.g., parents, other teachers, administrators, future employers, and other schools). Any kind of alternative to grades would have to consider their needs as well as the students'.

3. Research data suggests that students do not try as hard, or learn as much, in situations where pass/fail is used as an alternative to traditional grading.

4. The negative side effects she has noticed about grading may be real, and it is important to find ways to resolve those problems, even if a traditional grading system is continued.

5. It may be useful to appoint a committee to review the entire grading and reporting system. As someone who has strong feelings about grading, she might play an important role as a member of that committee.

#2

At least the following points should be included in your response to the friend who wants to enlist your support in discontinuing parent conferences.

1. Even though she has not felt very successful with previous parent conferences, many people find them to be very useful. Consequently, she may want to consider some alternative approaches to parent conferences before asking that they be eliminated.

2. Although it is clearly time-consuming, some advance preparation in terms of reviewing the student's file, assembling samples of the student's work, and listing specific issues she would like to discuss with each parent may help to make the conference more productive.

3. Reviewing the list of Do's and Don'ts contained in this chapter may provide some hints about improving the conference. It may even be useful to have a teacher who feels that conferences are beneficial to sit in as an observer on one or two conferences.

4. The use of a structured guide to summarize the results of the conference, along with specific activities that both parties have agreed to do, would be useful.

5. Parent conferences are effective only if true two-way communication occurs. It may be useful to collect some approximate data on how successful she has been in getting parents to talk in the conference. If she is doing most of the talking herself, it may explain why parents do not seem to enjoy the conferences.

6. Emphasize that since grades provide very limited information about a student's achievement, parent conferences and other means of communication are absolutely essential in helping parents understand what is happening in the school.

SECTION FOUR

Using Existing Measures: A Shopper's Guide to the Measurement Supermarket

The old adage about saving your energy by not reinventing the wheel is as relevant in measurement as anywhere. Educational measures abound; yet far too often educators labor to create their own tests and measures, only to find in some undiscovered test repository measurement "wheels" that would suit their purposes just as well, or perhaps even better.

In the preceding section we provided guidelines for designing your own measures when appropriate ones do not exist. In this section, we acquaint you with the veritable supermarket of tests and measures that are readily accessible to you. We also show you how to "browse around" to locate those measures that best fit your needs. We urge you, whenever you are faced with a situation that requires measurement, to look first at what is already on the shelves.

In Chapter 15 we discuss some of the more common criticisms of educational tests, examine whether those criticisms are legitimate, and look at how cautions against misuse of tests can reduce or solve many—if not all—the concerns posed by test critics. We also discuss alternative approaches to assessing student performance that have been proposed by critics of more traditional measurement approaches.

Chapter 16 tells you where to locate available instruments and how to choose intelligently among them.

Chapter 17 presents information on standardized achievement tests and batteries, including a discussion of how they are developed and how you can estimate their content validity. We also present, as examples, one comprehensive test battery and selected single-subject achievement tests.

Chapter 18 covers diagnostic tests, as well as elements necessary to integrate such tests into systems that support diagnosis, prescription, and instruction. Examples of some diagnostic measures are included, along with a description of a service that helps schools match selected measures to their curricula.

Chapter 19 defines aptitude tests and explains how they are used and what makes them valuable. This chapter covers the classification of aptitude tests, benefits of proper use, and potential dangers of improper use.

Chapter 20 covers ways of using measures of personal and social adjustment in the classroom, describes several such measures appropriate for your use, and cautions against potential misuses of personality inventories by those not specifically trained in their administration and scoring.

Collectively, the information in these six chapters will help you shop wisely in the educational measures marketplace and avoid the costly experience of creating tests no better than—and often not as good as—those already on the shelves.

CHAPTER 15

Avoiding Being Caught in the Crossfire between Standardized Test Supporters and Alternative Assessment Enthusiasts

Overview

How valid are the criticisms of educational testing? Is it true that standardized tests are unsuitable for measuring classroom learning? Is local control of education threatened by standardized testing programs? Do standardized aptitude and achievement tests categorize and label students in ways that cause damage to individuals? Are such tests racially, culturally, and socially biased? To what extent do tests invade the privacy of students and their families? Do widely used educational tests measure only superficial student knowledge and behaviors, often penalizing bright, creative students? Do such criticisms of tests result from flaws in the tests themselves or from instances where the tests are misused? What defenses can be mounted for tests in general, and for standardized tests in particular? Can criticisms be blunted by developing better tests or changing the ways tests are used? Does research show standardized tests to have beneficial or harmful effects on our schools? Are new forms of student assessment (e.g., *authentic, direct, performance,* or *portfolio assessment*) better alternatives than the more traditional tests? These are some of the questions we attempt to answer in this chapter.

We have organized this chapter into four major sections, dealing respectively with (1) criticisms of educational testing, (2) an analysis of the legitimacy of those criticisms and rebuttals to those criticisms that we find to be unfair or overdrawn, (3) the potential of recently proposed alternatives to standardized testing, and (4) possible classroom uses of one of those alternatives, portfolio assessment.

Objectives

Upon completing your study of this chapter, you should be able to

1. List at least 10 common criticisms of educational tests and the types of tests toward which each criticism is directed.
2. List five major rebuttals of these criticisms; explain whether you find the criticisms or the rebuttals more compelling.
3. List at least 10 common misuses of educational and psychological measures that contribute to criticisms of testing. For each, discuss how such misuse could be avoided.
4. Discuss the recent trends in the professional dialogue about testing, describing any changes you see in the nature or frequency of criticisms of tests.
5. Discuss the relative merits and potential utility of recently proposed *authentic assessment, performance assessment,* and alternative methods of assessing learning outcomes.
6. Explain how you might use portfolio assessment appropriately in your classroom.

CRITICISMS AND CAUTIONS CONCERNING EDUCATIONAL TESTS

In our overview of historical trends, we described briefly several waves of criticism that have washed across educational testing (and test makers) during the past 30 years. We now turn our attention to a more thorough examination of *why* educational tests have so frequently come under fire.

Common Criticisms of Standardized Tests

Norm-referenced, criterion-referenced, and minimum competency tests can all be standardized, but norm-referenced tests are by far the most common type of standardized test. Not coincidentally, most test criticism has been leveled at standardized, norm-referenced tests. But other types of testing receive their measure of invective also. Criterion-referenced tests are criticized not so much for what they are as for what they may lead to, such as arbitrary establishment of cutoff scores. Minimum competency tests have been not only targets of criticism but also of lawsuits. In this chapter, we focus primarily on 13 historically pervasive and thematic criticisms of standardized, norm-referenced achievement and aptitude tests we have drawn from the mass of literature produced by testing critics. Later we will add a new twist or two to this list as we discuss some recently emerging criticisms of standardized tests.

1. *Standardized achievement tests do not promote student learning.* Critics charge that standardized achievement tests provide little direct support for the "real stuff" of education—namely, what goes on in the classroom. They do nothing, critics contend, to enhance the teaching-learning process, provide diagnostic help to the teacher, or provide students the immediate feedback so essential to their learning.

2. *Standardized achievement and aptitude tests are poor predictors of individual students' performance.* Critics of testing argue that while some tests may accurately predict future performances of *groups,* they are often inaccurate predictors of individual performance. Examples such as "Einstein flunked sixth-grade math tests" are cited, showing where test scores earned by particular students were uncorrelated with later achievements in school or career.

3. *The content of standardized achievement tests is often mismatched with the content emphasized in a school's curriculum and classrooms.* Because standardized tests are intended for broad use, they make no pretense of fitting precisely and equally well the specific content being taught to third graders in Salt Lake City's public schools and their counterparts at the Tickapoo School downstate. That mismatch, which can result in discrepancies between what is being taught and what is being tested, provided much of the impetus for the criterion-referenced testing movement.

4. *Standardized tests are unsuitable for evaluating school programs or curricula.* If standardized tests do not reflect the goals or content of a particular curriculum, program, or instructional innovation, there would seem little point in using such test results as the basis for judging its success. Yet this is exactly what often occurs, to the distress of critics of standardized measures.

5. *Standardized tests dictate or restrict what is taught in ways that violate the principle of local control of education.* The claim that standardized tests dominate school curricula and result in "teaching to the test" are familiar allegations, and can be leveled at any standardized test that has serious consequences for the schools in which it is used. It may seem inconsistent to claim that standardized tests are mismatched with what is taught in the schools (see criticism 4 above) and also to complain that the tests drive the curriculum in many school systems, but those two allegations are not necessarily at odds. The first criticism is directed at the notion that schools ought to be free to vary in what they teach. The second merely acknowledges the flip side of the coin—that *any* case in which the tests intrude

into decisions about what is taught is unfortunate, for local schools have then partly lost their freedom to determine educational priorities.

6. *Standardized achievement and aptitude tests categorize and label students in ways that cause damage to individuals*. One of the most serious allegations against standardized tests is that their use frequently results in irreversible harm to students who are permanently categorized by test scores that follow them unrelentingly thereafter. Call it classifying, pigeonholing, labeling, or whatever, the result is the same, critics argue, as individual children are subjected to demeaning and insulting placement into categories. The issue is really twofold: (1) The fact that tests are not infallible (and that students can and do change) can result in tragic misclassifications of individual students; and (2) even when tests *are* accurate, categorization of students into groups that carry a stigma or negative connotation may cause more harm than any gain which could possibly come from such classification.

7. *Tests often represent an invasion of privacy for students and their families*. Even most critics recognize that *some* form of testing or observing performance is necessary to the educational process, but they oppose the proliferation of testing and unnecessary data collection as mere "snooping" conducted under the guise of legitimate measurement and evaluation. Tests that measure students' personalities, attitudes, or values, or that directly or indirectly probe family values and opinions, are viewed by many critics as the most offensive.

8. *Standardized achievement and aptitude measures are racially, culturally, and socially biased*. Critics claim that most published tests favor economically and socially advantaged children over their counterparts from lower socioeconomic families. Ethnic and cultural minority group members and women note that many tests have a disproportionately negative impact on their chances for equal opportunities in education and employment. (Because of the societal importance of these claims, we discussed them at greater length in Chapter 3.)

9. *Standardized tests often penalize bright, creative students*. By their very nature, critics suggest, standardized tests discourage creative and imaginative thinking. The emphasis on one "right" answer is wrong, they say, for it promotes simple choices rather than fostering reflective thought. As Shepard (1991) has thoughtfully observed, children may well conclude that their job is to get the correct answer that resides in the head of the test makers, even if they have to guess to do it.

10. *Test anxiety accompanying standardized achievement and aptitude testing interferes with student performance and distorts the test results*. Many educators are concerned that standardized testing creates so much anxiety for students that they "choke" and perform far below their true ability. Teachers tell of top students who excel in typical classroom quizzes but freeze when confronted with the formality of the Iowa Test of Basic Skills or the urgency of the state's test for determining promotion or graduation.

11. *Standardized achievement and aptitude tests measure only limited and superfi-*

cial student knowledge and behaviors. Critics censure tests for measuring only a narrow spectrum of the student abilities on which educators need information—and for failing to measure many of the most important human characteristics, like justice, humaneness, or love. Some critics (e.g., Frederiksen, 1984) have argued that multiple-choice tests seldom measure the more complex cognitive abilities, but the economy and efficiency of such tests have increased their popularity in schools, at the expense of measures better suited to assess higher level mental processes.

12. *Standardized achievement and aptitude tests are not based on sound psychological or educational theory*. Some measurement experts lament that "psychological" tests are often divorced from psychology, and "educational" tests often violate every principle of education. Anastasi (1967) and Glass (1986) have accused psychometricians of becoming so preoccupied with their techniques that they were losing track of what they had set out to measure.

13. *Standardized achievement tests do not promote quality or foster accountability in our schools*. Advocates of other types of testing (or even no testing at all) argue that standardized measures have very limited value for holding teachers, schools, or school systems accountable. If teachers' salaries are to consume large portions of the public purse, the argument goes, then teachers must be accountable for demonstrating what those expenditures have produced. Even properly used, however, standardized norm-referenced tests do not yield this information—thus failing to accomplish what many feel should be the primary function of testing programs.

CRITIQUING THE CRITICISMS OF TESTING

Are the criticisms of standardized testing we have listed all deserved? No, but that does not mean that we can afford to ignore them. As one of the foremost measurement experts in America has reminded us:

> Criticism of tests and testing practices is desirable. Tests obviously play an important part in the lives of many people. The tests, and more importantly, the uses that are made of them, deserve close scrutiny. Furthermore, criticism from within and from outside the profession has led to long-needed positive changes in testing practices, and more can be expected. (Linn, 1982, p. 279)

We agree. Moreover, there is legitimacy, in our opinion, to some of the concerns we have reported. Yet, many allegations aimed at standardized testing themselves deserve critique. Even thoughtful criticisms frequently turn out, upon further examination, to be overstated, unfair, or just plain wrong. For example:

- The concern that standardized tests do not reflect school curriculum is less an indictment of the tests than of those who chose inappropriate tests to begin with.

- The charge that standardized tests can damage students through labeling or mislabeling is more correctly a condemnation of those who use the tests unintelligently and/or unprofessionally.
- The accusation that standardized tests represent an invasion of privacy fails to note that test scores are far easier to keep confidential than teachers' verbal classroom questions, evaluations, or notations.
- The claim that standardized tests measure trivial information or require only low-level mental processes appears exaggerated at best, since close examination of actual tests shows that large proportions of test items measure more complex mental process. (See Rudman, 1977.)

While these preceding comments do not attempt to refute each criticism listed in the previous section, they serve to demonstrate that not *all* criticisms of standardized testing are unassailable. Let's look next at five reasons why the salvos of criticism fired by the antitest movement during the past quarter-century have not convinced us to join in the chorus of those who call for all standardized tests to be abolished.

1.   Standardized Tests Are Strongly Supported by Many Practitioners, Parents, and Policy Makers

Standardized testing has a strong contingent of supporters as well as an enthusiastic group of detractors. Predictably, many measurement experts are basically supportive of such tests, although many censure "measurement malpractice" and offer specific suggestions for improving testing efforts. But beyond the measurement community, many educational practitioners have registered strong support for testing programs. The debate is no longer between the "practitioner critics" and the conglomerate "testing industry" (including testing specialists), but rather between practitioners, parents, and policy makers who advocate testing and practitioners, parents, and policy makers who oppose it. For example, analysis of the positions of professional associations a decade ago showed that some groups of school principals and some teachers' associations had taken a strong stance against standardized tests, while other teachers' and principals' associations had spoken out just as strongly in their favor (*Educational Measurement*, 1982). Recently it appears that more professional associations are urging policy makers to slow down and rethink their use of such tests as indicators of school success or failure, but educational practitioners are still seriously divided on this issue.

And what of parents and policy makers? In a Gallup poll, some 81 percent of U.S. parents described standardized tests as very useful (Learner, 1981). Policy makers seem equally favorable. Darling-Hammond and Lieberman (1992) note that support for using standardized testing to improve education is increasing rapidly, especially at the federal level, where a national test is being devised for use in periodic pulse-taking to determine the health of the nation's educational system.

These examples should suffice to show that both testing supporters and critics exist in almost all groups, including teachers, principals, professors, parents, policy makers, and self-appointed school watchers.

2. Most Criticisms of Standardized Testing Have No Empirical Basis

We simply do not have a solid research foundation on which to base many of our claims—or counterclaims, for that matter—concerning standardized testing. We are left in that somewhat tenuous position where one person's opinion is just as good as another's. Some years ago, Airasian summed up the situation nicely:

> The rhetoric, and that is what it largely is, that produces claims and counterclaims about the uses and misuses of standardized tests has taken on a life of its own. Battle lines have been drawn and for many participants in the controversy there is no middle ground of uncertainty; if you're not for their position on testing you must be against it. In articulating their positions, both proponents and opponents of standardized testing have been guilty of distorting the historical development of testing and of failing to recognize that *there is precious little empirical evidence to support claims of test use or misuse.* (1979, p. 2, italics added)

Since then, substantially more research on the effects of standardized testing has been reported. Kellaghan and his colleagues (1982) summarized the limited empirical evidence then available on the *effects* of standardized testing in school-based programs as follows:

1. *School-level effects* of using standardized tests are not yet well understood, except that a majority of teachers polled in several studies reported that standardized tests have little influence on school curriculum.
2. *Teacher-level effects* of standardized testing primarily confirm judgments teachers have already made, based on their observations and other sources of data.
3. *Pupil-level effects* of standardized testing are overshadowed by feedback students receive from other sources (grades, verbal comments, written comments, etc.) and seem to have comparatively little impact on students' self-concepts, expectations, or attitudes.
4. *Parent-level effects* of standardized testing are virtually unknown.

In a study of their own, Kellaghan and his colleagues (1982) found that standardized testing does little to disrupt existing school and teacher practices and that standardized test results serve primarily to confirm the evaluations of pupils' ability and achievement that teachers have already formed.

Shortly thereafter, Haney (1984) summarized numerous studies that examined the *frequency* of standardized test use in schools and various *uses* to which such tests are put. Research studies dealing expressly with the *influence of testing on educational practice* were virtually nonexistent, however, and Haney's review unavoidably contained more opinion than evidence about the effects of testing on school practices.

More recently, however, some significant research on this topic has been reported. In Arizona, a state that had mandated annual use of standardized tests with all students in grades 2 through 11, surveys of school practitioners showed that the testing was having a dramatic impact on district curriculum (Haladyna, Haas, & Nolen, 1989; Haladyna et al., 1991). The common criticism that standardized tests "drive the curriculum" was confirmed, at least in Arizona, where the testing tail was clearly wagging the educational dog. Surveys of Arizona teachers also showed that pressure on educators to produce high test scores was resulting in a variety of doubtful practices teachers were using to achieve high scores. While many teachers engaged in "teaching to the test" or other ethically dubious methods to "prepare" their students for the test, others used blatantly dishonest techniques such as teaching the students the actual test items in advance, or dismissing low achieving students on testing day (Haas, Haladyna, & Nolen, 1989; Nolen, Haladyna, & Haas, 1989).[1] Similarly, based on teacher interviews and classroom observations, Smith (1991) reported that teachers determine to do whatever is necessary to avoid low scores, and that standardized testing programs *can* in fact narrow curricular offerings, reduce time available for instruction, and focus instruction on basic skills to the exclusion of more complex cognitive processes.

Two important points should be made here. First, these and other similar studies summarized nicely by Haladyna and his colleagues (1991) show that the negative effects of standardized testing on classroom practice occur when the test scores are perceived by educators as having important consequences, such as linking educators' continued employment or salary advances to students' test performance. In short, high-stakes use of standardized test scores seems to interfere with good curriculum and instruction. (Note that it is the misuse of tests, not the tests themselves, that cause these problems.)

Second, this research on the effects of standardized testing is relevant only to two of the common criticisms we have listed; on the remaining criticisms, the jury is still out. Despite the recent research, most criticisms and defenses of tests are still primarily "articles of faith," not scientifically supported positions. Much more empirical investigation is necessary before we will know unequivocally how much credence to give to each of the common criticisms of standardized testing.

3. Many Criticisms of Standardized Testing Assume Teachers and Other Test Users Are Naive and Credulous

In the dark scenarios developed by critics, promulgation of testing is the ploy by which greedy testing corporations extract excessive profits from schools, leaving them with precious little to show for their investment save disillusioned administrators, distressed teachers, and damaged students. The common theme of most such scenarios is that school practitioners are gullible and readily plucked by crafty charlatans whose hunger for profits prompts them to peddle measures that are at best unhelpful, and at worst, misleading and harmful. Our colleague Peter Airasian says it well:

---

[1] This topic is discussed in greater detail in Chapter 3 in a section on ethical problems associated with teaching to the test.

the mass of teachers and school administrators are often portrayed as lambs, innocently and uncritically accepting standardized test results as the most valid piece of evidence available about a child and, on the basis of that evidence, wreaking havoc—and worse—on pupils, their school experiences and future lives. In reality, teachers are neither as naive nor as blind to limitations of standardized tests as many commentators who purport to speak for teachers would have us believe. (Airasian, 1979, p. 5)

We agree. Those who operate our schools are not as credulous and naive as they are sometimes cynically portrayed to be. Indeed, we take vicarious offense at the insult to teachers and administrators implicit in many criticisms of test use in the schools.

4.   Even Though Standardized Tests Are Imperfect, They Still Seem Somewhat Better Than the Current Alternatives

All but the most rabid advocate of testing would concur that no test is perfect and that, taken as a whole, educational and psychological measurement is still (and may always be) an imperfect science. Why, then, promote imperfect measures? Because so far the alternatives have not proved to be any better, if as good. Ravitch offers this insightful comment:

In education, tests have grown more important to the extent that other measures have been discarded or discredited. Although it is easy to forget the past, we should recall that the tests helped to replace an era in which many institutions of higher education made their selections with due regard to the student's race, religion, class, and family connections. . . .

So long as there are educational institutions where there are more applicants than places, there must be an objective way to decide who gets in . . . [and] no other objective means has been discovered to take the place of ability testing. (1984, p. 23)

The authors of the 1974 *Standards* also cautioned that the call to abolish tests seems futile because:

it requires a corresponding but unlikely moratorium on decisions. Employers will continue to make employment decisions with or without standardized tests. Colleges and universities will still select students, some elementary pupils will still be recommended for special education, and boards of education will continue to evaluate the success of specific programs. If those responsible for making decisions do not use standardized assessment techniques, they will use less dependable methods of assessment. (APA et al., 1974, pp. 2–3)

While we oppose misuse of standardized tests, we generally support the correct use of such measures and will do so until more adequate alternatives emerge. (We discuss later in this chapter efforts to develop such alternatives.) In the meantime, existing measures must be improved and used properly. Which brings us to the final reason that criticisms of testing have failed to erode our (qualified) confidence in the value of traditional educational tests.

5. Most Criticisms of Standardized Tests Are Really Not Criticisms of the Tests but Rather of Their Misuse or Abuse

On their own, tests are incapable of harming students. It is the way in which test results can be misused that is potentially harmful. Yet critics of standardized testing seldom focus on test *misuse,* preferring to target the instruments themselves, as if they were the real culprits. (See, for example, Neill & Medina, 1989.) Such behavior is rather like condemning hammers because they have on occasions been used to commit mayhem. Or blaming the hemlock for Socrates's fate.

In short, it is nonsense to blame all testing problems on tests—no matter how poorly constructed—while absolving users of all responsibility. Not that bad tests should be condoned, of course. But eliminating test misuse would go far toward eliminating the criticisms currently directed against educational testing.

Standardized tests can be misused or abused in countless ways. We list below only a dozen of the more common misuses we have observed which, incidentally, can occur with other types of testing as well.

1. *Using the Wrong Tests.*   Schools often devise new instructional goals and curriculum plans, only to find their success being judged by tests that do not reflect those goals or plans but that are imposed nonetheless by some higher administrative level (e.g., district or state). Faced with such absurdity, two courses of action are open to teachers and local administrators: (1) Persuade higher levels of administration to select new standardized achievement or minimum competency measures that better match the local curriculum content and goals; or (2) supplement those tests with measures selected (or constructed) specifically to measure what the school is attempting to accomplish. Trying to measure goal attainment with tests insensitive to those goals is, as our colleague Jim Popham puts it, like trying to measure mileage with a tablespoon—it is simply the wrong measure.

    It is also "using the wrong tests" when schools employ tests for purposes for which they were never intended. Few would chasten the scalpel (or the neurosurgeon who wields it) just because it proves useless to the carpenter in driving nails. More subtle but equally absurd mismatches of purpose and instrument abound in educational testing. Misuse of tests would be largely eliminated if every test administered were carefully linked with the decision at hand.

2. *Assuming Test Scores Are Infallible.*   Every test score contains possible error; a student's *observed* score is rarely identical to that student's *true* score (the score he would have obtained had there been no distractions during testing, no fatigue or illness, no lucky guesses, and no other factors that either helped or hindered that score). Measurement experts can calculate (using techniques we described in Chapter 6) the probability of an individual's true score being within a certain number of score points of

the obtained score. Yet many educators ignore measurement error and use test scores as if they were highly precise measures.

Assume, for example, that a school sets a cutoff score of 100 on a math placement test, admitting students who score 101 and rejecting those who score 99. Yet such a test likely contains sufficient "measurement error" that a difference of two points on obtained scores reflects no real difference between the true scores of the admitted and rejected students. Forgetting that test scores all contain some error can result in serious abuses of tests, and of those who take them.

3. *Using a Single Test Score to Make an Important Decision.*   Given the possibility of error that exists for every test score, how wise is it to allow crucial decisions for individuals (or programs) to hinge on the single administration of a test? What about the basketball player who hits a miserable 15 percent of his shots in his first varsity game? Bench him for the season, right? Not if you have seen him hit 70 percent of his field goal attempts in practice and also learn he was informed of his grandfather's death just before game time. A single test score is too suspect—in the absence of supporting evidence of some type—to serve as the sole criterion for any crucial decision.

4. *Failing to Supplement Test Scores with Other Information.*   This misuse overlaps with the prior misuse, but adds a slightly different point. Supporting evidence for a *single* test score could be *another* test score (on the same or a corollary test), or it could be information from sources other than tests. For example, what about the student who can quote Chaucer and Shakespeare at ease in class, but when faced with a test is so terrified he cannot recall who said, "To be or not to be?" Doesn't the teacher's knowledge of the student's ability count for anything? In our judgment, it should. Though our individual perceptions as teachers and administrators may be subjective, they are not irrelevant. Though we would seldom trust them alone, because they *are* subjective (and therefore potentially biased), our private observations and practical awareness of students' abilities are essential supplements to more objective test scores.

5. *Setting Arbitrary Minimums for Performance on Tests.*   When minimum test scores are established as critical hurdles for selection and admissions, as dividing lines for placing students in special or regular education programs, or as the determining factor in awarding diplomas or certificates, then several issues become acute. Test validity, always important, becomes crucial; and the minimum standard itself must be carefully scrutinized. Is there any empirical evidence that the minimum standard is set correctly, that those who score higher than the cutoff can be predicted to do better in subsequent academic or career pursuits? Or has the standard been set through some arbitrary or capricious process? Setting and enforcing arbitrary minimum test scores to make critical decisions is potentially one of the most damaging misuses of educational tests.

6. *Assuming Tests Measure All the Content, Skills, or Behaviors of Interest.*   Every test is limited in the behaviors it elicits and the material it

covers. Seldom is it feasible—because of limited testing time, student fatigue on too-long tests, and other such factors—to measure all that is of interest, or to test more than a sample of the relevant content, skills, or traits the test is designed to assess. Sometimes students do well on a test just because they happen to have read the *particular* chapters or studied the *particular* content sampled by that test. Given another test, with a different sampling of content from the same book, the students might fare less well. When educators ignore the fact that test scores reflect only samples of behavior, they risk misleading conclusions about the individuals or groups being tested.

7. *Accepting Uncritically All Claims Made by Test Authors and Publishers.* Blind faith in any test can have unfortunate consequences. Most test authors and publishers are enthusiastic about their products, and some are downright zealous. Excessive zeal can lead to "overpromising" what the test can measure and how well it measures it. A so-called "creativity test" may really measure only verbal fluency. A math "achievement" test administered in English to a group of Inuit Eskimo children (for whom English is a second language) may test understanding of English much more than understanding of math. It is essential that the *user* check the publisher's claims about technical qualities of a test or its usefulness for particular purposes.

8. *Interpreting Test Scores Inappropriately.* There are many ways to interpret test scores inaccurately or inappropriately. For example, many educators fail to realize that the score per se tells us nothing about *why* an individual obtained that score. Or, a student's test score may erroneously be accepted as a qualitative evaluation of performance rather than as a mere numeric indicator that lacks meaning in the absence of some qualitative criterion defining what constitutes "good" or "bad" performance. Still, another common interpretive error is failing to consider the appropriateness of norms before using them to draw inferences about individual or group performance.

   Misinterpretation of test scores is far too pervasive a problem in our schools, and what makes this particular misuse especially harmful is not only its frequency but also the fact that such errors often go unnoticed. Once collected, test data may take on a life of their own, telling a story that turns out to be more fiction than fact.

9. *Using Test Scores to Draw Inappropriate Comparisons among Individuals or Schools.* Unprofessional or careless comparisons of achievement test results can foster unhealthy competition among classmates, siblings, or even schools because of ready-made bases for comparisons, such as grade-level achievement. Such misuses of tests can harm the schools and children involved, and also create a backlash toward the tests that might better have been directed toward their misuse.

10. *Allowing Tests to Drive the Curriculum.* If tests drive the curriculum, dictate subject matter content, and even curtail creative teaching, who is responsible? The test makers or marketers? The test users? Or the tests?

Isn't the conspicuously correct answer the *users*? In every instance, some individual or group has selected the tests and decided how to use the scores. If a test unduly influences what goes on in a school's curriculum, then someone has allowed it to override priorities that educators and the school board have established. When tests drive curricula, it is the flawed *use* of the tests that should be critiqued rather than the tests. Whereas using standardized tests to make high-stakes decisions results in a variety of negative influences on the quality of classroom instruction (see Haladyna et al., 1991; Nolen, Haladyna, & Haas, 1989; Smith, 1991), the tests would have no such detrimental influence if used properly.

11. *Using Poor Tests*.   Why use a poorly constructed or unreliable test if a better one is at hand? Tests can be flawed in a multitude of ways, from measuring the wrong content or skills (but doing it well), to measuring the correct content or skills (but doing it poorly). Some err in both directions. Every effort should be made to obtain or construct the best possible measures, and one of our primary purposes in this book is to help you in this effort.

12. *Using Tests Unprofessionally*.   Whether in medicine, dentistry, psychology, or education, professionals are expected to use the tools of their trade ethically and effectively. When educational tests are used in misleading or harmful ways, inadequate training of educators in test selection and use is often at fault. When test scores are used to label children in harmful ways, the fault generally lies with those who affix the labels—not with the test. When test scores are not kept confidential, that is the fault of the person who violated the confidence, not the test maker. Incompetent or unethical use of tests results in serious misuses that scar the image not only of testing but of education as a profession.

In Summary

There are clear misuses of standardized (and other) tests, and these account for much of the criticism aimed at educational testing. Not all criticisms of tests can be deflected, however, by claiming that they merely reflect test misuse. There are also apparent weaknesses in many specific measures, based in part on the fact that we have yet a good deal to learn about measurement. We know enough already, however, to state unequivocally that no test score will ever be unequivocal. Uncertainty and error will always be with us. No test of learning, mental ability, or other characteristics can ever be presumed absolutely precise in its measurements. The professional judgments of teachers and other educators will continue to be essential in sound educational decision making. Correctly used, tests produce for any educational enterprise a solid base of vital information that cannot—to this point—be obtained in any other way. Incorrectly used, they simply produce errors and problems. Unfortunately, misuse is likely to continue until society and the education profession provide resources sufficient to develop greater "assessment literacy" among our nation's educators.[2]

---

[2] The lack of assessment literacy was demonstrated by Stiggins (1991).

But important as traditional tests are, they are not the only potentially useful approach to assessing student outcomes.

THE POTENTIAL OF RECENTLY PROPOSED ALTERNATIVES TO STANDARDIZED TESTING

Few current movements have caught the attention of educators as quickly as the move toward more direct assessment of student performance.[3] Efforts to develop useful alternatives to standardized testing have proliferated during the past several years (e.g., Baron, 1989; Roeber & Dutcher, 1989). Major journals that serve educational practitioners have devoted large sections or entire issues to thoughtful analyses of assessment alternatives. (See, for example, *Phi Delta Kappan,* May 1989 & May 1991, and *Educational Leadership,* April 1989.) More and more state and national associations of professional educators are sponsoring symposia or special conferences to consider alternative ways to assess student performance. And not to be left behind, state legislatures are beginning to enact laws that mandate use of direct assessment of student performance as the means of determining how well individual schools, districts, and their statewide education systems are performing. According to Herman (1991), 25 states have passed or are considering passage of legislation in this area. In short, alternative assessment's rising tide has overflowed most of education's shoreline and schools are increasingly being flooded with calls for more direct assessment of student performance.

Despite the surge of interest in alternative assessment, criticisms of this movement by those who favor more traditional means of assessment create a strong undertow. Differences between proponents and opponents have sparked vigorous debates (e.g., Wiggins, 1991; Cizek 1991a and 1991b), resulting in cross-currents that leave many educators feeling rudderless as they attempt to direct their school on the optimal assessment course.

In this section, we propose to (1) describe briefly what alternative assessment is and how it differs from more traditional forms, (2) outline clearly our position concerning alternative forms of assessment, (3) identify some major issues that educators must resolve if alternative assessment is to reach its full potential in our schools, (4) suggest some criteria schools may use to determine how quickly to expand their use of and dependence on nontraditional methods of assessment, and (5) describe briefly how portfolio assessment might be useful in your school or classroom.

What Is Alternative Assessment?

Several labels have been used to describe alternatives to standardized tests, with the most common being *direct assessment, authentic assessment, performance assessment,* and the more generic *alternative assessment,* which we shall use

---

[3] This section draws heavily on a manuscript by one of the authors to be published soon in the *Phi Delta Kappan* (Worthen, in press).

hereafter.[4] Although these various descriptors reflect subtle distinctions in emphasis, the several types of assessment all reflect two central commonalities. First, they are all viewed as *alternatives* to traditional multiple-choice, selected-answer achievement tests. Second, they all refer to *direct* examination of student *performance* on significant tasks relevant to life outside of school.

Proponents of alternative assessment prefer it to more traditional assessment that relies on indirect, "proxy" tasks (usually test items). Sampling tiny snippets of student behavior, they point out, does not provide insight into how students would perform on truly "worthy" intellectual tasks. Conversely, they argue that student learning can be better assessed by examining and judging a student's actual (or simulated) performance on significant, relevant tasks. As McTighe and Ferrara (in press) have noted, the focus of such assessment can be on students' *processes* such as learning logs, "think aloud" observation sessions, or self-assessment checklists; *products* such as diaries, writing portfolios, art portfolios, or exhibits; or *performances* such as typing tests, dramatic or musical performances, or oral debates.

Do some of these sound familiar? They should, for direct assessment of student performance is no newcomer to the educational scene. Time-honored examples of direct performance assessment include:

- Language proficiency testing (conversation, translation)
- Competency testing (e.g., for pilots and dentists)
- Hands-on assessment in vocational programs (e.g., welding, auto mechanics, and carpentry)
- Holistic student products (e.g., examination of writing assignments)
- Measures of time-on-task
- Observations of cooperative learning
- Portfolios of student work
- Cumulative student record files
- Student live performances (e.g., music, athletics, or business education)
- Teachers' anecdotal records of student performance
- Interviews to assess responses to formal and informal questions
- Self-evaluation reports of achievement or learning difficulties
- Teachers' rating scales and checklists for specific performance levels
- Teacher-made achievement tests
- Teacher-made simulations or other projective or role-playing devices

To name only a few.

---

[4] Many authors place the now familiar label of *portfolio assessment* in this list, but that title refers more accurately to one of several ways that alternative assessment data can be recorded and reviewed, and thus is less a descriptor of this general *type* of assessment than it is of one of its *tools*, which we will describe later in this chapter.

Of course, insightful teachers recognize that alternative assessment has long constituted the core of their methods for assessing student learning. Elementary school teachers have kept anecdotal running records and folders of student work long before such records have been both legitimized and refined by recent attention to better ways to use portfolios of student work to assess student learning. Samples of student products or performances have long been the basis for teachers' evaluation of student outcomes in areas as diverse as music, drama, debate, art, shorthand, creative writing, and physical education. Many teacher-made tests present students with important, "real-life" tasks that they must perform correctly to receive passing scores. Creative teachers have had students engage in self-assessment and peer assessment. In short, our nation's classrooms have been quietly awash in such performance-based assessment for decades.

Then why the recent upsurge in calls for alternative assessment? Why the increasing urging that such assessments replace standardized tests (norm-referenced achievement tests, minimum competency tests, and the like)? Why propose them as the basis for judging not only how well individual students are performing, but also how well schools, districts, and states are fulfilling their educational mission? The answer lies in several forces that have flowed, in succession, through education's tangled tributaries in the past two decades. We will not expound on these forces here, for we have discussed them in earlier chapters. Instead, let us merely list for you the sequence of factors that have collectively sparked the increasing interest in alternative assessment.

1. *Demands for accountability in our schools.* Loss of public confidence in public schools led to a spate of new "educational accountability" laws (requiring test evidence that schools were performing adequately).
2. *Use of test scores to make high-stakes decisions.* Both minimum competency tests and standardized achievement tests were used to make high-stakes decisions. Not only have student promotion and graduation decisions been based on such test scores, but the test scores also have been increasingly used in unanticipated ways that have had far-reaching consequences for individual teachers, schools, and school districts.
3. *Negative consequences of high-stakes testing programs.* The pressures that accompanied high-stakes testing resulted more often in other, less beneficial practices and outcomes including measurement-driven instruction, the sometimes innocent but nonetheless insidious practice of teaching to the test, or the more pernicious problem of outright test cheating, where teachers coach students on actual test items.
4. *Increasing criticisms of standardized tests.* As scores on such tests began to be used for increasingly crucial decisions, the tests' limitations loomed larger.

This unscrolling of forces across the past two decades has set the stage for increased hopes that alternative assessment will prove helpful in improving student assessment—and classroom instruction. Yet sharp differences still divide advocates and opponents of such assessment methods. While consideration of all the potential benefits and drawbacks of alternative assessment is beyond the scope of this chapter,[5] there are several critical issues that must be discussed, for they will prove pivotal in tilting the balance either in favor of alternative assessment, or against it. Before addressing these issues, our position concerning alternative assessment should be made clear.

Our Position Concerning Alternative Assessment

In our view, alternative assessment holds great promise. It has the potential of enriching and expanding the very nature of the information that assessments provide. It should be the very backbone of assessment procedures within individual classrooms. Because content of high-stakes tests is unlikely to be ignored by educators, including more worthy and relevant assessment tasks on such tests should spur educators to develop more appropriate instructional emphases. Indeed, education's ultimate goals should be directly represented in the complex performances selected as the alternative assessment tasks. These tasks should provide *direct* measurement of *real* performance on important tasks. Whenever it is feasible to use valid, representative, direct assessment tasks, they are preferable to indirect measurement where inferences about student learning depend on performance on surrogate indicators. But this high potential of alternative assessment can be realized only to the extent to which the following issues are successfully addressed.

Critical Issues Facing Alternative Assessment

Each of the following 12 issues is a challenge that must be met before alternative assessment can reach its full potential. Of course, alternative assessment will continue, in the various forms listed previously as examples of prior and current uses of such methods, whether or not the following issues are addressed. Yet use of these nontraditional methods is unlikely to expand to play the pivotal role in education that alternative assessment's advocates propose for it unless these 12 issues can be resolved.

1. *Conceptual Clarity*

As yet, there is too little coherence to the concepts and language being used in both written and oral discourse about alternative assessment, performance assessment, authentic assessment, direct assessment, practical testing—have we made our point? Authors of various descriptors for these types of assessments have not carefully tacked down their definitional edges or delineated clearly what belongs to a particular label and what does not. For clear communication to occur, especially in technical and scientific endeavors, it is important to use language in which each concept is invariably described by the same term, and each term refers to only one phenomenon (Neurath, Carnap, and Morris, 1955). Until this occurs, the entire alternative assessment movement risks becoming trapped in thickets of

---

[5] For a more complete discussion of both advantages and disadvantages, see Maeroff (1991).

tangled terminology and conceptual clutter and confusion. Those who recall how interest in the "discovery" method of teaching surged through the schools in the 1960s will remember how quickly it slowed to a trickle in the 1970s when it became clear that one teacher's "guided discovery" method was identical to the "expository" method of another, while closely resembling the "independent discovery" method of a third, and so on. This promising field of instructional inquiry sank and was soon submerged in semantic swamps that no one had bothered to drain. If alternative assessment is to survive the decade and develop into a potent force for educational improvement, then its advocates must take time to clarify its concepts and terminology. It cannot continue to be, as one friendly critic put it, a movement whose only definition is that "it is everything that a multiple-choice test is not."[6]

2. Mechanisms for Self-criticism

No reform movement should be without those who are as skeptical of their own efforts as they are of the efforts they seek to change or displace. Yet such internal self-criticism is rather scarce among proponents of alternative assessment. Ironically, the future of alternative assessment could be threatened by its very popularity. The more broadly it is accepted, the less frequently it is challenged, and the more likely it is that anyone who questions or criticizes it will be dismissed as either a crackpot or an obstructionist. As voices of caution are drowned by the clamor for more rapid adoption of alternative assessment methods, advocates of those methods could easily forget that self-criticism is the only road to continuing improvement of any movement and, indeed, is essential if that movement is to make a lasting contribution.

Fortunately, some of alternative assessment's most articulate advocates have recognized this problem and urged that it be addressed:

> If the current interest in alternatives to standardized testing is to be anything but this decade's flurry, we have to be as tough-minded in designing new options as we are in critiquing available testing. Unless we analyze the workings of these alternatives and design them carefully, we may end up with a different, but perhaps no less blunt, set of assessment instruments (Linn, 1990). As with any form of assessment, the familiar, difficult, and nasty issues of efficiency, equity, and evidence persist. Whereas there is considerable criticism of the approaches taken by standardized tests, as yet we have no such critical tradition for new modes of assessment. And we cannot be without one. (Wolf, Bixby, Glenn, & Gardner, 1991, p. 60)

As yet, however, no mechanism or forum for such self-criticism has been established, and this urgent need is in danger of being ignored, for education is being flooded with an outpouring of enthusiasm and euphoria for assessment alternatives. If not channeled and filtered by careful and constructive self-criti-

---

[6] From comments made by Joan Herman in a speech delivered to the Consortium on Expanded Assessment (sponsored by ASCD), San Diego, November 5, 1991.

cism, this outpouring is as likely to wreak havoc with assessment as it is to improve it.

3. Training Educators in Using Alternative Forms of Assessment

The very nature of alternative assessment (and one of its major strengths) pivots on the close linkages of assessment with instruction. Thus the classroom teacher is the gatekeeper of effective alternative assessment. Indeed, it would be hard to imagine a successful large scale performance assessment taking place without teacher cooperation. To be feasible, large-scale alternative assessment would require teachers to help administer and score measures. Further, optimal performance assessments should be developed at least partly by the teachers from whose curricula the instructional targets are drawn.

Of course, alternative assessment's heavy dependence on teachers would require that they be competent to perform high-quality alternative assessments. To a much greater degree than in traditional assessment, the quality of alternative assessments will be directly affected by how well teachers are prepared in relevant assessment knowledge skills.

Good alternative assessment obviously requires a somewhat different set of assessment competencies than what is needed in traditional multiple-choice testing. But *different from* does not mean *less than*. Scoring rubrics and criteria necessary for several types of performance measures will prove as challenging for most teachers as have grade equivalent scores. Staff development programs to provide practitioners with confidence and competence to function effectively in all relevant areas of assessment is essential if the full potential of alternative assessment is to be realized.

4. Technical Quality and Truthfulness

There is currently little agreement about just what technical specifications and criteria should be used to judge the quality of alternative forms of assessment. Some assessment specialists would redefine or replace common conceptions of validity and reliability with alternative touchstones of acceptability (e.g., Wiggins, 1991), while others argue that alternative assessment will not be useful if its measures are not held to the same high standards of reliability and validity education has demanded of existing paper and pencil assessments (e.g., Cizek, 1991a).

The issue is not simple. Thorny technical questions abound. Can one generalize satisfactorily from specific performance assessment tasks to the broader domain of achievement needs? When students evidence that they can complete a specific hands-on, science project, does that evidence that they can "do science," do science projects of that type, or only that they can do that particular science project? Is performance task dependent or generalizable from task to task? If task dependent, how many tasks must students perform before one can generalize to meaningful levels of competence that transcend the specific task? How can assessment bias that has plagued traditional tests be kept from operating in alternative assessments that allow more subjectivity? What degree of interrater reliability should be required of scorers and judges of student portfolios, or is that really a relevant question? And these questions only scratch the surface.

The crux of the issue is whether the alternative assessment movement will be able to evidence that its assessments are able to reflect accurately a student's true ability in significant areas of behavior relevant to adult life. Whether called reliability, validity, or something else, some evidence that the technical quality of the assessment yields a truthful portrayal of student abilities is essential. To succeed, alternative assessment must show that its tasks and measures genuinely reflect authentic assessment (not merely authentic-*looking* assessment). Otherwise, the promise it holds for helping improve teaching and learning will be unfulfilled.

5. *Standardization of Assessment Judgments*

Some proponents of alternative assessment are excited by its potential to allow flexible, diverse assessment, tailored to the individual student. Wolf and her colleagues (1991) have argued persuasively that scoring rubrics for performance assessments, portfolios and exhibitions often assume erroneously that all students progress from novice to expert along the same unidimensional scale. They note that "as we move to different modes of assessment, the contest between idealized, universal descriptions of progress and differentiated but potentially divisive rubrics will be fierce" (p. 63). They make a convincing case that insistence on uniform standards would make a mockery of the important and time-honored role that educators' clinical judgments and diversity of opinions has played. Yet others are quick to note that insistence on such diversity, however ideal, could easily undermine the alternative assessment movement by rendering its results too variable to support comparisons that governing boards, legislators, and the public are demanding as part of educational accountability. It would be rather optimistic, if not naive, to assume that the clamor for accountability would be stilled simply by informing school patrons and key decision makers that alternative assessment is not intended to support such comparisons. Maeroff has addressed this issue in his excellent analysis of the alternative assessment effort in Rhode Island:

> Furthermore, there must be standardization of some sort, as Rhode Island hopes to achieve. Otherwise, there is no way to put the findings of an assessment in context. Even in Kentucky, which by 1995 is to have the first statewide assessment system that is completely based on performance, there is anguish over how to meet the state board's mandate that there be a way of comparing Kentucky students with those in other states. . . . And the work doesn't stop with declaring, for example, that students will submit portfolios. What should be in the portfolios? What should students be asked about the contents of their portfolios? How can some element of standardization be lent to the process so that one student's portfolio may be compared with another's? Putting less emphasis on comparisons is fine, but at some point a child and his parents have a right to know whether the child's progress is reasonable for his or her age and experience. (1991, pp. 275–276)

Resolving how to standardize criteria and performance levels sufficiently to support necessary comparisons without causing them to lose the power and richness of assessment tailored to the student's needs and achievements is a key issue to the future of this movement, especially if alternative assessments are to be used to support high-stakes decisions.

6. *Ability to Assess Complex Thinking Skills*

One of the key reasons for promoting alternative assessment is the conviction that such assessments can measure complex, higher-order abilities that are difficult, if not impossible, to assess with traditional measures (e.g., Bracey, 1989). Although there are examples of well-developed multiple-choice tests that *do* assess higher-order thinking skills (HOTS) and even have HOTS subscales (e.g., the Metropolitan Achievement Test, Sixth Edition), even supporters of standardized multiple-choice tests are unlikely to argue that measuring HOTS is a particular strength of such measures. Yet that is widely thought to be the signature of alternative assessment, and analyses of research data and surveys of professional educators' opinions concerning the relative utility of direct assessment versus objective tests (e.g., Suhor, 1985) seem to bear this out.

But do alternative modes of assessment *necessarily* require the use of more complex cognitive processes by students? Can we be assured that we are measuring reasoning ability, problem solving skills, or other HOTS just because we use some form of alternative assessment? Obviously not. As Linn and his colleagues remind us:

> The construction of an open-ended proof of a theorem in geometry can be a cognitively complex task or simply the display of a memorized sequence of responses to a particular problem, depending on the novelty of the task and the prior experience of the learner. (1991, p. 19)

If alternative assessment is to develop its full potential for assessing HOTS, great care must be taken to select and present assessment tasks in ways that require students to use—and show—complex thinking skills in their response, rather than simply *assuming* they are using such skills because they are responding to a hands-on task.

7. *Acceptability to Education's Stakeholders*

The earlier discussion of "standardization of assessment judgments" hinted at a critical issue to the future of alternative assessment, and that is the extent to which this movement proves acceptable to education's key stakeholders—legislators, school boards, parents, teachers, students, and associations of professional educators, to name only a few (we say more in a later section about how to judge key stakeholders' readiness for alternative assessment). Some schools may have stakeholders who readily accept the importance and usefulness of alternative assessment, while other schools may confront outright public rejection of any nontraditional forms of student assessment because their accountability-oriented stakeholders perceive that these forms will not provide them with readily manageable information. Most boards of education can, with little orientation, interpret test scores intelligently, whereas they will likely find it more difficult (though by no means impossible) to deal with summaries of student performance on other indices such as portfolios or anecdotal records. Useful as many of these methods are for describing student performance in meaningful ways to the teacher and perhaps to individual parents, most of these assessment methods are more difficult to summarize across individuals, making it difficult to use them for reporting learning outcomes for entire classes, schools, districts, or state systems. Yet, beyond the individual parent, these are precisely the levels at which educational administrators, policy makers, legislators, the lay public—and even many teachers—feel the greatest need for information. Public demand for evidence that teachers and schools are effectively educating students is increasing, and test scores are typically the kind of evidence the public finds most credible. Until and unless the public ceases to demand such assessment-driven accountability, proponents of alternative assessment must grapple with this simplistic view of educational reform and find ways to convince stakeholders that alternative assessment can play a pivotal role in improving teaching and learning that far transcends its inability to generate assessment data for decision makers.

A related key to the future of alternative assessment is the ability of its advocates to guide it along the narrow path that winds between the swamps of "underselling" and the pitfalls of "overpromising." It will take patience to persist on that pathway when the public and many educators clamor for immediate solutions to critical problems in our schools. Some leading proponents of alternative assessment have suggested privately that it will take a decade before these forms of assessment are sufficiently developed and tested to allow widespread dependence on them to support educational decisions. Given the recent trends seen in mandating of performance assessment by many legislative bodies and funding agencies, alternative assessment is unlikely to have very long to mature before being judged on its ability to solve some of education's thorniest problems.

It is critical that thoughtful proponents of nontraditional assessment help education's stakeholders see alternative assessment's *potential*, while adjusting and refining their expectations to align them with what is appropriate for a promising but still young movement. It may be too late to adjust expectations in Kentucky, where the legislature has mandated a statewide assessment system based completely on performance assessment by 1995. It can only be hoped this fledgling effort proves to be precocious and meets with at least modest success. If not, the entire alternative assessment movement may be seriously impeded because of the high profile of the Kentucky mandate.

This concern is echoed by Brewer in his thoughtful commentary entitled "Can Performance Assessment Survive Success?" He said:

> The good news is that performance assessment has succeeded: Policymakers from Maine to California and Washington to Florida have discussed it . . . . The bad news is that performance assessment has succeeded: Policymakers from Maine to California and Washington to Florida have discovered it. Until now, performance assessment has been nurtured, like tender shoots, in a greenhouse. The work being done by Project Zero and *Arts Propel*, the imaginative approach to assessment that has emerged in the Pittsburgh Public Schools, the slow and deliberate emergence of mathematics portfolios in California, and the development of science and mathematics assessment in Connecticut have taken place in sheltered environ-

ments, out of the public eye and the policy arena—stakes have not been attached to performance. No longer. In Kentucky, salaries and jobs are linked to the achievement of students, which is to be measured using performance assessment. However "voluntary" the national examination system proposed in "Raising Standards," states will be compared and there will be consequences for students and teachers. (1992, p. 28)

Wherever possible, therefore, promises to (and expectations of) stakeholders should be tempered to provide time to develop, pilot, and modify nontraditional forms of assessment before launching alternative assessment as the flagship of educational reform. Even then, as Cizek reminds us, it would seem wise to remember that "Performance assessment does have potential to make a positive contribution to reform efforts by providing unique information about student ability . . . [but] It should not be promoted . . . as *the* cure for what ails us" (1991a, p. 153).

8. *Appropriateness for High-stakes Assessment*

It is too early to be certain about the appropriateness of alternative assessment in high-stakes environments, but it is not too early to recognize this as a pivotal issue because of three unknowns about alternative assessment that raise questions about their usefulness in this context. First, does alternative assessment provide sufficient standardization to defend high-stakes decisions based on such measures? Second, will alternative assessment result in ethnic minorities scoring better than on traditional measures, or more poorly, as now appears quite possible (e.g., Darling-Hammond, 1991). Third, will the inevitable legal challenges aimed at high-stakes decisions based on alternative assessment be more difficult to defend because the validity of such measures may be less certain to psychometricians and thus less convincing to the courts? Until questions such as these are answered, it is unclear whether alternative assessments can simultaneously serve well the dual needs of assessment for instructional purposes and accountability purposes.

Brewer, who has been involved in Vermont's vanguard development of alternative assessment in the schools, sees this issue clearly:

The friends of performance assessment must understand that the tilt of the field has changed. Until now, performance assessment has been winning without having had to perform as a vehicle of assessment in an accountability system, and while performance assessment is not a "star wars" technology, as some have likened it, even its friends have been asking probing questions. . . .

Before the stakes grew it was possible to slough off the tough questions relating to consequences, equity, or reliability by pointing out that performance assessment was good because we were assessing real writing or real mathematics: This kind of assessment would lead to better instruction. This is no longer enough. We all need to agree that there are legitimate questions to be resolved as we proceed. . . . Nationally the questions are tougher and so is the environment for studying the results. In a different climate we could do evaluation work, improve approaches, let a hundred flowers bloom, picking the best where we found them. That luxury is gone. . . . When performance assessment moved into the high-stakes arena we lost our "license to fail." (1992, p. 28)

Yet, not all alternative assessments are proposed for use in high-stake settings. And not all alternative assessments are subjected to the scrutiny received by those that are high-stakes—and thus high-profile—assessments. For those who still have the luxury, there is wisdom and prudence in developing and testing alternative assessment approaches and measures in *low-stakes settings* where they can serve needs for better classroom assessment. Thus we would learn more about how to select worthy and representative tasks, how to set criterion levels and standardize scoring enough but not too much, how the assessment results could be used in improving instruction and stimulating reform, how to provide professional development to enable educators to use nontraditional assessment effectively, and how to obtain and maintain stakeholders' permission for its use. With that foundation, the effort to consider the use of alternative assessment in high-stakes settings seems more likely to succeed.

9. *Feasibility*

One of the most frequently debated issues is whether alternative assessment is feasible for large-scale efforts to assess student performance. (See, for example, "Test Experts See Pitfalls in Performance-Based Tests" in the April 29, 1992, *Report on Education Research*, p. 5.) No one, whether proponent or opponent of nontraditional assessment, would claim that its measures are as inexpensive, efficient, or as quick as scantron scoring of multiple-choice tests' bubble answer sheets. Obviously, scoring of students' constructed responses to performance assessment tasks costs enormously more by the time such responses (e.g., writing samples or art portfolios) are scored. The labor intensity of scoring and appraisers' observation of performance over extended periods are primarily responsible for the relatively high costs for performance assessments.

Cost should not be the only criterion, however, as supporters of alternative assessment are quick to point out. The more important criterion should be cost-benefit. Does alternative assessment produce sufficiently greater benefits to justify its increased costs? Are there benefits that are so intertwined with teaching and learning that it is naive to think they can be separated out by traditional cost-benefit analyses? No definitive answers can be given to such questions until considerably more research has addressed these issues. In the meantime, it seems reasonable to suggest that no assessment method will ever be rated high on its cost-benefit if it is unaffordable in the first place, as many assessment specialists contend (e.g., Popham, 1991).

Numerous suggestions have been offered for how to make alternative assessment more feasible beyond the individual classroom. Perhaps the most common is the use of sampling, where both the students and items (tasks) to be assessed are selected by precise scientific methods. The result might be a system where only a limited number of schools in a district or state would be sampled, within them only a small proportion of the students would be selected, and each student in the sample would receive only a sample of the assessment tasks. Obviously such a system would be far less costly to operate and, therefore, would be much more feasible.

For this strategy to succeed, however, school boards and legislatures would need to be convinced to test less and to be satisfied with very different reports on student performance—reports based on much more in-depth assessment of the performance of far fewer students, possibly at far fewer grade levels. Only additional time and experience will tell whether or not such a sampling approach will make alternative assessment affordable beyond the classroom and, if so, whether such a sampling approach is acceptable to educators and key educational policy makers.

A second proposal aimed at making the use of alternative assessment more feasible does so by restricting its scope to the classroom or possibly the school level, but in doing so, creates another issue concerning *continuity* of assessment.

10. *Continuity and Integration across Educational Systems*

If it is doubtful whether one assessment can—or should—be used to satisfy both instructional and accountability purposes, then why not use two separate assessments? And if traditional tests can more efficiently and inexpensively collect assessment data from large groups of students, then why not use them in appraising and reporting on student performance at national, state, district, and possibly school levels? Similarly, if alternative assessment is linked closely to teaching and learning, and is more feasible when closely integrated with the classroom curriculum, then why not use such assessment methods within the classroom? Why not use two "parallel" systems rather than forcing either to be used in an environment to which it is ill-suited? Such questions have led some schools or districts to propose a two-layer assessment system, where the first layer consists of performance assessment used to enrich classroom assessment, and the second depends on standardized, multiple-choice tests used to assess the performance level of larger groups of students, reporting on average achievement levels for the state, the district, or possibly the school.

Although such an approach may appear to be a case of simultaneous cakehaving and cake-eating, it poses some difficulty. Such a two-pronged system could easily become rather disjointed, with classroom (and possibly school) assessment dependent on intensive sampling of performance assessment and school district or state levels using standardized test programs. This may well create a dualistic view of student attainment, however, with standardized test data continuing to be as irrelevant to most classroom decisions as before, and the potential richness of alternative assessment data not extending beyond the local level to enhance the information available to those who make high-stakes decisions. In some ways this would formalize the presently disjointed situation where classroom teachers use their own methods of assessing students' learning (most often some type of performance testing), while high-stakes decisions would continue to be based on multiple-choice instruments not designed to assess student performance directly. Not many commentators argue that this disjointed approach to educational assessment is optimal. Thus, for the alternative assessment movement to be completely successful, it must find a way to link assessment for accountability more effectively to assessment for individual student diagnosis and prescription.

11. *Utilization of Technology*

The role that technology will play in alternative assessment is still largely unresolved. Although only technology enthusiasts are optimistic about technology's ability to resolve complex educational problems single-handedly, it would seem that better use of technology should be particularly helpful in solving some of the major challenges to alternative assessment discussed earlier. For example, use of computers would seem an obvious way to simplify now labor-intensive techniques and make them feasible. Kurland's (1991) "Text Browser" is a promising effort to use a network system to support highly individualized instruction and assessment, including portfolio management and scoring. Computerized adaptive testing is viewed by some (e.g., McBride, 1985) as so advantageous that such tests will eclipse most paper and pencil tests within this decade. And videotapes and audiotapes, already the core of some alternative assessment efforts, will doubtlessly become more practicable as those technologies advance.

One caution, however. Advancement of technology will not automatically lead to its use in improving alternative assessment. In commenting on the impact of computer technology on large-scale assessment programs, Haney and Madaus note that "At present, the major impact of computer technology on testing has been in the creation of more efficient multiple-choice tests rather than in the exploitation of computer technology to create real alternatives to standardized multiple-choice tests" (1989, p. 686). How to harness technology to make alternative assessment less labor intensive and, therefore, more feasible, is an important issue that will impact directly on the future of this assessment movement.

12. *Avoidance of Assessment Monopolies*

There is little sense in recreating the wheel by having every school attempting to develop all of its own performance assessment tools. As far back as 1975, the U.S. Office of Education had funded assessment and evaluation specialists in establishing a national clearinghouse for applied performance measures (Sanders & Sachse, 1975). Though funding for this program was later discontinued, this excursion into cataloging and exchanging fugitive performance measures was a valuable resource for schools and other agencies that wished to use performance tests but lacked the time and/or the expertise to develop their own. Resurrection of this approach today could provide an even more important service, in view of today's greater popularization of such measures.

There is also wisdom in drawing on existing expertise to develop high-quality performance assessments, such as some already produced by American College Testing and the Psychological Corporation (e.g., the battery of performance assessments contained in the College Outcome Measures Project). But there is also an element of risk if well-financed testing companies are allowed to become the primary source of alternative assessment instruments. Sole dependence upon measures developed in isolation from local curricula would clearly undermine one of alternative assessment's greatest strengths, namely the integration of instruction and assessment. While testing companies can and should provide well-developed, "common-denominator" performance assessments that would serve some assessment needs in the school, thoughtful and energetic efforts will be needed to develop locally relevant assessment alternatives as the core of any alternative assessment effort. Failure to do so would result in testing companies' current monopoly on standardized multiple-choice tests being extended to a monopoly on standardized alternative assessments. Much thought is needed about how to capitalize on the considerable assessment expertise of existing assessment corporations without abandoning to them responsibility for that which would better be served by local development of assessment measures.

Until the Issues Are Resolved

In the meantime, until the issues discussed above are resolved, what stance should educators take? In our view, schools should be quick to capitalize on alternative assessment, whenever appropriate, for it seems most clear that it offers much at the local level. District, state, and national assessment efforts should follow NAEP's lead in using performance assessment tasks whenever feasible, especially in low-stakes settings that are more permissive of experimentation. Educators should help shape the future direction of alternative assessment by gaining experience with it and continuing only that which works well. Where it proves to be unhelpful, urgings to use it should be ignored, unless it is clear how it can be changed to make it more useful. Finally, educators should be as slow to accept claims that alternative assessment is the panacea for all of education's ills as it is to believe critics who portray alternative assessments' pimples as terminal acne.

Such open-minded "neutrality" will not be easy, especially in a field where decisions about new approaches are more likely to be based on the zeal or passion of their supporters or critics than on any solid empirical base. In the absence of clear "proof" that these nontraditional methods will be beneficial in your assessment efforts, what criteria should be used to determine when (or whether) your school should move to expand its use of such measures? The next section attempts to answer that question.

Criteria for Determining Your School's Readiness for Expanding the Use of Alternative Assessment

Assuming you are convinced that you want to expand the use of alternative assessment in your school, how can you determine if you are ready to do so? How well prepared is your school to expand its use of this form of assessment, which requires teachers, administrators, students, and patrons to alter their views of student assessment and perform their various assessment roles rather differently?

What follows in Figure 15.1 is a presentation and brief discussion of a simple "self-check" profile of 10 considerations that your school may wish to contemplate carefully before embarking on any new alternative assessment effort. This profile is intended to help you identify the areas where your school is already well prepared, as well as areas that could threaten your efforts before they are well underway. (Obviously this profile may be less directly useful to schools already far along in their efforts to implement new modes of student assessment.)

Directions: **Check whether your school is high, medium, or low on each dimension listed below (each dimension is discussed briefly later in this chapter).**

	High	Med.	Low
1. Desire for better classroom and/or school assessment information than now exists			
2. Indications that current classroom/school assessment is creating negative side effects			
3. Openness of staff to new educational innovations			
4. Conceptual clarity about alternative assessment			
5. Staff "literacy" in relevant assessment concepts			
6. Clarity about desired student outcomes			
7. School emphasis/priority on content and curricula difficult to measure by traditional tests			
8. Existence of some good examples of local (in-class or in-school) alternative assessments to build on			
9. Willingness of staff to be constructively self-critical			
10. Patrons' and policy makers' openness to new forms of assessment more linked to instruction than to accountability			
SUMMARY			

FIGURE 15.1   A Profile of Considerations in Determining a School's Readiness for Expanded Use of Alternative Assessment

1. Desire for Better Assessment Information

Change seldom is spawned by contentment. If your school staff is satisfied that the information from current assessment activities is yielding all the information they need, then there would seem to be little reason to abandon present assessment efforts in favor of others that are less familiar. Be certain, however, that your present student assessment methods are really adequate. Do they provide you with a solid, defensible basis for deciding which students should be targeted for special help or challenged by placement in programs for the gifted and talented? Do your teachers have good diagnostic information about specific learning problems of each student? Does present student assessment information provide a good road map for day-to-day instructional decisions? Does it provide a foundation for decisions about the school curriculum? Answers to such questions should serve as a good barometer of your school's contentment with your present assessment system.

2. Indications of Negative Side Effects

The negative impact of high-stakes testing on our schools has already been discussed at some length in Chapter 3, and need not be repeated here. But if high-stakes testing has permeated your school and left a residue of such side effects in any of your student assessment efforts, it would surely signal a need to contemplate alternatives.

3. Staff Openness to New Innovations

It is not difficult to get innovative, forward-looking teachers and administrators to entertain new approaches to their jobs. Educators who keep themselves on the cutting edge are probably already well aware of alternative assessment and may even be experimenting with it. But the more critical issue is how your school's faculty and administrators would be rated on any "innovativeness" scale you may devise. If your administrators or key influence leaders on your faculty are resistent to new ideas, you may find promoting new modes of assessment an uphill struggle. If faced with such reactions, then before you try to immerse your school in alternative assessment activities, you would be well advised to use staff development, teacher mentoring, or other means to help spread the vision of how alternative assessment could enhance student assessment.

4. Conceptual Clarity about Alternative Assessment

This was one of the 12 issues we discussed previously, and we will not repeat that discussion here. But it is important that your school's staff members have clear ideas about what alternative assessment is and is not, how it differs from traditional modes, and how those differences impact on educational practice. They also should be able to articulate these differences and the potential advantages of proposed assessment innovations to patrons without too much tangled terminology.

5. Staff Assessment "Literacy"

Stiggins (1991) has reported that few educational practitioners are well informed about even the basics of student assessment, largely because university education programs are flawed. Good alternative assessment obviously requires a somewhat different set of assessment competencies than that needed in traditional objective testing. But *different from* does not mean *less than*. It will hardly be progress if a school switches from struggling with standardized tests to floundering with portfolio assessment. If competence in areas relevant to alternative assessment is insufficient to support such efforts, expanding the staff's assessment capability through staff development may be a necessary precursor to revamping your student assessment program.

6. Clarity about Desired Student Outcomes

Fuzzy targets are the bane of any assessment specialist. They are particularly problematic for those who propose to use alternative forms of assessment. The signature of most such methods is that the assessment task *is* the desired student outcome. This means that a school must have a clear idea of what they want students to be able to do, *specifically*, as a result of their schooling, before they can develop or select assessment tasks that will reflect those desired student outcomes. If higher order thinking skills are something your school hopes to develop in your students, for example, those skills need to be carefully identified and linked to assessment tasks. Otherwise, students may be assumed to be using complex thinking skills just because they are responding to an apparently complex task. The more clear your school is about desired student outcomes, the more probable it is that alternative assessment will prove useful.

7. *Content or Curricula Ill-suited to Traditional Tests*

If—heaven forbid—your school curriculum consists primarily of "drill them till you kill them" approaches to subject matter, then objective testing can probably track your students' achievement without difficulty. (That should not be misconstrued as meaning that objective testing is more *suitable* to assessing the results of drill and practice pedagogy than assessing other more valued educational outcomes, but only that it is *sufficient* to such a task.) The assessment challenges increase, however, with many types of curricula or instructional approaches that focus more on holistic performances than on those that can appropriately be subdivided into more atomistic components. A curriculum that emphasized the whole language approach and artistic visual expression could lead naturally to alternative assessment methods such as direct (holistic or analytical) writing assessment and judging student art portfolios. The more your school or classroom curriculum lends itself to—or perhaps requires—assessment by nontraditional techniques, the more important it is for your school to add such methods to your school's assessment arsenal.

8. *School Examples of Alternative Assessment*

It would be difficult to find a school bereft of instances of direct performance assessment, as we noted earlier with examples of typing tests, oral reading assessment, and so on. The challenges faced by most teachers or schools come, however, when they attempt to devise direct performance measures to assess student learning in areas traditionally assessed by traditional tests—areas such as reading vocabulary and comprehension, math computation, or math problem solving ability. It is helpful in times of transition if there are already a few local instances where new approaches have been implemented successfully, or at least tried, as long as the effort was enlightening. There is something deeply comforting about having someone nearby who "has been there" and can demonstrate new methods to neophytes or critique their embryonic efforts. The closer to home your school can find those who have implemented such alternative assessment efforts successfully (especially if *in* your school, district, or state), the better prepared you are to launch such assessment on a broader scale.

9. *Staff Willingness to Critique Their Assessment Methods*

This criterion is not aimed at *present* assessment methods, which were the focus of the first two points on this profile. Rather, it concerns the willingness of your school staff to be constructively self-critical of their efforts to implement better assessment alternatives (or supplements, since adopting alternatives does not require your school to drop appropriate use of traditional paper and pencil tests). As we argued earlier, it is important that those who launch new alternative assessment efforts must be careful that they do not allow the popularity of such methods to lessen the scrutiny to which they are subjected.

10.   Patrons' and Policymakers' Openness to New Forms of Assessment

Although increasing numbers of state legislatures and school boards are mandating use of alternative assessment, many policymakers and patrons continue to favor easily summarized test scores. Indeed, parents and politicians who are obsessed with notions of educational accountability are often unwilling to support any assessment approach unless it yields results that can be easily summarized into a numeric index that reflects the "success" of the schools. Moreover, the drift of our culture is toward competitiveness and away from cooperation, and this is nowhere more evident than in our schools, even putting athletics and other school-sponsored competition aside. Count the patrons of your school who would be as thrilled with the statement that "Your child is the most nurturing and cooperative learner in her class" as with the declaration that "Your child received the highest scores in her class in math and language arts."   Garrison Keillor's Lake Wobegon whimsy about a setting where "all the kids are above average" reflects a culture where "average" is no longer an acceptable label to most, yet where few seem willing to contemplate alternatives that would not allow comparisons among students or schools.

Of course, some schools do find their publics tolerant of noncomparative assessment methods, and many parents are enthralled by assessments that provide them with a rich array of their child's performances rather than a few test scores. And some alternative assessments provide a basis for comparing student attainments, if desired. But the critical question is whether your schools' patrons and policy makers have a fanatical fixation on achievement scales and scores that invite direct comparisons among students. If so, they may become apoplectic in attempting to determine how to rank students on the basis of their portfolios. It may be hard to convince parents who push to know their child's relative rank in a kindergarten class to throw their support behind an assessment system in which ranking is both less easy and less relevant.

As you contemplate launching an alternative assessment effort for your classroom or school, it will be useful to reflect on the preferences of your publics. If they tilt toward simple numerical indicators of what students have learned, then you may have a selling job to do before you can proceed very far. To garner the support of your policy makers and patrons, you must be able to convince them that alternative assessment can play a vital role in improving and reporting student learning sufficient to offset its inability to generate simple status snapshots.

Caveat Emptor

If you use this profile, there are a few "let the buyer beware" cautions that should be kept in mind. First, the ten considerations are not exhaustive and you may have others you wish to add. Second, with minor rewording, and slight refocusing of points 3, 7, and 10, the profile could serve as well for assessing your school's readiness to expand or revise a traditional assessment system based on paper and pencil tests, or shift to a different system of the same form. Third, no scoring mechanism has been suggested for fear it would be simplistic. Obviously one could assign a score of 3 to each "high," a 2 to each "medium," and so on, to produce a summary "readiness score" that could vary from 10 (low readiness) to 30 (high readiness). It seems more useful, however, to view this profile as a heuristic device to stimulate you to reflect on which of these, or other, considerations are likely to help or hinder your efforts to implement or expand alternative assessment efforts in your classroom or school.

POTENTIAL USES OF PORTFOLIO ASSESSMENT IN YOUR SCHOOL[7]

Portfolios are not new. They have been used by artists, architects, models, writers, and similar professionals for many years to provide a sample of their work that will demonstrate their skills and achievements. For example, an artist's portfolio would include samples of the artist's work that reveal the depth and breadth of the artist's experiences. Similarly, as mentioned in the preceding section, portfolios have long been used by teachers to document students' accomplishments in art, writing, vocational education, and the like.

What *is* new is that more and more schools are beginning to use portfolios as the primary means of assessing student outcomes in areas typically dominated by traditional paper-and-pencil tests. This increased and altered use of portfolio assessment has entered the educational arena in response to the demands for alternative assessment strategies, especially in light of the criticisms of traditional testing discussed in the preceding section. Before discussing uses of portfolios, however, it may be useful to define just what they are.

What Is a Portfolio?

Portfolios, coming from the word *port,* which means carry, and *folio,* which means paper, have also been called "school literary folders" (Wansart, Parsons, Pinkham, & Bailey, in Jongsma, 1989), "authenticity measures" (Valencia, 1990), and "collaborative assessment" (Valencia, 1990). The term *collaborative assessment* refers to the fact that well-conducted portfolio assessment can strengthen the relationship between student and teacher as they become partners in learning. The involvement of students in *assessing* their progress actively by reviewing and analyzing the performances documented in their portfolios is one of the greatest potential strengths of this method.

Paulson, Paulson, and Meyer define a portfolio as "a purposeful collection of student work that exhibits the student's efforts, progress, and achievement in one or more areas. The collection must include student participation in selecting contents, the criteria for the selection, the criteria for judging merit, and evidence of student self-reflection." (1991, p. 60)

---

[7] Appreciation is expressed to Vanessa D. Moss for sharing insights about portfolio assessment gained not only from reviewing literature on the topic but also, and more importantly, from extensive experience in using portfolios to assess students' learning. Many of the ideas presented in this section also draw on the writings of Vavrus (1990) and, to a somewhat lesser extent, on those of Valencia (1990).

Portfolios have also been called "authentic forms of assessment" because they represent real or actual learning activities occurring in classrooms (Vavrus, 1990). Portfolios are only one of the many types of authentic assessment, which is a much broader term that includes many types of nontraditional assessments in addition to portfolios.

What Does a Portfolio Look Like?

Unlike some common misconceptions, a portfolio is not merely some expandable, flexible file stuffed full of miscellaneous art sketches or snippets of writing. Those who view portfolios as merely containers full of aggregated stuff either have never seen a portfolio or, at best, have seen only poor examples. As Vavrus points out, "it is what's in the container, rather than the container itself, that becomes a student's portfolio" (1990, p. 48). Yet, unfortunately, some educators seem more preoccupied with the container than with what to put in it. Valencia (1990) has covered the essential concerns about the portfolio's physical dimension in saying that it must be larger and more elaborate than a report card, yet smaller and more ordered than a storage trunk filled with accumulated artifacts. Whether it is a large, expandable file folder or a segmented chest with styrofoam-lined compartments depends on whether the student's products are displayed on paper or sculpted in clay.

Vavrus (1990) has insightfully noted that the more important physical aspect of a portfolio is how the documents used to record student progress are actually arranged. Portfolios may be structured so that documents are ordered chronologically, by subject area, or by type or style of product. A portfolio could be focused entirely on a student's writing, for example, or it could be divided into sections, each containing the student's work in a different content area. Whatever the organizing scheme, the student should have a say in how the contents of the portfolio are arranged. Having students participate in the critical thinking that determines how the portfolio will be organized is one of the important reasons for using portfolios (Farr, in Jongsma, 1989).

In addition, Vavrus points out, each good portfolio also contains a less obvious but no less important conceptual structure, which reflects the teacher's (and perhaps the student's) underlying goals for student learning. We will say more about this later in discussing the philosophy underlying use of portfolios.

What Should a Portfolio Contain?

This question cannot be answered well here, for even the appropriate candidates for inclusion—let alone inappropriate items—are nearly as diverse as are the combinations of content and intent that lead to portfolios' being kept. The range of what to include is almost limitless. The key is to provide a variety of types of indicators of learning so that teachers, parents, students, and administrators can build a complete picture of the student's development.

The contents of a portfolio should contain whatever documentation is necessary to show changes and growth over time in the student's understandings, skills, and achievements. Examples of what might be placed in portfolios include, but are not limited to, the following:

1. Teachers' observational notes
2. Notes from parent-teacher conferences
3. Students' own periodic self-evaluations
4. Progress notes submitted by the teacher and student as they collaboratively review the student's growth
5. Samples of the student work selected by the teacher, student, teacher and student, or parent(s) in areas such as:
   a. Writing assignments that reflect student progress in writing
   b. Worksheets showing samples of complex math computations or calculations involved in solving increasingly complex story problems
   c. Science lab reports, including description of how findings were reached and interpreted
   d. Audiotapes of student reading
   e. List of books read by the student
   f. Audiotapes of the student talking about pictures in a book
   g. Renditions produced during a mechanical drafting class

And those are only a few of the items you might find useful to include in student portfolios. Rather than producing a long "laundry list" of likely ingredients in a portfolio, it may be more useful to provide you with several guidelines for how to decide what to include. Of course, the exact nature of the portfolio will vary depending on the student and the curriculum goals, making it difficult for us to prescribe what you should include in any particular portfolio. However, the following guidelines should prove helpful.

First, Vavrus has suggested several questions that can serve as a useful checklist for determining what goes into a portfolio. Before determining what to include, ask yourself:

• Who is the intended audience for the portfolios? Parents? Administrators? Other teachers?

• What will this audience want to know about student learning?

• Will the selected documents show aspects of student growth that test scores don't capture? Or, will they corroborate evidence that test scores already suggest about student performance?

• What kinds of evidence will best show student progress toward your identified learning goals?

• Will the portfolio contain best work only or a progressive record of student growth, or both?

• Will the portfolio include more than the finished pieces: for example, ideas, sketches, and revisions? (1990, p. 50)

Second, make certain that portfolios are not merely collections of each week's graded papers, tossed into the portfolio rather than into school or home wastebaskets. The process of determining what to include should be selective to be sure that the items selected reflect well the progress of the student in relation to what you and the student have agreed will serve as the benchmarks for measuring growth in knowledge or skill or both.

Third, periodically review with the student and parents the contents of the portfolio to determine if they are serving their purpose. Do they clearly portray how the student is doing? Are they helpful to you and the student in identifying both progress and areas in need of further work? If the answer to either of these questions is negative, adjust what you are putting into the portfolio until you can answer those questions affirmatively.

Fourth, use your key curriculum and instructional goals to guide your selection of the contents of each portfolio.

Fifth, have the student review the portfolio at regular intervals, focusing her attention on specific items or themes that run through the items, tracing either chronological or thematic growth. The student's written reflections about what the contents of her portfolio show about her growth can also become useful records to include for later review.

Sixth, do not select the contents of the portfolio from a single source, even if that source is the most obvious—the student. In addition to the student's products or descriptions of processes used, your own anecdotal records of the student's activities or behavior are important, as are observations of parents and other children (carefully selected to exclude any that would be inappropriate, of course). Information shared during parent-teacher conferences can be especially helpful.

Seventh, you may find it especially helpful to include a table of contents or a "summary form" in each portfolio to facilitate review and synthesis of the information it contains.

Where Should Portfolios Be Kept?

The answer to this question obviously depends on the size of the portfolios and the amount and location of available storage space. One general guideline to follow, however, is that portfolios should be placed in a spot in the classroom that is easily accessible to students as well as teachers. According to Valencia, "Unlike the secretive grade book or the untouchable permanent records stored in the office, these are working folders. Their location must invite students and teachers to contribute to them on an ongoing basis and to reflect on their contents to plan the next learning steps" (1990, p. 339).

It has been suggested that in addition to being accessible to both students and teachers, portfolios should be accessible to parents as well. Parents are encouraged not only to access materials from the portfolio but also to add items or to be an advisor to the student as to what should be placed in the portfolio.

Of course, a student's portfolio should not be accessible to other students unless she approves such access. All students should be taught to respect one another's portfolio privacy, even while being encouraged to share items in their portfolio with other students as they desire.

Now that we have described what portfolios are, what they look like, what they should contain, and where they should be kept, you might ask why one would choose to use an assessment tool that is obviously as time consuming as the portfolio. The question can only be answered in the context of a full understanding of the purposes and philosophy that undergirds and overarches the use of portfolios.

What Philosophy and Purposes Underlie Portfolio Assessment?

At the core of portfolio assessment is the recognition that instruction and assessment should be closely intertwined. Those who use portfolios are not concerned with the time they consume, for they recognize that portfolios are as much an instructional tool as they are an assessment device. Perhaps Valencia says it best:

> Portfolios represent a philosophy that demands that we view assessment as an integral part of our instruction, providing a process for teachers and students to use to guide learning. It is an expanded definition of assessment in situations before, during and after instruction. It is a philosophy that honors both the process and the products of learning as well as the active participation of the teacher and the students in their own evaluation and growth." (1990, p. 340)

Valencia also underscores the fact that portfolios are continuous, on-going, ever-changing instruments in which revisions are made frequently as teachers become more aware of student needs. Therefore, a central feature of portfolio assessment is that both the process and the outcomes (products) of learning are continually measured. Thus, "When we are positioned to observe and collect information continuously, we send a message to students, parents, and administrators that learning is never completed; instead, it is always evolving, growing, and changing" (Valencia, 1990, p. 338). This type of assessment tool is intended to "capture the authentic, continuous, multidimensional, interactive requirement of sound assessment" (Valencia, 1990, p. 339).

The use of portfolios also is an attempt to help students take greater responsibility for their own learning. Wiggins has urged that "Teachers need to rethink their relationships with students and consider their roles as coaches or enablers of student performance. . . . The whole point is to put the student in a self-disciplined, self-regulating, self-assessing position. Portfolios can help in this process" (Wiggins, 1990, p. 51). Viewed in this manner, assessment is not only a process that is within the teacher's control but also one that can be partially directed by the student, thus helping her identify how well she has learned and what she needs to learn next.

This process is facilitated by having students study their portfolios at various times during the year. When studying, students should ask themselves the following questions from Vavrus:

- What do I like most about this work?
- What was important to me when I wrote it?

- If I revised this, what would I change?
- How has my writing changed since I wrote this?
- How is it like other pieces of my work? Is it my best sample? (1990, p. 52)

As students reflect on such questions, it is important that frequent student-teacher discussions be held to review portfolio contents and to help guide students if they have difficulty in answering the questions. At least four or five sessions should be held with each student, and monthly sessions—or even more often, if possible—would be better. During such discussions the teachers can discern *how* students are accomplishing learning tasks, rather than simply viewing end products such as those produced by most traditional approaches to assessment. This is especially important in subjects in which the process is as important as the product, such as writing.

To summarize, portfolios can serve a variety of both instructional and assessment purposes. Specifically, portfolio assessment can serve as

- an instructionally linked way to assess student performance.
- a method for portraying a broad view of a student's achievements across a broad range of content.
- a way to document adequately a student's growth in a particular content area.
- a mechanism to enable students to identify their own strengths and weaknesses.
- a method for encouraging students to participate in and take more responsibility for their own learning.
- a valuable source of information for parents and administrators.

Does Portfolio Assessment Have Any Significant Weaknesses?

Portfolios obviously have numerous strengths, and nearly everything we have written so far points to inherent advantages that can be gained from their proper use. But are there any significant drawbacks in using portfolio assessment? Of course. Everything has some drawbacks, and portfolio assessment is no different. Even though we think it well worth your serious consideration if you are not already using portfolio assessment, there are several drawbacks we should mention.

First, portfolios obviously require an additional investment of time by already overextended teachers. While we agree with Wiggins (1990) that it may be possible to free up and redistribute some portion of teachers' total time, it seems unlikely that there will be major changes in the way teachers are currently spending their time (unless there are a lot more teachers than we think who are counting milk money and engaging in other tasks that are instructionally peripheral or irrelevant). There does not seem to be an easy answer for where to find the additional time to allow teachers to engage in the more labor-intensive portfolio assessment process. Perhaps the best answer is to leave it to each teacher, hoping that the vision of the potential advantages of this technique motivates her to identify other less important activities that can be jettisoned or streamlined to make room to use portfolio assessment in at least some subject areas.

Second, Valencia (1990) has pointed out that, ironically, one of the greatest strengths of the portfolio approach—its flexibility—could well lead to its greatest flaw. This flexibility could lead to unreliability, inconsistency, and inequity in classrooms, schools, and districts (Valencia, 1990). But the difficult task of finding appropriate ways to standardize portfolio-based student assessments still resists solution. Without some acceptable standards, it will be difficult for the schools in Maine to know how to interpret (or relate to their own placement standards) the Portfolio Assessment Summary that accompanies a newly arrived student from Virginia. As Valencia notes, the development of common instructional goals throughout the school and district could reflect consistency back into the portfolio approach, and the use of the nearly continuous measurement could add reliability and consistency to individual students' total scores or grades in an area. Yet the more one moves toward standardization, the more one risks losing the rich individualization that is one of the major reasons for opting for portfolio assessment in the first place. How to solve this conundrum is one of the daunting issues that still confronts portfolio assessment.

A closely related challenge is that of deciding how portfolios should be scored or evaluated. So far, very little useful information about this topic exists in the literature about portfolios. In essence, the whole concept of a portfolio lies in trying to get away from using a single score to determine a student's grade. Most evaluation of portfolios is subjective and qualitative, which does not necessarily mean *bad* but which seldom means *good*.

Vavrus has suggested that "The key to scoring a portfolio is in setting standards relative to your goals for student learning ahead of time. Portfolios can be evaluated in terms of standards of excellence or on growth demonstrated within an individual portfolio, rather than on comparisons made among different students' work" (1990, p. 53). Good advice, but not very well operationalized. As with most writers, Vavrus developed this section the least. Beyond general hints, little helpful counsel is provided on just how to evaluate portfolios. Unfortunately, we have no sudden wisdom in this area either. Just how to score and evaluate portfolios so as to retain their individuality while simultaneously permitting adequate standardization is a puzzle that awaits solution, a solution that we hope will come from the combined efforts and cooperation of assessment specialists, teachers, and other educational practitioners.

Finally, portfolios may prove too unwieldy to serve well as a means of providing information needed for educational accountability at district, state, or national levels. For example, a recent report states that "portfolios may be useful for teachers to gauge students' writing abilities, but a new Education Department study indicates they may prove unwieldy for national assessment" (Report on Education Research, 1992a, p. 1). The difficulties encountered by assessment specialists in using portfolios in this national assessment are likely to be found at state and district levels as well.

Steps to Take in Using Portfolio Assessment

The limitations just discussed do not suggest to us that portfolios should be abandoned but rather that their limitations should be honestly acknowledged even as we use them for the benefits they can provide. Vavrus (1990) has provided a simple but useful set of steps for using portfolios. In the remainder of this section we offer adapted excerpts of her very straightforward but powerful suggestions. We will not expand at length on each point but will offer only simple examples, since much of the activity that would be carried out under several steps has been suggested earlier in this section.

Step 1: Deciding What the Portfolio Should Look Like

This step would include (1) deciding on the physical aspects of the portfolio, including both the container and the structure or organization of its contents, and (2) deciding on the conceptual structure—that is, the learning goals and their linkage to instructional activities and assessment tasks.

Step 2: Deciding What Goes into the Portfolio

Here we refer you back to our prior section on this topic, including Vavrus's guidelines. What is essential is that you select the student's portfolio samples from the variety of daily and weekly learning activities and assessment tasks that are a part of your on-going instruction-assessment cycle. And be sure to add those "reflective records" in which students review and appraise their earlier efforts and progress.

Step 3: Deciding How and When to Select Portfolio Samples

Will your selection follow natural instructional cycles, such as end of unit, semester, or year? Who will select the contents? The teacher? The student? Or—and of course this is the preferable answer- both, working collaboratively? Answers to these questions may seem trivial, but failure to reflect on them early often results in a portfolio that is merely a hodgepodge. Even when it comes to items you select directly for inclusion, you need to establish some system of dating and providing explanatory captions to help you later remember the sequence of activities and products you selected and why they were chosen instead of other items. An error as simple as forgetting to date your own observations about a student that you file in her portfolio will rob those observations of much of their usefulness later on.

Step 4: Deciding How to Evaluate Portfolios

Although admittedly a difficult task, this step is still essential. Vavrus suggests you must set some standards, perhaps developing a scale that lists a progression of performance standards a student might be expected to attain over time. Sometimes it is useful to consult other teachers nearby who are using portfolios or even to contact schools featured in national media as deeply involved in portfolio assessment to learn how they are scoring and evaluating their portfolios. Although their systems are not likely to have resolved all the challenges we discussed earlier, they are likely to be far more advanced than your pioneer efforts would be without their greater experience to guide you.

Step 5: Deciding How to Pass Portfolios On

What do you do with a portfolio at year's end? Send it home with the student, or pass it on to the student's next teacher? Perhaps the answer should be yes, for both possibilities have merit. Parents can benefit from careful review of the student's year-end portfolio. But ideally that portfolio should find its way to the student's next teacher. Perhaps a careful selection can be made of key information to be retained for use by future teachers, and the remainder sent home with the student, thus also paring down the accumulating bulk of a multiple-year portfolio to a manageable size. Or, photocopying portfolio contents or printing duplicate copies if the product is on a computer disk is a way to have the best of both worlds. However you choose to decide this issue, it is an essential step if any portfolio is to have its optimal impact.

SUGGESTED READINGS

Airasian, P. W. (1979). A perspective on the uses and misuses of standardized achievement tests. *NCME Measurement in Education, 10*(3), 1–12.

This article contains a very useful description of the nature and common uses of standardized achievement tests. Against this backdrop, common claims and criticisms concerning standardized tests are examined, common misuses of tests noted, and much of the debate concerning standardized tests labeled as unsupported emotionalism.

Kellaghan, T., Madaus, G. F., & Airasian, P. W. (1982). *The effects of standardized testing.* Boston: Kluwer-Nijhoff.

This book summarizes many criticisms and defenses of standardized testing and reports on what empirical evidence is available on the effects of standardized tests. In particular, the authors report their study of the impact of a standardized testing program on school practices, teachers, students, and parents in Ireland.

Educational Leadership (1989). Redirecting assessment. *Educational Leadership, 46*(7), pp. 2–77.

This journal issue contains 17 articles, several of them excellent, dealing with various alternative assessment strategies and instruments. Although partisan in promoting non-standardized alternatives to standardized testing, the articles collectively provide excellent examples of real-life novel assessment techniques, mixed in with thoughtful reflections about the uses of such devices in today's schools.

Vavrus, L. (1990). Put portfolios to the test. *Instructor, 100*(1), 48–53.

This article is a relatively brief but very direct and useful exposition of practical and conceptual aspects of portfolio use.

SELF-CHECK QUIZ

1. One of the major arguments in favor of alternate assessment approaches is that they
   a. are less costly and less labor intensive than traditional tests.
   b. produce more reliable and valid results than traditional tests.
   c. can measure complex, higher order abilities more readily than traditional tests.
   d. lend themselves to establishing uniform standards of student performance more readily than traditional tests.

2. What is the primary basis for the claim that standardized tests too often influence school practice?

    a. Opinions of educational commentators   c. Results of curriculum evaluations

    b. Results of experimental research   d. Opinions of teachers

3. Norm-referenced measurements are primarily used to

    a. determine whether or not the student has mastered the material.

    b. compare a student's score with the scores of other students.

    c. describe what a student has or has not learned.

    d. set minimum standards of competency for certification purposes.

4. Which of the following represents the authors' opinion of novel (nonstandardized) assessment techniques?

    a. They ought to be avoided since they are overly susceptible to prejudiced evaluators.

    b. They should be used to supplement standardized school testing problems.

    c. They provide very little information not already available through standardized testing.

    d. They will soon replace standardized tests as general indicators of educational performance.

5. One relative advantage of standardized tests over novel (nonstandardized) tests is that they are

    a. better at measuring creativity and imagination.

    b. easier to match with the school's curriculum.

    c. less labor intensive for the school to implement.

6. Which of the following is a common error in using standardized tests?

    a. Assuming that they only measure a sample of the content

    b. Believing that the observed score is different from the true score

    c. Failing to enforce minimum performance standards

    d. Making an important decision based on a single test score

    e. Questioning the norms of the test publishers

7. In selecting contents to be placed in a student's assessment portfolio, the selection should typically be made

    a. by the teacher.

    b. by the student.

    c. by the school's assessment specialist.

    d. jointly by the student and the teacher.

    e. jointly by the teacher and the school's assessment specialist.

8. What is a commonly cited misuse of criterion-referenced measurement?

    a. Comparisons of individual person's scores with national averages

    b. Establishment of arbitrary cutoff scores

    c. The use of tests that are poorly matched with the school's curriculum

    d. The lack of criterion-related evidence of validity

9. Good portfolio assessment requires that

    a. access to the portfolio contents be restricted to the teacher and other professionals assisting in scoring, interpreting, and evaluating the student's performance.

    b. the contents of the portfolio be limited to student products or student descriptions of processes.

    c. joint teacher-student reviews of portfolio's contents be conducted no more frequently than once per semester.

    d. the portfolio contain documentation of changes over time in student understandings, skills, and achievement.

10. Which of the following best describes the two sides of the current debate over testing?
 a. The parents versus the practitioners.
 b. The parents versus the testing industry.
 c. The practitioners versus other practitioners.
 d. The practitioners versus the testing industry.

SUGGESTION SHEET

If your last name starts with the letter *P*, please complete the Suggestion Sheet at the end of the book while this chapter is still fresh in your mind.

CHAPTER 16

Finding and Selecting Measures That Can Help Solve Your Educational Problems

Overview

Educational measures can provide information and insights to help solve many classroom problems. What can I do to motivate John and Mark? What is at the root of Mary's reading difficulties? Does the class need more review in long division? These and similar questions can be better answered when good test information is added to the teacher's observations and experience.

Using an educational measure to help solve an educational problem requires four initial steps: (1) Define the problem, (2) identify possible causes and define variables that relate to these causes, (3) locate available measures of these variables, and (4) evaluate and select the most appropriate measures. The step-by-step sequence provided in this chapter should help you locate measures that can be used to help solve your educational problems.

Objectives

Upon completing your study of this chapter, you should be able to

1. Explain why results from educational measures should not be used as the only source of information to solve educational problems.
2. Given an educational problem, prepare a specific problem

statement, identify possible causes and variables related to these causes, and locate relevant measures.

3. Describe the most recent *Mental Measurements Yearbook* and the *ETS Test Collection Bibliographies* and explain how each is used to locate tests.
4. Briefly describe *Current Index to Journals in Education, Resources in Education,* and *Psychological Abstracts.*
5. Given an educational problem, describe the steps in conducting a manual search to locate appropriate available tests.
6. Explain how a computer search of the educational literature is planned and conducted.
7. Given an educational problem, plan and conduct a manual search and a computer search.
8. Using the Test Evaluation Form, locate and evaluate a test related to your area of interest.

DEFINING THE PROBLEM

There are thousands of measures that can help shed light on educational problems you want to address. Before you can select those most relevant to the problem, you must define the problem in precise terms. It is often helpful to put it in the form of a question, stating it and restating it until it is clear and specific. The usual school problem contains two or three concepts. Here are a few typical questions that educational measures can help answer.

1. Four students are failing my beginning algebra class. Why?
2. I never see Mary playing with other children in the class. Why?
3. My fifth grade students' arithmetic achievement test scores were well below the district average. In what specific areas do they need remedial work?
4. Bill, a tenth grader, seems to try hard but his progress in all academic subjects is well below average. What is his level of scholastic aptitude? How does it compare with his achievement level?

Valuable information that is relevant to each of these questions can be gathered by using appropriate educational measures. Educational measures can offer information that will provide better insight or simplify decisions related to virtually any educational problem. They should rarely be the sole basis of decision making, but their additional information should be combined with other perceptions and experience to *improve* decision making.

IDENTIFYING POSSIBLE CAUSES AND RELEVANT VARIABLES

Once you have stated the problem in specific terms, you're ready to identify possible causes and the variables that can and should be measured to determine their significance. A *variable* is a characteristic or kind of performance that a test measures. Music aptitude, test anxiety, mathematics achievement, vocational interest, intelligence, typing speed, and reading comprehension are a few of the many variables measured by educational and psychological tests. They are called *variables* because student performance or test scores *vary* from person to person.

Let's consider the first example of a problem cited above: Why are the four students failing algebra? Here are several possible causes, among the many that exist.

1. Their foundation in arithmetic is weak.
2. They have poor study habits.
3. They have negative attitudes about algebra, mathematics, the teacher, or school in general.

The variables you could measure to get more information on these possible causes include arithmetic achievement, study habits or study methods, and school-related attitudes—especially attitudes towards mathematics.

The three possible causes of failure in algebra listed previously could be explored by locating appropriate tests of the identified variables, administering them to the four students, and interpreting the results. Knowledge of arithmetic could be measured by an arithmetic achievement or diagnostic test. Several tests are available in this area. Similarly, there are measures of student attitude or study habits that can provide insight into these variables. However, the process of locating potentially useful measures, selecting those that are most appropriate for your specific problem, and interpreting the results requires information and experience. (Remember that even after appropriate measures are found, it is very important to supplement information obtained by these measures by interviewing the failing students or observing their behavior during class.)

LOCATING RELEVANT MEASURES

Three general approaches to locating tests will almost always enable you to find a test appropriate for your needs. These methods include (1) the use of test bibliographies, test catalogs, and journals; (2) doing a manual search of research data bases; or (3) doing a computerized search of research data bases.

Searching Test Bibliographies, Test Catalogs, and Journals

A variety of printed sources list educational measures. Some reference books are devoted entirely to listing and reviewing available measures. Publishers also distribute catalogs describing available tests. Additionally, because many educational measures are originally developed for use in research, much information on the development and validation of measures can be found in research journals.

Different sources are likely to list different kinds of tests. Thus, a single search will usually not uncover all potentially useful measures. Nevertheless, to keep things simple, we have decided to give you a simple step-by-step strategy that will usually be sufficient for locating measures relevant to most of the educational problems and questions you are likely to encounter.

The easiest procedures and those most likely to locate the tests you need are described first. You should not stop with the first test you find that seems to be appropriate. Instead, plan to identify at least two or three alternate tests for *each* variable to be measured. Then evaluate these tests to select the best measures for your specific problem. If you are dealing with a major educational problem or have an important decision to make, one that involves testing a large number of students for instance, you may choose to complete the entire sequence so as to locate most of the available relevant measures.

Step 1: Check the Most Recent **Mental Measurements Yearbook (MMY)**

Perhaps your best source is the most recent of a series of "yearbooks" that have been published 10 times during the past 50 years. The *Tenth MMY* (Conoley & Kramer, 1989) contains reviews of 396 commercially available tests that are new or significantly revised since the publication of the *Ninth Mental Measurements Yearbook* in 1985. The *Eleventh MMY* (Kramer & Conoley, 1992) has just come off the press at the time of this writing and reflects a substantial revision of the *Tenth MMY*. Most university libraries contain the entire set of *Mental Measurements Yearbooks*. For information on older tests, check the earlier yearbooks. The *Ninth MMY*, for example, covers 1,409 commercially published tests and provides critical reviews of most. These critical reviews are very useful in helping a teacher identify the strengths and weaknesses of the measures reviewed. (If you do not find a critical review of a measure that interests you in the *MMYs*, check *Test Critiques*, or one of the other references described in the Suggested Readings section at the end of this chapter).

The *Yearbooks* include basic information about each test such as the age or grade for which it is appropriate, the variables measured, the administration time, the cost, and the name of the publisher. In the "Tests and Reviews" section of the current *Yearbook*, tests are listed in alphabetical order by title and numbered consecutively. These numbers are called the entry numbers and are used instead of page numbers in the various indices.

To locate tests in a particular subject area, refer to the "Classified Subject Index." Here you will find tests classified under a number of broad categories: Achievement, Personality, Foreign Languages, Intelligence, and so on. Under each category are the titles and entry numbers of tests available in that area of interest. After locating tests in this index, note the entry numbers, check each number in the "Tests and Reviews" section of the book, and read the reviews to decide which test seems best for your needs.

The "Score Index" lists (in alphabetical order) all the variables for which scores can be obtained for all tests included in the *Tenth MMY*, for example. If you are looking for arithmetic measures, you will find five entry numbers after the word "arithmetic" in the "Score Index." Each of these numbers identifies a test that yields a score for arithmetic. You can look up each number in the "Tests and Reviews" section and scan the information to see whether the test is appropriate. If none appears suitable, you can check the "Score Index" of the *Ninth MMY* which lists an additional twenty measures. Measures included in the "Score Index" can be quite broad (like arithmetic) or rather narrow (like misplaced modifiers).

Many of the tests you locate will measure not only the variable in which you are most interested, but several others. Some of these additional variables may also be useful in addressing your problem or question. If not, the time devoted to measuring them would be wasted so look for a test or subtest that measures *only* the variables that are relevant to the problem you are addressing, or a test divided into subtests so that you can administer only the subtests you need.

In addition to the "Classified Subject Index" and the "Score Index," the following indices are sometimes useful:

1. "Index of Acronyms": Many tests are commonly referred to in the literature by their acronyms rather than their full titles (e.g., CAT for California Achievement Tests). If you know only the acronym, this index will give the full title and entry number.
2. "Index of Titles": gives the entry number if you know the title of the test. It also indicates whether the test is new (N) or revised (R). If revised, check earlier *Yearbooks* for information on earlier versions.
3. "Index of Names": lists names of all test authors, reviewers, and authors of cited references. This is useful if you know a test author's name but not the test title.
4. "Publishers Directory and Index": gives the names and addresses of the publishers of all tests included in the *Yearbook*. You can write to publishers for their catalogs or for additional information on tests you are considering.

When reviewing test information in the *MMY*, check for answers to the following questions, and record the data for each test on the Preliminary Screening section of the Test Evaluation Form included in Figure 16.1.

1. Does the test purport to measure the variable you want to test?
2. Is the test appropriate for the age or grade level of students you want to test?
3. Can the test be administered given the time and help you have available? Be sure to note whether the test is administered to individuals or groups, and whether special training is needed for test administrators.
4. Is the cost within your budget for the number of students you want to test?
5. Is the reading level satisfactory for your students? The test catalog and the test itself must usually be checked for this information.

Figure 16.2 is a test description from the *Tenth Mental Measurements Yearbook* showing where answers to most of the above questions may be found.

Test Evaluation Form

_____

TEST NAME _____   PUBLISHER/SOURCE _____
VARIABLES MEASURED: _____

PART I: <u>Preliminary Screening</u>: Generally, a test which does not meet any one of the following criteria should be eliminated.

1. Measures the variables needed to address your problem.   Yes No

2. Publisher claims test is appropriate for students to be tested and the purposes needed. Yes No

3. Test can be administered in the time and with the resources available.   Yes No

4. Cost of using the test is within available budget (this includes scoring costs
    if scoring must be done by publisher).   Yes No

5. Reading level is satisfactory for your students.   Yes No

PART II. <u>Test Evaluation</u>: Read all of the administration instructions, read each item, and mark your answers. As you take the test, write down potential problems. If the test can be hand-scored, go through the entire scoring process and grade your answers. Then answer the following items.

1. <u>Appropriate Content</u>: Rate whether the test items match the content you want to
    measure (1 [low] to 5 [high]).   _____

2. <u>Format</u>: Rate the format, organization, and appearance of the test from 1 (poor) to
    5 (excellent).   _____

3. <u>Ease of Administration</u>: Rate the administration procedures for the test from 1
    (different/complex) to 5 (easy/straightforward).   _____

4. <u>Scoring</u>: Rate whether the instructions for scoring are logical and understandable
    (1 [poor] to 5 [excellent]).   _____

5. <u>Interpretability</u>: Rate whether the test yields information which is specific and relevant
    to your needs (1 [poor] to 5 [excellent]).   _____

6. <u>Reliability</u>: Rate whether the evidence concerning test reliability is sufficient for
    your purposes <u>and</u> is supported by specific evidence (1 [poor] to 5 [excellent]). _____

7. <u>Validity</u>: Rate whether there is evidence that the results of the test will be valid for
    the students and purposes for which you will be using it (1 [poor] to 10 [excellent]). _____

8. <u>Norms</u>: If normative comparisons are needed, rate whether appropriate norms are
    provided for students similar to yours (1 [norms absent or inadequate] to
    5 {excellent norms]).   _____

TOTAL POINTS

Add up all of the points in Part II for each test evaluated. Tests with the most points are preferred, assuming all answers to Part I were affirmative.

FIGURE 16.1 Test Evaluation Form

Grade Levels

Number of Levels

Administration Time

[156]
Iowa Tests of Educational Development™ [Eighth Edition]. Purpose: "To assess intellectual skills that are important in adult life and provide the basis for continued learning." Grades 9-10, 11-12; 1942-88; ITED™; 9 scores: Correctness and Appropriateness of Expression (Test E), Ability to Do Quantitative Thinking (Test Q), Analysis of Social Studies Materials (Test SS), Analysis of Natural Science Materials (Test NS), Ability to Interpret Literary Materials (Test L), Vocabulary (Test V), Use of Sources of Information (Test SI), Composite, Reading Total; 2 forms: X-8, Y-8; 2 levels (Grades 9-10, Level I; Grades 11-12, Level II) in each form; 1988 price data: $44.40 per 25 test booklets with one Directions for Administration (specify Form X-8 or Form Y-8 and test level); $14.55 per 50 MRC answer sheets to be scored by publisher (includes materials needed for machine scoring; specifiy Level I or Level II); $7.80 per 50 parent communications brochures entitled "ITED Scores and What They Mean"; $1.23 per Directions for Administration ('88, 13 pages); $4.50 per Teacher, Administrator, and Counselor Manual ('88, 87 pages); $5.46 per Norms Booklet ('88, 111 pages); 250 (280) minutes; prepared under the direction of Leonard S. Feldt, Robert A. Forsyth, and Stephanie D. Alnot with the assistance of Timothy N. Ansley and Gayle B. Bray; The Riverside Publishing Co."

Purpose

Scores

Number of Forms

Cost

Norms

FIGURE 16.2 Test Description from *Tenth MMY*[a]

[a] Test coverage in *Tenth MMY* also includes test references and a review, and a listing of reviews in earlier editions of the test.

APPLICATION PROBLEM #1

Check the *Ninth MMY* and locate a group-administered test of attitudes toward school that can be used in testing sixth grade students. Write down entry numbers of appropriate tests. Now, check the *Tenth MMY*; is there an appropriate measure in this yearbook?

In most cases, the most recent two or three volumes of the *MMY* are the only test reference books you will need to consult for commercially published measures. They describe more published measures than other test reference books and usually provide more information about them. Unfortunately, they cover only commercially published tests. Having been published in 1989, the *Tenth MMY* is fairly current, and the *Eleventh MMY* (Kramer & Conoley, 1992) is just off the press. In the past, *MMY* information became increasingly out of date because volumes were published rather infrequently. Current *MMY* publishing schedules, however, aim at publishing "yearbooks" every other year, with updates being issued in the alternating years.

Many other test reference books describe measures in a specific area such as mental health, or for particular ages such as early childhood. Some of these are described in the suggested readings for this chapter. Before continuing, you should take time to scan these annotations and note any sources that are especially relevant to your own educational interests.

Step 2: Check ETS Test Collection Bibliographies

If you fail to locate the measures you need in the most recent two or three *MMYs*, the next step is to search the *Test Collection Bibliographies* published by the Educational Testing Service (ETS). There are 200 of these bibliographies in print. The following is a current list of the major areas covered in the Test Collection Bibliographies. Several examples are given for each area.

Achievement
   Fine Arts and Foreign Language
   Language Arts
   Mathematics
   Other School Subjects
   Reading
   Science
   Social Studies
   Miscellaneous Achievement Tests

Aptitude (e.g., Creativity, Intelligence, Memory, Reasoning)
Attitudes and Interests (e.g., Academic Interest, Attitudes toward Mathematics, Racial Attitudes)
Personality (e.g., Depression, Leadership, Projective Measures, Self-concept)
Sensory Motor (e.g., Auditory Skills, Sensory-motor Abilities, Visual Perception)
Special Populations (e.g., American Indians, Mentally Retarded, Spanish Speakers)
Vocational/Occupational (e.g., Business Skills, Professional Occupations, Vocational Interests)
Miscellaneous (e.g., Classroom Interaction, Environments, Piagetian Measures, Social Skills)

The ETS collection constitutes, by far, the most comprehensive compilation available, including information on over 11,000 measures. These bibliographies, which cover both published and unpublished tests, are frequently updated, thus overcoming the main limitations of the *MMYs*. However, they provide much less information than the *Yearbook*—usually including simply the name of the test, author, date the test was published, age or grade levels for which the test is appropriate, name and address of the publisher or developer, and a brief description of the variables the test is designed to measure. For experimental measures having no commercial publisher, the author is frequently listed as the publisher. Many such measures, which are not available from commercial publishers, can be obtained from ETS on microfiche,[1] which may be purchased for individual measures or in sets of fifty. Since many universities have purchased these sets, you should check with the reference librarians of universities in your area before purchasing them yourself.

To use the *Bibliographies* to locate a measure, do the following:

1. Check the list of *Test Collection Bibliographies* and decide which are most likely to list tests covering the variables you want to measure.
2. See if the *Test Collection Bibliographies* you need are available in any of the reference libraries in your vicinity. University departments of psychology and testing-counseling centers may also have these on file. If they are not locally available, order the bibliographies you need from ETS Test Collection, Educational Testing Service, Princeton, N.J. 08541-0001.
3. Read the selected bibliographies and identify measures that fit your needs. Fill out Part 1 (Preliminary Screening) of the Test Evaluation Form (Figure 16.1) for any measures that appear to meet your needs.
4. Obtain single copies of the measures you have identified from ETS or the test publishers.

If you have located the instruments you need, you are ready to evaluate the measures and make your final selection—and you can skip the following Steps 3 and 4. If you have not yet located an appropriate measure, you should check the other sources of test information as described in Steps 3 and 4.

Step 3: Search the Test Catalog File

Most commercial test publishers have catalogs describing the measures they offer. Frequent users of educational tests, such as counselors and psychologists, usually maintain a file of current test catalogs. If you want to use commercially published tests and cannot locate the measures you need in the most recent *MMYs,* or the *ETS Test Collection Bibliographies,* contact the testing center, department of psychology, or the library at your university to see if such a test catalog file is available.

The main advantage of the publishers' catalogs over the *Mental Measurement Yearbooks* and the *ETS Bibliographies* is that they are slightly more current, and are usually supplied to educators and psychologists free of charge. However, the

---

[1] A microfiche is a small sheet of film which contains up to 96 pages. Most libraries have readers that project the microfiche and enlarge each page to readable size.

Test Collection Bibliographies are nearly as current as publishers' catalogs and list both commercially published and unpublished measures.

Step 4: Search the Professional Journals

Many new measures developed for use in educational research are first reported in psychology and education journals. Thus, if you are trying to locate tests that measure a variable that has been a recent focus of educational research, professional journals may offer information on measures not yet listed elsewhere. Furthermore, since sources such as the *Bibliographies* do not list every new measure, professional journals should be searched to ensure more thorough coverage of available measures.

In locating articles or other publications related to any topic in education, the student must be familiar with relevant preliminary sources. These consist of periodical indexes, or abstracts that describe articles published in other relevant journals. In education, the most useful preliminary sources are the *Current Index to Journals in Education (CIJE)* and *Resources in Education (RIE)* published by the Educational Resources Information Center (ERIC). Since many new tests are reported in psychology journals, *Psychological Abstracts*, the principal preliminary source in that discipline, is also useful. CIJE currently indexes articles from nearly 800 journals, while *Psychological Abstracts* publishes abstracts of articles from over 850 journals, some of which overlap with CIJE. RIE publishes abstracts of other educational documents, such as research reports, papers read at professional meetings, and progress reports of ongoing studies.

Conducting a Manual Search

Tests may be located in journals through either a manual search or a computer search. Let us first outline the seven steps in conducting a manual search.

Step 1: Specify What Is to be Measured

First, list the specific variable you want to measure. Use the name commonly found in educational literature—such as achievement motivation, test anxiety, or intelligence. For example, many educational researchers have investigated how *locus of control* influences students' behavior. *Locus of control* refers to the individual's perception about whether such events as success or failure in school are determined internally (i.e., as a result of one's own behavior), or externally (i.e., by luck, fate, or other forces). Suppose you wanted to measure the locus of control of learning disabled students who had been mainstreamed into your ninth-grade homeroom. Because this area of investigation is progressing rapidly, it would be wise to search the professional journals for the most recent available information.

Step 2: Check the **Thesaurus of ERIC Descriptors**

Begin this step by checking the name of your variable in the latest edition of the *Thesaurus of ERIC Descriptors.* You can usually find this source at the reference desk of your library. Its purpose is to provide a standard set of terms that can be used to classify and describe the contents of educational publications. The terms listed in the *Thesaurus* are used to describe all the publications indexed in CIJE and RIE. Every publication indexed in these preliminary sources is read by a specialist who selects the descriptors that best describe its contents. These descriptors are then listed in RIE and CIJE, along with bibliographical data and brief abstracts of content. Figure 16.3 gives a typical reference from CIJE, with the various parts of the citation labeled to indicate what information each conveys. If your variable does not appear as a descriptor, try to locate a synonymous descriptor in the *Thesaurus*. A check of the current *Thesaurus* shows that *locus of control* is a descriptor, but if it were not, you should read about this concept in one or two general psychology textbooks, watching for related terms you could use, such as *attribution theory*.

FIGURE 16.3   Information about Each Article Included in *CIJE* Main Entry Section (CIJE. Feb. 1986, page 70)

Accession No.   EJ 326 040   TM 510 892   Clearinghouse No.

Article Title ——— The Reliability and Validity of Ideational Originality in the Divergent Thinking of Academically Gifted and Nongifted Children.

Authors ——— Runco, Mark A.; Albert, Robert S., *Educational and Psychological* ——— Journal Title *Measurement*: v45 n3 p483-501 ——— Pages

Publication Date ——— Aut 1985 ——— Issue Number ——— Volume Number

Major and Minor ——— Descriptors: *Academically Gifted; Descriptors   *Creativity Tests; Creative (major descriptors   Thinking; Divergent Thinking; are starred)   Elementary Education; Elementary School Students; Creativity; *Test Reliability; *Test Validity

Major and Minor ——— Identifiers: Teacher Indicator of Identifiers   Potential; Creative Activities (major identifiers   Checklist; Wallach and Kogan are starred)   Creativity Test Battery; Teachers Evaluation of Students Creativity; California Achievement Tests

Partial correlation procedures were ——— Descriptive Note used to compare the reliability of ideational creativity in 225 academically gifted and nongifted fifth to eighth grade children. The divergent thinking interitem and intertest correlations of the gifted children were significantly larger than the nongifted. Ideational originality was reliable only in the nonverbal tests. (Author/-GDC) ——— Annotator's Initials

***Step 3: Locate Descriptors in the* Current Index to Journals in Education**

An "EJ number" is assigned to each entry in CIJE. After you have selected descriptor terms for your variable in the subject index of the most recent volume of *Current Index to Journals in Education (CIJE),* write down the EJ numbers for articles listed under the descriptors for your variable. For example, if you look up *locus of control* in the subject index of the July–December 1985 volume of CIJE, you will find 22 references listed. Several are likely relevant to your problem and probably use *locus of control* measures you should consider. These include: EJ 316 174, EJ 317 654, EJ 318 457, EJ 321 942.

Step 4: Examine Abstracts in CIJE

Turn to each EJ number in the Main Entry Section of *CIJE,* where you will find bibliographical data, pertinent descriptors, and a brief abstract of the article. The article title and abstract often provide enough information to let you decide whether it is relevant to your variable. When we check the Main Entry Section for the EJ numbers related to *locus of control* noted in Step 3, we find that EJ 316 174 and EJ 318 457 appear most closely related to your problem. Here is the main entry data for these two articles:

EJ   316   174
TM510493
Causal Attributions of Learning Disabled Children: Individual Differences and Their Implications for Persistence. Licht, Barbara G., et al.
Journal of Educational Psychology; v77 n2 p108–16 Apr 1985 (Reprint: UMI)
Descriptors: Elementary Education; *Attribution Theory; *Locus of Control; *Learning Disabilities; Sex Differences; Reading Achievement; Persistence; Academic Failure; *Individual Differences; Individual Testing; Comparative Analysis
Identifiers: Intellectual Achievement Responsibility; Effort

This study compared the causal attribution by sex for academic failures of 38 learning disabled and 38 nondisabled elementary school students. The relationship between different attributional tendencies and a reading persistence task were also examined. (BS)

EJ   318   457
EC   172   663
Self-Concepts, Locus of Control and Performance Expectations of Learning Disabled Children. Rogers, H.; Saklofski, D. H. Journal of Learning Disabilities: v18 n5 p273–78 May 1985
Descriptors: *Learning Disabilities; *Self Concept; *Locus of Control; *Expectation; Elementary Education

Compared to 45 normally achieving students, 45 learning disabled six- to 12-year-olds had lower self-concepts, more external locus of control orientations, and lower performance expectations. Children new to the resource room had higher expectations for future success than Ss with experience in the resource room. (CL)

If an article appears promising, record the bibliographical data (i.e., author, title, name of periodical and the year, volume and pages where the article appears). Most people record information for each article on a separate three by five note-card, and keep cards in alphabetical order by the last name of the first author.

Step 5: Examine Articles that Seem Most Relevant

In the periodicals section of your library, locate each of the articles you have entered on notecards and scan it to see if a measure of your variable is described. In scanning, first read the abstract (if there is one). Then read the section headed "Method or Procedures," which usually gives a description of the measures used.

APPLICATION PROBLEM #2

Suppose you have been asked by the district superintendent to locate a measure that can be used to identify teachers who appear susceptible to teacher burnout, so they can be given counseling and other help.

1. Write down the definition of *teacher burnout* given in the *Thesaurus* (SN).
2. List all EJ numbers in the "Subject Index" of the July–December 1985 volume of *CIJE* under *teacher burnout*.
3. Check each EJ number in the Main Entry section of this volume, and copy bibliographical data for one article that appears to deal with a test of teacher burnout onto a three-by-five notecard.
4. Locate this article, scan it, and (a) name one test of teacher burnout described by the article, (b) list the variables measured by the test, and give the reliability coefficient for each variable, and (c) list bibliographic data for a reference by the authors of the measure.

If you locate a measure you believe may meet your needs, read the entire article and note any relevant information following the format given in the Test Evaluation Form (see Figure 16.1). Check the list of references at the end of the article to see if there are other articles you should locate. If so, make up a bibliography card for each. For example, the article by Licht et al. (1985) (EJ 316 174) that we located in our search for locus of control tests describes an experimental measure, the *EAX scale*, and reports reliability and validity data. This measure appears to meet the needs cited in our example. Another relevant measure, the IAR (Intellectual Achievement Responsibility Scale) is also described. Note that this scale is listed as an identifier in the CIJE Main Entry for the article. The article also lists 38 references, several of which are relevant to our problem.

Only a few articles include a copy of the test; usually, it is necessary to write to the author and request a copy. If you do so, be sure to explain the purpose for which you will be using the test and ask for a test key and other relevant information. Many journals list the author's address, but if not, check the membership directories of the American Educational Research Association or the American Psychological Association. If these directories are not available in your library, contact professors in education and psychology; many are members of these professional organizations and have copies of the membership directories.

Step 6: If Necessary, Check Earlier CIJE Volumes

If your search of the most recent volume of CIJE fails to locate a suitable test, repeat Steps 3 through 6 using the next most recent volume. It is sometimes necessary to check several years of CIJE before locating a test that meets your needs.

Step 7: Repeat the Process with Psychological Abstracts

Many educational topics, such as learning, attitudes toward teachers, and assessment of emotionally disturbed children, are also considered part of psychology. If your search of CIJE fails to produce a suitable measure, check in the *Thesaurus of Psychological Index Terms*, which contains the terms used to classify articles in *Psychological Abstracts*. After you have located the appropriate term(s), check the selected terms in the subject index of the most recent volume of *Psychological Abstracts* for sources related to your variable. A very brief description of each article will be given in the subject index, along with a number. Another volume of *Psychological Abstracts* will contain the abstracts. Look up each number taken from the index volume, read the abstract, and decide whether the article should be checked further. The relatively detailed abstracts in *Psychological Abstracts* usually make this decision simple. Review the selected articles, following the procedure described in Steps 5 and 6. See Figure 16.4 for a typical entry from *Psychological Abstracts*. Notice that this abstract contains much more information on the Licht et al. (1985) article than the CIJE abstract.

APPLICATION PROBLEM #3

Check the *Thesaurus of Psychological Index Terms* for *teacher burnout*. (1) Is this term included in the *Thesaurus?* (2) If not, what term could you use? (3) How would you locate articles in *Psychological Abstracts* that relate to teacher burnout? (4) Use *Psychological Abstracts*, vol. 71 (1984) Subject Index numbers 4, 5, 6 (April, May, June 1986) and list the abstract numbers of the first four abstracts that appear related to teachers' occupational stress or burnout. (5) Look up these abstracts, read them, and copy the bibliographic data for the first abstract.

Conducting a Computer Search

Computer searches can save a great deal of time if they are done correctly. Most universities and many state departments of education have terminals and conduct

20413.   Licht, Barbara G. et al. (Florida State U. Tallahassee).   Causal attributions of learning disabled children: Individual differences and their implications for persistence. *Journal of Educational Psychology*, 1985(Apr), Vol 77(2), 208-216.   --It has been shown that learning disabled (LD) children are likely to develop a maladaptive pattern of causal attributions.   However, it is unclear whether LD children are more likely to differ from their peers in terms of a greater tendency to attribute their difficulties to insufficient ability or in terms of a greater tendency to blame external factors. The authors investigated this issue in 24 LD boys and 14 LD girls in Grades 3-5 and in 38 age-, sex-, race-, and IQ-matched normal controls. Ss were asked to complete scales assessing attributions for academic difficulties: 2 wks later, Ss were presented with a reading task for which persistence was measured. It was found that LD girls were significantly more likely than nondisabled girls to attribute their difficulties to insufficient ability, but girls did not differ in their tendency to attribute their difficulties to external factors. In contrast, LD boys were significantly more likely than nondisabled boys to attribute their difficulties to external factors, but they did not differ from nondisabled boys in their tendency to attribute their difficulties to insufficient ability. Although the tendency to blame one's ability was negatively related to reading task persistence, the tendency to attribute one's difficulties to external factors did not show this negative relation. (38 ref) ---*Journal abstract*

Psychological Abstracts, 1985, 72:2253.

FIGURE 16.4 Sample Entry from *Psychological Abstracts*
SOURCE: *Psychological Abstracts*. 1985, 72:2253.

searches for public school teachers and administrators. The cost of searching the ERIC or PsycINF0 (the data base for *Psychological Abstracts*) data bases for measures of a given variable is usually very reasonable.

A computer search also gives you more complete coverage than you are likely to get from any manual search. While only one descriptor or test variable can be searched at a time using a manual search, the computer can search articles fitting any combination of descriptors—simultaneously. Suppose you want to locate a test that measured bilingual students' attitudes toward school. In a manual search, you would need to focus on one variable at a time—say school attitude—and check each abstract or article to see whether an attitude test were described and if so, whether it was suitable for use with bilingual students. In a computer search, however, you could search by multiple descriptors—say, *attitude test* and *school attitude* and *bilingual students*. The *And* connectors would tell the computer you only wanted references containing *all three descriptors*. This cross referencing spares the tedium of checking many irrelevant articles. In addition, the computer would supply a printout giving bibliographical data, an abstract, and other useful information for each article selected.

Here are the five steps for planning and conducting a computer search using the ERIC data base. Although other computerized data bases exist, the procedures are usually very similar.

Step 1: Identify the Specific Variable to be Measured

First, list the specific variable you want to measure and the level (i.e., preschool, primary, elementary, secondary, etc.) of students to be tested. If the students you plan to test belong to any special group (such as children with learning disabilities), list a term designating the group as well. Suppose, for example, you want to locate a test to diagnose the reading achievement of first grade pupils with learning disabilities. You might list *reading tests, reading diagnosis, first-grade*, and *learning disabilities*. Then, using the *Thesaurus,* find the correct descriptors for your test variable, student level, and special student group (if any). Be sure to copy the descriptors *exactly* as they appear in the *Thesaurus*. If you misspell a descriptor or even add an *s*, the computer will reply that it has no references for that descriptor; it can only work with the information *you* provide. It is faster and more thorough than you but *you* still have to do the thinking. In our example, the ERIC descriptors we selected are *reading tests, reading diagnosis, primary education*, and *learning disabilities*.

Step 2: Access the Computer Terminal Used for Searches

Usually it is best to discuss your search with the person who operates the computer search terminal in your library. This terminal is used to communicate with a computer located elsewhere (usually in another state) in which many scientific data-bases are stored.[2] Your search should be carefully planned before you are *on line,* that is, connected to that computer. Once you are connected, you are incurring long distance telephone charges as well as charges for computer time.

Usually, the operator enters your descriptors into the computer and the computer tells you how many references the ERIC data base has for each descriptor. In our example, the four descriptors entered were *reading tests, reading diagnosis, primary education*, and *learning disabilities*. We find that in the ERIC data base there are 1,997 references with the descriptor *reading tests*; 1,344 for *reading diagnosis*; 6,417 for *learning disabilities*; and 7,045 for *primary education*. Since new references are added to the ERIC data base each month, a repeat of this search would find more references than reported here.

Step 3: Adjust Your Search Parameters to Meet Your Needs

Usually it is best to begin by requesting information about all of the references in the database that contain all the descriptors you want. For example, the operator

---

[2] Some libraries now have CD ROM technology that allow on-line searches of data bases without being connected with an off-site computer.

may ask the computer to locate references using these four descriptors: *reading tests* <u>and</u> *reading diagnosis* <u>and</u> *learning disabilities* <u>and</u> *primary education*. Recall that the *and* connectors tell the computer to select only references that contain all of the descriptors joined by *and*. Only one reference has all four descriptors. However, it does appear to be exactly on target. Figure 16.5 shows the reference as printed out by the computer. Note that this reference has ED in front of its identification number. This means it is a reference from *Resources in Education*. Nearly all references from RIE are available on microfiche in most university libraries.

If we wanted more references, we could instruct the computer to locate sources that contained the descriptors (*reading tests* <u>or</u> *reading diagnosis*) <u>and</u> *learning disabilities* <u>and</u> *primary education*. This search produced eleven references, of which five appeared to be closely related to our problem. Using the *or* connector tells the computer that you want all references that contain *either* the descriptor *reading tests* or the descriptor *reading diagnosis*. Using *and* connectors tends to narrow the search and produce fewer references; while using *or* connectors tends to broaden the search and produce more references.

Step 4: Print Information about References that Seem Most Appropriate

If the number of references found in Step 3 is between 10 and 50, the operator should instruct the computer to print out the complete data (i.e., bibliographical

FIGURE 16.5 Sample Reference from a Computer Search of the ERIC Data Base

ED108405 EC072995
  Diagnostic Strategies in Reading for Primary Children with Special Needs.
  London, Maryland; Sismond, Mary V.
  Arlington County Public Schools, VA
  Jan 1975 37p.
  Sponsoring Agency: Office of Education (DHEW), Washington, D.C.; Right to Read Program
  Grant No.: 0EG-0-73-6130
  EDRS Price - MF-1/PC02 Plus Postage.
  Document Type: CLASSROOM MATERIAL (050)
  Journal Announcement: RIENOV75

  The teacher handbook is intended to provide a complete set of simple diagnostic testing materials in reading for children in kindergarten through third grade. Tests focus on such skill areas as visual discrimination and auditory memory. Included are lists of materials and strategies to be used after the students have been tested and their special needs determined. Also provided are suggestions on observations of behavior, classroom management and tutoring. A checklist for the observation of student behaviors and learning processes is presented along with a group screening form for recording results during the active testing process. It is recommended that folders be prepared for individual children and a prescription format is given. (GW)

  Descriptors: Exceptional Child Education; Kindergarten; Learning Disabilities, Primary Education; *Reading Diagnosis; *Reading Difficulty; *Reading Tests; *Teaching Guides.

data, descriptors, and abstract) for each reference.[3] The printed information can be mailed, or you can have the data printed out on the spot. Printing data at the computer is more expensive, however, since additional long distance telephone time is being used. If Step 3 yields more than 50 references, you might instruct the computer to print and mail only the most recent fifty which will usually be sufficient for locating two or three recent measures.

If the number of references found in Step 3 is fewer than 10, you may find that nothing of what is available is precisely on target for your problem. In this case, you might have the few references that have been located printed out on the terminal, reading them quickly as they are being printed. If they do not appear promising, it may be that you are searching too narrow a field. Broaden it. The easiest way to do this is to either drop one of the descriptors included in your initial plan or substitute a broader descriptor. For example, if we drop *primary education* from our search or use *elementary education* instead, we could get *more* references—but they would cover all grade levels and many might not be directly relevant to first grade reading. However, making some careful compromises is generally preferable to searching vainly for references that do not exist.

You can also ask the computer to search for variables that are more or less synonymous with yours. For example, let us say you are interested in locating measures of *Self-concept*. You notice in the *Thesaurus* that *self-esteem* and *self-congruence* are also listed as descriptors. These terms can all be searched using *or* connectors. In other words, the operator can instruct the computer to identify any articles with the descriptor *self-concept* or *self-esteem* or *self-congruence*.

Step 5: For "Difficult-to-Find" Items, Consider a Proximity Search

If you want to locate an article that describes a test that measures a recently discovered or researched variable, you frequently will find there are no appropriate terms for that variable listed in the *Thesaurus*. For example, the tenth edition of the *Thesaurus* does not list *comparable worth* as a descriptor because this concept is fairly new in educational literature. To locate measures of new variables such as *comparable worth*, the computer can conduct a *proximity search*, scanning all the words in its memory to see if the words *comparable worth* are present. If the words are present in a given article, there is a good chance that article deals with the variable you want to measure. Additions and changes to the ERIC controlled vocabulary since the last edition of the *Thesaurus* are listed in each number of RIE and CIJE. These should be checked if you cannot find a descriptor that fits your problem.

EVALUATING AND SELECTING MEASURES

Having located several measures that appear appropriate, you must now decide which is best for your specific needs. You have already begun this process in one

---

[3] These numbers are arbitrary but usually about right; you may of course, change them to fit your own needs.

sense, having carried out a preliminary screening. For the remaining measures, you should enter descriptive information at the top of the Test Evaluation Form and check the five items under *preliminary screening*. One form should be prepared for each measure you plan to evaluate (see Figure 16.1).

Table 16.1 summarizes the kinds of information needed to evaluate a test and the sources that are most likely to contain this information. Note that the *Mental Measurements Yearbooks* are the best sources for several kinds of data. In contrast, test manuals are often not available locally and must be purchased from test publishers. Professional journals are readily available in most university libraries, but are far more tedious and time-consuming to search than the latest *MMY*.

The column labeled "Other Sources" in Table 16.1 lists, in order of their probable value, the alternatives for helping to evaluate a test. Thus, if a test is not reviewed in the *MMYs*, other test reference books are likely to be the most productive source of critical reviews, followed by professional journals. Of course, Table 16.1 provides only general guidelines. Which sources really prove most useful depends on whether a given test is commercially published or unpublished, as well as on many other factors. Many of the types of data listed in Table 16.1 are self-explanatory, based on the previous chapters. However, some brief comments about validity, reliability, normative data, test administration, scoring, clarity of test content, and costs may be helpful here in the context of how they relate to evaluating the appropriateness of a particular test.

Test Validity

The most important characteristic of any test is the validity of the scores it produces. When evaluating a test, remember that content validity evidence is usually considered the most important for content-related tests such as achievement measures. Criterion-related validity evidence is most important for tests, such as aptitude tests, that attempt to estimate a criterion variable or predict future performance. The most useful source of information on the validity of published tests (except for content validity, which requires a match between test content and local curriculum content) is the *MMY*—provided the measure you are evaluating is reviewed in that source. Its critical reviews are useful and insightful, and should be read very carefully.

If the test you are considering is not reviewed in *MMYs*, the test manual is often a useful source—although this manual is usually written by the test author and it may be somewhat biased. Professional journal articles are also a useful source, but again, accept with caution articles written by the test developer.

Validity, especially criterion-related validity, is difficult to establish. As a result, many tests wind up being used even though there is little or no evidence to demonstrate that the resulting scores are valid. Absence of evidence does not mean that test scores are invalid. It may mean that the necessary research has not been done to determine how valid they are. Thus, while it is best to select tests for which validity has been demonstrated, one must sometimes use tests supported by little evidence of validity if they appear to be the best available.

TABLE 16.1 Sources of Information on Educational Tests

Kind of Data	Best Source	Other Sources
Variables or constructs measured	*Mental Measurements Yearbook*	Test Manual, professional journals, *ETS Test Collection Bibliographies*
Age or grade levels at which test can be used	*Mental Measurements Yearbook*	Test reference books other than *MMY*, publishers' catalog, test manual, *ETS Test Collection Bibliographies*
Cost	Publishers' catalogs	*Mental Measurements Yearbook*, test reference books other than *MMY*
Availability of alternate forms	Test manual	Publishers' catalogs, *Mental Measurements Yearbook*, test reference books other than *MMY*
Testing time	*Mental Measurements Yearbook*	Publishers' catalog, test manual
Validity	*Mental Measurements Yearbook*	Test manual, test reference books other than *MMY*, professional jounrals, the test itself
Reliability	Test manual	*Mental Measurements Yearbook*, professional journals, test reference books other than *MMY*
Critical reviews of test	*Mental Measurements Yearbook*	Test reference books other than *MMY*, professional journals
Normative data and statistical data such as $\overline{X}$ and SD	Test manual	
Administration and scoring procedures	Test manual	
Data on interpretation	Test manual	Professional journals, *Mental Measurements Yearbook*
Reading level	The test itself	*Mental Measurements Yearbook*, test manual
Clarity and relevance of content	The test itself	*Mental Measurements Yearbook*, professional journals
References to published sources related to the test	Professional journals	*Mental Measurements Yearbook*, test reference books other than *MMY*, test manual

Test reviews can be very useful in helping you evaluate data on validity. They are usually written by experts in the field, whose judgments are likely to be more sophisticated than those of an untrained critic. Reviews also discuss reliability and point out problems or difficulties in interpretation, administration, or scoring.

Test Reliability

In contrast to validity, test reliability is easy to determine. Reliability coefficients are reported in most test reference books and the test manual itself. If reliability data are not reported in the test manual, it may be assumed that it is low because it is an easy matter to compute some form of reliability. All of the methods for computing test reliability produce reliability coefficients that are reasonably comparable. It is desirable to have reports of reliability from several different studies, because such information helps you estimate the range over which reliability coefficients occur. Also, multiple studies increase the likelihood that students in one study will be similar to the students you plan to test—thus giving you a basis for predicting the approximate reliability level *you* can expect.

Keep in mind that tests with low reliability have large measurement errors and are thus of little value for diagnosis or assessment of individual students. Different kinds of tests differ in their typical reliability levels. For example, good standardized achievement tests usually have reliability coefficients ranging from .88 to .95. On the other hand, some of the best self-report personality inventories have reliabilities as low as .60.

Normative Data

Normative data provides a basis for comparing the performance of your students with that of the samples of students who were tested in developing the test norms. Although an increasing number of criterion-referenced tests are becoming available, most commercially published tests are norm-referenced and provide tables of norms to simplify test score interpretation.

In evaluating normative data, you should consider how appropriate the norms are for your students and for the specific question you are trying to answer. You may also be interested in norms obtained from samples of important national populations, such as "all fifth grade students in U.S. public elementary schools." For such samples to be truly representative of a national population, they must include students from different geographical areas, different socioeconomic levels, and different kinds of communities (e.g., rural, small city, large city).

In addition to the composition of the norm group, the size of the sample should be considered. Other things being equal, the larger the norm sample, the more accurately it represents the population from which it was selected.

Administration and Scoring

When evaluating a test, carefully review the procedures described in the test manual for administering and scoring. The administration instructions should be clear and detailed. For many measures, these procedures include

1. instruction on how to prepare for giving the test.
2. materials needed.
3. verbatim guidelines on what to say.
4. suggestions for responding to student questions.

Scoring instructions usually include instructions or procedures for

1. checking answer sheets for omissions and errors.
2. using the key (if the test is to be handscored).
3. dealing with unclear answers.
4. arriving at a raw score.
5. converting the raw score to some form of standard score, such as grade placement score, percentile score, or T-score.

In reviewing the administration and scoring instructions, consider carefully the level of objectivity. *Objectivity* is the degree to which the administration and scoring are independent of the persons doing these tasks. When the instructions are incomplete or unclear, or when inferences must be drawn or judgments made about the administration or scoring, then the procedures become less objective and the chance of error increases.

Some measures require special training for proper administration and scoring. Information on this training is usually given in the test manual, and may also be discussed in test reviews. If test administration or scoring requires training that you have not had and cannot readily obtain, you should look for another measure that you are qualified to administer, score, and interpret. Specific information on the *interpretation* of test scores should also be given in the test manual. These interpretation instructions are also discussed in test reviews.

Read interpretation instructions *very carefully* when evaluating a test. Are they clear and specific? Do they deal with those aspects of your problem or question that you want to explore? Does interpretation require special training or qualifications that you do not have and cannot readily obtain?

Many test manuals also report information on reading level. This is also discussed in many critical reviews. A good way to determine whether the reading level is acceptable for your students is to review the test and, if in doubt, administer it to a few students who are similar to those you plan to test. If the reading level is too high, you may well be measuring reading skills instead of the variable you want to measure. This is ample justification for rejecting a test, even if it appears to meet your needs in other respects. Alternatively, if your students are likely to have trouble with only a few words, and if an alternate measure is not available, you may choose to explain those words before administering the test. Remember, however, that such a procedure will probably change some students' scores and place in doubt the degree to which the test norms can be applied.

Clarity of Test Content

Clarity is best evaluated by studying the test itself and it can usually be considered at the same time you appraise the reading level. Here are some questions to ask in judging clarity:

1. Is the test organized in such a way that students can move quickly and easily from question to question, and section to section?
2. Are the questions written in clear, simple language, avoiding trick questions and complex sentences?
3. Are language or illustrations modern, timely, and recognizably familiar?
4. Is it clear what each question is asking for and precisely how students should respond?

You can learn a great deal about any test by administering it to yourself. Even if you are teaching first grade, the process of placing yourself in the role of a child and trying to see the test as he might see it will give you some valuable insights.

Cost of the Test

One important test selection criterion often not considered is that of cost. Anderson and her colleagues (1980) identify four categories of costs that comprise the actual cost of testing: (1) developmental costs, (2) test administration cost, (3) test scoring costs, and (4) costs of interpreting and disseminating test scores.

Test development costs
- Time required to determine the purpose of testing and the type of test needed
- Time to locate and review available tests
- Costs of purchasing test materials (booklets, answer sheets, manuals, etc.)
- Costs involved in developing tests (e.g., item writing, test validation)

Test administration costs
- Planning the test administration
- Training test administrators
- Coordinating distribution of materials
- Administering the test
- Collecting test results

Test scoring costs
- Time required to develop scoring procedures
- Time to train judges
- Time required to score items
- Costs associated with computer scoring or optical scanning

Costs of interpreting and disseminating scores
- Organizing and interpreting test scores
- Disseminating scores to decision makers

SUGGESTED READINGS

Borich, G. D., & Madden, S. K. (1977). *Evaluating classroom instruction—A sourcebook of instruments*. Reading, MA: Addison-Wesley.

This reference gives a comprehensive coverage of instruments used in teacher behavior research from 1954 through 1975. Measures are classified into nine categories according to who supplies information about whom. All the information normally used by a reviewer to make an evaluation is given; for example, a description of the measure, data on validity and reliability, and data on administration and scoring. Author and title indexes are provided for use in locating a specific measure you wish to evaluate.

Chun, K., Cobb, S., & French, J. R. P., Jr. (1975). *Measures for psychological assessment*. Ann Arbor, MI: Survey Research Center.

Many measures developed as part of research projects are published or referred to in professional journals. Tests of this sort are usually not available from regular test publishers and often are not covered in the *Mental Measurements Yearbooks*. Such measures can be located in the *ETS Test Collection Bibliographies*. However, *Measures for Psychological Assessment* can also be of help in locating unpublished measures and information about them. This book contains information on all measures located in a search of *Psychological Abstracts* plus several other important journals for the period 1960 to 1971. Over 3,000 measures are listed.

Keyser, D. J., & Sweetland, R. C. (1984–1988). *Test critiques*. Kansas City, MO: Test Corporation of America.

This seven-volume work dating from 1984 to 1988 contains critiques of tests selected by specialists in the given areas, and therefore the more widely used measures are usually reviewed. Each review includes five sections: a detailed description of the measure; a Practical Application/Uses section, which provides information on administration, scoring, and interpretation; a section on technical aspects, which is concerned primarily with reliability and validity; an overall critique, which is very useful in helping the potential user evaluate the test; and a brief list of references dealing with the measure and related topics. On average, seven to eight pages are devoted to each measure. Additional volumes are published periodically. In using these volumes, the best approach is to check the most recent volume, which will contain cumulative indexes covering all volumes. These volumes, along with the *Mental Measurements Yearbooks* are the best sources of evaluation information on available tests. The main advantage of *Test Critiques* is the thoroughness of the information provided for each measure. Its main limitation is the small number of measures covered thus far. As new volumes become available, this limitation will be largely overcome.

Levy, P., & Goldstein, H. (1984). *Tests in education—A book of critical reviews*. New York: Academic Press.

The measures reviewed in this reference are, for the most part, British in origin, although a few measures developed in the U.S. are reviewed. Perhaps the book is most useful in cases where a suitable measure cannot be located through American sources. The test reviews are organized under seven broad content areas.

Sweetland, R. C., & Keyser, D. J. (1987). *Tests—A comprehensive reference for assessments in psychology, education, and business* (2d ed.). Kansas City, MO: Test Corporation of America.

This reference provides information on more than 3,000 tests. Information on each test includes a description, statement of purpose, administration time, grade range, scoring information, cost, and publisher. Tests are listed under three major headings: Psychology, Education, and Business and Industry. Each of these sections is in turn divided into several specific subsections. For example, subsections under Education include Academic Subjects, Achievement and Aptitude, Intelligence, Reading, and Special Education.

SELF-CHECK QUIZ

1. What is the best source of information about correct procedures for administering and scoring a published test?
   a. *Mental Measurements Yearbook*
   b. Professional journals in the subject
   c. The test publisher's catalog
   d. The test manual

2. Measures based upon a new theory of learning are most likely to be described in
   a. commercial test catalogs.
   b. research journals.
   c. test reference books.
   d. standardized test manuals.

3. When trying to locate a measure of a specific variable related to your problem or question, the first source to check is
   a. *The Mental Measurements Yearbook.*
   b. publishers' current test catalogs.
   c. the *Current Index to Journals in Education.*
   d. the subject catalog of your college library.

4. The main advantage test publishers' catalogs offer over the *MMY (Mental Measurements Yearbook)* as a source for information about published tests is that the catalogs
   a. give more thorough critical reviews of tests listed.
   b. are more current.
   c. make it easier to locate all published tests on a given subject.
   d. are easier to obtain.

5. One advantage that the *ETS Test Collection Bibliographies* have over the *Mental Measurements Yearbooks* is that they
   a. contain descriptions of more measures.
   b. include complete copies of each test.
   c. list only published tests that are readily available.
   d. provide more detailed information on each test.

6. The *Thesaurus of ERIC Descriptors* is useful in literature searches because it
   a. lists all publisher's test catalogs.
   b. contains a standard set of terms that are useful in finding information.
   c. includes test reviews that are much more complete than those found in professional journals.
   d. contains abstracts of articles on standard tests published in *CIJE*.

7. In planning a computer search the student should remember that
   a. these searches are very expensive and should only be used as a last resort.
   b. the computer can search for several descriptors simultaneously.
   c. the computer can only supply bibliographical data.
   d. the computer is much less efficient than a well-planned manual search.

8. If a computer locates fewer than 10 references, the best recourse is to
   a. conduct a manual search.
   b. make the search more well-defined and specific.
   c. broaden the search by using *or* connectors.
   d. start over and select a new set of descriptors.

9. The most important characteristic of any test is
   a. the feasibility of the test.
   b. the reliability of the test scores.
   c. the validity of the test scores.
   d. whether normative data are available.

10. A test manual will often report several reliability coefficients. This usually indicates that
    a. reliability was computed using several different methods.
    b. the author is guessing at the actual reliability of the test.
    c. there is a broad range of reliability coefficients.
    d. the reliability coefficient has not been established using scientific methods.

SUGGESTION SHEET

If your last name starts with the letters *Q* or *R*, please complete the Suggestion Sheet at the end of the book while this chapter is still fresh in your mind.

ANSWERS TO APPLICATION PROBLEMS

#1

If you scanned the "Classified Subject Index" of the *Ninth MMY*, you found that attitude tests are classified under Personality. Two measures are listed, numbers 95 and 96 in the "Tests and Reviews" section. A check of the "Score Index" under "attitude toward school subjects" also lists entry 96, entitled "Attitude toward School K-12." Both 95 and 96 can be used for testing sixth grade students. Neither one of these measures is listed in the *Tenth MMY*.

#2

1. Teachers' syndrome caused by inability to cope with stressful occupational condition—characterized by low morale, low productivity, high absenteeism, and high job turnover.
2. Articles listed under "Teacher Burnout"
   EJ315 112, EJ316 006, EJ317 644, EJ319 751, EJ320 220, EJ320 564, EJ320 922, EJ320 930.
3. Judging from the abstracts in the Main Entry section, the most promising article is EJ320 564. The bibliographic data on this article is Gold, Yvonne, The Relationship of Six Personal and Life History Variables to Standing on Three Dimensions of the Maslach Burnout Inventory in a Sample of Elementary and Junior High School Teachers, *Educational and Psychological Measurement*, 45(2), 377–387, 1985.
4. The article provides the following information:
   a. Maslach Burnout Inventory
   b. Emotional Exhaustion—Frequency (reliability = .88) Emotional Exhaustion—Intensity (reliability = .87) Depersonalization—Frequency (reliability =

.72) Depersonalization—Intensity (reliability = .75) Personal Accomplishment—Frequency (reliability = .79) Personal Accomplishment—Intensity (An error by the author or publisher omitted the last reliability coefficient). However, since all others fall within a fairly narrow range, it is probably safe to assume the sixth is also in this range. If you decide to use this measure you should write to the author at California State University Long Beach for more information.

   c. From article's References section: Maslach, C. and Jackson, S. E. (1981). *Maslach Burnout Inventory: Manual.* Palo Alto, CA: Consulting Psychologists Press.

#3

1. The term *teacher burnout* is not included in the *Thesaurus.*
2. Check "Burnout" in the *Thesaurus.* You will find the note: "Use Occupational Stress." This is the term you should check.
3. Look up *Occupational Stress* in the subject index volume of *Psychological Abstracts,* read the brief descriptions and write down the abstract numbers of abstracts that appear to relate to teacher occupational stress or burnout. Then look up these abstracts in the abstracts volumes. Volume 71 includes four volumes of abstracts entered in numerical order.
4. Abstracts 5072, 21590, 7887, 7892 appear to deal with teacher burnout.
5. Abstract 5072: Schwab, Richard L. Teacher burnout: Moving beyond psychobabble." *Theory into Practice,* 1983 (Winter). Vol 22 (1) 21–26.

CHAPTER 17

What Have My Students Learned? An Introduction to Standardized Achievement Measures

Overview

Bettering students' academic achievement is generally considered the primary goal of the public schools. Achievement is generally measured by some type of test: teacher-made, curriculum-embedded, diagnostic, or standardized achievement, to name but a few. Although all different types of tests can provide important information, this chapter focuses on standardized achievement tests. Because of their widespread use in the public schools, standardized achievement must be well understood by all educators. The chapter covers the steps in developing standardized achievement tests, their major uses, and a simple process for estimating content validity. It also describes one of many important test batteries, the Comprehensive Test of Basic Skills, in some detail. Finally, it offers some comments on single-subject achievement tests and tests designed to measure the achievement of special groups.

Objectives

Upon completing your study of this chapter, you should be able to

1. Describe the characteristics of the typical standardized achievement test.

2. Briefly describe the major kinds of achievement measures used in schools.
3. Explain why a local school or district should determine content validity when selecting a standardized achievement test.
4. Describe the steps a teacher would take in estimating the content validity of a standardized test for the curriculum taught in her class.
5. Describe some of the ways that teachers, administrators, and counselors can use standardized achievement test information.
6. Briefly describe the limitations that must be considered in interpreting standardized achievement test scores.
7. State in your own words the steps a teacher should follow to gain an understanding of a standardized achievement test battery.
8. Review the steps taken in developing a standardized achievement test.

TYPES OF ACHIEVEMENT MEASURES

Parents and teachers generally agree that enhancing students' achievement in such subjects as mathematics, reading, and science is the schools' primary function. Several types of educational achievement measures have been developed to measure how well schools are teaching such academic subjects. The most frequently used achievement tests include

1. Teacher-made tests
2. Curriculum-embedded measures
3. Diagnostic tests
4. Single-subject tests
5. Special achievement measures
6. Standardized achievement test batteries

This chapter introduces you to all of these measures even though the main emphasis is on standardized achievement batteries. Throughout the chapter we have selected typical standardized measures to use as examples. Please note, however, that their inclusion does not mean that they are *superior* to others. Before discussing standardized achievement tests, let us discuss the other types of achievement measures briefly. A more detailed discussion of these measures is given elsewhere in this book.

Teacher-made Achievement Measures

Whether students are in the primary grades or studying for advanced degrees, most of the achievement measures they encounter are developed by their instructors. These can range from ridiculously easy to fiendishly difficult. The usefulness of some of these measures is questionable at best. However, a good teacher-made measure is often more useful than the standardized achievement measures available from publishers. Teachers who develop superior tests are skillful workers of test items, and use a variety of procedures to continually improve test quality. With the wide availability of microcomputers and word processors, it is becoming easier for teachers to develop a file of high quality test items.

The area where appropriately developed teacher-made tests are most often superior to standardized achievement measures is content validity. Content validity is the degree to which a test measures the content that has been taught. The classroom teacher knows best what she has taught her students, and can develop a test that is more appropriate than any standardized achievement measure is likely to be. Because teacher-made achievement measures can play a very important role in measuring students' progress and diagnosing learning difficulties, each teacher should attempt to master the skills needed to develop, evaluate, and interpret her own measures.

Curriculum-embedded Achievement Measures

Many of the curriculum materials available to today's schools include measures to monitor student progress, plan instruction, and assign grades. Curriculum-embedded tests are often made up for each unit of work so as to provide the teacher with frequent checks of students' progress. For example, in the DMI Mathematics Systems described in Chapter 18, a six-item mastery test is provided for each of the program's 170 instructional objectives. Such measures are typically criterion-referenced and measure whether a student has mastered the program's specific objectives. According to Dorr-Bremme (1983), curriculum-embedded tests are used extensively by teachers. Since the use of commercially developed curriculum programs is increasing, such tests are likely to become increasingly important.

Diagnostic Tests

Diagnostic tests differ from standardized achievement measures in several important ways. Diagnostic tests are typically criterion-referenced rather than norm-referenced; they focus on the low-achieving student rather than attempting to measure the entire achievement range; and, they measure learning objectives in greater depth and report individual student performance in more detail. Although diagnostic tests can be of value in such areas as mathematics and reading, most teachers do not make extensive use of such measures (Dorr-Bremme, 1983).

Single Subject Achievement Measures

The typical standardized achievement battery includes tests in mathematics, language arts, science, and social studies. Standard achievement measures are also available in a variety of other subject areas, including such traditional subjects as art and foreign languages, as well as less traditional subjects such as agribusiness and clerical skills. Since the potential market for single-subject achievement tests is much smaller than for achievement batteries, single-subject achievement tests tend to be less well developed and less frequently revised. Most such tests are published by groups with a special interest in a given subject area. For example, the Modern Language Association cooperates with the Educational Testing Service (ETS) in developing tests in several foreign languages. Similarly, achievement measures in business-related areas such as bookkeeping and typing are published by the National Business Education Association.

Many of the single-subject achievement measures are not commercially published, but are listed in the *Test Collection Bibliographies* published by ETS. These bibliographies list available achievement measures in such subjects as consumer competency, Hebrew, and sex education. Such measures vary greatly in their overall quality and their adherence to test development standards. If you teach subjects for which *Test Collection Bibliographies* are available, however, you will usually find them well worth their small cost, since they are likely to contain some useful measures or give you ideas to use in developing your own achievement tests.

Achievement Measures for Special Student Groups

Among the special student groups for whom achievement measures are available are the bilingual, disabled, and gifted.

Tests for Bilingual Students

The Spanish Edition of the Comprehensive Test of Basic Skills (CTBS) and the Spanish/English Reading and Vocabulary Screening (SERVS) test are among the standard achievement measures useful in schools having Latin American students. The SERVS is designed to determine a student's dominant language. If it indicates that a student should be tested in Spanish, then the CTBS Español can be used. This test is available in five levels, covering grades one through eight. The content is closely comparable to that of the English version of the CTBS.

Tests for Students with Disabilities

The identification and teaching of children with disabilities has been important in American education for years, and Public Law 94–142 (recently reauthorized as Public Law 101–476, Individuals with Disabilities in Education Act [IDEA]) has greatly increased the need for measures that can be used to screen and determine the progress of these children. CTB/McGraw Hill and Charles E. Merrill each list over 20 measures that can be used for children with disabilities. For example, the Stanford Achievement Test is available in large print and Braille editions for the visually disabled. There is also a special edition of this test for hearing impaired children. Regular achievement tests can sometimes be used for students with disabilities, but special attention should be given to problems that may arise (Jensema, 1980).

The *Wide Range Achievement Test (WRAT)* is an example of a test often used for students with mild disabilities to estimate their achievement level. Two levels of the test are available. Level I is designed for use with children ages 5 to 12, while Level II is intended for persons ages 12 to adult. Each test contains three subtests, in reading, spelling, and arithmetic. Although parts of each test, such as Level I spelling, may be administered to groups of children, all of the reading subtest and part of the arithmetic subtest must be administered individually. In practice the entire test is usually administered individually, by the special education teacher or the school psychologist. One of the advantages of the WRAT is its short testing time (20 to 30 minutes). Split-half reliability coefficients ranges from .94 to .98. A number of validity studies are reported in the test manual, with correlations between the WRAT and other achievement measures ranging from .74 to .93, suggesting reasonably good concurrent validity.

Tests for the Gifted and Talented

Standardized achievement test batteries are also useful in helping to identify academically talented students and in determining the specific areas in which their talents lie. While most early efforts to identify gifted children used intelligence test scores as the principal criterion, current definitions usually include children with demonstrated achievement and/or potential ability in any of the following areas, singly or in combinations: (1) general intellectual ability, (2) specific academic aptitude, (3) creative or productive thinking, (4) leadership ability, (5) visual and performing arts, (6) psychomotor ability. Note that "specific academic aptitude," which has usually been interpreted as outstanding performance on standardized achievement measures, is one of the criteria listed. Fox (1981) maintains that if the purpose of identifying academically talented students is to provide them with more challenging education programs, then achievement tests are more useful than intelligence tests.

A similar perspective emerged from Stanley's (1980) research on academically gifted students. To identify students with high levels of specific academic talent in a subject such as mathematics, Stanley recommended initial screening on an achievement test at the students' grade level. Those who score in the top 3 percent on this test would then be given a more difficult test at their functional level such as a mathematics achievement test designed for students several grades higher. Thus, academically talented students can be identified using regular standardized achievement tests, but two or more tests of increasing difficulty will usually be needed to identify students whose achievement is sufficiently above the norm for them to be classified as gifted.

Standardized Achievement Test Batteries

Standardized achievement test batteries have several characteristics that distinguish them from teacher-made tests and other achievement measures. The term *standardized* refers to the standard instructions, time limits, and materials used in administering and scoring. The goal of standardization is for each student to be exposed to the same testing situation so as to minimize errors and provide comparable information. Those who administer such measures must study the procedures carefully and motivate the students to make a maximum effort, since many important decisions will be influenced by these test scores. Research suggests that low motivation and careless test administration can significantly lower students' scores (Taylor & White, 1982).

Most standardized achievement tests are administered to large samples of students in different geographical areas to determine the average scores obtained by students at different grade levels. These data, called *norms,* are provided to test users to facilitate comparison of the norming sample with the performance of local students. Many of these tests are also criterion-referenced, since they provide data on students' mastery of specific objectives, based on criteria established by the test developers. Most standardized achievement measures available today also provide lists of objectives, individual student profiles, class record sheets, school district summaries, and guides for interpreting the test data.

Selecting a Standardized Achievement Battery

Selecting a standardized achievement battery is important because results from such tests are used to make many important decisions. Let's go back to the Test Evaluation Form in Chapter 16 and use it to consider some of the factors that are particularly relevant in the selection of standardized achievement measures. First, during the preliminary screening, be sure that subtests are available in all achievement areas you need. Not all batteries cover the same subject areas at the same grade levels. Also check the availability of alternate forms in case you want to give alternate forms in alternate years. Carefully review any evidence of the comparability of alternate forms. Assuming that alternate forms of a test produce closely comparable scores—when in fact they may not—can lead to serious misinterpretations.

Test validity, especially content validity is important for achievement measures. Review what the test manual says about content validity, but do not accept that evidence as sufficient. Test publishers usually establish content validity by studying a collection of curriculum guides, state courses of study, and popular textbooks, then developing test items that measure a sample of the content most frequently found in these sources. This approach aims at producing a test that is *reasonably well-suited* to the curricula of most local schools. However, because teachers stress different content, the objectives on a given standardized test may not be relevant to a particular situation. Therefore, it is also important to compare the test content with the content in your curriculum. Although all major test publishers use a similar approach, the objectives measured from test to test can differ considerably. Even in mathematics, where the curriculum tends to be most uniform, there are striking differences in the topics covered by different standardized tests (Freeman, Kuhs, Knappen, & Porter, 1979; also Floden, Porter, Schmidt, & Freeman, 1978).

Test reliability for most standardized achievement batteries is high, usually above .90 for each test in the battery. However, many of the tests will also provide several subtest scores. The mathematics test in the Stanford Achievement Test Battery contains three subtests: Concepts of Number, Math Computation, and Math Applications. If you plan to use scores from the subtests to evaluate your students' performance, also check their reliability. If subtest reliabilities are below the .80 to .90 range, scores for these subtests should be used cautiously in interpreting a student's performance.

Comparisons between norms and local students' performance are commonly used to estimate students' progress. Therefore, carefully review the characteristics of the norm groups and compare them with the characteristics of your own students to determine how valid such a comparison might be.

A Simplified Content Analysis

The only way to establish the content validity of a given standardized test *for your school* is to conduct a content analysis of the objectives covered in *both* the local curriculum and the standardized test. The following steps describe a process for determining how well a standardized test fits your local curriculum. Figure 17.1 gives the hypothetical results of such an analysis.

Step 1: Analyze the curriculum for each subject and grade level, and list the broad content objectives in column 1, and the specific objectives related to each broad objective in column 2. For example, a broad objective in your 6th grade mathematics curriculum could be "The student will multiply one-, two-, and three-digit numbers correctly for 80 percent of given problems." A related, more specific

Geography	6	18	Natl. Ach. Battery	Int.	A
Subject or Content Area	Grade Level	N Test Items	Standardized Test Name	Level	Form

A. Specific objectives not covered by any item: 3 of 8 = 37%
B. Test items not related to any curriculum objective: 7 of 18 = 39%
C. Curriculum Materials: 20 pages in "Our World"

Column 1	**Column 2**	Column 3	Column 4	Column 5		Column 6	
Broad Instructional Objectives or Content Areas	Specific Content Objectives or Concepts Covered in Local Curriculum	Items Related to this Objective	Items not Related to any Object; This Grade	Curriculum N	%	Test Emphasis N	%
Geography	1. Understand longitude and latitude	1, 8	(4, 5, 6, 12, 13, 14, 16)	11	5	2	11
	2. Locate points on map and give their long. and lat.	9, 10, 11		19	9	3	17
	3. Give examples of natural resources	7, 15		42	20	2	11
	4. Understand compass directions	2, 3		10	5	2	11
	5. Enter names of nations on a map of Western Hemisphere	0		28	14	0	0
	6. Identify sun, moon, and planets on solar system map	0		31	15	0	0
	7. Relate raw materials in a region to industry	17, 18		40	19	2	11
	8. Identify continents and oceans on a world map	0		26	13	0	0
		Total = 11 items	Total = 7 items				

FIGURE 17.1 Hypothetical Content Validity Analysis of a Standardized Achievement Measure Using the Content Analysis Form

objective could be "The student will multiply a two-digit number by a two-digit number." The hypothetical example in Figure 17.1, shows in column 2 the eight specific content objectives for geography from the district's curriculum guide.

Step 2: Read each test item and enter the item numbers of those items related to each given specific objective in column 3. In our example, test items 1 and 8 from the National Achievement Battery (NAB) social science geography subtest are related to the first curriculum objective. If an item does not fit *any* of the specific objectives for your grade level, or covers content not taught, enter the item number in column 4. Remember that since a given level of the achievement test will contain items related to more than one grade level, items in column 4 may fit specific objectives in higher or lower grades. Thus, it is desirable for teachers at all grade levels to work cooperatively in conducting the content analysis. In our example, 7 of the 18 items from the geography subtest do not relate to any of the objectives in the district's curriculum guide.

Step 3: Add the number of specific objectives listed in column 2. Then add the number of objectives for which no items are listed (column 3). Divide the number of objectives not tested by the total number of objectives and multiply by 100 to estimate the percentage of your curriculum *not* covered on the test. Enter the result in space A near top of form. In the example, three of the eight geography objectives (or 37.5 percent) were not tested. Since a given level of the test will often be designed for more than one grade level, and since students at a given grade level differ in achievement level, a satisfactory test must include items for more than one grade. However the approach described here will still provide a satisfactory estimate of how well a test fits your school's curriculum for your grade level.

Step 4: Add the number of items on the test that do not relate to any objective at your grade level (column 4). Divide this sum by the total number of test items in the subtest. Multiply by 100 to determine the percentage of the test that is not relevant to the curriculum taught at your grade level, and enter the result in space B at top left of the form. In our example, 7 of the 18 subtest items (or 39 percent) measured concepts not covered in the district curriculum.

Step 5: The results of Steps 3 and 4 will give you a reasonable basis for roughly estimating the content validity of different standardized achievement measures for your local curriculum, and for comparing the content validity of two or more tests.

Step 6: Estimate the emphasis given to each specific objective or concept in the curriculum. You might base this estimate on the amount of class time devoted to the objective, the number of pages in the text relating to the objective, or any other reasonable measure of emphasis. In our example, the textbook contains 207 pages on geography. The number of pages related to each of the eight specific objectives, is entered, and the percentage of pages relating to each objective is entered into column 5.

Another approach that will usually be sufficient is to rate the curriculum emphasis of each objective high (H), moderate (M), or low (L), and enter your estimates in column 5. Test emphasis can also be classified as high, moderate, or low, depending on the number of items listed for each objective in column 3. The purpose of this exercise is to compare the test emphasis, based on your estimate in column 6, to the curriculum emphasis, estimated in column 5. The closer these match, the more appropriate the test is for your curriculum. In our example, we have used another method by entering the number of test items related to each objective in column 6 and converting this to a percentage of the total eighteen items on the geography subtest.

APPLICATION PROBLEM #1

Using the Content Analysis Form (CAF) in Figure 17.1, select one broad instructional objective for a subject and grade level you teach. You may use an objective from a district curriculum guide or may develop one from a section of a textbook you use. Enter the broad objective into column 1 of the Content Analysis Form. Next write the specific objectives that relate to your broad objective into column 2 of the CAF.

Select a standardized test appropriate for your grade and subject area.[1] Read each test item in the section related to your subject area and decide if it is related to one of the specific objectives in column 2. Record the following information: total test items in your subject area, number of specific objectives covered by at least one test item, number of specific objectives not covered by any test items, and number of test items not related to any of your objectives. Based on the information you've compiled, decide how well the test content fits the curriculum content for this broad objective.

Even this simplified procedure to determine content validity requires considerable time, but it will provide an overall estimate of the content validity of each test the district is considering. It is probably best accomplished by a committee of teachers.

Probably none of the tests that are analyzed will provide a *fully* satisfactory match with the local curriculum. However, content validity can be increased by custom scoring—omitting test items not related to local instructional objectives.[2] The district may also supplement the standardized test items with locally developed items designed to measure local objectives not covered by the standardized test. This is a useful compromise solution but it does require substantial extra work. You must also remember that the national norms for the standardized test may not be used once the test has been changed.

---

[1] There are several ways you can obtain a standardized test for this application problem: (1) See if a nearby university maintains a test file from which you can borrow; (2) borrow a test copy from a local school district; (3) purchase a specimen set of an appropriate test from a test publisher.

[2] Some test publishers provide custom scoring in which schools may specify which items to score, based on the content of the local curriculum.

USING EDUCATIONAL ACHIEVEMENT DATA

Various types of standardized achievement tests provide information that can assist teachers, school administrators, and counselors in making a wide range of decisions. You may notice in reviewing the following uses of achievement tests that the uses tend to be related. For example, the evaluation of student performance on an achievement measure may provide information that can aid a teacher in diagnosing learning difficulties. Classifying the learning difficulties of different students will, in turn, help a teacher decide how many student learning groups are needed and which students should be assigned to each group. Reviewing the results of small-group instruction can help a teacher evaluate her instructional methods and plan future instruction—and so on.

Also note that our list is merely an aid to help you organize your ideas about standardized achievement tests. Following the lists, we will discuss each use of standard achievement data in more detail.

Teacher Uses
1. Evaluating student performance
2. Diagnosing student learning difficulties
3. Organizing student learning groups
4. Evaluating instructional methods
5. Developing individualized education programs
6. Planning instruction

Administrative Uses
1. Evaluation of student learning outcomes
2. Program and curriculum evaluation
3. Teacher evaluation
4. Identification of educationally deprived children, and selection of students for special classes or activities
5. Classification of students for purposes of funding or to provide special instruction
6. Provision of information to local, state, or federal agencies

Counseling Uses
1. Educational counseling
2. Vocational counseling

Teacher Uses of Achievement Data

Teachers use tests for many different purposes. Among the most frequent are evaluation of student performance, diagnosis of student learning difficulties, formation of student learning groups, evaluation of instructional methods, and development of individual education programs. Let us discuss each of those next.

Evaluation of Student Performance

Many instructional decisions made by teachers can be aided by the objective results of standardized achievement measures. Such information can be used to help assess students' learning needs, set priorities among curriculum objectives, and evaluate the results of instruction.

Standardized test batteries usually provide the teacher with an overview of each student's performance. For example, a careful study of the Class Record Sheet for the Comprehensive Test of Basic Skills (CTBS) in Figure 17.2 shows a great deal of information about the class as a whole and each child in the class. These forms, which are computer-generated, can be customized by the publisher to contain primarily that information required by the school.

Note that this example contains six different kinds of scores for each subtest. Although each of these scores provides useful information, a school district might want only one or two of them. Using the information in Figure 17.2, let's interpret the data available for Michael Fernandez. Note that his cognitive skills index (CSI), which is based on the Test of Cognitive Skills (TCS), is 122. Since all test scores are subject to error, the publisher has also given a range of 116–129 for the CSI, which indicates that Michael's true score is probably somewhere in this range. The Test of Cognitive Skills (TCS) is a scholastic aptitude test that can be used to compute anticipated achievement grade equivalent scores based on students' abilities. A comparison between these anticipated scores and the student's actual grade equivalent scores enables a teacher to estimate whether a student is performing consistent with her ability level.[3] In our example, Michael Fernandez's grade equivalent scores indicates that he is performing above his grade level (grade 5.4) on all the subtests in the battery. His grade equivalent scores range from 5.6 in spelling to 10.9 in vocabulary and total reading. This comparison between his obtained achievement (Row GE) based on the CTBS, and his anticipated achievement (Row AAGE) based on his TCS score helps the teacher estimate his strengths and weaknesses. Entries are made in row GED only when a student's performance is significantly higher (+) or significantly lower (−) than his expected performance. Note that Michael's actual achievement is significantly higher in reading vocabulary and science (indicated by plus marks) than would be expected based on his TCS score. To determine how well he is performing relative to the national average, the teacher can review the two rows that give the normal curve equivalent (NCE) and the national percentile (NP). The national percentiles show that he is above the 90th percentile in several areas, with a total battery average at the 91st percentile. His two weakest areas are spelling (53rd percentile) and language mechanics (58th percentile).

The group means given near the bottom of the record sheet show that although the class as a whole is above the national norms (62nd percentile), there is much variation from one subject to another, with the lowest performance relative to national norms being in language mechanics. Further insights can be obtained by comparing the class mean grade equivalent scores (GE) with the anticipated achievement grade equivalent scores (AAGE). Note that in language mechanics,

---

[3] Keep in mind the limitations of grade equivalent scores that we discussed in Chapter 5.

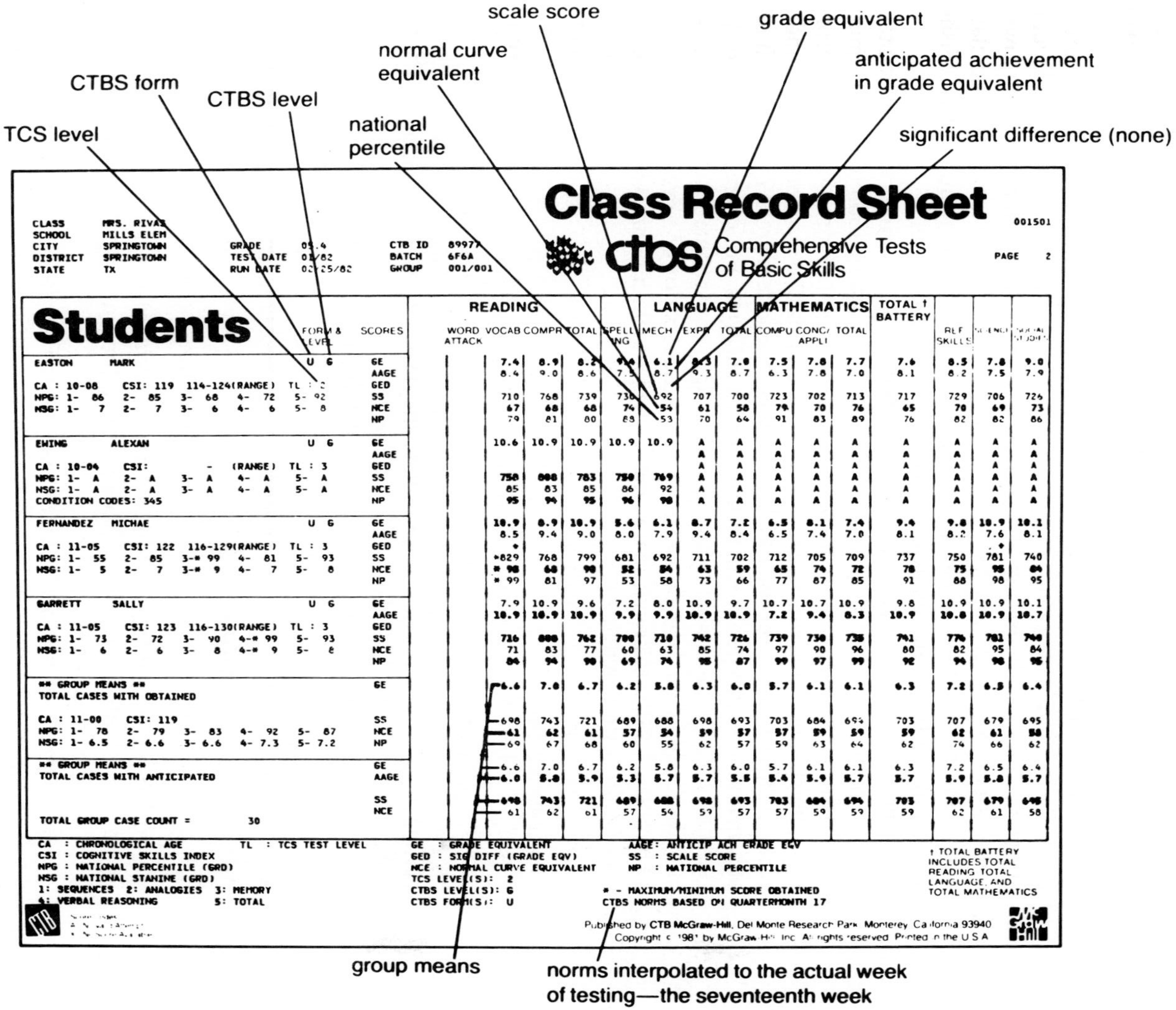

FIGURE 17.2 Class Record Sheet

SOURCE: *CTBS Classroom Management Guide*. 1981, CTB/McGraw-Hill, Monterey, CA. Reprinted with permission of the publisher.

the grade equivalent and anticipated grade equivalent scores are very similar, suggesting that the class is achieving in this area as would be predicted by their scholastic aptitude scores.

Based on the Class Record Sheet, the teacher may wish to examine the language mechanics area further. Although students are up to expectations in this area, their performance is somewhat lower in terms of national norms than for other areas. Thus, the teacher may ask whether this area is receiving adequate attention in the local curriculum. She may also question whether the local objectives differ from those being measured on the CTBS. If that were so, the relatively low score for the class might simply indicate that the content validity of that section of the test is not as high as for other parts of the test.

Single-subject achievement measures aimed at measuring performance in a specific subject area like algebra often provide more information than the relevant subtests in an achievement battery because they devote more time to measuring the subject. Such measures are especially useful in departmentalized programs such as those in most secondary schools, where teachers are typically interested only in how students perform in their particular subjects. For example, the Modern Geometry Test contains 48 items related to first-year geometry, and requires 45 minutes to complete. In contrast, the mathematics section of Level J (grades 8.6 to 12.9) of the CTBS, although containing 57 items, includes only 3 items concerned specifically with geometry.

Diagnosis of Student Learning Difficulties

Normative data on standardized achievement batteries can identify subject areas in which individual students and the class as a whole are not performing up to local or national norms. An individual's achievement is also often related to a set of objectives so the teacher can estimate the degree to which each objective has been mastered. Both kinds of information can be useful in helping to diagnose specific learning problems and plan remedial instruction.

APPLICATION PROBLEM #2

Examine Figure 17.2 and answer the following questions:

a. Which of the four students has the highest scholastic aptitude?
b. Which students are achieving above their anticipated achievement in social studies?
c. In terms of national percentiles, which student is lowest in the total reading score?

Although standardized achievement batteries and single-subject achievement tests provide a good overall picture of students' performances, they often do not offer sufficient detail for diagnosing and remediating specific student difficulties.

On most standard achievement tests, performance relevant to each objective is measured by very few items, which cannot provide a reliable measure of a student's mastery of even a very specific objective. For example, performance on five addition items would generally not provide conclusive evidence about whether a student had mastered an objective relating to addition.

Test reliability is largely determined by the length of a test. Thus, the overall percentile score a student obtains on a standard achievement battery will usually be based upon several hundred items and will be highly reliable. But the student's score on a *specific content objective* such as "Reduce a common fraction to its simplest form" is likely to be much less reliable because it will usually be based on only three or four items. Because of this limitation, diagnostic tests, many of which are criterion referenced, are often used to supplement achievement test data. Diagnostic tests typically cover a more narrow range of concepts and consequently provide more information on the student's mastery of specific concepts. For example, let's compare the mathematics section of the CTBS with a comparable level of the Diagnostic Mathematics Inventory (DMI). Level H of the CTBS covers grades 6.6 to 8.9, and includes two mathematics subtests containing a total of 85 items. In contrast, Level G of the DMI covers the same grade range but includes 168 items.

Formation of Student Learning Groups

Elementary schools often divide the class into a number of subgroups, each comprising students who are roughly comparable in their achievement relating to a given subject.[4] Many current diagnostic and achievement measures provide information to assist teachers in setting up such instructional groups. For example, a computer-generated Class Grouping Report available for the CTBS lists students who failed to master each instructional objective covered by the test. Teachers could use this information to organize student groups for related clusters of objectives. (See Figure 17.3 for a sample of this report.) Similarly, the Stanford Diagnostic Reading Test Instructional Placement Report enables a teacher to divide her class into several groups based on the specific reading deficiencies revealed by their test performance.

Evaluation of Instructional Methods and Strategies

Different instructional approaches are not equally effective for all teachers or students. To find the most effective teaching approaches for a given situation, teachers must constantly evaluate new approaches. Standardized achievement scores can help a teacher appraise the effectiveness of whatever approaches she is using. For example, a simulated United Nations General Assembly session might stimulate a great deal of student interest in current events. However, if an achievement test with objectives related to civics shows little mastery of the concepts the session was designed to teach, the teacher must consider carefully whether the simulation was worth the time, even if students enjoyed it. Teachers

---

[4] Although this approach is widely used, some researchers have questioned the value of the approach in general, as well as the wisdom of using standardized test results to group students (Culyer, 1982).

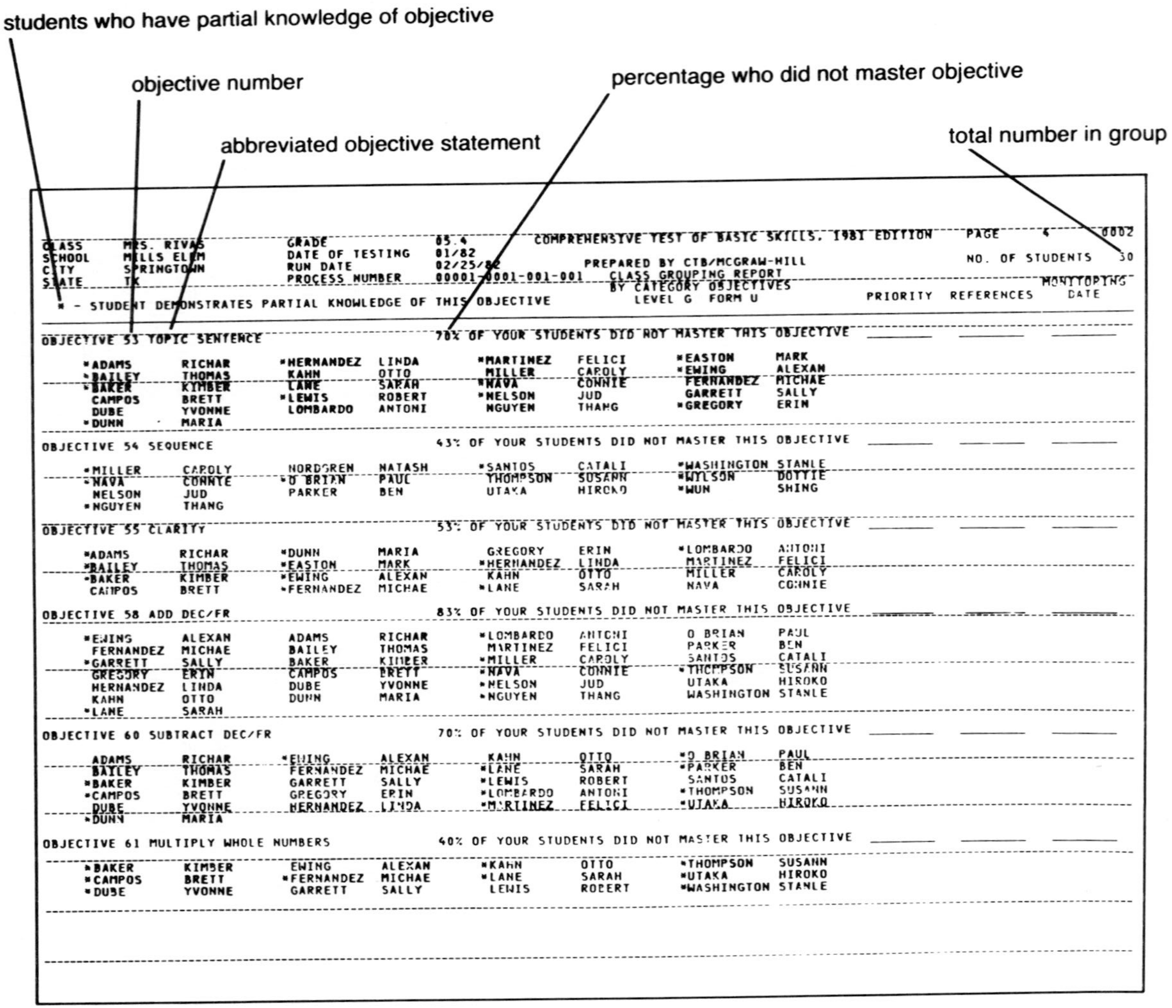

CLASS MRS. RIVAS — GRADE 05.4 — COMPREHENSIVE TEST OF BASIC SKILLS, 1981 EDITION — PAGE 4 0002
SCHOOL MILLS ELEM — DATE OF TESTING 01/82 — NO. OF STUDENTS 30
CITY SPRINGTOWN — RUN DATE 02/25/82 — PREPARED BY CTB/MCGRAW-HILL
STATE TX — PROCESS NUMBER 00001-0001-001-001 — CLASS GROUPING REPORT BY CATEGORY OBJECTIVES — LEVEL G FORM U

* - STUDENT DEMONSTRATES PARTIAL KNOWLEDGE OF THIS OBJECTIVE — PRIORITY — REFERENCES — MONITORING DATE

OBJECTIVE 53 TOPIC SENTENCE — 70% OF YOUR STUDENTS DID NOT MASTER THIS OBJECTIVE

*ADAMS	RICHAR	*HERNANDEZ	LINDA	*MARTINEZ	FELICI	*EASTON	MARK
*BAILEY	THOMAS	KAHN	OTTO	MILLER	CAROLY	*EWING	ALEXAN
*BAKER	KIMBER	LANE	SARAH	*NAVA	CONNIE	FERNANDEZ	MICHAE
CAMPOS	BRETT	*LEWIS	ROBERT	*NELSON	JUD	GARRETT	SALLY
DUBE	YVONNE	LOMBARDO	ANTONI	NGUYEN	THANG	*GREGORY	ERIN
*DUNN	MARIA						

OBJECTIVE 54 SEQUENCE — 43% OF YOUR STUDENTS DID NOT MASTER THIS OBJECTIVE

*MILLER	CAROLY	NORDGREN	NATASH	*SANTOS	CATALI	*WASHINGTON	STANLE
*NAVA	CONNIE	*O BRIAN	PAUL	THOMPSON	SUSANN	*WILSON	DOTTIE
NELSON	JUD	PARKER	BEN	UTAKA	HIROKO	*WUN	SHING
*NGUYEN	THANG						

OBJECTIVE 55 CLARITY — 53% OF YOUR STUDENTS DID NOT MASTER THIS OBJECTIVE

*ADAMS	RICHAR	*DUNN	MARIA	GREGORY	ERIN	*LOMBARDO	ANTONI
*BAILEY	THOMAS	*EASTON	MARK	*HERNANDEZ	LINDA	MARTINEZ	FELICI
*BAKER	KIMBER	*EWING	ALEXAN	KAHN	OTTO	MILLER	CAROLY
CAMPOS	BRETT	*FERNANDEZ	MICHAE	*LANE	SARAH	NAVA	CONNIE

OBJECTIVE 58 ADD DEC/FR — 83% OF YOUR STUDENTS DID NOT MASTER THIS OBJECTIVE

*EWING	ALEXAN	ADAMS	RICHAR	*LOMBARDO	ANTONI	O BRIAN	PAUL
FERNANDEZ	MICHAE	BAILEY	THOMAS	MARTINEZ	FELICI	PARKER	BEN
*GARRETT	SALLY	BAKER	KIMBER	*MILLER	CAROLY	SANTOS	CATALI
GREGORY	ERIN	CAMPOS	BRETT	*NAVA	CONNIE	*THOMPSON	SUSANN
HERNANDEZ	LINDA	DUBE	YVONNE	*NELSON	JUD	UTAKA	HIROKO
KAHN	OTTO	DUNN	MARIA	*NGUYEN	THANG	WASHINGTON	STANLE
*LANE	SARAH						

OBJECTIVE 60 SUBTRACT DEC/FR — 70% OF YOUR STUDENTS DID NOT MASTER THIS OBJECTIVE

ADAMS	RICHAR	*EWING	ALEXAN	KAHN	OTTO	*O BRIAN	PAUL
BAILEY	THOMAS	FERNANDEZ	MICHAE	*LANE	SARAH	*PARKER	BEN
*BAKER	KIMBER	GARRETT	SALLY	*LEWIS	ROBERT	SANTOS	CATALI
*CAMPOS	BRETT	GREGORY	ERIN	*LOMBARDO	ANTONI	*THOMPSON	SUSANN
DUBE	YVONNE	HERNANDEZ	LINDA	*MARTINEZ	FELICI	*UTAKA	HIROKO
*DUNN	MARIA						

OBJECTIVE 61 MULTIPLY WHOLE NUMBERS — 40% OF YOUR STUDENTS DID NOT MASTER THIS OBJECTIVE

*BAKER	KIMBER	EWING	ALEXAN	*KAHN	OTTO	*THOMPSON	SUSANN
*CAMPOS	BRETT	*FERNANDEZ	MICHAE	*LANE	SARAH	*UTAKA	HIROKO
*DUBE	YVONNE	GARRETT	SALLY	LEWIS	ROBERT	*WASHINGTON	STANLE

FIGURE 17.3 Class Grouping Report Provides Information on the Percentage of Students in the Class Who Fail to Master Each Objective on the CTBS

SOURCE: *CTBS Classroom Management Guide.* 1981, CTB/McGraw-Hill, Monterey, CA. Reprinted with permission of the publisher.

who use a variety of different forms of feedback to evaluate and improve their instructional methods are likely to become more effective than those who merely follow hunches.

Development of Individualized Education Programs

Most children with disabilities are now placed in regular classrooms for at least part of the school day. By law the school is required to prepare an *Individualized Education Program* (IEP) for each child with a disability that includes the following components:

a. A statement of the child's present levels of educational performance;

b. A statement of annual goals, including short-term instructional objectives;

c. A statement of specific special education and related services to be provided to the child, together with a description of the extent to which the child will be able to participate in regular educational programs;

d. The projected dates for initiation of services and the anticipated duration of the services; and

e. Appropriate objective criteria and evaluation procedures and schedules for determining, on at least an annual basis, whether the short-term instructional objectives are being achieved (Education of the Handicapped Act, 1977).

Standardized achievement measures as well as other standardized tests can be valuable in meeting several of the aforementioned requirements. For example, standardized achievement measures can be used to estimate a child's present level of educational performance and to determine whether instructional objectives are being achieved. Such measures, *when combined with other information*, are also useful in preparing annual goals and short-term instructional objectives.

Administrative Uses of Achievement Data

Just as teachers use tests for many different purposes, so do administrators. The most frequent ways in which administrators use test results include evaluation of learning for groups of students, program and curriculum evaluation, teacher evaluation, placement of students, classification of students, and provision of information to various constituencies. As you will see in the following discussion, results of tests are more useful for some of these purposes than others.

Evaluation of Student Learning

Teachers are generally most interested in the achievement of individual students in their classes, while school administrators are more interested in the overall pattern of achievement in the school, district, or state. The standardized achievement test battery is often used for appraising the overall progress of students and comparing this progress with students in other schools, districts, or states. Such comparisons are dangerous because there are differences in curriculum from school to school that make a given achievement test more or less appropriate for one school than another. In spite of this limitation, standardized achievement tests are often used as an overall measure of the quality of education.

Program and Curriculum Evaluation

Closely related to the overall evaluation of student learning is the use of standardized achievement measures to evaluate various curriculum areas. If a district's students score above the national norms in mathematics, science, and language arts, and below the national norms in social studies, school administrators should probably take a careful look at the social studies curriculum. A low district score in one subject area, however, may mean that the test is a poor match for the district's curriculum in that area, and a good match in the other areas. Thus, the school administrator may wish to conduct a content analysis of the local curriculum and the achievement measure being used to determine the degree to which the measure covered the content being taught.

If significant differences are found between local curriculum content and the standardized achievement test content, the administrator may be tempted to change the curriculum to better match what the test measures. This is probably unwise because it allows the test publisher to decide what will be taught in the local school or district. There are many valid reasons why the curriculum in a particular district might differ substantially from the content tested on a standardized achievement measure. It would be better to analyze the content of other standard achievement measures and determine whether another measure might have higher content validity for the local curriculum.

Two other approaches to increase content validity are (1) to develop a supplementary achievement test designed to measure local objectives not covered by the standardized achievement test, and (2) to use only those items on the standardized achievement test that fit local objectives, then compute an adjusted score. This approach, described by Wilson and Hiscox (1984), is gaining popularity in a number of areas.

Never assume that a standardized achievement test is valid for local curriculum evaluation until you have compared its content with local objectives. A recent study showed that, for a given district, the proportion of standardized achievement test items that matched local grade level mathematics objectives ranged from a low of 58 percent at sixth grade to a high of 66 percent at fourth grade. In other words, a *third* or more of the local objectives were not measured (Jolly & Gramenz, 1984).

Teacher Evaluation

Teacher evaluation takes many forms. In recent years many educators have advocated the use of standard achievement measures to evaluate teachers' effectiveness. If the main goal of the school is to educate students, they argue, then the standardized achievement battery is perhaps the most accurate measure of a teacher's success. The teacher whose students make the greatest achievement gain during the school year may reasonably be regarded as the most "effective" teacher.

The problem with this argument is that a great many factors influence student achievement—many of which have nothing whatever to do with the performance of the teacher. For example, students with a higher scholastic aptitude tend to achieve more in any environment, regardless of how effective the teacher is. Other factors, such as students' self-concept, motivation, and socioeconomic status are also related to academic achievement. It is easy to see how these variables can confuse the issue. Of course, results from standardized achievement tests may be used as a part of a teacher evaluation system. But any fair system of teacher evaluation based on student achievement must take all of these other variables into account. Designing teacher evaluation that is fair and accurate is a challenge with which education continues to wrestle.

Placement of Students

Standardized achievement measures are used, in conjunction with other measures such as scholastic aptitude test scores and teachers' judgment, as a basis for many placement decisions in public schools. Many schools employ some form of ability grouping to ensure that pupils in a given classroom are similar in ability or other important factors. For example, in assigning students to different sections of ninth grade algebra, educators might review students' eighth grade achievement test scores in arithmetic, then create three sections: those performing about on grade level, those requiring special help, and those ready for an extra challenge.

Classification of Students

State and federal laws often require the use of standardized test scores in conjunction with other assessment data for identifying and classifying children with disabilities. The first step in the classification process is usually administration of a screening test to alert school personnel of the *possible* existence of a disability. If a potential problem is suspected, more explicit diagnosis is made by a team of professionals from different disciplines, including at least one teacher (Wilson, 1980). Table 17.1 lists the various categories of children with disabilities and the assessment data that must be collected for each category. Note that a variety of assessment data, including measures of academic achievement, is needed to help the team identify a child's disabilities and determine whether special education or related services are required.

A child's score on a standardized achievement test is determined to a considerable degree by the match between curriculum and the standardized test. This is clearly illustrated in a study by Jenkins and Pany (1978) in which the words taught in the first- and second-grade books from five basal reading series were compared with the words tested in four standardized achievement subtests on word recognition. As shown in Table 17.2, large discrepancies were found among the grade placement scores a child who had mastered all words in a given reading program would obtain on different tests. For example, a child who mastered all the words in the grade 1 text of the SRA Reading Program would obtain a grade placement score of 1.0 on the SORT, but 2.1 on the WRAT. A score of 1.0 would probably qualify her for special education services while a score of 2.1 would not.

A close look at Table 17.2 will reveal many combinations of reading curricu-

TABLE 17.1   Classification Guidelines by Category of Exceptionality

Category of Disability	Assessment Data Should Be Collected in the Following Areas:
Mentally retarded	Intellectual functioning, adaptive behavior, academic achievement, medical/developmental, language
Hard of hearing/deaf	Audiological, intellectual, language, speech, academic achievement, social/emotional, psychomotor
Speech impaired	Audiological, articulation, fluency, voice, language, academic achievement, social/emotional
Visually handicapped	Ophthalmological, academic achievement, intellectual, social/emotional
Seriously emotionally disturbed	Intellectual, social/emotional, adaptive behavior, academic achievement, medical/developmental
Orthopedically impaired and other health impaired	Medical, motor, adaptive behavior, intellectual, academic achievement, social/emotional
Deaf-blind	Audiological, ophthalmological, language, medical, adaptive behavior
Multiply handicapped	Medical, intellectual, motor, adaptive behavior, social/emotional, academic achievement, language speech, audiological and ophthalmological (if appropriate)
Specific learning disabilities	Intellectual, academic achievement, language, social/emotional, classroom behavior
Gifted	Intellectual, academic achievement, social/emotional, creativity

SOURCE: Daniel P. Morgan, *A Primer on Individualized Education Programs for Exceptional Children.* Second Edition. 1981, The Foundation for Exceptional Children, Reston, VA. Reprinted with permission of the publisher.

lum and achievement tests that would produce drastically different achievement scores for children with identical reading skills. The authors offer this conclusion:

> It appears that achievement tests may not be capable of reliably discriminating handicapped children from those who have learned every word taught in a reading curriculum. Normally, achievement tests must make even finer discriminations; that is, they must discriminate between handicapped children who are achieving significantly below grade level and the approximately 45% of nonhandicapped children who are achieving below grade level. (Jenkins & Pany, 1978, p. 452)

The deficiencies illustrated by this study are due to the fact that tests differ in their content validity for various reading programs. Therefore, it is vital to use achievement measures that have *high content validity* for the *local curriculum* if the scores are to be valid for making classification decisions.

Many administrators assume that standardized test scores are more valid than teacher judgment. This assumption is often incorrect. When an achievement test score conflicts with other evidence, further information should be collected before making a decision.

TABLE 17.2 Grade Equivalent Scores Obtained by Matching Specific Reading Text Words to Standardized Reading Test Words

Curriculum	PIAT[a]	MAT: Word Knowledge	MAT: Word Analysis	SORT	WRAT
Bank Street Reading Series					
Grade 1	1.5	1.0	1.1	1.8	2.0
Grade 2	2.8	2.5	1.2	2.9	2.7
Keys to Reading					
Grade 1	2.0	1.4	1.2	2.2	2.2
Grade 2	3.3	1.9	1.0	3.0	3.0
Reading 360					
Grade 1	1.5	1.0	1.0	1.4	1.7
Grade 2	2.2	2.1	1.0	2.7	2.3
SRA Reading Program					
Grade 1	1.5	1.2	1.3	1.0	2.1
Grade 2	3.1	2.5	1.4	2.9	3.5
Sullivan Associations Programmed Reading					
Grade 1	1.8	1.4	1.2	1.1	2.2
Grade 2	2.2	2.4	1.1	2.5	2.5

SOURCE: J. R. Jenkins and D. Pany, "Standardized Achievement Tests: How Useful for Special Education?" *Exceptional Children*, 44(6), 1978. Reprinted with permission of the author.
[a] Test names: PIAT: Peabody Individual Achievement Test; MAT: Metropolitan Achievement Test; SORT, Slosson Oral Reading Test; WRAT: Wide Range Achievement Test.

The Education Consolidation and Improvement Act of 1981, designed primarily to help local and state education agencies meet the special needs of educationally deprived children, places further testing responsibilities on schools. This act, which consolidated funding from a number of previous federal assistance programs, requires an annual assessment to identify educationally deprived children and evaluate their needs with sufficient specificity to ensure useful remediation. It also requires annual evaluation to determine the effectiveness of programs designed to serve such children. Another section of the act requires that funded programs conduct a diagnostic assessment to identify the needs of all children in the school, and establish learning goals and objectives for those children. Procedures must be adopted for testing students, and for evaluating the continuity and effectiveness of services children receive.

Provision of Information

School districts are often asked to supply standardized achievement test information to local agencies (e.g., the school board or PTA), state agencies (e.g., legislature or department of education), and various federal agencies. Publishers of current standard achievement measures can provide virtually any summary information that may be required by the schools. If standard report forms do not provide the data needed, many publishers will customize the report for an additional fee.

Counseling Uses of Achievement Data

Results of tests are also used in counseling students regarding educational and vocational decisions, as summarized in the next two sections.

Educational Counseling

A student's achievement test scores are often useful in personal educational planning. Research has shown that the past achievement in a given subject area is usually the best predictor of a student's future performance in that same area. However, such predictions are not infallible. In most cases, a student should not be denied the right to take a given course purely on the basis of past achievement, but she should be warned that she may have difficulty.

Vocational Counseling

Various standardized measures—such as scholastic aptitude tests, vocational interest tests, measures of specific aptitudes, and standardized achievement test batteries—play an important role in appraising a student's potential for a given vocation. Research has revealed much about the academic demands of various occupations. Such information can be very valuable to a student in matching her own aptitudes with those of successful individuals in the vocation she is considering. Additionally, there are a number of standardized tests that can assist students in deciding how closely their interests are aligned with the typical activities in various occupations. By providing students with systematic information on both aptitudes and interests as it relates to vocational choice, the probability of the student making an appropriate decision is increased.

Cautions in Interpreting Standardized Achievement Test Data

Standardized achievement tests have certain limitations a teacher must keep in mind when interpreting scores. Let us consider a few of the most important.

Chance Scores

Since virtually all standardized measures employ multiple-choice items, the student is likely to get a certain number correct by guessing. If there are four alternatives to the multiple-choice questions, students who mark answers on a purely random basis will, on average, answer 25 percent of the items correctly. For example, the Reading Comprehension subtest of the Stanford Achievement Test (Intermediate 2—Grades 5.5–7.9) contains 60 multiple-choice items. On average, students who could not read a single word of English would still obtain a raw score of 15 on this subtest by randomly marking answers to all 60 items. A raw score of 15 equals a grade equivalent of 2.8. An uninformed fifth grade teacher might interpret this as meaning that a child receiving this score could read as well as the average child at grade 2.8—which in the case of our non-English speaking student would clearly be untrue. Another problem with the chance score is that there is no way to determine how many correct answers any given student obtained by chance. Like many chance events, guessing is normally distributed, which means that a few students will guess significantly more correct answers, and others significantly fewer than the average.

Chance scores are distorted by other variables, too. Most students can eliminate a few multiple-choice alternatives as clearly incorrect and guess among those that remain. If a student can eliminate one incorrect alternative for each question, she can—on average—guess correctly one-third of the time, instead of one-fourth.

Base Scores

Standardized achievement tests also have base scores below which a person cannot score. The base grade placement score of the aforementioned Reading Comprehension subtest is 1.0. This means that if a student does nothing except turn in a blank answer sheet with her name on it, she will receive a score that some might interpret as evidence that she reads as well as the average child at grade 1.0 level.

Time Limitations

Nearly all achievement measures have rigid time limits for each subtest. The time allowed is usually sufficient for most students. However, a few students at all levels of ability are much slower, more deliberate, and more thoughtful about their answers than their peers. Such students often receive spuriously low scores on timed tests because they do not finish. Culyer (1982) reports a case in which a student answered correctly 28 of the 30 items he attempted on a 60-item subtest, giving him a grade equivalent score of 7.2. On the following day he was given time to complete the test. His grade equivalent score increased from 7.2 to 10.0. This score was far more indicative of his actual achievement level.

In interpreting achievement test scores, the teacher should be alert to the scores obtained by students who work slower. Although the test norms are based on the time limits given, the teacher may want to follow the procedure described by Culyer to get a better insight into a student's actual achievement level.

Inadequate Content Validity

A good estimate of a test's content validity requires a careful comparison between local curriculum content and test content. In the absence of a rigorous content analysis, the teacher can make a rough estimate of content validity by reading each test item and checking those that are covered in the curriculum or by the procedure described earlier. For some standardized achievement batteries, the teacher can obtain detailed item-by-item reports on the performance of her class. The teacher who knows which and how many items in each subtest fit the local curriculum is in a better position to correctly interpret test reports and student test scores.

Steps in Developing a Standardized Achievement Test

If you have ever written a test yourself, you know something about how complex it is. And the process employed in developing standardized achievement measures is considerably more elaborate than that employed in preparing teacher-made tests. Educational Testing Service (ETS) reports that developing an entirely new test requires about two years (Educational Testing Service, 1983). During that time, the following steps are taken.[5]

Step 1: Defining the Test Characteristics and Objectives. First, the test developers must ask some important questions: (a) Why will the test be given and how will the results be used? (b) Who will take the test? (c) What specific content should be assessed? (d) What kinds of questions should be included in the test? (e) How long should it be? (f) How difficult should it be? Advisory committees are often employed to consider these questions. A committee for a standardized achievement test would likely include experts in the test content area, experienced teachers who teach the subject, and representatives from the test company staff.

Developing sound, relevant objectives is critical and demands careful, thorough examination of local curricula. In developing objectives for the Comprehensive Test of Basic Skills (CTBS), the developers examined current curriculum guides from state departments of education and large school districts throughout the country, as well as analyzing the content of recently published textbook series and instructional programs (Burket, Green, Yen, Guest, & Hunter, 1982). In the area of primary grade reading alone (K–3), 22 textbook series were reviewed (CTB/McGraw-Hill, 1982).

Step 2: Test Item Writing. Once test objectives and specifications have been clearly defined, test questions can be written. First-draft questions are typically prepared by teachers and subject matter experts. They are then revised and improved by item-writing specialists, without whose help many test items would have serious deficiencies. Since many items are rejected, it is usually necessary to write two to three times as many as will be required on the final form of the test. When the format and content of an item are judged satisfactory, the difficulty level of the vocabulary is checked and readability formulas are applied to assure appropriateness for the intended test takers.

Step 3: Assembling the Prototype. Once all test items have been written, a prototype test is assembled and administered to small samples of students similar to those for whom the test is intended and the results analyzed. Item analysis procedures (similar to those discussed in Chapter 11) are used to determine if items are ambiguous, incorrect, or need revision.

Step 4: The Tryout Edition. Following the initial prototype administration, a larger tryout sample of students at the appropriate grade levels in private and public schools is selected. This sample typically comprises several hundred students. Teachers who administer the "tryout edition" are asked to make suggestions concerning content, instructions, time limits, and illustrations. Their feedback is considered together with data from an additional item analysis in determining how the test should be revised.

Step 5: Conducting Sensitivity Reviews. During the initial development of test items, item writers follow guidelines designed to eliminate language that reflects racial, sexual, or other forms of bias. Editors also review for bias both before and after the tryout. Items are also reviewed by persons specially trained to identify

---

[5] These seven steps are a composite of those listed by several leading text publishers, and are indicative of current practice in the field.

and eliminate biased material, usually including professional educators who represent various racial and ethnic groups.

Step 6: Revising the Test. Based on evidence gathered from the tryout edition, necessary revisions are made to ensure that items appearing on the final form are relevant to the subject matter, are representative of the content to be tested, and are appropriate in difficulty. The revised test is again reviewed by content specialists, test specialists, and outside experts. Each reviewer answers all questions independently and prepares a list of correct answers.

Step 7: Developing Normative Data. Most standardized achievement tests now in use are norm-referenced. To establish test norms, the test publishers administer the revised measure, called the standardization edition, to a large national sample of students at the appropriate grade levels. Data from this large national testing are then used to develop tables of norms.

The Need for Flexibility

The typical standardized achievement measure is designed to measure student achievement over several grade levels: for example, the first three years of elementary school, or the middle school years. Because students at any grade level can be expected to vary widely in their achievement, the standardized achievement tests for use at the junior high school level must measure not only the concepts taught at that level, but also concepts typically learned at the elementary and senior high levels. To complicate the matter, the range of student achievement becomes larger as students advance through the grades, and standard achievement tests must be designed to accommodate this increase. For example, the Comprehensive Test of Basic Skills (CTBS) is available at 10 overlapping levels, covering achievement from the beginning of kindergarten to the end of grade 12. Early levels have an achievement range of about one grade, while levels aimed at the end of secondary school cover as much as 4.3 grades.

Because a standardized achievement test covers a wide range of achievement, as well as several different subject areas, the number of specific concepts tested in each area is limited. Therefore, the standardized achievement, although providing the schools with an overall picture of student achievement, may not provide enough information about the specific strengths and weaknesses of the individual student. Although the current batteries are more useful for individual student diagnosis than those available 10 years ago, both teacher-made tests and standardized diagnostic tests—which typically cover a much more narrow range more thoroughly—tend to provide more detailed information on specific student deficiencies, and to be more useful to the teachers in designing instruction to overcome these deficiencies.

APPLICATION PROBLEM #3

Select a small unit of work, such as a textbook chapter, on a subject you expect to teach. Follow steps 1, 2, and 3 for developing an achievement test. For step 4 (try out) administer the test to a colleague or, if you are teaching, to a small sample of your students. Conduct a sensitivity review of the test as described in Step 5. Then revise the test as described in Step 6.

A LOOK AT A WIDELY USED STANDARDIZED ACHIEVEMENT TEST

We will now examine a widely used standardized achievement test in some depth to help you understand what these measures contain and how they can be helpful. Let us again emphasize that our use of various measures as examples is not meant to be an endorsement of the measures.

The Comprehensive Tests of Basic Skills (CTBS)

The CTBS contains many interesting features not found in most of the older achievement batteries. The CTBS is available in 10 levels that cover grades K.0 to 12.9. Both the level and variability of student achievement increase as we move into the higher grades. Thus, Level A covers only .9 grades (K.0 to K.9) and requires only 1 hour and 8 minutes to administer, while Level J covers 4.3 grades (8.6 to 12.9) and requires 4 hours and 50 minutes to administer. This battery includes tests in only reading and mathematics at Level A, but Level D (grades 1.6 to 2.9) includes reading, spelling, language, mathematics, science, and social studies. A seventh area, reference skills, is added at Level F (grades 3.6 to 4.9).

As with virtually all standardized achievement tests, the CTBS provides a great deal of information. In addition to the number of items answered correctly, reports can also be provided that indicate which items *each student* answered correctly. Such information can help a teacher diagnose each student's instructional needs and plan for remedial instruction.

Since various CTBS levels overlap each other, a teacher may not be sure which level is most appropriate for her class. For example, students at the end of fourth grade could be tested either with Level F (grades 3.6 to 4.9) or Level G (grades 4.6 to 6.9). For a highly heterogeneous fifth grade class, the weakest students may best fit Level D (grades 1.6 to 2.9) while the strongest students might need Level H (grades 6.6 to 8.9). Starting with Level F, the format, instructions, sample items, subtests and time limits are the same for all levels, so different students in the same classroom may be administered different levels at the same time.

To help teachers select the correct test level for a given child, CTBS provides two locator tests (one for grades 1 to 6 and a second for grades 6 through 12). A *locator test* requires only a few minutes to administer, and yet greatly reduces the chances a teacher will select the wrong level for a given student.

Functional Level Testing

Until recently, most schools administered the same level of the standardized achievement battery to all students at a given grade level. Although this approach, referred to as on-level testing is satisfactory for most children, any on-level test will be too easy for some and too difficult for others. A test that is too easy will not adequately test the upper levels of the student's achievement, since she is likely to know more than it allows her to demonstrate. On the other hand, if a test is too difficult it will not reveal what lower level skills she has developed.

Such problems have encouraged many schools to use functional level achievement testing. While functional level testing provides a more accurate picture of what each student can do, it also requires that the school determine the level at which each child will be tested. In most cases locator tests are used for this purpose, but teachers' judgments and the results of prior achievement tests are also considered at some schools.

According to comparative research (Haynes & Cole, 1982), testing at the functional level allows all students to experience some success in the testing situation. It tends to reduce boredom for high-achieving students and causes them to try harder than on-level testing. At the same time, low-achieving students are less likely to experience frustration, and discouragement. Haynes and Cole (1982) also found that fewer children score below chance or above ceiling in functional level testing than when tested on-level. Such extreme scores are highly unreliable.

Learning to Use the CTBS

If your school purchases a new standardized achievement test, you should plan to devote several hours to studying the test, the objectives, the kinds of scores, and the various computer-generated record sheets available from the publisher. On the following pages we will use examples from the CTBS Forms U and V to help you understand the steps involved in getting to know any of the standardized achievement batteries now being used in the schools.

Step 1: Get an overview of the content and organization of the test. The first two sections of the Class Management Guide (in the CTBS) provide a good overview of the test and briefly describe the development process. The teacher should give particular attention to those subtests that will be used in her classroom. For example, in the area of reading achievement, items measuring visual recognition are included only at Level A (K.0–K.9), while word attack skills are covered at Levels B, C, D, and E. Thus, although all levels of the CTBS contain a reading test, the specific objectives measured will differ.

Step 2: Study the test objectives. The developers of most standardized achievement measures relate test items to a set of objectives based on their analysis of textbooks, and other curriculum materials. However, reviewing these objectives can be problematic. If a test claims to measure hundreds of specific objectives, can teachers hope to sensibly and systematically interpret test results? Alternately, if objectives are too broad, how can teachers know what specific content is tested or whether the test measures achievement in the same areas covered in the local curriculum? To solve this problem, test developers often write two or three levels of objectives, attempting a compromise between breadth and specificity—and usually achieving reasonable success.

Items on the CTBS are related to 90 content objectives in the areas of reading, spelling, language, mathematics, reference skills, science, and social studies. Each objective is measured only at certain levels of the test. For example, objective 1:

"The student will recognize the upper or lower case form of a letter," is measured only at Level A. However, objective 68, "The student will demonstrate an understanding of numeration," is measured at all levels, A through J. The teacher should note which objectives are measured by the CTBS subtests to be used in her classroom, and should compare the CTBS objectives to those in the local curriculum. Local objectives are often described in district or state curriculum guides or in the teacher's own curriculum planning materials.

If you were to examine the 90 objectives for the CTBS, you would notice that they differ considerably in breadth, clarity, and specificity. Objective 4, "The student will identify two words given orally as being identical or different," is very clear and specific. In contrast, objective 87, "The student will demonstrate an understanding of historical persons, events, or eras," is broad and general. When objectives are too general, the best recourse is to examine the text items themselves. This leads us to the next step.

Step 3: Review the test booklet. The Class Management Guide of the CTBS gives the information needed to relate specific test items at each level of the test to each of the objectives. For example, if a teacher's class were to be tested with Level F of the CTBS, she could consult Appendix B of the Class Management Guide to identify the eight test items designed to measure objective 87, which we discussed above. Reviewing the actual items is the *most important step* a teacher can take in ensuring that the test will provide useful information.

Step 4: Learn to interpret test results. Skillful test interpretation requires a basic understanding of the measurement process itself. Test developers often publish material that briefly describes measurement terms and concepts helpful in understanding a particular test. For example, Part 3 of the CTBS Class Management Guide, includes a description of the kinds of test scores available for the CTBS as well as a description of the various computer-generated report forms that organize and summarize the test data for both individuals and classes.

Step 5: Use the test results in the classroom. Standardized achievement test results can be used in a variety of ways—for identifying individual and class strengths and weaknesses with regard to national norms and specific test objectives, grouping students for certain instructional activities, planning instruction, monitoring individual and class progress and evaluating the success of instructional methods.

CTBS Report Forms

A knowledge of report forms available for particular standardized achievement tests can help you see how to make better use of test results. Let's continue to use the CTBS as an example of the kinds of report forms typically available.

Class Record Sheet (CRS).   This form, discussed earlier in this chapter (see Figure 17.2), is the basic report provided by CTB/McGraw-Hill's scoring service.

Class Management Guide (CMG).   This form contains guidelines for the various uses of the CTBS data. A section entitled "Reinforcement Activities" describes various instructional techniques useful in helping students attain objectives covered in the battery. For example, two group activities designed to help primary children improve sound recognition skills are described in Figure 17.4.

Right Response Record (RRR).   This form (Figure 17.5) indicates the number of items related to each learning objective that *each student* answered correctly. It

PRIMARY LEVEL

4 SMALL GROUP ACTIVITY   6 Rhyming Words
                                                                                    (objective)

Materials: 5 x 8 card with pictures of familiar objects

Draw or paste pictures of familiar objects on a set of 5 x 8 cards. Set the cards on the chalkrail and have students name each pictured object. Say a word and choose a student to find the card that illustrates a rhyming word. Ask the student to come and point to the picture, saying its name and repeating the given word, <u>such as bee. . . .me</u>.

Dr. Delwyn G. Schubert, <u>Reading games that teach</u> (Monterey Park, CA: Creative Teaching Press, 1968), Game #29.

5 SMALL GROUP ACTIVITY

Materials: Poster paper, pictures of rhyming nouns

Prepare a large poster with rows of pictured objects, such as <u>cat</u>, <u>boat</u>, <u>egg</u>, <u>ring</u>, <u>house</u>, and <u>hen</u>. Beside each picture, print its name. Fasten a pocket below each picture. Hang the poster where students can easily reach it. On the chalkrail, set pictures of things that rhyme with the poster words. Name the pictures aloud as they are set up. Ask a student to find a picture that rhymes with <u>cat</u> and put it in the pocket under the picture of the cat. Ask the student to pronounce the poster word and the name of the picture, to show that they rhyme (<u>cat. . .bat</u>). Continue until all the pictures have been placed in the correct pockets. Some poster words may have more than one rhyming picture. Suggested pictures: rat, mat, coat, leg, king, mouse, pen, men, ten.

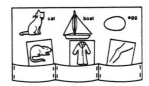

FIGURE 17.4 Sample Learning Activity from the CTBS Classroom Management Guide

SOURCE: *CTBS Classroom Management Guide.* 1981, CTB/McGraw-Hill, Monterey, CA. Reprinted with permission of the publisher.

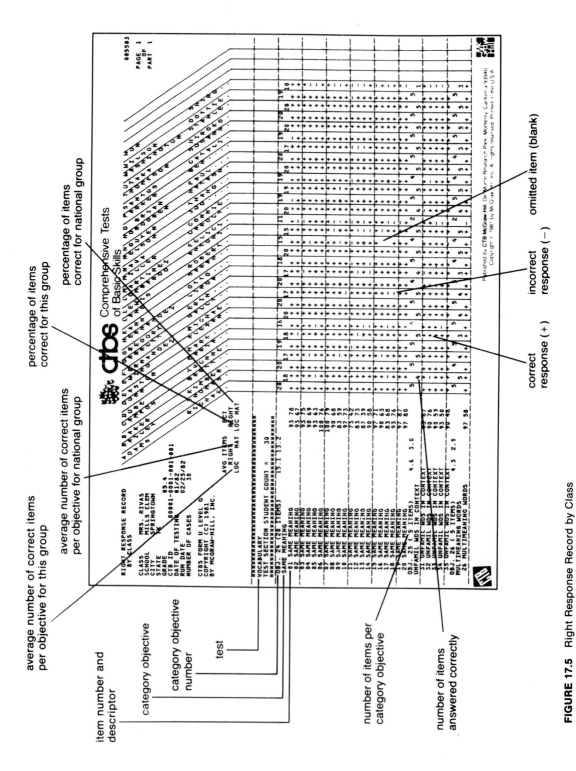

FIGURE 17.5 Right Response Record by Class

SOURCE: *CTBS Classroom Management Guide*. 1981, CTB/McGraw-Hill, Monterey, CA. Reprinted with permission of the publisher.

502

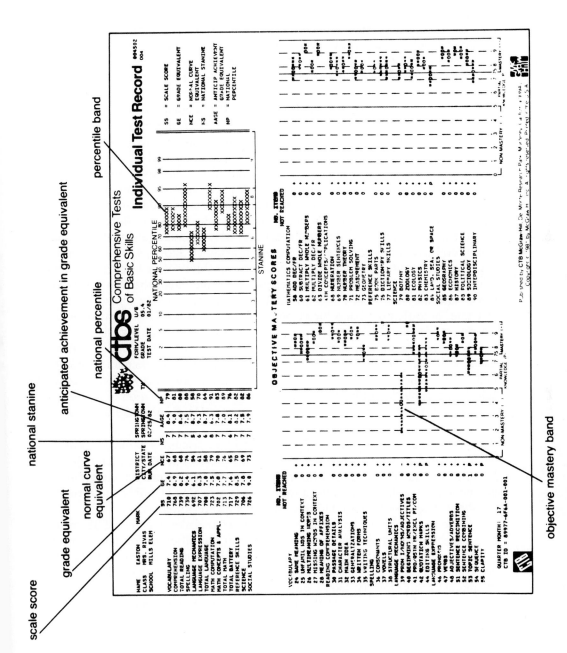

FIGURE 17.6 Individual Test Record Showing Objective Mastery Scores

SOURCE: *CTBS Classroom Management Guide*. 1981, CTB/McGraw-Hill, Monterey, CA. Reprinted with permission of the publisher.

also identifies the particular items each student answered correctly and incorrectly. For each item related to a given objective, the percentage of the class and the percentage of the national norm group responding correctly is given. By comparing these percentages, the teacher can identify the objectives on which her students are above or below national norms, as well as checking the specific test items on which her students performed above or below national levels.

Individual Test Record (ITR). This form provides a complete record of an individual student's performance on the test battery. Two forms of the ITR are available. One gives the student's mastery scores for each objective covered on the particular form of the test she took (Figure 17.6). The other gives her response to each item (right or wrong) on the test, organized by objective. The latter form gives essentially the same information as the Right Response Record (RRR). However, the objective mastery scores provide a one standard deviation confidence interval for each objective that is not provided on the RRR. Confidence intervals help the teacher remember that test scores are only estimates and that a student's true score may differ considerably from the obtained score. Also, the width of these bands permits the teacher to estimate the reliability of each score. Assuming that standard deviations are the same, the wider the band, the less reliable the score, and the more likely it is to fluctuate from one testing to the next. For example, note that the band for objective 27 (missing words in context) is very narrow, while the band for objective 42 (quotation marks) is very wide.

Note that the top of this form also summarizes an individual student's performance on the major test subdivisions, such as vocabulary, mathematics computation, and science. These scores give a quick overview of a student's general achievement, but are of limited value for diagnosis. One variation of this form is a home report that can be used when discussing a student's progress with parents.

Class Grouping Report. This report (Figure 17.3), discussed earlier, lists all students in the class who have failed to reach the mastery score on each objective. Its purpose is to help teachers who wish to organize their students into groups for instruction. Essentially the same information is provided in a different format on the Right Response Record and the Objective Mastery Report.

In summary, the computer-generated forms available for the CTBS overlap considerably in purpose and content. Although the different formats may save some time in interpreting test results, most useful information is likely to be given on or derived from the Class Record Sheet and the Right Response Record. And the moral of this story is: Don't waste time and money; study the forms offered by the test publisher very carefully and order only those you need and plan to use.

SUGGESTED READINGS

Arter, J. A. (1982, March). *Out-of-level versus in-level testing: When should we recommend each*? Paper presented at the Annual Meeting of the American Educational Research Association, New York, NY. (ERIC Document Reproduction Service No. ED 220507)

The author makes specific recommendations to aid school administrators in deciding whether to use functional level testing. A decision diagram for deciding when to use functional level testing is presented.

Mehrens, W. A. (1984). National tests and local curriculum: Match or mismatch? *Educational Measurement: Issues and Practices, 3*(3), 9–15.

The author reviews some basic facts about standardized achievement tests, discusses the amount of mismatch between standard tests and local curriculum and the implications of this mismatch. A good introduction to the topic of content validity written in clear, simple language.

Millman, J., & Greene, J. (1989). The specialization and development of tests of achievement and ability. In R. L. Linn (Ed.), *Educational Measurement* (3d ed., pp. 335–366). New York: Macmillan Publishing Company.

This chapter was written for the professional test developer, but it contains some interesting information for teachers about how standardized achievement tests should be developed. The content is much more technical than the material in the text. It proposes guidelines for specification of objectives, item writing, test assembly, and norming.

Peterson, N. S., Kolen, M. J., & Hoover, H. D. (1989). Scaling, norming, and equating. In R. L. Linn (Ed.), *Educational Measurement* (3rd ed., pp. 221–262). New York: Macmillan Publishing Company.

Comparing results from two or more different standardized achievement tests is not as simple as it might appear at first. This chapter provides a comprehensive, but somewhat technical, summary of the essential considerations in making such comparisons.

SELF-CHECK QUIZ

1. As compared with standardized achievement tests, teacher-made tests are usually superior in
   a. item quality.
   b. normative data.
   c. reliability.
   d. content validity.

2. Diagnostic tests differ from standard achievement tests in that they typically
   a. are norm-referenced.
   b. focus on a narrower range of content.
   c. measure a broader achievement range.
   d. focus on the average student.

3. The most important initial step in developing a standardized achievement test is to
   a. decide what type of test item will be used.
   b. develop the test objectives.
   c. decide how the test will be used for children with disabilities.
   d. determine how many items the test should include.

4. When selecting a standardized achievement test, consideration of content validity should focus on the degree to which the test content
   a. assesses the performance of minority students.
   b. avoids sexual or ethnic bias.
   c. remains consistent for all students at the appropriate grade levels.
   d. matches the school curriculum.

5. A curriculum-embedded test is best suited for
   a. making frequent checks of a student's progress.
   b. confirming the presence of a suspected learning disability.
   c. comparing a given student to national norms.
   d. assessing whether language ability interferes with learning the content.

6. Refer to Figure 17.2 (page 485). On which CTBS subtest did Sally Garrett obtain her lowest grade equivalent score?
   a. Reading comprehension
   b. Spelling
   c. Vocabulary
   d. Mathematics computation

7. For identifying and classifying children with disabilities, federal and state laws generally require that standardized achievement test scores
   a. be used with other assessment data.
   b. be used instead of other assessment data.
   c. be verified by readministering the test.
   d. not be used.

8. Base scores are a limitation of standardized achievement tests because they
   a. are distorted when students make "educated guesses."
   b. keep high achievers from knowing how well they really did on the test.
   c. may lead a teacher to think a low achiever did better than she actually did.
   d. tend to increase some students' scores and decrease other students' scores.

9. The purpose of a locator test is to
   a. identify sections of the local curriculum not covered by a standardized achievement test.
   b. classify students in terms of regional curriculum differences.
   c. identify curriculum materials that a teacher is not covering adequately.
   d. aid in selecting the correct level of a standardized achievement test to administer.

10. The main purpose of functional level achievement testing is to
    a. give each student an achievement test especially designed for her grade level.
    b. improve the morale of low-achieving students.
    c. give each student an achievement test appropriate for her actual achievement level.
    d. facilitate comparisons in performance of over- and underachievers.

SUGGESTION SHEET

If your last name starts with the letter *S*, please complete the Suggestion Sheet at the end of the book while this chapter is still fresh in your mind.

ANSWERS TO APPLICATION PROBLEMS

#1
Each student will select different curriculum material and a different standardized achievement test, so each student's work must be evaluated individually.

#2

a. Scholastic aptitude is estimated by the CSI. Sally Garrett, with a score of 123 is highest.

b. To determine this, compare each student's GE (actual achievement grade equivalent score) with his or her AAGE (anticipated achievement grade equivalent score). Students achieving above their AAGE in social studies are Mark Easton and Michael Fernandez.

c. Mark Easton is lowest with a national percentile score of 80.

#3

Each student will use different content, so each student's work must be evaluated individually.

CHAPTER 18

Keeping Your Finger on the Student's Pulse: Using Tests to Diagnose Strengths and Weaknesses

Overview

One of the greatest challenges a teacher faces is diagnosing student learning difficulties and providing useful remedial instruction. Diagnosing students' reading problems is especially crucial because reading is essential to other learning. Similarly, early diagnosis of student learning in mathematics is critical because of the sequential nature of this subject. Failure to master one step in the math process will make subsequent learning increasingly difficult. Teachers need good measurement tools to help them diagnose students' specific learning difficulties in these and other areas of the curriculum.

But isn't that exactly what standardized achievement test batteries do? Don't they provide a diagnostic profile that allows teachers to pinpoint a student's specific deficits in essential skills or knowledge? Not usually. Most standardized achievement tests include subtests in reading and math, and some include ''diagnostic'' subscales that attempt to show how each student performed in selected skill areas, but seldom is such information adequate for the teacher who needs to pinpoint precisely the nature of a student's learning difficulty. More specific diagnostic tools are needed, and providing these tools to teachers is the goal of this chapter.

We have organized this chapter into five major sections. In the first two, respectively, we define diagnostic testing more specifically and discuss steps for selecting diagnostic measures. In the third, we present examples of useful diagnostic reading and mathematics tests, together with information on other elements that integrate these tests into systems of diagnosis, prescription, and instruction. We also describe a service that provides schools with mathematics or reading measures that closely match local curriculum. In the fourth section, we contrast such a diagnostic system with standardized achievement tests. Finally, a brief description is given of a few diagnostic and screening measures for students with disabilities.

Objectives

Upon completing your study of this chapter, you should be able to

1. Explain why diagnostic tests are used and how they differ from other standardized achievement tests.
2. Describe some of the factors that should be considered in selecting diagnostic tests.
3. Discuss the relative advantages and disadvantages of individually administered diagnostic tests.
4. Briefly describe the Stanford Diagnostic Reading Test (SDRT), and interpret data provided in its Individual Diagnostic Report.
5. Briefly describe the DMI Mathematics Systems (DMI/MS), and interpret data provided in its Objective Mastery Report and Common Error Report.
6. Explain how teachers can develop diagnostic tests that closely fit their local mathematics or reading objectives.
7. Describe three types of measures used in the diagnosis and screening of students with disabilities.

WHAT ARE DIAGNOSTIC TESTS?

Diagnostic tests are tests designed to provide a precise picture of students' performances in a given subject area. Developers of such tests typically analyze a complex task such as reading, divide it into a series of specific skills, then develop items designed to measure a student's ability to perform each skill. These tests are not diagnostic in the medical sense—that is, they do not identify the underlying *cause* of the student's difficulty. For example reading difficulties could have many causes, such as poor vision or hearing, poor verbal fluency, low scholastic aptitude, short attention span, or emotional problems, to name just a few. Diagnostic reading tests do not identify such causes. They do, however, identify the *specific nature* of the difficulty so that the teacher can focus remedial work on a student's particular deficiencies.

Most diagnostic tests currently in use measure skills in reading and mathematics. Reading and math are generally regarded as the most basic of school subjects and are primarily process-oriented, as compared with such subjects as social studies, which are more content-oriented. Furthermore, because reading is essential to learning other school subjects, most educators feel it merits special attention. In process-oriented subjects, such as mathematics and reading, failure to master one step in the process can seriously affect mastery of subsequent steps. Most diagnostic reading and mathematics tests are designed to determine the specific deficiencies of low-achieving children in regular classrooms.

Diagnostic reading and math tests are intended to supplement information provided through standardized achievement tests. In fact, many current achievement test batteries have some characteristics of group-administered diagnostic tests. They divide complex tasks into components and provide test items to measure each component. They also compare each student's scores to criterion-referenced cutoff points to indicate which students have yet to master each specific learning objective. The current diagnostic tests that we will discuss, however, are better diagnostic tools than standardized achievement tests in mathematics and reading in several important ways.

1. First, they are aimed at the low achiever and can measure the performance of this group better than an achievement test—which must contain items appropriate for students across a wide achievement range. And after all, low achievers are clearly the group most in need of diagnosis and remediation.
2. Second, since they focus on a single subject and a narrow achievement range, diagnostic tests can include more items to measure each component of the process at hand, providing more detailed and more reliable information on each student's performance and facilitating identification of specific difficulties. Standardized achievement tests may identify students achieving below expectations, but typically do not provide enough specific information about students' difficulties to help teachers plan effective instruction.
3. Finally, the newer diagnostic tests are an integral part of a larger system of diagnosis and remediation that provides the teacher with a variety of instructional materials to help remediate problems revealed by the diagnostic measure. Although there is sometimes little evidence of the effectiveness of these remedial materials, they at least give teachers some ideas and instructional strategies to try.

Many diagnostic tests, especially in reading, are administered individually. Individual oral administration permits the examiner to observe and record many errors, such as mispronunciation, that are difficult to measure in group-administered tests. Listening to a child read or having him "talk through" his solution to an arithmetic problem can provide the trained examiner with a great deal of useful diagnostic information. The examiner can also estimate the student's level of anxiety, attention, and motivation. If the student is ill, emotionally upset, or antagonistic toward the examiner, the test results will be of little value. Thus, individual diagnostic tests do have some advantages over group-administered tests, where it is more difficult to discern such student variables.

On the other hand, administering many of the individual diagnostic tests requires skills and experience that the typical teacher has not developed; therefore, these tests must often be administered by a reading specialist or school psychologist. Further, because of the extensive time required for individual administration, a useful strategy is to identify *areas* of poor performance using a standardized achievement test, and then to administer a diagnostic test to determine specific steps in the learning process that need remediation. This strategy requires that the diagnostic measure be administered only to those students who show significant weaknesses on the standardized achievement measure.

As with other types of tests, a diagnostic test will be useful only to the extent that it is technically sound and suits the specific purpose for which you wish to use it. Therefore, we must consider how to select a diagnostic test that will serve you well.

SELECTING DIAGNOSTIC TESTS

In Chapter 16 we discussed the test characteristics that should be considered in selecting any test. All those are relevant when selecting a diagnostic test for classroom use. In addition, you should consider the following:

1. *Specific Skills:* Does the diagnostic test break down the broad skills of reading or mathematics into *specific subskills*? Are test items included to measure the student's mastery of each subskill? If not, the test will probably add little to what you can learn from a standardized achievement test.
2. *Subtest Reliabilities:* Because these tests are used for individual diagnosis, subtest reliabilities should be .85 or higher. Remember, as reliability declines, the standard error of measurement becomes larger, and the chance of your making a faulty diagnosis of an individual student's abilities increases.
3. *Administration Time:* Many diagnostic tests must be administered individually. They tend to be long because of the need for several items to measure each objective or step in the learning process. Can the necessary time be scheduled?
4. *Resources:* Administering and interpreting some diagnostic tests requires special training. Is someone available who is qualified to administer and interpret this measure?
5. *Linking Diagnosis to Remediation:* Can a student's deficiencies, revealed by the subtest scores, be translated into specific remedial strategies? In other words, can you decide what kind of remediation is needed simply by

reviewing the student's test performance? This link is essential to effective use of test results.

6. *Remedial Materials:* Does the test developer recommend or provide specific instructional materials or procedures that can be used to remediate student deficiencies revealed by the subtest scores? Although it is not essential, such material can be very helpful to the teacher. (Of course, you need not restrict yourself to remedial material supplied by the test developer.)

7. *Content Validity:* Does the test cover the reading or mathematics content and skills that your students have been exposed to? Students cannot be expected to have mastered skills not yet taught.

No diagnostic test is perfect, but if you find one that meets these criteria reasonably well, it will probably suit your purposes.

DIAGNOSTIC READING AND MATHEMATICS TESTS

In this section, we discuss diagnostic mathematics and reading tests used primarily with regular (i.e., nonhandicapped) students who are having difficulties in these subjects. These tests are aimed at diagnosing very specific deficiencies.

A common weakness of many diagnostic tests in the past has been their failure to give teachers guidance in designing instruction to help students overcome deficiencies identified by the test. Recently published measures, however, tend to provide teachers with more help—both in interpreting test results and in planning remedial teaching. The measures discussed in this section are designed to be used in conjunction with suggested remedial activities and supplemental teaching materials designed to help remediate each specific learning deficit.

In developing contemporary diagnostic tests, the first step usually is a detailed analysis of both the content and the processes related to a given area such as math or reading. A set of objectives is then developed to cover each specific step in the learning process, and test items are written to help determine the individual student's specific deficiencies. Such careful development leads to current diagnostic systems such as the two we describe below to give you a better understanding of how a diagnostic test can fit into a larger system of diagnosis, prescription, and instruction. These examples are only illustrative of the abundance of alternative diagnostic tests currently available.

Stanford Diagnostic Reading Test (SDRT)

The SDRT is based upon the view that reading is a developmental process that can be divided into four major components: decoding, vocabulary, comprehension, and rate. At different grade levels, the relative importance of these components and the specific skills related to each changes. The test is available at four levels (called Red, Green, Brown, and Blue) which collectively cover grades 1 through 12.

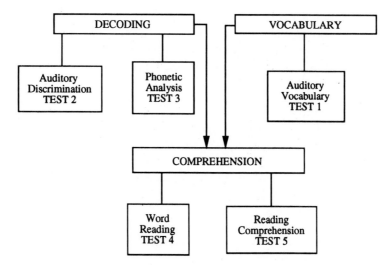

FIGURE 18.1   The Reading Process Measured by the Red Level
of SDRT

The structure of the SDRT Red Level (for grades 1 and 2 and low achievers in succeeding grades) is shown in Figure 18.1. There are five tests in this level. Note that *rate* is not measured since the authors believe that reading rate is not important at this level. Let's look at one of these SDRT tests, *Phonetic Analysis*, in some depth to show how the test is constructed and how it can be used in diagnosing both class and individual performance.

Phonetic Analysis

Phonetic Analysis measures the child's ability to relate sounds and letters, a skill essential to sounding out unfamiliar words. Two major objectives for this subtest, called *skill domain objectives*, relate consonant and vowel sounds to their most common spellings. Five *item cluster objectives* deal with specific aspects of the skill domain objectives. In Part A of this subtest, the pupil is asked to identify the letter or letter combination that matches the initial sound of a given word. For example, after administering the practice item, the examiner says, "Look at box number 1. You see a picture of a coat. Mark the space next to the letter that stands for the beginning sound of *coat*."

Part B is similar, except the pupil is asked to give the *ending* sound of each word. A total of 24 items in this subtest cover consonant sounds and 16 items cover vowel sounds. In turn, the 24 consonant sound items are divided into three item-clusters, which include eight items for single-letter consonant sounds, eight items for sounds represented by consonant groups, and eight items for consonant sounds represented by digraphs.[1] The 16 items on vowel sounds are divided into two item-clusters—short vowel sounds and long vowel sounds. The specific sound measured by each item is given in the *Manual for Interpreting* (Karlsen & Gardner, 1986). The other subtests are similarly divided into skill domain objectives and item clusters.

SDRT Information Provided to Teachers

Widespread use of computers has made it possible for major test publishers to provide teachers with a great deal of information useful in interpreting test results. For example, eight kinds of scores are available for the SDRT: content-referenced scores, raw scores, progress indicators, norm-referenced scores, percentile ranks, stanines, grade equivalents, and scaled scores. These can be used both for individual and class diagnosis.

In addition to a variety of scores, the SDRT also supplies the teacher with various reports containing profiles and summary sheets that can aid in diagnosis and interpretation.

The *Individual Diagnostic Report* (IDR) is the most useful of the report forms that are provided when the SDRT is machine scored by the Psychological Corporation. A separate copy of the form is provided for each pupil tested. It provides the teacher with the pupil's subtest raw scores and converts these to derived scores such as Grade Equivalent scores and National Percentile Rank so that the pupil's performance on each subtest can be compared with national norms. This form also gives a skills analysis for the pupil and progress indicators that tell whether the pupil's progress is satisfactory on each of the skills measured. Finally, it identifies the instructional group in which the pupil should be placed (see Figure 18.2).

The *Class Summary Report* combines the data from the Individual Diagnostic Reports to give a class overview. Mean raw scores, grade equivalent scores, scaled scores, percentile ranks, and stanines are given for the class on the first page (see Figure 18.3). A list of the pupils in each instructional group is given on the second page. Finally, specific suggestions are given for teaching the pupils in each group.

The *Instructional Placement Report* is filled out by the teacher when the SDRT is handscored. In this case, the Individual Diagnostic Report and the Class Summary, which cover the same information, would not be available. Space is provided on this form to enter each pupil's scores, the skill level of each pupil, and the progress indicator cutoff scores. Comparing the pupil's score on each test with the cutoff score indicates areas where the pupil's progress is satisfactory (+) and areas where he needs additional help.

Now, let's examine the Individual Diagnostic Report (IDR) in some detail. This report provides up to five different scores on each subtest for the pupil, indicates which of several reading groups is most appropriate for him, and gives *progress indicators*, telling whether he is above or below a critical cutoff score in the skill domains measured by the SDRT, such as vowel sounds, consonant sounds, and vocabulary (see Figure 18.2). For example, a look at the upper left corner of Figure 18.2 shows that Sam Rosen has a vocabulary raw score of 23,

---

[1] A digraph is a group of two letters whose phonetic value is a single sound.

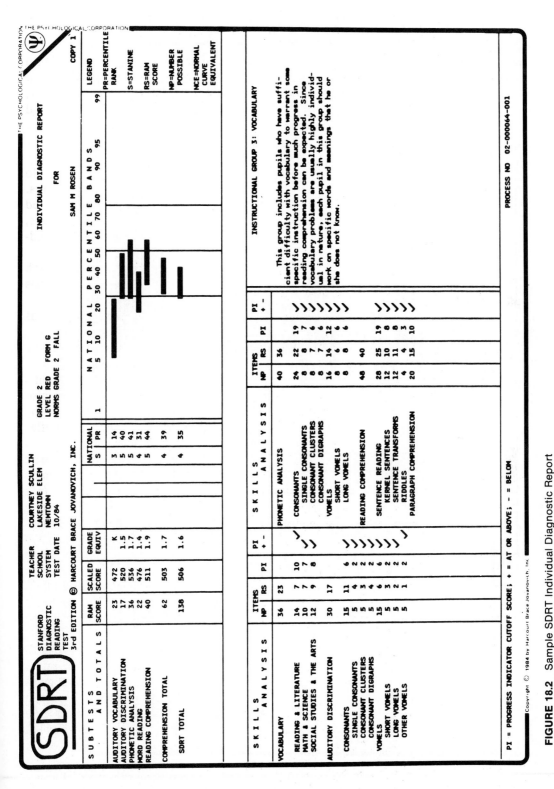

FIGURE 18.2 Sample SDRT Individual Diagnostic Report

SOURCE: Reproduced by permission from materials for the Stanford Diagnostic Reading Test: Third Edition. Copyright © 1984 by Harcourt Brace Jovanovich, Inc. Reproduced by permission. All rights reserved.

STANFORD DIAGNOSTIC READING TEST 3rd EDITION © HARCOURT BRACE JOVANOVICH, INC.

TEACHER	COURTNEY SCULLIN
SCHOOL	LAKESIDE ELEM
SYSTEM	NEWTOWN
TEST DATE	10/84

GRADE 2
LEVEL RED FORM G
NORMS GRADE 2 FALL

CLASS SUMMARY
WITH
INSTRUCTIONAL PLACEMENT REPORT

PAGE 1
COPY 1

SUBTESTS AND TOTALS	N'S	MEAN RS	SS OF MN RS	GE OF MN RS	PR-S OF MN RS	
AUDITORY VOCABULARY	35	26.9	506	1.6	34	4
AUDITORY DISCRIMINATION	35	19.5	535	1.9	46	5
PHONETIC ANALYSIS	35	36.1	536	1.7	41	5
WORD READING	35	22.6	486	1.6	35	4
READING COMPREHENSION	34	34.0	471	1.3	28	4
COMPREHENSION TOTAL	34	56.6	494	1.4	31	4
SDRT TOTAL	34	139.3	508	1.6	36	4

TOTAL TESTED = 35

	NUMBER	PERCENT
GROUP 1 REMEDIAL	0	.0%
GROUP 2 DECODING	8	22.9%
GROUP 3 VOCABULARY	7	20.0%
GROUP 4 COMPREHENSION	7	20.0%
GROUP 5 RATE	0	.0%
GROUP 6 DEVELOPMENTAL	12	34.3%
GROUP 7 ENRICHMENT	0	.0%
GROUP 8 INCOMPLETE	1	2.9%

SKILLS ANALYSIS SUMMARY

	PROGRESS INDICATORS			
	N+	%+	N-	%-
VOCABULARY				
READING & LITERATURE	25	71	10	29
MATH & SCIENCE	30	86	5	14
SOCIAL STUDIES & THE ARTS	26	74	9	26
AUDITORY DISCRIMINATION				
CONSONANTS	29	83	6	17
SINGLE CONSONANTS	29	83	6	17
CONSONANT CLUSTERS	29	83	6	17
CONSONANT DIGRAPHS	32	91	3	9
VOWELS				
SHORT VOWELS	29	83	6	17
LONG VOWELS	31	89	4	11
OTHER VOWELS	30	86	5	14
PHONETIC ANALYSIS				
CONSONANTS	32	91	3	9
SINGLE CONSONANTS	34	97	1	3
CONSONANT CLUSTERS	33	94	2	6
CONSONANT DIGRAPHS	31	89	4	11
VOWELS	33	94	2	6
SHORT VOWELS	29	83	6	17
LONG VOWELS	34	97	1	3
READING COMPREHENSION				
SENTENCE READING	28	82	6	18
KERNEL SENTENCES	31	91	3	9
SENTENCE TRANSFORMS	29	85	5	15
RIDDLES	24	71	10	29
PARAGRAPH COMPREHENSION	23	68	11	32

MN = MEAN RS = RAW SCORE PR = PERCENTILE RANK S = STANINE
NCE = NORMAL CURVE EQUIVALENT TNT = TEST NOT TAKEN
SS = SCALED SCORE GE = GRADE EQUIVALENT

PROCESS NO 02-000064-001

CONTINUED...

FIGURE 18.3 Sample SDRT Class Summary with Instruction Placement Report, First Page

SOURCE: Reproduced from Bjorn Karlsen and Eric Gardner (1986). *Stanford Diagnostic Reading Test, 3rd Edition Manual for Interpreting*, p. 19, by permission.

meaning he gave the correct answer on 23 of the 36 vocabulary items. This student has a grade equivalent score[2] of "K" indicating that his vocabulary level is lower than the typical first grade pupil tested in October. The next columns give his stanine score (3) and percentile rank (14) compared with the national norms. The top right corner of the IDR gives national percentile bands. These indicate the pupil's percentile rank plus or minus one standard error of measurement. Perhaps the greatest value of percentile bands is that they show the teacher that the scores obtained are only estimates that are subject to considerable error. The wider the percentile band, the greater is the standard error of measurement.

You will note that all of the scores on the upper half of the IDR tell the teacher essentially the same thing—that Sam's performance on all of the subtests is below average while the vocabulary subtest is much below average. Except for the raw score, these are all *norm-referenced* scores—that is, they tell Sam's performance *relative* to other students. Since these scores have very similar meanings, not all are needed and the school personnel may specify which scores are most useful to them. For most uses, the raw score, percentile, and stanine are sufficient.

Like most current diagnostic measures, the SDRT reports criterion-referenced information as well as norm-referenced scores. The progress indicators refer to a criterion—that is, the level of performance the student should attain to demonstrate mastery of each test objective. The skill analysis on the lower left side of the form gives criterion-referenced information, indicating the student's performance on specific subtest skills. For example, Sam correctly answered 11 of 15 items on consonant sounds, and 6 of 15 items on vowel sounds. Since both of these scores are checked in the plus (+) column, we can conclude that Sam reached the criterion or cutoff score in these areas, and remediation is not needed. Note that the progress indicator cutoff scores (PI column) for auditory discrimination, given at the bottom of the form, is 6 for consonant sounds and 6 for vowel sounds. Thus, Sam's scores of 11 and 6 are at or above the cutoffs. Scores at or above the cutoff are checked in the plus (+) column, those below the cutoff are checked in the minus (−) column. Note that in the lower right corner of the IDR, it is recommended that Sam be placed in Instructional Group 3: vocabulary. Students with low scores on the vocabulary subtest would be placed in Group 3, those with low comprehension scores in Group 4, and so on. Students may be classified into as many as eight groups.

In some cases, subgroup classifications are also given next to the student's name. For Group 2 students, a classification of 2A indicates general decoding problems, 2B auditory discrimination problems, and 2C phonetic analysis problems.

Now, for some practical experience in interpreting the Individual Diagnostic Report, try completing the following application problem using the data given in Figure 18.2.

---

[2] You will recall our caution in Chapter 5 concerning problems with grade equivalent scores and our suggestion that percentiles or other indices be used instead. Our statements did not rid the world of grade equivalents, however, so we discuss them here and hereafter in relation to their actual use by others.

APPLICATION PROBLEM #1

Study the report data for Sam Rosen and answer the following questions:

a. Under which instructional group is he classified?
b. On what subtest did this student earn his highest score relative to the test norms?
c. On what skill domains was this student below the progress indicator cutoff score?

Using the SDRT to Prescribe Learning

The SDRT comes with *Handbooks of Instructional Techniques and Materials* for each of the four test levels. The handbook for the Red Level (grades 1 and 2) describes skill areas covered at that level—such as consonant sounds, vowel sounds, word division, and blending. Instructional techniques appropriate for these groups are briefly described. The Class Summary Report also includes instructional suggestions. Here, for example, is the group definition and suggested classroom activities for the SDRT Red Level for Group 6: Developmental.

Group Definition

In general, pupils in this group earned average scores on all SDRT subtests. The main instructional objective for these pupils is continued development in all facets of reading. This overall objective is most efficiently achieved by means of a comprehensive and systematic reading program.

Suggestions

1. Make sure that the instructional program covers the basic skills taught at this level: auditory and visual decoding, eight-word development, vocabulary improvement, and reading comprehension.
2. Make deliberate efforts to help pupils transfer reading skills to the reading process.
3. Provide pupils with opportunities to use reading as a tool for problem solving by having them apply their reading skills to various situations such as following directions, playing games, cooking, assembling things, etc.
4. Encourage independent reading by making easy and interesting books readily available to pupils. (Karlsen & Gardner, 1986, p. 22).

In addition to the suggested instructional techniques, a selected bibliography and a list of commercially available instructional materials are also provided. While such materials may fall far short of detailed lesson plans, they do provide a great many ideas and resources that teachers can adapt to their own needs.

The Diagnostic Math Inventory (DMI) Mathematics Systems (DMI/MS)

Here is another example of a complete system for diagnosis, prescription, and instruction. Although the DMI was originally a diagnostic test, the DMI/MS has evolved into an objectives-based system designed to provide an integrating program for mathematics assessment and instruction. The system contains materials designed to assist in (1) placing students for assessment at their correct instructional levels, (2) diagnosing each student's mathematics strengths and instructional needs, (3) prescribing appropriate materials and activities, (4) teaching specific mathematics skills, (5) monitoring students' progress in the skills taught, and (6) reinforcing and enriching mastered skills.

The current system, introduced in 1983, includes a number of components under each of these six major functions. The first component in the system consists of two locator tests used to determine for each student the appropriate level on the Instructional Objectives Inventory (IOI)—the main diagnostic measure used in the system. The IOI, which diagnoses students' mastery of specific instructional objectives in mathematics, is available at seven levels (A through G), ranging from grade K.6 to grade 8.9 and above. The various levels of the IOI measure student achievement on 170 instructional objectives in mathematics. The IOI is not a timed test and each successive level includes more items and requires more time. The publisher estimates that level G, including the practice exercises, requires just over three hours. Level A, on the other hand, requires approximately one hour.

Several report forms available from the publisher summarize and organize score data on the Instructional Objectives Inventory. The *Objectives Mastery Report (OMR)* lists for each child the specific instructional objectives that child has mastered (+) or not mastered (−), and those for which he requires review (R). For example, there are eleven objectives related to whole numbers. As Figure 18.4 shows, John Brown reached mastery on six of these, needs review on one, and has yet to master five. Summary data are also given for each objective, indicating the percentage of children in the class who have mastered that objective, as well as the number who have yet to master the objective or who need further review.

The following application problem will give you experience in interpreting DMI data.

APPLICATION PROBLEM #2

Study Figure 18.4 and answer the following questions:

a. In Mr. Jones's class, how many students have not mastered Objective 15, Basic Multiplication Facts? How many need review?

b. What objective did the largest number of Mr. Jones's students not yet master?

c. Which students are weakest in Category 02, addition of whole numbers?

Development of the DMI was based on the publisher's experience with earlier tests, whose answer sheets gave test developers extensive information on the most common errors for each test item. Checking which incorrect response each child

DMI Mathematics Systems

OBJECTIVES MASTERY REPORT
BY CLASS

CLASS	JONES
SCHOOL	HANNAN
CITY	SMITHVILLE
STATE	IL
DISTRICT	FLORENCE
GRADE	3.0
TEST DATE	09/83
RUN DATE	10/12/83
TEST	DMI/MS, LEVEL C COPYRIGHT (C) 1983

NUMBER OF CASES = 20

	- NON MAS N	R REV N	+ MAS N	MAS PCT	ALLISON DEANA	BROWN JOHN	FENNEL JASON	GRAHAM MARY	HAMMERS RALPH	JACKSON TRAVIS	KLEIN MELVIN	MARKOWITZ CARL	MILLER KAREN	NOONAN TERESA	ORTEGA MANUEL	PARKER MARK	PORTER SUSAN	RODRIGUEZ SARA	SANCHEZ MARIA	SILVERSTEIN RON	SMITH WILLIAM	SCOTT LILY	TUTTLE ALLEN	WILLIAMS ROSALYN
I WHOLE NUMBERS																								
[01] NUMBERS AND OPERATIONS																								
02 NUM & NAMES FOR WHOLE NOS	7	5	8	40	R	-	R	-	-	-	+	+	-	R	-	+	-	+	+	R	+	+	+	R
03 COMPARE WHOLE NOS	6	3	11	55	+	-	-	+	R	+	+	+	+	+	R	-	+	-	+	+	R	-	-	+
04 PLACE VALUE IN WHOLE NOS	5	8	7	35	R	-	R	+	-	-	+	+	R	R	+	+	-	R	R	+	R	+	-	R
[02] ADDITION OF WHOLE NUMBERS																								
08 BASIC ADDITION FACTS	1	5	14	70	+	+	+	+	+	+	+	+	+	+	R	R	R	+	+	R	+	+	-	R
09 ADDITION WITHOUT REGROUP	5	7	8	40	R	-	+	+	-	R	+	+	-	-	+	-	R	+	R	+	+	R	R	R
10 ADDITION WITH REGROUP	7	6	7	35	R	+	+	+	+	+	-	-	+	+	R	-	R	R	-	R	R	-	-	-
11 ADDITION OF 3,4,or 5 ADDENDS	10	5	5	25	R	+	+	+	R	-	+	-	+	-	R	-	-	-	R	-	R	-	-	-
[03] SUBTRACTION OF WHOLE NUMBERS																								
12 BASIC SUBTRACTION FACTS	2	5	13	65	+	+	+	+	R	+	+	-	+	+	+	R	+	R	-	R	+	+	R	+
13 SUBTRACTION WITHOUT REGROUP	5	8	7	35	+	+	+	-	-	R	+	R	+	+	R	-	R	-	R	R	+	R	-	R
14 SUBTRACTION WITH REGROUP	12	2	6	30	R	+	+	+	-	-	+	-	+	+	-	-	-	-	-	-	R	-	-	-
[04] MULTIPLICATION OF WHOLE NUMBERS																								
15 BASIC MULTIPLICATION FACTS	5	7	8	40	+	R	+	R	+	+	+	+	-	-	R	R	+	+	-	R	R	-	R	-
INSTR OBJ MAS IN STRAND I - TOTAL POSSIBLE = 11					5	6	8	8	3	5	10	6	7	6	3	2	3	4	3	3	5	4	1	2
II FRACTIONS AND DECIMALS																								
[07] FRACTION CONCEPTS																								
23 ID/NAME FRACT PARTS	5	7	8	40	-	+	+	R	-	R	+	-	R	+	+	+	R	R	+	+	R	-	-	R
INSTR OBJ MAS IN STRAND II - TOTAL POSSIBLE = 01					0	1	1	0	0	0	1	0	0	1	1	1	0	0	1	1	0	0	0	0

INSTRUCTIONAL OBJECTIVES SCORES + MASTERY R REVIEW - NONMASTERY

CTB ID 90526-73C5-001-001

FIGURE 18.4 Sample of the Objectives Mastery Report Supplied with the DMI/MS

SOURCE: John Gessel, *DMI Mathematics Systems, Examination Materials.* 1983, CTB/McGraw-Hill, Monterey, CA. Reprinted with permission of the publisher.

made on a given item made it possible to diagnose the kind of error that led to the incorrect response. The resulting *Common Error Report* of the DMI/MS (Figure 18.5) identifies the errors made by each child in the class. For example, we can see from Figure 18.5 that 13 of the 20 pupils in Mr. Jones's class made errors that involved confusing two numerals. Note also that Susan Porter made all eleven of the common errors reported on this form. Working from this report, the teacher can check the *Guide to Correcting Common Errors,* which explains each error in detail. Then the teacher can refer to the *Teacher Resource Files* (Figure 18.6), which are also part of this system, to locate instructional activities designed to help remedy the common errors.

Each resource file states the objective with which the file is concerned and provides background information on the skills and vocabulary related to the objective and common errors students make relative to achieving that objective.

Another aid to prescribing remedial work for the student is the *Master Reference Keys*, keyed references to basal mathematics textbooks widely used in the public schools. The keys indicate for each DMI/MS objective the pages in each basal mathematics textbook and workbook that contain related instructional materials. Figure 18.7 shows a sample page from the Master Reference Keys.

As remedial instruction progresses, the teacher must monitor student progress. A set of mastery tests, for each instructional objective, is provided for this purpose. These tests provide a means for monitoring student progress on a continuous basis.

To reinforce and enrich each student's learning, *tutor activity sheets* and *common error worksheets* are provided with the DMI/MS. The activity sheets are designed for use with parents, tutors, or other students, though at higher grade levels they can also be used either as classroom work or homework assignments. For each instructional objective one or more activities are provided. These are labeled with the instructional objective number, level, and a brief explanation of the topic covered by the activity. A sample of a tutor activity sheet is shown in Figure 18.8.

The common error worksheets are designed to provide each student with practice in doing the kinds of problems that are currently giving him the most trouble. They also help determine whether instruction has been effective while providing additional practice to reinforce learning.

The Utility of Diagnostic Math and Reading Systems

In summary, the DMI/MS is an extensive system designed to assist the teacher in dealing with all aspects of mathematics diagnosis, prescription, and instruction, and the SDRT performs a similar function for reading. Because of the large public school market, publishers are encouraged to devote a good deal of time and energy to the development of such systems. Considerable study is necessary if a teacher is to make effective use of such diagnostic systems. However, when a teacher's knowledge of the children in his classroom is combined with conscientious use of one of these diagnostic-prescriptive systems, the teacher can probably do as good

DMI Mathematics Systems

COMMON ERROR REPORT
  BY CLASS

CLASS   JONES
SCHOOL   HANNAN
CITY   SMITHVILLE
STATE   IL
DISTRICT   FLORENCE
GRADE   3.0 (A)
TEST DATE   09/83
RUN DATE   10/12/83
TEST   DMI/MS, LEVEL C
             COPYRIGHT (C) 1983

NUMBER OF CASES = 20 (C)

	TRF* (D)	N (E)
I WHOLE NUMBERS		
COUNTING NUMBERS		
CN1 TRANSPOSE DIGITS	8C	6
CN2 OMIT A DIGIT	2C	12
CN6 CONFUSE TWO NUMERALS	2C	13
CN7 CONFUSE TWO WORD NAMES	2C	10
II FRACTIONS AND DECIMALS		
PICTORIAL FRACTIONS		
PF1 CHOOSE EQUAL PARTS	23C	11
PF4 CHOOSE WRONG NUMBER OF PARTS	23C	7
III MEASUREMENT AND GEOMETRY		
CLOCK		
CL1 READ ONLY ONE HAND	44C	11
CL3 MISREAD TIME BY ONE HOUR	44C	6
MEASUREMENT		
MS1 MISREAD A SCALE	47C	10
MS14 CHOOSE HIGHEST NUMBER	47C	9
GEOMETRY		
GM3 MISIDENTIFY 2-D FIGURE	55C	10
IV PROBLEM SOLVING AND SPECIAL TOPICS		
NO COMMON ERRORS WERE EVIDENT		

(Columns of the report are headed by individual student names, with X marks indicating which error each student made.)

*TEACHER RESOURCE FILES (TRF) CONTAIN ACTIVITIES THAT HELP REMEDY COMMON ERRORS

CTB ID 90526-73C5-001-001

FIGURE 18.5 Sample of the Common Error Report Supplied with the DMI/MS

SOURCE: John Gessel, *DMI Mathematics Systems, Examination Materials.* 1983, CTB/McGraw Hill, Monterey, CA. Reprinted with permission of the publisher.

DMI Mathematics Systems

By John Gessel

Teacher Resource File

OBJECTIVE 8: The student will be able to add pairs of addends from zero to ten.

TESTED AT LEVEL C: add addends from zero to ten

BACKGROUND INFORMATION

Foundation Skills

- counting (1A,B)
- numerals and names for whole numbers (2A–C)

Related Skills

- addition of whole numbers (9B,C; 10C,D; 11C–E)
- basic subtraction facts (12B,C)
- solving one-step word problems (62B–G)

Vocabulary

addition: Combining numbers to find out how many in all.

addend: A number to be added; given 4 + 5 = 9, 4 and 5 are addends.

plus (+): Symbol used to indicate the addition operation. For example, 4 + 5 = 9 is read as "4 plus 5 equals 9."

sum: The answer obtained by adding any set of numbers.

equals (=): A relation of being exactly the same.

equation: Mathematical sentence involving the use of the equality symbol (=).

solve: To find the number or numbers that make a given equation true.

commutative (order) property of addition: The idea that the order of the addends does not affect the sum. For example, 2 + 4 = 6 and 4 + 2 = 6.

Addition is the joining of groups of objects, usually shown by numerals, to find how many in all. The basic facts of addition are the sums of any numeral 0–10 and any other numeral 0–10. These basic facts form the foundation for all addition.

Students at this level should already be familiar with the basic facts with sums up to 20, introduced in Level B. They now need to review those facts to ensure an instant recall of them.

The review of the basic facts should begin with the simpler addition equations associated with real or pictured groups of objects. Once students have been reminded what the equations mean, these representations should be eliminated to leave only the addition equations. Emphasis should be placed on students gaining an instant recall of basic facts. To help them see the patterns in basic addition facts, all the facts may be reviewed initially with one addend remaining constant while the other varies from 0 through 10 (e.g., 0 plus all the numerals 0 through 10, then 1 plus all the numerals 0 through 10, . . .). The facts should then be mixed and practiced until students can readily recall them all. Both horizontal and vertical forms should be used.

Students should become proficient in reading the equation form as well. For example, 5 + 3 = 8 should be read as "five plus three equals eight." Students also need to understand and recognize the symbols + (plus) and = (equals) and to be able to set up addition equations for any given group of objects or numbers. They should understand that when the order of the addends is changed, the sum remains the same (e.g., 2 + 3 = 5 is the same as 3 + 2 = 5).

Common Errors

- **AW1:** obtaining a sum that is one or two more or less than the correct sum (See activity 9.)
- **AW4:** multiplying instead of adding (See activity 8.)
- **AW6:** subtracting instead of adding (See activity 3.)
- **AW15:** linking together some or all of the digits of the addends rather than obtaining a sum (See activity 4.)
- **CN1:** transposing digits in a numeral (See activity 11.)

See also the Guide to Correcting Common Errors.

 Published by CTB/McGraw-Hill, Del Monte Research Park, Monterey, California 93940. Copyright © 1983 by McGraw-Hill, Inc. All Rights Reserved. Printed in U.S.A.

FIGURE 18.6 Sample Page from the Teacher Resource File for the DMI/MS

SOURCE: John Gessel, *DMI Mathematics Systems, Examination Materials.* 1983, CTB/McGraw-Hill, Monterey, CA. Reprinted with permission of the publisher.

TITLE: HOLT MATHEMATICS
LEVEL: 1 GRADE: 1
DMI/MS LEVELS: 8   Copyright (C) 1983 by McGraw-Hill, Inc.   Page 2

PUBLISHER: HOLT, RINEHART AND WINSTON
SERIES: HOLT MATHEMATICS
COPYRIGHT: 1981

DMI/MS OBJECTIVE	CAT/C	CTBS/U	TEACHER'S EDITION	WORKBOOK	ORBIT
[1] NUMBERS AND OPERATIONS 1 Counting	75	68	1,2,14,23W,24,28W, 32W,123,124,133, 134W,184W,186W, 188W-192,209,223,		27000A 27000B 270100 270150 270160
3 Comparison of Whole Numbers	76	68 69	193,194W,203,204W		27000A 270100
[2] ADDITION OF WHOLE NUMBERS 8 Basic Addition Facts	69	57	37,38W-40W,41,42W, 45,46W-50W,51,52W, 53,54W,55,81-84W, 86W,88,98,148,166, 206W,220,223,228W, 301,304W		01000B 010030 010040
	69	57	85,86W,98,228W-230W, 283,284W-286W,288, 294		01000B 010050
9 Addition Without Regrouping	69	57	213,214		01000B 010110 010120
	69	57	215,216W-218W,232, 303		01000B 010110 010120 010160
[3] SUBTRACTION OF WHOLE NUMBERS 12 Basic Subtraction Facts	70	59	41,42W-44W,45,48,51, 52,54W,55,82		03000B 030030
	70	59	105,106W,129, 130W-132W,133,135, 151,152W-154W,158W, 176,307		03000B 030070 030080

FIGURE 18.7 Sample Page from the Master Reference Keys for the DMI/MS. Pages in each text that are relative to each CMI/MS objective are given.

SOURCE: John Gessel, *DMI Mathematics Systems, Examination Materials.* 1983, CTB/Mcgraw-Hill, Monterey, CA. Reprinted with permission of the publisher.

DMI Mathematics Systems

By John Gessel

Tutor Activities

Name

Date

(2)C

Category: Addition of Whole Numbers
Strand I: Whole Numbers

_____ is learning to add whole numbers. Some of the addition problems require carrying and some do not. Some problems have more than two numbers to add. The numbers to be added may have one, two, or three digits. Please do the circled activities as games or as part of relaxed conversation. Spend about ___ minutes doing them.

8C 1 Materials: playing cards.
Remove the face cards from a deck of playing cards. Shuffle the rest of the cards. Deal the student two cards at a time and ask him or her to add together the numbers that appear on the cards (aces count as one). If the student obtains a correct sum, he or she keeps the two cards; if not, the cards are returned to the deck. Continue until the student has "won" all the cards.

9C 2 Give the student nine toothpicks to use for adding each column of digits in a problem. Tell the student to use the toothpicks as counters if needed in working the problems you present. Give the student two- or three-digit addition problems which do *not* require carrying (i.e., the sum of any column is less than ten). Here are some problems to get you started:

34	49	234	577	193	632
+ 21	+ 50	+ 64	+ 21	+ 700	+ 147
(55)	(99)	(298)	(598)	(893)	(779)

10C 3 Materials: slips of paper.
Give the student ten slips of paper on which to write two sets of the numbers 5 to 9. Mix all the slips of paper together. Ask the student to draw six slips of paper each time and use these to set up three-digit word problems using the drawn numbers. Have the student add the problems step-by-step. If necessary, remind him or her to add the ones' column first, record the sum and write the carried digit above the tens' column; then add the tens' column, record its sum and write the carried digit above the hundreds' column; and finally add the hundreds' column and record its sum. Correct any errors as the student goes along. Here is a sample problem.

$$968$$
$$+ 785$$
$$1753$$

11C 4 Materials: 3"×5" cards.
Write the numbers 1 through 6 on 3"×5" cards and repeat until you have a set of 24 numbered cards. Have the student shuffle the cards and draw any three. Show the student how to add the numbers together by adding the first two numbers and then adding their sum to the third number. Take turns with the student each time drawing three cards and discussing how the numbers can be added together.

COMMENTS: These activities were too easy ☐; about right ☐; too hard ☐. Please write any additional comments on the back of this sheet and return it by

FIGURE 18.8 Sample Page from Tutor Activities for the DMI/MS*

SOURCE: John Gessel, *DMI Mathematics Systems, Examination Materials*. 1983, CTB/McGraw-Hill, Monterey, CA. Reprinted with permission of the publisher.

a job of diagnosis and remediation as the average clinician or content specialist.[3] Teachers have the advantage of observing their students every day. The use of adequately developed and field tested systems such as the SDRT and the DMI/ MS has great potential to enhance the effectiveness of teachers who already have a general sense of students' strengths and weaknesses.

Computerized Adaptive Testing (CAT)

A fairly recent innovation that combines some of the advantages of both achievement tests and diagnostic tests is called *computerized adaptive testing*. In conventional tests, all students are administered the same set of items. In a computerized adaptive test, different questions are administered to different students. The computer selects each question from a pool of items of known difficulty. The question is displayed on a TV screen, and the student either types the letter of the correct multiple-choice response or touches the screen at the location of the correct response. The computer records whether the response is correct or incorrect and selects the next question, based on the student's response to the previous question. If the student's response is correct, the next item selected will be more difficult; if the student's response is incorrect, the next item selected will be easier. As more items are administered, the computer considers the student's performance on all previous items in estimating his mastery level and selecting the next item to be administered. As a result, the items are adapted to the level of the student. That is, on the whole they will be neither too easy nor too difficult for the individual. The main advantage of this method over conventional testing is that CAT provides a more precise measure than a conventional test, while requiring fewer items to be administered to each individual. Another advantage of CAT is that, because each student is administered a different combination of items, the teacher cannot teach to the test, and the student cannot help his peers by passing on test items he remembers, because most of the items administered to other students will be different. In reviewing research on CAT, Weiss (1985) concluded that CAT decreases testing time by about 50 percent, while resulting in more precise measurement than conventional tests. In a more recent study, Olsen (1989) found that computerized adaptive tests provided a time saving of over 70 percent compared with paper and pencil tests.

It should be noted, however, that because each student is administered a different set of test items, the scores of different students are not comparable. On a CAT, each student will answer about 50 percent of the items correctly, regardless of his level on the trait or skill being measured. Thus, his mastery of the trait or skill is measured by *which* items he answers correctly, rather than *how many* he answers correctly. However, the difficulty level, discrimination level, and probability of guessing the correct answer must be known for each item in order to interpret his performance.

The main limitations of CAT are the needs for a large pool of test items, item analysis data on all items, and sufficient computer terminals to test students within

---

[3] There is some evidence that the reading specialist's and clinician's skill in linking diagnosis and remediation in reading is prone to considerable error; see Weinshank (1980).

a reasonable span of time. A software system is also needed to implement a CAT program. Several have been developed. The best known at this writing is the MicroCAT Testing System, marketed by Assessment Systems Corporation. Kingsbury (1989) reports that the CAT program used in the Portland, Oregon public schools is the MicroCAT system with IBM PC compatible computers at a cost of about $2,300 per station.

STANDARDIZED ACHIEVEMENT VERSUS DIAGNOSTIC TESTS

Now that you have learned something about diagnostic tests, let's review in greater depth some of the important differences between diagnostic and standardized achievement tests that we briefly outlined at the beginning of this chapter.

Standardized achievement tests include items that measure a sample of content related to each of the learning objectives in a given subject area; but they usually do not measure a student's ability to carry out each step within a process such as addition or subtraction. Therefore, the teacher may determine from a standardized achievement test that Mary is weak in word decoding, but he usually cannot determine from that test score the specific steps in the decoding process where Mary is making her mistakes.

In contrast, diagnostic tests divide broad content areas into specific learning objectives and report the student's performance relative to these objectives in considerable detail. Such detail gives the teacher a better understanding of each student's specific needs. However, in a broad content area such as long division, it takes more test items to reliably identify the specific steps in which the student needs help. This tends to make diagnostic tests considerably longer than achievement tests.

Because of the length of many diagnostic tests, it is often impractical to administer the entire test to all students. A good alternative is to identify a student's area of deficiency, using a standardized achievement measure, then administer only that part of the diagnostic test that explores that deficiency. Since most diagnostic subtests are related to very specific objectives, this is not a difficult task.

Another major difference between diagnostic tests and standardized achievement tests is that the former are aimed primarily at the low achiever while the latter are designed to measure achievement over the entire range of pertinent instruction at a given grade level. Thus, the diagnostic test contains a greater proportion of easy items. This not only provides more accurate assessment for low achieving students, but also makes it possible for most of them to obtain *some* correct answers. It is vital for low achievers to experience success since constant failure can be very destructive to the student's morale, self-perceptions, aspirations, and attitude toward school.

Although most report some normative data, diagnostic tests are primarily related to criteria. This means that specific learning objectives are spelled out, and cutoff points are established to determine whether the student has reached the criterion on test items designed to measure each objective. For example, progress indicators have been established for each cluster of items on the Stanford Diagnostic Mathematics Test (SDMT). If a student reaches this criterion he is given a plus (+) indicating mastery. The Brown Level of this test (grades 6 through 8) contains 21 items in the skill domain related to whole numbers and decimal place values. The seventh grade student must answer 14 or more of these items correctly to reach the criterion.

The value of a test such as the SDMT for diagnosis is clear when we see that the concept skill domain concerned with whole numbers and decimal place value is divided into six item-clusters that measure (1) naming numbers and counting, (2) reading numerals, (3) interpreting numerals, (4) working with place value and the operations, (5) ordering, and (6) rounding and estimating. A cutoff score (progress indicator) is established for each of these item clusters so the teacher can determine the specific areas in which the student needs remedial instruction.

In contrast, achievement batteries are primarily designed to provide a measure of general competence in the subject being tested, in relation to national (or local) norms. The Intermediate 2 Level of the Stanford Achievement Test (SAT) is comparable to the Brown Level of the SDMT. This test also has an objective related to whole numbers and place value, which is measured by 12 items (as compared with 21 on the SDMT). A single score is reported for this area on the SAT, while a score for each of six item-clusters is reported for the SDMT. Since the SAT is primarily interpreted against norms, the score for each pupil is classified as *below average, average,* or *above average,* instead of being weighed against a criterion or progress indicator. Although achievement measures such as the SAT provide the teacher with considerable information that can aid in diagnosis, they are much less useful for this purpose than a good diagnostic test.

Despite the fact that diagnostic tests contain more items than standardized achievement tests, and focus primarily upon the slow learner, scores on these two different types of tests are very closely related. Correlations between similar primary level subtests from the Reading Tests of the Stanford Achievement battery and the Stanford Diagnostic Reading Test range from .82 to .91.

DIAGNOSTIC AND SCREENING MEASURES
FOR STUDENTS WITH DISABILITIES

Because diagnostic tests such as those we have discussed are primarily concerned with diagnosis of students' remedial needs, and thus tend to focus on the low achiever, they may also be used for diagnosis of students with mild mental handicaps or learning disabilities. For example, the DMI/MS, although designed primarily for use with regular students, can also be used to diagnose the mathematics learning needs of students with mild disabilities. With some adaptation, such as use of a lower level of the test, most current diagnostic tests in reading and mathematics will provide useful information to the teacher who has children with disabilities in his class.

In addition, however, a number of tests have been developed specifically to diagnose various aspects of the performance of students with disabilities. Before we say more about such tests, however, we must provide an important caveat. Assessing students with disabilities is very complex, and although the regular classroom teacher often assists in the process, the main responsibility usually falls to specialists. For example, if such a student needs help with prevocational or daily living skills, usually a special education teacher or consultant will develop an individualized education plan (IEP) for the child and assist the classroom teacher in implementing that plan within the regular classroom. Consequently, it is the special educator who must learn a wide variety of specialized techniques for assessing these children. It is beyond the scope of this chapter (or this book, which is already challenged with covering in a single volume the entire field of testing and measurement) to deal with these specialized diagnostic techniques in any detail. Yet we are reluctant to omit entirely any mention of them, since most regular classroom teachers will be team members in working with special educators to meet the needs of students with disabilities who are mainstreamed into their classes. This section contains, therefore, brief descriptions of a few measures proposed for use in assessing special populations. Hopefully this overview will give you a sense of existing tools and processes in this specialized assessment area.

We wish to make clear that our use of some existing instruments as examples is not an endorsement of them. Tests for assessing students with disabilities are not nearly as well established or validated as are diagnostic measures like the SDRT or DMI/MS, and some we mention here have not yet been adequately validated. Also, there are other equally useful measures we do not have space to describe.

Most of these measures used with children with disabilities can be grouped into three major categories: tests that measure students' abilities to adapt to the demands of daily living, tests that assess or diagnose students' academic performances, and tests that measure abilities directly related to success in school. In addition, some comprehensive measures are concerned with performance in all three of these areas.

Tests of Adaptive Behavior

Measures aimed at diagnosing the skills needed for everyday living can be useful in helping the teacher and special education specialists identify which students need special instruction and guided experience in this area. Test results thus become the basis for developing individualized education plans (IEPs). As is the case with systems such as the DMI/MS, some of these measures are integrated with instructional materials. We examine in this section two such measures.

Social and Prevocational Information Battery (SPIB)

This battery consists of nine tests, using mostly a true-false item format, that may be administered orally to students in groups of 10 to 20. Designed for mildly retarded students at the secondary school level, each test requires from 15 to 25 minutes to complete. Not more than three tests should be given at a single sitting. Four sample items are provided for each test. These help familiarize students with the test format and also identify students who need additional practice before taking the test. Each test item is read twice by the examiner (Halpern, Raffeld, Irvin, & Link, 1975).

Table 18.1 lists the domains covered by the nine tests and briefly describes

TABLE 18.1 SPIB Goals, Domains, and Content Areas

Goal	Domain	Content 1	2	3
Economic Self-Sufficiency	Purchasing Habits	Methods and implications of comparative shopping	Relationship between type of store and type of merchandise available	Use of newspaper as a purchasing aid
	Budgeting	Time-buying and its relationship to budgeting	Impact of borrowing on a budget	Good judgment and arithmetic skills necessary for appropriate salary allocation
	Banking	Cost of checking and/ or savings accounts and where they may be opened	Procedures involved in deposit or withdrawal from bank accounts	How to write and/or cash checks
Employability	Job Related Behaviors	Role and duties of a supervisor	Appropriate job related communications	What constitutes job completion and its implications
	Job Search Skills	Relationship between types of jobs and job requirements	Functions and cost of public and private job assistance agencies	Why, when, and how to complete a job application form
Family Living	Home Management	Maintenance, repair and safe physical functioning of structural parts of living quarters	Safe and sanitary home living conditions	Proper food preparation and storage procedures
	Physical Health	Emergency health care	Common health care practices that prevent injury, illness, or infection	Proper use of medications
Personal	Personal Hygiene and Grooming	Need for regular health care	Need for body cleanliness	Consequences of poor health or inadequate personal hygiene and grooming
Communications	Functional Signs	Traffic and road signs	Safety signs	Emergency signs

SOURCE: Halpern, A., Raffeld, P., Irvin, L. K., and Link, R. *Examiner's Manual, Social and Prevocational Information Battery,*

Areas

4	5	6	7	8	9
Relationship between weight and cost	General purchasing terminology	Awareness of sales tax and the ability to compute it	Advantages and disadvantages of quantity buying	Ability to compare newspaper ads and determine best buys	
Concept, consequences, and prevention of overspending	Concepts and implications of credit ratings	Relationships between budgeting and savings	Impact of salary change on a budget	Distinctions between regular and irregular expenses	"Grace Periods" as they relate to payment of bills
Procedures and implications of properly recording and balancing check records	Basic concepts of interests and general inherent rates for savings accounts	Usefulness of checking accounts	Hazards of signing a blank check and problems with failure to sign completed checks		
Appropriate work relations with fellow employees					
Job sources	Proper use of telephone with potential employers	Appropriate interview behavior	Contents and purpose of job resume	Obtaining information from want ads	
Appropriate laundry procedures	Protective and utility agencies and their function				
Child health care practices	Importance of health care				
When and how to use body cleaning agents and grooming aids					
General information signs					

the content areas covered. Let us examine one of these measures, *Purchasing Habits*, in some detail. There are 36 items on this test, 31 true-false, and 5 requiring the student to select which of two newspaper ads shows the better buy for a product. A typical true-false item on this test might read as follows: "Store ads are not found on the same pages of the newspaper as the news." The true-false format allows the test taker to complete a large number of items in a short time and is reasonably valid for measuring specific knowledge or information. However, other types of items, such as that requiring comparison of two newspaper ads, require the student to apply knowledge in a much more realistic context.

The tests may be handscored or machine scored by the publisher. For each test, raw scores, percentile ranks, and percentage correct may be determined. Normative data are provided for students at the junior high and high school levels. Because there are relatively few items on each test, subtest scores for the various areas within each test would not be sufficiently reliable to form the sole basis for diagnosis, although they may help the teacher identify possible problem areas that warrant further exploration. A user's guide for the SPIB contains useful information on assessing students' needs, planning and implementing remedial programs, monitoring progress, and evaluating outcomes. An alternate edition of this measure, the SPIB(T) is designed for use with moderately retarded students.

Skills for Independent Living Resource Kit (SIL)

The SIL is a set of diagnostic and instructional materials covering many of the same skills tested by the SPIB. The kit includes a Teacher's Manual, 46 Teacher Resource Files that list specific objectives and briefly outline recommended learning activities, and a Resource Materials Guide, that (1) lists and briefly describes commercially available materials related to the skills covered in the kit, and (2) tells where these materials may be obtained. Several supplementary record forms are also available.

Although the Teacher Resource Files are not detailed lesson plans, they do contain many suggestions for lessons and class activities that the teacher can use to improve performance in any of the nine test areas in which the student appears weak on the SPIB (Lik, Halpern, & Becklund, 1981).

Assessment of Academic Performance of Students with Disabilities

In addition to the diagnostic measures for regular students, such as the SDRT and the DMI/MS, a few diagnostic measures and systems of diagnosis and instruction have been developed specifically to appraise the academic performance of special populations. One example here should suffice.

Criterion-referenced Curriculum (CRC)

The CRC is a comprehensive system of criterion-referenced tests and teaching materials in mathematics and reading designed for kindergarten through sixth grade students with mild disabilities. It may be used for individual tutoring or small-group instruction. It can be used either as a core curriculum or as a supplemental curriculum in which the teacher selects only those skills students are having difficulty learning. The system includes components designed to assist the teacher in diagnosis, teaching, evaluation, and development of teaching plans for IEP's (Stephens, 1982).

Scholastic Aptitude Measures for Students with Disabilities

Measures of special students' scholastic *aptitude* have also been developed; one such measure is described briefly here.

McCarthy Screening Test (MST)

This measure is aimed at children who are at or near the beginning of their schooling (ages 4–6.5) to measure abilities important to achieving school success. Two sections, right-left orientation and leg coordination, deal with sensorimotor abilities. The remaining four—verbal memory, draw-a-design, numerical memory, and conceptual grouping—are cognitive.

The purpose of the MST is to screen children as required by Public Law 94–142 in order to identify children who are "at risk," that is, likely to have difficulty in performing school tasks. The test is very short, requiring about 20 minutes to administer to a single child. It can be administered and scored by the classroom teacher. As is usually the case with short measures, time is saved at the cost of reliability. Reliability of the six subtests is low, ranging in one study from .32 for right-left orientation to .69 for numerical memory (McCarthy, 1978).

It should be remembered, however, that the purpose of the MST is to screen out quickly, for further assessment, children whose low scores indicate that they *may* be "at risk" of not being able to succeed in school. The MST is reasonably valid for this purpose. In one study, the MST was administered to 60 children who had been clinically diagnosed as "learning disabled" or "emotionally disturbed/behaviorally disordered." The MST correctly identified 67 percent of these children as being "at risk."

The MST is not designed to pinpoint specific reasons for low performance, but only to provide preliminary screening information. As such, it is the first step in the diagnostic process.

SUGGESTED READINGS

Beattie, J., & Algozzine, B. (1982). Testing for teaching. *Arithmetic Teacher, 30*(1), 47–51.

Teachers are encouraged to use test results to plan specific educational programs. Information is provided about the nature of diagnostic testing, with both content and process error analysis discussed. Prescriptive teaching is described to show how to devise remedial activities after student problems have been identified.

Freytes, C. E. (1982). *Procedures for assessing learning problems of students with limited English proficiency.* (FL 013 091) Washington, DC: U.S. Department of Education.

The author describes a procedure for identifying and assessing students with limited English proficiency who have special needs. A five-step identification process is recommended, which considers the child's task failure, identification of problems not primarily due to learning problems, the physiological component, intra-individual differences in performance, and discovery of the child's preferred learning style.

Fry, E. B. (1981). *Reading diagnosis: Informal reading inventories*. Providence, RI: Jamestown Publishers.

The reading diagnosis tests and observations in this book provide a systematic way of gathering information about a student. The first 10 chapters provide measures to test a variety of abilities in language arts and handwriting, as well as vision and student interests. The final three chapters explain how a teacher can obtain information through a structured parent/guardian interview, can summarize school records for maximum effectiveness, and can summarize the entire reading diagnosis process.

Melcher, J., McCoy, J., Lange, J., & Kammen, A. (1980, April). *A Review of assessment instruments and procedures for young exceptional children.* (Report No. WSDPI–Bull–0488) Washington, DC: Bureau of Education for the Handicapped.

Reviews are provided of approximately 60 assessment instruments useful with young exceptional children. The reviews are intended to provide descriptive information regarding the content, format, process of test construction, strengths, and limitations of a given test. A final section lists factors to consider when selecting an assessment instrument and suggestions for assessing young children with disabilities.

SELF-CHECK QUIZ

1. One advantage of recently developed diagnostic tests such as the Stanford Diagnostic Reading Test is that
   a. such tests are much shorter than standardized achievement tests in the same subject areas.
   b. one form of the test covers all grade levels.
   c. teaching materials are provided for use in conjunction with the test.
   d. since no norm-referenced scores are reported, the teacher can focus on criterion-referenced interpretations.

2. Referring to the Skill Analysis section of Figure 18.2, for which of the following skills did Sam get all items correct?
   a. Auditory discrimination—long vowels
   b. Phonetic analysis—single consonants
   c. Reading comprehension—sentence reading
   d. Vocabulary—math and science

3. A unique feature of the Diagnostic Mathematics Inventory/Mathematics System is the
   a. use of stanine scores.
   b. common error report.
   c. criterion for mastery of each skill area or objective.
   d. use of short-answer rather than multiple choice test items.

4. Referring to Figure 18.5, what is the most common error made by Mr. Jones's students in working with whole numbers?
   a. Confusing two numerals
   b. Choosing the wrong number of parts
   c. Omitting a digit
   d. Misreading a scale

5. A major difference usually found between standardized achievement tests and diagnostic tests is that
   a. standardized achievement tests use more test items to cover the same content.
   b. standardized achievement tests are primarily criterion-referenced.
   c. diagnostic tests do not report normative data such as percentile ranks.
   d. diagnostic tests are aimed primarily at the low achiever.

6. The Social and Prevocational Information Battery, designed for mildly retarded students, measures
   a. academic achievement.
   b. intelligence.
   c. self-sufficiency and employability.
   d. vocational preferences.

7. The McCarthy Screening Test is designed to
   a. measure the social skills of moderately retarded children.
   b. measure abilities related to school success.
   c. identify gifted children at the entry level.
   d. diagnose specific reasons for the low performance of preschool children.

8. An extensive diagnostic system, such as the Stanford Diagnostic Reading Test (SDRT), can be effectively used by
   a. a classroom teacher but not a content specialist.
   b. a content specialist but not a classroom teacher.
   c. either a classroom teacher or a content specialist.

9. Compared with paper and pencil tests, computerized adaptive testing has been shown to decrease testing time by about
   a. 10 percent.   c. 30 percent.
   b. 20 percent.   d. 60 percent.

10. Compared with standardized achievement test subscores, diagnostic test subscores generally cover skill areas that are
    a. more specific.
    b. less specific.
    c. at about the same level of specificity.

SUGGESTION SHEET

If your last name starts with the letter *T*, please complete the suggestion sheet at the end of the book while this chapter is still fresh in your mind.

ANSWERS TO APPLICATION PROBLEMS

#1
a. Instructional Group 3
b. Reading Comprehension, PR 44
c. Reading and literature, vocabulary. Other vowels, auditory discrimination

#2
a. Five students failed to master objective 15, and seven needed review.
b. Objective 14, subtraction with regrouping.
c. Susan Porter and Allen Tuttle are both at the nonmastery level on three of the four objectives, and need review on the fourth.

CHAPTER 19

Assessing Your Students' Potential: A Look at Aptitude and Readiness Measures

Overview

Every experienced teacher or parent knows that different children learn at different rates and are capable of mastering different materials. Because children are not all alike, instruction must be individualized if it is to be effective. To predict how well and in what ways students will learn, good teachers use many different kinds of information—they listen to parents' reports, observe the child in the classroom, and consider the child's past performance in similar areas. In addition, they may consider *aptitude tests* developed by educators and psychologists to predict how well a student will perform in a particular area.

Some people think only of intelligence or IQ tests when they think of aptitude tests; and it is true that intelligence tests are one form of aptitude test. But aptitude is much broader than what is measured by intelligence tests. Different types of aptitude tests are used to predict how well a person will do in a particular course, a vocation or profession, or whether she is ready to begin school.

This chapter will help you understand what aptitude tests are, how they are used, and what makes an aptitude test effective. We will give you a classification system for organizing information about aptitude tests. We will also discuss how the proper use of aptitude tests can assist you in being an effective teacher or school administrator, and point out the dangers associated with the inappropriate use of aptitude tests.

Objectives

Upon completing your study of this chapter, you should be able to

1. Compare and contrast aptitude and achievement tests.
2. Give examples of appropriate ways to use aptitude measures.
3. Describe the purpose and utility of culture-free aptitude tests.
4. Summarize the factors to consider in judging the appropriateness of an aptitude test for a given purpose.
5. Explain how genetic and environmental factors contribute to measures of intelligence.
6. Give examples of various types of aptitude tests.
7. Summarize the pros and cons of using individual and group administered aptitude tests.
8. Describe the rationale for Multiple Aptitude Batteries.
9. Explain how school readiness tests can be used to improve instruction.
10. Explain the purpose and usefulness of measures of creativity.
11. Give examples of how measures of specific aptitudes can be used.

THE USE OF APTITUDE TESTS

By predicting future performance, aptitude test results allow us to select students most likely to succeed, identify those needing help, or make our instruction more effective. If you knew that the students enrolled in your algebra course were the 15 brightest students in the school, you would approach the design and delivery of instruction differently than if they were the 15 slowest learners in the school. This example raises some major issues.

- Is aptitude the same as intelligence?
- How many different kinds of aptitude tests are there?
- What can you learn about someone from scores on an aptitude test?
- What are the characteristics of a good aptitude test?
- How useful are aptitude tests with culturally different children?

Let us look at these issues now.

What Is Aptitude?

An aptitude is a natural or acquired ability that is necessary or facilitative for a particular purpose or activity. No matter what the area—riding a bicycle, communicating effectively with other people, doing algebra, riding horses, eating large amounts of food, understanding how mechanical engines operate—some people have more aptitude than others. In other words, they learn it faster or do it better. Consequently, aptitude predicts how well a person will do some activity.

How an aptitude is measured depends on what is being predicted. You could not use the same test to measure aptitude for riding a bicycle and aptitude for solving word puzzles. If you wanted to know the aptitude of a particular child for learning the different subjects typically taught in school, you might give a test that measured the child's ability to perceive stimuli accurately, recognize and recall what had been perceived, think logically, abstract general principles from specific information, generalize knowledge from one situation to another, and identify relationships. Such abilities might be measured on a series of tasks in which the child was asked to detect similarities and differences, recall words and numbers, solve analogy problems, classify information, and recognize absurdities. Because such tasks are related to what we expect children to learn in school, but are not influenced much by the child's previous school experiences, her score on such a test would provide valuable information about how well and how quickly she would learn the material typically presented in school.

Alternatively, if you wanted to know about a child's aptitude for learning algebra, you would need a test more closely related to algebra than to general learning. Such a test might include some questions about her ability to think logically and recognize relationships, but it would focus more on how well she had performed in previous math classes. If you wanted to measure a person's aptitude for clerical work, you might devise a series of tasks that are similar to the work she would actually be doing on the job—tasks that would measure her attention to detail, ability to identify errors or inconsistencies, and skills in processing data. In short, the nature of the aptitude test will vary greatly depending on what is being predicted.

There is no such thing as an aptitude measure that indicates a person's general capacity to do any cognitive, physical, creative, or social activity. Although a person who has high aptitude in one area is more likely to have higher than average aptitude in another area, there is no way to measure general aptitude in the same way that we measure height or distance.

A difficulty with virtually all measures of aptitude is that they are imperfect predictors of whatever task is of interest. Not surprisingly, the more specific and closely related a measure is to the task being predicted, the more accurate the prediction. It is also important to recognize that any aptitude measure provides us with information about a student's aptitude *at a particular point in time*. That aptitude may change later as a result of maturation, learning, or experience.

To assist in understanding the many different kinds of aptitude measures, Sax (1980) proposed a framework in which aptitude tests are organized along a

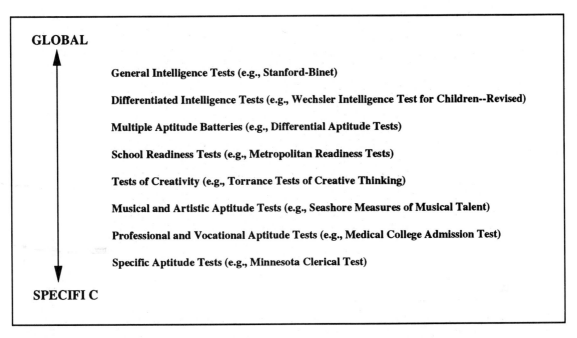

FIGURE 19.1   Arrangement of Various Types of Aptitude Tests along a Continuum of Global to Specific.

SOURCE: Adapted from Sax, 1980.

continuum ranging from global to specific as shown in Figure 19.1. Global measures, such as the Stanford-Binet Intelligence Test, are moderately good predictors about many different activities, whereas more specific measures, such as the Minnesota Clerical Test, are predictive only in a very narrow area. Tests at one end of the continuum are not necessarily any better than tests at the other, but are designed for a different purpose. For example, professional aptitude tests such as the Medical College Admissions Test (MCAT) focus on the specific aptitudes predictive of success in medical school, whereas a general aptitude test such as the Stanford-Binet Intelligence Scale includes items predictive of more general intellectual functioning. Consequently, the MCAT is more highly correlated with success in medical school, but it is not as good a predictor for general intellectual ability because of the way it was designed.

What Are Aptitude Tests Used For?

Using aptitude tests appropriately means using the right test for the right purpose. Let's consider some of the purposes for which aptitude tests are used most frequently.

Selecting Students for Special Programs

Often a school will have a special program for which it has more applicants than openings. In such cases, participation in the program may be limited to students who are most likely to succeed. No aptitude test can correctly identify all those who will succeed. But a good aptitude test can substantially increase the likelihood that the most appropriate candidates will be identified.

For example, consider Table 19.1, which shows the scores received by 111 students enrolled in a watch repair training school who took Differential Aptitude Tests (DATs) at the beginning of the school term and were graded on their performance at the end. There is a strong relationship between scores on the Space Relation subtest at the beginning and grades in the watch repair training school at the conclusion of the training. In fact, 88 percent of those scoring above the 76th percentile on the Space Relations test got an A or a B in the course. Similarly, 88 percent of those scoring below the 25th percentile got a C or lower in the course. If the school had limited openings, it would be more efficient to only enroll those who did well on the Space Relations subtest of the Differential Aptitude Tests. However, some mistakes would be made. For example, 12 percent of those who scored *below* the 25th percentile, obtained an A or a B in the course. In this case, aptitude tests scores led to good, but (as is always the case) not perfect, predictions.

Obviously, there are some ethical considerations in using a less than perfect test to select people who will be granted some educational opportunity. Our point here is not to argue whether such decisions *should* be made, but simply to indicate the ways in which aptitude tests *are* frequently used.

Aptitude tests are also used frequently to select children for gifted and talented programs. Since most classroom instruction is geared toward the needs of children with average ability, gifted children sometimes go unchallenged. As noted by Lyon:

> Prevented from moving ahead by the rigidity of normal school procedures, . . . the gifted youngster typically takes one of three tacks: (1) he drifts into a state of lethargy and complete apathy; (2) he conceals his ability, anxious not to embarrass others or draw their ridicule by superior performance; or, (3) not understanding his frustration, he becomes a discipline problem. (1974, p. 65)

TABLE 19.1   Percentage of 111 Students Receiving Various Grades as a Function of Scores on the DAT Space Relations Test

Score in Percentiles on Space Relations Test	Grades Received in Watch Repair Course		
	D or E	*C*	*A or B*
76–100	None	12%	88%
51–75	None	20%	80%
26–50	20%	40%	40%
1–25	58%	30%	12%

Appropriate aptitude tests can be very useful in identifying such gifted children—who may then be placed in accelerated or advanced programs.

Because even the best aptitude tests are imperfect, it is best to use such measures in conjunction with other information about students' motivation, past performance, and attitude. Always remember that a few students who score poorly on a given aptitude test will still be successful, and a few students who score well, will do poorly. Thus, aptitude tests can supplement—but never replace—sound professional judgment.

Identification of Children Needing Remediation

Many children experience difficulty in school. Unless difficulties are identified and remediated early, a child can become frustrated, and the problem becomes worse. Over the past three decades, many special education and compensatory education programs have been developed to help students succeed who need extra support. It is not always easy, however, to identify children who need special help. Children with the most severe handicaps are easier to identify, but the majority of children with handicaps are performing marginally. The sooner such children can be identified, the better their chance for success.

Although federal law prohibits the placement of children in special education programs based solely on aptitude tests, such tests can help make correct decisions. Because aptitude tests are not perfect predictors, the law requires that placement decisions be based on multidisciplinary evaluations, observations by teachers, information from parents, and consideration of the child's past performance. Aptitude tests are sometimes particularly useful, however, because they can help identify whether a student's achievement is consistent with her potential.

Tailoring Instruction for Individual Students

Given any task, students progress at different rates and achieve different levels of mastery. An important question is whether students are achieving their full potential. You would be appropriately concerned if you had a student who scored high on a test of general school aptitude, but was performing poorly in reading. You would want to check whether the student was experiencing health problems, having difficulty at home, felt unmotivated for some reason, or simply was not responding to current instructional methods. Without the aptitude test results, though, you might never get around to asking these important questions.

Note the distinction between what is measured on achievement tests and aptitude tests. Achievement tests assess very specific types of instructional outcomes such as the ability to spell certain words. How well a student does on an achievement test depends on how well she has mastered these specific instructional outcomes. By contrast, aptitude tests are designed to measure abilities that are not dependent on the particular instruction to which the student has been exposed. By comparing aptitude and achievement test scores, it is possible to know whether a student is performing at about the level you would expect. If she is performing much lower than expected, alternative instructional techniques may be needed or other problems may be interfering with her performance.

Unfortunately, aptitude tests can also be used inappropriately in this context.

If a student scores low on an aptitude test, it would be a terrible mistake for a teacher to conclude that since she obviously lacked the potential to learn, it would be a waste of time to even *try* to help her. Even though some teachers occasionally use aptitude test scores in such an inappropriate way, we should not blame the tests. As noted by Mehrens and Lehmann:

> The teachers in inner city schools who do not try their hardest because of preconceived ideas that their students cannot learn have not obtained their ideas of student deficiency primarily from aptitude tests scores. Such factors as the parents' educational level, socioeconomic status, race, and occupation, all contribute to teachers' opinions concerning a child's aptitude. (p. 337).
>
> *Aptitude tests can help teachers develop realistic expectations for their students.* While we do not condone—in fact we condemn—teachers who develop fatalistic attitudes toward the learning abilities of their students, we do not think aptitude tests should be made the scapegoat. (1991, pp. 337–338, *emphasis in original*)

Organizing Instructional Groups

Many educators believe that instruction can be more effective if students of similar ability are grouped together. While we are not arguing for or against this practice, aptitude tests can be a useful aid in deciding which children should be placed in which group[1]. Some people who oppose ability grouping blame the alleged problems of such practices on the use of aptitude tests. They have argued that the tests are unfair to different subgroups and consequently should be ignored in making decisions about ability grouping. While the pros and cons of ability grouping can be legitimately debated, it is inappropriate to blame the use of aptitude tests for any of the perceived problems with this instructional approach. In fact, research has demonstrated that the use of aptitude tests has provided beneficial opportunities to children from low socioeconomic groups who would likely have been denied had more subjective criteria been used as the basis for grouping (Findley & Bryan, 1971).

Of course, decisions about the organization of instructional groups, made with the help of aptitude test scores, should not be viewed as permanent. The whole point of instructional groupings is to provide children an opportunity to learn more efficiently. If instructional grouping is used to achieve this goal, it will be necessary to periodically restructure instructional groupings.

Counseling Students about Educational and Vocational Plans

Many different aptitude tests are used in counseling students about vocational and educational options. It is logical that someone who is considering a career in mechanical engineering will probably be more successful if she scores high on aptitude measures of space relations and mechanical reasoning, while someone who wants a job as a secretary should possibly reconsider if she scores poorly in clerical speed, spelling, and language usage.

---

[1] Indeed, many other educators are vehemently opposed to this practice. See for example, Esposito, 1973.

Aptitude test scores can be useful in predicting success in specific occupations, such as law enforcement or computer programming. This is often done by reviewing the average scores of successful people in various occupations on different aptitude tests, or by looking at the scores of those who successfully complete training courses for various jobs, professions, or vocations. Again though, it is important to consider scores from such aptitude tests in conjunction with other information.

Aptitude test scores should be used carefully in counseling. To see why, consider the data reported by Hopkins, Stanley, and Hopkins (1990, p. 369), where they noted that the average IQ of accountants, teachers, and lawyers was approximately 120, whereas the average IQ of welders, plumbers, and auto mechanics was about 105. Does this mean that anyone who has an IQ lower than 120 should not consider becoming an accountant or lawyer? Of course not. Even though the average IQ of accountants and lawyers was 15 to 20 points higher than that of welders, plumbers, and auto mechanics, approximately 20 percent of the welders, plumbers, and auto mechanics had IQs that were higher than those of about 25 percent of the accountants and lawyers. Thus, while aptitude scores can offer useful guidelines, we should not let them make decisions for us.

Measuring Aptitudes for Children from Different Cultures

Because aptitude tests are often used to make important decisions, many people worry about the influence of cultural differences on such test scores. Differences in language usage and mastery is one of the most obvious concerns. But other cultural differences may also affect performance on aptitude tests—differences in motivation and competitiveness, attitudes toward schooling, familiarity with test-taking procedures, and opportunities to learn the skills measured by the test.

Concern about bias in aptitude tests has led to the development of what are often referred to as *culture-free* or *culture-fair* tests. The goal of such tests is to eliminate the effects of extraneous cultural influences so that resulting scores are a pure measure of aptitude. Although many different tests purport to be culture fair, most share a number of characteristics.

1. Test materials are mostly nonverbal and include diagrams or pictures appropriate for the cultures in which the test will be used.
2. Additional time is provided beyond that thought to be necessary so that speed of completion will not be a factor.
3. Individualized testing or other motivational techniques are used to encourage participants to score as high as possible.
4. Simplified test procedures are used to eliminate the effects of the test-taking experience.

While all of the preceding are consistent with good test construction practices, most experts agree that culture-free testing is more an ideal than a reality (Hopkins, Stanley, & Hopkins, 1990).

The concern about having culture-free tests was a response to the recognition that African-American, Latin-American, and other minority children consistently received lower scores than Caucasian children. Because it is generally accepted that there are no genetic differences in intelligence among subcultures, such differences in scores were accepted as prima facie evidence that the tests must be biased. Efforts were consequently initiated to develop general aptitude measures that were predictive of later school success, but on which members of different ethnic groups did not score differently.

Unfortunately, the premise behind such test development efforts was flawed. As one African-American educator noted: "It is as incorrect to condemn tests for revealing inequalities between different ethnic groups as it is for the residents of Bismarck, North Dakota, to condemn the use of thermometers because it was minus 11 degrees in Bismarck when it was 73 degrees in Miami, Florida" (Clifford & Fishman, 1963, p. 87). The important point is that if inequalities exist, the measuring device should not be blamed. If, on the other hand, the measuring device is creating the appearance of inequalities when none exist, the measuring device should be blamed—and changed.

Obviously, tests can be biased, and some are. Consider a hypothetical item on a geography test where Latin-Americans score lower than Caucasians.

Which city is in the closest proximity to Los Angeles?

a. San Francisco   c. Chicago

b. New York   d. Atlanta

If the lower average scores of Latin-Americans occurred because fewer Latin-Americans knew that San Francisco was closest to Los Angeles, then the test is still a culture-fair test for those two groups. If the difference in average scores occurred because fewer Latin-Americans knew the meaning of the word *proximity*, then the test is biased against Latin-Americans.

In the same sense, consider the time it takes to run the 100-yard dash. If an electronically controlled stopwatch reveals that the average time for 10 African-American athletes is 2/10 of a second faster than the average time for 10 Caucasian athletes, is the measurement device biased against Caucasians? Of course not. The question in culture fair testing is whether the vocabulary, procedures, or tasks in any given test are biased against one subculture, not whether people in two groups score differently.

One of the best known efforts to develop culture free tests is the Culture-Fair Intelligence Test developed by R. B. Cattell. This test was developed after extensive review by experts from different cultures to eliminate those items that might be biased against one particular culture. Tasks are simplified and extensive verbal directions are given to make sure that the tasks are understood. Emphasis is on nonverbal tasks. In spite of this, there is no evidence that the Culture-Fair Intelligence Test is a better measure of intelligence than other widely used intelligence tests (Anastasi, 1988).

A somewhat different approach to developing a culturally fair measure of aptitude has resulted in the System of Multi-Cultural Pluristic Assessment (SOMPA) developed by Mercer (1977). This approach uses two different sets of norms—a national norm group, and a norm group that is similar to the examinee in social and cultural background. The assessment of aptitude is made by collecting information from two sources:

- A test session in which the child is given the Wechsler Intelligence Scale for Children-Revised (WISC-R), physical dexterity tasks, and the Bender Gestalt test
- Information from the child's primary caretaker, which is designed to measure the differences between the child's culture at home and the culture at the school

Using this additional information, statistical "corrections" are made to the WISC-R score as the best estimate of the child's intellectual aptitude.

Uncorrected scores are used to determine the child's immediate educational needs, while corrected scores are used to determine the child's "latent scholastic potential." So far, there is no evidence that this relatively elaborate procedure results in any better information than traditional measures of aptitude. In fact, Hilliard has concluded that the SOMPA "appears to have all the weaknesses of the old tests, plus a whole host of new weaknesses all its own, not the least of which is the absence of any construct validity" (National Institute of Education, 1979). Reynolds notes that "the SOMPA cannot be recommended for use at this time. Its conceptual, technical, and practical problems are simply too great. Nevertheless, it was an innovative, gallant effort . . . Current evidence would point to failure; however, it may serve as a springboard in some ways for future assessment systems" (1985, p. 1521).

Although culture-free testing has failed to demonstrate any advantage over traditional methods, the rationale behind the development of such tests is good. Children should be given an opportunity to demonstrate their skills and aptitude in a way that is free from extraneous influences. To the degree that tests are influenced by extraneous variables, we will be measuring something different from what we want to measure and the test will be invalid for that particular purpose. But, there is no such thing as an aptitude test that is totally independent of previous experience. The focus of any aptitude testing should be to make sure that the influence of extraneous variables is minimized and that every child who takes the test has an opportunity to score as high as possible.

COMPARING ACHIEVEMENT AND APTITUDE TESTS

Achievement tests measure what has been learned, aptitude tests predict the ability to learn, and intelligence tests measure one specific form of aptitude that may be described as general cognitive ability. Although the foregoing distinctions appear straightforward and simple, confusion arises because the three types of measures are interrelated. To some degree, all of them are a measure of what has been learned, and all of them can be used to make predictions about a student's ability to learn. They differ in the kinds of learning measured and the kinds of predictions each facilitates.

Achievement Tests

If you want to know how well a student has mastered the specific content presented in school, then you should use an achievement test. Some achievement tests (particularly locally developed tests) are very course-specific. Others, such as the Stanford Achievement Test, are measures of general educational development that provide information about a student's knowledge across several courses and learning experiences. Because achievement tests are designed as measures of what a student has learned, there should be consistency between what has been taught and what is being tested. In other words, you would not expect a student to get an item correct unless she had been given relevant instruction.

Even though achievement tests are primarily designed to describe what a student has already learned, they are also useful predictors. A student's performance in the first semester of social studies is usually a good predictor of how well she will perform in the second semester of social studies. However, the scope of such a prediction is usually quite narrow. Success in a specific area is a good predictor of success in that same area, but it is generally not as good a predictor of success in other school-related areas. For example, even though first-semester success in social studies is quite a good predictor of second-semester success in social studies, it is generally not as good a predictor of second-semester success in math.

So far, so good. But, some comprehensive achievement test batteries such as the Stanford Achievement Test predict future learning in a variety of school subjects almost as well as the best aptitude tests (Merwin & Gardner, 1962).

Aptitude Tests

Even though achievement tests are designed primarily as measures of what students have learned, if comprehensive achievement tests are such good predictors of future achievement, what is the role of aptitude tests? Let's consider that next. There are several reasons why aptitude tests are useful in addition to achievement tests.

- *Aptitude tests are relatively quick and economical to administer.* Whereas comprehensive achievement tests require as much as 10 to 12 hours to administer, most aptitude tests can be given in less than an hour.

- *Aptitude tests can be used before any instruction occurs.* It is very difficult to test a student for achievement in Spanish until at least some instruction in Spanish has occurred. One of the values of aptitude tests is that they can be used before any instruction.

- *Aptitude tests can be used to identify underachievers*. A student may be achieving poorly in an area for a variety of reasons. If we know that the student has potential to do better, then we may be able to identify the motivational problem, instructional deficiency, or competing influences responsible for the poor performance. Such a determination is difficult with an achievement test because we are measuring the same skills and knowledge in which we already know the student is weak.

- *Aptitude tests are appropriate for students from widely varied backgrounds*. Aptitude tests measure learning that occurs outside the classroom. Thus, a student is less likely to be penalized on the test because she has not been exposed to specific instruction.

Some people incorrectly assume that aptitude is a fixed innate characteristic. In reality, aptitudes change as a function of experience, learning, and maturation. Even though aptitude scores are useful as a way of predicting future success, it is best to interpret those scores as a measure of the student's *current* ability to learn. As Gronlund notes:

> [Aptitude] test performance reflects inherited characteristics to some (unknown) degree, but it also reflects the individual's experiential background, motivation, test taking skills, persistence, self-confidence, and emotional adjustment . . . Many of these factors can be modified by training, however, and therefore both learning ability and school achievement can be improved. It is when we interpret scholastic aptitude scores as direct and unmodifiable measures of learning potential that we are apt to misuse the results. (1985, p. 296)

Intelligence tests are one form of aptitude test, and, in fact, are often called *scholastic aptitude tests*. Figure 19.2 illustrates one way of thinking about the differences between aptitude and intelligence tests. Although the gentleman depicted in the picture has the necessary skills and abilities (i.e., aptitude) to be a good executive, he recognizes, based on his general intellectual ability, that he will probably not be happy as an executive.

Although many people use the terms *intelligence* and *aptitude* interchangeably, we believe it is better to avoid the term intelligence except in relation to those few tests specifically designed to measure general intellectual capacity.

Summary of the Differences between Achievement and Aptitude Tests

It should be clear by now that achievement and aptitude tests have many similarities, but they also have important differences. In general, aptitude tests measure broader skills such as verbal and numerical problem solving, abstract reasoning, and classification skills; whereas achievement tests are tied more closely to specific school subjects. Further, achievement tests generally focus on recent learning that has occurred at school, while aptitude tests measure learning that has occurred over an extended period—much of it outside of school. In addition, aptitude tests are designed to predict future learning, whereas achievement tests are designed

FIGURE 19.2 An Example of How Intelligence and Aptitude Differ

Copyright © 1976 by the National Council on Measurement in Education. Reprinted by permission of the publisher.

to describe current knowledge. Achievement tests are often good predictors of achievement within a narrowly focused range of related skill areas, but aptitude tests can often predict future learning across a wide range of skills or subjects. Both types of tests serve an important function in designing effective educational programs.

CHARACTERISTICS OF GOOD APTITUDE TESTS

The characteristics of a good aptitude test resemble those of most other tests used in education. They must demonstrate appropriate reliability and validity given their intended purpose and the students with whom they will be used. The most important type of validity for an aptitude test is predictive validity. It is particularly important that aptitude tests differentiate between people who are likely to be successful in a specific area and those who are not. Further, the test must be feasible to administer given the constraints that are present. A test that is too expensive or time consuming to administer given available resources will be of little use—no matter how impressive its data on reliability and validity. In many cases, the test must have appropriate norms that can be used in making selection, placement, or counseling decisions.

Because aptitude tests are frequently used to make decisions about individuals, the standards for acceptable reliability and validity are much higher than for tests used in making decisions about groups. This is because positive and negative errors of measurement tend to balance out among groups of people, whereas it is more difficult to know whether an individual's score is truly indicative of ability, or whether it might also be reflecting motivation, attitude, or general physical or psychological well-being at the time of testing. How, when, and in what manner the test is administered can also influence performance. Test givers, like test takers, have good and bad days. The point is, these advantages and disadvantages tend to balance out for groups of people but not for individuals.

In judging whether a particular aptitude test is suitable for your purposes, it is important that you adopt a "show me" attitude, as noted by Salvia and Ysseldyke:

> Do not expect test authors to admit in the manuals that the test was poorly normed because there was no money to pay testers or that the test had inadequate reliability because they didn't develop enough test items. Test authors put the best possible face on their tests, as might be expected. You simply cannot accept the claims made by test authors and their colleagues who write the technical manuals. If you accepted them at their word, they would only have to say that they had a "good, reliable, valid, and well normed test." Test authors must **demonstrate** that their tests are reliable, valid, and well normed . . . demand numbers; do not settle for statements as to the test's [appropriateness]. Make the authors show you the proof. (1988, pp. 549–550, *emphasis in original*)

EXAMPLES OF DIFFERENT TYPES OF APTITUDE TESTS

There are many types of aptitude tests, all designed to predict which students will be most successful in various activities. The examples in the next section should help you use the techniques and procedures described in Chapter 16 to identify an appropriate test for your specific needs.

Intelligence Tests

Almost everybody has an opinion of what intelligence tests measure. Unfortunately, many of these opinions are incorrect. So before we move on to specific examples, it is important to clarify some key concepts about intelligence tests.

What Do Intelligence Tests Measure?

People have been trying to measure intelligence systematically since the latter part of the nineteenth century. Francis Galton, an English biologist, was one of the first to try. Encouraged by the work of his cousin, Charles Darwin, regarding the natural variation within species, Galton believed that intellectual ability could be measured using various tests of sensory discrimination and reaction time. Building on the work of Galton, James McKeen Cattell (1890) first used the term *mental test*. His test consisted of a variety of tasks requiring muscular strength, speed of movement, sensitivity to pain, reaction time, and sensory discrimination. Although Galton and Cattell found that such characteristics could be measured accurately, they were disappointed that measures of such characteristics were not consistent with other observations about mental ability.

Binet and Simon (1905) used a very different and more successful approach. Binet believed that characteristics such as memory, attention, and comprehension were more directly related to mental ability than the type of variables proposed by Galton and Cattell. Using this approach, Binet developed a scale consisting of 30 tasks of higher mental processes, and used this scale to successfully identify mentally retarded children in the Paris school system. Based on his work, Binet characterized intelligence as a single attribute that was demonstrated by *inventiveness* dependent on *comprehension* and marked by *purposefulness* and corrective *judgment* (Binet, 1911).

Since Binet, others have characterized intelligence as consisting of multiple factors or components. Spearman (1927) suggested that intelligence could not be defined by a single factor and suggested that it was composed of a general factor (*g*) and many specific factors. Thurstone (1938) extended this rationale and argued that intelligence consisted of many different primary mental abilities. He argued that a person could have high scores in one area such as spatial relations and low scores in another area such as verbal reasoning. Guilford (1969) extended this reasoning in proposing his "structure of intellect" model, in which intelligence is comprised of 120 different factors described by the operation performed, the product involved, and the material or content involved (see Figure 19.3).

Disagreement over the nature of intelligence is far from new and will likely continue. In 1921 the editor of the *Journal of Educational Psychology* asked 14 prominent psychologists to define the nature of intelligence. Fourteen clearly different conceptions of intelligence were presented. Some psychologists stressed acquired learning, some the ability to think abstractly, while others focused on the adaptive nature of intelligence or the ability to learn.

In response to the confusion produced by these articles, Peak and Boring (1926) suggested that one should define intelligence as "that which an intelligence test measures." The suggestion is not a bad one. As Jensen pointed out many years later:

> Intelligence, like electricity, is easier to measure than to define. . . . There is no point in arguing the question to which there is really no answer, the question of what intelligence *really* is. The best we can do is to obtain measurements of certain kinds of behavior and look at their relationships to other phenomena and see if

these relationships make any kind of sense and order. (1969, p. 6, *emphasis in original*)

Older definitions of intelligence regard it as an innate and unchangeable capacity. More recent definitions, such as that given by Cleary, Humphreys, Kendrick, and Wesman (1975, p. 19), emphasize acquired behaviors rather than innate capacity. This definition states that intelligence is "the entire repertoire of acquired skills, knowledge, learning sets, and generalization tendencies considered intellectual in nature that are available at any one period in time." As Mehrens and Lehmann (1984, p. 362) point out, "Intelligence is not something people have, like brains and nervous systems. Rather it is a description of how people behave."

Even though experts do not agree on how to define intelligence, it is clear that whatever is measured by intelligence tests is predictive of many other academic behaviors. Operationally, we can define intelligence as whatever it is that intelligence tests measure, but we must do so with an understanding that there are many different types of intelligence tests. Therefore, it is important in selecting and

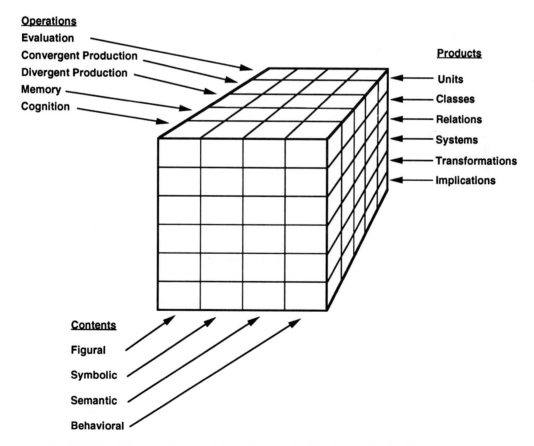

FIGURE 19.3 A Graphic Representation of Guilford's Structure of Intellect Model

interpreting the results of any intelligence test, to understand clearly the author's definition of intelligence.

Further, it is important to note that not everyone agrees that intelligence can or should be measured (see for example Garcia, 1981; Gould, 1981; Houts, 1976). Others suggested that intelligence can be measured, but radically different definitions and approaches should be used (see for example Gardner, 1984; Sternberg, 1981). Even the legal system has become mixed in contradictory rulings, suits, and countersuits over "intelligence" issues such as those summarized in Chapter 3. For the time being however, it is clear that intelligence tests continue to be widely used in our educational system. It is therefore important for educators to have a basic understanding of what intelligence tests measure and how they can be used most appropriately.

Is Intelligence Acquired or Inherited?

The argument over whether intelligence is inherited or acquired (often referred to as the nature-nurture controversy) has raged for years. Until the early twentieth century, most experts believed that intelligence was mostly, if not totally, inherited. Today most agree that it is a combination of inheritance and acquisition. Believing that intelligence is partly an acquired behavior does not rule out an important genetic influence. For example, a great basketball player has many *acquired* skills, even though inherited abilities are likely to have influenced the speed of development and the maximum level of skill achieved.

Hundreds of research studies have examined the issue of heredity versus environment with respect to intelligence. Erlenmeyer-Kimling and Jarvik (1963) reviewed 52 studies examining the correlation of intelligence test scores between identical twins, fraternal twins, siblings, relatives, and genetically unrelated children who had been raised together or apart. Based on over 30,000 correlational pairings, they produced average correlations, some of which are shown in Table 19.2. These data provide strong evidence that both environment and heredity contribute to a person's score on intelligence tests. For example, if heredity did not contribute, the correlation for identical twins reared apart would be close to 0; instead, it is .75. If environment did not contribute, the correlation between genetically unrelated children reared together would be close to 0, but it is .23.

Both heredity and environment are important contributors to a child's score on intelligence tests. Obviously, educators cannot change the inherited component

TABLE 19.2 Correlations of IQ Scores for Pairs of Children of Differing Genetic and Environment Circumstances

Correlation between:	*r*
Genetically unrelated children, reared apart	−.01
Genetically unrelated children, reared together	.23
Siblings, reared together	.49
Identical twins, reared apart	.75
Identical twins, reared together	.87

that contributes to intelligence test scores. We can, however, structure the environment so that it facilitates learning. Of course, individual differences in how children learn will not be eliminated by changes in the environment. Finally, even though the influence of inherited components cannot be eliminated, it is important to recognize that intelligence is not unchangeable.

How Useful Are Intelligence Test Scores?

The main purpose of aptitude tests, of which intelligence tests are one example, is to predict future performance. How well do intelligence test scores do that? Although a complete answer would fill a book, we can give you a number of examples to provide the basic understanding needed to appropriately use the results of intelligence tests in educational settings.

Hundreds of research studies show that intelligence test scores become more stable as children grow older. Kubiszyn and Borich (1987) estimated that the correlation among IQ tests given at ages 10 and 14 would be about .90; the same tests given at ages 6 and 14 would correlate .70, and at ages 2 and 14 only .20.

It is now generally accepted, that results from infant "intelligence" tests have little predictive validity. By the time children reach age 6, however, measures of intelligence are relatively stable. The stability of group-administered intelligence tests is somewhat lower than for individually administered tests, although the gradual increase in stability as children grow older is the same. Dozens of studies demonstrate that for school-aged children, results of individualized or group intelligence tests are highly correlated with scores on academic achievement tests. Most of those studies demonstrate correlation coefficients of .70 to .80 (see Hopkins, Stanley, & Hopkins, 1990).

Based on work reported by Wechsler (1955), many people believe that measured intelligence tends to increase until about age 30, and then begins to gradually diminish. However, Wechsler's data were based on a cross-sectional sample in which many variables were not controlled. Other work by Bayley (1955), Hopkins, Stanley, and Hopkins (1990), and Jarvik, Eisdorfer, and Blum (1973) suggests that there is continued intellectual growth until at least age 50. The environment in which a person lives may contribute to increases or decreases in intellectual performance, but unless there are health problems or other disrupting circumstances, a fifty-year-old will have as much or more intellectual ability as she had at age 25.

Some interesting evidence about the validity of intelligence test scores is found in the results of a study conducted during World War II, in which over 90,000 recruits were tested on the Army General Classification Test (see Stewart, 1947). Intelligence test scores of these people, averaged for each occupation, are partially summarized in Figure 19.4. These data indicate clearly that in the 1940s intelligence test scores were clearly related to occupational level. For example, the median IQ for accountants is over 30 points higher than that for miners. These differences are consistent with what one would logically expect. However, there is wide variability within groups. For example, even though the average IQ of barbers was only 94, 25 percent of the barbers had IQs over 106. Similarly, even though the average IQ for accountants was 123, 25 percent had IQs less than 117. The average intelligence score for different occupations can be somewhat

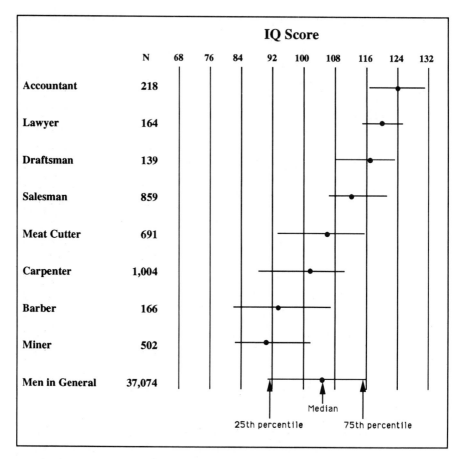

FIGURE 19.4   Median Intelligence Test Scores from the Army General Classification Test for Men Having Different Occupations

SOURCE: Kenneth D. Hopkins, Julian C. Stanley, and B. R. Hopkins, *Educational and Psychological Measurement and Evaluation*, 7th Edition. Copyright © 1990. Adapted with permission of Allyn and Bacon. All data converted to deviation IQ equivalents.

misleading. As pointed out by White (1982) and the Educational Testing Service (1980), the correlation between occupational level and IQ is only about .30—much lower than most people assume. Furthermore, there are people with very high IQ scores in every occupation. Nonetheless, the fact that average IQ varies by occupation lends strength to the position that intelligence tests are measuring something important.

Individually Administered Intelligence Tests

Most intelligence tests used in an educational setting are group-administered tests. Individually administered intelligence tests are used primarily for clinical applications such as deciding whether children need special education services. Individualized tests require more training to administer, provide greater flexibility in testing, can be used with younger children, and depend less on the child's ability to read. Although they are more costly and time consuming to administer, individually administered tests provide a number of benefits. The examiner is able to observe the respondent's approach to problem solving and is better able to control extraneous influences that might affect performance. Thus, individualized administrations generally result in more reliable measurement and a better understanding of which factors contribute to the child's score.

The most widely used individual intelligence tests are the Stanford-Binet and the various Wechsler tests. Other frequently used individually administered tests include the McCarthy Scales of Children's Abilities, the Columbia Mental Maturity Scale, the Bayley Scales of Infant Development, the Merrill-Palmer Scales, and the Leiter Adult Intelligence Scale. Because there are so many different intelligence scales, it is important for you to carefully consider the reliability and validity data for a particular test before using it. One excellent source is the *Mental Measurements Yearbook*, which offers critical reviews of many tests. As examples, we'll give you a brief overview of several widely used individually administered intelligence tests.

Stanford-Binet Intelligence Scale.   The fourth edition of Stanford-Binet Intelligence Scale (S-B) (Thorndike, Hagen, & Sattler, 1986) is the latest edition of the intelligence scale first developed by Alfred Binet in 1905 and later revised for use with American children in 1916. The S-B is designed for persons between ages 2 and 23 and yields a single score based on how well the subject performs a variety of tasks requiring responses to concrete pictorial stimuli at younger ages and abstract verbal stimuli at higher ages. The following lists are tasks included on the test.

Verbal Reasoning
Vocabulary: Identifying pictures or selecting from among orally presented words
Comprehension: Explaining why something is done—for example, why do people have umbrellas
Absurdities: Explaining why certain pictures are absurd
Verbal Relations: Presented with four objects, explaining in what way one is different

Quantitative Reasoning
Quantitative: Demonstrating computational skills
Number Series: Given a series of numbers, identifying the rule that defines it
Equation Building: Logically arranging a sequence of numbers and symbols; for example, 2 2 4 + =, should be 2 + 2 = 4

Abstract/Visual Reasoning
Pattern Analysis: Arranging materials to match or make a pattern
Copying: Copying designs of increasing complexity

Matrices: Completing missing sections of 2x2 or 3x3 matrices

Paper Folding and Cutting: Predicting what a folded piece of paper will look like after it is cut and unfolded

Short-term Memory

Bead Memory: Identifying or reproducing designs or patterns of different colored beads

Memory for Sentences: Repeating a sentence

Memory for Digits: Repeating a sequence of digits

Memory for Objects: Selecting previously shown pictures in correct order
The Stanford-Binet emphasizes verbal rather than quantitative tasks. The test has excellent psychometric properties, with reliability coefficients over .90 and a great deal of research supporting predictive and concurrent validity.

Wechsler Intelligence Scale for Children-Revised (WISC-R). Published by the Psychological Corporation, this is the most popular intelligence test for six- to sixteen-year-old children. The test yields verbal, performance, and full-scale IQ scores, in addition to these twelve subtest scores.

Verbal	*Performance*
Information	Picture Completion
Similarities	Picture Arrangement
Arithmetic	Block Design
Vocabulary	Objective Assembly
Comprehension	Coding
Digit Span (optional)	Mazes (optional)

Bortner noted that the WISC-R was "the best standardized, most objectively administered and scored test of its kind. . . . The manual is a model for other test makers" (1985, p. 1713). Norms are based on a sample of 2,200 children stratified on the basis of age, sex, race, geographic region, occupation of head of household, and urban-rural residence, based on the 1970 census. Reported reliabilities are in the .90s, but very little validity data are reported in the test manual. WISC-R scores do correlate highly with S-B scores and its popularity is probably based partly on its excellent organization and ease of administration.

A new version of the WISC-R has recently become available. Known as the WISC-III, it is still too recent for much information to be available about how it compares to the WISC-R. However, based on the excellent track record of the WISC-R, it would be very surprising if the WISC-III does not continue as an excellent measure.

Bayley Scales of Infant Development. This test was developed for two- to thirty-month-old children. Scores are provided for a mental scale (which includes items measuring perception, memory, learning, problem solving, vocalization, the beginnings of verbal communication, and rudimentary abstract thinking), and a motor scale (which includes items measuring gross motor skills and manipulatory skills of hands and fingers). Norms are based on 1,262 children equally distributed across ages and representative of the U.S. population. Published by the Psychological Corporation, the scale has been used widely since it was first published in 1969. Although it is one of the better tests of infant intelligence and has high reliability, little evidence is available for its predictive or construct validity.

Group-administered Intelligence Tests

Although the data they yield are not as precise, group-administered intelligence tests are used more extensively in educational settings because they cost substantially less to administer and teachers, who have received basic in-service training, can give them. Most group intelligence tests provide both verbal and nonverbal scores. Following are brief descriptions of several of the more widely used tests.

Cognitive Abilities Test.   Published by Houghton-Mifflin, this test was developed as a companion to the Iowa Tests of Basic Skills for children in grades K through 13. The test consists of a nonreading test for kindergarten and first grade children and provides verbal, quantitative, and nonverbal scores for older children. The Cognitive Abilities Test was standardized in 1977 to 1978 concurrently with the Iowa Test of Basic Skills so as to facilitate the comparison of aptitude and achievement. According to Ansorge (1985), the test has high reliability and correlates between .65 and .78 with the Stanford-Binet and in the .70s to .80s with the ITBS. Administration requires about an hour and forty minutes, although no time limit is imposed. According to the manual, correlations with end-of-year grade-point average for grades 7, 9, and 11 are about .50.

The Otis-Lennon School Ability Test.   This test, published by Harcourt Brace Jovanovich, can be administered in as little as 30 minutes at lower grade levels, and about 50 minutes at the higher grade levels. It is designed for use with children in grades K through 12. Though designed to measure verbal, numerical, and abstract reasoning abilities, it yields a single IQ score. It consists of six levels, with the first three requiring no reading ability. Norms are based on a nationwide standardization sample and were done concurrently with the Stanford Achievement Test and the Metropolitan Achievement Test. Reliabilities are generally above .90. Evidence for validity is based on correlations with achievement tests that are mostly in the .70s, correlations with teacher's grades are between .50 and .75, and correlations with other aptitude tests are between .70 and .90.

APPLICATION PROBLEM #1

You are having a conference with the parents of a third grader who has just moved into your district. The parents tell you that the child was given an IQ test at the end of last year in the school district from which they just moved. The results indicated she had an IQ in the lowest 25 percent of all the children tested. The principal of the last school reportedly told the parents they should not ever expect much from their daughter since IQ determines how much a child is able to learn in school and IQ does not change. What advice would you give them?

Multiple Aptitude Batteries

Some experts believe that an adequate representation of aptitude requires a profile of scores that describe relatively independent abilities. The earliest multiple aptitude test batteries (the Chicago Test of Primary Mental Abilities) were developed by Thurstone (1938) using factor analysis techniques. Mehrens and Lehmann (1991) suggest that the development of the multiple aptitude test batteries was due to the growth of vocational and educational counseling because these tests provided information that counselors were seeking when guiding people into different vocations, professions, and schooling options.

The rationale for multiple aptitude batteries is seductively simple, as described in the administration manual for the Differential Aptitude Tests:

> Let us suppose that two students have taken a . . . test which is comprised equally of verbal and numerical items. John answers only a few of the verbal items correctly, but gets almost every numerical item right. Jim, on the other hand, picks up very few points on the numerical part, but answers almost every verbal item correctly. If John and Jim are the same age, they will be classed, by this test, as having the same IQ—yet they are *not* the same in their abilities. . . . The need for differential measurement—and multiple scores—is self-evident. (p. 2)

Although the rationale for multiple aptitude batteries is appealing, existing research does not provide many examples of where the differential prediction, which is supposedly made possible by multiple aptitude batteries, has been useful. Generally, the different aptitudes measured by these tests are highly correlated, and there are few activities that require very high skill in one aptitude and low skill in other aptitudes. However, multiple aptitude batteries are still used frequently. Examples of several multiple aptitude batteries are given below.

Differential Aptitude Tests (DAT)

First published in 1947, the DAT has been revised periodically, most recently in 1982 (Bennett, Seashore, & Westman, 1982). The DAT yields scores for students in grades 8 through 12 in verbal reasoning, numerical ability, abstract reasoning, clerical speed and accuracy, mechanical reasoning, space relations, spelling, and language usage. Norms for the test are based on over 60,000 public and private school students in 64 districts from 32 states. Percentile and stanine norms are given in the manual for male and female students in each grade from 8 through 12. Reliabilities for the test are typically in the .90s, and there are dozens of studies that demonstrate that DAT scores are predictive of high school achievement in both academic and vocational programs. According to Anastasi (1988, p. 394), the evidence is less encouraging with regard to differential prediction.

The General Aptitude Test Battery (GATB)

The GATB was developed by the U.S. Employment Service and is used frequently in State Employment offices for counseling and job referral and is available to public school programs. Although the original norms are quite old, hundreds of recent studies provide evidence of the test's reliability (high .80s to low .90s) and validity. The 12 tests included in the GATB yield a total of nine factor scores. The following list is adapted from a description of them by Anastasi (1988):

- *General learning ability*—the sum of scores for vocabulary, arithmetic reasoning, and three-dimensional space.
- *Verbal aptitude*—measured by the respondent's indicating which two words in each set are either the same or opposite in meaning.
- *Numerical aptitude*—combines scores from the computation and arithmetic reasoning tests.
- *Spatial aptitude*—a measure of the ability to comprehend two-dimensional representation of three-dimensional objects and the ability to visualize the effects of movement in three-dimensions.
- *Form perception*—requires the respondent to match identical drawings of tools in one test and of geometric forms in the other.
- *Clerical perception*—requires the respondent to match names rather than pictures or forms.
- *Motor coordination*—requires the respondent to make specified pencil marks in a series of squares.
- *Finger dexterity*—requires the assembling and disassembling of rivets and washers.
- *Manual dexterity*—requires the respondent to transfer and reverse pegs in a board.

School Readiness Tests

Readiness tests, used most frequently at kindergarten and first grade, are a type of aptitude test designed to determine if children are ready to begin formal instruction. According to Anastasi, "School readiness refers essentially to the attainment of prerequisite skills, knowledge, attitudes, motivations, and other appropriate behavioral traits that enable the learner to profit maximally from school instruction" (1988, pp. 441–442). In most cases, readiness tests emphasize the prerequisites necessary for reading instruction; however, some tests also measure readiness for numerical computation, writing, and behavioral prerequisites for school, such as the ability to pay attention for sustained periods.

For many years, people believed that readiness was a maturational characteristic, and tests were designed to determine if children had matured sufficiently to begin school. It is true that some sorts of maturation are essential for academic learning. For example, to learn to write, a child must have developed sufficient motor skills to be able to hold a pencil. However, the notion that school readiness is strictly a function of maturation may lead to the inappropriate conclusion that when a child scores low on a school readiness test, there is nothing that can be done except to wait. In reality, low scores on a school readiness test suggest that the child has not yet acquired the prerequisite skills; *and*, that the teacher needs to design appropriate instruction to assist the child in developing those skills. As Mehrens noted, "Aptitude test scores should be used in helping teachers form realistic expectations of students; they should not be used to help teachers develop fatalistic expectations" (1982, p. 140).

Two cautions are in order. First, there is little data substantiating the predictive validity of school readiness tests in general. The prerequisites measured may be logical enough, but there is not sufficient evidence to show that children who score low cannot be successful. This is particularly true for those readiness tests that can be administered in a very short time. Thus, decisions about individual children based on school readiness test scores should be made carefully, and only in conjunction with other information. Second, school readiness tests are sometimes used as measures of current functioning or to document student progress. Because the tests were not designed as achievement measures, such uses are generally inappropriate and should be avoided.

Since the early 1970s, a large number of school readiness tests have been developed. Excellent discussions of the criteria for selecting readiness tests and analyses of several available tests are presented by Salvia and Ysseldyke (1988) and Meisels (1978). Two of the more widely used readiness tests are described below.

Metropolitan Readiness Tests

The fifth edition of the Metropolitan Readiness Test (MRT) is a "group administered test designed to assess a diverse range of prereading skills . . . and more advanced skills that are important in beginning reading and mathematics" (Nurss & McGauvran, 1986, p. 7). Level I, preschool through mid-kindergarten assesses: immediate recall of words; discrimination of initial sounds; recognition of upper- and lowercase letters; ability to match a series of letters, words, numbers, and other symbols; and mastery of basic cognitive concepts and complex grammatical structure. The second level, middle of kindergarten through beginning of first grade, has 10 subtests: quantitative language, beginning consonants, sound-letter correspondence, visual matching, finding patterns, school language, listening, quantitative concepts, quantitative operations, and copying. Within Levels I and II, separate norms are provided for fall, mid-year, and spring. Reliabilities are generally in the high .80s and low .90s, and the test is an unusually good predictor of achievement on the Stanford Achievement Test (with correlations as high as .83 between the prereading composite score on the MRT and the total SAT scores) and a modest predictor of achievement on the Metropolitan Achievement Test.

Boehm Test of Basic Concepts—Revised (BTBC-R)

The BTBC-R (Boehm, 1986) assesses a child's knowledge of 50 abstract, relational concepts that occur frequently in preschool and early primary curricula. According to Boehm, these particular concepts are "both fundamental to understanding verbal instructional and essential for early school achievement" (1986, p. 1).

The test was designed to identify those children who do not understand these essential concepts and consequently are at risk for later learning problems. The test requires approximately 40 minutes to administer. In taking the test, the child is required to mark the picture that best answers the question read by the teacher (for example, "Mark the one where the boy is *next* to the horse"). Reliability of the test is somewhat lower than for many readiness tests (.65 to .82), with test-retest coefficients after one year being about .70. BTBC-R scores correlate modestly (about .40) with achievement after one year.

Tests of Creativity

Some experts believe that creativity is a part of intelligent behavior and is adequately measured with existing tests of intelligence. Others believe that creativity is a distinct ability. It is logical that to be creative one must be reasonably intelligent, but it is not necessarily true that one must be creative to score high on an IQ test.

It is easy to think of words that are related to creativity—*ingenuity, originality, inventiveness*—but to operationally define creativity without using such words is a formidable task. For example, when we speak of creativity, are we talking about a creative process or a creative product, or both? Is creativity more closely aligned with divergent thinking or inductive logic? Who is more "creative"—the person who comes up with a multitude of unworkable solutions to a problem, or the person who comes up with one highly effective solution?

The most widely known and best documented tests of creativity are Guilford's Aptitudes Research Project Test of Divergent Thinking (Guilford & Hoepfner, 1971) and the Torrance Tests of Creative Thinking (Torrance, 1965). Current tests of creativity should be viewed as experimental efforts and should be used very carefully, if at all, by practitioners. Predictive validity tends to be low (Hoepfner, 1967), and the tests are usually too unreliable—about .65—for individual use (Yamamoto, 1962). In fact, in her review of creativity tests, Crockenberg states, "Therefore, while it may be imminently reasonable to study the processes that appear to be involved in creativity production, it is conceptually unjustifiable to call these tests 'tests of creativity' " (1972, p. 40). As an example of the types of tests available, a brief description of one of the most popular is given next.

Torrance Tests of Creative Thinking (TTCT)

This is really a series of tests consisting of Thinking Creatively with Words (a series of seven verbal subtests), Thinking Creatively with Pictures (a series of three pictorial subtests), Thinking Creatively with Sounds and Words (two subtests administered using a record which provides both instructions and stimuli), and Thinking Creatively in Action and Movement (in which all responses are limited to motor responses). As an example of the kinds of items included on the tests, consider the subtests of Thinking Creatively with Words. In this battery, respondents are shown a picture and are asked to write all the questions they would ask to find out what is happening, list the possible causes of the action shown in the picture, and list all possible consequences of the action. Another item asks the respondent to list all the unusual uses of a common object she can think of. The individual test items are described as activities, and the instructions emphasize that respondents are to have fun with the test.

The tests are designed to be used at kindergarten through adult levels, but below the fourth grade these tests have to be administered individually and orally. Two equivalent forms of each battery are available, and speed is an important component of scores on most activities. Typically reported test-retest reliabilities range from .60 to .80 (Haensly & Torrance, 1990).

There are four possible scores for each activity: fluency (the number of relevant responses), flexibility (the number of different categories of response), originality (whether responses are routine or unique), and elaboration (the amount of detail used in responses). Scoring can only be done by people who have been trained, and tentative norms are available in current editions. In his review of the TTCT, Chase notes:

[T]he tests are engaging to take. However, the theory of this trait is loosely formed and is not well equipped to become the basis for generating hypotheses. The TTCT, therefore, does not have a firm base in construct validation. Reliabilities are adequate, especially for assessing group changes or differences, but the sub-areas in the test—flexibility, fluency, originality—are clearly overlapping and suggest that a single total score might be appropriate. . . . Torrance originally presented the tests for the purpose of 'research and experimentation.' It appears that this reservation still is an appropriate one for users and potential users of the TTCT. (1985, p. 1632)

Tests of Musical and Artistic Aptitudes

Relatively few measures of musical and artistic aptitude are available. The most commonly used musical aptitude tests are the Seashore Measures of Musical Talent and the Wing Standardized Tests of Musical Intelligence. The Seashore uses a record or tape in which respondents are asked to discriminate between two stimuli with respect to pitch, loudness, time, timbre, rhythm, or tonal memory. For example, on the time subtest, the respondent indicates which of two intervals is longest, and in the tonal subtest, the respondent is asked whether two sequences of notes are the same or different. Reliabilities (internal consistency) range from .55 to .85, but evidence for validity is sparse.

The Wing Standardized Test of Musical Intelligence consists of seven subtests—chord analysis, pitch discrimination, memory for pitch, harmony, intensity, rhythm, and phrasing. Unlike the Seashore, the Wing requires the respondent to evaluate the aesthetic quality of chords. Reliability (both split-half and test-retest) is generally in the .90's. Validity data for both tests is meager, although the Wing reports correlations with teachers' grades of .60 or higher.

The most widely used measure of artistic aptitude is the Meier Art Judgment Test. On this test, the respondent is shown one hundred pairs of pictures. In each pair, one is a masterpiece, and the other is a slight modification of the original. The respondent is asked to select the better picture. Reliability for the Meier is about .75, and scores on the test correlate about .50 with grades given in art classes.

Professional and Vocational Aptitude Tests

Many academic, professional, and vocational training programs have a limited number of openings. To make placement as fair as possible, aptitude tests are used to identify those individuals most likely to succeed. Examples of such tests include the Graduate Record Examination (GRE) for admission to graduate school, the Scholastic Aptitude Test (SAT) for admissions to undergraduate colleges and universities, and the Law School Admission Test (LSAT) and the Medical College Admission Test (MCAT) for admission to training in those respective specialties. All are secure measures that are only administered by licensed centers, and the contents of the test are not available to the public. A brief description of three such tests follows.

Graduate Record Examination (GRE)

Originally developed in 1936, the GRE is available throughout the United States and in many other countries. The test consists of a general test, which reports verbal and quantitative scores, and subject area tests in various fields of specialization such as biology and computer science. The verbal subtest requires verbal reasoning and comprehension of reading passages from several different fields. The quantitative subtest require mathematical reasoning, and interpretation of graphs, diagrams, and descriptive data. Success on the GRE depends substantially on the student's past achievement. Reliabilities are generally at .90 and above for the various subtests. Predictive validity has been assessed using graduate school grade point average, performance on departmental comprehensive examinations, overall faculty ratings, and attainment of the Ph.D. as criteria (Anastasi, 1988). Scores on the GRE are a better predictor of graduate school performance than undergraduate grade point average.

Scholastic Aptitude Test (SAT)

The SAT consists of verbal and mathematical subtests. All items are in a multiple-choice format with five options, and the test requires about three hours. Scores are reported in standard score units, with a mean of 500 and a standard deviation of 100. Reliability coefficients are in the low to mid .90s. Samuda claims "the evidence about college entrance tests as predictors is no longer a subject of legitimate dispute. The studies have been widespread, they number in the thousands, and the results are consistent. By and large, the higher the test scores, the more successful the students are in college" (1975, p. viii).

There have been claims that tests like the SAT are biased or overemphasized in educational decision making, or that scores can be affected by coaching (Crouse & Trusheim, 1988). However, Mehrens (1982), in his review of aptitude measurement, claims that such concerns are not supported by the available evidence.

Law School Admission Test (LSAT)

This test is required for applicants to virtually all American law schools. A total test score, ranging from 10 to 48 with a mean of 30.5 and a standard deviation of 8, is computed based on four subtests: reading comprehension, analytical reasoning, issues and facts, and logical reasoning. The test requires approximately two and a half hours to administer. Reliability of the LSAT is in the low .90s, and most validity studies have involved prediction of either law school grades (yielding relatively low correlations of about .30) or performance on the examinations for admission to the Bar (with correlations of about .50). Melton, in his review of the LSAT for the *Mental Measurements Yearbook,* concluded that it was:

> a moderately valid predictor of law school grades, especially when used in combination with undergraduate GPA . . . The [LSAT] provides law schools with far more systematic admissions data . . . than they would probably be able or willing to generate on their own. However, particularly in view of the small proportion of variance in law school performance now predicted by the LSAT, attention should be given to the possibility that other verbal aptitude tests would be better predictors (1985. p. 825).

Specific Aptitude Tests

Many aptitude tests have been developed to predict success in specific areas. The most widely used are probably clerical and mechanical aptitude tests, but there are many others—such as the Purdue Pegboard Tests, which measure manual dexterity, and the Computer Aptitude, Literacy, and Interest Profile, designed to predict success in computer-related activities. The skills measured by these specific aptitude tests often overlap with skills measured by multiple aptitude batteries such as the Differential Aptitude Tests.

Specific aptitude tests have advantages: They can be longer, better normed, and better validated for specific applications. One of the most widely used is the Bennett Mechanical Comprehension Test, in which respondents look at pictures and respond to questions that assess their understanding of how mechanical principles apply in everyday life. For example, one picture shows two men carrying a weight on a bar suspended over their shoulders. The weight is closer to the one man than the other, and the question asks which man carries the most weight. Reliability coefficients range from the high .80s to low .90s. Ghiselli (1966) claimed that there was good evidence for the test's concurrent and predictive validity for mechanical traits and engineering. In fact, Guilford and Lacey (1947, p. 843) claimed this test was one of the best predictors of pilot success in World War II.

APPLICATION PROBLEM #2

You are on a committee at your school to select criteria for identifying children to participate in a gifted and talented program. The committee is currently working on the criteria to be used for first and second grade children, and has decided that only one standardized test can be used. The following standardized measures have been suggested as one basis for selection.

Which one would you recommend? Why?
- Stanford Binet Intelligence Scale
- Cognitive Abilities Test
- Torrance Test of Creative Thinking
- Metropolitan Readiness Tests

SUGGESTED READINGS

Anastasi, A. (1988). *Psychological testing* (6th ed.). New York: Macmillan.

Now in its sixth edition, this is one of the classic textbooks in psychological measurement. The book devotes substantial attention to aptitude tests as well as providing extensive discussion of the psychometric properties of all psychological tests.

Crouse, J., & Trusheim, D. (1988). *The case against the SAT*. Chicago: University of Chicago Press.

Based on existing research literature, this book builds a case for why the SAT should not be used for making admissions decisions to postsecondary educational institutions, and proposes an alternative method using high school course work and grades. The perspective presented in this book demonstrates that assessment issues have a political as well as a scientific dimension and emphasizes the need to carefully consider alternative points of view before making a decision.

Jensen, A. R. (1980). *Bias in mental testing*. New York: The Free Press.

Although many people disagree with his conclusions, no one can argue that this is not the most comprehensive treatment ever done of bias in mental testing. Most of the book deals with aptitude tests and it is *must* reading for anyone who is seriously interested in the issue of bias in aptitude tests.

Reynolds, C. R., & Kamphaus, R. W. (1990). *Handbook of psychological and educational assessment of children: Intelligence and achievement*. New York: The Guilford Press.

This book provides a more in-depth assessment of the issues related to measuring intelligence than was possible in the text. Included are chapters on measuring infant intelligence, the value of nonverbal and psychological measures of intelligence and extensive discussions of the Wechsler, McCarthy, Kaufman, and Stanford-Binet scales.

Salvia, J., & Ysseldyke, J. E. (1988). *Assessment* (4th ed.). Boston, MA: Houghton Mifflin Company.

Written primarily for educators involved with remedial and special education, this book is an excellent reference for obtaining a brief critical review about frequently used aptitude tests as well as other tests. Each chapter contains a brief section on issues and problems with using that particular type of test.

SELF-CHECK QUIZ

1. When compared to a standardized comprehensive achievement test battery, most group-administered scholastic aptitude tests for elementary age school children
   a. are less biased against minority children.
   b. are relatively quick and economical to administer.
   c. require a licensed psychologist to administer.
   d. are better at identifying specific content areas that need remediation.

2. For educational applications, the best operational definition of intelligence is
   a. whatever it is that is measured by intelligence tests.
   b. the top 10 percent of the scores on comprehensive achievement tests.
   c. the inherited ability to successfully master educational materials.
   d. a person's performance on tasks requiring sensory discrimination and reaction time.

3. Aptitude tests listed in the *Mental Measurements Yearbook (MMY)*
   a. have all been certified as having acceptable reliability and validity.
   b. can be obtained free by writing to MMY editors.
   c. should only be used by nonprofit organizations.
   d. may be appropriate for your needs but should be checked carefully before use.

4. Culture-fair aptitude tests
   a. require two or three times as long to administer as other aptitude tests.
   b. have generally replaced other aptitude tests in today's schools.
   c. are usually no more unbiased than other well-developed aptitude tests.
   d. yield more accurate estimates of aptitude than other aptitude tests.

5. Group-administered scholastic aptitude tests are best for
   a. deciding when students are ready to progress to the next instructional unit.
   b. determining which curriculum objectives to emphasize during the next year.
   c. calculating grades, if used in conjunction with teacher observations.
   d. assisting with the selection of students for special programs.

6. Aptitude tests administered to children younger than age three
   a. are excellent predictors of future academic performance.
   b. are more reliable than aptitude tests for older children.
   c. are poor predictors of future academic performance.
   d. have a smaller standard error of measurement than aptitude tests for older children.

7. Which of the following types of questions would be *least* likely to appear on a scholastic aptitude test?
   a. Given four objects, explain in what way one is different.
   b. Given a series of numbers, identify the next number in the series.
   c. Repeat a sequence of digits.
   d. Name the capital cities of a group of states.

8. Scholastic aptitude tests scores obtained in the third grade
   a. almost never improve.
   b. are very poor predictors of achievement in sixth grade.
   c. may change later as a result of learning, experience, or maturation.
   d. are correlated highly with ethnicity.

9. Compared to group-administered IQ tests, individually administered IQ tests
   a. require more training to administer.
   b. can be administered in a shorter time.
   c. are less reliable and consequently less valid.
   d. are more biased against minority children.

10. Tests of creativity
    a. are generally correlated .80 or higher with IQ.
    b. predict later scholastic success better than past grades.
    c. are still experimental and should be used mostly for research purposes.
    d. are biased against people who are mechanically oriented.

SUGGESTION SHEET

If your last name starts with the letter *S,* please complete the suggestion sheet at the end of the book while this chapter is still fresh in your mind.

ANSWERS TO APPLICATION PROBLEMS

#1

Before giving any advice, it would be wise to learn more about the situation at the last school. For example, had their daughter been having difficulty in school before she was given an IQ test? What kind of an IQ test was it—group or individually administered? Has she been checked for vision or hearing loss? Have there been any unusual health or behavior problems? Was this the first IQ test she had been given; and, if not, how did it compare to previous tests? The answers to these questions would affect any advice given. Certainly if the results of the IQ test contradict other information, another test should be given. A second test should be an individually administered IQ test since these are more reliable and valid. Before the next test, the parents should be sure that there are no other factors that may be inappropriately lowering their daughter's score, (e.g., health, vision, or behavior problems).

You should also inform the parents that although IQ tests are a good predictor of future academic performance, many variables can affect an IQ score at any given time. If it is established that their daughter does score relatively low on a measured IQ at this time, that will affect how instruction is designed and may suggest that consideration be given to having her participate in special programs. However, it is incorrect to assume that she will never be successful in school. It should also be noted that an IQ in the lowest 25th percentile is not dramatically low, and that the school will continue to work with her to enable her to achieve her potential.

#2

It is important to emphasize that the standardized test should only be a part of the selection criteria for the gifted and talented program. In considering which one test should be used (we are assuming here that there are financial or time constraints that preclude the use of more than one test), the following issues should be considered.

- As a standardized test of intelligence, the *Stanford-Binet* is one of the best. However, it requires highly trained test administrators and must be administered individually to children. It requires from one to two hours to administer and yields a single IQ score. Thus, if the committee is considering a test that can be given to every child in the school, it would probably be prohibitively expensive and logistically difficult.

- *The Cognitive Abilities Test* is a group administered IQ test that yields verbal, quantitative, and nonverbal scores for children in grades K to 13. It can be administered in a group setting in less than an hour and was normed concurrently with the Iowa Test of Basic Skills so it would be good for comparing the match between achievement and aptitude. It would be much less expensive and more feasible to administer to all children in the school, and it yields appropriate information.

- *The Torrence Test of Creative Thinking* is one of the best measures of creativity available. However, it is still considered to be an experimental research instrument. There is not yet much evidence that scores on the TTCT are a good way to select children for a gifted and talented program.
- *The Metropolitan Readiness Test* is a good screening measure to assess readiness for first grade and prereading skills. As a measure to select children for a gifted and talented program in first and second grade, however, it would be inappropriate. The test measures basic prerequisites and children who are gifted would "top out" on the test.

Based on this information, the Cognitive Abilities Test would be the most appropriate choice if only one standardized test can be used. However, it should be emphasized to the committee that using a single test to select children for the gifted and talented program is indefensible.

CHAPTER 20

Being Sensitive to Your Students' Personal Problems: Measures of Personal and Social Adjustment

Overview

Unless a teacher fosters the personal and social adjustment of students, optimum learning cannot be achieved. Learning can be dramatically enhanced or impeded by children's patterns of friendship, their isolation or rejection by other students, and the frictions, favoritism, and competitiveness they feel in the classroom. Learning is also affected by a student's self-concept—the way she perceives herself—as well as the degree to which she believes she is responsible for her successes or failures, as opposed to attributing them to luck or the action of others. Test anxiety, which is vexing, can be dwarfed by more persistent and pervasive anxiety or other personality disorders that can be debilitating to a student's success in school.

The classroom environment should be conducive to enhancement of students' social and personal adjustment, and creating such an environment is one of the most important responsibilities of the teacher. You can hardly fulfill this responsibility, however, if you have only your own instincts to guide your efforts to identify students whose personal or social development has lagged. Many students have needs that are not apparent; many hide deep hurts, frustrations, and fears behind polite and placid exteriors. As a teacher, you need tools that magnify your own insights and help you see where individual students—and the class as a whole—can be helped to grow in these important affective dimensions. This chapter is intended to provide you with such tools.

In the first section, we discuss briefly the importance of social acceptance and adjustment in the classroom, and the teacher's role in facilitating growth in these areas. In the second section, we briefly describe how measures of personal and social adjustment can be used to assist teachers. The remaining six sections of the chapter deal respectively with measures of: sociometric choice (social choices or perceptions of social desirability); classroom climate; self-concept; locus of control (attribution of responsibility to self or others); test anxiety; and personality/personal adjustment.

Objectives

Upon completing your study of this chapter, you should be able to

1. Describe how the teacher can use measures of personal and social adjustment in the classroom.
2. Describe two kinds of sociometric choice measures and briefly explain how each could be used in the classroom.
3. Explain how a sociogram or sociometric target is constructed.
4. Define *classroom climate,* describe three specific aspects of classroom climate, and explain how measures of this variable can give you insights into your students' perceptions of your classroom.
5. Define *self-concept* and *locus of control* and explain how measures of these variables can provide insights into student motivation and achievement.
6. Describe the two factors that appear to make up test anxiety.
7. Give three reasons why personality inventories are seldom used by teachers.

SOCIAL ACCEPTANCE AND ADJUSTMENT IN THE CLASSROOM

The classroom is viewed by educational sociologists as a microcosm of adult society. Its primary function is learning, which is achieved by interactions between teacher and student, between students, and between the student and the curriculum or learning materials.

The effectiveness of these interactions is, to a large degree, related to the personal and social characteristics that students and teachers bring to the classroom. The different attitudes, interests, values, experiences, and social class backgrounds, that they bring can significantly affect the classroom social climate, friendship patterns, and learning.[1]

The teacher must try to understand the characteristics of her students and adjust her behavior to provide an accepting atmosphere that will enhance both positive interactions and learning. Conflicts between teacher's and students' values can hinder communication and leave students feeling at best unsuccessful, and at worst, rejected.

Developing an effective classroom atmosphere devoted to learning is one of the teacher's most important and difficult tasks. The greater the differences in the social background and values of teacher and students, the more difficult and more important this task becomes. It is beyond the scope of this book to teach you how to accomplish this task, but the measures described in this chapter (and Chapter 13) can help you understand your students. This is the first step in creating a congenial environment in which students want to learn. Because success in the classroom society is related to success in the larger society, you can give this task nothing less than your best effort.

USES FOR SOCIAL AND PERSONAL ADJUSTMENT MEASURES

Social and personal adjustment measures can help the classroom teacher understand students who appear to have noncognitive problems. Some of these measures, such as sociometric choice questionnaires, concern the students' social adjustment or status in the society of the classroom. Others, such as self-concept measures, concern the student's personal adjustment.

Measures have been developed for literally dozens of variables related to personal and social adjustment. A few may be found in source books such as the *Tenth Mental Measurements Yearbook*. Many more are described in several *ETS Test Collection Bibliographies*. Still others are described in professional journals and can be located using computer search procedures described in Chapter 16. However, we will focus on only a few of these variables that are especially relevant to the classroom situation.

A word of caution: For the most part, measures of personal and social adjustment are direct self-report measures that can easily be faked or distorted. Further, there is little evidence of validity for most such measures. Thus you should never accept the results of these measures at face value.

For example, suppose a measure you administer indicates that a student is socially isolated from other students. You might decide to observe her interactions in the classroom and on the playground, talk with her about her relationships with other class members, and discuss the problem with the school psychologist or counselor. Only after gathering this kind of supporting evidence should you take steps to help the student gain social acceptance. The school psychologist can usually suggest how you might help her improve her social or personal adjustment.

---

[1] Students interested in the classroom as a social system may refer to Richardson's (1986) text in educational sociology.

Some of the sources listed in the Suggested Readings also describe strategies a teacher can use to help students make a better adjustment. However, it is unwise to take any action until you have obtained expert advice, since there is a real danger in an area as sensitive as personal and social adjustment that actions taken without sound advice will do more harm than good. Although the teacher may help a student adjust in some areas, students sometimes have problems that should only be treated by a qualified clinical psychologist.

SOCIOMETRIC CHOICE MEASURES

A great many things go on in the average classroom that everyone *except the teacher* knows about. Awareness of the minidramas that play out within the social structure of your classroom can be extremely important in developing a good learning environment for *all* of your students, for helping them gain recognition and social acceptance, and overcoming problems such as social isolation, rejection, intimidation, and prejudice. Measures of sociometric choice are useful in helping teachers understand the status of each student with respect to other students in the class.

Specifically, sociometric measures can help the teacher

1. Identify students who need help building social relationships.
2. Identify interpersonal conflicts she can help resolve and student factions she can help integrate.
3. Organize and rearrange classroom groups, remembering that groups organized along sociometric lines tend to work together more effectively.
4. Determine the best placement for exceptional children.

Several methods have been developed for measuring social distance, social acceptability, and other perceptions of individuals in social settings. The most common methods are the *nominating* technique and the *guess who* technique.

Nomination Measures

The nomination method, developed by Moreno (1953), usually asks each student to name other classmates whom she prefers (on some specific criterion). She may be asked to list the three students she would most prefer to study with, or to work with on a class project, or play with during recess. For example, a nomination item administered to a group of fifth grade girls might be:

Write the names of the *two* girls in the class you would most like to have as your best friends.
1. _____
2. _____

Based upon the responses of all students in the class, the teacher can plot a *sociogram* that shows patterns of choice for each student. The sociogram identifies the *most* popular students as well as students not chosen by anyone. It also shows cliques or small exclusive groups.

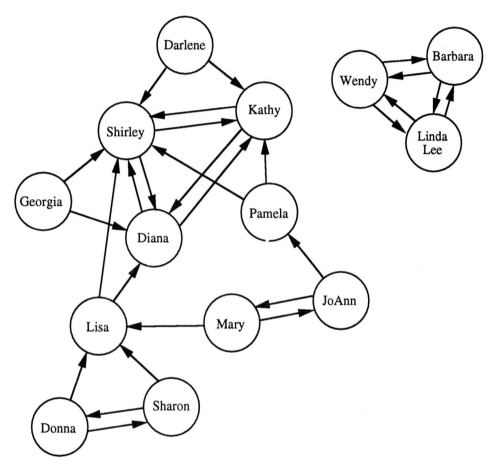

FIGURE 20.1 Sociogram of a Group of Fifth Grade Girls Asked to Nominate Two Girls They Would Most Like to Have as a Best Friend

A simple visual summary of responses, such as the sociogram shown in Figure 20.1, is constructed to reflect within-class social structure and identify social isolates who may need special attention.

The following classifications are frequently used in interpreting the results of sociometric choice measures:

1. *Star:* An individual who is frequently chosen
2. *Isolate:* An individual who is never chosen
3. *Neglectee:* An individual who receives few choices
4. *Rejectee:* An individual who receives negative choices, such as "least liked," but no positive choices
5. *Mutual Choice:* An individual chosen by the same student(s) she herself selected
6. *Cross-Sex Choice:* A boy chosen by a girl or a girl chosen by a boy

7. *Clique:* A small group of students who choose one another and make few if any choices outside the group
8. *Cleavage:* Two or more groups within the class who never choose someone from the other groups

In Figure 20.1, for example, Shirley would be considered a *star,* Georgia and Darlene *isolates,* Pamela a *neglectee,* Mary and JoAnn *mutual choices,* and Wendy, Barbara, and Linda Lee a *clique*. There is also a *cleavage* between these three girls and the rest of the class. Perhaps, unknown to the teacher (but not to other students), these three belong to a misunderstood religious minority. This sociogram could enable the teacher to discretely try to ascertain reasons for the cleavage and create opportunities to correct misunderstandings and eliminate prejudice.

There is another clique in the classroom—Shirley, Kathy, and Diana. Although each of them was chosen by one or more girls outside of their threesome, they restricted their nominations to one another.

By using different criteria—such as, "person I would most like to study with," or "person I would most like to have on my team at recess,"—different social patterns can be explored. In some cases, students are asked to identify least preferred individuals, which helps teachers perceive rejection patterns in classroom social structures. Although some practitioners have raised ethical questions about the use of negative selection criteria, research (e.g., Hayvren & Hymel, 1984) indicates that sociometric testing has no effect on children's peer interactions. Negative perceptions exist whether or not the teacher measures them. By using negative selection criteria, the teacher can identify which children are rejected and take steps to reduce the negative perceptions. In any case, it is wise to consult with the principal, other teachers, and possibly parents before using negative sociometric criteria.

APPLICATION PROBLEM #1

Assume the same group of fifth grade girls were asked the following question: "Write the names of the *two* girls in the class you would most like to have on your softball team at recess," with the results displayed below. Convert these data into a sociogram and interpret any similarities or differences you may see between it and the sociogram in Figure 20.1.

Respondent:	Chose A	and	B
Wendy:	Barbara		Linda Lee
Barbara:	Wendy		Linda Lee
Linda Lee:	Wendy		Barbara
Darlene:	Shirley		Barbara
Shirley:	Linda Lee		Barbara
Kathy:	Shirley		Diana
Georgia:	Linda Lee		Diana

Diana:	Linda Lee	Barbara
Pamela:	Linda Lee	Kathy
Lisa:	Linda Lee	Georgia
Mary:	Lisa	JoAnn
JoAnn:	Georgia	Pamela
Donna:	Lisa	Sharon
Sharon:	Donna	Georgia

There are other, already developed, sociometric nomination measures available, some of which use more sophisticated scoring and visual displays. Of the measures that are available in the sources outlined in Chapter 16, we have selected one to serve as a typical example.

The L-J Sociometric Test

This measure is typical of the nomination type of sociometric measure. Each student is asked to give a first and second choice to the following questions:

1. Who do you like most in this class?
2. Who do you like least in this class?
3. What students in this class can make others afraid of them?

Teachers are often reluctant to collect negative sociometric data such as questions 2 and 3. But as noted earlier, students know, with great clarity, whom they like and dislike and therefore such nominations do not create new attitudes but make the teacher aware of these attitudes, making corrective measures possible.

After the nominations are collected, each student's first and second choices for Question 1 (most liked), are recorded on a matrix table such as that in Figure 20.2. To obtain a student's weighted score, the student is given three points for each first choice received and two points for each second choice. For example, Andy was Ed's first choice and Frank's second choice. Thus, Andy's weighted score is five (i.e., 3 for first choice plus 2 for second choice).

Once weighted scores are computed for each child, this score is used to place the child on the sociometric target (Figure 20.3), as follows:

Band 1: Students with weighted score of zero (i.e., students 3, 7, 9, and 10)

Band 2: Students with weighted scores of 1 to 4

Band 3: Students with a weighted score of 5 (i.e., the expected score of all students)

Band 4: Students with weighted scores from 6 to 10

Band 5: Students with weighted scores of 11 or higher

MATRIX TABLE 1: Liked the Most

Group:
Date:

CHOICES

	1 (Andy)	2 (Bob)	3 (Carl)	4 (Don)	5 (Ed)	6 (Frank)	7 (Gary)	8 (Harold)	9 (Ian)	10 (Jon)
1 (Andy)						2		1		
2 (Bob)						2		1		
3 (Carl)						1		2		
4 (Don)					1	2				
5 (Ed)	1			2						
6 (Frank)	2				1					
7 (Gary)		2						1		
8 (Harold)		1			2					
9 (Ian)		1			2					
10 (Jon)				2	1					
No. of times selected	2	3	0	2	5	4	0	4	0	0
Weighted Score	5	8	0	4	13	9	0	11	0	0

FIGURE 20.2 Matrix Table Used with the L–J Sociometric Test

SOURCE: P. S. Popeil, "A Sociometric Approach to Understanding Interpersonal Relationships in a Classroom for Emotionally Disturbed Pupils." *Pointer*, Vol. 27, No. 3, Spring 1983, pp. 6 and 7. Reprinted with permission of the Helen Dwight Reid Educational Foundation. Published by Heldref Publications, 4000 Albemarle St., N.W., Washington, D.C. 20016. Copyright © 1983.

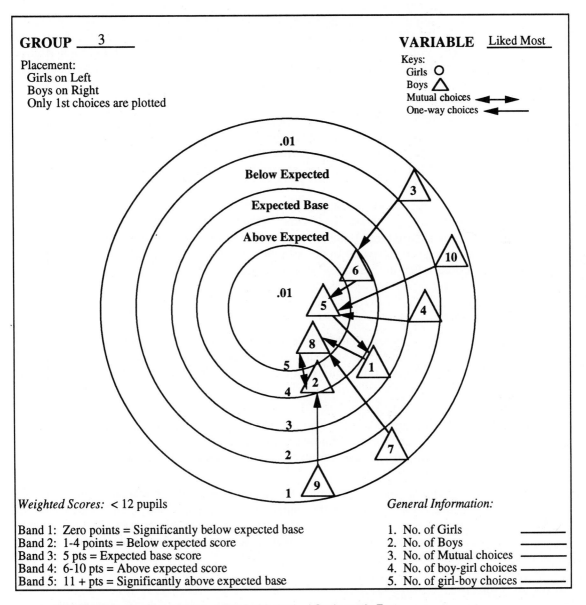

FIGURE 20.3 Sociometric Target Used with the L–J Sociometric Test

SOURCE: P. S. Popeil, "A Sociometric Approach to Understanding Interpersonal Relationships in a Classroom for Emotionally Disturbed Pupils." *Pointer*, Vol. 27, No. 3, Spring 1983, pp. 6 and 7. Reprinted with permission of the Helen Dwight Reid Educational Foundation. Published by Heldref Publications, 4000 Albemarle St., N.W., Washington, D.C. 20016. Copyright © 1983.

Once all students are placed on their correct bands on the target, arrows are drawn to indicate each choice. For example Andy (1) chose Harold (8) as his first choice and in turn was chosen by Ed (5). Only first choices are shown on Figure 20.3 to simplify the example. However, the teacher will obtain a more informative picture of the class structure if second choices are shown as well. In practice, girls would also be recorded on the matrix table and target. The teacher can then study the target to gain better insights into questions such as these:

1. Which students are most often chosen as "liked most"?
2. Which students are least often chosen or not chosen at all?
3. Which students make mutual choices?
4. What cross-sex choices are made?

The teacher can then make up matrix tables and sociometric targets for the other two items (i.e., "least liked" and "feared") to gain a more complete picture of the social structure. Teachers can easily make up their own nomination questions which can be designed to get information on specific aspects of the class social structure that are important in a given classroom.

Guess Who Measures

Another sociometric approach employs the *guess who* technique. Brief descriptions are given to the students and they are asked to write down the names of students (usually one to three) who best fit the description. For example, descriptions such as the following can be used:

1. This student is the best person to work with on class projects.
2. No one seems to know this student very well.
3. This person is often angry at other students in the class.

Scoring consists of simple frequency counts. If the teacher is interested in locating children with specific characteristics, as perceived by classmates, she can make up brief guess who descriptions for these characteristics. Many available instruments use the guess who technique; again, we have selected but a single representative example.

The Revised PRIME Guess Who Measure

This is a typical guess who instrument that was developed for use in Project PRIME, a large-scale study of educable mentally retarded (EMR) and learning disabled children who had been partially integrated into mainstream classrooms (Kaufman, Semmel, & Agard, 1974). The original measure, consisting of 29 questions, was administered to 13,045 pupils in the third, fourth, and fifth grades. A factor analysis of these data identified four major factors: "disruptive," "bright," "dull," and "well behaved." A revised scale, containing the five items contribut-

TABLE 20.1   Factor Structure of the Revised PRIME Guess Who Items

Item	Loading	Item
Factor I:	Disruptive	
14 .80		Who does the teacher have to scold all the time?
1 .79		Who is always bothering other children?
20 .78		Who makes too much noise in class?
2 .77		Who breaks the rules?
26 .74		Who bothers the teacher all the time?
Factor II:	Bright	
6 .87		Who is the smartest in the class?
18 .85		Who always knows the answers to the teacher's questions?
4 .84		Who is the best in math (arithmetic)?
24 .76		Who always gets their school work done on time?
25 .74		Who is the best in reading?
Factor III:	Dull	
8 .76		Who is the worst in math (arithmetic)?
15 .75		Who never knows the answers in class?
10 .66		Who is the worst in reading?
21 .66		Who learns new things very slowly?
28 .62		Who never gets their school work done on time?
Factor IV:	Well-Behaved	
5 .68		Who doesn't talk much to other children?
17 .66		Who is the best behaved?
22 .63		Who never talks in class discussions?
19 .63		Who never gets mad at other children?
13 .46		Who is friendly to everyone?

SOURCE: D. J. Veldman and John R. Sheffield, "The Scaling of Sociometric Nominations." *Educational and Psychological Measurement* 39 (101), 1979. Reprinted with permission of the publisher.

ing most to each factor is shown in Table 20.1. These 20 items can also help teachers think of good guess who items for their own use.

Veldman and Sheffield (1979) report reliability coefficients for the four factor scores ranging from .56 to .77. They also report strong concurrent validity correlations of the guess who items with teacher ratings, but only moderate correlations with self-reports.

CLASSROOM CLIMATE MEASURES

Research on classroom climate has its foundations in the social climate research of Murray (1938). He hypothesized that individuals have specific needs, such as achievement needs and affiliation needs. Although the strength of these needs largely determines individual behavior, another strong influence is the composite of pressures in a person's surroundings, which Murray called *environmental press*. The pressure a student perceives within the classroom has been called *classroom climate*. Although classroom climate can be measured by carefully structured classroom observation, this method is very costly and does not give us information about students' *perceptions* of that classroom environment. Group administered low-cost paper- and pencil measures have therefore been developed that provide information about students' perceptions. If students answer truthfully, measures of this variable can be very useful. We will briefly describe three measures of classroom climate selected from the available classroom climate measures to provide examples across school levels.

The Learning Environment Inventory (LEI)

This measure, initially developed and validated for use at the secondary school level, has seen wide use and several revisions. It is intended to measure individual student perceptions, and provide an overall picture of the classroom learning environment.

The current LEI version contains 15 scales (each with seven statements) that elicit student perceptions of the classroom environment. These are four-choice Likert-type scales using the response options *strongly disagree, disagree, agree,* or *strongly agree*. Table 20.2 provides a brief description and sample item from each LEI Scale.[2]

Reliability estimates for the 15 scales include alpha coefficients ranging from .58 to .86 and test-retest coefficients ranging from .43 to .73. These low coefficients are probably due primarily to the fact that each scale contains only seven items, making the reliability of most scales too low for use in individual diagnosis. The class means are generally more reliable, however, so teachers can be moderately confident in using LEI results to estimate overall classroom climate.

A review and analysis of 12 correlational studies (Haertel et al., 1981) indicates that achievement or learning measures in a variety of subjects are positively related to seven of the LEI scales (cohesiveness, satisfaction, difficulty, formality, goal direction, democracy, and material environment) and negatively related to four others (friction, cliquishness, apathy, and disorganization). This, and research reported in the test manual suggests that the LEI has good predictive validity.

My Class Inventory (MCI)

This simplified form of the LEI (also contained in the LEI test manual) is designed for use with children between eight and twelve years of age. In this measure, item wording has been simplified and a yes-no response format adopted. Only five of the LEI Scales are included, namely cohesiveness, friction, satisfaction, difficulty, and competitiveness. The authors report alpha reliabilities for the five scales ranging from .62 to .78. However, since the reliabilities and normative data are based on a sample of seventh grade Australian children, their applicability to American elementary school pupils is unknown. Some evidence of predictive validity reported in the LEI test manual suggest that the MCI is a useful measure of classroom climate.

---

[2] The LEI test manual (Fraser, Anderson, & Walberg, 1982) contains detailed descriptions and technical information.

TABLE 20.2 Scale Description and Sample Item for Each LEI Scale

Scale	Scale Description	Sample Item
Cohesiveness	Extent to which students know, help and are friendly toward each other	All students know each other well. (+)
Diversity	Extent to which differences in students' interests exist and are provided for	The class has students with many different interests. (+)
Formality	Extent to which behavior within the class is guided by formal rules	The class is rather informal and few rules are imposed. (−)
Speed	Extent to which class work is covered quickly	Students do not have to hurry to finish their work. (−)
Material Environment	Availability of adequate books, equipment, space, and lighting	The books and equipment students need or want are easily available to them in the classroom. (+)
Friction	Amount of tension and quarreling among students	Certain students in the class are responsible for petty quarrels. (+)
Goal Direction	Degree of goal clarity in the class	The class knows exactly what it has to get done. (+)
Favoritism	Extent to which the teacher treats certain students more favorably than others	Every member of the class enjoys the same privileges. (−)
Difficulty	Extent to which students find difficulty with the work of the class	Students in the class tend to find the work hard to do. (+)
Apathy	Extent to which students feel no affinity with the class activities	Members of the class don't care what the class does. (+)
Democracy	Extent to which students share equally in decision making related to the class	Class decisions tend to be made by all the students. (+)
Cliquishness	Extent to which students refuse to mix with the rest of the class	Certain students work only with their close friends. (+)
Satisfaction	Extent of enjoyment of class work	There is considerable dissatisfaction with the work of the class. (−)
Disorganization	Extent to which classroom activities are confusing and poorly organized	The class is well organized and efficient. (−)
Competitiveness	Emphasis on students' competing with each other	Students seldom compete with one another. (−)

Items marked (+) are scored 1, 2, 3, and 4, respectively, for the responses Strongly Disagree, Disagree, Agree, and Strongly Agree. Items designed (−) are scored in the reverse way.

SOURCE: Reprinted from B. J. Frazer, G. J. Anderson, and H. J. Walberg, *Assessment of Learning Environments: Manual for Learning Environment Inventory and My Class Inventory.* 1980, Western Australian Institute of Technology. Reproduced with permission of the authors.

The Classroom Environment Scale (CES)

This measure, consisting of 90 true-false items grouped into nine subscales, was designed for use at junior and senior high school levels. The subscales provide scores on classroom order and organization, involvement, affiliation, teacher support, task orientation, competition, rule clarity, teacher control, and innovation. Internal consistency coefficients range from .67 to .86 and test-retest reliability ranges from .72 to .90. Some validity data are also reported in the test manual. Average intercorrelation among the nine scales is .25, indicating that they measure reasonably independent aspects of the social environment in the classroom.

There are four forms of the CES. Form R asks teachers and students how they perceive the *current* classroom climate. Form S, a shortened version of Form R, is useful only in research and for total *classroom* diagnosis (i.e., *not* for individual student diagnosis). Form I measures the students' conception of the *ideal* classroom environment. Form E asks *prospective* class members what they expect the classroom environment to be like. Specific information about the CES can be found in Moos and Trickett (1987).

SELF-CONCEPT MEASURES

Each of us has a complex, multifaceted set of perceptions about ourselves. There is evidence in the psychological literature to indicate that these perceptions, which combine to form our self-concept, have an important impact upon our behavior in a wide range of situations. As a rule, when faced with a situation that requires us to act, we act in a manner that supports or enhances these perceptions. If we behave in a manner that is in conflict with our self-concept, then a change in some aspect of our self-perception must be faced. If such reappraisal involves facets that are important and central to the picture we have constructed of ourselves, it can be a very stressful experience. Consider, for example, the soldier whose self-concept includes the perception that he will be brave when facing danger on the battlefield. If he then runs away in terror when facing enemy fire, a serious psychological trauma may well result. Maintaining his self-concept requires that he either change his behavior to be in harmony with his self-concept, or change his self-concept to fit his behavior.[3]

Self-concept can be divided into broad categories that show how different facets of this construct relate to different kinds of experience or behavior. One group of investigators divides self-concept into four major categories: academic, social, emotional, and physical (Shavelson, Bolus, & Keesling, 1980). For teachers, academic self-concept is clearly of major importance in understanding students' behavior. However, academic self-concept is really a complex construct that may vary in relation to different subjects and different aspects of academic performance. Many studies have shown significant relationships between academic self-concept and achievement, and there is some evidence that self-concept

---

[3] For a fascinating analysis of this phenomenon, called *cognitive dissonance,* see Festinger (1962).

is causally linked to achievement (Shavelson et al., 1980). In other words, low self-concept can lead to lower achievement than one might expect, given the child's ability level. Furthermore, raising self-concept may raise achievement.

Many measures of self-concept are listed in the ETS Test Collection Bibliographies. Here, we briefly describe two of the more widely used measures appropriate for public school use.

Dimensions of Self-concept (DOSC)

The DOSC is a Likert scale designed to measure five noncognitive factors associated with self-concept in school: (1) level of aspiration, (2) anxiety, (3) academic interest and satisfaction, (4) leadership and initiative, and (5) identification versus alienation (Michael, Smith, & Michael, 1984). The DOSC contains 14 items for each of these five dimensions. Two forms are available, one for grades 4 to 6 and the other for grades 7 to 12. Like most self-concept measures, the DOSC uses direct self-report items such as these:

11. I believe my teachers are pleased with the quality of my schoolwork.
22. I worry about how well I am doing in my classes.
42. Talking in front of class makes me nervous.
54. I can solve problems faster than anyone else in class. (DOSC Test Booklet, Form S, grades 7–12)

Reliability coefficients (internal consistency) reported for the five subscales range from .70 to .84 for the elementary form, and from .83 to .90 for the secondary form. There is some evidence of concurrent validity for the five DOSC scales, with validity coefficients (using total grade point averages as the criterion) generally the highest and most consistent for "level of aspiration," while those for "anxiety" were lowest and least consistent. Some evidence of construct validity, based on factor analyses of the DOSC, is also reported in the test manual.

Self-esteem Inventories (SEI)

Three forms of this measure are available. The school form, containing 50 self-esteem[4] items plus an eight-item "lie" scale, is the most appropriate for use in the schools. This form may be used for students ages 8 to 15: The adult form is recommended for people over age 15. The "lie" scale measures the students' defensiveness or tendency to create a favorable impression. Such scales (often found in self-report measures) are useful in identifying the student who is not accurately describing herself.

For each item the student indicates whether the item is "like me" or "unlike me." The total score provides an overall measure of self-esteem. Four sub-scores—general self, social self-peers, home-parents, and school-academic—may be obtained.

---

[4] The terms *self-concept* and *self-esteem* are essentially synonymous as typically used in the relevant literature.

Several reliability studies are reported in the test manual (Coppersmith, 1981). Internal consistency (KR_{20}) for the overall score is around .90, varying slightly from grade to grade. Several studies of test-retest reliability over periods of as long as three years demonstrate that self-esteem is a moderately stable characteristic with coefficients reported from .42 to .70. The stability of self-esteem increases as age increases. (This suggests that efforts to help children increase low self-esteem should begin as early as possible; Coppersmith suggests some strategies teachers can try). Reliability data are provided for the four subscores. Except for the "general self" subscore (26 items), however, the subscales are too short (eight items each) to be sufficiently reliable for diagnosing the self-esteem of individual students. Thus, it is recommended that only the total score and lie score be considered when interpreting this measure.

Evidence of validity is also provided, suggesting that the SEI is sufficiently valid to be a useful measure of self-esteem.

Cautions in Using Self-concept Measures

The test manuals for self-concept measures usually provide useful suggestions for helping students who score low on these scales. However, low scores on the SEI, DOSC and similar measures should be regarded as *tentative* indicators that some aspects of a student's self-concept *may* be low. If a student obtains a low score on one of the scales, the teacher can check that result against another test or scale purporting to measure the same variable—and against her own observations of the student's behavior. Advice from the school counselor or psychologist may be helpful, too. Remember that noncognitive measures are difficult to validate conclusively and should only be acted upon when the results they yield are supported by other evidence.

LOCUS OF CONTROL MEASURES

It has been found that people differ considerably in the degree to which they believe that they control their own lives and destiny. The person who believes that her own actions largely determine the rewards and punishment she receives is said to be functioning under *internal* locus of control, while the person who believes that luck, fate, or powerful other persons control the reinforcements she receives is said to be operating under *external* locus of control. Research has shown that there are many important differences between people who attribute their successes and failures to themselves and those who believe luck or other people largely control their lives. Research has also shown a relationship between self-concept and locus of control, suggesting that locus of control is an important component in the individual's perception of self. Internal locus of control is generally related to favorable self-concept and achievement.[5]

---

[5] See Lefcourt, 1981; Findley & Cooper, 1983; and Gordon, 1977 for more information on locus of control.

Locus of control seems to influence many aspects of the person's personality, attitudes, and behavior. For example, the child who believes that her failure in school is due to bad luck or discrimination by the teacher can see little reason to work harder or change her own attitude. On the other hand, the child who regards her successes and failures as a direct result of her own behavior is much more likely to change her behavior to increase her chances of success.

Several general locus of control measures have been developed, including Rotter's (1966) well known I-E Scale. Teachers and educational psychologists, however, have been mainly interested in possible applications of this construct to education. Therefore, we will describe briefly two representative locus of control measures that are aimed primarily at the school environment.

The Intellectual Achievement Responsibility Questionnaire (IAR)

The IAR (Crandall, Katkovsky, & Crandall, 1965) limits the source of external control to people with whom the child comes in face-to-face contact, such as peers, parents, and teachers. The scale is composed of thirty-four forced-choice items. For each item stem there is an internal (I) and an external (E) choice. The choices indicating internal locus of control are of two kinds. The I+ items indicate that the respondent believes her *successes* are due to her own behavior, while the I− items indicate acceptance of responsibility for her *failures*. Half the items are designed to measure internal versus external responsibility for successes (I+) while half are concerned with internal versus external responsibility for failure (I−).

Here is an example of an I+ item, with labels added in parentheses:
1. If a teacher passes you to the next grade, would it probably be
    _____ a. because she liked you (E), or
    _____ b. because of the work you did? (I+)

Here is an example of an I− item:
15. When you forget something you heard in class, is it
    _____ a. because the teacher didn't explain it very well (E), or
    _____ b. because you didn't try very hard to remember? (I−)

Three scores are obtained: (1) the I+ score (total number of items in which the student attributes success to internal alternatives), (2) the I− score (sum of items in which the student attributes failure to internal alternatives), and (3) the total I score (the sum of the I+ and I− scores).

Normative data for this measure, provided for grades 3 to 12, indicate that self-responsibility (i.e., internal locus of control) is already established by third grade.

Test-retest reliability coefficients after a two-month interval ranged from .65 to .69 for the overall I score, with reliability of I+ and I− subscores falling in about the same range. Internal consistency (split-half) coefficients ranged from .54 to .60 for both I+ and I− subscores.

Concurrent and predictive validity studies have shown that the IAR total I score correlates positively and significantly with almost all achievement measures used, but the correlations were low, ranging from the .20s to .50s. Correlations were inconsistent across grade levels, but were generally higher for the elementary grades. The low reliability and validity of this measure suggests that the scores be considered only rough indicators of locus of control and be used cautiously.

The Academic Achievement Accountability Scale (AAA)

The AAA (Clifford, 1976) is a five-choice Likert-type scale, consisting of 18 items designed to measure locus of control related to academic activities. Twelve of the items are phrased so that agreement indicates internal locus of control, while for the remaining six, agreement indicates external locus of control. Here is an example of an "internal" item:

When you make up your mind to work hard, does your schoolwork get better?
YES!   yes   ?   no   NO!

Here is an "external" item:

When a teacher gives you a low mark is it because she doesn't like you?
YES!   yes   ?   no   NO!

Each response is weighted from 1 to 5; thus total scores range from 18 to 90. A high score indicates that the student accepts responsibility for academic outcomes—she is behaving under internal locus of control. The items deal primarily with luck and effort, thus providing a measure of a different aspect of locus of control from that of the IAR.

The author reports reliability coefficients (KR_{20}) ranging from .63 to .85 for different grade levels and student groups, with a median internal consistency of .74. Limited evidence of construct validity (Clifford, 1976) and concurrent validity (Rahe, 1975) suggests that teachers should regard AAA scores as highly tentative. However, when combined with observations and other available evidence, this locus of control measure can provide useful insights about how students view responsibility for their own fate—and how they are likely to respond to success or failure in school.

TEST ANXIETY MEASURES

The test-anxious student is one who knows the course material but, because of anxiety, cannot demonstrate her knowledge on a test. Test anxiety received major attention through the classic investigations of Mandler and Sarason (1952) and Spielberger (1966). Many subsequent studies, including Spielberger's programmatic research (Spielberger, 1972, 1979, and Spielberger & Vagg, 1984), have shown that people with high test anxiety differ from those with low test anxiety across a number of characteristics.

First, research has indicated that test anxiety is actually made up of two components: worry and emotionality. The *worry* component includes such elements as lack of confidence, feelings of inadequacy and insecurity, poor self-evaluation, thinking about the consequences of failure, feeling unprepared, feeling helpless, and feeling there is not enough time to complete the test. The *emotional* component includes feelings of tension, apprehension, nervousness, and panic, and somatic symptoms such as rapid heartbeat, sweating, and upset stomach (Salame, 1984).

It appears that emotionality is not significantly related to examination performance. However, several studies have found that worry is significantly related to lower test performance. Correlations between test anxiety and either examination performance or course grades are typically low (i.e., −.47 to −.14), although statistically significant.[6] This suggests a moderate tendency for students with high test anxiety to perform less well on examinations and earn lower grades.

Although there are a dozen measures of test anxiety listed in the *ETS Test Collection Bibliography on Anxiety,* we will examine briefly only two classic anxiety scales especially relevant to classroom settings.

Test Anxiety Scale

The first instrument developed to measure test anxiety was the Test Anxiety Questionnaire, designed primarily for use with college students. Its authors (Sarason & Ganzer, 1962) revised some of its items to develop the Test Anxiety Scale, which consists of 16 items in true-false format. Although designed primarily for college students, this scale appears appropriate for secondary school students use. Here, for example, are two typical items on this scale: "I feel very panicky when I have to take a surprise exam" and "I usually get depressed after taking a test."

Most test anxiety measures use direct self-report questions, and you will recall that such measures can be faked if the student has some reason to deceive the investigator. Therefore, it is important that you try to reassure students who will take this scale that there are no "correct" answers.

Test Anxiety Scale for Children (TASC)

The TASC, developed by Sarason, Hill, and Zimbardo (1964), has been used extensively in the public schools. It has been recommended for use in grades 1 through 9, but some investigators have administered it to students at the senior high school level. Both a "nervous form" (Do you worry a lot while you are taking a test?) and a parallel "relaxed form" (Do you feel relaxed before you take a test?) have been developed.

The nervous form of the TASC is more widely used, probably because it focuses on the student's worries, the aspect of test anxiety that seems to interfere

---

[6] For a brief review of this research see Tryon, 1980.

with test performance. A short 7-item version of the relaxed form of the TASC has been developed and extensively tested at grades 4, 8, and 11 (Harnisch, Hill, & Fayans, 1980). Copies of the 30-item TASC (both nervous and relaxed versions) and the 7-item short form may be found in this reference, which also contains item analysis, reliability, and validity data on the short form.

APPLICATION PROBLEM #2

Describe the kind of measure you could use to get more information on each of the following problems:

a. Mary does good work in class, contributes to class discussions, and turns in excellent homework assignments, but her test scores are always lower than you think they should be.

b. Fred seems to have a very low opinion of himself. Sometimes it appears that he won't try to answer a question even though you're pretty sure he knows the correct answer. He often makes remarks such as "I just don't have what it takes to do math."

c. You have just taken over a fifth grade class from a teacher who has had a heart attack and you are concerned about some of the children. Everyone seems to ignore Maria and she seems to be slowly going into a shell. Four of the girls are constantly together and seem to exclude everyone else from their group. How can you learn more about what's going on in this class?

PERSONALITY INVENTORIES

Personality inventories are self-report questionnaires that ask the respondent direct questions related to the various "personality traits" the inventory purports to measure. Some of these measures are designed primarily for use with normal individuals, while others are aimed at individuals seeking therapy. In the past, such measures were widely used in the public schools to help counselors and teachers learn more about students and to help make decisions about students. However, serious questions have been raised about their use in the schools. And, as a result, personality measure are rarely used in today's schools.

One major question concerns the validity of these instruments. A large number of validity studies have been done on the more widely used measures such as the California Psychological Inventory and the Minnesota Multiphasic Personality Inventory. For most subscores, there is some research evidence on their level of construct validity. That is, they appear to measure the constructs they purport to measure. However, concurrent validity against external criteria is generally low (.2 to .5), which limits the value of such inventories for individual diagnosis.

Interpretation of the scores and profiles obtained from personality inventories is a complex task that very few teachers are qualified to undertake. Therefore, the use of these measures should be restricted to clinical psychologists who have been trained in interpreting the results.

Perhaps the major reason that personality inventories are no longer used extensively in the public schools is that such measures have been challenged as an invasion of privacy.

Personality inventories, are, however, still used by clinical psychologists, largely as an aid to diagnosis. If you have an emotionally disturbed student in your class who is referred to a clinical psychologist for treatment, it is likely that one or more personality measure will be administered to the student.

In one of the methods used in developing a scale to measure a given personality trait, the trait is first defined so as to explicitly describe its nature and the characteristics of people having the trait. Then items are written that the developer believes will differentiate between those who strongly manifest the trait and those who do not. To estimate the validity of the measure, the test developer compares the scores of people believed to differ on the trait as indicated by some independent criterion measure, such as diagnoses by clinical psychologists.

California Psychological Inventory (CPI)

This measure was developed primarily for use with normal individuals, ages 13 and older. It contains 18 basic scales focusing on interpersonal behavior or social interaction. Among the variables measured are dominance, sociability, self-acceptance, self-control, and flexibility. Six additional scores can be obtained when the measure is scored by the publisher. This measure has been on the market since 1956. Excellent reviews and extensive references may be found in the *Mental Measurements Yearbooks*.

Minnesota Multiphasic Personality Inventory (MMPI)

This measure is the most widely used of the personality inventories. It was first published in 1942 and since then the various forms and revisions have been used in literally thousands of psychological studies. It is used primarily by clinical psychologists as an aid in screening and diagnosing emotionally disturbed adult patients, although it is sometimes administered to patients as young as 13. Fourteen scores are obtained from 399 items (new Group Form) that measure such variables as depression, hysteria, and paranoia. Extensive training and a considerable degree of psychological sophistication is required to interpret this measure. Several excellent reviews and over 3,000 references may be found in the *Mental Measurements Yearbooks*.

Several other widely used personality inventories are described in the *Ninth* and *Tenth Mental Measurements Yearbook*. In addition, there are several *ETS Test Collection Bibliographies* that describe personality and adjustment measures that can be used at different grade levels in the schools. Students interested in learning more about personality measurement are referred to the Suggested Readings.

SUGGESTED READINGS

Angleitner, A., & Wiggins, J. S. (Eds.) (1986). *Personality assessment via questionnaire.* New York: Springer-Verlag.

This reference covers a number of important topics that acquaint the reader with the current state of knowledge about personality questionnaires. The theoretical formulations of the personality inventory are explored, methods of developing such inventories are analyzed, and problems of validation are discussed.

Asher, S. R., & Gottman, J. M. (Eds.) (1981). *The development of children's friendships.* New York: Cambridge University Press.

The first chapter provides a good historical perspective of peer interaction research. Other chapters deal with a variety of topics such as advances in sociometry, social skills and peer acceptance, and friendships between retarded and nonretarded children.

Frazer, B. J. (1989). Twenty years of classroom climate work: Progress and prospect. *Journal of Curriculum Studies, 21*(4), 307–327.

Fraser's review provides an excellent framework on classroom climate. The paper highlights the historical background, gives an overview of classroom environment instruments, and synthesizes research in the area. Many references are included to further direct readings of interested students.

Gronlund, N. E. (1959). *Sociometry in the classroom.* New York: Harper.

This remains the classic source for teachers who are interested in using sociometric measures. The sociometric nomination technique is described in detail along with examples. Evidence on the reliability and validity of such measures is reviewed. Guidance in using sociometric results to improve social relations in the classroom is provided.

Lefcourt, H. M. (Ed.) (1981). *Research with the locus of control construct, Vol. 1: Assessment methods.* New York: Academic Press.

The initial chapter gives an overview of locus of control measures. Subsequent chapters describe a variety of locus of control scales currently in use and describe relevant research and applications. Several measures are included in this book.

March, H. W., Byrne, B. M., & Shavelson, R. J. (1988). A multi-faceted academic self-concept: Its hierarchical structure and its relation to academic achievement. *Journal of Educational Psychology, 80*(3), 366–380.

This paper explores the notion of *academic self-concept* and how it relates to academic achievement. Additional citations on self-concept are included in the reference list.

Smith, C. P. (Ed.) (1969). *Achievement-related motives in children.* New York: Sage.

These vintage chapters by Smith, Feld and Lewis, and Sarason contain useful information for the student who wants to learn more about test anxiety. The Feld and Lewis chapter also lists all the original and reversed questions that make up the Expanded Test Anxiety Scale for Children.

Tryon, G. S. (1980). The Measurement and Treatment of Test Anxiety. *Review of Educational Research, 50*(2), 343–372.

A very useful review that briefly discusses correlates, measures, and the treatment of test anxiety. Four tables provide very comprehensive summaries of the research results obtained from different treatment strategies. Bibliographic data for over 100 references related to test anxiety are also provided.

SELF-CHECK QUIZ

1. One advantage of most personal and social adjustment measures is that
   a. available measures focus on a wide range of variables important to the teacher.
   b. these measures have very high predictive validity and concurrent validity.
   c. since there are no right or wrong answers, these measures cannot be faked.
   d. they do not rely on self-report data.

2. Sociometric choice measures are useful for determining
   a. a student's locus of control.
   b. friendship patterns among students.
   c. how a student perceives herself.
   d. how a student will act in a given situation.

3. *Guess who measures* are made up of brief descriptions that
   a. are more effective than sociometric choice measures in identifying stars and isolates.
   b. identify students perceived by their peers as fitting each description.
   c. are mainly designed to identify the highest achievers in a class.
   d. are so broad they cannot really be linked to any individual student.

4. Students maintain their self-concept by
   a. refusing to accept any negative information about themselves.
   b. forcing themselves to achieve at levels beyond their perceived capability.
   c. behaving in ways that harmonize with their current self-concept.
   d. separating their feelings about themselves from the way they behave.

5. The student who operates under internal locus of control believes that her successes and failures are mainly due to
   a. her won good or bad luck.
   b. environmental influences.
   c. the actions and behaviors of influential persons in her life.
   d. her own attitudes and behaviors.

6. Studies of test anxiety have shown that
   a. the *emotionality* component of test anxiety is significantly related to test performance.
   b. the *worry* component of test anxiety is significantly related to test performance.
   c. there is no significant correlation between test anxiety and test performance.

7. Research on classroom climate indicates that
   a. information about students' perceptions is best obtained through classroom observation.
   b. most classroom climate measures have adequate validity and reliability for individual student diagnosis.
   c. some measures of classroom climate are positively related to achievement.

8. Personality inventories are generally used by
   a. classroom teachers.
   b. clinical psychologists.
   c. parents of students.
   d. school counselors.

9. Which of the following is an important limitation of personality inventories?
   a. Virtually no validity studies are available, even for the most widely used measures.
   b. They are inappropriate for students younger than ninth grade.
   c. Valid interpretation of the scores and profiles usually requires special training.
   d. They are inappropriate for students with major psychological problems.
10. Which of the following is a characteristic of a sociometric target?
   a. Arrows indicate where each student would prefer to be located.
   b. Isolates are grouped together below the target.
   c. Students at the center are those chosen most frequently.
   d. The students' gender is concealed by using identification numbers.

SUGGESTION SHEET

If your name starts with the letter *V*, please complete the Suggestion Sheet at the end of the book while this chapter is still fresh in your mind.

ANSWERS TO APPLICATION PROBLEMS

#1

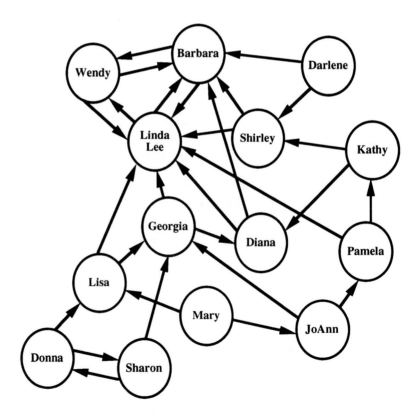

Of course, yours might look different, but it should contain the same information. The trick is to try to position as many girls as possible near other girls they have chosen; so the arrows will not be tangled and confusing.

There are many differences between this sociogram and Figure 20.1. Although Wendy, Barbara, and Linda Lee are still a clique, the cleavage has disappeared completely, and Linda Lee and Barbara are now stars. Shirley is not nearly as popular a choice for a teammate as she was for "best friend." While Darlene is still an isolate, Georgia is not, but Mary now has become isolated on this social dimension. We shall not comment further on every difference, but our interpretation would be that softball talent and desirability as a best friend are rather different, especially for some girls. Interest in winning intramural games may cause some girls to extend beyond their normal friendships and provide an opportunity for the teacher to form teams in a way that would allow new friendships to emerge and eliminate the previous cleavage. Of course, great care must be taken so that new problems are not crested in attempts to solve existing ones; sociograms are useful tools but the teacher's observations and judgment will continue to be central to solving social adjustment problems in the classroom.

#2
a. Test Anxiety Measure
b. Self-concept Measure
c. Sociometric Choice Measure

Beyond the Classroom: Setting Up School Measurement and Evaluation Programs

So far, our major focus has been on the use of educational measurement and evaluation at the classroom level. In this section, we explicitly address how to develop schoolwide or districtwide systems for measurement and evaluation.

In Chapter 21, we focus on how to set up a school (or district) testing program. We discuss the advantages of developing a comprehensive testing program and list essential ingredients and necessary steps to ensure a sound program. We describe ways to evaluate and select tests to be included in a testing system and discuss important considerations in scheduling, administration, scoring, analysis, and reporting. We also describe how microcomputers can be used to improve testing programs.

Finally, in Chapter 22, we describe how to obtain and use evaluation information in making wise decisions about curricula, programs, and instructional materials. Here we help you look beyond the beam of light cast by a good testing program to observe and evaluate *all* the outcomes of a school or district curriculum or program, something that even the best testing program cannot do. This chapter also introduces you to a series of practical guidelines for setting up and operating a school evaluation program.

These two chapters are directed not only to educational administrators and others with schoolwide or districtwide responsibilities, but also to classroom teachers who are asked to serve on committees that assist in setting up testing and evaluation programs that transcend the boundaries of single classrooms.

CHAPTER 21

Setting Up a School Testing Program

Overview

When people think of testing in schools, they typically think about either teachers' classroom tests or standardized tests administered districtwide. It is often assumed that all the tests administered in a particular school district are part of a comprehensive district plan for testing. Frequently, however, tests do not relate to any overall plan for collecting and using data about student performance to improve the education provided to these students. On the contrary, many school districts lack any testing *program* deserving of that title; the tests used may duplicate one another, may fail to collect vital information, may be technically inadequate, or may be selected more because of convenience—or ignorance—than for any sound educational purpose.

Obviously, some districts have invested the time and effort necessary to develop a systematic testing program and have outlined how both teacher-made and selected standardized tests can work together to provide pivotal information educators need to improve teaching and learning. Such districts are, unfortunately, rare. Teacher-made tests are seldom integrated effectively into overall district testing programs, and teachers typically receive little guidance from the district to help make their classroom tests more effective. Often districts choose standardized tests because of their popularity or reputation, or the persuasiveness of the publishers' sales pitches, rather than because they are necessary parts of a well-conceived testing program. Many classroom teachers have become resigned to the current situation, and make use of their own classroom tests and those tests that the school psychologist might administer at their request to individual students, while viewing other district or statewide testing programs as intrusive or irrelevant.

School administrators, school psychologists, and other school district staff such as curriculum or testing specialists have historically been responsible for planning school district's testing programs. However, in today's atmosphere of shared responsibility for educational planning and policy, it is increasingly likely that classroom teachers will be invited to provide input into a districtwide testing program. District testing committees that review and revise existing district testing policies and programs frequently include classroom teachers. In addition, teachers often play a major role when individual schools are allowed to develop their own testing programs. This chapter is intended to give you information you can use effectively when and if you have an opportunity to shape district or school testing programs in positive ways.

Also, given the increasing dependence on computer technology, our discussion of districtwide testing programs necessarily includes a brief discussion of ways that microcomputers can be used to improve school testing programs.

Objectives

Upon concluding your study of this chapter, you should be able to

1. Discuss why it is important for each school district to develop a comprehensive testing program, including the major purposes such a program can serve.
2. List the essential ingredients common to any good school testing program.
3. List eight steps necessary to develop and implement a sound districtwide or schoolwide testing program.
4. Discuss the relative advantages of establishing a districtwide testing program or having individual schools develop individual schoolwide testing programs.
5. Describe ways to evaluate and select tests.
6. Discuss important considerations in scheduling and administering tests.
7. Discuss important considerations in test scoring, analysis, and reporting.
8. Briefly describe how microcomputers can be used to improve testing programs.

THE IMPORTANCE OF A COMPREHENSIVE TESTING PROGRAM

Tests serve many purposes. Teachers use tests because they need to know how well their students have mastered specific learning objectives. Comprehensive diagnostic testing is used by some teachers as a tool for helping lower achieving students. Districts and individual schools depend on tests to guide instructional management decisions, to inform student placement or certification decisions, and to evaluate the effectiveness of existing curricula. At the state level, legislators or state school officials frequently mandate minimum competency testing or other forms of assessment to determine how well schools are accomplishing their goals. Test scores are often the primary tools used by legislators to evaluate special state-funded programs. At the national level, tests are mandated as the primary means of evaluating many categorical federal aid and other entitlement programs in education, such as Chapter I.

So many tests, initiated for so many different reasons, by so many different parties may leave us with a hodge-podge of test results that are redundant on the one hand, while failing to assess important educational objectives on the other. To everyone who has endured the frustration of this paradox, the need for a well-planned, orderly, and systematic testing program is obvious.

A well-organized and carefully developed testing program—incorporating a combination of teacher-made, curriculum-embedded, and standardized tests—can serve the following purposes:

Instructional Purposes

Diagnosis of individual student performance/attitudes

Evaluation/grading of individual student performance

Determining achievement gains of groups of students

Within-classroom grouping of students for instruction

Identification of under- or overachievement

Determining mastery of specific content or learning objectives

Administrative Purposes

Admissions and selection decisions

Placement or certification decisions

Curriculum or program evaluation

Public accountability

Compliance with legal mandates

Guidance Purposes

Career counseling

Solving of individual problems

Research Purposes

Conducting or replicating research relevant to the school/district

Identifying and solving educational problems

Until a district or school has settled on the purposes of testing, it is difficult to establish a testing program or select specific tests. Yet the unfortunate practice of selecting and scheduling tests without first thinking through the purposes is widespread. Further, many districts trustingly—even naively—adopt another district's testing program. This approach may work—especially in cases where districts have such similar goals, organizations, and curricula that the adopted testing program requires only fine tuning. In most cases, however, a ready-made program cannot hope to suit your district's purposes as well as one tailor-made to meet your needs.

IMPORTANT INGREDIENTS IN A GOOD TESTING PROGRAM

A well-conceived testing program should possess the following 14 characteristics.

1. Congruence with the Purposes for Testing

A testing program obviously should fulfill the purposes for which it is intended, yet so many fail to do so. For example, if the purpose is "to measure relative achievement levels across the entire student population," then minimum competency testing is ill-suited for the task, since such testing primarily is pertinent for low-achieving students and provides little useful information about above-average students.

Similarly, good testing programs provide the precise information administrators and teachers need to determine whether district and school goals are being achieved.

Thought should also be given to possible use of norm-referenced and criterion-referenced measurement, for each plays a different role and achieves different purposes. As Shepard (1979) notes, most good testing programs depend upon a combination of both types of measures.

2. Coverage of the Most Important Outcomes

Far too many district or school testing programs are narrowly focused, overlooking many important outcomes. No testing program can measure everything, but the measurement of certain areas, such as attainment of basic skills, should be included as the core of any program. At the same time, it is easy to allow a preoccupation with basic skills to narrow not only testing but the curriculum itself.

For example, a survey of a nationwide sample of school principals and teachers (Herman & Dorr-Bremme, 1984) revealed that more time is spent teaching the basic skills—mathematics, English, and language arts—than other subjects because of mandatory testing in those areas. Nevertheless, testing programs should also measure other important areas.

How do we strike a good balance? Sax (1989) proposes a *minimum* testing program for *all* students (focused largely on achievement tests in common core curriculum areas), with a *supplemental* program that would allow teachers to request that attitude and interest measures, or achievement measures in specific subject areas be administered to specific students or groups.

3. Feasibility

As important as it is for a testing program to provide comprehensive coverage, it must be tempered by a consideration of what is possible. It makes little sense to try to cover all the important outcomes of a school or district if the resources available for testing are inadequate to permit good coverage in basic areas of the curriculum. There are numerous ways to make comprehensive testing economical. For example, a school can avoid testing that is too repetitive within the same subject areas, can eliminate redundancy among tests, and can test samples of behavior in all important outcomes, rather than testing intensely in some areas while leaving others totally untested. Yet, inexperienced educators often attempt to undertake too large a testing effort at one time. A testing program should be built incrementally, thereby allowing district personnel to incorporate each test into the district's decision-making structure before additional tests are added.

4. Cooperative Development

If testing programs are to succeed, they must be developed cooperatively with teachers, educators, testing specialists—and possibly parents. Otherwise, these groups may tend to view such programs merely as another imposition being "handed down" to classroom teachers. Many teachers criticize districtwide achievement tests for being insensitive to their classroom or school's instructional objectives. Therefore, establishing good district and school testing programs may require development of tests representative of local curricular objectives.

In an individual school (or in a very small school district), it may be possible to involve all teachers and administrators in developing the testing program. Subject matter specialists in relevant areas (e.g., district curriculum specialists) should also be included. In a large school or district, it is seldom possible to involve all teachers or administrators directly, but that is no excuse for failing to include representative teachers and principals on a testing committee charged with tailoring a program to the district's needs.

5. Linkage of Testing and Instruction

If testing programs are to provide valid data about how well instructional programs are producing desired ends, there must be a match between test content and the content of classroom instruction. Nothing very useful is learned by extensive, thorough testing of objectives students have not yet been taught.

Linking districtwide tests with the districtwide curriculum is a challenging undertaking, especially where there is wide variation in textbooks, tests, and instruction. Even when districts adopt a common curriculum, linking it to typical standardized tests can be tricky. This difficulty can be minimized if the commercial or districtwide curriculum materials come with good curriculum-embedded tests. Along with self-constructed tests, teachers most often use curriculum-embedded tests for assessing student learning and for grading (Dorr-Bremme, 1983).

Leinhardt and Marseewald (1981) proposed four possible approaches a district might use for improving the linkage between curricula and tests: (1) Build new criterion-referenced tests, (2) modify existing tests by removing items not related to the curricula, (3) construct taxonomies of tests and curricula to serve as guidelines in selecting the most appropriate measure, and (4) measure the degree of overlap between curricular and test content, using the result as a way of assessing the extent to which the test is an appropriate measure of the curriculum. The last two approaches are potentially the most workable in the typical school district, although districts whose staff have high levels of psychometric expertise may find the first two solutions just as workable.

6.   Support of Instructional Functions

Even when tests match curriculum content, a testing program still may not support all the important instructional functions society expects of schools. Most of us agree that testing should *facilitate* learning, *assess* basic skills, and *detect* learning difficulties. A systematic, functional school testing program indicates how well classes of students are progressing in school at different stages, shows the extent to which important learning objectives are being met, and suggests ways teachers can improve instruction.

7.   Support of Diagnostic Functions

Testing programs that fail to provide information useful in diagnosing individual student learning difficulties, aptitudes, interests, and attitudes are of limited value. A good school testing program helps schools match individual students to the curriculum—and vice versa.

Good testing programs rely on the diagnostic services of school psychologists, who use a wide array of formal standardized tests, informal assessments, diagnostic interviews, and observations to provide teachers and school administrators with information about individual students.

In addition, many teachers use comprehensive diagnostic systems of their own, particularly in basic skill areas such as math and reading. Such classroom diagnostic systems typically use teacher-made and/or curriculum-embedded tests. Good testing programs should accommodate and incorporate such localized diagnostic testing efforts.

TABLE 21.1 Possible Timing for Administering Tests in an Overall Testing Program

Type of Test	K	1	2	3	4	5	6	7	8	9	10	11	12
Achievement Batteries			X			X			X			X	
Readiness Tests	X	or X											
Academic Aptitude Tests				X	or X								
General Aptitude Tests											X	or X	
Interest Inventories												X	or X
Diagnostic Tests, as needed	X	X	X	X	X	X	X	X	X	X	X	X	X
Individual Classroom Tests	X	X	X	X	X	X	X	X	X	X	X	X	X
Minimum Competency Tests										X	or X		X

Year in School

8. Parsimony and Efficiency

Many district testing programs are driven more by external forces (e.g., state or federal legislative or executive requirements for information) than by a well-conceived plan for improvement. The consequence is frequent redundancy in testing efforts.

For example, many districts are guilty of overtesting by administering the same test more frequently than necessary. It is seldom if ever necessary to administer achievement test batteries at both the beginning and end of the school year. Yet many districts adhere to this practice. For many tests that measure stable characteristics, such as *general* academic aptitude, there is seldom a need to test more than once or twice during the student's first twelve years in school. Table 21.1 suggests possible times for the administration of different types of tests, as part of an overall testing program. Each district would need to tailor such a schedule to their needs by examining the nature of each test and its relationship to the district's overall purposes for testing. But whatever the schedule, avoid overtesting. You will save much time and money, as well as reducing the time testing takes from instruction.

9. Interpretability of Test Results across Grade Levels

Perhaps the best way to accomplish this end is to use the same series of examinations throughout grade levels, wherever possible, to ensure that norms and subtests are comparable. Further, test interpretations and comparison of scores are generally facilitated if forms of the same battery are used across all grades, since the norms will remain more or less constant.

10. Effective Use of Technology Capabilities

It seems foolhardy to administer, score, and report tests in a horse and buggy fashion when advanced technology permits doing so more efficiently and effectively. In addition, technology can link a district's test results with other data in such a way that the true impact of various educational programs can be creatively and thoroughly explored. Sensible use of technology in a district's testing program provides the means to determine why a given student, group of students, or program succeeds, or what needs a particular student has.

11. Relevance to Public Needs for Information

Few people would deny that the public has a right to know what schools are accomplishing with the resources—and students—entrusted to them. Unfortunately, many schools fail to collect test data that bear directly on key concerns expressed by parents and other publics. If a testing program is to help a school district to be appropriately accountable, the district must take into account the type of test information that would be accepted by their constituencies as trustworthy indicators of school performance.

Also, *all* legitimate audiences should be recognized and served. Well-designed testing programs can provide parallel and simultaneous reports of (1) *individual* test data to teachers, administrators, parents, and where appropriate, students, and (2) *aggregated* data to governing bodies and funding agencies. Restrictive and underutilized reports of testing typically signal inadequacies in the testing programs.

12. Timeliness

No testing program is adequate if it fails to communicate test results to all relevant audiences in an effective and timely fashion. Tardy test information is a patent waste of both opportunity and resources. For example, if a particular standardized testing program suffers from too slow turnaround time in test scoring and reporting, then districts may be well advised to opt for an alternative.

13. Use Restricted to Legitimate, Agreed-upon Purposes

A well-conceived testing program will reduce or eliminate the possibility of misuse. Further, no testing program should be subverted to serve illegitimate purposes or ends that were not intended when the program was designed. For example, a school board that decrees that the results of the district's achievement test results be used as a covert mechanism for teacher evaluation is *at best* misguided.

14. Periodic Evaluation and Improvement

It would be foolhardy to allow any testing system to stagnate. Tests become outdated, curriculum and goals change, school populations shift, and new technology prompts new testing practices. Consequently, any testing program should be periodically evaluated and, where necessary, revised.

However, testing programs ought not to be revised willy-nilly, without regard for the consequences of change. Remember that frequent changes in achievement test batteries and other standardized testing programs will make comparability of scores across grades difficult, if not impossible. Such changes should occur only when they are clearly in the best interest of the school and not simply to comply with new fads.

STEPS IN DEVELOPING AND IMPLEMENTING A SCHOOL TESTING PROGRAM

Setting up a well-integrated school testing program requires eight steps, which we discuss in this section, giving greater attention to those that require more elaboration and have not already been discussed in connection with topics covered earlier.

Step 1: Determining What Purposes Your Testing Program Is to Serve

Although discussed earlier in this chapter, the importance of this first step cannot be overemphasized. When the purposes for testing are unclear, unknown or poorly defined, there is every likelihood that limited testing resources will be wasted, and that test results will either not be used at all, or—worse yet—will be used in making decisions they were never designed to support.

Step 2: Choosing the Level of the Testing Program

School districts attempting to set up a testing program face a quandary: whether to establish one testing program for the entire district or to allow individual schools to develop independent testing programs. Districtwide testing programs have obvious advantages—greater efficiency and the support and technical capability of district central office staff. On the other hand, individual school testing programs have the advantage of being tailor-made to meet informational needs at the building level.

Districtwide testing programs (frequently called district assessment programs) should link testing with district curriculum. For districtwide achievement tests to be useful, the *core* curriculum and supporting materials must be consistent across schools in the district. A testing program for an individual school, by contrast, is more likely to exhibit sensitivity to particular innovations and learning objectives held by that school.

It is easy to fall into the trap of setting up a false dichotomy where one must choose between two alternatives: districtwide or school-based testing. Yet it is usually feasible for districts both to have their cake and eat it by developing a basic district testing program with essential tests required of all students at specified grade levels, while simultaneously allowing individual schools to develop their own programs to supplement districtwide efforts. Most districts allow considerable autonomy to individual schools, with decisions about additional tests left primarily to teachers and principals. Given such autonomy, some schools may do extensive testing beyond what the district requires, while others do little or none.

Step 3: Developing a Structure for the Overall Testing Program

Earlier, we discussed 14 characteristics important to a good testing program. Those ingredients represent the building blocks that must be carefully combined to construct a solid framework for an overall testing effort. Space does not permit our discussing at length how each of them might fit together in a particular testing program, since the possibilities for combining them is almost infinite. Suffice it to say here that careful reflection on each of those 14 characteristics is necessary to provide structure for the overall testing program and will greatly enhance the probability that the remaining steps in developing a testing program will prove fruitful.

Step 4: Determining the Specific Behaviors and Content to Be Measured

No testing program will have much impact on educational improvement unless the specific behaviors and content to be measured have been well defined. It is hard to hit fuzzy targets. When desired learning outcomes are vague, one can hardly fault a test for failing to determine how well they have been attained. It is important, therefore, to define the instructional content to be measured, and the specific behaviors students are expected to demonstrate. Imprecision at this level can render test results useless.

Step 5: Choosing or Developing the Tests to Be Used

Not only must a testing *program* meet the purposes for which it was established, but any test selected as part of that testing program must also serve those purposes. It is a clear case of confusing cart and horse to select tests too early, before deciding exactly what you want those tests to accomplish. A test that is superbly suited to one purpose may be a total waste for another. Test selection should not proceed without regard for the four steps outlined above. Far too many schools choose and administer tests without adequate attention to each of the "important ingredients" discussed earlier.

Perhaps one reason many educators pay too little attention to test selection is their innocence about the consequences of selecting the wrong tests. They fail to realize that tests that do not measure what the school is trying to teach cannot be of much use in determining whether the school is accomplishing its intended goals. Worse yet, a mismatch between tests and curriculum can encourage teachers and students to concentrate on content that is irrelevant.

In determining which specific tests should be used, four questions must be answered: (1) Who should be involved in test selection? (2) From what sources can information about specific tests be obtained? (3) What procedures should be used in test selection? (4) What criteria and standards should be used to guide the final choice? Although we have answered each of these questions somewhat earlier in this chapter or in Chapter 16, we will touch each again briefly in this context.

Who Should Be Involved in Test Selection?

Earlier in this chapter we discussed the need for teachers, principals, school psychologists, central office staff, and other specialists to work cooperatively in developing a testing system. The same need for cooperative involvement exists in test selection. Few teachers will enthusiastically administer and use the results of an achievement test they (or their colleagues) played no role in selecting. Involving them in the selection process pays more than shared-ownership dividends, however, for teachers may well be the most expert in determining how well the *content* of achievement tests matches that of the curriculum. But teachers and administrators are less often qualified to judge the technical adequacy of such a test without the assistance of a school psychologist or psychometrician. Similarly, selection of academic aptitude tests, interest inventories, and other nonachievement measures may require assistance from people trained in the development and use of such instruments. Even in such cases, however, it is wise to elicit the opinions of teachers and other educators regarding the acceptability of each measure.

What Are the Best Sources of Information about Specific Tests?

It is not feasible to try out every existing test to determine which one best suits your purposes. Practicality forces most of us to depend upon secondary sources of information, such as those we described in Chapter 16. Here we only stress the importance of drawing on these sources to learn all you can about a test before you use it or make decisions based on the results it gives you.

What Procedures Should Be Used in Test Selection?

It is important to follow some systematic evaluation procedure in choosing a test. There is seldom room in any educational endeavor for haphazard and slipshod procedures. There is never any room for such casualness in selecting instruments that will be used to measure important student behaviors and characteristics. We refer you to Chapter 16 for a more complete discussion of procedures for selecting from among existing tests.

What Criteria Should Be Used in Test Selection?

In Chapters 6, 7, and 16, we discussed technical and practical characteristics that should be considered in judging the quality of educational and psychological tests. We developed lists of criteria and worksheets that could be used to select from among alternative tests under consideration. Here we will simply underscore the importance of applying such criteria to *each test* considered for inclusion in a district's testing program.

What If You Want to Develop Your Own Tests?

You will not always find an appropriate test, even if you search carefully. If no good measure exists, you may need to construct one to fulfill the purposes of your testing program. This is often true for teacher-made tests designed to measure how well students have mastered specific learner outcomes. When careful evaluation suggests there are no tests well suited to your needs, it is comforting to have the knowledge—supported by the help of specialists where necessary—to develop your own home-grown instrument, tailored for your use. (We have described ways of constructing and validating instruments in Chapters 9 to 13.)

Step 6: Developing Testing Schedules and Guidelines for Test Administration

Once tests have been selected, it is necessary to plan the testing schedule and establish guidelines for administration. We turn our attention first to the issue of scheduling.

Planning a Testing Schedule

With the exception of teachers' classroom tests, most tests can be administered at preappointed times. Your district (or school) testing program will not be well coordinated until you have decided when each test should be given and aggregated those specific dates into an overall testing schedule. With standardized tests, for example, the biggest issue is typically whether to test in the spring or fall. Both have advantages, as the following lists show:

Advantages of Fall Testing
- Provides information about new students (summer "move-ins")
- Provides information needed at the beginning of the next school year
- Is useful in diagnosing learning difficulties
- Assesses achievement after the usual decline in retention across the summer vacation
- Allows the remainder of the school year to focus on content or skills in which tests reveal students to be deficient
- Avoids covert use of tests to evaluate teachers
- Avoids teachers "teaching to the test" because of concerns about their classes' performance

Advantages of Spring Testing
- Offers useful information for decisions about promotion, placement, or grouping of students at the next grade level

- Provides summative information about achievement gains and other educational outcomes for each year
- Provides information about the cumulative effects of a particular school curriculum (e.g., a junior high curriculum) through "exit testing" of those about to graduate
- Provides useful information for most program or curriculum evaluations

Deciding which of these is most compelling is only illustrative of decisions that must be made about when to schedule particular tests and how to fit them together into an overall testing schedule.

Deciding How Much Time to Spend on Testing

It is important to consider how much time students spend taking tests. Rather than presuming to suggest how much time is appropriate, it seems wiser to report what most districts are doing. Dorr-Bremme reported that for secondary school teachers, "Case study findings indicate that testing, across all subjects, takes up about 10% of students' annual classroom time" (1983, p. 12). Of that time, the teachers reported about one fourth was spent taking tests mandated by federal or state agencies or by the district.

Herman and Dorr-Bremme (1984) found that high school teachers reported spending about twice as much time testing as did elementary school teachers, primarily because secondary teachers are more prone to perceive tests as motivational. Of the time elementary school teachers reported their students spent taking tests, about half was consumed by responding to tests mandated at higher levels (district or above).

Planning for Test Administration

It is not our purpose here to discuss *how* to administer tests since we dealt with that topic at some length in an earlier chapter. But we think it useful to remind you that there are several important considerations when planning to administer any test. To whom should the test be administered? How long will it take to administer it? How will standardization in administration be guaranteed? Who will administer the test? When? Unless such questions are thoughtfully answered, it is unlikely that tests will be administered under standardized or controlled conditions. And without standardization, interpretation of test results is challenging, at best. Flawed test administration frequently leads to badly distorted test scores.

One additional thought. It is often not as easy to administer a test as the test manual makes it appear. Districts that depend on teachers to administer standardized tests would be well advised to schedule a practice administration before the actual testing. (For further information concerning the specifics of test administration, we refer you back to Chapter 11.)

Step 7: Developing Procedures for Test Scoring, Analysis, and Reporting

Without repeating Chapter 11, in which we discuss specific techniques in these areas, we need to touch on several general issues important in setting up a districtwide testing program.

Test Scoring Procedures and Standards

First, it is necessary to plan carefully how tests will be scored, keeping such criteria as feasibility, cost, and scoring reliability in mind. Careful attention to standardizing test administration is of limited value if the scoring of those tests is slipshod or scoring standards are suspect. Minimum competency testing programs are creating scoring problems because educators are being asked to set standards for large numbers of students *as a group,* rather than individually. Setting an unreasonably high passing score on an extremely important minimum competency test can have dire consequences for many students. On the other hand, society is the loser in the end if the minimum competency standards are set too low.[1] One reason minimum competency tests were developed was to stop the depreciation of the high school diploma. Clearly, if standards are set too low, depreciation will be increased rather than decreased.

Analysis of Test Results

It is also important to make certain that the analysis of test scores fits the purposes for which the tests were given. As Anderson and Pipho point out:

> Different types of analyses can greatly influence the reporting of scores and their ultimate use. . . . Conducting analyses that show changes by subgroups of students will highlight issues different from those revealed by reporting total groups averages. (1984, p. 212)

Reporting of Test Results

In Chapter 14 we describe several methods for reporting individual test results. But it is also important to think about overall reporting strategies. Reporting comparative achievement data school by school will have a far different impact from reporting districtwide test results.

Reporting must also be timely. Test results that are reported too late to affect the decisions for which they were intended signals a poorly conceived (or operationalized) testing effort. The practice of collecting results from all tests administered during a school year and issuing them in a single report at the end of the school year is lamentable, for such results typically come too late to influence any of the decisions that prompted test administration in the first place.

A well-developed testing program also provides reports of testing results to all "stakeholders"—those affected in some way by those test results. Students—obviously the most directly affected stakeholders—should be informed appropriately about how well they have performed on various measures. The schools' tacit responsibility to inform parents is also well-understood, but many district testing programs fail to incorporate effective reporting procedures to ensure that appropriate information about test results gets to parents.

For purposes of accountability, it is also important that test reports reach governing boards and other representatives of the general public, whose interests

---

[1] See Glass (1978) for a very thoughtful analysis of dilemmas encountered in setting standards and criteria.

the schools serve. Yet such reports are likely to be valued more by administrators than by teachers (Dorr-Bremme, 1983). Conversely, comparing achievement across classrooms or schools is one of the principle interests of district administrators and program coordinators and reporting such scores to the school board may be of considerable importance to principals or superintendents.

Teachers and school administrators are the chief consumers for test results, since they consider those results in designing educational programs and addressing the learning needs of specific students. Reporting format is just as important as promptness if test results are to be used. According to Herman and Dorr-Bremme (1982, 1984), required tests (e.g., standardized tests, minimum competency tests, and tests referenced to district objectives) are used less by teachers than by administrators in making curriculum evaluation decisions and in communicating with other school personnel and parents. Recent innovations in reporting formats for standardized achievement tests have made the results of these tests more useful to teachers in making individual instructional decisions, and should encourage them to make greater use of such results than in the past.

Step 8: Developing Procedures for Periodic Review and Evaluation of the Testing Program

Any testing program needs periodic review and evaluation to assure its continuing quality and relevance. Chapter 22 describes in detail procedures that can be used to evaluate any educational program, including a districtwide or individual school testing program.

USING MICROCOMPUTERS IN YOUR TESTING PROGRAM

No discussion of a testing program would be complete without some attention to the use of computers in educational testing. As far back as 1980, 90 percent of nearly 1,000 school districts studied were found to be using computers in instructional settings (Chambers & Bork, 1980). But it is a long leap from simply using a computer to using it effectively. As Hiscox laments,

> Unfortunately, many advocates treat the microcomputer as the end in itself. Too often microcomputers wind up in classrooms not because they are the most cost-effective way to increase students' reading achievement but because of educators' belief that any modern school should have several. This end in itself approach already is wearing thin in some locations, particularly where educators lack the training and direction to make good use of new technology, and one wonders how many classroom microcomputers will be collecting dust in storerooms 5 years from now. (1984, p. 29)

The answer, unfortunately, is "quite a few." But, used properly, computer-assisted testing can support or even take over many valuable functions, including: administering, scoring, and interpreting tests; providing students with diagnostic feedback; presenting instructors with summaries of individual student and group progress; and providing statistical analyses of test results, including information on individual test items. Our purpose in this section is to provide a brief overview of some recent trends in computer-assisted testing and to describe how microcomputers can be used to improve testing programs. Before doing so, however, it may be useful to address briefly a significant impediment to full utilization of computers in education, namely, computer anxiety.

The Problem of "Computer Anxiety"

Not typically a problem for students, timidity about using computers has been a frequent phenomenon among teachers and administrators. This is not surprising, given the relatively recent rise in computer usage. Many of today's classroom teachers had several years of teaching experience under their belts before they ever heard computer enthusiasts speak their esoteric bits-and-bytes jargon. The language was foreign to many. And even teachers of math, science, and other technical subjects often found themselves intimidated by this new electronic wizardry. While optimists predicted that computers would resolve most educational problems, skeptics questioned whether schools and teachers would ever embrace the new technology with open arms or use it effectively. Coburn, Kelman, Roberts, Snyder, Watt, and Weiner (1982) observed that some skeptics felt educational computer programs used in schools might fall as far below their potential as had educational television programming.

In retrospect, this view is too pessimistic. While computers may not be a panacea for education's problems, neither are they a passing fad. Computers are here to stay but that does not make them less threatening and alienating to many teachers. As Coburn and his colleagues remark, to some, "the news that 'the computers are coming' sounds more like an ominous warning than the announcement of a bright new day" (1982, p. 4).

Those who experience "computer anxiety" are quick to find innumerable criticisms of computers—or their users—to excuse their faintheartedness. Microcomputers are not an indiscriminate solution to every educational ailment, as Hiscox (1984) points out. But that should not dissuade us from capitalizing on the many advantages microcomputers can offer in educational testing. The real culprit lurking behind poor use of computers in the classroom is often simple fear of new-fangled gadgetry. We can offer no sophisticated solution to computer anxiety; after all, we are measurement specialists not therapists. Perhaps the most simple suggestion is also the most effective—*try it!* You are likely to find what many new users have already discovered. The computer program developers and handbook writers of today are far more sensitive to users' needs and anxieties than ever before. The language, the instructions, the steps have all been greatly simplified in the last few years, as computer capabilities have been expanding dramatically. It now takes less effort and skill to get better results. And there is plenty of support to guide you, structured in language designed not to bore, antagonize, intimidate, or mystify you. But trying is believing. Usually a brief exposure to the simplicity of most of today's microcomputers and a realization of their power and utility can make quick converts, if not addicts, of most educators.

The Use of Microcomputers in School Testing Programs

Microcomputers serve many purposes in school testing. They can be used to develop, administer, score, and interpret tests, to mention only some potential applications. Before we discuss specific applications, however, let us consider trends in the use of microcomputers for testing that make such applications possible.

The Evolution of Microcomputer Testing Applications

Microcomputers have been used for some time to serve educational testing. Their helpfulness in this function has increased dramatically during the past few years, and changes continue to occur rapidly. Inouye and Bunderson (1986) provide an excellent summary of prior—and projected—developments in computerized measurement. They trace this development through four stages,[2] each of which they see as more sophisticated and powerful than its predecessor.

Computerized Testing (Stage 1). Perhaps the most common—and certainly the most primitive—use of microcomputers in testing involves adapting traditional paper and pencil tests to a computerized format. This type of testing is not adapted or tailored to the student, since the number, sequencing, content, and timing of the items do not depend on student responses but are programmed to be the same for all students.

Computerized Adaptive Testing (Stage 2). This more advanced use of microcomputers provides adaptive or tailored testing for students. In contrast to simple computerized testing, computerized adaptive testing presents items based on the student's performance on previous items. The difficulty or content of each test item, as well as the timing of the next item, depends directly on the examinee's responses. Tests presented in this form can be shorter since they provide more precise estimates of the student's ability. (This type of testing was discussed in greater detail in Chapter 18.)

Continuous Measurement (Stage 3). A yet more sophisticated stage in microcomputer use involves using adaptive tests embedded within a computer-based curriculum. Such testing is relatively unobtrusive, using carefully constructed measures, embedded in a curriculum, to estimate significant changes in each student's achievement profile. Continuous measurement can be particularly useful in mastery learning, where progress to the next phase of instruction depends upon mastery of previous instruction.

---

[2] These authors refer to the stages as *generations*, but we chose to substitute *stages* to avoid possible confusion with *generations* of computer equipment development.

Intelligent Measurement (Stage 4).   This most sophisticated use of microcomputers in testing involves developing computer systems that teach essential knowledge in an interactive fashion, with the computer serving as a consultant or advisor. In such applications, the computer produces intelligent scoring, interprets individual profiles, and provides advice to learners and teachers, using expertise implanted within the system by instructional specialists and psychometricians. Closely related to the more familiar *artificial intelligence,* intelligent measurement attempts to capture the knowledge and expertise of measurement professionals in such a way that it can be disseminated broadly to practitioners who can thus draw on that expertise to obtain benefits of the more powerful measurement techniques typically not available to school practitioners.

Against this backdrop of evolving and increasingly powerful testing applications for microcomputers, let us now turn our attention directly to some of the specific testing uses that microcomputers can serve in your testing program.

Specific Microcomputer Testing Applications

Developing Tests and Test Items.   There are a variety of software programs that can help you construct classroom tests and test items. Such programs have proliferated and diversified widely since the early computer-developed spelling tests (Fremer & Anastasio, 1968). Now microcomputers are often used to store items in collections called *item banks.* From these, items can be selected by the computer in a random or predetermined manner to construct individual tests. Alternative forms of such tests can be developed at specified difficulty levels or to match specific instructional objectives. Forms that measure common content can be constructed at the same level of difficulty to provide parallel forms of a test that may be useful for pretest-posttest data collection. Microcomputers are also powerful tools for analyzing tests or evaluating individual test items—which may later be revised or deleted from the test, as appropriate. Such analysis of items is critical. In Chapter 11, we describe a manual process for doing item analyses; the use of computers can make this process much more efficient and informative.

A promising new technology of interest to many teachers is authoring systems—programs that guide teachers through test construction, allowing them to design their own tests based on their own instructional objectives.

Test Administration.   Microcomputers can serve a variety of test administration functions. At the most basic level, they can be used to administer standard tests to students. But the microcomputer is capable of far more than simply serving as an expensive "page turner." It becomes most valuable in test administration when computerized adaptive testing techniques are used. Roid lists five advantages of computer adaptive test administration:

(a) increased precision of measurement,
(b) improved efficiency and time savings for the examinee,
(c) increased breadth of trait or achievement levels assessable, resulting in more accurate decision making (e.g., identification of students who have mastered a unit of instruction),
(d) improved examinee motivation due to the perceived objectivity of computers or fairness in the choice of items selected for a given examinee, and

(e) possible technical improvements in the selection of test items having desirable statistical properties for certain subjects. (1986, p. 37)

Test Scoring and Interpretation. The computer is a very efficient tool for scoring tests. Computer scoring is quick and error-free. The teacher can have scores converted into any scale he wishes. Microcomputers can also be used to administer and score the answer-until-correct tests championed by Wilcox (1982), if one views such tests as having utility.

Statistical Analysis of Test Results. In addition to statistical uses of the microcomputer in item analysis and direct summaries of student scores, the statistical capability of the computer lends itself to a variety of other purposes, such as preparing descriptive statistics to compare students' relative achievement in different academic subjects, to compare the effectiveness of alternative teaching methods, or to adjust such comparisons to account for differences in students' ability levels, socioeconomic levels, and so on.

Providing Feedback to Students. If computer adaptive testing is used, students can receive immediate feedback on performance after each item, or at the end of an exam. As instructional scientists have long argued, feedback—especially immediate feedback—is an excellent way to increase learning, and computer testing that provides such feedback assures that taking exams is a learning experience. Microcomputers can also serve useful functions in summarizing student scores on exams (and other measures) and translating them into grades or other performance indicators. Unless maliciously programmed to be unfair, microcomputers grade totally without bias or favoritism.

There are probably other useful applications of the microcomputer in testing that you can find by exploring on your own the many ways in which microcomputers can be useful in your school testing program.

Deciding What Microcomputer System Fits Your Needs

Whether you are serving on a district committee to select microcomputers for a districtwide testing program or selecting one to help you with your own classroom testing, it is important to select hardware and software that fits your particular needs. For example, suppose you were asked by your principal to pilot test feasibility and cost-effectiveness of a computer-assisted testing program in your classroom curriculum. Many alternatives are open. In determining the best alternative for your school, you need to answer such questions as the following:

- Do I currently know enough about microcomputers to choose intelligently, or do I need to obtain expert help?

- What purpose (or purposes) would this computer assisted testing program serve?

- Would the microcomputer be used to develop tests, administer tests, score and interpret test results, or all of the above?
- What type of existing computer-assisted testing software would best suit my needs?
- What type of hardware would be compatible with the most useful software, and would provide the greatest flexibility and power in my computing system?
- Does my school (or district) have sufficient budget allotted for the computer hardware and software I would prefer? Does it have the funds to maintain the system? If not, what computer system could the budget afford? Would it suit my needs?
- Does the district have purchasing agreements with particular hardware and software vendors that would either constrain or facilitate my selection of hardware and software?
- What alternative locations should I consider for placement of the computer? What are the advantages and disadvantages of each location? How can I set up the system to keep student information secure?

While space does not permit us to provide answers to those questions here, the annotated references at the end of this chapter provide excellent resources for such a task. Instead, we turn our attention to two thought-provoking lists that should be useful to you as you think about using a microcomputer system to aid in your testing program.

A Checklist for Analyzing Your Proposed Microcomputer System

Hiscox provides an excellent checklist of questions you should ask yourself as you review the overall adequacy of your microcomputer-based testing system:

1. Have you carefully matched memory, storage, and processing speed of the hardware to your application?
2. Have you verified that the system will hold the necessary data and will retrieve information fast enough to be practical?
3. If you use a hard disk, how will you ensure that users perform adequate backup procedures?
4. Are your users sophisticated enough to perform . . . [necessary] activities?
5. Does your application require many graphics and, if so, how will you display them?
6. Can your disk drive system provide adequate space for the graphics you need to store?
7. Will the printer(s) you plan to use provide acceptable print quality for your application?
8. Is the speed and reliability of the printer(s) you plan to use adequate for the amount of printing you will be doing?
9. Are there impending developments that would significantly change the way you design your system?

10. Is the software you are considering for your system adequately tested and supported?
11. Will you need special programming and, if so, do you have a cost-effective way of getting any programming you need completed?
12. Have you investigated what existing packages might meet your need before initiating your own program development?
13. If you are developing programs, will they run rapidly enough to be practical for routine use?
14. [If you are developing testing-related software] . . . Have you realistically estimated the development costs and found them acceptable?
15. Is your [technological] design sufficiently robust to withstand some problems caused by . . . uncontrollable factors?
16. Have you conducted the surveys and task force meetings necessary to permit you to design your system so you know it will be accepted?
17. Do you have the global picture of what you're trying to accomplish and the specifics on how it will be done?
18. Have you allotted enough time before your system has to be operational?
19. Have you based your plans on vaporware [hardware and software announced before it is actually available for purchase] that may or may not be available when you need it?
20. [If you broaden the audience for your system] . . . Do the benefits to the broader audience offset the increased effort required for their training and support? (1984, p. 34)

A Checklist for Evaluating Microcomputer Software and Hardware

Coburn and others (1982) also provide an excellent checklist for evaluating microcomputer software and hardware. We excerpt here only the major headings in that list, which we think are instructive in themselves, and refer you to their full reference if and when you need additional help in applying the steps they suggest.

Evaluating Software
1. Look for local sales and service.
2. Buy software that does what you need it to do.
3. Obtain and read the documentation for the software.
4. Thoroughly test the software.
5. Look for good error checking.
6. Demand fast and flexible data retrieval.
7. Buy software that makes the computer do the work.
8. Look for software that runs on different hardware.

Evaluating Hardware
1. Look for local sales and service.
2. Beware of new products.
3. Look for durable construction and engineering.
4. Allow for expansion.
5. Look for good and well-documented systems software.
6. Choose a system with more than one language available.
7. Look for systems with a lot of available applications software.
8. Talk to owners and users of the systems you are considering.

  9. Don't rush anything.
  10. Remember that all rules have exceptions [including the rules in this list]. (1982, pp. 89–94)

These authors also make an excellent point that we think you should keep in mind as you evaluate hardware and software options for your microcomputer system:

> Although we have separated the questions of hardware and software evaluation and implied that the software comes first, in actuality the evaluation of hardware and software must happen simultaneously. Identification of a wonderful software package is of little use to you if it only runs on computers that are practically unavailable to you. (1982, p. 91)

In selecting software, one needs to be thoughtful about the use of prepackaged computerized tests. Such tests may or may not match the objectives of the teacher or curriculum. Once such tests have been purchased, they can become increasingly obsolete as textbooks and other curriculum materials change, as there are changes in teachers, and so on. Purchasing software that will allow changes in the test themselves is the only way to maintain content validity of prepackaged computerized tests over a long period of time.

Without doubt, microcomputers can enhance a school or district testing program. Before actually investing in such a system, however, we advise you to peruse some of the references provided at the end of this chapter to obtain more specific information. At the same time, do not let fear of computers prevent you from enjoying the benefits that they can provide.

SUGGESTED READINGS

Airasian, P. W., & Madaus, G. F. (1983). Linking testing and instruction: Policy issues. *Journal of Educational Measurement, 20*(2), 103–118.

  This article discusses the importance of linking testing and instruction and provides an overview of methodologies that have been applied to link these two educational activities. The authors describe strategies that can be used to assess the overlap between instruction and tests, along with the use of post hoc techniques that can be used to identify test items that differentiate among groups.

Coburn, P., Kelman, P., Roberts, N., Snyder, T. F. F., Watt, D. H., & Weiner, C. (1982). *Practical guide to computers in education.* Reading, MA: Addison-Wesley.

  This guide is the basic primer for a series of Addison-Wesley texts on the use of computers in education. It is an excellent introduction to computers in the general setting of schools, aimed especially at the novice. It includes information on the workings of computers, their potential educational applications, and practical suggestions on how to establish a computer resource in a school. The book will be very useful to anyone who wishes to better understand microcomputers, their uses in educational settings, and the advantages and disadvantages they might have as part of a school districtwide testing program.

Dorr-Bremme, D. W. (1983). Assessing students: Teachers' routine practices and reasoning. *Evaluation Comment*, 6(4), 1–12.
This article reports a series of interesting results from a survey of teachers and administrators conducted by the UCLA Center for the Study of Evaluation. This survey focused on testing practices and preferences reported by those surveyed.

Roid, G. H. (1986). Computer technology in testing. In B. S. Plake & J. C. Witt (Eds.), *The future of testing*. Hillsdale, NJ: Lawrence Erlbaum Associates.
This chapter provides an excellent overview of the current status in relation to computer testing technology, as well as providing a perspective on future directions in relation to computer testing. The utility of computers is discussed in detail in relation to (1) test development, (2) test administration, (3) test scoring, and (4) interpretation of test results.

SELF-CHECK QUIZ

1. Approximately what percentage of secondary school students' annual classroom time is taken up by testing?
   a. 2 percent
   b. 5 percent
   c. 10 percent
   d. 20 percent

2. When deciding what time of year to schedule a standardized test, the primary factor to be considered is its
   a. length.
   b. purpose.
   c. level of difficulty.
   d. type (norm vs. criterion-referenced).

3. Teachers should be involved in test selection because they are often the most expert in determining
   a. how well the test content matches the curriculum.
   b. where to find the most inexpensive testing materials.
   c. whether or not the test is technically adequate.
   d. which types of tests yield highly reliable scores.

4. The practice of administering standardized tests in the spring is advantageous because it
   a. avoids teachers "teaching to the test."
   b. provides summative data about achievement gains.
   c. provides information about declines in retention of learning.
   d. provides information about summer "move-ins."

5. One advantage of giving standardized tests in the fall is that the resulting information is useful for
   a. diagnosing learning difficulties.
   b. evaluating individual programs.
   c. grouping students at the next grade level.
   d. measuring the cumulative effects of a school's curriculum.

6. Which stage of computerized testing is characterized by interactive instruction where the computer interprets individual profiles and provides advice to learners and teachers,

using expertise implanted within the system by psychometricians and/or instructional specialists?

   a. Computerized testing

   b. Computerized adaptive testing

   c. Continuous measurement

   d. Intelligent measurement

7. For a typical school district, which of the following approaches is potentially the most workable for linking testing and instruction?

   a. Design and produce new criterion-referenced tests that match the curriculum well.

   b. Find and use existing tests that have a high degree of overlap with the curriculum.

   c. Modify existing tests by removing items not related to the curriculum.

   d. Modify the curriculum to more closely match the content of existing tests.

8. What is the authors' advice to those who suffer from "computer anxiety?"

   a. Avoid using computers whenever possible.

   b. Enroll in a course in computer programming.

   c. Give computers a brief try at least.

   d. Grit your teeth and commit yourself to computers.

   e. Let colleagues handle computers for you.

9. In general, achievement test batteries should be administered

   a. at the beginning and end of each school year.

   b. once a year.

   c. every other year.

   d. as needed, but usually about every third year.

10. In general, academic aptitude tests should be administered

   a. at the beginning and end of each school year.

   b. once a year.

   c. every other year.

   d. once or twice during the first twelve years of school.

SUGGESTION SHEET

If your last name starts with the letter *W,* please complete the Suggestion Sheet at the end of the book while this chapter is still fresh in your mind.

CHAPTER **22**

Setting Up a School Evaluation Program

Overview

Many school administrators believe that when they have established a good testing program, they have done all that is necessary to make wise decisions about the curricula, programs, and instructional materials and techniques used in their schools. Not so: There are many steps between summarizing test scores and drawing correct inferences about the aspects of schooling that influence students' test performance. Further, many important educational outcomes, such as students' attitudes and values, may not be measured within the typical school testing program; yet they are central to any complete evaluation of a school program or curriculum.

Imagine, for a moment, that a teacher, who believes that drill and competition are key essentials in learning, introduces a method of teaching math that incorporates her beliefs. A review of her students' math test scores shows tremendous increases since her new ''drill-em-till you-kill-em'' and ''post-the-poor-test-scores'' teaching methods were introduced. Looking only at test scores, she judges her innovation a great success. Never mind the fact that kids in her classes cry more now, and that more are absent on test days, or dropping out of school completely. A testing program, used without sufficient thoughtfulness, might appear to support her self-congratulations. A broader evaluation would raise some red flags, warning that her new creation might be causing some very undesirable side effects not disclosed by typical testing programs.

Evaluation of a classroom or schoolwide curriculum requires looking beyond the beam of light cast by a good testing program to observe *all* the important outcomes of that curriculum. This chapter provides an overview of educational evaluation, what it is, and how it can be used to improve classroom and schoolwide curriculum.

We have organized this chapter into four major sections. In the first, we distinguish evaluation of school programs from evaluation of individual student performance. In the second, we introduce some basic evaluation concepts and discuss how systematic evaluation efforts can be used to improve all aspects of school programs. We also consider the centrality of measurement as an evaluation tool. In the third section, we provide a series of practical guidelines for setting up and operating a school evaluation program and carrying out individual evaluation studies. Finally, we touch briefly on some cautions and suggestions for how to obtain *useful* evaluation help from sources outside your school.

Objectives

Upon completing your study of this chapter, you should be able to

1. Discuss the role of evaluation in improving our schools.
2. Compare and contrast *internal* versus *external* evaluation and *formative* versus *summative* evaluation. Discuss the advantages and disadvantages of the following four combinations of these dimensions: internal formative, external formative, internal summative, external summative.
3. List and discuss important considerations and guidelines for deciding
   • When to conduct an evaluation
   • What should be evaluated
   • Whom the evaluation is intended to serve
   • Who should conduct the evaluation
   • What questions and issues the evaluation should address
   • How to plan and conduct the evaluation study
   • How to report results
   • How to deal with political, ethical, and interpersonal issues in evaluation
4. Explain the circumstances under which it is wise (or necessary) to obtain outside help in planning and conducting evaluations.
5. Identify sources to help school practitioners identify well-qualified evaluators.

EVALUATION OF PROGRAMS, NOT OF INDIVIDUAL STUDENT PERFORMANCE

In Chapter 4, we defined *evaluation,* at its most general level, as the determination of worth, value, or quality. We distinguished it from measurement and testing, two of the tools used in evaluation. We also distinguished between two distinct ways the term *evaluation* is used in education—evaluation of individual pupil performance and evaluation of educational programs, projects, products, processes, goals, or curricula. So far in this book, we have used the term *evaluation* to refer to evaluation of individual pupil performance—the observation of pupil behavior and the interpretation and conversion of test scores or other measurement devices to enable qualified persons to judge the quality of individual students' performance. Such a focus is both appropriate and necessary in a book devoted primarily to measurement and the evaluations that can follow from such measurement. But we cannot ignore the broader connotation of the term *evaluation*. We are interested not only in the quality of *individual* performance, but also in the quality of *institutional* or *programmatic* performance. It is not enough to say that Mary and Johnny can't read. Educators must also find out why, and ask how to correct the problem. Evaluation must also focus on the merit of particular curriculum materials, the utility of instructional approaches or organizational patterns, and the overall effectiveness of educational programs or practices. And so we use the term evaluation in another sense, to refer to efforts that are not limited in attention to individual student evaluation, but also answer broader questions such as:

- Do students in my classroom learn writing better when computer-assisted writing programs are used? If so, are the increases in writing ability sufficient to warrant the costs of the computer hardware and software?
- How well did the school district's compensatory education project attain its intended objectives?
- In terms of building self-confidence, is team teaching preferable to self-contained instruction for primary children?
- What are the relative advantages and disadvantages of year-round schools, in terms of student achievement, parental acceptance, and economy?

Answers to these questions will usually require measurement and evaluation of *individual* student performance, aggregated across individuals as one indicator of program or product effectiveness. But evaluation of particular programs or curricula not only aggregates across individuals, but also goes beyond the type of measurement and evaluation of students that we have discussed so far. Thus, unless otherwise noted, *evaluation* will be used throughout this chapter to refer to this broader scrutiny of the worth or merit of particular educational curricula, programs, projects, and methods.

USING EVALUATION TO IMPROVE SCHOOL PROGRAMS[1]

Widespread public perceptions that something is amiss in our educational system have sparked a continuing national debate about the quality of education in the United States.

---

[1] Portions of this and subsequent sections in this chapter draw on prior writing by one of the authors (in Worthen & Sanders, 1987, which treats the subject comprehensively).

Even when critics of our schools are patently unfair in their criticism, schools are seldom able to launch credible or effective rebuttals. That is because very few schools have any solid evaluative data they can use to prove how well they are doing. Without careful, systematic evaluation of the effectiveness of either current school practices or new programs, our schools are ill-equipped to defend their practices; in fact, they cannot even be very certain that what they believe they have accomplished is actually so.

Evaluation perhaps holds more promise than any other approach in providing schools with information they need to improve their practices. Awareness of this fact has led many educational and governmental leaders, along with most educated lay persons, to support the evaluation of school programs. Parents increasingly ask schools about the teaching methods and the curricula used to instruct their children, and other citizen groups question the results being achieved through schools' expenditures of public funds. Because evaluation can help provide this information, educators have begun turning to it more and more as a vehicle for improving school programs.

Informal and Formal Evaluation

Every school teacher and administrator has engaged in informal educational evaluation. Consider, the sixth grade teacher who reviews alternative mathematics books for use in the classroom and chooses one because she prefers the format and type style, while overlooking the fact that the teaching of algorithms is confusing. Such informal evaluation occurs whenever one chooses from available alternatives without systematically collecting evaluation information to determine which alternative is truly best. Because it is based on highly subjective *perceptions* of which alternative is best, informal evaluation has limited decision-making value in education. Our focus is on more formal approaches to evaluation, therefore, where choices are based on *systematic* efforts to collect and weigh *accurate* information about alternatives, thus allowing the most objective possible evaluation of those alternatives.

Many classroom teachers have never undertaken or participated in a formal evaluation study; therefore, they may not realize the advantages in doing so. The evaluation *process* described in this chapter can help solve many problems and answer many questions important to classroom teachers. Such problems or questions may be too narrow or specific to justify a major, schoolwide evaluation effort, but a teacher's decision based on a small-scale, formal classroom evaluation is almost certain to be more sound and defensible than one based on subjective judgment alone. As for schoolwide evaluations that look at broader issues, teachers obviously benefit from any activity that can lead to educational improvement. It is to every teacher's advantage, therefore, to understand something of schoolwide evaluation and to participate cooperatively in such studies.

Two Basic Distinctions in Evaluation

Two distinctions in evaluation are important. The first has to do with two major purposes evaluation can serve, the second with the locus of the evaluator.

Formative and Summative Evaluation

Formal evaluation studies can serve either a *formative* purpose (such as helping to improve a mathematics curriculum) or a *summative* purpose (such as deciding whether that curriculum should be continued). Although these distinctions may blur somewhat in practice, they are useful nonetheless.

Formative evaluation is conducted during the planning and operation of a school program to provide those involved with evaluative information they can use in improving the program. For example, assume a school district is attempting to develop a local curriculum package on the history of their particular county. During development of the new curriculum unit, formative evaluation might involve content inspection by history experts' early tryouts with small numbers of children in one school in the district, and so forth. Each step would provide immediate feedback to the curriculum developers, who could use such information to make necessary revisions.

Summative evaluation occurs after a curriculum or program is considered ready for regular use, and provides potential consumers evidence about the program's worth. In our example, after the local history program was developed, a summative evaluation might determine how effective the program was in teaching local history, using a broad sample of the schools, teachers, and students in the district for which it was developed. The findings of that summative evaluation could be made available to all schools in the district who could then better determine whether to use the history unit in their schools. Summative evaluation is also used to make ''go/no go'' decisions, such as whether to continue or terminate a particular curriculum.

Notice that the audiences and uses for formative and summative evaluation are very different. In formative evaluation, the audience is whoever is involved in planning or implementing whatever is being evaluated and, therefore, are in the position of being able to make improvements. In summative evaluation, the audience includes other teachers, administrators, school boards, or anyone who will make decisions concerning the adoption, continuation, or termination of whatever is evaluated.

Formative and summative evaluation are both essential because decisions are needed early in the development of a school program, to improve it, as well as when it has stabilized, to judge its final worth. Unfortunately, summative evaluations are more common in our schools than are formative evaluations. Failure to use formative evaluation can be costly, however, for considerable time, money, and effort are frequently channeled into educational innovations that turn out ultimately to be unproductive. Formative evaluation can often alert educators to potential problems when there is still time to do something about them.

Internal and External Evaluation

The terms *internal* and *external* refer to whether the evaluation is conducted by someone employed within the school or school system where the program is based, or by someone outside it. For instance, a school district's new extended-day program might be evaluated by a member of that school district's staff (internal) or by an evaluator appointed by the State Board of Education (external).

In some cases, the distinction is not quite so clear-cut. Let's create an imaginary Banner Middle School to use as an example. Assume that the PTA called for an evaluation of the mathematics curriculum. Assume that the superintendent assigned Valene Laytor, an evaluator in the district central office, to evaluate the Banner School curriculum. Valene is external to the school, but internal to the district. Will her evaluation be an internal or an external evaluation? Obviously the answer depends on the referent, but it points out some important advantages and disadvantages of internal and external evaluation. If Banner's teacher, Lotta Smart, were assigned to conduct the evaluation, she would probably know more about the math curriculum than Valene, but she also might be too close to the program to be completely objective about it. Indeed, Lotta might be so preoccupied with certain unimportant details that she would unintentionally overlook important information.

Conversely, an evaluator coming from outside the district might never know as much about program details as Lotta, but should be more objective in judging the math curriculum. Valene would likely have more detailed information about the program than would a completely external evaluator, but would also probably be somewhat more objective in judging it than would a complete insider, such as Lotta. Whether Valene might be considered an external evaluator might best be determined by deciding who the evaluation is for. If it is for the Banner PTA, then her employment outside Banner School would seem to qualify her as external. However, if the evaluation had been commissioned by an outside group, such as the state school board, her employment within the district makes her "internal" to the agency of which Banner is a part, and anything she said about its curriculum may be compromised by perceptions that she cannot be objective about that of which she is a part.

Evaluation Roles and Locus of the Evaluator

Combining the dimensions of formative and summative evaluation with those of internal and external evaluation yields the following four classifications:

1. Internal formative evaluation
2. External formative evaluation
3. Internal summative evaluation
4. External summative evaluation

Internal formative evaluation has clear merits. The internal evaluator's knowledge of the school program is valuable, and the possible lack of objectivity is not nearly the problem it would be in a summative evaluation. The fact that internal formative evaluations may not be as objective or credible as those conducted by external evaluators should not discourage their use, but only make educators sensitive to the importance of making them as objective and credible as possible.

External formative evaluation is unfortunately rare in education. Internal evaluators may have serious blind spots because they come to share the perspectives of colleagues with whom they work closely. They may neglect even to entertain negative questions about a program or curriculum. The external evaluator is much less likely to be influenced by close association with either the program or its implementors. A fresh outside perspective can be very useful in identifying potentially serious flaws before they prove fatal to the program's effectiveness and continuation.

Internal summative evaluation is usually the weakest and least credible type of evaluation. We should not underestimate the impact that making tough summative judgments can have on objectivity—or even truth. Would you purchase a new computerized curriculum just because the vendor issues an evaluation report concluding that its curriculum is far better than its competitors'? The credibility of such potentially self-serving evaluation studies is very suspect. In cases where it is impossible to obtain external help with a summative evaluation, some semblance of externality can be obtained by choosing an internal summative evaluator who is as far removed as possible from the actual development of the program or curriculum being evaluated.

External summative evaluation is generally the most credible, since external evaluators should have no vested interest that would make it difficult for them to be completely objective in judging the worth or merit of the curriculum or program.

APPLICATION PROBLEM #1

Assume Banner School's Lotta Smart wishes to improve her students' writing skills and has recently begun to use in one of her two English classes a new Computer-assisted Writing Program (CAWP), which provides students with immediate feedback on both mechanics and language patterns typical in good writing. Students seem to enjoy the computers and the convenient word processing program, and they frequently use CAWP's feedback to check their writing performance. But Lotta worries that students' creativity in writing may be lessened by strict adherence to CAWP's criteria. She also wonders if students write better, overall, as a result of using CAWP, whether the program influences student writing beyond the actual period when they are using it, and whether any gains in writing skills attributable to CAWP are worth the additional costs of the computer hardware and software. Given such questions, rank the four types of evaluation described above (internal formative, etc.) from *most useful* to *least useful* in helping Lotta answer her question. Justify your rankings in terms of the applicability of each type of evaluation to Lotta's situation and their advantages in answering the questions she has raised.

Measurement as a Key Evaluation Tool

Although measurement is used to collect data on which evaluative judgments are made, it is not in and of itself an evaluative activity.

Moreover, measurement is not the only way to collect evaluative data, since many data are collected without the evaluator's following specified rules or procedures. For example, teams sent to evaluate a high school would know something was amiss if they observed obscene graffiti covering the hall walls, litter in the classrooms, and frequent rudeness to the teachers. And they would not need to *count* the number of candy wrappers, slimy scrawlings, or rude behaviors in order to reach this conclusion. It is not necessary to engage in formal measurement to evaluate. Sound professional judgment, for all of its subjectivity, has a legitimate role in evaluation. One need not measure an alligator's girth or length to reach the compelling conclusion that it is not a cuddly companion. Unfortunately, educational "alligators" are not often as obviously ill-suited to the uses for which we employ them. For that reason, we take a risk when we rely on subjective judgment alone to tell us the real nature and character of our various educational innovations. And here is where measurement becomes pivotal. Indeed, in most credible evaluation studies with which we are familiar, measurement has played a key role and, in many instances, serves as the primary or sole basis for collecting the data on which evaluative judgments depend. In short, without good educational measurement, it would be virtually impossible to conduct useful evaluations of school programs.

GUIDELINES FOR SETTING UP
A SCHOOL EVALUATION PROGRAM

Entire doctoral curricula are devoted to preparing educational evaluators. We make no pretense of condensing the scope of that training into an individual chapter. But we do want to give you an overall picture of the evaluation process, since most teachers will participate, at least occasionally, in an evaluation. Evaluations of school programs would improve if more people knew the importance of

- Deciding *when* to evaluate
- Deciding *what* precisely to evaluate
- Deciding *whom* the evaluation is intended to serve
- Deciding *who* should conduct the evaluation
- Deciding *what* questions the evaluation should address
- Planning the evaluation study
- Deciding *how* to report the evaluation study
- Dealing effectively with the political, ethical, and interpersonal issues in evaluation

Guidelines and important considerations for each area are discussed in the

TABLE 22.1 Example of Curriculum Evaluation Cycles

Curriculum to Be Evaluated	1994	1995	1996	1997	1998	1999	2000
Mathematics	X					X	
Language Arts		X					X
Social Studies			X				
Music				X			
Physical Education					X		

following sections. At the end is an application problem that invites you to try your hand at applying these various guidelines.

Deciding When to Conduct an Evaluation

Sometimes a system or schedule has been established for evaluating particular facets of a school program. Many districts have developed long-range curriculum evaluation plans that are cyclical, with periodic reviews scheduled in a staggered fashion so that some curriculum areas are evaluated every year and every curriculum area is evaluated at reasonable intervals, as shown in Table 22.1.

More than one curriculum area might be evaluated each year, depending on time and personnel resources available; and noncurriculum areas such as facilities, fiscal management, and the like could be incorporated into such a cyclical evaluation system.

The advantages inherent in cyclical evaluation systems often offset any possible disadvantages, and it would be easy to urge schools to simply set up such a system and thus eliminate the need to worry further about when to conduct an evaluation, since the schedule would automatically answer that question. We resist that temptation for three reasons:

- Some districts experience practical or political constraints that prevent them from establishing a regular evaluation schedule.
- Other issues can arise that require changes in original schedules.
- Even when long-range cyclical evaluation schedules have been established, it may still be appropriate to consider whether such schedules are continuing to be effective.

Determining when an evaluation is to be conducted requires first determining whether it should be conducted at all. To determine whether an evaluation is appropriate, it is necessary to understand what prompted it, including the exploration of such questions as:

1. Why is this evaluation being requested? By whom? What is its purpose? What questions will it answer?

2. What use will the findings serve? Who will use them? Who else should be informed of the results?
3. What is to be evaluated? What does it include? Exclude? What are its objectives? What need is it intended to address? During what time period? In what settings? Who will participate? Who is in charge of it?
4. Who is available to help with the evaluation? How much time and money are available for it?
5. What is the political climate surrounding the evaluation? Will any political factors preclude a meaningful and fair evaluation?

Answers to questions such as these may reveal circumstances in which evaluation would be, at best, of dubious value and, at worst, harmful. For example, it would be inappropriate to conduct an evaluation study if

- The evaluation would produce trivial information.
- The evaluation results would not be used.
- The evaluation could not yield reliable and valid information.
- The evaluation was premature (e.g., a summative evaluation before a program's development was complete).
- No qualified evaluators were available.
- The evaluation was intended to embarrass particular individuals.

Conversely, it *would be* appropriate to evaluate a program if

- There were a legal requirement to evaluate it.
- That which was to be evaluated had enough impact or importance to warrant formal evaluation.
- There were human and fiscal resources for the evaluation.
- That which was to be evaluated was well enough defined, implemented, and managed to permit a fair evaluation.
- There were an important decision for which the evaluation results would be relevant.
- It was likely that the evaluation would provide dependable information.
- The evaluation was likely to meet acceptable ethical standards.
- The decision was likely to be influenced by the evaluation data, rather than being made on other bases.

Deciding What (Precisely) to Evaluate

It seems reasonable to presume that no educational evaluation would be conducted without a clear idea of what was to be evaluated. Reasonable, but wrong. Many educational evaluations are aimed at blurry targets. No wonder so many miss the mark.

Evaluators are frequently asked to help evaluate entities as vague as "our school math program." Does that include the districtwide mathematics curriculum for all grade levels, the districtwide math curriculum at a particular grade level, a particular school's total curriculum in math, a school's fourth-grade math program, or the mathematics curriculum in a particular fourth-grade classroom? Should the evaluation focus on the instructional materials, instructional procedures, or both? Answering such questions establishes boundaries that help make the evaluation manageable and useful.

No evaluation is complete without a detailed description of the program, process, or curriculum being evaluated. Poor or incomplete descriptions can lead to faulty judgments—sometimes about entities that never really existed. For example, the concept of team teaching has fared poorly in several evaluations, resulting in the general impression that team teaching is ineffective. Closer inspection, however, shows that what is often labeled as "team teaching" provides no real opportunities for staff members to plan or work together in direct instruction. Obviously, a better description would have precluded these misinterpretations. One can only evaluate adequately that which one can describe accurately.

Deciding Who the Evaluation Is For

An evaluation is adequate only if it collects information from and reports information to all the legitimate evaluation audiences. An evaluation of a school program that answers only the questions of the school staff and ignores the questions of parents, children, and community groups is simply a bad evaluation. Each legitimate audience must be identified, and the evaluation plan should include their objectives or evaluative questions in determining what data must be collected. But how does one identify all legitimate audiences?

Usually important evaluation audiences include

- The agency or individual who authorizes the evaluation and provides the necessary fiscal resources for its conduct
- The specific agency or individual who requests the evaluation, if different from the authorizing agent
- Those directly affected by the evaluation (e.g., school administrators, teachers, and students in a program being evaluated)
- Those indirectly affected by the evaluation (e.g., parents or other taxpayers who support the school).

Too frequently, evaluation studies are targeted to satisfy those who are most strident, or powerful, ignoring equally important groups with vital—though perhaps somewhat different—informational needs. While the evaluator must be reasonable in deciding how many audiences can be well served, the following checklist might be useful as a starting point. Probably no one evaluation can serve all these audiences, yet the most appropriate audiences for any given evaluation are very likely to be listed here:

- Funding agencies/sponsors
- Teaching faculty
- Students
- Others who might benefit from the program
- Supporters
- Professional colleagues

- Educational administrators
- Other staff members
- Parents of students
- Public/community members
- Advisory groups
- Opponents
- Potential adopters

Deciding Who Should Conduct the Evaluation

Internal evaluations are most often conducted by whoever has the talent, time, and willingness to do so. In internal evaluations, one is seldom faced with large numbers of well-qualified evaluators. Thus, commonly, a reasonably willing teacher or administrator is pressed into service.

Not so with the external evaluation. Here one can usually select from among a variety of persons or agencies who purport to be qualified. Claims are not enough, of course. Selecting an external evaluator is neither simple nor trivial, and obtaining competent evaluation help is obviously pivotal to producing useful evaluation information.

Deciding What Questions the Evaluation Should Address

Evaluations are conducted to answer questions about the value of educational programs, utility of educational practices, or educational issues that need to be resolved. If such evaluative questions are not clearly identified, the evaluation will lack focus, and the evaluators will have considerable difficulty explaining what is to be examined, how, and why. The process of identifying and selecting evaluative questions requires careful reflection and investigation, if important questions are not to be overlooked, nor trivial questions allowed to preoccupy the evaluator's attention.

This task encompasses two phases: (1) *identifying* all potentially important questions, and (2) *selecting* the most critical questions to be addressed.

Identifying Evaluative Questions

The most important thing in identifying evaluative questions is to be open-minded so that potentially important questions are not arbitrarily ruled out just because they do not immediately strike your fancy. Remember that good questions come from many sources, including

1. Persons affected by the evaluation
2. Relevant educational literature
3. Expert consultants
4. Professional standards or guidelines
5. The professional judgement of the evaluator

Perhaps the single most important source is the one listed first—individuals and groups affected by the evaluation. We call such persons *stakeholders*, since they have a legitimate stake in the outcomes of the evaluation.

Stakeholders are likely to include

- *Policy makers,* such as legislators or governing board members
- Program or project *administrators* or *managers*
- Program or project *developers,* if they differ from managers
- *Practitioners,* those who operate the program
- *Primary consumers,* students, parents or whoever is meant to benefit
- *Secondary consumers,* such as citizen and community groups affected by the influence on primary consumers

If a school curriculum is to be evaluated, for example, the evaluation should address questions of the school board, the school administration, teachers, parents, and so on. It is wise to ask each group what they would accept as evidence that the school curriculum is working well. Different groups and individuals will often have different questions they would like to see addressed. This phase of evaluation planning is no time for a critique of proposed questions. Some may strike you as unanswerable. Don't worry about that now. This is the time for generating all of the evaluation questions possible. Selecting the subset of questions to be addressed comes in the next phase.

Selecting Evaluative Questions

No evaluation can responsibly answer all the questions one might want addressed. Fortunately, there are many techniques for identifying those questions most pivotal to the present study (e.g., see Worthen & Sanders 1987, Chapter 14). For our purposes, we simply urge the evaluator to work carefully with stakeholders or their representatives in identifying those questions that have the highest priority. Remember, when you think you have your final list in hand, assess the feasibility of answering all the "top priority" questions in a quality manner. It is also important to ensure that selected questions address all the major concerns of stakeholders.

Planning the Collection and Analysis of Information

Once the evaluation questions are known, the next logical step is to determine what information the evaluator needs to answer each question. The evaluation plan should specify what information will be collected and from which sources. These steps may seem routine, but they are critical.

Identifying Needed Information

The evaluator and stakeholders should work together to examine each evaluative question, asking, "What information would enable us to answer this question adequately?" Needed information might include existing records; data on students' performance, abilities, or attitudes; or opinions of parents.

Identifying Appropriate Sources of Information

Once everyone knows what's needed, it's simple to figure out where to look. Most often the sources of information will be people (e.g., participants, consumers, governing boards, content specialists) from whom information about their performance or perceptions will be elicited by varying means. Evaluators are wise, however, to see if any needed information has already been documented. For example, existing evaluation reports, status reports, or data collected for other purposes may provide complete or partial answers to some evaluation questions. Student performance records, existing data bases, or public documents can help preclude duplication of effort.

Identifying Appropriate Methods and Arrangements
for Conducting the Evaluation

The next step is specifying methods and instruments for collecting the information, and determining how it will be analyzed and interpreted.

Use a simple worksheet to summarize the evaluation plan. One might use a matrix such as shown in Table 22.2, with the first column listing the evaluative questions and subsequent column headings corresponding to each important element of the plan. There is no need to use every column in the matrix. Nor is there anything magical or immutable about the headings; they can be modified to suit your needs. Or you can add columns and other details. What is important is to create a manageable, concise summary, for it will prove a very useful tool for summarizing or communicating the evaluation plan, not only to others, but to yourself.

Conducting and Reporting an Evaluation

The guidelines we have discussed so far cover activities leading up to the actual study. That is fitting for two reasons. First, while many books describe how to conduct an evaluation, relatively few provide useful information about planning and focusing an evaluation. As a result, far too many evaluations fail to answer the critical questions of important stakeholders. Second—and it's a closely related issue—many school programs or curriculum evaluations are launched without adequate forethought about what issues they should address or how results should be used. Relying on a clear, comprehensive set of guidelines during planning helps ensure that all the critical pieces will be in place before the evaluation itself gets underway.

It is beyond the scope of this book to provide guidelines for actually collecting, analyzing, interpreting, or reporting evaluation information. Those who want such guidelines are referred to texts cited previously in this chapter.

Dealing with Ethical Issues in Evaluation Studies

Few educators would purposely bias evaluation outcomes, even in judging the merit of a curriculum or program they had developed or operated. But intention to avoid bias does not—unfortunately—make one immune to it. Bias, inadvertent

TABLE 22.2   Sample Worksheet for Summarizing an Evaluation Plan

Evaluative Questions	Information Required	Information Source	Method for Collecting Information	Arrangements for Collecting Information (who, when, under what conditions)	Analysis Procedures	Procedures for Interpreting Data and Reaching Conclusions
1.						
2.						
3.						
4.						
.						
.						
.						
.						
.						
.						
.						
.						
.						
.						
.						
.						
.						
.						
.						
.						
n.						

or conscious, can intrude subtly into nearly every choice one makes in planning or conducting an evaluation, from selecting an evaluation approach to designing a report. Indeed, the portrait of the completely dispassionate, unbiased evaluator probably belongs alongside that of the unicorn.

Questions would be raised if someone were asked to evaluate a curriculum developed by her sister-in-law. But is there less cause for concern if a school district evaluator is assigned to evaluate a program being piloted by her weekly tennis doubles partner? Or what about the staff member assigned to evaluate an instructional program developed by a colleague who shares office space, coffee breaks, and membership on the school bowling team?

An evaluation would also be biased if the evaluator could realize any financial advantage from the results (whether pro or con). Similarly, bias is hard to avoid if an evaluator is employed within the school or organization that operates the program or curriculum being evaluated. It would be challenging, to say the least, for any panel of teachers to objectively evaluate a curriculum known to be the pet project of the new superintendent, and enthusiastically endorsed by district principals.

Such potential problems have led several individuals and professional organizations to propose ethical issues surrounding the evaluation of educational programs (e.g., Joint Committee on Standards for Educational Evaluation, 1981; Worthen & Sanders, 1987). We simply add to this existing body of literature a footnote that ethical compromises or distortions can destroy an otherwise well-designed and technically impeccable evaluation. It is imperative that the highest ethical standards be used in each evaluation to avoid any taint of self-congratulation, whitewashing, or compromising of results to fit personal prejudices or preconceived notions.

APPLICATION PROBLEM #2

Assume that you are a fourth grade teacher and have been asked to serve on a districtwide committee charged with the task of evaluating the district's fourth grade reading curriculum. The school board has suggested that such an evaluation would be useful because the fourth grade students were found, on the average, to be reading somewhat below grade level norms on standardized tests used to measure the student's reading ability. Go back through the section of this chapter on "Guidelines for Setting up a School Evaluation Program" and examine how each guideline might apply to this particular evaluation problem. Although we cannot provide you with enough information about this hypothetical setting to allow you to apply the guidelines as fully as you could in real life, you will gain much more understanding of the guidelines if you will list questions that you would ask and/or steps you would take in applying the guidelines proposed within each of the following decisions or steps:

1. Deciding when to conduct an evaluation
2. Deciding precisely what to evaluate
3. Deciding whom the evaluation is intended to serve
4. Deciding who should conduct the evaluation
5. Deciding what questions the evaluation should address
6. Planning the evaluation study
7. Conducting and reporting the evaluation study
8. Dealing with the political, ethical, and interpersonal issues

Now try listing what you think would be the appropriate results of applying the guidelines within each of the preceding decisions/steps. (We recognize these responses will be hypothetical because you are lacking sufficient information, but you will find this process instructive nonetheless.)

SUGGESTIONS FOR OBTAINING USEFUL EVALUATION HELP FROM OUTSIDE SOURCES

Although some large school districts and other educational agencies have sufficient resources to employ a staff of well-trained evaluation specialists, this is not the norm. In most public and private schools, evaluations are either conducted by staff members (e.g., administrators, teachers, and curriculum specialists) who do not have specialized training as evaluators, or by individuals from outside the school. Although an internal evaluation may be an appropriate choice for some internal formative evaluations (as discussed earlier), even there it may be more desirable to obtain outside help to provide *additional* expertise to an evaluation conducted primarily by school staff. There are many advantages in combining the efforts of internal and external personnel. For example, an external evaluator's unfamiliarity with the program is not likely to be a serious problem if she works in tandem with an internal evaluator. Travel costs can be greatly reduced if internal school staff collect the bulk of the necessary data, working under the "supervision" of the off-site external evaluator to increase impartiality and credibility. Similarly, external evaluators can assist in key tasks where bias might inadvertently occur, such as designing the evaluation, selecting and developing instruments, drawing conclusions from data, and the like. Such partnerships yield the advantages of external evaluation without requiring that the entire evaluation be conducted externally. Perhaps even more important, through the resulting team work, external evaluation specialists can help increase the skills of school teachers, administrators, and curriculum specialists, by preparing them to conduct better future evaluation activities.

When it comes to conducting summative evaluations, however, the task is best left solely to the external evaluator, for reasons discussed earlier. But whether one is seeking an external evaluator to assist with an internal evaluation or to conduct an external "third-party" evaluation the selection task is neither simple nor trivial. It is important that the evaluator who is selected have the necessary competence and sensitivity to do the job well. There is no better way to guarantee a bad evaluation than to turn it over to someone who is inept. And the resulting misleading or incorrect information is easy to generate and disseminate, but difficult to eradicate.

Unfortunately, there are no widespread certification or licensure systems for evaluators (with the exception of some jurisdictions, such as the State of Louisiana). The absence of such systems allows *anyone* to claim she has evaluation competence, even if she possesses little or no genuine qualifications—or scruples. This leaves educational agencies vulnerable to being "ripped off" by incompetent but crafty charlatans who manage to pass themselves off as evaluators because the field of evaluation does not include any analogue to the professional "seal of approval'' provided by licensure or certification in other professions. In this context, where *caveat emptor*—let the buyer beware—has become an altogether too familiar motto, schools are frequently victimized by incompetent ''evaluators'' who leave educators disenchanted with evaluation, when indeed they have never really seen *real* evaluation at all.

This unfortunate situation has led to suggestions (e.g., Worthen & Sanders, 1987) of several criteria for judging prospective evaluators' qualifications. You may wish to peruse this reference to learn simple steps that can protect you from wasting time and resources on an abortive external evaluation effort, when the same resources could obtain highly qualified, affordable help that would be of genuine benefit to your school.

SUGGESTED READINGS

Brinkerhoff, R. O., Brethower, D. M., Hluchyj, T., & Nowakowski, J. R. (1983). *Program evaluation: A practitioner's guide for trainers and educators (Sourcebook/Casebook)*. Boston, MA: Kluwer-Nijhoff.

Brinkerhoff, R. O., Brethower, D. M., Hluchyj, T. & Nowakowski, J. R. (1983). *Program evaluation: A practitioner's guide for trainers and educators (Design Manual)*. Boston, MA: Kluwer-Nijhoff.

These two companion volumes are intended as ''how to'' books to help individuals plan and conduct their own evaluation studies. The sourcebook contains chapters of guidelines, resources, and references. The casebook (bound with the sourcebook) is a collection of twelve stories about evaluation, applied to real life projects and programs. The separate design manual contains sets of worksheets, examples, and checklists to help design your own evaluation. These two volumes are intended to be useful to classroom teachers, other educators, including professional evaluators. Many practical examples, checklists, and forms are provided to assist individuals in carrying out actual evaluations.

Walberg, H. J., & Haertel, G. D. (Eds.) (1990). *The international encyclopedia of educational evaluation*. Oxford, England: Pergamon Press.

This is a comprehensive and up-to-date treatment of educational evaluation theory, practice, and research. Containing over 150 articles by internationally recognized evaluation specialists and examples of evaluation studies from many countries, this volume is thematically arranged around the following topics: evaluation approaches and strategies, conduct of and issues in evaluation studies, curriculum evaluation, measurement theory and application, types of tests and examinations, research methodology, and educational policy and planning in relation to evaluation.

Worthen, B. W., & Sanders, J. R. (1987). *Educational evaluation: Alternative approaches and practical guidelines*. White Plains, NY: Longman.

This book is designed to accomplish two general goals. First, it helps educators to understand what evaluation is, describes how it can be useful to them, and explains six of the most popular approaches for evaluating educational programs, along with discussing their relative strengths and weaknesses. Second, this volume includes practical guidelines on how to plan, conduct, report, and evaluate educational evaluation studies. The book includes a case study that shows how the practical guidelines can be applied in real life. It has been judged by users as very beneficial to the educator wanting a single book that will give them enough information to understand what evaluation is all about and how to do it in their setting.

Worthen, B. W., & White, K. R. (1987). *Evaluating educational and social programs: Guidelines of proposal review, on-site evaluation, evaluation contracts, and technical assistance.* Norwell, MA: Kluwer-Nijhoff Publishers.

This book is intended to be narrower and deeper than the Worthen and Sanders book, dealing extensively with four specific topics within educational evaluation: (1) the evaluation of educational proposals; (2) the use of on-site evaluation to judge educational programs and curricula; (3) how educators can obtain technical assistance in evaluation when they need additional expertise beyond that which they possess; and (4) how evaluation agreements and contracts can be used to assure that evaluations conducted by external persons will be conducted appropriately in a way that is mutually beneficial to all parties.

SELF-CHECK QUIZ

1. Educational evaluation is the process of
   a. improving instructional materials, programs, and curricula.
   b. deciding which teaching method yields the best results.
   c. monitoring expenditures of public funds for educational systems.
   d. determining the worth or merit of whatever educational entity is being evaluated.
   e. justifying existing or planned programs, materials, or curricula.

2. Choosing from among alternatives without systematically collecting information to determine which of those alternatives is best is an example of what type of evaluation?
   a. Biased
   b. Informal
   c. Internal
   d. External

3. Which of the following is typically the most flawed evaluation arrangement (assuming the evaluations were all conducted as well as possible, given the arrangement)?
   a. Internal formative
   b. Internal summative
   c. External formative
   d. External summative

4. An evaluation that is conducted by a member of the program staff while the program is in operation is an example of which type of evaluation?
   a. Internal formative
   b. Internal summative
   c. External formative
   d. External summative

5. The most important decision when using an external evaluator is deciding
   a. who will conduct the evaluation.
   b. how to interpret the results of the evaluation.
   c. how to analyze the data.
   d. which instruments to use to collect the data.

6. An evaluation study with the goal of helping improve a district's science curriculum is an example of
   a. external evaluation.
   b. formative evaluation.
   c. internal evaluation.
   d. summative evaluation.

7. It is usually *inappropriate* to conduct an evaluation study when
   a. the primary reason for doing so is to satisfy a legal requirement.
   b. program consultants are found to lack necessary expertise.
   c. the evaluation will not produce reliable or valid information.
   d. the selected evaluator is found to have no formal training in evaluation.

8. In planning an evaluation, which of the following is the *least* important?
   a. Describing procedures for analyzing evaluation data
   b. Describing how the evaluation's results will be used
   c. Selecting methods for collecting information
   d. Identifying major evaluative questions to be addressed

9. A good program evaluation will
   a. provide information that is relevant to an important decision about the program.
   b. carefully restrict distribution of its results to those who will participate in making the decision(s).
   c. prevent evaluation findings from falling into the hands of program opponents.
   d. provide interim summative evaluation information to guide the program's development.

10. The best example of a stakeholder in an evaluation study would be
    a. a member of the local evaluation certification board.
    b. a person owning stock in a company being evaluated.
    c. an evaluator bidding for the contract to do the evaluation.
    d. a meta-evaluator called in to critique the evaluation study.

SUGGESTION SHEET

If your last name starts with the letters *X*, *Y*, or *Z*, please complete the Suggestion Sheet at the end of the book while this chapter is still fresh in your mind.

ANSWERS TO APPLICATION PROBLEMS

#1

Rank 1. The most useful type of evaluation here would be *internal formative* evaluation. Lotta's innovation in teaching writing is still embryonic and hardly ready for a summative evaluation, either internal or external. Lotta can do much of the evaluation herself, *if* she is not already so sold on CAWP that she has lost her objectivity. She could assess students' creativity by having fellow teachers or writing experts judge the creativity of "creative writing" samples her students produce. She could determine whether CAWP results in overall better writing by randomly selecting half of her writing classes to use CAWP (with the other half promised a turn next) and comparing holistic writing samples of CAWP-taught students with those of students not yet exposed to

CAWP. Such steps would yield information that could be useful to Lotta in direct proportion to how unbiased she could be in submitting CAWP to rigorous evaluation. There is much to learn that is useful in evaluating one's own education programs.

Rank 2. External formative evaluation would also be very useful, for it would serve to (1) check whether Lotta has been adequately objective or whether she has unwittingly allowed enthusiasm to color her evaluation; and (2) examine questions and evaluation issues beyond those Lotta thought to pose. It is important to have someone with no vested interest in a program examine it during its formative stage to assure that there is no unintentional bias in the evaluation. If CAWP were proposed for districtwide adoption, external formative evaluation might well have ranked 1.

Rank 3. External summative evaluation may be appropriate later, but not now. At that time, it would be asking a great deal of Lotta to render an unbiased judgment about continuation of CAWP. A better choice would be for her to ask for an external review from someone detached enough to do that job. The district's language arts coordinator *may* be a semi-outsider, but he approved payment for Banner's purchase of CAWP and has "bought in" to that extent. It is better to get someone, when the time comes, who is skilled in evaluation and who is completely detached from the school district.

Rank #4. Internal summative evaluation is not only not a good idea now, since Lotta only recently started the CAWP program, but high potential of bias seldom makes internal summative evaluation a good idea.

#2

Because there are so many questions and steps you could apply for each of the eight areas listed, and so many different results you could specify, it seems unwise to try to give a single response to this question. If you wish to assess your responses to similar questions, you might wish to examine Chapters 13 to 21 of the Worthen and Sanders text described under Suggested Readings above.

References

Abramson, T. (1969). The influence of examiner race on first-grade and kindergarten subjects' Peabody Picture Vocabulary Test scores. *Journal of Educational Measurement*, *6*, 241–246.

Ace, M. C., & Dawis, R. V. (1973). Item structure as a determinant of item difficulty in verbal analogies. *Educational and Psychological Measurement*, *6*, 241–246.

Aiken, L. W. (1980). Attitude measurement and research. In D. A. Payne (Ed.), *Recent developments in affective measurement.* (pp. 1–24). San Francisco: Jossey-Bass.

Airasian, P. W. (1979). A perspective on the uses and misuses of standardized achievement tests. *Measurement in Education*, *10*(3), 1–12. (ERIC Document Reproduction Service No. ED 187 730)

Airasian, P. W., & Madaus, G. F. (1983). Linking testing and instruction: Policy issues. *Journal of Educational Measurement*, *20*(2), 103–118.

Alderman, D. L., & Powers, D. E. (1980). The effects of special preparation on SAT-Verbal Scores. *American Educational Research Journal*, *17*, 239–251.

Allport, G. W. (1935). Attitudes. In C. Murchison (Ed.), *Handbook of social psychology* (pp. 798–844). Worchester: Clark University Press.

American Educational Research Association, American Psychological Association, and National Council on Measurement in Education. (1985). *Standards for educational and psychological testing.* Washington, DC: American Psychological Association.

American Federation of Teachers, National Council on Measurement in Education, and National Education Association. (1990). Standards for teacher competence in educational assessment of students. *Educational Measurement: Issues and Practices*, *9*(4), 30–32.

American Psychological Association. (1981). *Ethical principles of psychologists.* Washington, DC: Author.

American Psychological Association, American Educational Research Association, & National Council on Measurement in Education. (1966). *Standards for educational and psychological tests and manuals.* Washington, DC: American Psychological Association.

American Psychological Association, American Educational Research Association, & National Council on Measurement in Education. (1974). *Standards for educational and psychological tests.* Washington, DC: American Psychological Association.

Anastasi, A. (1958). Heredity, environment, and the question "How?" *Psychological Review*, *65*, 197–208.

Anastasi, A. (1967). Psychology, psychologists and psychological testing. *American Psychologist, 22,* 297–306.

Anastasi, A. (1988). *Psychological testing* (6th ed.). New York: Macmillan.

Anderson v. Banks, 540 F. Supp. 761 (S.D. Ga. 1982).

Anderson, B., & Pipho, C. (1984). State-mandated testing and the fate of local control. *Phi Delta Kappan, 66*(3), 209–212.

Anderson, B. L., Stiggins, R. J., & Gordon, D. W. (1980). *Educational testing facts and issues: A layperson's guide to testing in the schools.* Portland, OR: Northwest Regional Educational Laboratory and California State Department of Education (contract #400–79–0059).

Anderson, L. W. (1988). Attitudes and their measurement. In J. P. Keeves (Ed.), *Educational research, methodology, and measurement: An international handbook* (pp. 421–426). Oxford, England: Pergamon Press.

Anderson, R. C., Kulhavy, R. M., Andre, T. (1971). Feedback procedures in programmed instruction. *Journal of Educational Psychology, 62,* 148–156.

Anderson, R. E., Welch, W. W., & Harris, L. J. (1982). Methodological considerations in the development of indicators of achievement in data from the national assessment. *Journal of Educational Measurement, 19*(2), 113–124.

Anderson, R. H. (1966). The importance and purposes of reporting. *National Elementary School Principal, 45,* 6–11.

Angleitner, A., & Wiggins, J. S. (Eds.). (1986). *Personality assessment via questionnaire.* New York: Springer-Verlag.

Angoff, W. H. (1982). Norms and scales. In H. E. Mitzel (Ed.), *Encyclopedia of educational research* (5th ed., pp. 1342–1355). New York: The Free Press.

Ansorge, C. J. (1985). Review of cognitive abilities test, form 3. In J. V. Mitchell, Jr. (Ed.), *The ninth mental measurements yearbook,* (pp. 351–352). Lincoln: Buros Institute of Mental Measurements, University of Nebraska.

Arter, J. A. (1982, March). *Out-of-level versus in-level testing: When should we recommend each?* Paper presented at the Annual Meeting of the American Educational Research Association, New York (ERIC Document Reproduction Service No. ED 220507.)

Asher, S. R., & Gottman, J. M. (Eds.). (1981). *The development of children's friendships.* New York: Cambridge University Press.

Austin, G. R., & Garber, H. (1982). The implications for society. In G. R. Austin & H. Garber (Eds.), *The rise and fall of national test scores* (pp. 247–255). New York: Academic Press.

Baglin, R. F. (1981). Does "nationally" normed really mean nationally? *Journal of Educational Measurement, 18*(2), 97–107.

Bailard, V., & Strang, R. (1964). *Parent-teacher conferences.* New York: McGraw-Hill.

Baird, L. L., & Feister, W. J. (1972). Grading standards: The relation of changes in average student ability to the average grades awarded. *American Educational Research Journal, 9,* 431–442.

Bajtelsmit, J. W. (1977). Test-wiseness and systematic desensitization programs for increasing adult test-taking skills. *Journal of Educational Measurement, 14,* 335–341.

Bakeman, R., & Gottman, J. M. (1986). *Observing interaction. An introduction to sequential analysis.* New York: Cambridge University Press.

Baker, F. B. (1982). Item analysis. In H. E. Mitzel (Ed.), *Encyclopedia of educational research* (5th ed., pp. 959–967). New York: The Free Press.

Baron, J. B. (1989). Performance testing in Connecticut. *Educational Leadership, 46*(7), 8.

Bayley, N. (1955). On the growth of intelligence. *American Psychologist, 10,* 805–817.

Beattie, J., & Algozzine, B. (1982). Testing for teaching. *Arithmetic Teacher, 30*(1), 47–51.

Becker, H. S., Geer, B., & Hughes, E. C. (1968). *Making the grade: The academic side of college life*. New York: Wiley.

Beckham, J. C. (1986). Objective testing to assess teacher competency: Emerging legal issues. In T. N. Jones & D. P. Semler (Eds.), *School law update*. Topeka, KS: National Organization on Legal Problems in Education.

Bellanca, J. A., & Kirschenbaum, H. (1976). An overview of grading alternatives. In S. B. Simon & J. A. Bellanca (Eds.), *Degrading the grading myths: A primer of alternatives to grades and marks* (pp. 51–62). Washington, DC: Association for Supervision and Curriculum Development.

Belson, W. A. (1981). *The design and understanding of survey questions*. Aldershot, England: Gower.

Benbow, C. P., & Stanley, J. C. (1980). Sex differences in mathematical ability: Fact or artifact. *Science, 210*(4475), 1262–1263.

Benjes, J., Heubert, J., & O'Brien, M. (1980). The legality of minimum competency test programs under Title VI of the Civil Rights Act of 1964. *Harvard Civil Rights and Civil Liberties Law Review, 15*(3), 537–622.

Bennett, G. K., & Doppelt, J. E. (1956). Item difficulty and speed of response. *Educational and Psychological Measurement, 16*, 494–496.

Bennett, G. K., Seashore, H. G., & Westman, A. G. (1982). *Differential aptitude tests: Administrator's handbook*. San Antonio, TX: Psychological Corporation.

Berdie, D. R., & Anderson, J. F. (1974). *Questionnaires: Design and use*. Metuchen, NJ: Scarecrow Press.

Berk, R. A. (1984). Selecting the index of reliability. In R. A. Berk (Ed.), *A guide to criterion-referenced test construction* (pp. 231–266). Baltimore, MD: Johns Hopkins University Press.

Berk, R. A. (1986). Minimum competency testing: Status and potential. In B. S. Plake & J. C. Witt (Eds.), *The future of testing* (pp. 89–144). Hillsdale, NJ: Lawrence Erlbaum Associates.

Berk, R. A. (1988). Criterion-referenced tests. In J. P. Keeves (Ed.). *Educational research methodology, and measurement: An international handbook* (pp. 365–370). Oxford, England: Pergamon Press.

Bernard, J. (1966). Achievement test norms and time of year of testing. *Psychology in the Schools, 3*, 273–275.

Bersoff, D. N. (1981a). Testing and the law. *American Psychologist, 36*(10), 1047–1056.

Bersoff, D. N. (1981b). Test bias: The judicial report card. *New York University Education Quarterly, 3*, 2–8.

Bester v. Tuscaloosa City Board of Education, 722 F. 2d 1514 (11th Cir. 1984).

Binet, A. (1911). *Les idees modernes sur les enfants*. Paris: Flammarion.

Binet, A., & Simon, T. (1905). Methodes nouvelles pour le diagnostic du niveau intellectuel des anormaux. *Annee Psychologique, 11*, 191–244.

Black, H. (1962). *They shall not pass*. New York: Random House.

Blessum, W. T. (1969). *Annual report 1968–1969, Medical Computer Facility*. Irvine: University of California, Irvine, California College of Medicine.

Bloom, B. S., Engelhart, M. D., Furst, G. J., Hill, W. H., & Krathwohl, D. R. (1956). *Taxonomy of educational objectives: Handbook I, The cognitive domain*. New York: David McKay Company Inc.

Bloom, B. S., Hastings, J. T., & Madaus, G. F. (1971). *Handbook on formative and summative evaluation of student learning*. New York: McGraw-Hill.

Boag, A. K., & Nield, M. (1962). The influence of the time factor on the scores of the Triggs Diagnostic Reading Test as reflected in the performance of secondary school pupils grouped according to ability. *Journal of Educational Research, 55*, 181–183.

Board, C., & Whitney, D. R. (1977). *The effect of selected poor item-writing practices on test difficulty, reliability, and validity* (Research Report 55). Iowa City: University of Iowa, University Evaluation and Examination Service.

Board of Education of Northport—East Northport Union Free School District v. Ambach, 436 N. Y. S. 2d 564 (Sup. Ct., Albany County, 1981).

Boehm, A. E. (1986). *Boehm test of basic concepts—Revised.* San Antonio, TX: Psychological Corporation.

Boersma, W. C. (1967). *The effectiveness of the evaluative criteria as a stimulus for school improvement in eleven Michigan high schools.* Unpublished doctoral dissertation, University of Michigan.

Borg, W. R., & Gall, M. D. (1989). *Educational research: An introduction* (5th ed.). New York: Longman.

Borg, W. R., Worthen, B. R., & Valcarce, R. W. (1986). Teachers' perceptions of the importance of educational measurement. *The Journal of Experimental Education*, *55*(1), 9–14.

Borich, G. D., & Madden, S. K. (1977). *Evaluating classroom instruction: A sourcebook of instruments.* Reading, MA: Addison-Wesley.

Bortner, M. (1985). Review of Wechsler Intelligence Scale for Children— Revised. In J. V. Mitchell, Jr. (Ed.), *The ninth mental measurements yearbook*, (pp. 1713–1714). Lincoln: Buros Institute of Mental Measurements, University of Nebraska.

Bowman, C. M., & Peng, S. S. (1972). *A preliminary investigation of recent advanced psychology tests in the FRE program—an application of cognitive classification system.* Unpublished Educational Testing Service report, Princeton, NJ.

Bracey, G. W. (1989). The $150 million redundancy. *Phi Delta Kappan*, *70*(9), 698–702.

Brewer, W. R. (1992, April 15). Can performance assessment survive success? *Education Week.*

Brickell, H. M. (1978). Seven key notes on minimal competency testing. *Educational Leadership*, *35*(7), 551–552, 554–557.

Brinkerhoff, R. O., Brethower, D. M., Hluchyj, T., & Nowakowski, J. R. (1983). *Program evaluation: A practitioner's guide for trainers and educators* (Design Manual). Boston, MA: Kluwer-Nijhoff Publishing.

Brinkerhoff, R. O., Brethower, D. M., Hluchyj, T., & Nowakowski, J. R. (1983). *Program evaluation: A practitioner's guide for trainers and educators* (Sourcebook/Casebook). Boston, MA: Kluwer-Nijhoff.

Brookhart v. Illinois State Board of Education, 697 2d. 179, 187 (7th Cir. 1983).

Brown v. Board of Education of Topeka. (1954). 347 U.S. 483.

Brown, F. G. (1976). *Principles of educational and psychological testing* (2nd ed.) New York: Holt, Rinehart and Winston.

Burba, K. V. (1976). A computerized alternative to grading. In S. B. Simon & J. A. Bellanca (Eds.), *Degrading the grading myths: A primer of alternatives to grades and marks* (pp. 64–69). Washington, DC: Association for Supervision and Curriculum Development.

Burket, G. R., Green, D. R., Yen, W. M., Guest, M. E., and Hunter, W. H. (1982). *Preliminary technical report.* (Available from CTB/McGraw Hill, Del Monte Research Park, Monterey, CA, 93940.)

Buros, O. K. (1938). *The 1938 mental measurements yearbook.* New Brunswick, NJ: Rutgers University Press.

Buros, O. K. (1974). *Tests in print II: An index to tests, test reviews, and the literature on specific tests.* Highland Park, NJ: The Gryphon Press.

Burrill, L. E. & Wilson, R. (1980). Fairness and the matter of bias. *Test Service Notebook*, *36.* New York: The Psychological Corporation.

Burstein, L. (1983). A word about this issue. *Journal of Educational Measurement, 20,* 99–101.

Cangelosi, J. C. (1982). *Measurement and evaluation: An inductive approach for teachers.* Dubuque, IA: Wm. C. Brown Company Publishers.

Cannell, J. J. (1988). *Nationally normed elementary achievement testing in America's public schools: How all 50 states are above the national average.* Daniels, WV: Friends for Education.

Cannell, J. J. (1989). *How public educators cheat on standardized achievement tests.* Albuquerque, NM: Friends for Education.

Carlson, R. E. (1990). An alternative methodology for appraising the job relatedness of NTE Program tests. *Applied Measurement in Education, 2*(3), 243–253.

Carlson, S. B. (1985). *Creative classroom testing: Ten designs for assessment and instruction.* Princeton: Educational Testing Service.

Carter, R. S. (1952). How invalid are marks assigned by teachers? *Journal of Educational Psychology, 43,* 218–228.

Cashen V. M., & Ramseyer, G. C. (1969). The use of separate answer sheets by primary school children. *Journal of Educational Measurement, 6,* 155–158.

Cattel, J. McK. (1890). Mental tests and measurements. *Mind, 15,* 373–381.

Chadwick, E. (1864). Statistics of educational results. *The Museum, 3,* 480–484.

Chambers, J. A., & Bork, A. (1980). Computer-assisted learning in U.S. secondary and elementary schools. *The Computing Teacher, 8*(1), 50–51.

Chapman, M., & Hill, R. A. (Eds.) (1971). *Achievement motivation: An analysis of the literature.* Philadelphia, PA: Research for Better Schools.

Chase, C. I. (1985). Review of Torrance Test of Creative Thinking. In J. V. Mitchell, Jr. (Ed.), *The ninth mental measurements yearbook* (p. 1637). Lincoln: Institute of Mental Measurements, University of Nebraska.

Christen, W. (1976). Contracting for student learning. *Educational Technology, 16,* 27.

Chun, K., Cobb, S., & French, J. R. P. Jr. (1975). *Measures for psychological assessment.* Ann Arbor, MI: Survey Research Center.

Cizek, G. J. (1991a). Confusion effusion: A rejoinder to Wiggins. *Phi Delta Kappan, 72*(2), 150–153.

Cizek, G. J. (1991b). Innovation or enervation? Performance assessment in perspective. *Phi Delta Kappan, 72*(9), 695–699.

Clark, D. C. (1969). Competition for grades and graduate student performance. *Journal of Educational Research, 62,* 351–354.

Cleary, T. A., Humphreys, L. G., Kendrick, A. S., & Wesman, A. (1975). Educational uses of tests with disadvantaged students. *American Psychologist, 30,* 15–41.

Clemens, W. V. (1971). Test administration. In R. L. Thorndike (Ed.), *Educational measurement* (2nd ed.), (pp. 188–201). Washington, DC: American Council on Education.

Clifford, M. N. (1976). A revised measure of locus of control. *Child Study Journal, 6*(2), 85–90.

Clifford, P. I., & Fishman, J. A. (1963). The impact of testing programs on college preparation and attendance. *The impact and improvement of school testing programs. LXII yearbook.* National Society for the Study of Education.

Clingman, J., & Fowler, R. L. (1976). The effects of primary reward on the IQ performance of grade school children as a function of initial IQ level. *Journal of Applied Behavior Analysis, 9,* 19–23.

Coburn, P., Kelman, P., Roberts, N., Snyder, T. F. F., Watt, D. H., & Weiner, C. (1982). *Practical guide to computers in education.* Reading, MA: Addison-Wesley Publishing Company.

Code of Fair Testing Practices in Education. (1988). Washington, DC: Joint Committee on Testing Practices.

Coffman, W. E. (1971). Essay examinations. In R. L. Thorndike (Ed.), *Educational measurement* (2nd ed., pp. 271–302). Washington, DC: American Council on Education.

Cohen, S. A., & Hyman, J. S. (1991). Can fantasies become facts? *Educational Measurement: Issues and Practice, 10*(1), 20–23.

Cole, N. S. (1981). Bias in testing. *American Psychologist, 36*, 1067–1077.

Cole, N. S., & Moss, P. A. (1989). Bias in test use. In R. L. Linn (Ed.), *Educational Measurement* (3rd ed., pp. 201–219). London: Collier Macmillan.

Coleman, J. S., Campbell, E. G., Hobson, C. J., McPartland, J., Mood, A. M., Weinfeld, F. D., & York, R. L. (1966). *Equality of educational opportunity*. Washington, DC: Government Printing Office.

College Entrance Examination Board. (1968). *Effects of coaching on Scholastic Aptitude Test scores*. New York: Author. (ERIC Document Reproduction Service No. ED 169 130.)

College Entrance Examination Board. (1979). *Taking the SAT: A guide to the Scholastic Aptitude Test and the test of standard written English*. New York: Author.

Conklin, J. E., Burstein, L., & Keesling, J. W. (1979). The effects of date of testing and method of interpretation on the use of standardized test scores in the validation of large-scale educational programs. *Journal of Educational Measurement, 16*, 239–246.

Conklin, R. C. (1985). Teacher competency testing. *Education Canada, 25*(1), 12–15.

Conoley, J. C., & Kramer, J. J. (Eds.). (1989). *The tenth mental measurements yearbook*. Lincoln, NE: University of Nebraska Press.

Conroy, M. (1987, November). Coaching for SAT tests: Could it help your child get into college? *Better Homes and Gardens*, pp. 105–106.

Coppersmith, S. (1981). *SEI, self-esteem inventories*. Palo Alto, CA: Consulting Psychologists Press.

Cornehlsen, V. H. (1965). Cheating attitudes and practices in a suburban high school. *Journal of the National Association of Women Deans and Counselors, 28*, 106–109.

Crandall, V. C., Katkovsky, W., & Crandall, V. J. (1965). Children's beliefs in their own control of reinforcement in intellectual-academic achievement situations. *Child Development, 36*, 91–109.

Crockenberg, S. B. (1972). Creativity tests: Boon or boondoggle? *Review of Educational Research, 42*, 27–48.

Crocker, L., & Algina, J. (1986). *Introduction to classical and modern test theory*. New York: Holt, Rinehart & Winston.

Crocker, L., & Benson, J. (1976). Achievement, guessing, and risk-taking under norm referenced and criterion referenced testing conditions. *American Educational Research Journal, 13*, 207–215.

Cronbach, L. J. (1946). Response sets and test validity. *Educational and Psychological Measurement, 6*, 475–494.

Cronbach, L. J. (1951). Coefficient alpha and the internal structure of tests. *Psychometrika, 16*, 297–334.

Cronbach, L. J. (1984). *Essentials of psychological testing* (4th ed.). New York: Harper and Row.

Cross, L., & Frary, R. (1977). An empirical test of Lord's theoretical results regarding formula scoring of multiple-choice tests. *Journal of Educational Measurement, 17*, 313–322.

Crouse, J., & Trusheim, D. (1988). *The case against the SAT*. Chicago: University of Chicago Press.

CTB/McGraw-Hill. (1982). *Comprehensive tests of basic skills: Class management guide.* Monterey, CA: Author.

Culler, R. E., & Holahan, C. (1980). Test taking and academic performance: The effects of study-related behaviors. *Journal of Educational Psychology, 72,* 16–20.

Culyer, R. C. (1982). Interpreting achievement test data: Some areas of concern. *Clearing House, 55*(8), 374–380.

Cureton, L. W. (1971). The history of grading practices. *National Council on Measurement in Education: Measurement News, 2,* (Whole No. 4), 1–8.

Dadourian, H. M. (1925). Are examinations worth the price? *School and Society, 21,* 442–443.

D'Agostino, R. B., & Cureton, E. E. (1975). The 27 percent rule revisited. *Educational and Psychological Measurement, 25,* 41–50.

Darling, H. L., & Wise, A. E. (1985). Beyond standardization: State standards and school improvement. *The Elementary School Journal, 85,* 315–336.

Darling-Hammond, L. (1991). The implications of testing policy for quality and equality. *Phi Delta Kappan, 73*(3), 220–225.

Darling-Hammond, L., & Lieberman, A. (1992, January 29). The shortcomings of standardized tests. *Chronicle of Higher Education,* pp. B1–2.

Dawis, R. V. (1980). Measuring interests. In David A. Payne (Ed.), *Recent development in affective measurement.* San Francisco, CA: Jossey-Bass.

Debra P. v. Turlington, 474 F. Supp. 244, 265 (M. D. Fla. 1979).

DeCecco, J. P. (1968). *The psychology of learning and instruction: Educational psychology.* Englewood Cliffs, NJ: Prentice-Hall.

Diana v. California State Board of Education, No. C-70 37 RFP, District Court of Northern California, 1970.

Dobbin, J. E. (1984). *How to take a test.* Princeton, NJ: Educational Testing Service.

Dolly, J. P., & Williams, K. S. (1983). *Teaching testwiseness.* Paper presented at the annual meeting of the Northern Rocky Mountain Educational Research Association, Jackson, WY.

Dorr-Bremme, D. W. (1983). Assessing students: Teachers' routine practices and reasoning. *Evaluation Comment, 6*(4), 1–12.

DuBois, P. H. (1970). *A history of psychological testing.* Boston: Allyn and Bacon.

Dunkleberger, G. E., & Heikkinen, H. (1982). A review of computer-generated repeatable testing. *AEDS Journal, 15*(4), 218–225.

Dwyer, C. A. (1982). Achievement Testing. In H. E. Mitzel, (Ed.), *Encyclopedia of educational research,* (5th ed., pp. 13–21), New York: The Free Press.

Ebel, R. L. (1954). Procedures for the analysis of classroom tests. *Educational and Psychological Measurement, 14,* 352–364.

Ebel, R. L. (1956). Obtaining and reporting evidence on content validity. *Educational and Psychological Measurement, 16,* 269–282.

Ebel, R. L. (1965). *Measuring educational achievement.* Englewood Cliffs, NJ: Prentice-Hall.

Ebel, R. L. (1979). *Essentials of educational measurement* (3rd ed.). Englewood Cliffs, NJ: Prentice-Hall.

Echternacht, G. J. (1976). Reliability and validity of item option weighting schemes. *Educational and Psychological Measurement, 36,* 301–309.

Education of the Handicapped Act. (1977). *Federal Register, 42,* 42474–42518.

Educational Leadership. (1989). Redirecting assessment. *Educational Leadership, 46*(7), 2–77. Author.

Educational Measurement: Issue and Practices. (1982). How other organizations view testing, *1*(1), 17–19. Author.

Educational Testing Service. (1963). *Multiple choice questions: A close look*. Princeton, NJ. Reprinted in G. H. Bracht, K. D. Hopkins, & J. C. Stanley, (Eds.), 1972. *Perspectives in educational and psychological measurement*. Englewood Cliffs, NJ: Prentice-Hall.

Educational Testing Service. (1980). *Test scores and family income: A response to changes in the Nader/Nairn report on ETS*. Princeton, NJ: Author.

Educational Testing Service. (1981). *Public interest principles for the design and use of admissions testing programs*. Princeton, NJ: Author.

Educational Testing Service. (1983). *Developing a test*. Princeton, NJ: Author.

Educational Testing Service. (1985). *Creative classroom testing: 10 designs for assessment and instruction*. Princeton, NJ: Author.

Educational Testing Service. (1987). *ETS standards for quality and fairness*. Princeton, NJ: Author.

Edwards, A. L. (1957a). *The social desirability variability in personality assessment and research*. New York: Dryden Press.

Edwards, A. L. (1957b). *Techniques of attitude scale construction*. New York: Appleton Century-Crofts.

Eells, W. C. (1930). Reliability of repeated essay grading of essay type questions. *Journal of Educational Psychology, 31*, 48–52.

Epstein, J. L. (Ed.). (1981). *The quality of school life*. Lexington, MA: Lexington Books.

Epstein, J. L., & McPartland, J. M. (1976). The concept and measurement of the quality of school life. *American Educational Research Journal, 13*(1), 15–30.

Erlenmeyer-Kimling, L., & Jarvik, L. F. (1963). Genetics and intelligence: A review. *Science, 142*, 1477–1479.

Esposito, D. (1973). Homogeneous and heterogeneous ability grouping: Principal findings and implications for evaluating and designing more effective educational environments. *Review of Educational Research, 43*, 163–179.

Evans, W. (1984). Test wiseness: An examination of cue-using strategies. *Journal of Experimental Education, 52*, 141–144.

Evertson, C. M., & Green, J. L. (1986). Observation as inquiry and method. In M. C. Wittrock (Ed.), *Handbook of research on teaching* (3rd ed., pp. 162–213). New York: Macmillan.

Faggen, J. (1990). The profession's evolving standards. *Educational Measurement: Issues and Practices, 9*(4), 3–4.

Feldmesser, R. A. (1971). *The Positive Function of Grades*. Paper presented at the Annual Meeting of the American Educational Research Association, New York.

Festinger, L. (1962). *A theory of cognitive dissonance*. Stanford, CA: Stanford University Press.

Findley, M. J., & Cooper, A. M. (1983). Locus of control and academic achievement: A literature review. *Journal of Personality and Social Psychology, 44*(2), 419–427.

Findley, W. G. (1963). Purpose of school testing programs and their efficient development. In W. G. Findley (Ed.), *Sixty-second yearbook of the National Society for the Study of Education, Part II*. Chicago: University of Chicago Press.

Findley, W. G., & Bryan, M. M. (1971). *Ability grouping: 1970 status, impact, and alternatives*. Athens, GA: University of Georgia, Center for Educational Improvement. (ERIC Document Reproduction Service No. ED 060 595.)

Fiske, E. (1981a, April 14). Pyramids of test question 44 open a pandora's box. *New York Times*, p. C-3.

Fiske, E. (1981b, March 24). A second student wins challenge on math test. *New York Times*, p. B-1.

Flanders, N. A. (1970). *Analyzing teaching behavior*. Reading, MA: Addison-Wesley.

Fleming, M. (1982). *Standardized testing under court ordered desegregation: Developing a compliance plan.* Paper presented at the annual meeting of the National Council on Measurement in Education. (ERIC Document Reproduction Service No. ED 221 577)

Fleming, M. & Chambers, B. (1983). Teacher-made tests: Windows on the classroom. In W. E. Hathaway (Ed.), *Testing in the schools: New directions for testing and measurement,* (Vol. 19, pp. 29–38). San Francisco, CA: Jossey-Bass.

Floden, R. E., Porter, A. C., Schmidt, W. H., & Freeman, D. J. (1978). *Don't they all measure the same thing? Consequences of selecting standardized tests.* East Lansing, MI: Michigan State University, National Institute for Research on Teaching (ERIC Document Reproduction Service No. ED 167632.)

Fox, L. H. (1981). Identification of the academically gifted. *American Psychologist, 36*(10), 1103–1111.

Frazer, B. J. (1989). Twenty years of classroom climate work: Progress and prospect. *Journal of Curriculum Studies, 21*(4), 307–327.

Frederiksen, N. (1984). The real test bias: Influences of testing on teaching and learning. *American Psychologist, 39,* 193–202.

Freeman, D., Kuhs, T., Knappen, L., & Porter, A. (1979). *A closer look at standardized tests* (Research Series No. 53). East Lansing, MI: Michigan State University, Institute for Research on Teaching (ERIC Document Reproduction Service No. ED 179581.)

Fremer, J., & Anastasio, E. J. (1968). *Computer-assisted item writing: I. Spelling items.* Princeton, NJ: Educational Testing Service.

Frey, J. H. (1983). *Survey research by telephone.* Beverly Hills, CA: Sage Publications.

Freytes, C. E. (1982). *Procedures for assessing learning problems of students with limited English proficiency.* (FL 013 091) Washington, DC: U.S. Department of Education.

Fricke, B. G. (1975). *Report to the faculty: Grading, testing, standards, and all that.* Ann Arbor: University of Michigan, Evaluation and Examination Office.

Fry, E. B. (1981). *Reading diagnosis: Informal reading inventories.* Providence, Rhode Island: Jamestown Publishers.

Fuchs, D., & Fuchs, L. S. (1986). Test procedure bias: A meta-analysis of examiner familiarity effects. *Review of Educational Research, 56,* 243–262.

Furst, E. J. (1958). *Constructing evaluation instruments.* New York: David McKay, Inc.

Gaffney, R. F., & Maguire, T. O. (1971). Use of optically scored test answer sheets with young children. *Journal of Educational Measurement, 8,* 103–106.

Garcia, J. (1981). The logic and limits of mental aptitude testing. *American Psychologist, 36*(10), 1172–1180.

Gardner, H. (1984). Assessing intelligences: A comment on 'testing intelligence without I.Q. tests.' *Phi Delta Kappan, 65*(10), 699–700.

Gardner, P. L. (1975). Attitude measurement: A critique of some recent research. *Educational Research, 17,* 101–109.

Gay, L. R. (1980). The comparative effects of multiple-choice versus short answer tests on retention. *Journal of Educational Measurement, 17,* 45–50.

Geisinger, K. F. (1979). A note on grading policies and grade inflation. *Improving College and University Teaching, 27,* 113–115.

Geisinger, K. F. (1980). Who are giving all those A's? *Journal of Teacher Education, 31,* 11–15.

Geisinger, K. F. (1982). Marking systems. In H. E. Mitzel (Ed.), *Encyclopedia of educational research* (5th ed., Vol. 3, pp. 1139–1149). New York: The Free Press.

Geisinger, K. F., & Rabinowitz, W. (1979). Grading attitudes and practices among college faculty members. In H. Dahl, A. Lysne, & P. Rand (Eds.), *A spotlight on educational problems* (pp. 145–172). New York: Columbia University Press.

Geisinger, K. F., Wilson, A. N., & Naumann, J. J. (1980). A construct validation of faculty orientations toward grading: Comparative data from three institutions. *Educational and Psychological Measurement, 40*, 413–417.

Georgia Association of Educators v. Nix, 407 F. Supp. 1102 (N.D. Ga. 1976).

Ghiselli, E. E. (1966). *The validity of occupational aptitude tests*. New York: Wiley.

Glaser, R. (1963). Instructional technology and the measurement of learning outcomes: Some questions. *American Psychologist, 18*, 519–21.

Glass, G. V (1978). Standards and criteria, *Journal of Educational Measurement, 15*(4), 237–261.

Glass, G. V (1986). Testing old, testing new: Schoolboy psychology and the allocation of intellectual resources. In B. S. Plake, J. C. Witt, & J. V. Mitchell (Eds.), *The future of testing*. Buros-Nebraska Symposium on Measurement and Testing, Vol. 2, Hillsdale, NJ: Lawrence Erlbaum Associates.

Glasser, W. (1969). *Schools without failure*. New York: Harper & Row.

Glazer, N. (1970). Are academic standards obsolete? *Change in Higher Education, 2*, 38–44.

Gold, R. M., Reilly, A., Silberman, R., & Lehr, R. (1971). Academic achievement declines under pass-fail grading. *Journal of Experimental Education, 39*, 17–21.

Goldberg, L. R. (1965). Grades as motivants. *Psychology in the Schools, 2*, 17–24.

Golden Rule Insurance Company v. Washburn, 419–76 Illinois Circuit Court, 7th Ind. Cir Ct. (1984). Consent Decree.

Gonzalez, M. (1985). Cheating on standardized tests: What is it? In P. Wolmut & G. Iverson (Eds.), *National association of test directors 1985 symposia* (pp. 4–16). Portland, OR: Multnomah ESD.

Goodwin, W. L. (1966). Effect of selected methodological conditions on dependent measures taken after classroom experimentation. *Journal of Educational Psychology, 57*, 350–358.

Gordon, D. A. (1977). Children's beliefs in internal-external control and self-esteem as related to academic achievement. *Journal of Personality Assessment, 41*(4), 383–386.

Gould, S. J. (1981). *The Mismeasure of Man*. New York: Norton.

Graziano, W. G., Varca, P. E., & Levy, J. C. (1982). Race of examiner effects and the validity of intelligence tests. *Review of Educational Research, 52*, 469–497.

Green, B. F. (1981). A primer of testing. *American Psychologist, 36*, 1001–1011.

Green, B. F. (1983). Adaptive testing by computer. *New Directions for Testing and Measurement, 17*, 5–12.

Green, D. R. (1983). *Content validity of standardized achievement tests and test curriculum overlap*. Symposium conducted at the annual meeting of the National Council on Measurement in Education, Montreal.

Green, K. E., & Stager, S. F. (1985, April). *Teachers' attitudes toward testing*. Paper presented at the annual meeting of the National Council on Measurement in Education, Chicago, IL. (ERIC Document Reproduction Service No. ED 253–588.)

Grier, J. B. (1975). The number of alternatives for optimum test reliability. *Journal of Educational Measurement, 12*, 109–113.

Gronlund, N. E. (1959). *Sociometry in the classroom*. New York: Harper.

Grisafe, J. (1979). *Occupational assessment handbook* (Resources in Education ED 187879).

Gronlund, N. E. (1985). *Measurement and evaluation in teaching* (5th ed.). New York: Macmillan.

Gronlund, N. E. (1988). *How to construct achievement tests* (4th ed.). Englewood Cliffs, NJ: Prentice-Hall.

Gronlund, N. E., & Linn, R. L. (1990). *Measurement and evaluation in teaching* (6th ed.). New York: Macmillan.

Gross, M. (1962). *The brain watchers*. New York: Random House.

Guilford, J. P. (1965). *Fundamental statistics in psychology and education* (4th ed.). New York: McGraw Hill.

Guilford, J. P. (1969). *Intelligence, creativity and their educational implications*. San Diego: Educational and Industrial Testing Service.

Guilford, J. P., & Hoepfner, R. (1971). *The analysis of intelligence*. New York: McGraw-Hill.

Guilford, J. P., & Lacey, J. I. (Eds.) (1947). *Printed classification tests. Army Air Forces aviation psychology research program report, Report 5*. Washington, DC: U.S. Government Printing Office.

Gullickson, A. R. (1984). Teacher perspectives of their instructional use of tests. *Journal of Educational Research, 77*(4), 244–248.

Gullickson, A. R., & Ellwein, M. (1985). Post hoc analysis of teacher-made tests: The goodness-of-fit between prescription and practice. *Educational Measurement: Issues and Practice, 4*, 15–18.

Gulliksen, G. (1986). Perspective on educational measurement. *Applied Psychological Measurement, 10*, 109–13.

Gustav, A. (1963). Response set in objective achievement tests. *Journal of Psychology, 56*, 421–427.

Haas, N. S., Haladyna, T. M., & Nolen, S. B. (1989). *Standardized testing in Arizona: Interviews and written comments from teachers and administrators* (Tech. Rep. No. 89–3). Phoenix, AZ: Arizona State University West Campus.

Hadley, S. T. (1954). A school mark—Fact or fancy? *Educational Administration and Supervision, 40*, 305–12.

Haensly, P. A., & Torrance, E. P. (1990). Assessment of creativity in children and adolescents. In C. R. Reynolds & R. W. Kamphaus (Eds.), *Handbook of psychological and educational assessment of children: Intelligence and achievement* (pp. 697–722). New York: The Guilford Press.

Haertel, G. D., Walberg, H. J., Junker, L. K., & Pascerella, E. T. (1981). Early adolescent sex differences in science learning. *American Educational Research Journal, 18*(3), 329–341.

Hakstian, A. R., & Kansup, W. (1975). A comparison of several methods of assessing partial knowledge in multiple-choice tests: II. Testing procedures. *Journal of Educational Measurement, 12*, 231–240.

Haladyna, T., & Thomas, G. (1979a). The affective reporting system. *Journal of Educational Measurement, 16*(1), 49–54.

Haladyna, T., & Thomas, G. (1979b). The attitudes of elementary school children towards school and subject matters. *Journal of Educational Measurement, 48*(1), 18–23.

Haladyna, T. M., & Downing, S. M. (1989a). A taxonomy of multiple-choice item writing rules. *Applied Measurement in Education, 2*(1), 37–50.

Haladyna, T. M., & Downing, S. M. (1989b). Validity of a taxonomy of multiple-choice item-writing rules. *Applied Measurement in Education, 2*(1), 51–78.

Haladyna, T. M., Haas, N. S., & Nolen, S. B. (1989). *Test score pollution* (Tech. Rep. No. 1). Phoenix, AZ: Arizona State University West Campus.

Haladyna, T. M., Nolen, S. B., & Haas, N. S. (1991). Raising standardized achievement test scores and the origins of test score pollution. *Educational Researcher, 20*(5), 2–7.

Haladyna, T. M., & Roid, G. (1981). The role of instructional sensitivity in the empirical review of criterion-referenced test items. *Journal of Educational Measurement, 18*, 39–53.

Haladyna, T. M., & Roid, G. H. (1983). A comparison of two approaches to criterion referenced test construction. *Journal of Educational Measurement, 20*(3), 271–282.

Halpern, A., Raffeld, P., Irvin, L. K., & Link, R. (1975). *Social and prevocational information battery examiners manual, and user's guide.* Monterey, CA: CTRB/McGraw-Hill.

Hambleton, R. K., & Cook, L. L. (1977). Latent trait models and their use in the analysis of educational test data. *Journal of Educational Measurement, 14*, 75–96.

Hambleton, R. K., & Traub, R. E. (1974). The effects of item order on test performance and stress. *Journal of Experimental Education, 43*, 40–46.

Haney, W. (1981). Validity, vaudeville, and values: A short history of social concerns over standardized testing. *American Psychologist, 36*(10), 1021–1034.

Haney, W. (1984). Testing reasoning and reasoning about testing. *Review of Educational Research, 54*(4), 597–654.

Haney, W., & Madaus, G. (1989). Searching for alternatives to standardized tests: Whys, whats, and whithers. *Phi Delta Kappan, 70*(9), 683–687.

Harnisch, D. L., Hill, K. T., & Fayans, L. J. (1980, April). *Development of a shorter, more reliable, and more valid measure of test motivation.* Paper presented at the Annual Meeting of the National Council on Measurement in Education, Boston (ED 193 273).

Harris, A. (1980). Bias in mental testing. In A. Jensen (Ed.), *Bias in mental testing.* New York: The Free Press.

Hassencahl, F. (1979). Contract grading in the classroom. *Improving College and University Teaching, 27*, 30–33.

Hatch, J. A., & Freeman, E. B. (1988). Who's pushing whom? Stress and kindergarten. *Phi Delta Kappan, 69*, 145–147.

Hattie, J. (1983). The tendency to omit items: Another deviant response characteristic. *Educational and Psychological Measurement, 43*, 1041–1045.

Haynes, L. T., & Cole, N. S. (1982, March). *Testing some assumptions about on level versus out-of-level achievement testing.* Paper presented at the annual meeting of the National Council on Measurement on Education, New York.

Hayvren, M., & Hymel, S. (1984). Ethical issues in sociometric testing: Impact of sociometric measures on interaction behavior. *Developmental Psychology, 20*(5), 844–849.

Heberlein, T. A., & Baumgartner, R. (1978). Factors affecting response rates to mailed questionnaires: A quantitative analysis of the published literature. *American Sociological Review, 43*, 82–101.

Henerson, M. E., Morris, L. L., & Fitz-Gibbon, C. T. (1978). *How to measure attitudes.* Beverly Hills, CA: Sage.

Henrysson, S. (1971). Gathering, analyzing, and using data on test items. In R. L. Thorndike (Ed.), *Educational measurement* (pp. 130–159). Washington, DC: American Council on Education.

Herman, J. (1991, November). Speech delivered at a meeting of a Consortium on Expanded Assessment, Sponsored by Association for Supervision and Curriculum Development, San Diego, CA.

Herman, J. L., & Dorr-Bremme, D. W. (1982). *Assessing students: Teachers' routine practices and reasoning.* Paper presented at the annual meeting of the American Educational Research Association, New York.

Herman, J. L., & Dorr-Bremme, D. W. (1984, April). *Teachers and testing: Implications from a national study.* Paper presented at the annual meeting of the American Educational Research Association, New Orleans, LA.

Hicklin, N. J. (1962). *A study of long-range techniques for predicting patterns of scholastic behavior.* Unpublished Ph.D. thesis, University of Chicago.

Hill, K. T. (1984). Debilitating motivation and testing: A major educational problem, possible solutions, and policy applications. In R. Ames & C. Ames (Eds.), *Research on motivation in education: Student motivation*. New York: Academic Press.

Hill, K. T., & Wigfield, A. (1984). Test anxiety: A major educational problem and what can be done about it. *The Elementary School Journal, 85*(1), 105–126.

Hills, J. R. (1986). *All of Hills' handy hints*. Washington, DC: National Council on Measurement in Education.

Hiscox, M. D. (1984). A planning guide for microcomputers in educational measurement. *Educational Measurement: Issues and Practice, 3*(2), 28–34.

Hobson v. Hansen, 269 F. Supp. 401 (D.D.C. 1967), off'd sub nom. Smuck v. Holson, 408 F. 2d 175 (D.C. Cir. 1969).

Hoepfner, R. (1967). Review of the Torrance tests of creative thinking. *Journal of Educational Measurement, 4*, 191–192.

Hoffmann, B. (1962). *The tyranny of testing*. New York: Crowell-Collier Press.

Hogan, T. P. (1975). *Survey of school attitudes, Manual for administering and interpreting*. New York: Harcourt Brace Jovanovich.

Hopkins, K. D. (1964). Extrinsic reliability: Estimating and attenuating variance from response styles, chance, and other irrelevant sources. *Educational and Psychological Measurement, 24*, 271–281.

Hopkins, K. D., & Glass, G. V (1978). *Basic statistics for the behavioral sciences*. Englewood Cliffs, NJ: Prentice Hall.

Hopkins, K. D., & Stanley, J. C. (1981). *Educational and Psychological Measurement and Evaluation* (6th ed.). Englewood Cliffs, NJ: Prentice Hall.

Hopkins, K. D., Stanley, J. C., & Hopkins, B. R. (1990). *Educational and Psychological Measurement and Evaluation* (7th ed.). Englewood Cliffs, NJ: Prentice Hall.

Houston, J. P. (1976). Amount and loci of classroom answer copying, spaced seating, and alternate test forms. *Journal of Educational Psychology, 68*, 729–735.

Houts, P. L. (1976). Behind the call for test reform and abolition of the IQ. *Phi Delta Kappan, 57*(10), 669–673.

Hoyt, D. P. (1970). Rationality and the grading process. *Educational Record, 41*, 105–109.

Hu, C. T. (1984). The historical background: Examinations and control in pre-modern China. *Comparative Education, 20*(1), 7–26.

Ingle, R. B., & de Amico, G. (1969). The effect of physical conditions on the test room on standardized achievement test scores. *Journal of Educational Measurement, 6*, 237–240.

Inouye, D. K., & Bunderson, C. V. (1986). Four generations of computerized test administration. *Machine-mediated learning, 1*, 355–371.

Jacobson, R. (1981, March 30). "Discovery of second error poses threat to test," College Board Chairman says. *Chronicle of Higher Education*, 4.

Jaeger, R. M. (1982). The final hurdle: Minimum competency achievement testing. In G. R. Austin & H. Garber (Eds.), *The rise and fall of national test scores* (pp. 223–246). New York: Academic Press.

Jaeger, R. M. (1989). Certification of student competence. In R. L. Linn (Ed.), *Educational measurement* (3rd ed., pp. 485–514). London: Collier Macmillan.

Jaeger, R. M. (1990). Establishing standards for teacher certification tests. *Educational Measurement: Issues and Practices, 9*(4), 15–20.

Jarvik, L. F., Eisdorfer, C., & Blum, J. E. (Eds.) (1973). *Intellectual functioning in adults: Psychological and biological influences*. New York: Springer.

Jencks, C., & Riesman, D. (1968). *The academic revolution*. New York: Doubleday.

Jenkins, J. R., & Pany, D. (1978). Standardized achievement tests: How useful for special education? *Exceptional Children, 44*(6), 448–453.

Jensema, C. (1980). Considerations in utilizing achievement tests for the hearing impaired. *American Annals of the Deaf, 125*(4), 495–498.

Jensen, A. R. (1969). How much can we boost IQ and scholastic achievement? *Harvard Educational Review*, *39*, 5–28.

Jensen, A. R. (Ed.) (1980). *Bias in mental testing*. New York: The Free Press.

Jessell, J. C., & Sullins, W. L. (1975). The effect of keyed response sequencing of multiple choice items on performance and reliability. *Journal of Educational Measurement*, *12*, 45–48.

Johnson, F. W. (1911). A study of high school grades. *School Review*, *19*, 130–24.

Joint Committee on Standards for Educational Evaluation (1981). *Standards for evaluations of educational programs, projects, and materials*. New York: McGraw-Hill.

Jolly, S. J., & Gramenz, G. W. (1984). Customizing a norm-referenced achievement test to achieve curricula validity: A case study. *Educational Measurement: Issues and Practice*, *3*(3), 16–18.

Jongsma, K. S. (1989). Portfolio assessment. *The Reading Teacher, 43*(3), 264-265.

Kahn, S. B. (1968). The relative magnitude of speed and power in SCAT. *Journal of Educational Measurement*, *5*, 327–330.

Karlsen, B., & Gardner, E. F. (1986). *Stanford Diagnostic Reading Test. Red level, forms G and H* (3rd ed.). San Diego, CA: Harcourt Brace Jovanovich.

Kaufman, M. J., Semmel, M. I., & Agard, J. A. (1974). PRIME: An overview. *Education and Training for the Mentally Retarded*, *9*, 107–112.

Kellaghan, T., Madaus, G. F., & Airasian, P. W. (1982). *The effects of standardized testing*. Boston, MA: Kluwer-Nijhoff.

Kelley, T. L. (1939). The selection of upper and lower groups for the validation of test items. *Journal of Educational Psychology*, *30*, 17–24.

Keyser, D. J., and Sweetland, R. C. (1984–88). *Test critiques*, Kansas City, MO: Test Corporation of America. (A total of six volumes have been published as of November, 1989.)

Kingsbury, G. G. (1989). *Usage of computerized adaptive testing as a school based tool for student and program evaluation*. Paper presented to the annual meeting of the American Educational Research Association, San Francisco, CA, March 31.

Kirkland, K., & Hollandsworth, J. (1979). Test anxiety, study skills, and academic performance. *Journal of College Personnel*, *20*(5), 431–435.

Kirschenbaum, H., Simon, S. B., & Napier, R. W. (1971). *Wad-ja-get? The grading game in American education*. New York: Hart.

Klosner, N. C., & Gellman, E. K. (1973). The effect of item arrangement on classroom test performance. *Educational and Psychological Measurement*, *33*, 413–418.

Kramer, J. J., & Conoley, J. C. (Eds.). (1991). *The supplement to the tenth mental measurements yearbook*. Lincoln, NE: Buros Institute of Mental Measurements.

Kramer, J. J., & Conoley, J. C. (Eds.). (1992). *The eleventh mental measurements yearbook*. Lincoln, NE: Buros Institute of Mental Measurements.

Koretz, D. (1988). Educational practices, trends in achievement, and the potential of the reform movement. *Educational Administration Quarterly*, *24*(3), 350–359.

Kramer, J. J. & Conolen, J. C., (Eds.) (1992). *The eleventh mental measurements yearbook*. Lincoln, NE: University of Nebraska Press.

Krathwohl, D. R., Bloom, B. S., & Mazia, B. B. (1964). *Taxonomy of educational objectives: Handbook II: Affective domain*. New York: David McKay.

Kubiszyn, T., & Borich, G. (1987). *Educational testing and measurement: Classroom application and practice* (2nd ed.). Glenview, IL: Scott, Foresman and Company.

Kuder, G. F., & Richardson, M. W. (1937). The theory of the estimation of test reliability. *Psychometrika*, *2*, 151–160.

Kuehn, P. A., Stallings, W. M., & Holland, C. L. (1990). Court-defined job analysis requirements for validation of teacher certification tests. *Educational Measurement: Issues and Practices*, *9*(4), 21–24.

Kulik, J. A., Kulik, C-L. C., & Bangert, R. L. (1984). Effects of practice on aptitude and achievement test scores. *American Educational Research Journal, 21*, 435–447.

Kunder, L. H., & Porwoll, P. J. (1977). *Reporting pupil progress: Policies, procedures, and systems.* Arlington, VA: Educational Research Service, Inc.

Kurland, D. M. (1991, April). *Text browser: A computer-based tool for managing, analyzing, and assessing student writing portfolios.* Paper presented at the annual conference of the American Educational Research Association, Chicago, IL.

LaBenne, W. D., & Greene, B. I. (1969). *Educational implications of self concept theory.* Pacific Palisades, CA: Goodyear.

Lambert, N. M. (1981). Psychological evidence in Larry P. v. Wilson Riles: An evaluation by a witness for the defense. *American Psychologist, 36*(9), 937–952.

LaPiere, R. T. (1936). Type-rationalizations of group antipathy. *Social Forces, 15*, 232–237.

Larry P. v. Riles, 343 F. Supp. 1306 (N.D. Cal. 1972) (preliminary injunction), affirmed, 502 F. 2d. 963 (9th Cir. 1974), opinion issued No. C-71–2270 RFP (N.D. Cal. October 16, 1979.)

Lasden, M. (1985). The trouble with testing. *Training, 22*(5), 79–86.

Lavin, D. E. (1965). *The prediction of academic performance.* New York: Wiley.

Lavisky, S. (1975). Invited address. In J. R. Sanders & T. P. Sachse (Eds.), *Problems and potentials of applied performance testing: Proceedings of the National Conference on the Future of Applied Performance Testing* (pp. 35–54). Portland, OR: Northwest Regional Educational Laboratory.

Learner, B. (1981). Representative democracy, "men of zeal," and testing legislation. *American Psychologist, 36*, 270–275.

Lefcourt, H. M. (Ed.). (1981). *Research with the locus of control construct, Vol. 1 Assessment methods.* New York: Academic Press.

Leinhardt, G., & Marseewald, A. (1981). Overlap: What's tested, what's taught? *Journal of Educational Measurement, 18*(2), 85–96.

Lenke, J. M., & Keene, J. M. (1988). A response to John J. Cannell. *Educational Measurement: Issues and Practice, 7*, 16–18.

Lennon, R. T. (1982). The abiding agenda of measurement. *Educational Measurement: Issues and Practice, 1*(1), 10–11.

Lessinger, L. M. (1970). Engineering accountability for results in public education. *Phi Delta Kappan, 52*, 217–225.

Lessinger, L. M., & Tyler, R. W. (Eds.) (1971). *Accountability in education.* Worthington, OH: Charles A. Jones.

Levy, P., & Goldstein, H. (1984). *Tests in education—A book of critical reviews.* New York: Academic Press.

Licht, B. G., Kistner, J. A., Oz Karegoz, T., Shapiro, S., & Clausen, L. (1985). Causal attributions of learning disabled children: Individual differences and their implications for persistence. *Journal of Educational Psychology, 77*(2), 208–216.

Light, R. J., & Smith, P. V. (1969). Social allocation models of intelligence: A methodological inquiry. *Harvard Educational Review, 39*(3), 484–510.

Lik, I., Halpern, A. S., & Becklund, J. D. (1981). *Skills for independent living, Teacher's manual and resource materials guide.* Monterey, CA: CTB/McGraw-Hill.

Likert, R. (1932). A technique for the measurement of attitudes, *Archives of Psychology,* #140.

Linn, R. L. (1979). Issues of reliability in measurement for competency-based programs. In M. A. Bunda & J. R. Sanders (Eds.), *Practices and problems in competency based measurement.* Washington, DC: National Council on Measurement in Education.

Linn, R. L. (1982). Admissions testing on trial. *American Psychologist, 37*(3), 279–291.

Linn, R. L. (1990, June). *Cautions about performance assessments*. Paper presented at the Education Commission of the States, Boulder, CO.

Linn, R. L., Baker, E. L., & Dunbar, S. B. (1991). Complex performance-based assessment: expectations and validation criteria. *Educational Researcher, 21*(8), 15–21.

Linn, R. L., & Drasgow, F. (1987). Implications of the Golden Rule Settlement for Test Construction. *Educational Measurement: Issues and Practice, 6*(2), 13–17.

Linn, R. L., Graue, M. E., & Sanders, N. M. (1989). *Comparing state and district test results to national norms: Interpretations of scoring "above the national average"* (Technical Report, Grant No. OERI-G-86–0003). Los Angeles: UCLA, Center for Research on Evaluation, Standards, and Student Testing.

Lippman, W. (1922). The mental age of Americans. *New Republic, 32*, 213–215.

Livingston, S. A. (1988). Reliability of test results. In J. P. Keeves (Ed.). *Educational research methodology, and measurement: An international handbook* (pp. 386–392). Oxford, England: Pergamon Press.

Longstreth, L. E. (1979). Pressures to reduce academic standards. In K. F. Geisinger (Chair), *University grade inflation: Documentation, causes, and consequences*. Symposium presented at the annual meeting of the American Psychological Association, New York.

Lord, F. M. (1980). *Applications of item response theory to practical testing problems*. Hillsdale, NJ: Erlbaum Associates.

Lutz, S. W., & Richards, J. M., Jr. (1967). *Predicting student accomplishment in college from the ACT assessment*. Iowa City, IA: American College Testing Program.

Lyon, H. C., Jr. (1974). The other minority. *Learning: The Magazine for Creative Teaching, 2*(5), 65.

Madaus, G. F. (Ed.). (1983). *The courts, validity, and minimum competency testing*. Boston, MA: Kluwer-Nijhoff.

Madaus, G. F. (1985a). Test scores as administrative mechanisms in educational policy. *Phi Delta Kappan, 66*, 611–617.

Madaus, G. F. (1985b). Public policy and the testing profession: You've never had it so good? *Educational Measurement: Issues and Practice, 4*(4), 5–11.

Madaus, G. F., Airasian, P., & Kellaghan, T. (1980). *School effectiveness*. New York: McGraw-Hill.

Madaus, G. F., & Pullin, D. (1987). Teacher certification tests: Do they really measure what we need to know? *Phi Delta Kappan, 69*(1), 31–38.

Maeroff, G. I. (1991). Assessing alternative assessment. *Phi Delta Kappan, 73*(4), 272–281.

Magnusson, D. (1967). *Test theory*. Reading, MA: Addison-Wesley.

Maller, J. B., & Zubin, J. (1932). The effect of motivation upon intelligence test scores. *Journal of Genetic Psychology, 41*, 136–151.

Mandler, G., & Sarason, S. B. (1952). A study of anxiety and learning. *Journal of Abnormal and Social Psychology, 47*, 166–173.

Mann, H. (1845). Report of the annual examining committee of the Boston grammar and writing schools. *Common School Journal, 7*, 326–336.

March, H. W., Byrne, B. M., & Shavelson, R. J. (1988). A multi-faceted academic self concept: Its hierarchical structure and its relation to academic achievement. *Journal of Educational Psychology, 80*(3), 366–380.

Marso, R. N. (1985). *Testing practices and test item preferences of classroom teachers*. (ERIC Document Reproduction Service No. ED 268 145.)

Martin, D. V. (1986). Teacher testing: I'm O.K., You're O.K., But Somebody's Not! (ERIC Document Reproduction Service No. ED 169 130.)

Matter, M. K., & Ligon, G. D. (1984, April). *Preparing students for standardized testing:*

Everybody's business. Paper presented at the annual meeting of the American Educational Research Association, New Orleans, LA.

McBride, J.R. (1985). Computerized adaptive testing. *Educational Leadership*, *43*(2), 25.

McCall, W. A. (1936, December). *The test newsletter*. Teacher's College, Columbia University.

McCarthy, D. (1978). *Manual for the McCarthy Screening Test*. New York: Psychological Corporation.

McKellar, N. A. (1986). Behaviors used in peer tutoring. *Journal of Experimental Education*, *54*(3), 163–167.

McMorris, R. F., Brown, J. A., Snyder, G. W., & Pruzek, R. M. (1972). Effects of violating item construction principles. *Journal of Educational Measurement*, *9*, 287–295.

McTighe, J. J., & Ferrara, S. (in press). A process for planning more thoughtful classroom assessment. In A. Costa & J. Bellanca (Eds.), *Mind matters*. Palatine, IL: Skylight Publishing.

Mehrens, W. A. (1982). Aptitude measurement. *Encyclopedia of educational research* (5th ed., Vol. 1, pp. 137–144). New York: Macmillan.

Mehrens, W. A. (1984). National tests and local curriculum: Match or mismatch? *Educational Measurement: Issues and Practice*, *3*(3), 9–15.

Mehrens, W. A., & Kaminski, J. (1989). Methods for improving standardized test scores: Fruitful, fruitless, or fraudulent? *Educational Measurement: Issues and Practice*, *8*(1), 14–22.

Mehrens, W. A., & Lehmann, I. J. (1984). *Measurement and evaluation in education and psychology* (3rd ed.). New York: Holt, Rinehart and Winston.

Mehrens, W. A., & Lehmann, I. J. (1991). *Measurement and evaluation in education and psychology* (4th ed.). New York: Holt, Rinehart and Winston.

Meisels, S. (1978). *Developmental screening in early childhood*. Washington, DC: National Association for the Education of Young Children.

Melcher, J., McCoy, J., Lange, J., & Kammen, A. (1980). *A Review of assessment instruments and procedures for young exceptional children*. (Report No. WSDPI-Bull-0488) Washington, DC: Bureau of Education for the Handicapped.

Melton, G. B. (1985). Review of Law School Admission Test. In J. V. Mitchell, Jr. (Ed.), *The ninth mental measurements yearbook* (pp. 824–826). Lincoln: Buros Institute of Mental Measurements, University of Nebraska.

Menacker, J., & Morris, V. C. (1985). Intelligence testing, civil rights, and the federal courts. *The Educational Forum*, *49*(3), 285–296.

Mercer, J. (1977). *SOMPA, system of multicultural pluralistic assessment*. New York: Psychological Corporation.

Merrell, K. W. (1993). *Measurement and evaluation in the schools: A practical guide. Student Workbook*. New York: Longman.

Merwin, J. C., & Gardner, E. F. (1962). Development and application of tests of educational achievement. *Review of Educational Research*, *32*, 40–50.

Messick, S. (1981). Evidence and ethics in the evaluation of tests. *Educational Researcher*, *10*(9), 9–20.

Messick, S. (1982). Issues of effectiveness and equity in the coaching controversy: Implications for educational and testing practice. *Educational Psychologist*, *17*, 67–91.

Messick, S. (1989). Validity. In R. L. Linn (Ed.). *Educational measurement* (3rd ed.), pp. 13–103. New York: American Council on Education and Macmillan Publishing Company.

Messick, S., & Jungeblut, A. (1981). Time and method in coaching for the SAT. *Psychological Bulletin*, *89*, 191–216.

Metfessel, N. S., & Sax, G. (1958). Systematic biases in the keying of correct responses on certain standardized tests. *Educational and Psychological Measurement*, *18*, 787–790.

Meyer, M. (1908). The grading of students. *Science, 27*, 243–50.

Michael, W. B., Michael, J. J., & Zimmerman, H. S. (1980). *Study attitudes and methods survey: Manual of instructions and interpretation.* San Diego: Educational and Industrial Testing Service.

Michael, W. B., Smith, R. A., & Michael, J. J. (1984). *Dimensions of self concept (DOSC) technical manual.* San Diego, CA: EDITS.

Millman, J. (1978). *Strategies for constructing criterion-referenced assessment instruments.* Ithaca, NY: Cornell University.

Millman, J., Bishop, C. H., & Ebel, R. (1965). An analysis of test-wiseness. *Educational and Psychological Measurement, 25*, 707–727.

Millman, J., & Harrington, P. J. (1982). Standards for tests and ethical test use. In H. E. Mitzel, J. H. Best, & W. Rabinowitz (Eds.), *Encyclopedia of educational research: Vol. 4* (pp. 1767–1769). New York: Macmillan.

Moore, J. C., Schutz, R. E., & Baker, R. L. (1966). The application of a self instructional technique to develop a test-taking strategy. *American Educational Research Journal, 3*, 13–17.

Moos, R., & Trickett, E. (1987). *The classroom environment scale manual* (2nd ed.). Palo Alto, CA: Consulting Psychologists Press.

Moreno, J. L. (1953). *Who shall survive?* New York: Beacon.

Moynihan, P. (1971). Seek parity of educational achievement, Moynihan urges. *Report on Educational Research, 3*, 4.

Mueller, D. J. (1986). *Measuring social attitudes.* New York: Teachers College Press.

Mueller, D. J., & Shwedel, A. (1975). Some correlates of net gain from answer changing on objective test items. *Journal of Educational Measurement, 12*, 251–254.

Mullis, I. V. S., Dossey, J. A., Owen, E. H., & Phillips, G. W. (1991). The state of mathematics achievement: NAEP's 1990 assessment of the nation and the trial assessment of the states (Executive Summary). Princeton, NJ: Educational Testing Service (20-ST-04); Washington, DC: National Center for Education Statistics (91-1259).

Murray, H. A. (1938). *Explorations in personality.* New York: Oxford University Press.

Naccarato, R. W. (1988). *A guide to item banking in education.* Portland, OR: Northwest Regional Educational Laboratory.

Nairn, A. (1980). *The reign of ETS: The corporation that makes up minds.* Washington, DC: Ralph Nader.

National Commission on Excellence in Education (1983). *A nation at risk: The imperative for educational reform.* Washington, DC: U.S. Government Printing Office.

National Institute of Education (1979). *Testing, teaching and learning.* Washington, DC: Author.

Neill, D. M., & Medina, N. J. (1989). Standardized testing: Harmful to educational health. *Phi Delta Kappan, 70*(9), 688–697.

Nell, W. (1963). A comparative investigation of teacher assigned grades and academic achievement in the Aztec Junior High, New Mexico. In Society for the Study of Education. *Educational Research Bulletin*, 15–16.

Neurath, O., Carnap, R., & Morris, C. (Eds.). (1955). *Fundamentals of the unity of science: Toward an international encyclopedia of unified science.* Foundations of the Unity of Science Series (Vol. 1–2). Chicago, IL: University of Chicago Press.

Nevo, B. (1985). Face validity revisited. *Journal of Educational Measurement, 22*(4), 287–293.

Nevo, D., & Shohamy, E. (1984, April). *Applying the joint committee's evaluation standards for the assessment of alternative testing methods.* Paper presented at the annual meeting of the American Educational Research Association, New Orleans, LA.

Nitko, A. J. (1984). Book review of Roid and Haladyna's *A technology for item writing*. *Journal of Educational Measurement, 21*, 201–204.

Nitko, A. J. (1989). Designing tests that are integrated with instruction. In Linn, R. L. (Ed.), *Educational measurement* (3rd ed., pp. 447–474). London: Collier Macmillan Publishers.

Nolen, S. B., Haladyna, T. M., & Haas, N. S. (1989). *A survey of Arizona teachers and administrators on the uses and effects of state-mandated standardized achievement testing* (Tech. Rep. No. 89-2). Phoenix, AZ: Arizona State University West Campus.

Noll, V. H., Scannel, D. P., & Craig, R. C. (1979). *Introduction to educational measurement* (4th ed.). Boston, MA: Houghton Mifflin.

Nungester, R. J., & Duchastel, P. C. (1982). Testing vs. review: Effects on retention. *Journal of Educational Psychology, 74*, 18–22.

Nurss, J. R., & McGauvran, M. E. (1986). *Metropolitan readiness tests*. San Antonio, TX: Psychological Corporation.

Oakland, T., & Laosa, L. M. (1977). Professional, legislative, and judicial influences on psychoeducational assessment practices in schools. In T. Oakland (Ed.), *Psychological and educational assessment of minority children* (pp. 21–51). New York: Brunner/Mazel.

Oakland, T., & Parmelee, R. (1985). Mental measurement of minority-group children. In B. B. Wolman (Ed.), *Handbook of intelligence: Theories, measurements, and applications*, (pp. 699–736). New York: Wiley & Sons.

O'Leary, B. S. (1980). *College grade point average as an indicator of occupational success: An update* (PRR-80-23). Washington, DC: U.S. Office of Personnel Management, Personnel Research and Development Center.

Olsen, J. (1989). *Applying computerized adaptive testing in schools*. Unpublished manuscript.

Osgood, C. E., Suci, G. J., & Tannenbaum, P. H. (1957). *The Measurement of Meaning*. Urbana, IL: University of Illinois Press.

Osterlind, S. J. (1989). *Constructing test items*. Boston: Kluwer Academic.

Page, E. B., & Paulus, D. H. (1968). *The analysis of essays by computer: Final report*. Storrs, CT: U. S. O. E. Bureau of Research (contract #OEC-16 001318-1214).

Palmer, O. (1962). Seven classic ways of grading dishonestly. *English Journal, 51*, 464–67.

PASE v. Hannon. 506 F. Supp. 831 (N.D. Ill. 1980).

Paulman, R. G., & Kennelly, K. J. (1984). Test anxiety and ineffective test taking: Different names, same construct? *Journal of Educational Psychology, 76*, 279–288.

Paulson, F. L., Paulson, P. R., & Meyer, C. A. (1991). What makes a portfolio a portfolio? *Educational Leadership, 48*(5), 60–63.

Payne, D. A. (1982). Measurement in Education. In H. E. Mitzel (Ed.), *Encyclopedia of educational research* (5th ed., Vol. 3, pp. 1182–1190). New York: The Free Press.

Peak, H., & Boring, E. G. (1926). The factor of speed in intelligence. *Journal of Experimental Psychology, 9*, 71.

Perkins, M. R. (1982). Minimum competency testing: What? Why? Why not? *Educational Measurement: Issues and Practice, 1*(4), 5–9, 26.

Peterson, N. S., Kolen, M. J., & Hoover, H. D. (1989). Scaling, norming, and equating. In R. L. Linn (Ed.), *Educational Measurement* (3rd ed., pp. 221–262). New York: Macmillan.

Phillips, B. N., & Weathers, G. (1958). Analysis of errors in scoring standardized tests. *Educational and Psychological Measurement, 18*, 563–567.

Phillips, G. W., & Finn, C. E. (1988). The Lake Wobegon effect: A skeleton in the testing closet? *Educational Measurement: Issues and Practice, 7*, 10–12.

Pike, L. W. (1978). *Short-term instruction, test-wiseness, and the Scholastic Aptitude Test: A literature review with research recommendations* (Research Bulletin RB-78-2). Princeton, NJ: Educational Testing Service.

Plake, B. S., Ansorge, C. J., Parker, C. S., & Lowry, S. R. (1982). Effects of item arrangement, knowledge of arrangement, test anxiety and sex on test performance. *Journal of Educational Measurement, 19*(1), 49–57.

Popham, W. J. (1978). The case for criterion-referenced measurement. *Educational Researcher, 7*, 6–10.

Popham, W. J. (1984a, April). *Action implications of the Debra P. decision.* Symposium presented at the annual meeting of the American Educational Research Association, New Orleans, LA.

Popham, W. J. (1984b). Specifying the domain of content or behaviors. In R. A. Berk (Ed.), *A guide to criterion-referenced test construction* (pp. 29–48).

Popham, W. J. (1987). The merits of measurement-driven instruction. *Phi Delta Kappan, 68*, 679–682.

Popham, W. J. (1990). *Modern educational measurement* (2nd ed.). Englewood Cliffs, NJ: Prentice-Hall.

Popham, W. J. (1991, June). *Circumventing the high costs of authentic assessment.* Paper presentation at the annual Education Commission of the States/Colorado Department of Education Assessment Conference, Breckenridge, CO.

Popham, W. J., & Husek, T. (1969). Implications of criterion referenced measurement. *Journal of Educational Measurement, 6*, 1–9.

Popham, W. J., & Kirby, W. N. (1987). Recertification tests for teachers: A defensible safeguard for society. *Phi Delta Kappan, 69*(1), 45–48.

Pullin, D. (1982). *Minimum competency testing, the denied diploma and the pursuit of educational opportunity and educational adequacy.* (ERIC Document Reproduction Service No. ED 228 279.)

Pyrczak, F. (1973). Validity of the discrimination index as a measure of item quality. *Journal of Educational Measurement. 10*, 227–231.

Raffeld, P. (1975). The effects of Guttman weights. *Journal of Educational Measurement, 12*, 179–185.

Rahe, D. F. (1975). *Locus of control and preferences of children for skill versus chance tasks.* Unpublished Masters Thesis, University of Iowa.

Ramseyer, G. C., & Cashen, V. M. (1971). The effect of practice sessions on the use of separate answer sheets by first and second graders. *Journal of Educational Measurement, 8*, 177–182.

Ravitch, D. (1984). The uses and misuses of tests. *The College Board Review, 130*, 23–26.

Reed v. Rhodes (1978, February). C-73–1300, *Remedial order*, 73.

Report on Education Research. (April 29, 1992a). NAEP study casts doubt on national portfolio assessment. *Report on Education Research*, 1–2.

Report on Education Research. (April 29, 1992b). Test experts see pitfalls in performance-based tests. *Report on Education Research*, 5–6.

Reschly, D. J. (1980). *Nonbiased assessment.* Des Moines, IA: Iowa State Department of Public Instruction; Iowa State University of Science and Technology, Department of Psychology. (ERIC Document Reproduction Service No. 140 324.)

Reschly, D. J. (1981). Psychological testing in educational classification and placement. *American Psychologist, 36*(10), 1094–1102.

Reynolds, C. R. (1981). *In God we trust, all others must have data* (Report No. TM8 10684). Paper presented at the Annual Meeting of the American Psychological Association, Los Angeles. (ERIC Document Reproduction Services No. ED 209 252.)

Reynolds, C. R. (1985). Review of system of multicultural pluralistic assessment. In J. V. Mitchell, Jr. (Ed.), *The ninth mental measurements yearbook* (Vol 2, pp. 1519–1521). Lincoln: Buros Institute of Mental Measurement of The University of Nebraska-Lincoln.

Reynolds, C. R., & Kamphaus, R. W. (1990). *Handbook of psychological and educational assessment of children: Intelligence and achievement.* New York: The Guilford Press.

Rice, J. M. (1897a). The futility of the spelling grind: I. *Forum, 23,* 163–172.

Rice, J. M. (1897b). The futility of the spelling grind: II. *Forum, 23,* 409–419.

Richards, J. M., & Lutz, S. W. (1968). Predicting student accomplishment in college from the ACT assessment. *Journal of Educational Measurement, 5,* 17–29.

Richardson, J. G. (Ed.) (1986). *Handbook of theory and research for the sociology of education.* New York: Greenwood Press.

Roeber, E., & Dutcher, P. (1989). Michigan's innovative assessment of reading. *Educational Leadership, 46*(7), 64–69.

Rogers, W. T., & Bateson, D. J. (1991). Verification of a model of test-taking behavior of high school seniors. *Journal of Experimental Education, 59*(4), 331–350.

Roid, G. H. (1986). Computer technology in testing. In B. S. Plake & J. C. Witt (Eds.), *The future of testing* (pp. 29–69). Hillsdale, NJ: Lawrence Erlbaum Associates, Publishers.

Roid, G. H., & Haladyna, T. M. (1982). *A technology for test item writing.* New York: Academic Press.

Rossman, H. E. (1970). Graduate school attitudes to S-U grades. *Educational Record, 41,* 310–313.

Rotter, J. B. (1966). Generalized expectancies for internal versus external control of reinforcement. *Psychological Monographs, 80*(1), 1–28.

Rudman, H. C. (1977). The standardized test flap: An effort to sort out fact from fiction, truth from deliberate hyperbole. *Phi Delta Kappan, 59,* 179–185.

Salame, R. F. (1984). Test anxiety: Its determinants, manifestations and consequences. In H. M. Vander Ploeg, R. Schwarzer, & C. D. Spielberger (Eds.), *Advances in test anxiety research* (Vol. 3, pp. 83–119).

Salmon-Cox, L. (1981). Teachers and standardized achievement tests: What's really happening? *Phi Delta Kappan, 62,* 631–634.

Salvia, J., & Hughes, C. (1990). *Curriculum-based assessment: Testing what is taught.* New York: Macmillan.

Salvia, J., & Ysseldyke, J. E. (1988). *Assessment* (4th ed.). Boston, MA: Houghton Mifflin Company.

Samuda, R. J. (1975). *Psychological testing of American minorities.* New York: Dodd, Mead.

Sandefur, J. T. (1985). Competency assessment of teachers. *Action in Teacher Education, 7*(1–2), 1–6.

Sanders, J. R., Hathaway, W. E., Johnson-Lewis, S., Madaus, G. F., & Worthen, B. R. (1987). Final report. NCME task force on certification of measurement professionals.

Sanders, J. R., & Sachse, T. (1975). Problems and Potentials of Applied Performance Testing. *Proceedings of the National Conference on the Future of Applied Performance Testing.* Portland, OR: Northwest Regional Educational Laboratory.

Sarason, I. G. (1980). *Test anxiety, theory, research, and applications.* Hillsdale, NJ: Erlbaum.

Sarason, I. G., & Ganzer, V. J. (1962). Anxiety, reinforcement, and experimental instructions in a free verbalization situation. *Journal of Abnormal and Social Psychology, 65*(5), 300–307.

Sarason, S. B., Hill, K. T., & Zimbardo, P. G. (1964). A longitudinal study of the relation of test anxiety to performance on intelligence and achievement tests. *Monographs of the Society for Research in Child Development,* Serial No. 98, *29*(7).

Sax, G. (1980). *Principles of educational and psychological measurement and evaluation* (2nd ed.). Belmont, CA: Wadsworth.

Sax, G. (1989). *Principles of educational and psychological measurement and evaluation* (3rd ed.). Belmont, CA: Wadsworth.

Sax, G., & Cromack, T. R. (1966). The effects of various forms of item arrangements on test performance. *Journal of Educational Measurement, 3,* 309–311.

Schriesheim, C. A., & Hill, K. D. (1981). Controlling acquiescence response bias by item reversals: The effect of questionnaire validity. *Educational and Psychological Measurement, 41*, 1101–1114.

Scriven, M. (1970). Discussion. *Proceedings of the 1969 Invitational Conference on Testing Problems* (pp. 112–117). Princeton, NJ: Educational Testing Service.

Scruggs, T. E., White, K. R., & Bennion, K. (1986). Teaching test-taking skills to elementary-grade students: A meta-analysis. *The Elementary School Journal, 87*, 69–82.

Seashore, H. G. (1980). *Methods of expressing test scores* (Test Service Notebook #148). New York: The Psychological Corporation.

Selden, R. W. (1985). Measuring excellence: The dual role of testing in reforming education. *Curriculum Review, 25*(1), 14–32.

Selden, S. (1982). Promotion policy. In H. E. Mitzel (Ed.), *Encyclopedia of educational research* (5th ed., pp. 1467–1474). New York: The Free Press.

Sesnowitz, M., Bernhardt, K. L., & Knain, D. M. (1982). An analysis of the impact of commercial test preparation courses on SAT Scores. *American Educational Research Journal, 19*, 429–441.

Shanker, A. (1985). A national teacher examination. *Educational Measurement: Issues and Practice, 4*(3), 28–31.

Shavelson, R. J., Bolus, R., & Keesling, J. W. (1980). Self-concept: Recent developments in theory and methods. In D. A. Payne (Ed.), *Recent developments in affective measurement*. San Francisco, CA: Jossey-Bass.

Shepard, L. A. (1979). Purposes of assessment. *Studies in Educational Evaluation, 5*, 13–26.

Shepard, L. A. (1980). Definition of bias. *Test item bias methodology: The state of state of the art*. Washington, DC: The Johns Hopkins University National Symposium on Educational Research.

Shepard, L. A. (1990). Inflated test score gains: Is the problem old norms or teaching the test? *Educational Measurement: Issues and Practice*, 15–22.

Shepard, L. A. (1991). Interview on assessment issues with Lorrie Shepard. *Educational Researcher, 20*(2), 21–27.

Shepard, L. A., & Kreitzer, A. E. (1987). The Texas teacher test. *Educational Researcher, 16*(6), 22–31.

Shimberg, B. (1990). Social considerations in the validation of licensing and certification exams. *Educational Measurement: Issues and Practices, 9*(4), 11–14.

Shulman, L. S. (1987). Assessment for teaching: An initiative for the profession. *Phi Delta Kappan, 69*(1), 38–44.

Simon, A., & Boyer, E. G. (1974). *Mirrors for behavior III: An anthology of observation instruments*. Wyncote, PA: Communications Materials Center.

Simpson, R. H. (1944). The specific meanings of certain terms indicating different degrees of frequency. *Quarterly Journal of Speech, 30*, 328–330.

Slack, W. V., & Porter, D. (1980). The Scholastic Aptitude Test: A critical appraisal. *Harvard Educational Review, 50*, 154–175.

Slakter, M. J. (1969). Generality of risk taking on objective examinations. *Educational and Psychological Measurement, 29*, 115–128.

Smith, A. Z., & Dobbin, J. E. (1960). Marks and marking systems. In C. W. Harris (Ed.), *Encyclopedia of educational research* (3rd ed., pp. 783–792). New York: Macmillan.

Smith, C. P. (Ed.) (1969). *Achievement-related motives in children*. New York: Sage.

Smith, E. R., & Tyler, R. W. (1942). *Appraising and Recording Student Progress*. New York: Harper & Row.

Smith, I. L., & Hambleton, R. K. (1990a). Content validity studies of licensing examinations. *Educational Measurement: Issues and Practice, 9*(4), 7–10.

Smith, I. L., & Hambleton, R. K. (1990b). *Curriculum-based assessment: Testing what is taught*. New York: Macmillan.

Smith, M., White, K. P., & Coop, R. H. (1979). The effect of item type on the consequences of changing answers on multiple choice tests. *Journal of Educational Measurement, 16,* 203–208.

Smith, M. L. (1991). Put to the test: The effects of external testing on teachers. *Educational Researcher, 20*(5), 8–11.

Snyderman, M., & Rothman, S. (1987). Survey of expert opinion on intelligence and aptitude testing. *American Psychologist, 42*(2), 137–144.

Spearman, C. (1927). *The abilities of man*. New York: Macmillan.

Spielberger, C. D. (1966). Theory and research on anxiety. In C. D. Spielberger (Ed.), *Anxiety and behavior*. New York: Academic Press.

Spielberger, C. D. (1972). Anxiety as an emotional state. In C. D. Spielberger (Ed.), *Anxiety: Current trends in theory and research*. New York: Academic Press.

Spielberger, C. D. (1979). *Understanding stress and anxiety*. New York: Harper & Row.

Spielberger, C. D., & Vagg, P. R. (1984). Psychometric properties of the STAI: A reply to Ramanaiah, Franzen, and Schill. *Journal of Personality Assessment, 48*(1), 95–97.

Stanley, J. C. (1980). On educating the gifted. *Educational Researcher, 9*(3), 8–12.

Starch, D. (1913). Reliability and distribution of grades. *Science, 38,* 630–636.

Starch, D., & Elliot, E. C. (1912). Reliability of grading high school work in English. *Scholastic Review, 20,* 442–457.

Starch, D., & Elliot, E. C. (1913a). Reliability of grading high school work in mathematics. *Scholastic Review, 21,* 254–259.

Starch, D., & Elliot, E. C. (1913b). Reliability of grading high school work in history studies. *Scholastic Review, 21,* 676–681.

Steinkamp, M. W., & Maehr, M. L. (1984). Affect, ability, and science achievement: A quantitative synthesis of correlational research. *Review of Educational Research, 53*(3), 369–396.

Stephens, T. M. (1982). *Criterion-referenced curriculum guide*. Columbus, Ohio: Charles E. Merrill.

Sternberg, R. J. (1981). Intelligence and nonentrenchment. *Journal of Educational Psychology, 73,* 1–16.

Stewart, N. (1947). AGCT scores of army personnel grouped by occupation. *Occupations, 26,* 5–41.

Stiggins, R. J. (1991). Assessment literacy. *Phi Delta Kappan, 72*(7), 534–539.

Stiggins, R. J., & Bridgeford, N. J. (1985). The ecology of classroom assessment. *Journal of Educational Measurement, 22,* 271–286.

Stiggins, R. J., Conklin, N. F., & Bridgeford, N. J. (1986). Classroom assessment: A key to effective education. *Educational Measurement: Issues & Practices, 5,* 5–17.

Strickland, G. P. (1970). *Development of a school attitude questionnaire for young children* (CSE Report #59). Los Angeles: University of California, Center for the Study of Evaluation.

Strickland, G. P., Hoepfner, R., & Klein, S. P. (1976). *Attitude toward school questionnaire manual*. Hollywood, CA: Monitor.

Subkoviak, M. J. (1988). A practitioner's guide to computation and interpretation of reliability indices for mastery tests. *Journal of Educational Measurement, 25,* 47–55.

Sudman, S., & Bradburn, N. M. (1982). *Asking questions: A practical guide to questionnaire design*. San Francisco, CA: Jossey-Bass.

Suhor, C. (1985). Objective tests and writing samples: How do they affect instruction in composition? *Phi Delta Kappan, 66*(9), 635–639.

Super, D. E., Braasch, W. F., & Shay, J. B. (1947). The effect of distractions on test results. *Journal of Education Psychology, 38,* 373–377.

Sweet, R. C., & Ringness, T. A. (1971). Variations in the intelligence test performance of referred boys of differing racial and socioeconomic backgrounds as a function of feedback or monetary reinforcement. *Journal of School Psychology, 9,* 399–409.

Sweetland, R. C., and Keyser, D. J. (1987). *Tests: A comprehensive reference for assessments in psychology, education, and business.* (2nd ed.) Kansas City, MO: Test Corporation of America.

Tallmadge, G. K. (1985). Normalizing the NCE. *Educational Measurement: Issues and Practices, 4*(1), 30.

Tate, M. W. (1948). Individual differences in speed of response in mental test materials of varying degrees of difficulty. *Educational and Psychological Measurement, 8,* 353–374.

Taylor, C. (1981). *The effect of reinforcement and training on group standardized test behavior.* Unpublished doctoral dissertation, Utah State University, Logan.

Taylor, C., & White, K. R. (1982). The effect of reinforcement and training on group standardized test behavior. *Journal of Educational Measurement, 19,* 198–209.

Taylor, C., White, K. R., Bush, D., & Friedman, S. (1982). *Training teachers in test administration.* Logan: Exceptional Child Center, Utah State University.

Terwilliger, J. S. (1966). Self-reported marking practices and policies in public secondary schools. *National Association of Secondary School Principals Bulletin, 50,* 5–37.

Thorndike, E. L. (1904). *Introduction to the theory of mental and social measurements.* (pp. 560–620). New York: Teachers College, Columbia University.

Thorndike, R. L. (1951). Reliability. In E. F. Lindquist (Ed.), *Educational measurement.* Washington, DC: American Council on Education.

Thorndike, R. L. (1969). Marks and marking systems. In R. L. Ebel (Ed.) *Encyclopedia of Educational Research* (4th ed., pp. 759–766). New York: Macmillan.

Thorndike, R. L. (1988). Reliability. In J. P. Keeves (Ed.). *Educational research methodology, and measurement: An international handbook,* (pp. 330–342). Oxford, England: Pergamon Press.

Thorndike, R. L., & Hagen, E. (1977). *Measurement and evaluation in psychology and education.* New York: Wiley.

Thorndike, R. L., Hagen, E. P., & Sattler, J. M. (1986). *Stanford-Binet Intelligence Scale* (4th ed.). Chicago, IL: Riverside Publishing.

Thorndike, R. M., Cunningham, G. K., Thorndike, R. L., & Hagen, E. P. (1991). *Measurement and evaluation in psychology and education* (5th ed.). New York: Macmillan.

Thurstone, L. L. (1938). Primary mental abilities. *Psychometric Monographs, 1.*

Tittle, C. K. (1978). *Sex bias in testing: A review with policy recommendations.* (ERIC Document Reproduction Service No. ED 164 623.)

Tittle, C. K., & Zytowski, D. G. (Eds.) (1978). *Sex-fair interest measurement: Research and implications.* Washington, DC: National Institute of Education.

Tobias, S. (1984). *Test anxiety: Cognitive interference or inadequate preparation?* Paper presented at the American Educational Research Association, New Orleans, LA.

Tolar, A. (Ed.) (1985). *Effective interviewing.* Springfield, IL: Charles Thomas.

Torrance, E. P. (1965). *Reward creative behavior.* Englewood Cliffs, NJ: Prentice Hall.

Towle, N. J., & Merrill, P. F. (1975). Effects of anxiety type and item-difficulty sequencing on mathematics test performance. *Journal of Educational Measurement, 12,* 241–250.

Traub, R. E., Hambleton, R. K., & Singh, B. (1968). *Effects of promised reward and threatened penalty on performance of a multiple choice vocabulary test.* Unpublished manuscript, The Ontario Institute for Studies In Education.

Travers, R. M. W. (1983). *How research has changed American schools.* Kalamazoo, MI: Mythos Press.

Triandis, H. C. (1971). *Attitude and attitude change.* New York: Wiley.

Tryon, G. S. (1980). The Measurement and Treatment of Test Anxiety. *Review of Educational Research, 50*(2), 343–372.

Tufte, E. R. (1983). *The visual display of quantitative information.* Cheshire, CT: Graphics Press.

Turnbull, W. W. (1985). *Student change, program change: Why SAT scores kept falling.* (ERIC Document Reproduction Service No. ED 266 189.)

United States v. South Carolina 445 Supp. 1094 (S.C. 1977).

Valencia, S. (1990). A portfolio approach to classroom assessment: The whys, whats, and hows. *The Reading Teacher, 43*(4), 338–340.

Vasta, R., & Sarmiento, R. F. (1979). Liberal grading improves evaluations but not performance. *Journal of Educational Psychology, 71*, 207–221.

Vavrus, L. (1990). Put portfolios to the test. *Instructor, 100*(1), 48–53.

Veldman, D. J., & Sheffield, J. R. (1979). The scaling of sociometric nominations. *Educational and Psychological Measurement, 39*, 99–106.

Waetjen, W. B. (1977, September). *Sex differences in learning: Some open questions.* Paper presented at the Fourth Annual Meeting of the International Society for the Study of Behavioral Development, Pavia, Italy.

Wainer, H. (1986). Can a test be too reliable? *Journal of Educational Measurement, 23*(2), 171–173.

Walberg, H. J., & Haertel, G. D. (Eds.). (1990). *The international encyclopedia of educational evaluation.* Oxford, England: Pergamon Press.

Warren, J. R. (1971). *College grading practices: An overview* (Report No. 9). Washington, DC: ERIC Clearinghouse on Tests, Measurement, and Evaluation. (ERIC Document Reproduction Service No. ED 117 193.)

Warren, J. R. (1979). The prevalence and consequence of grade inflation. In K. F. Geisinger (Chair), *University grade inflation: Documentation, causes, and consequences.* Symposium presented at the annual convention of the American Psychological Association, New York.

Waters, B. K. (1981). *The test score decline: A review and annotated bibliography.* (ERIC Document Reproduction Service No. ED 207 995.)

Webb, E. J., Campbell, D. T., Schwartz, R. D., & Sechrest, L. (1966). *Unobtrusive measures: Nonreactive research in the social sciences.* Chicago: Rand McNally.

Wechsler, D. (1955). *Wechsler Adult Intelligence Scale, Manual.* New York: Psychological Corporation.

Weinshank, A. B. (1980). *An observational study of the relationship between diagnosis and remediation in reading. Research series No. 72.* East Lansing, MI: Institute for Research on Teaching, College of Education, Michigan State University.

Weiss, D. J. (1985). Adaptive testing by computer. *Journal of Consulting and Clinical Psychology, 53*(6), 774–789.

Weiss, R. H. (1980). *Effects of reinforcement on the IQ scores of preschool children as a function of initial IQ.* Unpublished doctoral dissertation, Utah State University, Logan.

Werts, C., Linn, R. L., & Joreskog, K. G. (1978). Reliability of college grades from longitudinal data. *Educational and Psychological Measurement, 38*, 89–96.

Western Institute for Research and Evaluation (1982). *An evaluation of the humane education curriculum guide.* Logan, UT: Author.

Wexley, K. N., & Thornton, C. L. (1972). Effect of verbal feedback of test results upon learning. *Journal of Educational Research, 66*, 119–121.

White, E. E. (1886). *The elements of pedagogy.* New York: American Book Company.

White, K. R. (1976). *The relationship between socioeconomic status and academic achievement.* Unpublished doctoral dissertation, University of Colorado.

White, K. R. (1982). The relationship between socioeconomic status and academic achievement. *Psychological Bulletin, 91*, 461–481.

White, K. R., & Carcelli, L. (1982, March). *The effect of item format on computation subtest scores of standardized achievement tests.* Paper presented at the annual meeting of the American Educational Research Association, New York.

White, K. R., Taylor, C., Friedman, S., Bush, D., & Stewart, K. (1982). *An evaluation of training in standardized achievement test taking and administration* (Final Report of the 1981–82 Utah State Refinements to the ESEA Title I Evaluation and Reporting System). Logan: Exceptional Child Center, Utah State University (ERIC Document Reproduction Service No. ED 238 931)

Wiggins, G. (1990). A conversation with Grant Wiggins. *Instructor, 100*(1), 51.

Wiggins, G. (1991). A response to Cizek. *Phi Delta Kappan, 72*(9), 700–703.

Wilcox, R. R. (1982). Some new results on an answer-until-correct scoring procedure. *Journal of Educational Measurement, 19*(1), 67–74.

Williams, P. L. (1988). The time-bound nature of norms: Understandings and misunderstandings. *Educational Measurement: Issues and Practice, 7,* 18–21.

Williams, R. H., & Zimmerman, D. W. (1984). On the virtues and vices of the standard error of measurement. *Journal of Experimental Education, 52*(4), 231–233.

Williams, R. L. (1972). *The BITCH test (Black Intelligence Test of Cultural Homogeneity).* St. Louis, MO: Author.

Willingham, W. W. (1974). Predicting success in graduate education. *Science, 183,* 273–278.

Wilson, R. (1980). *Early childhood screening under Public Law 94-142.* New York: The Psychological Corporation.

Wilson, S. M., & Hiscox, M. D. (1984). Using standardized tests for assessing local learning objectives. *Educational Measurement: Issues and Practice, 3*(3), 19–22.

Wine, J. (1971). Test anxiety and direction of attention. *Psychological Bulletin, 76,* 92–104.

Wolf, D., Bixby, J., Glenn, J., & Gardner, H. (1991). To use their minds well: Investigating new forms of student assessment. In G. Grant (Ed.), *Review of research in education* (Vol. 17, pp. 31–65). Washington, DC: American Educational Research Associates.

Womer, F. B. (1973). *Developing a large scale assessment program.* Denver: Cooperative Accountability Project.

Wood, R. (1976). Inhibiting blind guessing: The effect of instructions. *Journal of Educational Measurement, 13,* 297–307.

Worthen, B. R. (1987, April). *Certification of measurement professionals: Arguments pro and con.* Paper presented at the annual meeting of the National Council of Measurement in Education, Washington, D.C.

Worthen, B. R. (in press). Critical issues that will determine the future of alternative assessment. *Phi Delta Kappan.*

Worthen, B. R., & Sanders, J. R. (1987). *Educational evaluation: Alternative approaches and practical guidelines.* White Plains, NY: Longman.

Worthen, B. R., & White, K. R. (1987). *Evaluating educational and social programs: Guidelines for proposal review, onsite evaluation, evaluation contracts and technical assistance.* Boston, MA: Kluwer-Nijhoff.

Yamamoto, K. (1962). *A study of the relationships between creative thinking abilities of fifth-grade teachers and academic achievement.* Unpublished doctoral dissertation, University of Minnesota, Minneapolis.

Yeh, J. (1978). *Test use in the schools.* Los Angeles: University of California at Los Angeles, Center for the Study of Evaluation.

Zastrow, C. H. (1970). Cheating among college graduate students. *Journal of Educational Research, 64,* 157–160.

Zeller, R. A. (1988). Validity. In J. P. Keeves (Ed.). *Educational research methodology, and measurement: An international handbook* (pp. 322–330). Oxford, England: Pergamon Press.

Answers to Self-check Quizzes

Chapter 1   1:a, 2:c, 3:c, 4:b, 5:a, 6:b, 7:a, 8:c

Chapter 2   1:d, 2:a, 3:f, 4:a, 5:c, 6:e, 7:a, 8:b, 9:d, 10:b

Chapter 3   1:a, 2:c, 3:a, 4:c, 5:a, 6:e, 7:b, 8:c, 9:a, 10:b

Chapter 4   1:c, 2:f, 3:b, 4:c, 5:e, 6:d, 7:a, 8:c, 9:a, 10:a

Chapter 5   1:b, 2:b, 3:d, 4:d, 5:c, 6:b, 7:e, 8:b, 9:a, 10:c

Chapter 6   1:a, 2:b, 3:c, 4:a, 5:d, 6:a, 7:c, 8:a, 9:a, 10:a

Chapter 7   1:a, 2:b, 3:c, 4:d, 5:b, 6:b, 7:c, 8:d, 9:d, 10:c

Chapter 8   1:b, 2:d, 3:d, 4:a, 5:c, 6:a, 7:c, 8:c, 9:d, 10:d

Chapter 9   1:b, 2:d, 3:c, 4:c, 5:a, 6:e, 7:a, 8:a, 9:e, 10:b

Chapter 10   1:d, 2:a, 3:b, 4:a, 5:d, 6:a, 7:d, 8:b, 9:b, 10:b

Chapter 11   1:c, 2:b, 3:b, 4:b, 5:d, 6:d, 7:a, 8:c, 9:c, 10:c

Chapter 12   1:a, 2:c, 3:c, 4:d, 5:b, 6:d, 7:b, 8:a, 9:c, 10:a

Chapter 13   1:c, 2:c, 3:a, 4:d, 5:a, 6:d, 7:c, 8:d, 9:c, 10:b

Chapter 14   1:b, 2:a, 3:b, 4:c, 5:d, 6:c, 7:a, 8:c, 9:b, 10:c

Chapter 15   1:c, 2:a, 3:b, 4:b, 5:c, 6:d, 7:d, 8:b, 9:d, 10:c

Chapter 16   1:d, 2:b, 3:a, 4:b, 5:a, 6:b, 7:b, 8:c, 9:c, 10:a

Chapter 17   1:d, 2:b, 3:b, 4:d, 5:a, 6:b, 7:a, 8:c, 9:d, 10:c

Chapter 18   1:c, 2:b, 3:b, 4:a, 5:d, 6:c, 7:b, 8:c, 9:d, 10:a

Chapter 19 · 1:b, 2:a, 3:d, 4:c, 5:d, 6:c, 7:d, 8:c, 9:a, 10:c

Chapter 20   1:a, 2:b, 3:b, 4:c, 5:d, 6:b, 7:c, 8:b, 9:c, 10:c

Chapter 21   1:c, 2:b, 3:a, 4:b, 5:a, 6:d, 7:b, 8:c, 9:d, 10:d

Chapter 22   1:d, 2:b, 3:b, 4:a, 5:a, 6:b, 7:c, 8:b, 9:a, 10:b

Author Index

Subject Index

Instructions: The purpose of this suggestion sheet is to get student feedback that can be used to improve the next edition of this book. We have asked for your comments on only one chapter in order to minimize the time needed for you to respond. All comments and suggestions will be greatly appreciated.

Items 1–3: The first four questions are aimed at learning more about the students who use this book. Please circle appropriate alternatives.

Item 4: Be sure to indicate the chapter you are evaluating.

Items 5–9: These are the most important questions. Please be as specific as possible.

When you complete the suggestion sheet, cut along the dashed line, fold and place in a stamped envelope, and mail. Thanks very much for your help.

Blaine Worthen and Karl White

SUGGESTION SHEET

1. Degree you are seeking (circle one): **BA, BS, MA, MS, other:** _____ .
   (specify)

2. Graduate major (circle one): **elem educ, sec educ, spec educ, educ adm, other:** _____ .
   (specify)

3. Have you taken elementary statistics: (circle): **yes, no;** any other educational measurement or psychometries courses: **yes, no;** computer science? **yes, no**

4. Chapter commented on _____ .

5. What specific ideas, definitions, descriptions, or examples in this chapter are not clear? (Please give page number and brief description.)

   _____

   _____

6. Should the book include more information on any of the sections in this chapter? (Please give page number and subheading.)

   _____

   _____

7. What sections should be shortened or omitted? (Give page number and subheading.)

   _____

   _____

8. Other comments about this chapter:

   _____

   _____

9. Any other general comments about this book:

   _____

   _____

9 8 7 6 5 4 3 2 1

(suggestions, *continued*)

Please place in envelope and return to:

Longman Publishing Group
Attn: Education Editor
10 Bank Street
White Plains, NY 10606